T0386763

THE LIFE OF A

UNION ARMY SHARPSHOOTER

THE LIFE OF A
UNION ARMY SHARPSHOOTER

THE DIARIES AND LETTERS OF JOHN T. FARNHAM

WILLIAM G. ANDREWS

FONTHILL

Fonthill Media LLC
www.fonthillmedia.com
office@fonthillmedia.com

First published 2016

Copyright © William G. Andrews 2016

ISBN 978-1-62545-077-7

Typeset in 10pt on 13pt Sabon
Printed and bound by CPI Group (UK) Ltd, Croydon, CR0 4YY

Contents

Preface

The purpose of this book is to document through his diaries and newspaper reports the Civil War experiences of a Union Army soldier. A number of diaries of Civil War soldiers have been published. However, I know of none that combines diary entries with newspaper reports. Also, Farnham's diaries are unusual in that he almost never skipped a day. Moreover, he consistently wrote substantial entries. I find no one-liners. Farnham's handwriting is clear. Illegible words are infrequent, usually the result of moisture damage. I doubt that such a complete account of the daily life of a Civil War soldier exists.

This is not to say that his accounts convey very much important "high history". He rarely participated in major historical events, though he was a near witness to Lincoln's assassination, attended Lincoln's second inauguration, met Lincoln and his wife, roomed with the feminist journalist Jane Gray Cannon Swisshelm, saw Grant, Vice President Johnson, numerous generals, Sojourner Truth, etc.

The diary entries begin on August 21, 1862, when Farnham traveled from his home in Brockport to Rochester to enlist. The diary for June 1—October 9, 1864, is missing, if, indeed, it ever existed. My transcription of them ends on June 21, 1865, with his arrival in Brockport after his discharge.

I have collated the diary entries with the chronologically-corresponding newspaper reports. Rarely are they duplicative. Where they are, I have deleted the less interesting duplication. I have inter-lined brief notes placing Farnham's writings in the context of the official accounts of his unit's activities and of major events in the war. The diaries are in light-face roman, the newspaper reports are indented in smaller type and the contextual and editorial notes are in italics.

Acknowledgements

I am grateful to the staff of the Wichita State University Library's Special Collections Department and to Dr. Blaine V. Houmes for permitting me to transcribe Farnham's diaries and to publish them. My son, Bill, as usual, has been indispensable as my tech support. I have exploited the resources of the Drake Memorial Library at the State University College at Brockport, especially its very helpful Archivist, Charles Cowling. Also, Alan Sutton of Fonthill Media has been very patient and helpful with the editing of the book. His counsel has made this a much more interesting book, I believe. Especially, I am grateful for his suggestion that I add explanatory endnotes. Finally, those electronic miracles, Google and Wikipedia, have been amazing sources of information for those endnotes. I have copied from them shamelessly.
The sources of the illustrations are:

Abbott, John S.C.*The History of the Civil War in America*, Henry Hill, NY, 1866, 2 volumes (Abbott)
Battles and Leaders of the Civil War, Century, NY, 1887, 4v. (B&L)
Coffin, Charles Carlton, *Drum-Beat of the Nation*, Harper, NY, 1888, 478p. (Coffin)
Elson, Henry W., *The Civil War Through the Camera*, McKinley, Stone & Mackenzie, NY, 1912, pages unnumbered. (Elson)
Google and Google Images
Harper's Pictorial History of the Civil War in the United States, McDonnell, Chicago, 1866, 2 volumes (HPH)
Harper's Weekly, 1861, 1862, 1863, 1864 volumes. (HW)
Library of Congress Digital Collection (LoC)
Losing, Benson J., *Pictorial Field Book of the Civil War*, Belknap, NY, 1868, 3v. (Lossing)
Millet, Francis Trevelyan, ed., *The Photographic History of The Civil War*, Review of Reviews, NY, 1911, 10 volumes (Miller)
Wikipedia

A Note Relating to the Transcription

I copied Farnham's words exactly, except where illegible. However, to improve clarity, I have filled in most of his abbreviations *[in italicized brackets]*. Although his writing is remarkably free of misspellings and grammatical errors, I have not corrected any that did occur, and I have not modernized his vocabulary or spelling and, in the interest of preserving authenticity, I have not bowdlerized his occasional racist language. Nor have I repaired inconsistencies in such things as underlining. The endnotes provide information about people and places that Farnham mentions and terms he uses that might be unfamiliar to the general reader. The numerals in bold type (**1a**) in the text are cross-references to the illustrations to be found between pages 128 and 129.

Abbreviations: NYVI = New York Volunteer Infantry, ACWRD = American Civil War Research Database, a website.

Introduction

Biographical Note on John T. Farnham

John Tyler Farnham was born in Union Springs, Cayuga County, New York, on March 25, 1842. He was named for the incumbent President of the United States. His parents were Charles and Lucy Kirtland Farnham.[1] His father was a physician, born in New York State about 1810. His mother's occupation in the 1860 census report is difficult to read, but appears to be milliner. She was born in New York State about 1817.

John was the eldest of seven children. Charles Jr. was three years younger and Cordelia was four years younger. Alonzo followed her in two years and Harvey in two more. Edward, the youngest, was born about 1855. Also, a daughter named Kate died at age two in 1867.[2] All were natives of New York State.

The 1850 census has the family residing in the Town of Phelps in Ontario County. By the 1860 census (1) the family had moved to the Town of Union (later Hamlin) in Monroe County with a post office address of North Clarkson. However, the Andrew Boyd *Six County Business Directory* for 1863-64 and the 1864 *Monroe County Directory* list Charles Farnham, physician, residing at 11 College Street (2), Brockport.[3] The 1869–70 *Monroe County Directory* has no Farnham listed for the Towns of Sweden, Hamlin, or Clarkson. In 1869, the *Brockport Republic* reported that Charles was residing in Hamlin. When John enlisted in August 1862, he gave his residence as Brockport. He also lived with a Smith family in Medina in 1857–58.[4]

The Farnhams seem to have had close affectionate relations, as shown by the lively correspondence they exchanged during his service in the Union army. Also, John records much mail and many visits exchanged with cousins, aunts, and uncles. He seems to have had many relatives in the Brockport area, but also in Elmira.

John reports in his diary that he "commenced the Printing profession at Newark, Wayne Co., N.Y." on January 26, 1853, at which time he was not yet eleven years old.[5] Later, he worked as a typesetter for the *Brockport Daily Advertiser* for "about three years" *c.* 1858–60[6] and on January 1, 1861, he records in his diary that he "Commenced this year as compositor in Brockport for Mr. H. N. Beach",[7] publisher of the *Brockport Republic*. By the time he enlisted in August 1862, he had been promoted to shop foreman.

Farnham seems to have been an exemplary employee. According to his diaries and death notices, he worked for four newspapers. When he enlisted, the *Brockport Daily Advertiser* described him as "a young man in whom we have much confidence—having always found him honest and prompt in the discharge of duty",[8] even though he had left its employ after three years to defect to its rival. At the same time, the *Brockport Republic* said that Farnham "by his fidelity, energy and industry demonstrated his qualification for any responsible pursuit in which he may engage, and we have all confidence that he will make a worthy soldier." After his discharge from the Union army, Farnham returned to the *Brockport Republic* for a time, then left for the *Elmira Daily Advertiser*. Yet, when he died (of tuberculosis at age 27)(3), the *Brockport Republic* called him "a rapid and accurate workman, and a faithful and obliging employee".[9] His death notice in the Elmira paper said that he "was an excellent workman, and one of the most exemplary and reliable men ever in our employ … His many friends here will regret to hear of his death, and all will drop a silent tear that one so amiable, talented and worthy should be called away so early in life."[10] The death notice in the *Rochester Evening Express*, where he worked after the Elmira paper, said, "Whilst at work in the *Express* office, he gained the respect and confidence of all his associates. He was a quiet, unassuming young man, well-read and intelligent. He had many warm friends in this city and vicinity who will regret to hear of his death."[11]

Indeed, his diaries reflect a personality that was gregarious and attracted many friends of both genders. The entries after his enlistment but before his unit departed for Elmira report a very active social life in the Brockport area and in Rochester. During that time, he reports at least one social activity every day. He resumed an active social whirl when home on leave and after his discharge.

One name in particular recurs often, Mary A. C. French (4). She was the only child of a carpenter–joiner and lived in Brockport. He notes in his diary seeing her socially 26 times between August 26 and November 13, as he was entering the service and in training in Rochester. While home on Christmas furloughs,[12] he attended a party at her home in 1863 and spent time with her at least fifteen times in fifteen days in 1864. While serving away from Brockport, he wrote 70 letters to her, sent her 21 newspapers, and received 57 letters from her—not counting their correspondence during the four months covered by the missing diary. He called on her his first day home after his discharge.

As I have not transcribed Farnham's diaries after his return home, I do not know what happened to their romance in the period before his death in 1869. I suspect that he was too ill from tuberculosis to contemplate marriage. In any case, he did not marry—and neither did she. I have traced her through the decennial censuses. Her father had died by 1880 and her mother by 1900. She remained alone in their 82 Park Avenue home until she moved to Coldwater, Mich., in 1912[13] to stay with cousins. She died there in 1917[14] at age 78. All the censuses record that she had "no occupation".

During his service in the army, Farnham made many friends. He names at least 108 friends while he was on field duty. They were all fellow soldiers, except for three "contrabands".[15] He even had many good friends among the officers. Often, the friendships, both officers and enlisted men, crossed the unit lines.

Physically, Farnham was frail and sickly. When he was first examined by a recruiting medical examiner, he was told that his "chest was too small" for him to be enrolled.[16] The next day, another doctor accepted him. He was 5 feet and ⅞ of an inch tall.[17] He constantly expressed concern about his weight, which fluctuated between 108 and 132 pounds.

Although he was a member of a sharpshooter company, he was not a very sharp shooter. He records several instances of target practice when he was unable to hit the target. The only times that he fired at rebels, he missed.

Farnham often reported that he had been unable to keep pace with his unit on long marches and wound up with officers carrying his rifle or knapsack or he rode in an ambulance. In January 1865, his company commander said in a letter to the Assistant Adjutant General that Farnham's "constitution physically, is slight, and renders him unable to endure the fatigue of campaign, and carry the heavy target rifle now used by this Batt."[18] As a result, he was transferred to duty in the War Department's Printing Office.

On 163 days, he complains in his diary about being sick, not feeling well, etc. He was in a hospital 134 days, though his diaries reflect activity suggesting that he was not really incapacitated much of the time. He was the hospital's librarian and served, in effect, as clerk/secretary/errand boy and general factotum to its staff and some of its patients. He also was a very attentive nurse for one patient. In 45 diary entries, he complains about being tired.

Despite his frailty, sickliness, and fatigue, Farnham was a surprisingly energetic and enterprising young man. He pursued cultural activities with ardor. His diaries report his attendance at 23 theatrical performances, six concerts, two public speeches, and the state fair. He reports having read 22 books and several magazines. Besides the *Brockport Republic*, he subscribed to the *Rochester Evening Express* and the *Philadelphia Inquirer*. Also, nearly every day that he was able, he bought one or another newspaper. He also attended religious services most Sundays when he was able. He did not seem to discriminate among denominations and he commented critically on the sermons.

He was attending a play at Grover's Theater in Washington when the word came that Lincoln had been shot. The play was stopped and the audience repaired to Ford's Theater. He was a member of a social circle that included the wife of the Rev. Phineas D. Gurley, pastor of the F Street Presbyterian Church and Lincoln's spiritual counselor who comforted him in his death throes. Another member of that circle was a servant in the White House.

Other evidence of his enterprising character were instances of his self-promotion. He knocked on the White House door one day and asked to see President Lincoln. When told that the President was not receiving that day, he arranged to return on a reception day and did meet Lincoln and his wife. He campaigned for a job in the War Department's printing office and, when it was not forthcoming, went to the home of his Congressman one evening, knocked on the door, was admitted, and persuaded the legislator to intervene for him—which was successful. He also contrived to be assigned to the headquarters of the Iron Brigade for a time.

His energy also produced a prodigious amount of writing. It would be difficult to find a more disciplined diarist. In 850 days from August 22, 1861, until April 14, 1865, not counting the period of his missing diary and his fifteen days on leave (February 14–29, 1864), he wrote 848 entries, 99.7 percent of the days. He wrote on days when he had been in battle—once for ten consecutive days—sick in the hospital, exhausted after a hard march, in any kind of weather.

Not only did he keep up his diary incessantly, he also wrote at least 63 long articles for the *Brockport Republic*, about one every two weeks until on April 20, 1865, when he "concluded to have no more to do with the *[Brockport]* Repub*[lic]* establishment". Of that number, 48 survive, have been transcribed, and are reproduced below. He mentions the other fifteen in his diary, but they have not survived because the file of the *Brockport Republic* is missing from October 1864 until October 1866. His editor at the *Republic* said in print that some of his articles had been reprinted in other newspapers, but a search of the *Rochester Evening Express* and the *Rochester Daily Democrat*, the most likely newspapers to use his letters, did not discover any letters from the period when the *Republic* is not extant. In his diaries, he mentions having sent articles to the *Albion (N.Y.) Republican*, the *Brockport Daily Advertiser*, the *Washington Chronicle*, and the *Philadelphia Inquirer* and having excerpts from his *Brockport Republic* articles reprinted in the *Rochester Evening Express* and the *Rochester Daily Democrat*. However, I have been unable to locate them.

In Farnham's diaries, he records having written at least 490 letters, mostly to family and friends, more than one every other day. I have been unable to learn if any have survived.

Besides his other activities, he became actively involved in politics. He was an ardent supporter of President Lincoln and campaigned for him among his fellow soldiers. He was also a fervent Unionist and got into several arguments on the issue.

Farnham's relationships with African-Americans deserve comment. One of his closest friends was a soldier named Shedrick J. Jackson, whom Farnham identifies as "colored".[19] He mentions Jackson at least nineteen times in his diaries. Jackson was so close a friend that he accompanied Farnham when he went on leave to attend to his brother's grave.[20] This friendship was the more remarkable that Jackson was not even a member of his unit, being a private in the 140th NYVI. Nor was he in the Brockport company of that regiment.[21] Also, Farnham became close friends of a couple, Hetty Copeland and Nelson Ely, who were living in a camp run by the Union Army for escaped slaves, that was located near his encampment at Suffolk, Va. He recorded in his diary at least 38 visits to them. He sent home for a reader and a spelling book to use in teaching them to read and write and he helped build a school for the camp residents. He often brought them food and just as frequently had meals with them in their dwelling. He also reported a very pleasant encounter with a young African-American girl, writing of her in quite complimentary terms.[22]

The Background to this Publication

While writing the section on the 1861–65 period of my *Early Brockport* book[23], I discovered some 189 letters from Brockport soldiers in the Union Army that the *Brockport Republic* published. I thought that they might be the basis for another book. So, I omitted any material on the village's involvement in the Civil War from *Early Brockport*. However, when I tried to use those letters to form a cohesive narration, I found that they did not lend themselves to such use.[24] But the 48 extant letters by Farnham seemed a possibility by themselves.

On a whim, I Googled "John T. Farnham" and learned of five of his wartime diaries in the Wichita State University Library. I traveled to Wichita twice and transcribed them. Then, I Googled him again and learned that a sixth diary of his had been sold at auction the previous November for $23,900. It had been accompanied by a blood-stained shirt cuff that had been taken from the body of the assassinated Abraham Lincoln. A diary entry explained how Farnham had acquired the shirt cuff. I called the auction house, leaving a message and wrote it a letter asking that they let the buyer know that I would like to transcribe the diary. I received no answer from either my phone call or my letter.

The very next week, the *New York Times* ran an article about a Jewish physician named John Lattimer who had collected Nazi memorabilia and whose estate had been sold at auction. It also mentioned that he had collected Lincoln memorabilia, including the Farnham diary, and gave the name of Lattimer's daughter who was the executor and lived in Topeka, Kansas. I called her, left a message, wrote her a letter, enclosing another letter to the buyer of the diary, asking her to forward it to the buyer. In the buyer's letter, I offered to transcribe the diary for him and collaborate with him in any way he wished. Again, no answers.

Again, I Googled Farnham. This time, I learned that the sixth diary and the shirt cuff had been displayed as part of an exhibit on the bicentennial of Abraham Lincoln's birth at the Herbert Hoover Memorial Library in West Branch, Ia., and that it belonged to Dr. Blaine V. Houmes, of Cedar Rapids, Ia. I called Dr. Houmes and left a message. I wrote him a long letter, offering to come to Cedar Rapids and transcribe the diary. No answer. Six weeks later, Dr. Houmes called to tell me that I need not come to Iowa. He would copy the diary for me and send me the copy. He did so and the result is part of this document.

Incidentally, I was able to return a favor to Dr. Houmes by identifying for him Farnham's friend who had given him the shirt cuff.

Farnham's Military Unit

Company 6 of the 1st New York Sharpshooters
From Frederick Phisterer, New York in the War of the Rebellion,
1861-1865, 1912 3rd ed., pp. 1,689–90.

Major W. S. Rowland received, October 10, 1862, authority from the War Department to recruit a regiment of sharpshooters in the States of New York and Pennsylvania; the regimental organization failed and only a battalion was recruited, which as finally organized consisted of four companies, the 6th, 7th, 8th and 9th; another company, the 10th, was contemplated, but not completed. The companies left the State February 3, 1863, and served at Washington, D.C., from the time of their departure; at Suffolk, Va., in Terry's Brigade, Peck's Division, 7th Corps, from March, 1863; on the Peninsula, Va., in 1st Brigade, 1st Division, 7th Corps, from June, 1863; in the defenses of Washington, D.C., 22nd Corps, from July, 1863; in the 1st Brigade, 1st Division, 1st Corps, Army of the Potomac, from July, 1863; in the 1st Brigade, 4th Division, 5th Corps, Army of the Potomac, from April, 1864; in the 3rd Brigade, 3rd Division, 5th Corps, from August, 1864; in the 1st Brigade, 3rd Division, 5th Corps, from September, 1864; and, unattached, in the 3rd Division, 5th Corps, from November, 1864. Captain Joseph S. Arnold succeeded Major Rowland in command.

Sixth Company; Flank Company, 108th N.Y. Volunteers: This company was organized and recruited at Rochester, under Capt. Abijah C. Gray; it was mustered in the United States service for three years September 13, 1862; and honorably discharged and mustered out, under Lieut. Philip Hysner, June 3, 1865, near Washington, D.C. The company lost by death six enlisted men killed in action, four enlisted men of wounds received in action, nine enlisted men by disease, etc., a total of 19 of whom four died in captivity.

Rowland commanded the battalion only until succeeded by Capt. Thomas S. Bradley, age 37, on November 19, 1862. In fact, Phisterer says that Rowland rendered "no service", but also says that he was commissioned a major on March 5, 1863. Bradley's command ended April 7, 1863, and he died of cancer of the stomach on June 28, 1863.

Farnham's 6th company was organized by Capt. Abijah C. Gray and commanded by him from August 30, 1962, until February 19, 1863. Capt. Volney J. Shipman succeeded him until September 23, 1864, after having been its first lieutenant from its formation until his promotion. First Lt. Alphonso W. Starkweather succeeded him until the company was discharged on July 26, 1865. He had been the second lieutenant from the formation of the battalion until he took command. The only other officer of the 6th company was Philip Hysner, who was second lieutenant from February 19, 1863 until June 3, 1865.

From Farnham's Diaries and Phisterer[25]

The officers of the 1st NYSS were:

William S. Rowland	major and battalion commander, October 22, 1862,[26] colonel and battalion commander at least until March 22, 1863.[27]
Thomas S. Bradley	age 37, captain and battalion commander, November 19, 1862, to April 7, 1863.[28]
Warren Blinn	quartermaster from March 1 to June 27, 1863.[29]
Abijah C. Gray	captain and company commander, August 30, 1862, discharged Februray 19, 1863.[30] On January 24, 1863, he "suddenly appeared from imprisonment in Fort Lafayette to take command of the Co[mpany]".[31] He does not appear in the 1860 census, but in 1870, he is a 57-year-old stone quarry worker in Venalhaven, Maine, with a wife and 11-year-old daughter.

Volney J. Shipman	age 23, 1st lieutenant, August 30, 1862, to February 19, 1863, acting quartermaster, December 4, 1862,[32] captain and company commander, December 25, 1862,[33] or February 19, 1863[34] to *ca.* February 25, 1864, battalion commander by February 12, 1864;[35] wounded at Piney Branch Creek, May 8, 1864,[36] and discharged for disability on September 23, 1864.[37] He was court-martialed June 1863 and hospitalized or on sick leave June–August 1863,[38] "received a slight scratch on the hand from bullet.[39] He does not appear in the 1860 census, but in 1870, he is living in State Center, Iowa, as a merchant of sundries with a 25-year-old wife and four-month-old son. James K. McDonald, 1st Lieutenant and acting battalion commander, March 11–20, 1864 while Shipman was on furlough.[40]
Alphonso W. Starkweather	age 31, 2nd Lieutenant, 6th Company, August 30, 1862, 1st Lieutenant February 19, 1863, mustered out July 26, 1865,[41] quartermaster,[42] captain,[43] acting company commander June 20–August 14, 1863,[44] while Shipman was hospitalized and on leave, hospitalized with a broken leg suffered in a fall from a horse.[45]
Philip Hysner	age 25, sergeant, September 13, 1862, promoted to 1st sergeant no date, to 2nd Lieutenant, February 19, 1863, (despite a company vote for Orderly A. L. Root),[46] mustered out June 3, 1865.[47] Commanded the company until mustered out.[48] He does not appear in the 1860 census, but in 1870 he was a 32-year-old carriage painter with a 28-year-old wife and two small children, having been born in Prussia, Germany.

Summary of Farnham's Military Career

August 21–November 13, 1862	In training at Camp Fitz John Porter in Rochester, 6th Company attached to the 108th NYVI.

November 14, 1862–January 6, 1863	In training at Camp Weehawken, N.J.
January 6–February 5, 1863	In staging area at Camp Sprague, New Dorp, Staten Island, N.Y.
February 8–26, 1863	In staging area at Camp Casey/Seward, Arlington Heights, Va.
March 1–June 18, 1863	Participated in the successful defense of Suffolk, Va., much skirmishing.
June 27–October 9, 1863	Hospitalized at Chesapeake General Hospital, except August 15-29, on leave.
October 25, 1863–June 20, 1864	6th Company attached to the Iron Brigade, October–November much marching, some skirmishing. December–April, winter quarters near Culpepper, Va., Farnham serving as a clerk at brigade headquarters from March 8, 1864. During May and June 1864, the Iron Brigade, with the 6th Company attached, was engaged in a series of pitched battles.
June 21–December 22, 1864	Activities for June 1–October 9 are unknown as diary and newspaper reports are missing, but apparently he remained a clerk at brigade headquarters.
December 23, 1864–January 10, 1865	On furlough to Brockport.
January 13–February 21, 1865	Back at brigade headquarters.
February 22–March 31, 1865	Hospitalized at Carver Hospital, Washington.
April 1–June 16, 1865	Clerk in office of the Adjutant General of the War Department.

THE LIFE OF A UNION ARMY SHARPSHOOTER

The Diaries and Letters of John T. Farnham

VOLUME I
1861

Jan. Tuesday 1 1861
Commence this year at work as compositor in Brockport for Mr. H. N. Beach.
Worked part of this day. Wrote to Aunt C. in Medina. Father called at office
this noon.

Front matter

Whoever finds this will please send it to me at Brockport Monroe Co. N. Y.
or to me directed to Sharpshooters, 108th NYV Washington–DC to receive
thanks of John T. Farnham
To Co. A. 1st Regt NYS Sharpshooters

 J. T. Farnham
Gray's S. S. 108th N.Y.S.V. Brockport N. Y. Washington, D. C.
1st Reg. NYS Sharpshooters

Diary—1862 J. T. Farnham Brockport, N. Y.
Gray's S. S. 108th NYV

[Tipped in at entry for Friday, August 22, 1862, is a newspaper clipping
reading:]

*For the war:—One more representative of the Brockport press responds to
the call for more volunteers in defence of the old Constitution and flag.*

John T. Farnham, *for about three years employed in the office of the Daily
Advertiser, but for the past year employed as foreman of the Brockport
Republic, enlisted last evening in Capt. Gray's Rifle Company of
Sharpshooters, in Rochester, to be attached to the 108th Regiment.—He is a*

*young man in whom we have much confidence—having always found him
honest and prompt in the discharge of duty.—Daily Advertiser.*

August 1862
Context—Farnham enlisted in the aftermath of the failure of McClellan's ill-
fated Peninsular Campaign, March–July 1862, that was supposed to result in
the capture of the Confederate capital of Richmond.

Thursday, 21st.—At office before break[fast]. Paper worked at 4 P.M. Father
up. Let him have 25c. Started for Roch[ester]. At 4:45—Met two Lieutenants.
at depot there. Dr. Backus refused to give me certificate of soundness
on account of my chest not being large enough. Went to the surgeon who
examined me yesterday & after another examination he pronounced me all
right & signed my papers. The adjutant then administered oath of support
& to U.S. obedience to superior officers &c. Signed order for $25½ of state
bounty & also enlistment money $2 but got no money. Had my name enrolled
on company roll of Capt A[bijah]. C. Gray's Sharpshooters. Found friend J.
C[hauncey] Parker[49] who has enlisted in same co[mpany]. Went to supper at
National [Hotel]: was introduced to the Capt[ain] (Gray) & got reassurance
of leave to go to B[rockport]. C[hauncey] P[arker] & I examined revolvers
& bo't water filter 40c. Home at 9 P.M. train. Found N.D. at depot & after
calling to let Mr. [Horatio N.] B[each] know I had enlisted, went with him to
his house where I found besides the girls belonging there, Cousin C., N.R.,
Miss [Mary] Judd, & sister. Had a gay time generally & it was late when we
went home. Rain to-night. Paid $1.33.

Friday, 22d—Let blank tuition bills for college, & at work on the paper.
Rain this A.M. Took my exemption papers from Town clerk's office. Called
on [William H.H.] Smith Editor of the Daily Advertiser & told him of my
volunteering when he gave me the flattering notice on the following page in
his Daily. Got a dozen extra copies. Sent paper to Capt[ain] Gray, Aunt C. &
Mrs. M. down st. & called at Mrs. S[mith]'s not at home. Came home early.
Very warm to-night M[ary A. C. Fr]ench] & E.D. called at our house. Feel
pretty tired. Was congratulated & wished a safe return from war by several of
young ladies.

Saturday, 23d.—*[illegible word]* trouble me this A.M. Father gave me medicine.
Cousin H[enry C. Murray] at office just after I wrote to him. Lent paper to
Uncle J. Outside "up" at 11. A.M. & "made up" immediately. Cleaned up in
P.M.—C[hauncey] P[arker]. agreed to telegraph to me from Roch[ester]. if
my uniform had come. Got some "necessary" $6 of Mr. [Horatio N.] B[each],
[illegible word] & my aged horse $3 & buggy at livery for tomorrow. Bo't

almonds 25c. Show *[?]* for about the last time. Took supper at home with Misses M. & E. D., Miss Mary Judd, & my own "family" & spent a pleasant evening. Had a walk, saw C*[hauncey]* P*[arker]*. Got meat at market 5c with M*[other]*. & left the splendid northern lights after leaving my "charge". Rec*[eive]*d $6 Paid 34c.

Sunday, 24th.—*[Entry has no military interest]*

Monday, 25th.—Diarrhoea very hard all day. Laid abed till 9 taking medicine, eating crackers & drinking scalded milk. Cha*[u]*n*[cey]* P*[arker]* called & I sent word to Roch*[ester]*. Well enough to go to the depot with mother & sister to see Capt*[ain]* *[Nathan P.]* Pond's cav*[alry]*. Co*[mpany]*.[50] leave. At office; Darling is at work in my place till I come back from the war. Mr. *[Horatio N.]* B*[each]* asked me to send him communications for the *[Brockport]* Republic; he to send me the *[Brockport]* R*[epublic]*. Laid down till dark at home. Mother has made me needle "housewife"[51]—took & filled it with pins, needles, buttons, a comb, &c. & is to make me a Havelock[52]. Min. & bro. called; M. & I went to depot to see C*[hauncey]* P*[arker]*. but not come. Called at M's. Abed early. Tired. Cool today. Paid 47c.

Tuesday 26th.—Diar*[rhea]*. no better. Took some med*[icine]* ate a little breakf*[as]*t & started for Roch*[ester]*. On cars at 6:40. 34c Occupied part of two seats. At R*[ochester]* bought morning paper. Slowly walked along. Saw private Jack*[son P.]* N*[ichols]*. who gave me a good dose of "Bone Liniment"[53]. Surprised to see at recruiting office boys from Kendall Mills acquaintances. Hector Butler, Henry Murray, Nelson Miller, Chauncey Parker, Jack Nichols, Mr. Hughes are also from Kendall Mills. Capt*[ain]* G*[ray]*. kindly gave me leave of absence till Friday & paid me $2 enlistment money. Also paid for a "dose" of brandy & sugar. It is understood that we are to furnish our own rifles at $45 each, in order to make sure of being an independent blank *[or flank?]* Co*[mpany]*. goes to camp today at 11. Lieut*[enant]*. gave me furlough[54]. Bo't reader for sister at Gift Store & drew silver butter knife. Bo't portfolio 50c & paper 50c & drew fine breastpin. At Dewey's bo't camp screw top inkstand 3c, thin writing paper 1 q*[uire]* 24c, pens ½ gross 50c, holders, pencils 4, 12c, rubbers 3c, Hardee's tactics[55] 25c, health book 10c, War map 6c &c. Found friend Bennie Davis at h*[ea]*dq*[uarte]*rs & after taking another dose of Jack's "warmer" *[Hector]* B*[utler]* went to depot with me; met his father. & bro*[ther]*. at train, & left them. I taking a seat in a luxuriantly cushioned car getting to B*[rockport]* at 11:45. Made mother present of butter knife & sister the pin. Nap after dinner. Aunt B. Allen, Kate Ackerson & Christine Webb called. I went to *[Brockport]* R*[epublic]*. office, printed cards got *[Brockport]* Daily *[Advertiser]* at D*[aily]* office, called at Mrs. S*[mith]*'s, home & laid down. Eddie[56] got eve. paper for me. Father came up. Very warm day. With M*[other]* & sister saw Mr. & Mrs. Cook M.'s C. has left a bad *[illegible word]* & enl*[isted]* in Mack's rifle battery 108th. Home early. Diar*[rhea]* much better. Rec'd $2. Paid $4.20.

Wednesday 27th.—Up early, slight d*[iarrhea]* took dose of alcohol, sugar & water, also tannin hem*[lock]* bark. Got order for sister's tuition 6.35 & slate 34c. Rode down st. with F*[ather]*. Took horn of brandy 6c & sug*[ar]*. Saw sister off to col*[lege]*[57]. With M*[ary A. C. French]* went to depot with mother to see Capt. *[Milo]* Starks's co*[mpany]*. leave at 9:45 for Camp Porter; many of them friends. Left black berries at Mr. Austin's for mother. Rec*[eive]*d letter from Aunt C. for sister. ...

Thursday 28th—... Mr. *[Horatio N.]* B*[each]*. has given me a very flattering notice in the Weekly *[Brockport]* Repub*[lic]*. To be correspondent.

Context—The Union Army suffered a humiliating defeat in the Second Battle of Bull Run, August 28-30.

Friday 29th.—At office before breakfast, got ink sent paper to Aunt C. & Mrs. Marshall 2c. Paid box rent 13c at P.O. to Jan. 1, 1863, & got rec*[eip]* t. Got ready for camp. Left watch to have it fixed again. Bo't comb 2c At Dr. S*[mith]*'s office talked with him; took letter for Roch*[ester]*. Got *[Horatio N.]* B*[each]*'s check cashed Rec*[eive]*d $27.44. Called & got letter for B.D. Mother went to 9:45 train with me. Sorry to see her shed tears. At recr*[ui]*ting office got cert*[ificate]*. of enlistment—to get clothes.—Gave *[Brockport]* Repub*[lic]* paper to Lieut]enant]. Bo't 12c for plenning *[?]* button. Walked to camp part way with Che*[s]t[er]* Van Tine of 13th *[NYVI]*. Camp at noon. Went in on pass. Had soldier's dinner first in camp, with friend *[Charles]* Thompson of Clarkson. Found Jack*[son]* N*[ichols]* & Mr. Hughes. Good dinner of boiled potatoes, ripe tomatoes in vinegar, beans, salt pork with bre*[a]*d, &c. Gave letter to B*[rockport]* D*[aily Advertiser]* writer. Drilled under Benj*[amin]* P. Hutson. Lots of fun among the boys. Found Ja*[me]*s Case, who went to school with 14 y*[ea]*rs ago in Orleans; in our Co*[mpany]*. Bo't *[illegible word]* Drew clothes in P.M. *[illegible word]* cap, dark blue dress coat, lighter pants (too large) thick serv*[ice]* shoes, l. blue overcoat—2 p*[ai]*rs und*[er]* shirts d*[itt]*o drawers, d*[itt]*o stockings blankets & knapsack. Wore overcoat in eve. The Mills boys came up in the eve. We have a California hunter in our co*[mpany]* & all pretty good boys. Bo't eve. paper;. No encouraging news. Reb's driving our men to Washington. Abed not far from 9 P.M. Lantern in barracks till 9, then out. Bunk with "uncle" Hughes. The boys joking & having lots of fun. One Dutchman[58] couldn't "find a feather" under him. Long while getting asleep; then rested good. Wooden barracks, 3 rows of bunks, 2 tiers, one above the other, accommodating 96 men in all; filled with straw; 2 men a bunk.

Saturday, 30th.—Up at 5½. Frosty. Washed; about 7 marched to the table. Break*[fast]* of boiled steamed potatoes. Steamed beef, Bread, coffee, all pretty good. Got pass at 9 to city rode down 10c & took knapsack & blankets & left them at National Hotel. Found Cap*[tain]* & Lieut*[enant]* gave C*[aptain]* paper *[Brockport]* Repub*[lic]* & got furlough till Mond*[ay]*. Noon. Bo't 108th numbers for cap paid 37½ for 3. Subscribed for Roch*[ester]* Ex*[press]* for 6 mo*[nth]*s. $2. Got receipt. Took knaps*[ack]*. & things to depot & checked to B*[rockport]*. Saw A*[l]*b*[ert]*. Allen & *[Heber]* Fuller. Bo't picture of *[illegible word]* Pope 25c & little Zouave[59] for *[brothers]* Eddy & Harvey. Took cars at 11. Soon in B*[rockport]*. House to dinner. Mother cut & sewed blue pants over. Fixed up & went down st*[reet]*. *[Horatio N.]* Beach gave me paper & *[illegible word]* letter directed also a general letter appointing me a regular corres*[pondent]* to *[Brockport]* Republic. Bo't shoestring. Shoemaker put nails in shoes. Printed labels for clothes, &c. Father at home. At depot, 4:50, again at 6:20. Made mistake & took Hughes coat knapsack instead of my own. Mr. Kimball at supper. Bo't 2 towels 25c 1 yar*[d]* each. Sister & I called at Mrs. S*[mith]*'s also at M*[ary A. C. French]*. Abed early.

Sunday 31st.—A splendid day. At the depot at 8:17 Called at *[illegible word]* boarding place. Rec*[eive]*d letter from bro*[ther]* Charley in camp at Washington. Attended Pres*[byterian]* Church with mother & sister. Henry R. Aunt C. & Miss Judd (at M*[ary A. C. French]*'s) attended Pres*[byterian]* Church with us to hear sermon by Rev*[erend]* Kimball, soldiers. Good. After supper packed up my things & in eve. went to depot & saw *[Nathan P.]* Pond's cav*[alry]*. Co*[mpany]* leave for good. Took leave myself of several young ladies. Called on M*[ary A. C. French]*. Seems like rain.

Monday, Sept 1st.—Rain all day. Took knapsack to depot. At the office. Bo't paper, Tax on R.R. ticket of 2c R.R. ticket 36c. bid some friends good by, mailed letter to Charley. Mother, Eddy & Harvey saw me off at the depot also friends rush at cars. At Roch*[ester]* met Lieut*[enant]* at R*[ochester]* depot—rain. Wrote to Roch*[ester]* *[Evening]* Ex*[press]*. Saw *[Brigadier]* Gen*[eral John H.]* Martindale Rode to camp 10c & got there at 12. Dinner. Unpleasant & damp, cloudy. In barracks all the P.M. & had knapsack marked 10c. No parade today. Angel threw *[illegible word]* on the table fun. Stay in hospital tonight. Steward B. Davis 2 men sick.

Tuesday, 2d.—Chilly night & cold the A.M. Up at 5 every morn. Took double quick before break*[fas]*t. Friends from K*[endall]* Mills brought provisions for us. Good. At noon was requested by Lieut*[enant Volney J.]* Shipman to present sword, sash & belt to Capt*[ain Abijah C.]* Gray at 3 P.M., which was bought by his Co*[mpany]* & have only short time to prepare for it. Got up a short speech, & in presence of some friends & the co*[mpany]*, made the presentation. Capt*[ain]* made short reply. Pass to Roch*[ester]* till 7 P.M. & took supper with Mr. Brook. Back to camp 1 min*[ute]* after 7; 4 *min[ute]s* more would have got me into guard house. Bunked with *[illegible name]* after talking *[with]* Lieut*[enant]*. Fine evening. Cold.

Wednesday, 3d.—A splendid day. Am to do table waiter duty from this A.M. & like it. Commenced at break*[fast]*. Rush for food. Wash dishes &c after meals. Those entitled to the Monroe county bounty of $100 marched to co*[mpany]* clerk office at Roch*[ester]* & got it. Bo't paper 2c. Saw cap. Got my $100 in cash. Friends in *[illegible word]* at dinner. Soup. Wrote my own furlough & Lieut*[enant]* signed. Ready to leave camp at 3 to get carriage to Roch*[ester]*. For Mrs. Cook & M*[ary A. C. French]* & rode 50c to R*[ochester]* had soda water 15c. bo't oil cloth cap 12.5c. cap cover 50c; peaches, apples, brush broom, ticket. Saw Gid Allen & *[illegible name]* on cars after M*[ary A. C. French]* & I left Mrs. C. Pleasant ride in cars. Father at sup*[per]*. Down st*[reet]* & called at Mr. *[Horatio N.]* Beachs home early & had social time. Fine eve. Rec*[eive]*d $100.

Thursday, Sept. 4th.—Mother sewed things for me. Gave Mr. H*[oratio]* N. Beach $70 & took his note int*[erest]* 1 y*[ea]*r from today. Had photographs. Life insured for benefit of Mother in Mutual Benefit L*[ife]*. Ins*[urance]*. Co. Newark N.J. for $500 ($9.87) 3 y*[ea]*rs paying about $38 a y*[ea]*r. quarterly. Mr. *[Horatio N.]* Beach answered question also father. Called at Mrs. S*[mith]*'s & bid E*[mma]* & Mrs. S*[mith]* good bye. Hand put on watch & got strings & key 12c. Eng*[aged]*. horse & buggy $1.50 to take mother & sister to Uncle *[Albert]* Allen's & Rand's & we started after dinner. Fine ride & good time; *[illegible word]* melons & other fruit. Good supper with R*[and]*'s & Grandmother. Home then sister & I called at Miss A. Clark's & took a ride with her stopping at M*[ary A. C. French]*'s taking her & all to A.C's & had fine time little …

Friday, 5th.—Up early; wrote. Down st*[reet]* & had boot fixed, paid Mr. *[Sanford]* Goff for extra livery. At the office bid the boys good bye. Bo't ball twine 10c. Mother, sister & Harvey & Eddy went to Depot with me at 9:45 train. Bo't ticket to R*[ochester]* 36c. Good bye again & left in good spirits. Glass of brandy 12c in R*[ochester]* with *[Ezra]* Hutson. Rode to camp in co. 10c with Mrs. Beach & Mrs. I. B. King. Put them thro guard. Mrs. B*[each]*. gave me cake and peas for dinner which I divided with Capt*[ain]*, Lieut*[enant]*

& ladies at table where had a good time. Gave Capt*[ain]* copy of speech at sword presentation. On table duty for last time. Saw skull of man buried 20 years ago just dug up near hospital. Miss El. D. & others from B*[rockport]*. Out on dress parade. In bed early to-night after having won discussion with driller *[Ezra]* Hutson.

Saturday, 6th.—Detailed for guard duty. Two hours on & 6 off. Went on at 11 till 1; relieved at noon; waiter gave me glass ale. Rainy A.M. & slight shower in P.M. Mrs. Courtney & husband, Misses *[Mary A. C.]* French, Butler, Bradford, Mrs. Cook & others here 3 lemonade 15c; got pass on dress parade; Lon *[brother Alonzo]* came while I was there & took supper with me, leaving at 7. Peaches. A good crowd of people at eve. On guard from 7½ till 10; had lots of fun, am to sleep in guard house, with rest of relief guard, till 3 A.M. 7th. Splendid evening.

Sunday, 7th.—On guard from 3½ till 6, & helped with 3 men for running guard. Very fine sunrise. Roll call break*[fast]* & at 9 discharged from g*[uard]*. duty. Pretty tired & think of taking a nap. Warm. Ordered out to sign pay roll for $50 state bounty. Out after supper to see parade. A great many people in camp, band. Helped Lieut*[enant]* about month's pay roll till 10 P.M., then signed it. A little rain to-night.

Monday, 8th—Up at 3½. Looking for paymaster. Wrote to Aunt C. & home. Rec*[eive]*d $13, 1 mo*[nth]* pay. Sent letter to P.G. by Capt*[ain]*. G*[ray]*. Wrote notice of Co*[mpany]* to Albion Repub*[lic]* for Serg*[ean]*t *[James C.]* Noble. Soup (extra) for dinner. Saw Martha Kendrick on the grounds. Drilled a considerable in P.M. Bo't peaches (4 for 3c). Laid down a while before supper. On drill at 6. Fine eve. Am thirsty to-day. In bed in good season. Rec*[eive]*d $13 paid 9c.

Tuesday, 9th—Roll call after washing. Then on table guard. B*[enjamin B]* Davis gave me tin button cleaner. Capt*[ain]*. & others shooting at target with revolver. Capt*[ain]*.centered 3 in sq*[uare]* at 18 paces. Made shot myself & shot two in*[ches]* below. Table guard duty at noon. Life Ins*[urance]*. Policy No. 17,768. Mark Webster up & I showed him about, saw Miss Rice; also Ch. Allen at supper. Stranger lady gave me fine boquet, left it in water at officers quarters. At parade & walked about with B.D. In P.M. Parks came & had lemonade. Fine eve. Abed early.

Wednesday, 10th.—Table guard, break. Father & Harvey came & bro't ins*[urance]* note & policy for me to sign & did so. Target shooting with revolver. Showed F*[ather]* & H*[arvey]* about. Let F*[ather]*. have $50 to take home at 10.

Read morn*[ing]* paper. Laid down. Bo't cakes for B.D. sick. 4c. Orders to leave for Washington as soon as ready. Miss Ag*[gie]* J*[ohnso]*n at camp Wrote to B*[rockport]* Republ*[ic]*. Also home. Received blouse haversack[60], canteen, choker & ordered to pack our knapsacks. Capt*[ain]* here. We voted to buy our guns Nat*[ional]* tel*[escope]* target rifle, to cost about $45; to be ord]ered] immediately & the boys who wish to help make them a little give *[?]* presented us with pincushions. Won't start till guns are ready. Rev*[erend]* Kimball & 2 Miss Frye from B*[roc]*kp*[or]*t int*[roduced]* to two gentlemen. Showed Mrs. Miller about & to supper; on table guard then parade. Peaches 4c. Chat finished supper with guard. Fine eve.'s continue. Paid 7c.

Brockport Republic, September 11, 1862

Camp Porter, Sept. 10, 1862. Mr. H. N. Beach—Visitors continue to pour into this camp, which you know is situated 1½ miles from the city of Rochester, opposite Mt. Hope, overlooking the Genesee Valley Railroad, Genesee River, and the Genesee Valley Canal, on high grounds, the location being a very healthy one.

The 140th regiment makes a very good appearance when on parade, and the camp presents a lively aspect; many visitors make us daily calls, Brockport sending her quota. On Sunday last 15,000 people are estimated to have been on the ground. Perkins[61] Band are present each day at evening parade. Capt. Starks' company being Co. A, take the first position on the right of the battalion on parade; they are being well drilled.

The principal order of exercises of the camp are: Reveille at 5 A.M.; squad drill from 5:30 to 7; breakfast 7:15; officer drill, 8:30 to 9:30; company drill, 9:30 to 11:30; dinner, 12:15. In the afternoon, officer drill, 1:30 to 2:30; company drill, 3 to 5; supper, 5:30; evening parade, 6:30; taps, (to bed) 9:30.

The companies were paid $13, (one month's pay to those who enlisted before Aug. 22) on Monday last, and the State and government bounties are hourly expected.

Capt. Mack's rifle battery, and Capt. Gray's company of Sharpshooters, flank companies, to be connected with the 108th, now at Washington, are in barracks here, and have orders to leave for the regiment as soon as ready, and are anxious to be in the field. The Sharpshooters are to buy their own rifles, and are waiting to have them made. They probably will not go under two weeks.

Sword presentations, &c,. are of almost daily occurrence. The commissioned officers of the Sharpshooters, Capt. A. C. Gray, 1st Lieut. V. J. Shipman and 2nd Lieut. A. W. Starkweather, have each been presented with a sword, sash and belt, the latter also having received, in addition, a fine uniform. The members of Capt. Gray's Co., as a testimonial of respect to their noble leader, contributed and bought for him the articles enumerated above. The presentation was made by J. T. Farnham, of that company, the captain replying appropriately and briefly.

The men at camp sleep in wooden barracks in bunks filled with straw, two men in each bunk, every barrack accommodating over one hundred men. The cooking is done by steam on contract. The food consists mostly of potatoes, beef, pork and beans, good baker's bread, a kind of coffee with milk and sugar, good soup occasionally, and sometimes fresh tomatoes.— Butter is had only by the men subscribing for it and buying of the regimental sutler,[62](5) who has almost everything for sale. Friends of the soldiers who visit us are hospitably entertained.

Very truly, J.T.F.

Thursday, 11th.—Used tooth brush before breakfast & had drill. Wear blouse which is more comfortable than dress coat. Helped Lieut*[enant]* copy rolls. A splendid day. Had task for this P.M. of copying rolls. Had glass wine & piece pie 6c. Peaches 3c. Int*[roduced]* to Mrs. Tripp. Boys made fuss about cold meat bread and a kind of coffee for supper. Not on drill but with B.D. & had fun skedaddling a couple from a seat at table. Had pint of milk for dinner. Warm. Paid. Marked things 15c. Returned blouse. 26c. Wrote paper by order of Lieut*[enant]*.

Friday, 12th—Headache. Put on guard after drill & break. Ceremony of guard mounting. Received *[Brockport]* Repub*[lic]* with my letter published, read it while on guard duty; gave it to Lieut*[enant]*. Peaches from H*[enry C.]* Murray. Subscribed for white gloves. 12c. Had coat marked & paint taken from it. Rainy. Off post till 11. Man's jaw broken by being kicked. Nap after dinner. On duty from 3 till 5 & had work to keep people outside the beat. Mrs. Courtney & Mrs. Gordon of B*[rock]*port at dress parade with Mr. G. On g*[uar]*d 9 till 11. Colder.

Saturday, 13th—Duty from 3 to 5 A.M. Counter sign "Bull Run". No one run past No. 13. Asleep till after break. Bo't paper 3c. Also green cord for pants 6c. Disch*[ar]*g*[e]*d from guard. Paymaster came at 9½. Cold raw wind. Great excitement. At noon friends at dinner & little fixings, int*[roduced]* to Mrs. Parker. Brockport people in camp. Peaches 6c. Sent letter home by Mr. Davis. At 5 formed for pay & before 8 were mustered into U. S. service (two men refusing to swear were put into the guard h*[ouse]* & are to be transferred) Paid $25 Gov*[ernment]*. bounty & $50 state. I made an allotment of $9 monthly to mother. Scored names on roll as fast as paid. No pass to-night & no chance to eat till 9 then bo't quart milk 5c & gr*[ape]* pie 3c. To bed early. Rec*[eive]*d $75. Paid 22c.

Sunday 14th—Splendid day. Just right. Came near going by co[*mpany]* to city but stopped by officer of the day. Breakfast. Lots of the soldiers running the guard. Many people in camp. Man arrested for selling liquor & 4 women for bringing liquor into camp. On duty: viz. Friend *[Lewis B.]* Courtney gave his bride formerly El. Long into my charge while he was on guard; promenaded had lemonade, int[*roduced]* her to Capt[*ain]* & Lieut[*enant]*.—In cook room, &c. Bo't milk for supper 3c. In bed after being on bank. Had oysters[63] & pie. Paid 34c.

Monday, 15th—Detailed for guard & went on at 9. Nothing unusual till P.M. when we marched with 140th Reg[*imen]*t to Roch[*ester]* received colors. Marched about 5 miles in heavy rain. Rather disagreeable. Had glass lemon beer &c coat wet through & changed for overcoat; guard duty. Sup[*per]*. Bunk with C[*hauncey]* P[*arker]*. Out at 6 till 11 then & had fun with a fellow who tried to run guard. Drunk. Paid 12c.

Tuesday, 16th—Cloudy. Tried to get nap. Cramp in stomach at 5 A.M. *[illegible word]* Disch[*arge]*d from guard duty. Rich man here. Com[*mittee]* appointed to receive funds for rifle. Paid $30 for rifle to com[*mittee]*. Sent money belt by Ch[*arles]* Miller to bro[*ther]* Charley in 108th NYVI Reg[*imen]*t. Aunt B. & others in camp Mr. Barlow also; got furlough till 18th 12 P.M. & rode to R[*ochester]* with B. Bo't gilt buttons $1, got dinner for 2, 40c papers. Started in buggy at 1:40, stopped in S[*pencerport]* & in B[*rockport]* at 4½, after a pleasant ride with jolly driver. Father in st[*reet]* at home to supper, had buttons sewed on by sis[*ter Cordelia]*. Let F[*ather]* have $25 making $50 in all. Down st[*reet]*, int[*roduced]* to Miss Thompson, called at Miss Butler, at Mrs. S[*mith]*'s saw sickish Miss Julia Ch. & Miss Richmond, also at Mr. Smiths, the Misses S. & L. Bradford. Saw Em[*ma]* S[*mith]* & F. Moore also at *[illegible word]* then home. Paid $56.57.

Brockport Republic, September 18, 1862

Camp Porter, Sept. 16, 1862. Editor Republic—Saturday and Sunday last were eventful days in camp. The former was pay-day, so anxiously hailed by the men, most of whom received the state and Government bounties, excepting those who were obliged to wait until another pay-day, by previous order from Washington, not having enlisted within a certain time. Before being paid, the men were mustered in by a U.S. officer. Part of one company hesitated to take the mustering oath, (the same as the enlisting oath,) because they had not received all the bounties; in one company where every other man stood true, two foolish ones refusing to perform the ceremony, were ordered in double irons, and were since transferred to the regular U.S. service—an example to those few who *volunteer* more from love of of *bounty* than patriotic devotion to the Union. After being paid, an opportunity was given prudent "boys" to send from camp in the future to some relative or friend at home, a portion of monthly pay, easily spared in health. Many enrolled their names on the allotment papers and designated the person and address of the one to whom they wished the money entrusted. In this case the Government manifest a worthy benevolence; they give a check for the amount and ensure its safe transmission, and if the check is lost, another is given.

There was much "skedaddling" since pay-day, by those adventurous enough to run the guard rather than take a chance of going out under the regimental order which allows each company to issue but eight furloughs per day.

On Sunday the grounds are thronged, and the guard doubled. Camp presented a holiday appearance. Guard house full of prisoners, among whom were four "ladies," arrested for smuggling a contraband article called whiskey; two of these females had bottles nicely packed in a "baby cart". Liquor in outside eating tents was confiscated and tents closed.

On Monday afternoon all turned out and marched through mud and rain, to witness a banner presentation (which, after all, they could not "see") to the 140th. The presentation would have been more appropriate at camp.

Company pictures are fashionable, and Brockporters are this season making peaceful "war" excursions to the banks of the Genesee, and Camp Porter's patriotic attractions throw into the shade, for the present, Ontario's ancient but none the less pleasant grounds at Troughburgh [*Troutburg?*]. Friends of the rifle Sharpshooters are to give a social dinner on Saturday. Capt. Gray invites a general attendance at the festival. This company and the Rifle Battery stay in camp some time yet, the former waiting for rifles to be finished at Canandaigua.

After our fellow soldiers of the 140th have the order "onward," probably on Friday, the barracks vacated will partly be occupied by companies of cavalry.

Members of the 108th flank campanies, R[*ifle*] B[*attery*] and S[*harp*] S[*hooters*], should not be surprised if, in case the 108th should meet with a loss in action, they are called for immediately.

Wishing success to our agreeable brothers of the 140th—especially, those of Co. A.—please accept thanks of,

Yours, for the war, J.T.F.

Context—Union forces won the Battle of Antietam, first major Union victory in the East, on September 17.

Wednesday, 17th.—Fixed up; Down s[reet] & got 4 photographs, paid $1 for 6. Sewed cord on pants, &c. At 9 started with F[ather] to ride to the [Kendall] Mills. Stopped at Goodrich & took good dinner &c. Left photo. Called on almost all my friends & to see ladies picking lint at sch[ool]. house. Home at 5 & down st[reet] & talked with many. Saw Helen Somes [sp?] & Mary Parker. Home early & had good time. Paid $1.

Thursday 18th.—Wrote & set up letter at office. Rec[eive]d papers from Mrs. M. Called at [Horatio N.] Beach & Mrs. Parker, &c. Windy last night & to-day. After dinner went to bank & paid 38c on ins[urance]. Got 2 papers with my letter in [Brockport] Daily [Advertiser] office. Barber shop. A M[ary A. C. French]'s a short time. Met Miss Shepard; haircut at home; inv[ited] to Dr. Clark's by mischievous Miss Peeley. At depot saw boys going to camp; wrote to Lieut[enant]; saw boys on cars; F[ather] up with peaches; After supper down st[reet] after reading news, bo't candy 2cts. bo't ticket at R.R. depot to R[ochester]. 38c., almonds 13c; called at Dr. Clark's Miss Amelia & Eva Clark, Miss Alice Sealey & Miss Van Tine; first rate time, music &c Int[roduced] to Mrs. Dr. Clark & other lady. Time passed swiftly till 11 P.M. Letter, A.M., &c. Paid $1.39.

Friday, 19th.—At office got paper, about town 6c; Miss Aggie Johnson asked for photograph; home after read morn[ing] paper. Harvey arrived. Saw Rev[erend L. Clark. Haversack to depot for me & I left on 9:45 train, in co[mpany]. with Miss Mary [A. C.] French, also Mr. & Mrs. B. Randolph, all took carriage ($1) at R[ochester]. rode to camp, met the 140th marched on road, visited camp, lemonade 20c, & back to depot & in the rush bid good bye to soldiers; all had first-rate dinner & fun at Clinton Hotel 50c; walk about town, bo't swords 25c for Harvey & Eddy, & a ring for Mrs.. R[andolph], Misses [Mary A. C.] French, G., J. & sister 5c; bo't papers 6c. At hotel a while having a good visit; & went to see the folks on the 5:40 train. Saw Miss Happell a sister of Mrs. S[mith], & found a seat for her, got overcoat & stopped at Nation[al Hotel], gave Capt[ain] a B[rockport] paper, & rode to camp 25c with Lieut[enant] [Volney J.] Sh[ipman]. No guard. Boys agreeing to stay in camp unless passed out.—Bo't supper at sutlers & soon in bed; guard about barracks at night: Rec[eive]d $1 Paid $2.43. Cloudy in A.M. Pleasant in P.M. Warm.

Saturday, 20th.—At roll call appointed on table duty; served till 10 o'c[lock] & cleaned floor & tables for picnic. Cleaned self for the P.M. A fine day. Not quite so lively in camp. Great preparations for dinner, which was had at 3; waited on table; oysters & other meaties. Drill. Corporal Albert Adams died last night; Pair of white gloves. No regular supper. Had lots of dishes to wash.

Sunday 21st:—Breakfast earlier than usual, to attend funeral of 1st Corps A*[lbert]* Adams of our co*[mpany]*. who died of typhoid fever & taken to Churchville. (crape & white gloves) Tramped to depot & took cars at 7½. Saw Dr. Clark; soon in C*[hurchville]* at hotel; paid 62c R.R. fare; invited to parlor of Mr. Bangs & had peaches &c. Attended Bapt*[ist]* Ch*[urch]* & heard sermon from Rev*[erend]* Balcom, good dinner at J. Dunn's hotel 25c. Funeral at 3; escorted corpse; house crowded; ex-Col*[onel]* Fuller preached sermon from Tim*[othy]* & over 1,000 saw the corpse; the last duties were performed & A*[lbert]* A*[dams]* slept in his last earthly resting place. No supper, but a boy gave *[Sampson W.]* Fry⁶⁴ & I peaches. Arrived in camp at 9 after riding to R*[ochester]* & marching to the grounds in camp. Had pie cheese & cake; milk. Paid $1.04. A pleasant day, this.

Monday, 22d.—Not a cloud to mar the A.M. On table duty till 9. Table duty at noon, then at night; Laid down in P.M.—Two laughing ladies at opposite table. Wrote a pass by permission of Lieut*[enant]*. Two int. ladies on ground. Nothing unusual. Read eve. paper. Paid 10c almond.

Tuesday, 23d.—More fine weather. Elected head table waiter (awful) & had things through at 9½ A.M. Wrote letter to *[Brockport]* Repub*[lic]* 3c & home. Have lots of peaches. Most of Co*[mpany]* gone to attend funeral of a 13th *[NYVI Regiment]* boy. After dinner washed dishes & cleaned table alone & was visited by Miss Coo*[ley]*, Mrs. Douglas & daughter Francis⁶⁵. Had pass to Roch*[ester]* till 9 P.M. countersigned. Waited for the three ladies & at past 5½ we all went to R*[ochester]* in a farmer's buggy. At P.O., Mrs. D*[ouglas]* asking me to bring her home; had 15c soda; *[Sampson W.]* F*[ry]* had nose bleeding & we called at Osburn house rings at store. Left Mrs. C. & esc*[ort]* F*[ry]* home to 79 North st*[reet]*, *[illegible words]* went in, saw family pictures, &c. Inv*[ited]* to call again. Pleasant time. Half ap*[ple]* pie, cakes, glass milk on Main st*[reet]* all for 8c. Saw Geo*[rge]* Lewis. Bo't Union 2c. Reg*[istered]*. name at National *[Hotel]*. At depot, then walked to camp before 9. Paid 31c.

Wednesday, 24th.—Windy early. Drizzling rain. & detailed to supply table waiters; 4 now on table duty. 3 assistants. Everything settled at 9. Arranged bunk. Rain stopped just before noon, & we had a drill. Dinner passed without anything unusual. Drill at 3. Young lady of 22nd here again in all her vicious beauty. Ladies (one with straw hat & smiling countenance) here. Supper through in good season. Spoke for furlough to-morrow night. Day closes finely, tho' cold, frosty. Talk with H*[enry C.]* Murray, & we had boiled eggs, cake, In bed at 8½.

Brockport Republic, October 2, 1862

Camp Porter, Sept. 24, 1862. Editor Republic:—The 140th Regiment left this ground last Friday, escorted by military companies from Rochester, the city authorities, the Rifle Battery and the Sharpshooters, their camp associates. Friends were present to bid many, perhaps, a last adieu, and a parting grasp which all hoped will be renewed. The boys departed in good spirit, and as the long train left the depot, hearty cheers were replied to by the brave men nobly given by loved ones at home, to save the Union. Thus they go from us. May success attend their vigilance in duty.

The camp is not so dull and lonesome as might be supposed after sending out 1,000 men. Several companies of cavalry are quartered here; also a company recruited for Monroe's 13th; these together with the two 108th flank companies, sustain the reputation of this camp for activity.

The picnic given to the Sharpshooters on Saturday, was a hearty affair, shared in by the Battery boys, who furnished oysters for the festival. All the substantials and dainties considered necessary for such an occasion were poured upon the tables. Rare boquets were abundant, and the scene would have been a more merry one had not death just taken from our company its first Corporal. Most of those who furnished the dinner knew not this melancholy occurrence until they arrived on the ground. The kindness of our friends in thus making light, for a time, the duties of camp, then were and ever will be appreciated.

Last Sunday morning the Sharpshooters had a very early breakfast, marched to the depot and took cars to Churchville, to attend the funeral of Corporal Albert Adams, who died on the 19th inst., of typhoid fever, at the National Hotel in Rochester. On arriving at C[hurchville], the company, marching by the house where lay the body, uncovered, (saluted,) as they passed. Upon invitation from Rev. Mr. Balcome, (formerly a Lieut. Col. of State militia, now pastor of the Baptist church,) we listened to a sermon from him, which proved very appropriate, coming from one of his experience.

In the P.M. we attended the funeral of our departed comrade. Nearly 2,000 people there. The sermon was good, delivered by Rev. Col. Fuller, of Le Roy, after which the remains were escorted to the grave by his fellow soldiers. The last sad offices were performed, and the green sod covered out brother's clay. Sorrowful were the faces, and fearful were many eyes, as leaving the cemetery, the thought came up, "Who shall go next?"

Thanks are due to Mr. Bangs and others of pleasant Churchville, for hospitality to the Sharpshooters, who were pleased with the trip.

Here at camp there is nothing of unusual importance to-day. The boys are playing ball, writing to friends, and some are target shooting—others are in bunks reading or sleeping. No dullness here, and were it not for urgent calls from those now in the field we'd wish to stay near Genesee. Farmers are constantly supplying us with peaches and other nice fruit.

Ever holding in grateful remembrance kind Brockport friends,

I remain, Respectfully,

J.T.F.

Thursday, 25th.—Splendid weather. Table work done up at 8½; blanket shaken, no one to drill after guard detailed. Ball playing. Partly promised furlough today. After dinner, nap; blacked boots, saw Miss D. & made engagement to Theatre. Then after seeing target-shooting found a carriage for her to R[ochester] 25c. Supper & found substitute; cup milk 3c pass for self & K.M. till 29th; left in hurry, found carriage 10c, rode to R[ochester] to P.O. left coat at National, bo't almonds 12c, Bo't papers, called at Mr. D[ouglas]'s talked with Mrs. & Francis D[ouglas] & went with latter to Theatre 73c. Play of Female American Cousin[66] &c. Talked with Sornburger (pistol) & enjoyed play well. Out at 10½. Stopped at Howard's oysters 5c & wine 12c then saw F[rancis R. Douglas] home. Back to Nat[ional Hote]l & roomed at 38 with H[enry C.] M[urray][67]. Paid $1.83.

Friday, 26th.—Up at 5 paid 25c bill. Bo't Dem[ocrat] 3c On cars & rode to B[rockport] 27c. Splendid morn & so all day. Break[fast] at home. All well except Lon. Fixed up. F. came. Bo't meat. Paper at office. Called at Dr. [R. G.] L[owery]'s office. At the Fair in P.M. with Cordelia. 10c. Free pass. Not many people. Passable show. Saw many friends as usual. Watermelon 15c. Mrs. Court[ney] & Miss [Mary A. C.] F[rench] home to supper; Miss Raleigh. Called at M[ary A. C. French]'s. Paid 77c.

Saturday, 27th.—Read paper 3c. At [Brockport] Daily [Advertiser] office, fixed letter from A.O. At Mrs. S[mith]'s at dinner. Wrote to Capt[ain] Cutler 6c. Also to Capt[ain] Gray 6c, B[orrowe]d h[an]d[ker]c[hie]f of Mrs. S[mith]. Called at Miss [Mary A. C.] French's she Miss Searle & Mrs. Courtney there. Grand time left photo there. Music. F. at home. At depot found Lucy & Melissa Benedict who called at our house; found F. & a ride for L. Called at Miss [Aggie] Johnsons; not at home almonds. Home early & read paper. M's staid. Pleasant day. .

Sunday, 28th.—At depot P.O. & stable. Break[fas]t. Pres[byterian] Ch[urch]. With mother. Rev[erend] Kimball, front seat. Looked two hours for horses, found one & buggy at 2. $1.50. Took sister & M.R. to K[endall] Mills. Supper at B's. K. Murray & wife there. Rode to T[rout] Burgh with M. B. & saw Father a minute. Stroll on beach. Lake never so calm. Lemonade 17c. Then back to K[endall] M[ills]. Girls & boys at B's; Music. Staid till 10. Pleasant ride home with sis[ter]. Everything all right.—Hostler cheated me out of a quarter. Fine day. Very warm. P[ai]d $1.70.

Monday, 29th.—After break[fast] in the house till 8. Cloudy this A.M.—At the office, read Dem[ocrat] & at 8½ went to work on paper, fair premis [?]; quit at 11½, & at depot saw [Ezra] Hutson. In P.M. at work till 4½ altogether set 5,000 ems[68]; at 4:45 train. Some of the boys left; Father at supper & we went to P.O.; letter from Capt[ain] G[ray] & extension of furlough till Oct[ober] 2. Cal[le]d at Mr. French's; int[roduced] to 2 Mr. French's & Mrs. F. Illinois & Boston. To depot with them & Mrs. Courtney; on cars saw Lieut[enant Volney J.] S[hipman].—Back & home early. Rainy to-night.

Tuesday 30th.—Misty & cloudy. Wrote to Miss F[rancis] R. D[ouglas] 3c Rode to office with Father. At work most of the day. Called at Mrs. S[mith]'s a minute. Cold. Wore great coat. Harvey & Eddy brought [Rochester] Eve[ning] Ex[press]. Cordelia & I called at Mrs. French's & M[ary A. C. French]. Mrs. C. & we called at Miss [Aggie] Johnson. Left photo with Aggie &c. Saw Joe, who is dying with consumption.[69] Had a pleasant time till 9 P.M. P[ai]d 6c.

Wednesday. Oct. 1.—Still cloudy & rainy. In the office till noon. Have set altogether 12,500 ems at 20c, $2.50. Stove set up in office. Set up my letter written last week. Saw cousin H.P.R. at canal collector's office. Ready for Roch[ester]. After dinner worked a short time. Called at M[ary A. C. French]'s. Run to the 5 o'c[lock] train after supper. Got there 36c. Mr. Crabb on train promised to let me take his rifle. Saw Mr. [Horatio N.] Beach. Letter at P.O. from H.R. Called there & int[roduced] to F's sister; pre-engagement. Bro't Ex[press]. Saw Capt[ain]n G[ray] & Mrs. C. & agreed to meet him at 8 A.M. to-morrow. Roch[ester] to B[rockport] on 8:15 train, met Miss G. & Mrs. C. at Depot. Saw Mr. [Horatio N.] Beach at office & he wrote me letter to Capt[ain] G[ray]. Dr. Smith invited me to call at his house. Rather pleasant to-night. Home & had a bite at 10. P[ai]d 75c.

State Fair commenced 30th 4 days

Thursday, 2nd.—Willie C. & Wes. L. at our house & we went to Roch[ester] on 6:40 train 36 Capt[ain] & Lieut[enant] in parole belong in 28th [or 128th] NYV also others on train. Delivered letter to Capt[ain] G[ray] & he gave me furlough to 4th. In Union office saw press work with Hipman. Wrote to H[oratio] N. B[each] & Mr. Crabb. Left overcoat at Nat[iona]l [Hotel]. Miss Raleigh at Depot. Then to Kent st[reet] & called on Mary Renine [sp?] No 12c Dinner 38c. Roch[ester]. To State Fair 15c paid 25c to go into grounds. Saw many fine articles & many people. Miss M. Adams, Miss Steves & int[roduced *to]* Miss Crouch. Rode to Roch*[ester]* after waiting for ride (before this had ice cream & cake 29c saw ex-mayor Long John Wentworth of Chicago[70]. Hurried to find Miss S. but forgot number of house. Tho' found it at last 19 Howell st[ree]t Mr. Crouch's. Mrs. S*[mith]* & daughter to theatre; crowded. Poor plays . Out at 11 & had room 38c at hotel on S*[outh]* St. Paul st*[reet]*. Pleasant latter part of P.M. P*[ai]*d $3.33.

Friday, 3d.—Up at 6, too late to take 1st train. Overcoat at Nat*[iona]*l Hotel. Bo't Dem*[ocrat]* 3c. At depot ticket 36c—read on train for B*[rockport]*. Saw wounded Col*[onel]* Butler of 6th Wis*[consin VI Regiment]*. In Bat*[talion]* 8.17 *[?]*. break*[fas]*t at home; *[Sampson W.]* F*[ry]* there. At work in office till 5½ P.M. Sent paper to Aunt C. Mrs. M., Miss F*[rancis]*R. D*[ouglas]*, Mr. Bangs. Supper at Mrs. S*[mith]*'s Miss Shepard there at depot; down st*[reet]* & left S. called at Miss *[Mary A. C.]* F*[rench]*'s not at home. Then on Miss Colden a few minutes; home & had peaches ind. bread & cake. Not a pleasant day, but very warm. Paid 42c.

Saturday, 4th.—In office & set 2000 ems making 6000 ems yesterday & to-day. Altogether making $3.70. Read Dem*[ocrat]* at *[Brockport]* Daily *[Advertiser]* office. Home. Rainy this morning. After dinner called at Dr. Smith's & was shown over the well furnished house. Had boot mended. Supper & Cordelia 2 tickets went to depot 4:45 saw F. Mrs. Courtney & Miss *[Mary A. C.]* F*[rench]* bid me good bye at depot. Mrs. & Jane Parker in cars. Boys at depot In R*[ochester]* left coat in Nat*[iona]*l. Called at 79 N*[orth St.]* & saw H. Beals, printer. At 19th *[illegible word]* No one at home. Went to camp with 3 boys at 8½ P.M. Paper to Lieut*[enant]*. Very windy to-day. In bed early.

Sunday, 5th.– On table duty for break*[fast]*. Marched to funeral of Maj*[or George B.]* Force, 108th *[NYVI Regiment]* then to Mt. Hope & back in all 6 miles. Double quick. In city saw Nel*[son]*. Borodaile. (19 al) Had oysters, &c 15c At supper had milk. On guard at 5. Girls in barracks. Pleasant evening to be on guard. Moonlight but cold. Paid 18c.

Monday, 6th.– Up at 1 A.M. till 3 on guard then off till 7 on till 9. Shot at target with 1 inch from rim. After dinner heard song by Jerry Tillotson, formerly held by rebels in Alabama. (Mobile) Drill in skirmishings from 2 till 5. Saw Album of the Nel*[son]* Boroda*[ile]* & after supper tried to get furlough to Brockport, but no go. Bo't papers. Windy & rainy tonight. In bunk read news, & to bed early.

Tuesday, 7th..—Rainy A.M. No furlough. Telescope. Fired at target. Nap from 11 till 1. Dinner. Drill in P.M. Skirmishing. Passed guard by P. & went by canal to N*[elson]* B*[órodaile]*'s made short call. Int*[roduced]* to B. Morgan, serg*[ean]*t in 13th *[NYVI Regiment]*. Very good time. Back safely at 10 ½. Fine day. Windy.

Wednesday, 8th.—Had a run about 1 A.M. Late breakf*[as]*t. Another fine day. Fired at target. Misses D. here int*[roduced]* to Miss Case 13 Rome. Fine picnic with R. Battery. Parade, grapes & shot. Saw men on guard in west. Warm. Walk about the guard. In bed early after visiting sutler's. Paid 20c.

Thursday, 9th.—Cloudy & little rain, warm & spring like. Nothing unusual. Less lively in camp. Officers mostly away. Drill by *[Ezra]* Hutson. Toothache like fury. After supper read. Pass to Roch*[ester]*. Till 8 10th. Left overcoat at Nat*[iona]*l Hotel. Oil of cloves for tooth. Bo't tickets to Theatre, called at 19 Alex*[ander St.]* & to T*[heater]* with Bd B'e. Play of "Extremes", Mr. & Mrs. Richings. Good play & singing. Alarm of fire. Out at 11:20. Pie & lemonade; bed at Nat*[iona]l Hotel]* 25c Pd $1.09. Rains.

Friday, 10th.—Up at 6. Called at dentist. Dem*[ocrat]* 3c Walk to camp in time for breakfast; milk; 2c drill; face swelled from toothache. Letter from bro*[ther]* C*[harles]* & Mother. At dinner got furlough to B*[rockport]*. Rode to Roch*[ester]* & walked about. Had peaches pie, peanuts, lemonade, &c. Saw Hoe's cylinder press[71], printing 10,000 per hour; Union office, Also folding machine at Const. Saw Capt*[ain]* G*[ray]*. Saw lady looking for husband eloped. On 5:40 train to B*[rockport]* with Capt*[ain]* Mc T. Routson *[sp?]* Awful pain in jaws. Supper at home; at Dr. Smith's office got powder gratis & liquid for ulcer in tooth. At old boarding place a few minutes. Home & had face done up. This has been a rainy day. Paid 21c.

Saturday, 11th.—Face very much swelled; waiting for Father; wrote to Bella B. 3c at P.O. & *[Brockport]* Repub*[lic]* office. Beach wrote to Lieut*[enant Volney J.]* S*[hipman]* to have my furl*[ough]* ext*[ende]*d & I took it to depot for Roch*[ester]*. At house & laid down. Almost crazy with toothache. At two dentists but found no one. Father came at 5 & pulled it. Felt so much better that I called on Miss *[Mary A. C.]* French borrowed "Life among the Pines" by Edmund *[Kirke]*[72] A good book. Paper at P.O. Dark & rainy. Home early.

Sunday, 12th.—Attended M*[ethodist]* E*[piscopal]* church with Harvey after going to 8 o'c*[lock]* train & taking cup coffee at Mrs. S*[mith]*'s. Rev*[erend]* Wentw*[ort]*h Called at Geo*[rge]* Parker's at Pres*[byterian]* Ch*[urch]*. With Eddy in P.M. Read "Life in Pines" In eve. went to Mrs. S*[mith]*'s with sister then to S*[unday]* S*[chool]* concert at Pres*[byterian Church]*. Home early.

Monday, 13th.—Finished reading "Pines" At office & worked 2 hours. Rather a pleasant day. Mr. B*[each]* rec*[eive]*d letter from Lieut*[enant]* Sh*[ipman]* extending my furlough—Returned book to Miss *[Mary A. C.]* French. Saw letter from A*[ndrew]* Boyd,[73] 108th *[NYVI Regiment]* at A*[ggie]* J*[ohnson]*. Family at prayers.

Tuesday, 14th.—Promised to work to-day & do so. At night have 7500 ems altogether $5.17. Ambrotype[74] taken for father & lent him 75c change. A very pleasant day. Saw H*[enry C.]* Murray & the S*[harp]* S*[hooters]*. After sup*[per]* bo't almonds, called at office, then to Dr. Clark's house. Misses Am. E. & Al. S. had another very pleasant time; music, autographs, almonds, albums, &c. Very dark night, P*[ai]*d 88c.

Wednesday 15th.—Wrote to L*[ieutenan]*t Sh*[ipman]* & correspondence at office. *[Horatio N.]* B*[each]* paid me $5.15. At *[Brockport]* Daily *[Advertiser]*. Promised rifle to practice. Bo't powder ½ lb. 25c. lead 2 lbs 12c box caps &c. Couldn't find rifle. Home & had lemonade. Called on Charley B*[ar]*kly. After dinner rode to Clarkson & near there met cousin H*[enry C. Murray]* with buggy & rode with him to his house. Mike Judd there also. Intr*[oduced]* to Miss Isabella McMahon, music teacher from Lima. Heard good playing on melodeon[75] & singing. After sup*[per]* H*[enry]* & I with the girls drove to B*[rockport]* to Old Folks concert 50c Long had C*[?]* After that all called at home; found company there. Then called at D's. Fine moonlight ride driving back to R's. horses scared & whip played by Isa. P*[ai]*d 93c Rec*[eive]*d $5.15.

Thursday, 16th.—Wakened by music & heard more by Isa. M. Grapes for break*[fas]*t, then the girls went home. Read &c. Bread & milk. Grapes for home. Henry took me to B*[rockport]*. Got rifle. Run bullets. Gun lock gave out after firing three times. Rode to Main st*[reet]* with H*[enry C. Murray]* & left him. Boot mended 10c. almonds 6c. Home to sup*[per]*. Ready & called at Dr. Clark's accom*[panied]* Am. to Old folks concert 45c. Very good. Fun with Mrs. King. "Axes grind". Out early. Dark, & a little rain, today. Pd 61c.

Friday, 17th.—Went before break*[fas]*t to see Gordon of 13th *[NYVI]* reg*[imen]*t who called to see me last eve. now on his way to Wash*[ington]*. Did not find him. Home to break*[fas]*t. A pleasant day. Wrote to Aunt C. 3c. Saw R.J. Gordon at depot. Acted as p*[all]* bearer at funeral of little Edith Stafford. Stephen (Lieut*[enant]*) *[Stafford]*[76] in 129th *[NYVI Regiment]* came. Prof*[essor]* Williams preached good sermon from Psalms 23.4. After dinner called at Mr. Pease's. Saw M.A. Adams in buggy. At *[Brockport]* Daily *[Advertiser]* office. Mrs. Richards at our house. Father came up. Mother went with him to *[Kendall]* Mills. Cordelia did an errand for me at Am. C.'s. Called at Miss A*[ggie]* J*[ohnson]*'s grapes & a pleasant time.

Saturday, 18th—Reading till 9. Called at Mary *[A. C.]* F*[rench]*'s & made arrangements for to-morrow eve. Read Dem*[ocrat]*. Bo't almonds ¼ lb. Engaged horse & buggy $1.25 for P.M. At Dr. C.'s office haircut 13c at Mrs. S*[mith]*'s. Home to dinner. Got livery at 12½ . Sister & I called for Miss Am. C.'s; while waiting took Alice S. around the square. Drove to Uncle R.'s grapes & waited for Cous*[in]* H*[enry C. Murray]*; left sister drove to Mr. Royces near Parma Corners. Int*[roduced]*. to Mrs. Royce on to Mr. Clarks; int*[roduced]* to Mrs. C. & Miss Rall; also Mr. C. Henry Brockway put out horse & we staid to supper, pleased with the people. Miss R. rode with us to Mr. Judd's. Miss McM. there; sister & H*[enry C. Murray]* came, we could not get rid of another supper & afterwards had a splendid time; music, piano, melodeon and vocal; fortune telling, &c. after staying late we started homeward, stopped to warm by fire, kindly by the good Mrs. Clark, went on to Uncle R.'s, sister then rode with us home where we all arrived safely after enjoying hugely a splendid visit or visits on a day never more pleasant & lovely. Long will it live in memory. P*[ai]*d $1.45.

Sunday, 19th.—Cloudy & Fall like. In the house all the A.M. reading. In P.M. at Mrs. S*[mith]* a family gathering—Dr. S*[mith]* Mr. Hubbard Mr. Ryer &c. Rec*[eive]*d letter from Gordon at Albany. Had grapes at home till 6. With Miss M*[ary A. C.]* F*[rench]* called for Miss G. & went to Miss *[Aggie]* Johnson's where we had a pleasant time. Windy & cold. Pleasant in P.M.

Monday 20th.—Raw cold. Wrote to Bro*[ther]* Charley & Andrew Boyd. Bo't 25c worth of stamps. Rec*[eive]*'d letter from "Canary" & ans*[wer]* it. After supper called at Chester Van Tine's. Home early. Father up today & paid me 75c bor*[rowe]*d. Saw Mr. Crabb's *[illegible word]* at Mr. Smith's. Rec*[eive]*d 75c. P*[ai]*d 23c.

Tuesday, 21st.—Worked in office part of the day. Rode to Clarkson at noon. Wrote to Henry R. 3c. Back at 2½ & worked till 5, rode in livery to get Cous*[in]* H.P.R. eat supper & brought H. back at 7½. Bo't almonds 25c. Expected company but they did not come. H. & I went to the depot &c. Saw light of barn burning in Adams Basin. Lots of fun. Rec*[eive]*d letter & paper from Aunt C. Rain & looks like a heavy storm. P*[ai]*d $1.

Wednesday, 22nd .—Bo't Dem*[ocrat]*, & went to work at 9 till 12.—Dark & gloomy. Congressional convention in Brockport.[77] Attended & saw a regular Tammany Hall row. Helped Father put up two stoves. Rain. At P.O.

& attended speech by Lawyer Hyde of Rochester. Rec*[eive]*d letter from "Canary". Home read news aloud.

Thursday, 23d.—In the office at work from 7 till 11. Set over 3000 ems in all 10,000; $2. At P.O. Home & wrote to R.J. Gordon. Pleasant awhile then cloudy. Cold. Rode to Clarkson & listened to the laughable testimony of a witness in a petty trespass suit case. Walked home. Fired at target with Smith with his five barreled Colt rifle,[78] made some good shots but S*[mith]* rather beat me. Rode with Henry P.R. a short distance & with Miss*[Mary A. C.]* French called at several places & found no one. Then at Mr. Butler's found Miss A*[ggie]* J*[ohnson]* Miss Stule *[sp?]* & Mrs. B. Packard; went with A*[ggie]* J*[ohnson]* to Mr. Boyd's to borrow corn popper read letter from A.B. Popped corn & found Mr. Steele & Miss *[Emma]* Smith; we all went to depot to see the 151st (Lockport) reg*[imen]*t pass; too early; saw Miss N. Seaves also Miss & Mrs. Steves. All walked back, I to Mr. *[Horatio N.]* B*[each]*'s with A*[ggie]* J*[ohnson]* then back to N.S.'s heard letter & saw M*[ary A. C.]* F*[rench]* home. Thus passed a pleasant eve. & a fine starlight. On the way home heard train & went to the depot found Henry Fuller of the Battery, Capt*[ain]* Anthony, & bid him good bye.

Friday, 24th.—At work most of the day. Set 6,000 ems, $1.20. In all, $3.20. Wrote to Lieut*[enant]* Sh*[ipman]*. Father up. After supper down st*[reet]* got paper & called to see soldier B*[enjamin]* C. Davis just from camp. All of the boys off till 28th.—Home & found the Clark girls & Seeley. Very glad to see them & passed the evening very pleasantly. Gave the girls their albums & saw them home. Heavy rain to-night. Double quick home.

Saturday, 25th.—Rainy morning.—At work from 9 till 12, after reading the news at home. Rec*[eive]*d furlough. Called at Miss *[Mary A. C.]* French's to make arrangements for Monday night. Met Cha*[u]*n*[cey]* P*[arker]*. with a new telescope rifle. After dinner got ready to go to Parma. Fired at target short distance with telescope rifle after running bullets. Made the best shot & hit the bull's eye. Rode to Clarkson. Saw Henry R. Almost a fight with a rabid young democrat. Rode to B*[rockport]* with H*[enry C. Murray]*. Bo't can oysters 50c., also paper 6c. Home to supper & after bo't oil can for G. Bo't crackers 16c. Home early. Snow storm to-night. P*[ai]*d 72c.

Sunday, 26th.—Snow quite deep in A.M. & continued all day.—At the office & set 3,000 ems. At Mrs. S*[mith]*'s had some good pumpkin pie. Saw a nice boquet picked from the snow. Oysters for supper. B. C. Davis & sister here. At M*[ethodist]* E*[piscopal]* Church with Lon. No one there. Then called at M*[ary A. C.]* F*[rench]*'s & found Mary] & Nell S. there. N*[ell]* writing letters to soldiers. Had a good time, peaches & grapes. Poetry &c. On way home heard branches breaking from trees, being so loaded with damp snow, branches hanging so low on sidewalk that one can hardly pass. Snow enough has fallen to make good sleighing if ground was frozen. Wrote note to A[ggie] J[ohnson].

Great snow storm

Monday, 27th.—Snow fell until 5 this A.M.—34 hours altogether. Mailed paper to [brother] Charley. At work most of the day. 26,000 in all. Mr. [Horatio N.] B[each] paid me $5.20. Invited C[hester] V[an Tine] & sister to Mary [A. C.] F[rench]'s. Bot almonds, candy &c. At depot 4.50. Saw Mary G'n, also M[ar]y P[eas]e. At home to tea. Ready for party. At P.O. engaged carriage. At Dr. C[lark]'s & in carriage took A.E.H. to M[ary A. C.] F[rench]'s 25c. Bro't Cordelia there also. After having a very agreeable time. Cousin H.P.R. & Mary J[ud]d came. Present also Misses G'n J[ohnso]n S[mith]'s & C[lar]k & Chester Van Tine disch[ar]g[e]d from 13th NYIV wounded. Never had a much better time. Wine, grapes, peaches, almonds, candy, music & home with the fair feminines thro' the snow. Rec[eive]d $5.20. P[ai]d 61c.

Tuesday, 28th.—Cold & cloudy look like snow. In the house busy till 10 o'c[lock]. Note to A.E.C. Called at Mrs. S[mith]'s. Dr. S[mith]. there. Wrote notice of marriage of Miss Janette Chappell & Mr. John Hubbard; No [Brockport] Daily [Advertiser] office set up. Notice of same for publication. Rode to Clarkson. Saw any quantity of liquor going down the throats of a bar-room crowd. Rode back [honey] & stopped at Dr. C[lark]'s & put off the arrangement for to-night. At [Brockport] Daily [Advertiser] office sent paper to Lieut[enant] Sh[ipman] & wrote to H.P.R. 10c. Tea at Mrs. S[mith]'s. Gse'd [?] Em[ma] S[mith] & Frank Rich'd to F[rench]'s then got letter for sister & home early. Read papers. Dismal day. Not much if any yet till last night. Leaves yet on the trees & robins still here & other birds. P[ai]d 13c.

Wednesday, 29th.—Sun shines today. Very muddy. Snow disappearing. Read morning paper at home till 10 o'c[lock]. Made arrangements for going to Parma. Called at M[ar]y [A. C.] French's & she agreed to go. Engaged horse & buggy $1.20 Bo't nuts &c. 11c. At the [Brockport] Daily [Advertiser] office. Home. Invited to dinner at Mrs. S[mith]'s. Accepted & had nice sweet potatoes. At livery stable got rig;—"hollow back". With Mary [A. C.] F[rench] stopped for Am. C[lar]k then with a rush we all started on our pleasure excursion "in the mud", tho' the sky was clear & the air nice—mild & spring like. At Uncle R.'s agreed to be back in a short time & went on to Parma. Saw Uncle Jonah's folks. Stopped at Mr. Royce's & was int[roduced] to Miss E. Royce, also Mr. Clark R. In co[mpany]. with them started for Spencerport to the Teacher's

Institute horse balked or refused to go on for 15 minutes & then would go on only by backing him first. Put him through & got to S*[pencerport]* about 3 minutes after they did; watered horse & drove back to Mr. R.'s to tea, after being int*[roduced]* to Miss Connie R. All left at 6½, horse again refusing to move till he was smartly backed, then "O.K." At Uncle Randall's put out horse & staid the eve*[nin]*g. Henry & Miss Mary J*[ud]*d there, also visited with Aunt P. & Uncle H. Walter & Stell baby. Very pleasant. Agreeable ride home discussed pea-nuts & muff. Mary *[A. C. French]* kindly driving. Home all right after waiting for the old hostler to dress. P*[ai]*d $1.37.

Thursday, 30th.—Morning opened pleasant, then cloudy. Not very cold. Read the morning news, Had nap from 10 till 12. At *[William H.H.]* Smith's daily *[Brockport Daily Advertiser]* office & got paper . Called at Dr. Smith's; had currant wine, grapes & saw almonds raised on the D*[octo]*r's place. On farm saw fish-pond, &c. In eve. called at Mrs. S*[mith]*'s for Cordelia.

Friday, 31st.—About 8 o'clock went to work in the office. Worked ½ day. In P.M. from 2 till 4 attended reading of composition & declamation at Brockport Collegiate Institute. Aunt P. & Cous*[in]* H. were here at tea. Rec*[eive]*d letter from Capt*[ain]* Gray. At Miss *[Mary A. C.]* F*[rench]*'s, Clark & with A*[ggie]* J*[ohnson]* & M*[ary A. C.]* F*[rench]* to Nettie Searles. Home early. Fine day.

November 1862

Saturday, Nov. 1.—Worked in office from 7 A.M. till 4:30 P.M. Set (cast) in all 5,000 $1.60. Wrote to Capt*[ain]* G*[ray]*. A fine day. At 4:15 rode to Clarkson & most of the way from there to Uncle R.'s. After supper H & I walked to Uncle Allen's & staid the evening. Back. A splendid evening & has been a nice day.

Sunday, 2d.—After break*[fast]* & riding horse a few steps had lunch at noon, then H*[enry C. Murray]* & I rode to Uncle *[Albert]* Allen's got grapes, drove to Parma Corners. Had wine. Drove to Judd's found Izzie McMahon & Mary Judd. After supper all rode to Parma to church. After that had a ride home in the pleasant moonlight. A few minutes after we got back to J*[udd]*'s a storm of rain broke out. Had music & rather late went back to Randall's. Another lovely day. P*[ai]*d 10c.

Monday, 3d.—Slept till 10. Breakfast & rode most of the way to Brockport. Stopped to make arrangements for this eve. but some circumstances in the way. At the boarding place called at M*[ary A. C.]* F*[rench]*'s home read the news & wrote. A cold raw wind to-day. Cloudy. Looked for cousin H*[enry*

C. *Murray]* but he did not come till 9, with Miss McM. & Mary J*[udd]*. staid only a short time. Cold & windy to-night.

Tuesday, 4th.—State Election. & for a wonder a pleasant day. In the office from 7 A.M till 4 P.M. Set 6½ thousand altogether, making 14,335 ems $2.86. Posted letter for Izzie McM*[ahon]* After getting thro' work at 4, went to old place & plagued Em*[ma]* S*[mith]* a while. Then called at Davis. Home to supper. With Cordelia to P.O. & got paper. At French's & with Mary called at Am. C*[lar]*k's a few minutes & had pleasant moonlight walk. Home & had glass cider.

Context—Lincoln replaced McClellan by Burnside as commander of the Army of the Potomac on November 5.

Wednesday, 5th.—Rather a pleasant morning for Nov*[ember]*. tho' cold. Put on my camp trip*[?]* & made to leave for Camp Porter. Sent papers to Charley at the office of the *[Brockp[ort]* Repub*[lic]* & *[Brockport Daily]* Adv*[ertiser]*. Bo't stamps 10c. Had $10 bill changed. Took leave of folks at home. Lon gave me a neck tie. At depot saw several friends. Rode free to Roch*[ester]*. with boys of the co*[mpany]* who came up to vote. Sat in seats with two ladies. ... At Rochester with Cha*[u]*n*[cey]* P*[arker]*. went to several photograph galleries & at last found & ordered photograph of Capt*[ain]* Gray & lady.... Walked with C*[hauncey]* P*[arker]* to camp, got there, had cheers & just in time for dinner. Fired at target. Read letter from Aunt C. & ans*[were]*d it, sending by J. C*[hauncey]* P*[arker]*. On guard from 3 till 5. Any number of men run the guard & lots of whiskey drank. Supper by the lights. A co*[mpany]* of cavalry left for Washington in the eve. Boys talking politics around the coal stove in the barracks. Storm of rain to-night. This has been a pleasant day.

Thursday, 6th—Quite a pleasant day. Two of our boys in camp drunk. Tried to get a daily but could not. Boys in the eve. Telling stories around the stove. Colder this eve....

Friday, 7th—Heavy wind and cold, the wind has a full speech about the camp. All huddled around the stove. Gave 10 cts. towards buying soap. Appointed head waiter at noon. Bo't apples & cider 7c. Just after dinner Mrs. D's came in buggy & I drove to R*[ochester]* with her. Cold. Called on Mike Doug's & Miss B's. Had *[illegible word]* pie on treat. Paper from P. At P.O. At Mr. Delano's but did not go in. Walked back to camp after buying photograph of Capt*[ain]* Gray & wife. 13c. Back just as supper was eaten & helped clear off table. Candle & read papers having bo't *[Rochester Evening]* Ex*[press]* 2c. Coldest day of the season. Cold & biting to-night.

Saturday, 8th.—Snow fell last night 3 or 4 inches deep, but the weather is more mild than yesterday. Swept snow from eating room & after break*[fas]*t helped clear off table, &c. Had permission to go to K. & C. J. *[illegible name]* & I walked to the city. Bo't ticket for concert to *[illegible word]* horse & saddle, took two bottles of liniment. Bo't paper 3c. Saw list *[illegible words]* depot the *[illegible word]* rather surrounded one. Then H*[enry C.]* M*[urray]* & I walked to his mother's by canal, had supper then walked to Spencerport, mostly by R.R. Got to S*[pencerport]* at 5:30 P.M. I had bo't ticket to S*[pencerport]*. from R*[ochester]*. & we got on 6 o'c*[lock]* train & I rode on that ticket to B*[rockport]*. Supper at home & changed wet stockings. Go in the eve.*[illegible word]* at M. D.'s. Splendid moonlight. Very pleasant day.

Sunday, 9th.—A raw, cold day. At Pres*[byterian]*. Ch*[urch]* with mother. At home till 5, at old boarding place. At M*[ary A. C.]* F*[rench]*'s with Em*[ma]* S*[mith]* at J. Hub's grapes & apples.—Home early. To-day wrote a camp letter.

Monday, 10th.—At the Post office heard of McClellan being removed, & Burnside substituted.—At P*[rintin]*g office set up com*[position]*. In all 15,500 ems $5.30. At Mrs. S*[mith]*'s to dinner. Heard there was a regular stampede after me by Lieut*[enant]* Shipman & a small army. Saw F*[ather]* at 6. At Mr. *[Horatio N.]* Beach's. Cordelia & I called at Dr. Cl*[ar]*'ks & spent a pleasant evening. Em V.Y. there. Music as usual. Pleasant most of the day.

Tuesday, 11th.—Up early & break*[fast]*. Bid all good by & took 6:10 train to Roch*[ester]*. 36c after getting 3. In Roch*[ester]* wrote to Aunt C. Bo't Dem*[ocrat]* 3c. Registered my name at National *[Hotel]*. At the camp all right. Paid $1 expenses. Read papers in the bar racks. Fiddling & card-playing there. Rather a dark day.

Brockport Republic, November 13, 1862

Camp Porter, Rochester, Nov. 11, 1862. Editor Republic.—It is some time since I informed you of the dullness and monotony of soldier life here. The companies of 8th cavalry for a time quartered with us, are here no longer, and the frequent order, "Right turn," which we so often heard at drill, is now given in the vicinity of Baltimore. The last company, Capt. Smith's, (formerly Barry's,) were escorted to the Genesee Valley depot on Friday last, en route to a milder climate.

The only companies now here are the Rifle Battery and Sharpshooters, and I am sorry to inform you that these companies no longer consider themselves attached to the 108th, for an official dispatch informs us that, in some manner as mysterious as many other inexplicable government moves, we are *transferred*, not entirely out of the service, but to an unformed regiment (!) of Sharpshooters to be raised in this state for nine months, and that we are, probably this week, to be removed to winter quarters or rendezvous, on Staten Island, near New York City.

We all enlisted intending to join the 108th, and of course are disappointed. It is useless to grumble, and we quietly submit to "powers that be," and go to the field of "oysters and clams near the Jersey shore." If we have the good fortune to comfortably quarter for the winter in this State instead of camping amid the howlings of war on the bloody field, our feelings and sympathies for friends in that regiment, while *they* may be doing the hard work, will be none the less because we are not with them—for we shall eagerly watch for tidings of valorous deeds performed by those so closely endeared to us. What will become of our red-trimmed Battery brothers I cannot say.

"Our rifles" are progressing, so we are told—the only trouble is in procuring good lenses for the telescopes.

After bidding farewell to Camp Porter, the recollection of its many pleasant three months associations will live long in our memories, and in after time, should we return, a visit to Fitz John's once lively and warlike camping-ground will be gladly made, as, while enjoying the silent loveliness of its adjacent landscape, we think of some comrade given up to a glorious battle-death, a victim to the *Confederate's treasonable ambition*.

Should Staten Island or "any other" place, be our destination, Mr. Editor, I shall not forget the Republic and its readers, but will endeavor to keep you posted upon matters in the locality of the transferred Sharpshooters, for there is now no prospect of our being allowed to damage the rebel cause this winter. But "Little Mac" has served *his* time of "masterly inactivity," and we patiently await the sure *Burn*-ing of not only the rebels *side*, but their very hearts and substance.

In the meantime allow me to remain,

Yours truly,   J.T.F.

Wednesday, 12th.—Up very early on. Rather a sudden call. Rain early & the latter part of day pleasanter & mild. Detailed on table duty. Packed knapsack. Our new major, *[William S.]* Rowland, inspected us & ordered to be ready to march early to-morrow for Wehawken, N.J. Partly agreed to let my pay for 2 mo[nth]s partly apply towards pay in bal[ance] $13.00 on telescope rifle. Just after dinner took boots to Roch[ester] & left them for Father at Kings d[ru]gstore 96 Buff[alo Road] & now have Gov[ernment]t shoes. Wrote home. Called at Mr. Douglas & bid the girls good bye.....

Thursday, 13th.–Cloudy & cold in the A.M. & warmer in P.M.—Everything made ready for a march. Father came up & bid me good by. Also Mr. Johnson.

Sent cap. figures home. Rec[eive]d 2 days rations & at 4½ o'clock bid adieu to & started from camp Porter, esc[orte]d by R. Battery. At depot saw Father & gave him bottle &c. Bid adieu to Misses Douglas also sev[era]l others. Started at 6:30 & at Canandaigua—7:45 changed cars to Elmira 11 p.m. & then on same cars on N.Y. & Erie riding all night, but everything looked dreary.

Friday, 14th.—Rode all night. Early we saw Susquehanna River & later the Delaware & canal, high, rocky hills, &c. Thro' Port Jervis (Point St. Peter) 7:00 Goshen, Orange Co[unty]. 8:35 A.M. Patterson, N.J. 10:20 here a woman waved a flag. Passaic 10:30, here saw schooners on river. Extensive hay fields in Jersey. Bergen. Slaughter house. Great tunnel 7/8 of a mile long. At Jersey City took ferry boat (Niagara) to N[ew] Y[ork] City 11:30 A.M. Met Col[onel] W[illiam] S. Rowland at N[ew] Y[ork] dock. Marched to White st., stopped ½ hour, passed around the monument to Gen[eral] Worth to pier at foot of 42nd st[reet] took ferry to Weehawken, where we arrived in camp at Palisade Park, on the top of hill on the Jersey shore, at about 4 P.M. Got ready to sleep on floor of hotel upstairs, & eat of Camp P. rations. Commenced writing home. In bed early.

Saturday, 15th.—Up at 5 o'clock & finished writing letter home, after *[illegible word]* mail carrier, & sent letter by him. Picked walnuts in grove over Hudson river, after rations. Pitched tents then laid on rocks upon river bank & looked at vessels in N[ew] Y[ork] Bay, seeming like forest of masts. Saw iron clad Monitor[79] & many other interesting things from this romantic spot. Filled straw tick with leaves for sleeping. No rations dealt out here till late after we had all waited about dark, when we got coffee bread & cheese. Roll call, then bunked in, 5 of us in one tent. Change of weather to colder. This has been a very pleasant one.

Sunday, 16th.—Cold as fury & windy. Up at roll call, 6. Commissary dealing out rations, & cooks appointed for cooking break[fas]t, which we had at 8½ o'c[lock]. consisting of coffee, bad, steak, & hard bread. Shooting on grounds. Some flakes of snow. Ticks filled with straw. Commenced writing. Visited by the Col[onel] who is to take our letters over to-day. Beaching at 2 by McDougal of our co[mpany]. Wrote to [Brockport] Republic also to M[ar]y [A. C.] F[renc] h. A good meal at 3½ P.M. Coffee, soup & crackers. In eve. sat in eating room alone reading. Had a walk on the platform in front of house. In tent early (8). Weather milder. Bro[ther] Charley died in hospital at Warrenton, Va., today.

Brockport Republic, November 20, 1862

Camp of Instruction, Weehawken, New Jersey, Nov. 17, 1862. Editor Republic—Capt. Gray's Sharpshooters, Co. A. of 1st Regiment N.Y.S

Sharpshooters, Col. W. S. Rowland, left Camp Porter, Rochester, on Thursday, 13th, at 6:30 P.M., after being escorted to the Central depot by Mack's Rifle Battery.—After parting with friends at the depot, we started for the above camp via New York Central Railroad. This journey could hardly be called a pleasure excursion, for most of it was made under cover of night. We changed cars but once, and that at Canandaigua, and at Elmira, came upon the New York & Erie railroad track. In the darkness everything looked bleak and much of the way appeared swampy. Nothing unusual happened and sleep would have been enjoyed but for the continual bouncing and jerking of the cars over the rough way, but the boys were merry and light enough to pass the time happily.

After two or three hours sleep, your correspondent awoke early and found that we were passing the Susquehanna river, an occasional glimpse of which could be obtained in the dim moon and starlight through the engine smoke. We next came alongside the Delaware river (much like the Genesee,) and the adjoining canal. For a long distance only a few feet separate the former from the canal, which in many places is walled with stone. As for rocks, the numerous lofty hills on the route are walled with them, and present a very stony aspect. Houses in the hilly region must be built upon a solid foundation—many are certainly backed with granite; in one place trees appeared to have sprung from the hard substance. We passed many pleasant villages: Port Jervis, under a mountain called Point St. Peter; Goshen, Orange county; Patterson, N.J.; at the latter lovely village a lady standing in a fine dwelling near the railroad waved the American banner, and was cheered by the boys. Soon after leaving Passaic we came upon the immense New Jersey hay fields, a tract of level land covering thousand of acres upon which nothing grows but grass; much of the grass is now cut and piled, but much is still standing; there are no fences upon the whole hay field. In the farther end of this grass plot we could see a large schooner under full sail, and some of the boys spoke of it as sailing upon dry land, but as we neared it, it was found to ride in the channel of a stream. The next "institution" we passed was labeled "Bergen Slaughter-House, now open." We did not go in, although we stopped for a broken rail. Next came the celebrated Bergen tunnel, nearly a mile long, and dark enough to remind one of the subject of negro emancipation. Entering Jersey City we crossed to the city of New York by ferry boat Niagara, to Chambers street to Broadway, through which we marched after stopping at the headquarters of the Sharpshooters' regiment, 82 White street. We were met at the ferry by Col. Howland. Going through Broadway we marched around the monument in memory of Gen. Worth.—Passed down to foot of 42nd street, took passage on ferry to Weehawken, N.J., and marched up the hill to Palisade Park, where we are to be instructed in drill and shooting. A battalion of four companies are immediately to be organized to go with Banks' expedition to Texas, and may stay here two or three weeks. Two other battalions are to be organized here afterwards, the whole to compose a regiment under Col. W. S. Rowland, formerly Major in Berdan's Sharpshooters. We are in a splendid location, opposite New York city, overlooking that city and Hudson River.

I am in haste now, but soon will more fully describe this place, the scene of Aaron Burr's duel with Alexander Hamilton.

All wishing to address any one in this company should direct in care Capt. A. O. Gray, Co. A, 1st regiment NYS Sharpshooters, New York City. This is our address. J.T.F.

Monday, 17th.—Slept better than usual except poor head rest. After a harangue by the Capt*[ain]* & a little drill wrote to Aunt C. sending sprig of cedar, same to M*[ary A. C.]* F*[rench]*. Sent letter by carrier, also sent for stamps, out at the P*[ost]* O*[ffice]*. They would take nothing except U.S. Treas*[ur]*y notes. Most of the day sitting in the bar room, reading & it is raining & dark as regular so after had glass of wine & apples 8c & paid *[William]* Hues 15 cts. I borrowed. Rather dull here this day. Have cheerful reflections upon home & scenes of past three months of which the time passed more pleasant than ever before. In the hotel heard singing. In bed early.

Tuesday, 18th.—Rather a pleasant day. Boys washing clothes. Wrote to Am. C*[lar]*k & sent to B*[rockport]* by *[Theron]* Ainsworth. Looked at vessels in bay & picked walnuts. Company B came from Albany. Rather mild weather. Cracked nuts & had company in tent. Singing by *William]* Hues. Read N.Y. paper in morning. Also saw target shooting.

Wednesday, 19th.—Rainy all day. Bo't 50c worth of stamps.—Co*[mpany]* B pitched tents. Privilege to go to N.Y. City, but not till to-morrow. In the officer's room reading most of A.M. Read also after dinner. Some 7 or 8 are on sick list. A dark & foggy day. Read letter from Father, Mother, & sister. Also papers. Very glad to *[be]* rec*[ei]*ving them. In the hospital room to see some of the sick. Detailed for guards, then discharged. A *[illegible word]* raised to guard put on because a few got drunk.

Thursday, 20th.—At 1 A.M. called out to go on guard from 1 till 3. Abed at 3, then on again from 7 till 9, being relieved to go to break*[fast]*. Bo't N*[ew]* Y*[ork]* Sun. 2c Read. Filled canteen. Did nothing more of importance.

Friday, 21st.—A rainy day. Bo't *[illegible word]* of pie, 5c. On table duty. Have a cold in my head. In P.M. rec*[eive]*d letter from Mate F*[Mary A. C. French]*

& a good long one too. By the stove in the hospital all the eve*[ning]*. Bo't N.Y. paper 3c. Abed early. Cap*[tain]* in the tent. Wrote letter home.

Saturday, 22d.—Pleasanter but cold. Had a good wash early. Walnuts. Drill by a new drill-master. Capt*[ain]*. Nash, twice each day. Done washing dishes about 7 P.M. Rec*[eive]*d *[Brockport]* Republic with my letter. Man with hole in his head.

Sunday, 23d.—Bad cold in my head & all over. Sore throat. After wash of break*[fas]*t things relieved from duty. On sick list. Wrote letter for a man. Wrote to cous*[in]* H.P.R., also Al*[bert]* A*[llen]*. Col*[onel]*/*[William S.]* R*[owland]* here. A little supper. Left paper in Capt*[ain]*'s office. Rather sore tonight. In the hospital room all the evening.

Monday, 24th.—It was decided this morning that a person troubled with the sore throat & cold in the head was not entitled to hospital privileges. Had a pretty lively drill in A.M. & P.M. Rec*[eive]*d paper from home stating that Charley was not expected to live in a hospital near Warrenton, Va. In the tent early.

Tuesday, 25th.—Detailed for guard. On at 11 till 1, 5 till 7, 11 till 1. Drill. Letter from Aunt C., a kind one. A fine day this & yesterday. Nothing of any consequence for supper. So I bo't 7 piece pie. 5c. Rain at 11 P.M.

Wednesday, 26th.—Off guard at 7. Pass to New York City till night. Went over on ferry boat in rain with Capt*[ain]* G*[ray]*. Bought pair boots $3.50. With *[Charles W.]* Spaulding bugler & Brackett, went all around the dock thro' markets & saw ships of different kinds laying about. Had nice dish of oysters 12 pie 3c &c. 2 Again pie 10c. Thro' Fulton Market–saw everything in the grocery & market line & people buying poultry of all kinds. Stopped at Barnum's Museum 25c. Saw *[P. T.]* B*[arnum]* himself & performing bears, other fish reptiles wax figures Com. Nutt the dwarf. Albino family & many other curiosities, play of Victorine or "I'll Sleep on it".[80] Took st*[reet]* car at 5 o'c*[lock]* & rode to 40th st*[reet]*. Walked to 8th Av*[enue]*. Got old shoes then to ferry just in time to get the boat. Good dish of oysters, &c. 27c then in camp 7:30 P.M. Gave my boots a good trial to-day & my feet feel rather sore. Rec*[eive]*d a letter from Father, stating that Bro*[ther]* Charley died in hospital without any care, no one near when he died. Never felt so discouraged in my life.

Thursday, 27th.—My cold was so bad this morning that I could hardly speak aloud. Made out to get up in time to get breakfast. Then went into hospital &

staid all day, but could get no medicine. Rec*[eive]*d papers from home & read N.Y. paper. Wrote to Father. Co*[lone]*l R*[owland]* gave us a fine Thanksgiving dinner. Turkey, ham, celery, apples, &c.—First rate dinner. Bro't tick & blanket to hosp*[ita]*l to stay to-night. Read & finished writing. Quite a pleasant day. Cold to-night.

Friday, 28th.—Some rain today. In the hospital all day. Sent letter home. Bo't piece pie 5c. Rec*[eive]*d Brockport *[Daily]* Adv*[ertiser]* from home noting of Bro*[ther]* C*[harles]*'s death. Cooking done outdoors.

Saturday, 29th.—Rather a pleasant day. Wrote to Aggie J*[ohnson]*. A little something to eat at noon. In P.M. went for crackers for Nel*[son]* Miller & bo't dish of stewed oysters {12} & pie 3c. Papers from home & *[Brockport]* Repub*[lic]*. Wrote letter to *[Brockport]* Repub*[lic]*. Tea & hard crackers for supper. Rain poured down at eve*[ning]*. D*[octor]*r came & prescribed croton oil outside on my breast. Exch*[ange]*d Ex*[press]* for Dem*[ocrat]* with Orderly. In bed early in the hospital after living a sociable time by the fire.

Brockport Republic, December 12, 1862

Camp Weehawken, N.J. December 1, 1862. Dear Republic:—Two weeks have passed since I last wrote, and we are still here at camp of instruction where we are drilled in skirmishing in the woods and among the rocks every day by Capt. Nash, formerly a captain in Bordann's, and now commander of this camp. In this drill, at command of "cover," all fall flat on the ground, as though expecting a rebel fire, no matter whether mud or dry gound is before us, it's all the same, and down we go; you may judge what an appearance our clothes will soon make. If the mud gets plastered on thick enough to render us ball proof, all right.

Company B came here from Albany on the 18th, and are *enjoying* camp life with us. Their commissioned officers are Capt. T. S. Bradley, Lieuts. Warren Blinn and Wm. H. Woodin. Capt. B. was formerly a Presbyterian clergyman; and he, together with Robert McPherson, of Parma, in company A, conducted Sabbath religious services in camp. Rev. Mr. Blackmer, of N.Y. city preached to the men yesterday.

In regard to sickness, hospital, &c., I will say that three of Capt. Gray's company died before we left Rochester; Adams, Cook and Teal. Some seven are in charge of our Hospital Steward J. Nickolson, and nurse L. L. T. Smeadley, but complaints are mostly of colds, though our tents are water proof, they sometimes are damp and the wind will find its way through them, and all the boys are not yet toughened to camp life. Capt. Gray had a severe attack at the lungs. Three of our men were brought here on the sick list and are pronounced unfit for duty. They have received discharges. Their names are Amos Robinson and D. O. Sornberger of Rochester, and Alexander Ross of Caledonia.—No doubt some of the boys wish they were in the boots of the fortunate trio, as regards the discharge, but keep cool, we will soon be in—with Banks' expedition, unless the war caves in before we get there.

In this company there have been promotions. 1st Lieut. V. J. Shipman is acting Quartermaster; his activity and business capacity will enable him to discharge promptly the duties of this department, so perplexing in a new regiment. Our commissary is B. P. Hutson; F. J. Bray is Colonel's Orderly; Jas. Capwell mail carrier; C. W. Spaulding is bugler. These are unexceptional appointments.

We often have an incident of some kind. One night a week ago, Lieut. Starkweather was knocked down while coming to camp, but not much hurt. The perpetrator of this fiendish act was not seen distinctly in the darkness, but reliable suspicions traced it to a rough customer in Co. B. by the name of Van Slyck. As soon as the boys learned of the unprovoked assault they were enraged and "Phil," ever ready to avenge an insult to the company, soon found the assassin and gave him one ponderous blow with his fist, which severely punished him, for in a few minutes he came in to the hospital bleeding from a wound in the temple. This man is not liked in Co. B and they say he deserved the blow. A few days afterwards this same Van S. was tied to a tree for getting drunk and tearing things in another spree. Smuggled whiskey causes some disturbance.

On Thanksgiving day we were about as well served as you all are at home. Col. Rowland kindly ordered turkeys and other nice "fixins," which were served to us in good order, and you may believe we enjoyed it. Our dessert was apples. Three cheers for the Col. testified to our appreciation of the dinner.

Of our time of departure and destination you know as well as we, for we hear all sorts of reports, one of which is that in a few days we will go on board a transport to await the departure of Gen. Banks' expedition, looked forward to with so much anxiety.—By the way, we had a visit from three Rifle Battery boys on Friday. They were to embark on a transport off New York on that day, to go with the great expedition. They have five of their own batteries and five six pounders. Health good.

I wish to say here this if friends of soldiers wish to keep them posted in the news of the day, and enable them to pass many a gloomy hour less lonesome, send a good paper or two often. No one but the recipient of such favors can know how welcome they are. They are the next thing to a friendly letter from home. To be sure we can get New York dailies, but they seem dry and tell us nought of local interest to us.

Weather while we have sojourned here has been 'mixed'; that is, one day pleasant and the next two rainy. When favored with sunshine, we take the benefit of our fine encampment. On the high rocks, 200 feet above the Hudson, we see vessels of all kinds. Across and down stream we have a good view of New York city and harbor in the distance—a forest of steeples and masts, ferry boats plying back and forth constantly, with barges and steamboats up and down the river. Frequent booming of cannon is heard. A Monitor, iron-clad, the Passaic[81], passed here a few days ago on trial trip and looked like a picture of the old Monitor.

I obtained a furlough on Wednesday and visited the river docks in the city, saw the numerous fleet lying up, and observed the immense amount of business which the running of thse vessles make, visited the markets, where people were busy purchasing poultry &c., for a Thanksgiving dinner. Washington market, the principal one, is a perfect bee hive, and a person can purchase anything in the line of eatables there. Also visited Barnum's Museum. If you wish to see a good natured man; look at P. T. Barnum.

I will impose upon your valuable space no longer, so good bye for the present, while we still cling to Weehawken. J.T.F.

Sunday, 30th.—Late breakfast of coffee & hard crackers. Read papers awhile. Sent letters to Aggie & [Brockp[ort] Repub[lic]. Took a walk with D. C. Sornburger along the river bank, found oysters in the shell and ate them, also found other shells. Saw the place where Aaron Burr & Alex[ander] Hamilton fought celebrated duel, now marked by a stone. Had a pleasant walk and view and had good dish of fresh oysters 12c raw & pie 12c. Back at 3 o'clock. Had supper of good beef soup. No better of my cold. In the hospital again to-night & it seems like a bar room.

Monday, December 1.—Rainy. A heavy blister on my breast feels rather sickly. Put on guard from 11 till 1. Paid 2c towards buying paper. At 4½ o'[clo]ck carried my things back to tent. Guard from 5 till 7. Kept in tent again.

Tuesday, 2d.—Last night heard that an armistice of 6 mo[nth]s is reported, Delighted to hear it but nothing is said in the papers. Pres[iden]ts message. No news. No rain, but mud. Chilly & a few flakes of snow. Carried 12 pails water. Looked at vessels on the river. Cold as fury. In bed at 6:30.

Wednesday, 3d.—Froze harder last night than usual. Breakfast & short drill. Appointed guard for hospital & read papers. In the hospital till 6 P.M. Rec[eive]d good letter from Aunt C., also sister C[ordelia] Mother & brother Alonzo. A pretty cold night. Nel[son] M[iller] bunks with us. Salt beef, hard crackers & tea outdoors for supper. Had game of dominoes. Pay 1 ct. for each letter received. Some flakes of snow to-night.

Thursday, 4th.—Capt*[ain]* G*[ray]* spoke to me about anonymous letter. Had a long drill A.M. & P.M. Jumped a picket fence. Bean soup & hard tack for dinner. A pleasant day. Did a washing. Wrote to Mother & rec*[eive]*d letter from Father. Supper salt beef tea & h*[ard]* tack[82]. In eve*[ning]*. wrote to Mrs. S*[mith]*. by a fire in the tent. A fiddle going & some one singing in one tent. Cold night.

Friday, 5th.—On guard. Rather a pleasant day till 5 P.M. Then rain followed by snow. Had drill at 2. Bean soup for dinner. Had lots of fun on guard. Sent letter home this morning. Rice for supper. Had game of dominoes. In bed early & got called out for a minute & the snow was falling to 3 or 4 inches deep. Up & on guard at 11 in guard tent.

Saturday, 6th.—In bed till 10. Very cold & snowy. Carried stick of wood to woman. At sutler's bo't 1 gr*[ape]* pie 5c & got my feet warm. Beef soup for dinner. Freezing around a stove all the P.M. In bed early. That is the only warm place for this cold night.

Sunday, 7th.—O, what a cold morning. Breakfast of coffee & hard tack. Helped pile wood. The boys have got a nice little stove in our tent, which makes it quite comfortable. Brought water. Commenced a letter to Mr. *[Horatio N.]* Beach of Brockport & one home. Wind blows hard. A very cold night. Saw a barn burn. Ate a cracker, then to bed.

Monday, 8th.—Cook our own provisions to-day. On guard.—Cold, but pleasant. Rec*[eive]*d 2 papers from home. Lieut*[enant]* S*[hipma]*n told me to keep on writing to the B*[rockport]* R*[epublic]*. Sleighs running.

Brockport Republic, December 11, 1862

Camp Weehawken, N.J., December 7, 1862. Mr. H. N. Beach:—We are in the midst of winter. During Thursday night snow fell to the depth of four or five inches, and yesterday morning the camp presented an appearance of a Greenland Scene. Everything was covered with snow and looked much like the first storm in Brockport this season, which destroyed so many trees.—Last night was very cold, and to-day the boys think it is rather tough. Many of the tents rest upon boards staked up and banked up with earth, thus giving more room; and there are small stoves in most of them, which the boys bought at their own expense—costing from $3 to $4 with pipe— cooking is done in tents and out doors, many choosing to draw their rations and cook their own fare. Of course there is more or less grumbling about everything. If we knew we were to stay here all winter the tents would be made quite comfortable—for what a soldier cannot turn to good account, is worthless.

Our battalion, (four companies,) is not yet made out, but probably will be by consolidating companies not full. Part of a company from Buffalo came yesterday—they will be the starting point of Company C.

Those telescope rifles of ours are finished and in New York, and we expect to see them in a day or two. Then we will be nearer ready to start. Bank's expedition, or a portion of it, started, as you know, last Friday, and we are told that the balance are to go on the 15th. One would suppose that if we go with Gen. Banks at all, we will go then. A summer hotel bar room here is occupied as our hospital, and although several are on the sick list, none are considered dangerous. Two or three who are expecting discharges are still here.

Our sutler, S. S. Eyre, (formerly in the Crimean war, and since through the Potomac campaign,) supplies us with such dainties as pies at 20 cents each, cider 5 cents per glass, tobacco 7 cents a paper, candles 4 cents each, and other things in proportion. But with most of us money is getting scarce, and among other things expected is the paymaster.

Among the incidents of camp life a few days since was a man who for drunkenness was sentenced to stand on the head of a barrel four hours each day for two or three days. He made a good target and bore his wristlets with fortitude, and very gracefully.

Yours, &c., J.T.F.

Tuesday, 9th.—Pleasant. Most of the boys go for their guns.—Off guard at 7. Good breakfast of beef potatoes, coffee & h[ard] tack Read N.Y. paper. Washed up & served. Brought a pail of water. Had glass cider & gr[ape] pie 10c. On guard a short time for Nel[son] M[iller]. Good supper.

Wednesday, 10th.—A splendid day. Water carrier ¼ of a mile, up hill, from a spring. Had glass cider. Rec[eive]d 2 Ex[presses] from home. No drill in several days. Everything goes loosely. Expected letter from home, but none came.

Thursday, 11th.—Water carrier again. A pleasant day & muddy. Nothing unusual today. But I did have an apple for dessert. Rec[eive]d letter from Aunt C. & ans[were]d it in a paper.

Friday, 12th.—Drew a rubber blanket. Asked Capt[ain] G[ray] for a pass & he gave me an ungentlemanly answer, then Lieut[enant] S[hipman] said that he would see that I had one. Had clothes washed. 10c. Sent paper to Aunt C. cleaned up in front of tent. Read papers from R[ochester]. Wrote home.

Saturday, 13th.—Voted by the Co[mpany] to allow the Capt[ain] to resign on account of bleeding at lungs. Lieut[enant] gave me pass. Sent letter. Went to N.Y. with C[harles] S[paulding] bugler, on ferry. No changes 8th Av[enue] st[reet] car & Barnum's Museum 5c. then to P.O. Nothing there. Great rush for stamps. At Am[erican] Ex[press] office sent rub[ber] blanket to Father 30c. Down to Fulton market & had pie & oyster stew. Strolled about & saw the sights. At Bar[num] Museum saw part of play &c. Colleen Baron[83] & took st[reet] car back to ferry. Back all right. O, what mud in camp.

Sunday, 14th.—Mud mud! After break[fast] Cha[u]n[cey] Parker came & I was very glad to see him. He bro't me from mother two nice pies, cakes, a night cap & paper. Very glad to receive them. This is a cloudy day. Had some butter on bread. Preaching in the grove on bank of river. Wrote letter to Mother. No candle to-night.

Monday, 15th.—On guard first thing after breakfast & this is a lovely day. Sunshine & warm. My pie has it well & is just as good as when first made. Rec[eive]d Repub[lic] from Mr. [Horatio N.] B[each] & 2 [Rochester Evening] Ex[presses] from home. Heard joyful news that [Major General Nathaniel P.] Banks has taken Richmond. Too good to be true[84]. Not much sleep to-night, 4 hours. Looks like rain & the moon once in a while looks through the clouds on me as I am standing sentry.

Context—Union forces occupied Fredericksburg on December 11, but were driven out by the Confederates on the 13th.

Tuesday, 16th.—A rainy, blue day.—Staid in my tent all the A.M. & ate no breakfast. Read papers part of the time. Not very favorable news from the seat of war. Burnside retreated from Fredericksburg.

Wednesday, 17th.—Pretty cold; otherwise pleasant. Drill. Rec[eive]d six letters by mail from home (mother, father, Lon, Cordelia & Harvey) cous[in] Alb[ert] Allen, Mrs. Smith & Em., Aggie J[ohnso]n & Mate [Mary A. C.] F[rench] Boston. Ans[were]d Cordelia's to-night. In bed early.

Thursday, 18th.—Very cold still. Wrote to M[ary A. C.] F[rench] & Lon & Harvey; in the eve[ning]. Rec[eive]d letter from Aunt C. stating that she had sent me gloves & stockings by Ex[press]. Rec[eive]d [Brockport] Rep[ublic] & 2 [Rochester Evening] Ex[presses]. Wrote to Aunt C. Had pie &c of sutler. In C[hauncey] P[arker]'s tent to-night a while.

Friday, 19th.—On guard & supernumerary[85] to lead out the boys. Pleasant day. Sent letter home & paper to Aunt. Nothing by mail. New Co*[mpany]* Com*[mander]* this P.M. Boys sparring. Guard taken off at 9:30. Freezing cold.

Saturday, 20th.—Suffered more from cold this A.M. than ever before. Paid $1 toward a stove in the tent; which was put up in the P.M. & feels nice. In a tent most of the day. Rec*[eive]*d a Roch*[ester]* Ex*[press]* & notice from Am*[erican]* Ex*[press]* Co*[mpany]* that my things have come. Company in tent & we cracked walnuts. Abed in good season.

Sunday, 21st.—After breakfast finished writing to Brockport Republic, just as Capt*[ain]* came into the tent. Cold & rather windy. In the eve*[ning]* attended preaching by McDougal. Capt*[ain]* G*[ray]* placed under guard.

Brockport Republic, December 25, 1862

Camp Weehawken, N.J., Dec. 20, 1862. Editor Republic:—When I wrote last the ground was covered with snow, the snow has long since melted, followed by a week of sunshine and pleasant weather. To-day the wind howls and rushes by with almost force enough to carry off our tents, and the cold is intense. The boys begin to think this a time that not only "tried men's souls," but bodies too, and many and loud are the curses because we are kept so long out in the cold. The reverses before Fredericksburg have, if anything, rather a discouraging effect on the spirits of men long anxious to do something for the country except lying idle. Still we look for better times coming.

Our captain, A. C. Gray, is supposed to have sent in his "resignation," caused, apparently, by ill health, "bleeding at the lungs" &c.—The real or principal causes will probably soon appear. Capt. G. undertook without cause, among other prohibitions, to prohibit your correspondent from writing to the Republic, but failed, for no one has a right to stop communications that are perfectly harmless; and I have no disposition to make any hurtful personal allusion, although the truth ought to be told occasionally. Our present first Lieut. V. J. Shipman, will undoubtedly be our captain, and will make a good one, too. Other promotions will be made soon.

Co. D, from Columbia county, N.Y., came yesterday. There are still only between two and three hundred men here. Our guard arrangements and other things have been rather slack, but are becoming daily more brief.— Not much is yet done in the way of target shooting, and only a part of our guns have been received here.

A change has been made in our postoffice address, and now, in addition [to] the usual direction, those who write to any in our company, should be particular to direct as follows: Co. A, 1st Reg't N.Y. Sharpshooters, Station F, 8th Avenue, New York. Many letters have been delayed by being directed to no particular station; although our wideawake postmaster has managed to bring them around.

Some time ago I spoke of Robert McPherson as assisting to conduct religious services; that was a mistake—It should have read M. D. McDougal, of Parma.

Christmas is near at hand. With us it may pass the same as other days, unless some generous person kindly furnishes us with those extras which tend to make the day go on agreeably to the stomach. Although we in camp may have only our usual "hard tack," we will think of those near the home fireside and hope the holidays may be merrily happy to you all. Perhaps you do not think we "enjoy" life here in Jersey, among the Dutch and rocks, if you don't, come down and stay with us one night. Most of the business done here seems to be getting out paving stone for the streets of Havana, Cubas.

Dec. 21—an election held this morning, decided that the choice of the company for 2nd Lieut., is our present orderly A. L. Root. 2nd Lieut. Starkweather will probably be our 1st Lieutenant.

J.T.F.

Monday, 22d.—Pleasanter today. Furlough & went to N.Y. city with mail carrier in st[reet] car to P.O. & rec[eive]d B[rockport] Rep[ublic] then to Am[erican] Ex[press] office to get package Aunt C. sent me—2 p[ai]r stocking & lined mittens. At Wash[ington] market, 34 & wrote letter to Aunt C. Bo't 75c worth of stamps & rambled about the city. In Bank Note Engravers office; saw people passing on cor[ner] Broadway & Fulton st[reet]s in front of Knox's hat store. At Fulton Market had oyster & pie, coffee, &c. Met Cha[u]n[cey] P[arker], had oysters & rode on st[reet] car to 42nd st[reet] 8th ave[nue] took boat to Weehawken, & to camp. All right again.

Tuesday, 23d.—On guard & a pleasant day. Do cooking in tent altogether now. Nothing very new, only at dress parade the Adjutant was tight & after that the co[mpany] voted to not [to] try to get away from here till the Gov[ernment] order us. Coffee & hard tack for supper.

Wednesday, 24th.—Off guard at 9 salt pork for break[fas]t Cut wood. Another fine day. No snow on the ground but frozen quite hard. Wrote to Miss F[rancis] R. D[ouglas]. [A. L.] Root. Sent J.C[haucey] P[arker] 25c. Rec[eive]d 2 Roch[ester] [Evening] Ex[presse]s.

Christmas.

Thursday, 25th.—A warm spring like day. Battalion marched to Guttenbery, N.J. breweries & had three glasses beer given by proprietors. Bo't lb. nails to raise & fix tent with boards. Had a house warming & celebrated Christmas by eating turkey pie, honey, &c. sent to J[onas H.] K[ocher] & J[ackson P.] N[ichols] from home. Goods.—Helped bank tent, & drew rations then in eve[ning] made requisition & "Jay Hawked[86]" boards. Not much like regular Christmas.

Friday, 26th.—Mild weather & overcoat not needed. Tent almost fixed. Bo't N[ew] Y[ork] Sun. Read most of the A.M. Steak for breakfast. The P.M. went to N[ew] Y[ork] with [Chauncey] P[arker] & received letter from home. Rode in st[reet] car passed by City Hall & Tribune office. At Fulton Market oysters & coffee. Rode back to 42nd st[reet] in car, & stopped a short time before taking the ferry boat, at which we arrived just in time. Back all right. Wrote to mother Cordelia & Harvey. Slight rain to-night.

Saturday, 27th.—Warm and muddy. Laid down most of the day with heavy cold. Sent papers to Lon. Rec[eive]d Repub[lic] & [Rochester Evening] Ex[presse]s— Dress parade. Bro't water. Bo't candle. Rec[eive]d papers & went to bed early.

Sunday, 28th.—Knapsack parade. Have a taste, often, of knicknacks by the boys in our tent. Bro't water. Wrote letter to Miss A.E.C. Weather mild. At 4 o'clock a fatal accident happened to James Case, an old schoolmate of mine, was shot in the breast with a revolver in the hands of Benton Tuttle, as they were fooling in their tent. He hardly spoke a word afterwards but died in about five minutes. The ball passed just over his heart. A case of carelessness & recklessness in handling firearms. In the evening everything was stiller than usual. Rec[eive]d an apple outside the lines.

Monday, 29th.—Took the place of Brown at guard mounting. On duty carrying water. Read paper & washed dishes. Rec[eive]d letter from Corporal R[obert] J. Gordon [of the 13th NYVI Regiment], near Fredericksburg. Borrowed N[ew] Y[ork] paper to send to G. Had lots of fun in the tent before & after going to bed. Rather a nice day.

Tuesday, 30th.—On guard 3rd relief. Bo't N[ew] Y[ork] Herald. Sent paper. Cloudy but mild. At 3½ P.M. battalion escorted remains of Ja[me]s Case to ferry on way to his friends in the west. Another fellow soldier departed. Ezra Hutson a member of this Co[mpany] came to-night & bunks with us. Had a family supper of beef, bread & rice.

Wednesday, 31st.—Snow fell last night to the depth of 3 inches. Not very cold. Guard left off during night. I was on from 7 till 9. Some wind. After break*[fas]* t washed dishes. In Butler's tent read N*[ew]* Y*[ork]* paper. At my own tent most of the P.M. Bro't water &c. A box of provisions came from home for Nel*[son]* M*[iller]* & I had a share. In tent all the eve*[ning]* & in bed in good season. Thus has passed this, to me, eventful year. Passed through fires, & spent over 4 months in the service of the U.S., together with many other incidents of less importance. My principal hope is that peace may soon come to us.

Context—President Lincoln signed the Emancipation Proclamation on January 1 declaring liberated all slaves in the states under Confederate control.

Thursday, Jan. 1.—A new year brightly dawns upon a land in arms. A sunny day with a trifle of snow upon the ground and rather cold. At roll call, then an early breakfast of potatoes, beef, bread and a piece of pie from N*[elson]* M*[iller]*, a contribution from home. Then helped bring a pail of water from the spring. Mr. *[William]* Hues is sitting in the corner, smoking a nasty black pipe. Jack*[son P.]* Nichols is washing dishes. Jonas *[H.]* Kocher and N*[elson]* Miller are snoozing or reading in bunk. Had my hair cut closely in the eve*[ning]*. Went with two or three others to see a Dutch dance. Saw lots of fun and our boys were well represented. Almost two fights. Home all night.

Friday, 2d.—In my bunk most of the day with sick headache. Ate nothing till eve*[ning]*, scarcely. In P.M. received a letter from home and Aunt. Ans*[were]*d it, also wrote to B*[rockport]* Republic. To bed early. A fine moonlight.

Brockport Republic, January 8, 1863

Camp Weehawken, N.J., Jan. 3, 1863. Editor Republic:—The holidays have passed. On Christmas day the weather was of a spring mildness; the proprietors of two breweries in the village of Guttenburg, N.J., near here, invited the soldiers of the camp to partake of their foamy beverage, which invitation was accepted and resulted in the destruction of several masked Batteries in the shape of casks of ale. The boys, seeing this was their first "charge" in Jersey, drank lightly; as a consequence they came back to the camp in a good condition, after cheering the German proprietors, one of them made a patriotic speech, mixed with the brogue of "faderlands." New Years was a pleasant day; sleighs were run over the three inches of snow which fell the day before, and bells jingled merrily. Some of the boys had received during the week, boxes of provisions from home, and celebrated the day by partaking thereof. Altogether we live like princes, compared to the accounts of the "living" of the 140th and 108th. In the evening of New Years most of the boys attended a German dance at Union Hill, and there were hardly enough left at camp to form a corporal's guard, during the evening. We are "learning German" fast, and talk "nix fur stay" and "yaw yaw," with great volubility.

Nothing in regard to our time of leaving is yet known with certainty. The battalion seems to fill up slowly We already have men formerly in battles of this war, veterans discharged, and prisoners paroled, whose experience will be made available if we ever go into action. A son of Com. Tatnall, (now in the confederate service and long a naval officer in the U.S. service, but who clung to Georgian "States rights,") is a private in Co. C. Young Tatnall held a commission in the naval service at the breaking out of the rebellion; his father going with the South, the U.S. government, without waiting for Tatnall Junior to prove his loyalty which they suspected at the time, took away his commission. Now he is doing duty as a private, in a nine months company of Sharpshooters, thus modestly proving true to the Union in happy contrast to his father's course. Capt. Bradley of Co. B is commander of the camp. Capt. Gray is still here waiting for something to "turn up".

On Sunday evening last a sad and fatal accident happened in camp, and threw a gloom over us all. James Case, a private in Co. A. was "carrying on" with some others in a tent, when one of the boys playfully pointed a revolver towards Case, saying, "you had better be careful," then the revolver went off, the ball, a small one, entering Case's breast just above the heart, and killed him almost instantly. An inquest was held and a verdict rendered. In accordance with the above facts. The body was kept till Tuesday, to go through a legal process in order to take the body from the State, when the whole camp turned out and attended the remains to the ferry, whence they were sent to his friends at Orleans county, from which place Case enlisted, and where he was brought up, and was schoolmate of the writer of this. Case was thought very much of by all in the company, for his lively disposition, and his loss will long be deeply felt. His parents now live in Illinois. This accident will serve as a lesson to those in the company who use firearms carelessly.

J.T.F.

Saturday, 3d.—Another warm splendid day. Bo't paper. On guard. Had piece of mince pie and toast for dinner. Rec[eive]d B[rockport] papers and Roch[ester Evening] Ex[press]. Also Curriers. Address of the two B[rockport] papers by Father. Fine moonlight evening. Clear and cold.

Sunday, 4th.—Good news this morning of battle and victory in Tenn[essee].[87] Co[mpany] E from Buffalo came with band, helped bring their baggage from ferry. Had glass wine. Snow thaws; cloudy and chilly. Dress parade. After we have got nicely fixed for winter quarters, then talk of moving us. Late supper. Read papers to the boys. In bed early.

Monday, 5th.—Fine day. Thawing and muddy. Bro't water. Showed my correspondence to Capt*[ain Thomas]* Bradley, commanding camp. Had nap and dreamed of seeing brother Charley. Skirmish drill and visited a tower. Rec*[eive]*d letter from Aunt C. and Mate *[Mary A. C.]* French. Washed dishes and soon after orders were opened to cook two days rations, preparatory to leaving for Staten Island, N*[ew]*Y*[ork]* tomorrow. Go*[ve]*r*[nment]* meat ready and packed up some things.

Tuesday, 6th.—Struck tents, packed knapsacks &c. ... Muddy & very foggy. At 1 bid good bye to camp Weehawken and at 2½ steamed from the dock. Rode to Staten island. Waited a long time, then took cars for destination after dark. Slept in a long barracks on wet ticks in New Dorp, Staten Island, after a bite of something to eat. Mud*[d]*y.

Wednesday, 7th.—Awoke early & lots of confusion. Bo't something to eat at store. Wrote to Father & Aunt C. Fixed up bunks & got somewhat straightened. Bunk with Ezra Hutson. Abed early.

Thursday, 8th.—On guard all alone but off after 10 P.M. Rec*[eive]*d letters from home & Miss Frank *[Francis R.]* Douglas Roch*[ester]*. Also Roc*[hester Evening]* Ex*[press]*. Some snow. Wrote to mother & commenced a letter to *[Brockport]* Republic, also to Mate *[Mary A. C.]* F*[rench]*.

Friday, 9th.—Cold day & little snow. No breakfast till 11½. Everything behind. Had to buy something to eat at sutlers. Sent letter home. After washed up. Nothing by mail for me today. Wash dishes too.

Saturday, 10th.—Helped fix up a cook house. Made soup for supper. Rain tonight. A dance in the barracks. Almost made up my mind not to write any more except home. No good place to write & everything in confusion.

Brockport Republic, January 15, 1863

New Dorp, Staten Island, N.Y. January 10, 1863. Editor Republic:—Again we are in York State, and about where we expected to go just before we left Camp Porter. On Monday evening we had orders to prepare rations for two days, which we did. On Tuesday morning we packed knapsacks and struck tents, packing up stoves and such things as we would need in "keeping house" in our future place of destination. The mud was deep, and boards and broken articles lay scattered about in great confusion: then I was reminded of the appearance of Main street after the Brockport fire in May last.[88] About 1 o'clock we marched to the ferry, where we had to wait a long time for the tug engaged to take us away. Soon we were on boards and steamed away from Weehawken and landed at a dock on Staten Island, where after waiting till after dark to get our baggage changed to the railroad, we took the cars, riding about 5 miles, where we landed in the mud about 9 o'clock, took our wet ticks and slept in a long barrack as well as circumstances would allow. Wednesday morning we found ourselves in one of three different barracks, 3,000 feet of them in all, and new, capable of holding 15,000 men; they form three sides of a square. We are one mile from the water, and in sight of Sandy Hook. A little place of a few houses, hotel, store and postoffice, is called New Dorp, and is only a few rods from us. Our post office address is "New Dorp, Staten Island, N.Y." company and regiment the same as before. Everything is confusion as yet unsettled. If we can have a decent place to write I may soon give some particulars of our condition—otherwise I shall be obliged to "lay off" a while; for about all we want to attend to now is to keeping warm and getting enough to eat. J.T.F.

Sunday, 11th.—A fine day overhead but very muddy. Attended Epis*[copal]* Ch*[urch]* at Richmond, 1½. Came back & had oyster stew. Then a leg of chicken killed this morning. After dress parade nothing unusual happened. Wrote to Mrs. S.T.E. ...

Monday, 12th.—Pleasant & not much like January weather. Rec*[eive]*d papers from home. Bro't water & washed dishes. Sent letter. Nothing of importance today. A late supper. Part of a Co*[mpany]* of Zouaves came to-night.

Tuesday, 13th.—Bro't pail water in after break*[fast]*. Washed dishes. Drill. Cooking to be done now in the cook house. Not cold, but cloudy. At eve. rec*[eive]*d letter from Mother & sister, also a photograph of Bro*[ther]* Charley.

Wednesday, 14th.—On guard, late relief. Cloudy & misty. Good dinner of b*[ean]* soup. Commenced writing to sister. Quite pleasant in P.M., but rainy in eve. Felt unwell in eve. Wrote letter to mother.

Thursday, 15th.—Laid abed till noon, unwell. Rec*[eive]*d papers. At a miserable dinner & bo't a piece of pie. Paid for washing, but did not get my own. On dress parade were told that we would be mustered for pay on Monday. Finished letters home to sister & M*[other]*. Misty but warm. Half baked beans for supper. A perfect mess after we got to bed, things thrown about, loud talking, &c. Pain in my bowels and was obliged to get up.

Friday, 16th.—Rain all day. Made out to get up to breakfast tho' I could not eat, then to bed & slept till most noon, when we were inspected by Brig*[adier]* Gen*[eral]* *[John C.]* Brown of Gen*[eral]* *[Thomas J.]* Wood's staff. Rice soup dinner. Dark & unpleasant. Supper of beef, bread & coffee. Had a nice coal fire in barracks. To bed early.

Saturday, 17th.—Very cold night. Slept alone & had cold feet. Ready for inspection of barracks but inspection did not come. Rec*[eive]*d a *[Brockport]* Republic of this week. Got rid of a shin plaster for pies & oranges. Pleasant overhead but cold. Women here with apples &c. trading & having some fun. Got shirt washed & got woman to wash drawers. Pistols taken from all the Co*[mpanies]*. Food poorest since enlisted. *[George]* Bennett sleeps with me on account of cold.

Sunday, 18th.—Slept comfortably. Very cold but a pleasant day. Attended Moravian Ch*[urch]* services similar to Episcopal. Steak dinner for a wonder. Scoured buttons &c. & tore off cord from pants. Commenced a letter to Ag*[gie. J[ohnso]n* but stopped for dinner, then it was dark & I looked on to see a game of chequers. All kinds of games going on. Sleep alone to-night.

Monday, 19th.—On guard (3rd relief) A fine day. Col*[onel William S.]* Rowland consolidated 2 Co*[mpanie]*s & spoke highly of us (Co*[mpany]* A). Wrote & sent letter to A*[ggie]* J*[ohnson]*. Expect to be mustered in for pay. No very unusual thing happens except that we are coming under stricter regulations. A cold clear night & I manage to keep warm by constantly moving on guard (sentinels cry the hours). Sleep with Mr. *[William]* H*[ues]*, & more comfortably than before in a long time. Keep fire in coal stove all night.

Tuesday, 20th.—Off guard at 9. Cloudy & moderate, ... a pleasant sunrise. Fixed bunk. Passed out *[got a pass]* & got a drink of cider & pie & lost 0.0.0 Read to the boys &c. After supper went to bed early tired & sleepy.

Wednesday, 21st.—Rainy all day. In bunk most of the forenoon. Rec*[eive]*d a letter from Mother, Father, Cordelia & Harvey, Aunt C & also paper from Aunt. Disagreeable day. To bed about 7 P.M.

Thursday, 22d.—No rain, but cloudy, mild. Pass & went to store & wrote to Father, Mother & Aunt. Rec*[eive]*d paper from home. Bo't pie & paid for washing. Baked beans for dinner. Worked on cook house in P.M. Mud deep. Cup of milk for supper. Read news after dark &c.

Friday, 23d.—Fog early. Very mild. Almost like summer. On guard, 1st relief. Saw fleet of boats going out to sea. Coal stoves. Promotion of P*[hilip]* Hysner *[to 2nd Lieutenant]*.

Saturday, 24th.—Had doughnuts & apples. On guard 3 to 5. Cloudy & windy in P.M., tho' mild. Rec*[eive]*d *[Brockport]* Rep*[ublic]*. Wrote home &c. Stood guard for N*[elson]* M*[iller]*. About 4 P.M. Capt*[ain]* Gray suddenly appeared from imprisonment in Fort Lafayette to take command of the Co*[mpany]* (saluted!) Great sensation. Read in eve. & bro't water. Masticated my first clam.

Sunday, 25th.—Warm but cloudy. Break*[fast]* at 9. Fixed up. Attended Episcopal Ch*[urch]* at Richmond & came back over hills where I could see the ocean & ships. Had piece of pie &c. at hotel. After dress bro't canteen of water & had talk of politics.

Brockport Republic, January 29, 1863

Camp Sprague, Staten Island, N.Y. *[n.d.?]* Editor of the Republic:—While you in Monroe are enjoying winter and sleighing, we here are having almost summer weather, and bare ground, with any quantity of mud; in fact, during the time we have been here, over two weeks, with the exception of a heavy storm of wind and rain last Wednesday, we have generally a clear sky and warm sun. The ground has occasionally been frozen quite hard, but remaining so for only a short time.

In summer this Island must be a pleasant place indeed; even now, on a clear day, we can see some of its advantages of location in a fine view of the salt water with the white winged vessels coming from and passing out to sea. Long Island can be seen in the distance. The boys often go to the beach and gather clams, of which an abundance may be found at low tide.

A railroad, the only one on the island, passes close to us, and four trains a day connect with the New York city ferry at Clifton. This road is only about 14 miles long, and there are several heavy grades, which give the cars an appearance of running up or down hill. Like other railroads, this is subject to accidents one of which detained the mail several hours a few days ago, but no heavy damage was done.

Richmond, 1½ miles from here, is a small village, and besides the usual places of business for a town of its size, contains three churches: Episcopal, Dutch Reformed and Catholic. Most of the people appear well-to-do, and live in style. Unlike its Virginia namesake, there are no appearances of secession in the place. We had no idea of leading Gen. Burnside's army, but it is an indisputable fact that the Monroe Sharpshooters have "been to Richmond."

Some of us, with Captain Shipman, attended what is called a Moravian church, or "Church of the United Brethren," on Sunday last. The services were similar to the Episcopal, and we heard a good sermon.

Last week we were inspected by Brig. Gen. Brown, of Gen. Wool's staff. Gen. Wool has command of all the troops in this state. Some Zouaves, just recruited, are in camp, and with their shaggy trowsers, look quite Turkish.— They are called the "Lost Children." On Monday last companies D and E were consolidated—neither being full. In company E are some musicians who form a very good brass band, and furnish us often with music second only to Perkins' Band, of Rochester. A member of Co. C, of Buffalo, Henry Scott, died recently of crysipolas[89], and was buried here.

Co. A, (now Capt. Shipman's,) were highly complimented lately by Col. Rowland, for diligence, good behavior, obedience to orders, &c., and said he was astonished that there were no desertions among us, recruited at a time when so many volunteered for nothing but bounty. Altogether, this is a singular company in many respects. He also spoke of Capt. Gray being in Fort Lafayette, undergoing punishment—one offense being for receiving money from and attempting to discharge a private on his own responsibility; the man, Geo. Marcellus, is now in Canada. This is not the only offence of which Capt. G. was guilty. He undertook to speculate every member of his company out of five dollars, by making a private contract with the makers of our guns to have the rifles manufactured for $30 and $40; then a contract was afterwards made by which $35 and $45 was to be paid for the guns, the latter contract being between the manufacturer and a committee from the company, of which the Capt. was one, and by a secret understanding, unknown to the other members of the committee, Capt. G. was to pocket the extra five dollars. This transaction was exposed, and the guns will probably be obtained at the lowest figure, and over four hundred dollars saved to the company. Every man of us had the utmost confidence in the Captain when we enlisted, but subsequent acts of his proved that he was undeserving of it. Such acts sho'd be exposed, as too much evil exists in the army already.

Yesterday, on dress parade, an order was read that Sergeant Philip Hysner should act as 2nd Lieutenant; it was supposed that Orderly Root would be appointed, after a company vote had been taken, which indicated him as the man. A. W. Starkweather is promoted to 1st Lieutenant.

We have two large coal stoves in our part of the barracks, and they make us comfortable. Pay day, a very slow coach, has not yet arrived. Next Saturday is the time now set. We have been fooled so often in regard to different matters that we are prepared for anything. Greenbacks, however, would be acceptable.

By the amount of coal stored, among other indications, I should think we were to stay some time, although it is said we will be ready to start by Jan.

31. There are a few sick ones in hospital, but no serious cases. A surgeon attends regularly. There are three or four candidates for discharge in this company. J.T.F.

Monday, 26th.—Signed payroll. Drew pair of l[igh]t blue pants. Ready for inspection. Rec[eive]d papers from home & Aunt. Inspection by Gen[eral] [blank space]. Rain in P.M., but warm. Playing cards & other amusements going on in the evening. Weighed 128½ lbs.

Tuesday, 27th.—Dark & misty. Still warm. On guard (1st relief); good breakfast, coffee crackers beefsteak & potatoes. Rainy in P.M. Rec[eive]d letters from M[other] & sister & fine comb. A debating society was got up by the Co[mpany] (6th Co. NYSSS)—Capt[ain] [Volney J.] Shipman Pres[ident], M.D. McDougal V.P. & myself Sec[retar]y selected questions for the debate & adj[ourne]d. Had piece of pie & the Corp[ora]l passed around with countersign[90].

Wednesday, 28th.—At [my] last time out snow was falling & continuous all day, very fine & growing cold. In bed most all day. Made report to Soc[iety] meeting last eve. Very stormy. Splendid bread for supper. Had game of euchre with M[atthew] Hennes[s]ey before S[ociety] debated, then adj[ourne]d till to-morrow eve. same subject. Snow & sleet.

Thursday, 29th.—1 or 2 in[ches] of snow on ground & fell during the day, pleasant. Wrote report & read N[ew] Y[ork] Herald which says talk now is that if the war is not fought out by the 1st May a separation will be made. Read magazine. Commenced letter home. Mended stockings. Medicine of surgeon for sore throat. At meet[ing] of Debating Society.

Friday, 30th.—Ground 2 in[ches] snow froze. Pleasant & just cold enough to be comfortable. Ready for pay. Rec[eive]d papers from home & one from Aunt C. Soup for dinner. Paymaster paid the whole Co[mpany]. I received $43.76 which pays to Jan[uary] 1 & received a globe sighted rifle[91] & paid $5, which makes $35 paid for it. It looks like a good one, No.1009. Sent $10 home by letter. Wiped out my gun & examined it. Bo't piece pie. In the eve. troubled by sore eye. Read papers. Rec[eive]d letter from Aunt C. Wrote letter for Mr. C[harles] P. Tinker about gun. Some of the boys got drunk to-night. A bandage, wet, on my eye.

Saturday, 31st.—Got med[icine] for eye which stuck tight together. When I got up, bo't ball starter for gun & molds. Molded some bullets. Bo't some apples of a woman. Shook blankets. Pleasant. Took gun out to shoot but shooting was prohibited, fired a blank charge & found there was a hole clear thro' the barrel head. Freezing to-night.

Sunday, Feb*[ruary]* 1st.—Muddy, mild. Eyes better. Saw (Cavalry) Capt*[ain]* Ira Holmes[92] formerly of Brockport & sent home (to Mother) $20, & took receipt, he to send Mother cert*[ificate]* of deposit in "Holmes Banking House". Knapsack parade. Put on new pants to go to Ch*[urch]* but did not. On guard, 3rd relief. 2 meals per day. Rain in eve. Guard march around the camp. Wrote home.

Monday, 2d.—Fine day, but muddy. Rec*[eive]*d *[Rochester Evening]* Ex*[press]* from home & Dem*[ocrat]* from Aunt. I molded bullets. Sent letter home. Mud drying fast in P.M. Washed some things & feet. Euchre in eve.

Context—The first five companies of the 1st Battalion left NYS February 3 to serve in the defense of Washington.

Tuesday, 3d.—Colder & mud frozen. Windy. Battalion *[drill]*. Bo't New York paper. Sent it home. Also bo't apples &c. Skirmish in the P.M. In barracks by the stove all day. Reported that we are going to-morrow.

Wednesday, 4th.—Knapsack inspection by Col*[onel William S. Rowland]* who said we are going to Washington to-morrow. Wrote home & sent home some things with the boys. Packed knapsack. Stood guard for M*[atthew]* H*[ennessey]*. Very cold. In the eve. helped carry barrel beef out to store. Had wine & cherry brandy. Bo't 2 pies &c. The coldest night we have had yet.

Brockport Republic, February 12, 1863

Camp Sprague, Staten Island, N.Y. February 4, 1863. Mr. Beach: Please announce, if not too late, that it is understood here in camp, that the battalion of Sharpshooters, (the Rochester company included), are ordered to leave for Washington on Thursday or Friday of this week. It is rumored that we are to go to Chain Bridge, near Washington, and it may or may not be true.—Co. A were paid off on Friday last, and received the remainder of the telescope and globe rifles. The other companies in the battalion are not yet armed.

There are several outside companies of Zouaves and Cavalry in camp; among the latter, Capt. Ira Holmes, of Brockport, brought down and quartered here thirty recruits for his company from Buffalo. He has gone to Rochester for men recruited there, and some of the boys in this company from Brockport and vicinity sent home by him some greenbacks, which he kindly consented to carry for us. We were glad to welcome him to camp.

Corporal Raymond, of Parma, in company A was discharged last week, and has gone home. Two or three others will soon be discharged.

You will probably hear from us when we get to our destination, wherever it may be. Letters or papers which come directed to us here will be forwarded to us. J.T.F.

Thursday, 5th.—Snowing all day. Very cold in A.M. Saw some of the Brockport boys in Cav*[alry]* Co*[mpany]*. Things all ready to leave—knife, fork, plate, cups, and spoon. Helped wash dishes. Sold partnership stove; got 70c, divided & 25c remained. Took some pure cherry brandy. Marched to cars at 1, not ready & went back. Then left on cars at 3, rode to Tottenville, staid 2 or 3 hours in snow & rain on steamer to S. Amboy. There took cars, rode to Camden & by ferry across Del*[aware]* river *[to]* Philadelphia. Had lunch at Cooper Shop Volunteer Refreshment Saloon[93].

Friday, 6th.—At lunch 3½ in A.M., furnished by citizens of Philadelphia to all volunteers passing through the city. Found a boy who gave me information. Left & went (in rain) to Depot of Phila*[delphia]* Wilmington, and Balt*[imore]*, R.R., laid on the floor a few minutes & was ref*[reshe]*d by *[it]*. Went indoors & wrote letters home putting let*[ter]* in box. Drew water from hydrant. Talked with conductor who gave me a check from P*[hiladelphia]* to Balt*[imore]*. Did not sleep. Saw gov*[ernment]* arms in depot. Left Phila*[delphia]* at 8 via Balt*[imore]*, rain all the way. Saw negroes on the way. Cars crossed on ferry boat at Susq*[uehanna]* R*[iver]* and arrived at Balt*[imore]* 2½ P.M.; rain stop*[pe]*d. Marched thro' st*[reet]*s. to "Yankee Doodle"; lunch at Vol*[unteer]* Relief. To Fort Federal Hill[94] with others, then saw boys from K*[endall]* Mills; fine view of the city of Balt*[imore]* W*[ashington]* Mon*[ument]* &c. Cannon, mortars, shells & balls. Parade back to depot. Dan & Simon W. with us. Started for Wash*[ington]* at 8 P.M. Fine moonlight; am in W*[ashington]* at 10 (10). Lunched at Sold*[ier's]* Relief,[95] poor coffee, good bread, salt beef. Slept in building near the Capitol on the floor upon blanket, tired.

Saturday, 7th.—A splendid sunny day. View of only the dome of Cap*[itol]*; city (outside) appears scattered, ground broken (break*[fast]* at S*[oldiers]* R*[elief]*). Inspections of rifles after cleaning; fine wash in tank where water flows all the time. Cav*[alry]* here. Bo't illustrated (writing) paper & wrote home. Dinner at *[Soldier's Relief]* same as break*[fas]*t. Went to visit Capitol with Serg*[ean]*t—hastily. A noble work & dome uncompleted, marble continually going up & men polishing fine marble statues. Entered & saw large paintings of events & celebrated persons. In House of Representatives heard debate on internal improvements, a splendid place, & most of the members present. As one sat down, others wishing to speak jumped up & shouted "Mr. Speaker, Mr. Speaker." Messenger boys. Staid only a *[few]* minutes. In Senate Chamber a Sen*[ator]* from Kentucky, Mr. *[Garrett]* Davis,[96] speaking on the bill to appropriate $20,000,000 to buy & emancipate all slaves in Missouri; interesting. Nice furniture, &c. Vice Pres*[ident]* H*[annibal]* Hamlin. From window saw forts & Arlington Heights. Came back to camp by poor sidewalks; passed thro' park. Stopped & had raw oyster &c. Supper eatables same. See baggage wagons, 4 horses, (driver) man riding one & driving with 1 line. In bed early, prospect of leaving tomorrow. Rather cold to-night.

Sunday, 8th.—Warm, sunny. Better break*[fas]*t at S*[oldiers]* R*[elief]*. Ham. Saw lots of soldiers. Filled canteen, bo't ginger bread—ready to bake. About noon (ambulance) teams & baggage wagons being drawn, they took our knapsacks. We had lunch at S*[oldiers]* R*[elief]*, also rations, then marched through Penn*[sylvania]* Avenue with our rifles, haversacks & canteens, over Long Bridge in mud to camp Casey in Arlington Heights. Stopped, very tired, & put up tents. Ate from haversack. Pleasant camp 4 or 5 miles from Capitol & in sight of it. In a peach orchard, near Forts Richardson & Albany & in sight of Reb Gen*[eral Robert E.]* Lee's (former) residence. Saw lots of crows on the way here; get water at spring. Sleep on blanket spread on damp grounds. Cold. Managed to get my things together. Quite tired & sleepy. Abed early.

Monday, 9th.—Fine day. Break*[fas]*t from haversack; bread & meat. Orderly sick. Took walk with R.R. to Fort R*[ichardson]*. Large guns. Bo't gingerbread. On hill overlooking convalescent camp. Rifle pits & men throwing up embankments under the guns of the Fort. Commenced a letter to Brockport R*[epublic]*. Did not finish. Fire at target, 80 rods. Commenced letter home. Coffee & beef for supper. Not in very good humor & go to bed early to sleep it off.

Tuesday, 10th.—After breakf*[as]*t, sent letter home. Changed my quarters to tent with S*[ampson]* W. Fry. Got hay. Cleaned up in front of tent. Washed up after dinner, shoveled, clearing for parade grounds. Sent card to Henry Fuller (Artilllery) Miners Hill. Capwell bro't me $1 in stamps & bottle oil. Bo't paper of boy this morning. Read tonight. Cold nights.

Wednesday, 11th.—Cold & a few flakes of snow. Sent paper home. Cleaned rifle & oiled it. Put on new (old fixed) stockings. Sewed on buttons, &c. Read in this Diary. Hear report of fighting in Fredericksburg[97] (7, 8, 9) so we ordered to get knapsacks ready & have 1,400 lbs. of lead (bro't here to melt into bullets. Read paper in tent; damp & cold nights. Roll call at 8 P.M.

Thursday, 12th.—Some rain. Read Washington Chronicle. In P.M. a brigade of 141st New York *[VI]* & other reg*[imen]*ts encamped near us. Wrote to Republic. Heard rapid firing to the South. Rec*[eive]*d letter from Aunt C. & from R*[obert]* J. Gordon 13th *[NYVI]* Reg*[imen]*t. Wrote to Amer*[ican]* Ex*[press]* Co*[mpany]* about box. Heavy wind took part of our tent down & threw back pole over *[Sampson W.]* Fry & I. Wind blew on our heads, but at last we covered our heads & slept.

Context—The Federal troops were defeated in their Fredericksburg operation on February 13.

Brockport Republic, February 19, 1863

Camp Casey, Arlington Heights, Va., Feb. 13, 1863. Editor Republic:—We are, at last, on Dixie's sacred soil on the road to Richmond.—Whether we will ever reach that rebel nest, remains to be seen. Perhaps something like a description of our journey here would be acceptable, although brief. Soldiers' travels to the seat of war generally afford but limited chance of observation, especially if the soldier be a private.

Company A (the Rochester company) now called the sixth company of the 1st battalion, 1st regiment N.Y.S.S., were paid to Jan. 1st, on the 31st of Jan., and received the remainder of our guns. Last Thursday, 5th, having had marching orders to Washington, we, three companies in all, slung our heavy knapsacks and left New Dorp, S.I., at 3 P.M., rode on the cars to Tottenville, where we waited in snow and rain for transport, which came after dark. Steaming to South Amboy, N.J., we took cars to Camden. Here we ferried the Delaware about 2 A.M., arrived in Philadelphia in the rain, and marched, escorted by Mr. L. W. Thornton, to the "Cooper Shop Volunteer Refreshment Saloon," (6) of which institution he is an active member, where we found awaiting us, a lunch in the shape of good coffee, bread, cold meat, cabbage, cheese, &c.—On one side of the room were set the eating tables; the opposite side was occupied as a cooper shop. This institution was started by the coopers[98] of Philadelphia, May 26, 1861, and is now kept on by the generous-hearted Philadelphians; many a regiment of soldiers on the way to battle have been fed here. On the second floor is a free hospital retreat where wounded soldiers are taken care of in a comfortable suite of rooms. Dr. Nebinger of Philadelphia, volunteers his services in caring for any who are "lucky" enough to get in there. As we march through the streets the rain poured down in torrents, and we had a poor view of the "City of Brotherly Love."—We went to the Philadelphia, Wilmington and Baltimore Railroad depot, and laid on the floor from 4 A.M. till daylight. This depot is large and well arranged. To the vigilant and accommodating watchman, George Tetter, your correspondent is indebted for information.

Leaving Philadelphia at 8, on the above road, the most direct route, we reached Baltimore at 2½ P.M. What might be a pleasant scenery in good weather was then made dreary by clouds and falling rain. As we passed thro' Maryland, negro faces at every farm house reminded one of the existence of slavery in that State. As Baltimore was reached, the rain ceased and the sun came forth. The threatening guns of Forts Federal Hill, Albany, and McHenry could be seen in the distance. Thro' the streets of this rebel nested city we marched without disturbance, to the tune of "Yankee Doodle," over the same ground where two years ago federal troops were stoned on passing. Crowds of white and black faces swarmed into the streets as we passed. Nothing unusual in the appearance of that part of the city through which we passed, could be discovered, different from that of any city of the age of Baltimore. A soldier's relief here furnished us with a lunch; though not of as good a quality as Philadelphia.

As we could not leave until evening, several visited friends in the 129th and 151st N.Y. regiments. The former have been transferred, and are called the "8th N.Y. Heavy Artillery," Col. Porter—from Lockport. They occupy Fort Federal Hill, which is well defended by heavy breastworks; large cannon and mortars, on an eminence commanding a splendid view (from that place) of the pleasant city. We met with a good reception by our friends in the fort, who appear well pleased with their comfortable situation.. A correspondent of the Roch. Express, W.W., is here, and his contenance looks familiar. Co. K were ordered to the city on some duty just before we came away, and made a good appearance. After showing us about, Lieut. S. Webster and the Drum Major escorted us back to the depot.

At 8 o'clock we left Baltimore for Washington; arrived there about 11 P.M. The pleasant moonlight revealed to us the Capitol dome as we marched to the Soldiers' Relief; here were tables containing corn beef, bread, and a very poor sort of coffee. This institution is almost continually supplying soldiers with meals of this kind. The city appears to be filled with volunteers, and tents can be seen in every direction, though there are less in the city now than formerly. We slept that night on the floor of a building near the depot, then partly occupied by cavalry, and while remaining in the city, took our meals at the Relief.

Marching orders were hourly expected, consequently we could not go about the city, and many were disappointed. Within a few rods of the public buildings, and scarce permission to visit them; the military patrols constantly on the look-out for stragglers. However, in company with a sergeant I visited the nearly finished capitol. Approaching the building at one and, one might think it but a common structure. It is only as seen by a close front view that the beauty of the grand marble edifice can be appreciated. I will not attempt to describe this solid work of art; a rough idea of it may be formed from pictures except the dome, which is yet unfinished. The grounds in the rear are covered with pieces of marble and blocks of that material are constantly being drawn to the dome. Numerous designs of finely carved statuary adorn the grounds and steps; inside are fine paintings of prominent men and scenes recorded in American history; tasty decoration and furniture add to the comfortable appearance of the Senate Chambers and Representative Hall. A visit so hurried as this unavoidably was, admits of no time to notice everything. In the House, most of the members appeared to be present. The subject of discussion seemed to be Internal Improvements of some kind. Mr. Grow,[99] the dignified Speaker, appeared to understand himself, and when that part of the debate where one member closes and others wishing to speak jump up and shout, "Mr. Speaker! Mr. Speaker!" was played, he brought them to order immediately, and "the gentlman from New York" had the floor. In the Senate a Kentucky member was speaking upon the bill to appropriate $20,000,000 for the emancipation of Slaves in Missouri. In both Houses some of the members were lounging around, while others were busy conversing, &c., among the latter was the Hon. Alfred Ely,[100] of Monroe. Reporter's pens were flying glibly. Vice President Hamlin occupied the presiding chair of the Senate. Besides citizens occupying the galleries, were many soldiers attentively listening to the debates.

I had not the satisfaction of visiting the other public buildings, but am sure Washington has very poor streets, no pavements generally and from rough observation appear irregularly formed. On Sunday afternoon, we marched through Pennsylvania Avenue's business *[illegible word ending "ing"]* thoroughfare, and attracted crowds of people; our ambulance and baggage wagons bro't up the rear, all making an "imposing" appearance. Crossing the Long Bridge into Virginia, after a good march for men unused to it, we pitched tents on Arlington Heights, about five miles from Washington, near Camp Casey, in a once thriving peach orchard, not many rods from Forts Albany and Richardson; a fine location with a good view of the Capitol and Potomac. So now it appears we are "in for it," and may soon be "on to glory" or Richmond. There is much to write, but no time now.—Letters, &c., should be directed to us at Washington, D.C. J.T.F.

Friday, 13th.—Sunny & warmer. Fixed text, bro't water & drilled. At a negro house to get washing done. Oiled my gun. *[Sampson W.]* Fry washed for me. Run bullets. Drill with rifles, parade & battalion drill & bank. Saw Tom *[illegible name]* or *Cha[rle]s* Stratton & lady ride by in carriage. A cold night. To bed just after 8 o'c*[lock]* roll call.

Saturday, 14th.—St. Valentine's Day—Cold, but pleasant. Had set screw changed in my rifle & sight changed. Run bullets. Aired clothes. Bo't paper. Commenced writing to mother. Received papers from home. Rec[eive]d breast & should[er] belts, brass plates, bullet & cap boxes; getting well loaded up. No coffee for supper. By the fire in eve.

Sunday, 15th.—Rain most of the day. No breakfast cooked. Bread & raw pork. Finished letter & wrote to Aunt C. Bro't water. Had rice & molasses & tea in the P.M. Drill & dress parade with equipment. Pleasant in the P.M. Read paper till roll call.

Monday, 16th.—Pleasant & quite warm. After breakfast [Sampson W.] Fry & I went out to shoot at target. Lighted my rifle at 40 rods, but no extra shots; wind blew. Saw rabbit shot. Wiper stuck in gun twice. Staid till 3 o'c[lock]. Back through (Camp Casey) fort. Bean soup. Bo't nut cakes & pie. Parade afte cleaning gun. Rec[eive]d 3 letters from F[ather]; Mother has been very sick, now better; also letter from sister & Aunt C.—Wrote to F[ather]. Quite mild to-night.

Tuesday, 17th.—Winter again—snow falling fast & getting colder. Good breakfast. Sent letter. Snow fell nearly all day. Nothing cooked after breakfast. Found Esq[uire] Carter formerly of Medina [NY] now sutler here. Had talk with him. Coffee, pie & oysters. In eve. had cider at N.E. House. Gave man p[ostage] $1 to send for box at New York. At gun house awhile. Cold to-night.

Wednesday, 18th.—Snowy & rain most of the day. Had breakfast of coffee, pie & bread at N.E. house with [Sampson W.] F[ry]. With J[ohn] D. Campbell, bo't small stove, pipe & fry-pan, for $1.50—50c each. Put up stove & it's a nice thing, in this damp weather. Cooked a piece of beef for sup[per]; bro't water had soup made outdoors & sugar for 4 days. Good news of general draft.[101] Borrowed papers. Another in tent to-night. Rainy.

Thursday, 19th.—Some pleasanter but misty. Made cup coffee & had fried pork. Cleaned snow. Read. In tent most of day as yesterday. Made cup coffee. Awkward dress parade. Rec[eive]d letter from Aunt C & sister. M[other] gaining. Reclined by pleasant light of fire in stove till dress parade.

Friday, 20th.—Sunshine & very windy. On guard, 1st relief. Jangle[102] in regard to time. Run bullets, washed up. Bo't paper. Looked through telescope at vessels on the Potomac & at the Capitol in Washington. Read papers & went on guard to-night.

Saturday, 21st.—Sun shines, very mild; bro't water; breakfast & washed dishes. Cleaned gun. Aired clothes. Wrote. Rec[eive]d [Brockport] Republic with my letter. Feel not very well to-night (colder in P.M.).

Sunday, 22d.—Washington's Birthday—Heavy snow storm, piling drifts. Cut wood. Had cup coffee, bread & pork. In the tent all day. Wrote to sister & Aunt C. Supper about the same as breakfast. In dealing out sugar, we are not given as much as we are entitled to. Fire in the stove makes it cheerful. Abed early.

Monday, 23d.—Thawing in the sun but a very cold north wind. Had tent raised by putting log under it. Coffee & pie at sutlers. Heard that the box sent from home 3 weeks ago is in Washington. Speak for a pass to-morrow, doubtful. Supped on coffee & bread, sitting on the ground. Seems rather tough. Found a soldier's paper. Made out to get a bed made after roll call.

Brockport Republic, March 5, 1863

Camp Seward, Feb. 21, 1863. Editor Republic:—In view of the National Capitol, the silent Potomac with its busy fleet of transports, the city of Alexandria on the right, Fairfax Seminary[103] steeple towering farther to the South, in sight of the flag floating from Arlington house, former residence of the rebel General Lee, and Fort Corcoran on the left; a line of forts and rifle breastworks for miles on either side, and near the western line of the District of Columbia, here lie a battalion of N.Y. Sharpshooters, sixth company of which represent Monroe and Orleans. A splendid location for a camp—a side hill, ground sandy, good spring water near—and only five miles from Washington. Monroe troops have quartered here before. A few traces of a once thriving peach orchard remain; but were rendered useless by the horses of a cavalry regiment, who, in the absence of forage, stripped the bark from them, and those remaining are fast disappearing by the axe when the regular supply of wood runs short. Timber and fences are scarce articles in these parts, of the latter but a vestige remains, and the absence of timber land gives the country rather a desolate appearance. There are large tracts of new land unbroken by the plow and darkened by stumps, the soil bearing evidence of once being the camping ground of soldiers, where ditches were dug about the tents for draining. Springs are numerous. Houses and outbuildings of the "F.F.V."[104] have a dreary and forsaken look, and everything once showing the presence of civilization, now attests the blasting effects of war and its ravages. If such are the appearances on comparatively the outside border of secession, how much more changed must be the once pleasant country where war is actually raging. Destruction of home comforts appear to fall as heavily in general, upon loyalists as traitors; for everything movable seems destined to minister to the wants and add to the comfort of the army. Near us, the 25th Maine regiment are building a fort; a large force of contrabands are drawing logs for the breastworks; a small army of blacks pass here daily, driving teams, and cutting wood for the government; one dollar per cord is said to be paid them for the latter work. Our boys are just building stockades for putting up logs, on which the tents are set, making a comfortable house "for a soldier." A few uneasy persons deserted us just after pay day. It is gratifying to get rid of such weak-minded ones, who are unthinking enough to bring disgrace upon themselves and trouble to their friends.— Their services are needed, and it is hoped they will be properly punished. The eighth and ninth companies, (the seventh is recruiting at Staten island,) received Sharp's improved rifles[105] last week, and we all received cartridge and cap boxes, belts, &c. As we of the sixth company run our own bullets, loading our telescope and globe rifles with ball and patch, powder flasks are yet to be given us; then we will be ready to follow those who have gone before and given up their lives, notwithstanding the disloyal exertions of Northern secession-aiding "Copperheads,"[106] who cry "peace on any terms." We are bound to *fight* it out; there is now no honorable way to obtain peace but for us to assist with the bullet, on the battle field to

"Push on! Push on *our banner* proud!
Its glorious folds shall ever waive;
Black Treason's flag long cannot cloud
The sky o'er Monticello's grave;
And there redeem this classic land
Where old Virginia's sages lie—
Redeem, redeem that noble band—
Redeem their graves from infamy!"

At all hours of the day baggage wagons with teams of four and six horses, pass too [sic] and from Washington, going after and bringing provisions for the army. Every wagon as well as every person must submit to a search on passing Long Bridge, which is strictly guarded. Passes to Washington are not easily obtained.—Changes of weather are as sudden here as in N.Y. We have much rain. Tuesday and Wednesday last we had a regular Northern snow storm, ahead of anything we saw in New York city, and very tedious; snow fell to the depth of nine inches; a rain storm followed and the snow disappeared fast. Now the sun shines brightly, and milder weather could not be asked for. "Everything is lovely." The rainy season has not yet passed, however.—Cold nights are extremely fashionable. A few are on the sick list, caused perhaps by sleeping in proximity to the damp ground. (It is with pleasure, however, that I inform any anxious friends that your correspondent is all right, well and hearty, and has not forgotten Brockport and its inhabitants.)

Sutlers are numerous hereabouts, and generally charge double price for everything. R. Garter, Esq., formerly a Medina lawyer, is acting as sutler near the 25th Maine. The honorable gentleman appears still attached to "court" reminders, for while he politely dispenses necessaries to the soldiers at his "bar," a cobbler occupies the "bench" on the opposite side of the room. The Medina Battery, Capt. Anthony, are said to be six miles from here. I will now close by saying that our honored Capt. Gray has been "honorably" discharged from service. V. J. Shipman is now our captain.

Feb. 23.—Another heavy storm yesterday piled up the drifts in regular northern fashion. Air last night was *very cold* This morning the sun comes forth brightly, and the snow may soon be gone. The "sacred soil" looks bleached. J.T.F.

Tuesday, 24th.—A cold (freezing) night & we slept with front of tent open. Made coffee & had that & bread. Could get no pass to W*[ashington]* but sent for box. Fixed tent, banked up. Rec*[eive]*d letter from home (mother). At roll call had order to have everything packed & ready to strike tents Thursday morning as we might expect, just as our tents are well arranged. Saw Ch*[auncey]* P*[arker]* & am getting box to-morrow.

Wednesday, 25th.—Sent papers home to let them know we are to leave. Pleasant, as yesterday. Snow melting some. Getting ready for marching. Fried pork for sandwiches. Some bad smelling salt beef drawn. Mending, &c. Got bottle ink filled. Bo't cakes. Sold stove (3 in Co*[mpany]*) for $1. Made hominy & coffee for 2 teamsters & coffee for canteens. No box in Wash*[ington]*. Rec*[eive]*d dagger, had lots of fun. Washed dishes. All ready at a moments notice.

Thursday, 26th.—Woke at 5, got up, made coffee at fire out doors. Packed knapsack & at 7 stacked tent & packed it up. Rainy. Waited in the rain till 9 or after (knapsacks carried in wagon), then marched to Wash*[ington]* in the mud & rain, back over Long Bridge. At a pier go on board steamer "Planter"[107] & when everything was taken on at 2 o'clock started down the Potomac. As we got to Alexandria (4 m*[iles]*) stopped & sky cleared. Rec*[eive]*d letter from Cous*[in]* Mary. At VP also bo't cake & pie & paper. Secured bunk on boat, felt wet & damp & no place to dry. Lots of boats at Alexandria also below. At 6 (P.M.) passed Mt. Vernon & saw it with its pillars in front & negro houses. Supper—dry bread & cake with (cold) coffee in canteen. Quite early I made up bunk (which I was lucky to get) & retired. Boat stopped for the night at 10 & I slept well.

Friday, 27th.—Foggy this A.M. but about 10 cleared off. Rain last night. Laid abed till 9. Then ate from haversack. Oiled gun. Saw Aquia Creek. Lots of ducks but not often shot. Commenced writing home. At 3 fog cleared & sun shone pleasant. Halted at a gun boat to have papers examined. At 4 cast anchor for the night. Oyster boat ran near us. Soon a man with an oyster boat ran to us & I bo't a pail (nearly a bushel) of them in the shell for 14c. *[Sampson W.]* Fry & I opened them & F*[ry]* made me a cup of meat. Ate part of them raw with bread & saved the rest till morning. We are anchored near the mouth of St. Mary's river, near Chesapeake Bay. A pleasant sunset & rebels near. In my bunk again in good season.

Saturday, 28th.—Late getting up—8. Bread & raw oyster. Boat started about 2 A.M. In Chesa*[peake]* Bay, blue water, sea gulls flying, & ducks. Cloudy. Cleaned gun. On guard. Knapsack packed & all ready to march. Wrote letter home. Vessel rocks some. Off Fortress Monroe[108] about 12, large guns. 'Rip Raps'[109] opposite. Iron clad & men of war. Rainy. Seagulls. Steamed on to Norfolk, passed Servall's Point & Craney Island. Model light house. Arrived at Norfolk 6. Clean city. Marched thro' st*[ree]*s to a negro church & slept on the floor with overcoat on. Hear frogs croak.

March

Context—The battalion served at Suffolk, Va., in Terry's Brigade, Peck's Division, 7th Corps, from March until June 1863.

Sunday, March 1st.—Felt quite as well as could have been expected on floor. In the grave yard found lilys in bud, green grass & heard robins. At brick court house, also residence of Roger A. Pryor, now rebel Gen*[eral]*. Got daffodil in bloom to send him. Saw gunboat on Nansemond river, & steamb*[oat]*. Canteen filled at pump. Nig*[ger]* scraped his heel & bent his head. Left the city & marched east on Portsm*[outh]* M*[ain]* R*[oad]* 1½ m. to bridge in cornfield, nice & sandy. Just stopped raining as we got there. Tired. Put up tent & put boughs on floor. Filled tick with spruce boughs, & got tent rigged. Washed for first time in 3 days. Fine weather. Frogs croaking. A good bed & slept well. In with *[Sampson P.]*Fry & *[Charles]* Collamer.

Monday, 2d.—Heavy dew & frost. Gun wet. Oiled it. Birds singing. Bound & do no guard except at night. None till we get flasks. Saw *[Brigadier]* Gen*[eral Michael]* Corcoran & staff ride by. Wrote home & to M*[ary A. C. French]*, Aunt & H*[arvey]* & it took me all day. Great rush for meat, &c. before dress parade. Colder to-night & warm to-day. Dew. Roll call in hurry. Moon.

Tuesday, 3d.—Fine day. A few sprinkles of rain in P.M. Detailed to get wood for cooking. Cook house built.—Wrote to *[Brockport]* Republic. Cannon bro't on fort. A good supper. Tide on.

Brockport Republic, March 12, 1863

Camp near Suffolk, Va., March 4, 1863. Editor Republic.—I am happy to inform you that this battalion has made another "excursion," and is now encamped in the southeast part of Virginia, near the great Dismal Swamp,[110] and in the region of the Blackwater river, where only a few days ago our forces had a brush with the rebels and drove them back. Now we may be considered in the heart of rebeldom.

Having received marching orders while at Arlington Heights, after the usual preparations for a trip, on Thursday monrning, Feb. 26, we took down our tents, and marched in rain and mud back to Washington, over the Long Bridge again. (It is generally unusual for an excursion to be made in the rain, but we are as sure to get a storm when on a move as the Orleans county people are at Fair time.) At the city we took passage on board the government steamboat "Planter," Capt. Curtis, and when our baggage wagons, horses, &c., were on board, we steamed down the Potomac about 2 P.M., stopped a short time at the busy city of Alexandria, and then on down the river past Fort Washington, and at 6 came in view of the Washington Mansion at Mt. Vernon; could see the pillars in front, and the outbuildings of this sacred burial place. The air was very foggy, and of course we could not see much.—Boat anchored at 9, as government boats are not allowed to run at night. The Planter is a very neat boat. Some slept in the upper cabin, and others in the hold. On Friday the weather was no better till P.M. We had passed Acquia Creek (**11**), and halted near a gunboat to have papers examined near Piney Point, and at 4 came to anchor for the night in the mouth of St. Mary's river. The weather was clear as we stopped, and we had a beautiful sun set. Oyster boats were numerous; oysters were piled on their decks, they came alongside and we bought them in the shell for fifty cents a bushel. The boys had during the day been amusing themselves by shooting at seagulls and ducks which were numerous on the water, but as they had a wonderful facility for diving at each flash, were rarely hit. The boat started again at 2 o'clock Saturday morning, and made good headway down the Chesapeake Bay, past the mouth of the Rappahannock and York rivers, and about noon came to anchor between Fortress Monroe (**12, 13**) and the Rip Raps opposite where, without our going on shore the officers reported to Gen. Dix at the fort; many of us had friends at the fort and would liked to have visited them. Fortress Monroe is built well up with smooth stone, and its many guns, among which are two heavy ones outside, command the passage between it and the Rip Raps; the latter is a stone fort built upon a foundation of large stones thrown into the water.— Many vessels were at anchor here—steamers, an iron clad gunboat, a French and English man-of-war, &c. Waiting till 4, we had orders to go on to Suffolk, via Norfolk. Rain was pouring down as we steamed on past a long line of schooners, across the mouth of the James river, by Sewall's Point and Craney Island and just at dark came to the city of Norfolk, opposite Portsmouth. Norfolk, as we rode in made a fine appearance, and is the cleanest looking city I have seen; here a navy yard was burned about the time the rebels occupied it. It was dark when we at last got out ourselves and baggage, and took passage in new freight cars and rode over the Dismal Swamp to Suffolk, Va. In the latter place the first thing we heard was the croaking of frogs, and they were having a nice spring shower.—We took possession of an old church and slept on the floor till morning. On going to the church yard Sunday morning the rain had ceased; the air was mild, everything was mild, everything appeared green, birds were singing and buds of plants in the grave yard were just ready to blossom. Down in the city the darkies had on their best rig, and many of the Dinahs were arrayed in crimson, prepared for church and "Sunday night." A brick court house is now occupied by provost guard. A fine brick dwelling and nice grounds, formerly occupied by the rebel General Roger A. Pryor, is now the headquarters of Gen. Peck, commanding here; in the yard of this dwelling I found some nice flowers in bloom; daffodils were said to have been in blossom a month. The Nansemond river, very narrow here, is navigated by vessels from Fortress Monroe and a gunboat is guarding a bridge here. Suffolk is a respectable appearing city; soldiers are most numerous of anything except "darks."

We are encamped one and a half miles east from the city, on the railroad running to Portsmouth, near the track, in a nice sandy cornfield, opposite an unfinished fort which we guard, and expect soon to occupy. A small creek called "Jericho" running close by, comes from the great Dismal Swamp, one end of which is near us. A long line of rifle pits protect us on one side, and we are prepared for the rebels who are said not to be many miles in advance. The "Mounted Rifles" are here, who were recruited in Rochester, also men from all parts of New York. We were mustered for pay yesterday, which may be significant of greenbacks soon. Gen. Corcoran's brigade is in the vicinity, and his men are finishing our pits. The general and staff galloped by here on Monday, he sits very erect, has a light hair, but is not of quite so commanding an appearance as I supposed.

The weather is fine, as warm as we could wish, but a heavy dew makes the nights chilly; otherwise everything is decidedly lovely. I will perhaps give you more news next time. Letters, &c., should be directed to Suffolk, Va. J.T.F.

Wednesday, 4th.—Air was filled with snow for an hour in A.M. but went right. Pretty cold. N[orth]. wind. Drill. Cleaned brass. Took walk to military burying ground & among others found a grave marked Luther Farnham. Near N[egro] town, a new negro village. [illegible words] of pine trees all about. Bro't water. A wench went by with white bandana on her head. Bo't pie &c in A.M. Dress parade. Some of our boys went after spy—gone. Others out on picket in the woods. Fire on the hill. Cold night.

Thursday, 5th.—Ice froze in tent ¼ of inch. Sun shone warm about noon. On guard at spring, darkies after water. Gave [Timothy H.] Babbitt buttons. At Unionville, negro village crossed a swamp to get there saw some blacks splitting pine for boards. One, a slave from N[orth] C[arolina]. One old "Uncle" making mortar. Little "pickaninnies" playing, old lady with wen on eye. Back 10 m[inutes] after time to go on guard & found Corp[oral] on my post at spring. Steak sup[per]. Freezing cold, still at eve. On guard front till 11, in moonlight—guinea hens cackling. Joe Pratt & negores bobbing in & out.

Friday, 6th.—[Sampson P.] Fry took my place at 3 Good sleep till 7½. Clean gun every morning. Out by stream of water with [Sampson W.] F[ry], saw shells in sand, &c. Staked down tent tighter. At Unionville among the darkies with [Sampson W.] F[ry]. Mounted rifle corp[oral]. Bo't pint large oysters at negro house for 10c. Woman told us about slavery. Agree to bring some washing at another place, lady with wen on eye & black gals, also Irish soldier. Back to camp first time for supper (coffee) & had a good dish of oysters, with all. Parade. Jumping. Hurt my hand this A.M. Windy & cold till 5, then in eve. warm. Called in shanty of colored people Hetty Copeland & Nelson Ely, formerly slaves. Pleasant talk. Invited to biscuit on Sunday morning.

Saturday, 7th.—A little rain then pleasant. Bro't boughs & set out trees in between tents. No parade. Out in rain watching for furs on the bank of creek. In eve. called a few minutes at [Nelson] Ely's.

Sunday, 8th.—A rain shower prevented knap[sack] parade. At Nathan's [no Nathan in 6th Company after 10/28/62. Is this Nelson Miller?] he fixed [Sampson W.] F[ry] & I a good breakfast of corn cake biscuit, fresh fish & coffee all well cooked. Had talk with them in cabin. Walk about fort. A fine day, warm. At negro meeting in Uniontown black preacher & praying ones & woman had the "power"—"Yah"—Some 300 colored all ages sexes & hues— some yellow, others black as jet. All fed by Gov[ernmen]t & paid $10 a month for work. Dress parade. A bag of letters & papers for our 3 Co[mpanie]s, which had been sent from Washington came. I rec[eive]d 5 papers & a letter from mother, sister, and Aunt C. Feel better. Read news to those across the way & gave them b[rea]d—Read papers in tent &c.

Monday, 9th.—Cloudy, then pleasant. Reading. Powder flasks come, also powder. Contrabands about for clothes to wash. Boys building stockade. After dress parade rec[eive]d flasks & papers from home, also [Brockport] Repub[lic] with letter in it. Took washing across the R.R. staid till roll call, 8. Heard of black beans & sparks. From 11 till 1 stood on guard for S[ampson] W. F[ry], Grand Rounds (Rome [countersign]) moonlight, lightning.

Tuesday, 10th.—Pass to Suffolk for S[ampson] W. F[ry] & I. Rain all day but went to Suffolk. Watch crystal put in at store of Jews—a good looking girl. Found a printing office but without a pass. At Adjutant Gen[eral]s office presented Mr. [Horatio N.] Beach's letter, the A[djutant] gave me a pass to the Pr[inting] O[ffice] & I with [Sampson W.] Fry went back & in; all the material was old & not much of. Wash[ington hand] press Chautauqua Co[unty] foreman. Dish of oysters stewed (nice) for 15c. Then back to camp in rain. Powder in flask & cotton for patches. Papers from home. Carried b[rea]d &c. to Hett[y Copeland] & Nels[on Ely] & read the news to them & they seemed to enjoy it. Still raining at 9.

Wednesday, 11th.—Abed late. Nelson [Ely] & Hetty [Copeland] gave me a warm hoe cake[111] or Johnny cake (white meal) for breakfast—nice—. On guard 1st rel[ief]—stood from 9 till 11 in rain at fort. At noon cleared off & sun shone pleasant P.M. Saw black women making or baking hoe cakes in kettles by coals—funny way. Children playing. In P.M. wrote letter to mother while in the fort, also while there Corp[oral]. Cha[rle]s R. Sikes of 1st NY Mounted Rifles & Sup[erintenden]t of contrabands of Uniontown had talk with him. Letter from M. C. & H. Finished letter to M[ary A. C.] F[rench]. Stood guard from 9–11.

Thursday, 12th.—Headache & laid abed till 7½. Finished letter to Cordelia & being too late for our carrier, Nelson [Ely] kindly took a letter for me to P.O. Practiced shooting in water. Satisfied with my rifle. Cleaned gun. In P.M. Cha[u]n[cey] [Parker] was in tent with me. Wrote letter to [Brockport] Republic. Rec[eive]d paper (Ex[press]). Cold & windy. At Hetty [Copeland]'s, read paper &c. Wrote to Harvey.

Brockport Republic, March 19, 1863

Camp Jericho, near Suffolk, Va., March 12, 1863. Mr. Editor:—We are just far enough South to have an occasional sample of all phases of weather, but it is generally mild, except quite cold nights, although we had an hour of winter the other day, and the air was filled with those heavy snow flakes which indicate in the North, a "right smart chance" as the negroes would say, for good sleighing, but the flakes melted in the succeeding *[illegible word]* rays of the sun sooner than they came. Since then we have had a drizzling March rain and now the bright warm sun again cheers us. The chirp of frogs in the marshes, the cackling of Guinea hens as they call for "buckwheat," and the wind sighing through the pine woods, is part of the music we hear, and all this occasionally varied by the firing of guns by soldiers in practice. The latter frequently reminds us that the rebels may be about, but that is not often the case, except as an occasional gray-back[112] is bro't in prisoner by the Mounted Riflemen, or "robbers," as the "Chinese" term them.

We hear all sorts of rumors; but you no doubt get the news of events about here as soon as we. Heavy skirmishes often occur.—We have at last received our powder and flasks, and are practicing at targets; probably will soon have a chance to pick off the traitors.—We are in Gen. Terry's division. There is no sickness of account, and the boys have lately completed comfortable stockades and built fire places in them with a wood and clay chimney running up the outside, as is the fashion here in common houses. Another evidence of their enterprise and good taste—as though preparing for visits from friends—is evident in the smoothing over of the ground in the streets between the rows of tents of each company, and the fine young pines shading and adorning the same, which they selected in the forest.— You would think a canvas city (**14**) had sprung up under a thrifty growth of evergreens. Then some have placed on the side of the earth banking the tents a covering of moss, in which is tastily placed an occasional small stone or shell. In the absence of other witness, I must assure you that we are enjoying a comfortable camp indeed. And I believe, we are justified in making ourselves as happy as possible under adverse circumstances, for at any hour we may be ordered to handle lead and powder.

We should be thankful that Providence and the government sent us here, among the comparatively ignorant contrabands, for we get from them a great amount of information concerning the evils and miseries of the cursed institution which has so long kept a people in bondage who are evidently anxious to breathe the air of freedom and get a common education as well as to earn a respectability. Between our camp and Suffolk, near us, is a negro, or contraband village (**16, 17**), and it is decidedly a great and benevolent institution. For an account of the rise and progress of the settlement, called Uniontown, I am indebted to the energetic Superintendent or Director, Corporal Charles R. Sikes, of the 1st N.Y. Mounted Rifles, who formerly lived in Troy, N.Y. The town now consists of some 150 houses hastily put up by the contrabands, of whom there are in all about 900 men, women and children—some 300 of the former. Contrabands escape from their masters and bring with them all their fellow servants they can manage, which is usually done on overhearing the masters talk of sending them farther South; then the slaves escape in the night and come through our picket lines but not so many come now as formerly, on account of the watchfulness of the owners, who are loth to see their human property take legs and walk away. On these blacks presenting themselves to the Provost Marshall here, they are sent to the Supt. of contrabands, who takes the names of the men, and the name and condition of the women or children who come with them, and the name and residence of the master; they are furnished then with comfortable quarters and each man allowed two weeks to build a house for his family, with help to do so if necessary.—At the expiration of this time the men are put in squads and employed to work for the government on fortifications or otherwise, at $10 a month, with rations of food for themselves and families; no authorized provision has yet been made as to clothing, although two requisitions have been made on the government by Mr. Sikes, for shoes; anything in the clothing line captured from the rebels is applied to those contrabands. There are new arrivals daily.—The village is laid out in streets, some of the houses having a fence in front. Everything looks as neat and clean as could be expected, and all things pass smoothly. The inhabitants are remarkably polite and well behaved. In going through there the other day, I came upon two black females, and one of middle age was teaching an old lady to read in a spelling book of an ancient date; the old lady was just advancing into the rudiments, and seemed delighted at her success. This is an illustration of the eagerness of all to master reading and writing, and there is here an extensive field for an exercise of that generous benevolence which characterizes the friends of advancement and education in the North. Will not some person or persons in New York State interest themselves in helping to furnish these now mostly ignorant people with means or tools to bring them from their present darkness to the light which they would obtain even by a mere knowledge of reading and writing.— Under the supervision of their friend and hard-working benefactor, Corporal Sikes, lumber is being made ready to build a commodious school house, (a rare object in this region) and any persons having second hand or other primers, spelling books, and readers of a primary character will confer a great kindness upon those people by getting them together and sending them in a box, directed to "Corporal Chas. R. Sikes, care Provost Marshall, Suffolk, Va." There are in almost every house in the North second hand books of this kind, (and only the most common sort are needed.) and I am sure Brockport might send her share to help this object for she is never behind in charitable works—all necessary to start the matter being a movement by some of the many warm hearted frinds of the down trodden, who are not afraid of an opposing spirit, fit only as a relic of crushing barbarism. Meetings are held at Uniontown on Sundays, in the open air—a black preacher officiating—and are attended by a large congregation, of all hues, sexes, ages and conditions.

Not wishing to impose upon the space of the Republic, I will leave further notice of matters about here, and close, in the hope that the above object will meet with the approbation of the kind-hearted. Those sending letters and papers to us should be particular to write the company number [*illegible words*]. J.T.F.

Friday, 13th.—Out with all our harness on at roll call & had slight drill before breakfast. Some of Hetty [*Copeland*]'s hoe cake, warm, which she gave me. Finished letter to Harvey. Target shooting—60 rods—one of 5 best. A cold, raw day. In P.M. visited camp of Mounted Riflemen thro' the woods. Fine camp; brass howitzers;[113] in gun shop & saw their dress parade. Battalion of 9th Army Corps just off from cars & more coming. Back to parade—Rec[*eive*]d letter from Cousin H. Took b[*rea*]d to H[*etty Copeland*]'s & had a good supper— fritters & molasses, &c. Sat by the fire in fireplace & talked with the family. Bo't shirt. Paper from home. Have had cold.

Saturday, 14th.—Usual performances & target shoot; windy & no extra sheets, but I am satisfied. Gathered boughs for floor of hospital & had some med[*icine*] for my cold. Cut bullet matches for rifle. My cold is worse. To tent with Mr. [*William*] Hues, also with Cha[*u*]n[*cey*] Parker. Letter from Aunt C. Sitting by fireplace, talking &c. Guard from 9 till 11 for S[*ampson*].W. Fry & heard officers singing, &c. Pleasant, starry.

Sunday, 15th.—Weather variable; some wind. Knapsack parade. Medicine last [*evening*] & this A.M. pills today. Break[*fast*] at Hetty [*Copeland*]'s. Cough some today. In the tent most all day & wrote to Cousin Henry [*C. Murray*]. Rice & molasses for supper. In eve. Hetty [*Copeland*] 's, good fire awhile. Went to bed quite early to-night. I do not feel well.

Monday, 16th.—Up a 8; & had cup coffee for break[*fas*]t. Reported on sick list & went to hospital at 9. D[*octo*]r there; took haversack there & had coffee & roast. Wrote to Mrs. Smith & Em[*ma Smith*]. Cloudy, damp & misty. Read papers. Across the R.R. a few minutes, got my blanket & went back to the hospital to stay to-night; a good place to sleep; dose of medicine.

Tuesday, 17th. (St. Patrick's Day)—Pleasant but cold. A good rest but coughed hard near morning. Up & washed. At my tent a few minutes then breakfast at the hospital—coffee & toast. Cleaned gun &c. Surgeon came & gave me some medicine which made me sick at my stomach. Beans, coffee & toast for dinner. Report of firing out near the lines. Wrote to M[ary A. C.] F[renc]h. Went over to see seven rebels prisoners (15) mostly in gray suits, 1 or 2 Kentucky jean[114] coats, white felt hats & looked lank & dirty; one sergeant (41st N[orth] C[arolina] Cavalry) all are guerillas, leader Capt[ain] Brown, Dutchman, a spy & a hard looking customer; long hair & whiskers yellow. All taken away to Suffolk in a wagon. 25th N[ew] J[ersey] V[olunteers] camping in small shelter tents in the woods near our camp, saw their dress parade. Dr. [John] Snevely is the hospital physician or steward. Drew my bread for hospital. Pleasant evening.

Wednesday, 18th.—Sun blood red. Feel rather weak, after taking medicine. Breakfasted on coffee & toast. Pretty hard cough yet. Read papers. Surgeon Nasbrond came & talked some secesh—that the South had a right to secede & if they gain the victory, all right—but if they are whipped they must submit!! Pretty bold for a man who gets $120 a month from the *Gov[ernmen]t*. Run some bullets & put on patches. In the hospital; sup[per], rec[eive]d [Brockport] Repub[lic] paper with my letter in & it was read by some of the boys; across the R.R. a few minutes with [Sampson W.] Fry. Sat up awhile in the hosp[ital] tent—then to bed.

Thursday, 19th.—Rainy. Hail. Cloudy & damp. Capt[ain] Volney J. Shipman read my paper, is going to send for the Republic to be sent to his home. Left the hospital at noon & went back to my tent. Feel well except some cough yet. Rain all day & snow fell in eve. Letter from Father, sister & Lon. Also papers & scraps. At the good old fire across the R.R. & read.

Friday, 20th.—Regular old Northern storm all day, thick & heavy. Tedious. No cooking for the co[mpany] & rations divided among us. [Sampson W.] Fry took ours & Hetty [Copeland] cooked us some steak, coffee, biscuits, &c. From Father's letter I found that new tent mate [Sampson W.] Fry is a relative of mine & that I have a cousin, Geo[rge] Farnham, from Victor, N.Y., in the 1st N[ew] Y[ork] Mounted Rifle Co[mpany] "K', so in the storm I posted over to their camp & found him. Helped him eat some bread with Victory butter & dried beef. After visiting with him & talking with the boys awhile, I came back by way of the camp of the 25th N[ew]J[ersey] in shelter tents. Wrote letter to Father, sis[ter], & Lon. Made cup coffee by fire in next tent & fried a piece of pork for my supper. Rec[eive]d package of reader & sp[elling] b[oo]k from home. Took them over to the cont[raband]s who were delighted; heard Sarah spell &c. A pleasant time by the fire. In Capt[ain Volney J.] Shipman's tent & showed him his printed letter & Father's poetry &c. Saw his pictures, then to bed. Still snowing at 9.

Saturday, 21st.—Storm closed about 10. Mild but snow about 4 or 5 in. makes slush. Nat cooked us some break*[fast]*. We ate with 2 boys from the Mounted Riflemen. Cleaned snow from around the tent. Mailed letters. Sent paper back home yesterday. Cleaned gun &c. Mended clothes. Snow melts. Letter from orderly Serg*[ean]*t Andrew Boyd Co*[mpany]* H 108th N.Y. near Falmouth. Ans*[were]*d it. Read papers in *[William]* Hues' tent. Got onions today, raw—a rarity. Rain tonight.

Sunday, 22d.—Polished buttons & made ready for inspection at 9 o'c*[lock]* *[Jonas H.]* Kocher shaved the sides of my face. A regular wash up & change of clothes. *[illegible word]* wood in wagon & stood guard for *[Sampson W.]* F*[ry]*. Carried clothes to Hetty *[Copeland]* & heard her & Sarah read; also a young black. A splendid day, warm & nice. Soldiers lounging all about. After parade rec*[eive]*d *[Brockport]* Republic & *[Rochester Evening]* Express. On guard from 7 till 9 in *[Sampson P.]* F*[ry]*'s place.

Monday, 23d.—Pleasant & warm. Pass & already to go to Suffolk & just started when I met Cousin Geo*[rge]* Farnham coming to see me. Gave my pass to *[Sampson W.]* Fry & Geo*[rge]* & I went out to shoot at targets. Back, cleaned gun & got dinner for me & Geo*[rge Farnham]*; coffee, pie (fried & warm) & we visited all the P.M. Fifteen of our boys & Capt*[ain]* V*[olney]* J. Shipman went to the Dismal Swamp on a hunt, but nearly all came back wet above their knees. Supernumerary on guard, stand from 3 till 5 to-morrow morning (*[Sampson P.]* F*[ry]* standing 9 till 11). Papers & read across the R.R. Cold to-night.

Tuesday, 24th.—Fine day. Boys gone out again to D*[ismal]* Swamp. Pass again & go to Suffolk. Town looks pleasant—flowers in bloom also some trees. Officers, soldiers & some ladies promenading the st*[reet]*s. At the market—fish (4 for 25c) & provisions. At the depot saw & heard *[Brigadier]* Gen*[eral Michael]* Corcoran talking to a Major Gen*[eral]*. C*[orcoran]* is light complexion, sandy hair, moustache & chin whiskers. His looks do not flatter him as a noted Gen*[eral]* of Bull Run & Richmond. At print*[ing]* office. At a store bought of a Dutch female clerk a comb—matches, also tobacco for Brackett. At saloon bo't oyster stew which made me a good dinner. Plenty butter & crackers. Went about with *[James R.]* Fisher to a drug store. At dock on Nansemond river boat unloading army stores. Gun boat 6 guns (2 brass). Passed negro houses, court-houses, jail. Stopped at Provost Marshall[115] J. F. Smith's office, found Corp*[oral]* Sikes who introduced me to Major & Prov*[ost]* M*[arsha]*ll (M Smith, 112th reg*[imen]*t of Chamb. Co*[mpany]*). The latter told story of selling his shoes in Brockport when a boy. Gave me general pass to contraband camp, also signed B.S. Res. Visited with S*[mith]* in his office & had interesting conversation with him & he gave me old papers. At P.O., saw the pile of papers to be distributed & read paper myself. At camp [symbol], in time for dress p[arade]. Late supper 7 at Hetty [Copeland's] int[roduced] to her dau[ghter] girl & read awhile. Back abed early, tired. To-nite warm, the warmest night yet.

Wednesday, 25th.—My twenty-first birthday. Light sprinkle of rain. Commenced my celebration of this important day by washing some little articles before breakfast, which we had rather late. My colored friend Hetty [Copeland] made me a hoe cake, a "royal" breakfast, with fried pork, potatoes, & coffee. Shot at target, Lieut[enant] of 120th NY[VI Regiment] [Andrew W.] Wilkin to see [Sampson W.] Fry. At camp of contrabands, Uniontown, saw a negro who had just died—feet laying in the ashes in a hut, crowd looking in. Talked with the blacks. In company with W[illia]m Anderson, Quartermasters Log't 9th Mass. Walked to hospital of Mich[igan] artillery—fine dwelling once occupied by Virginia "quality." In back yard found printed secession documents of Richmond, also letters of men now in the Confederate lines & ambled about some. Back by way of Uniontown. In a colored house saw cavalry man & black woman. Saw peach trees in bloom. Back to camp & swept up. Found "mistletoe boughs." No parade. Sugar for 6 days dealt out. Had quite a gay time at Hetty [Copeland]'s, then in [Rice H.] Eaton's tent. Thus passes my birthday.

Thursday, 26th.—Pleasant. Across the R.R. Drill before break[fast]. Bo't apples. Wrote to [Brockport] Republic. Quite sultry. Drill skirmish 2 P.M. Mended my coat, then laid down. After supper had a "confab" with Serg[ean]t [James C.] Noble about contrabands. Lent my letter [to him]. At H[etty Copeland]'s with [Sampson W.] Fry. Let Capt[ain Volney J.] Shipman have secesh Gov[ernor] of Virginia's 1861 messages to read. A fine, starry eve.—cold.

Brockport Republic, April 2, 1863

Camp Jericho, near Suffolk, Va., March 26, 1863. Editor Republic.—We have been in this pleasant camp about four weeks, which is as long a time as we generally stay in one place. A heavy snow storm last Friday, left the snow 4 or five inches deep; all that day we expected orders to move west of Suffolk as we generally go in a storm—but the snow fled and fine weather finds us still here. Peach trees are in bloom. A great many troops came on here lately, and we looked for a stirring time. But everything in the army line appears stagnant and the rebels on the Blackwater seem to dislike the idea of disturbing us. Both sides appear to act on the defensive—a singular way to end this great controversy, and seemingly a favorite plan in Virginia.

The greatest excitement in our camp lately was occasioned a few days ago by the getting up of an exploring party under our stirring captain, V. J. Shipman. Some 25 men, under the guidance of [a] negro, with their guns, ammunition, rubber and woolen blankets and some rations, started for lake Drummond, in the interior of the Dismal Swamp. They started out boldly at 5 P.M., and bid the remaining ones adieu, and departed to—"see what they could see." The water in the swamp at this season of the year moistens and covers almost every spot of ground, and it seems the party had not proceeded far when they found the water so "numerous" that proceeding on "shanks Horses"[116] was almost out of the question, and there was a "right smart chance" for swimming. Most of the party, taking a sensible view of the uncomfortable situation, wisely concluded to come back and try it earlier on some other day.—They came back to camp, their lower garments dripping, and we concluded the pickets had been driven in. But they told us that on the morrow they would surely investigate the "Lake of the Dismal Swamp." They had left several who had obstinately refused to "back out" but were bound to and did remain in the swamp. This was the first attempt of the party to go on a "scout," and their limited knowledge of that business would not be supposed to give them a great success.—However, the next day the remainder of the first day's party started for the Lake, but this time took small boats and rowed up the can [?] which runs from this vicinity to the lake, which is ten miles from here. The Lake is 7 miles long and 5 miles wide. They represented it to be a pleasant place, much more so, probably, later in the season. The party who remained over night were compensated by the glimpse of what they called a bear, and the other party killed a huge "snaik." A large hut was inhabited by two families of mixed blood; a white father and mother had two sons in the rebel army. This being their first visit there and the weather rather unfavorable, our expedition did not push their investigation, but returned that day; it will be resumed soon, in dryer weather, and I hope to give you a personal account of the trip. All returned uninjured.

In a skirmish with the enemy near the Blackwater last week the 11th Penn. Cavalry lost a Lieutenant killed and several wounded, also a number were taken prisoners. About the same time 12 of the Mounted Riflemen captured 7 guerilla cavalry who had just taken breakfast at a house outside our pickets; I saw these dusty looking secesh in the guard house of the Mounted Rifles; most of them wore a gray coat, others a coat of Kentucky jean, white slouched hats, pants of different quality and color, poor shoes, and they looked lean and dirty; one, quite a young boy, wore a good gray overcoat. One of them, Brown, was a noted bushwhacker spy, and seemed to defy all opposition to the confederacy—knew our strength here, and did not deny having been inside our lines; he paraded any quantity of confederate scrip, probably received by him fresh from the rebel treasury, for valuable services as a spy. He with the rest was taken before the Provost Marshall, thence to Fortress Monroe.

In the pleasant city of Suffolk is a small printing office, where once was published a religious paper. At the time the city came into our possession, a good share of the material was left, and the proprietor remained a short time, but is now in the rebel lines. No one is allowed inside the office without a pass; obtaining one from Adjutant Gen. Foster, I visited the establishment and found soldier printers at work doing government jobs exclusively.—The foreman of the office is from Chatauqua Co., N.Y. A sight of a Washington press, type cases and other implements of our art, reminded me of old times before the war. A paper would long since have been started here, had the material in this office been sufficiently abundant to do so.

An order was lately issued that no soldiers would be allowed to visit the contraband camp without a pass from the provost Marshall; Major J. F. Smith, of the 112th N.Y.V., formerly of Chautauqua Co. This was necessary because of disturbance made by some reckless, riotous soldiers about here. Through the politeness of Supt. Sikes and the gentlemanly Major and Provost Marshall, I obtained a general pass to the contraband village, which is flourishing, and a large school house is being erected, and will be ready by the time primary books are sent. There are 12 government farms worked by contrabands between this and Portsmouth, worked by contrabands, who are funished with goods, &c, and get one-half the crop. A plantation of Gov. Wise, who hung John Brown, is confiscated, and what is singular about it is this: The land is now worked by contrabands and is under the supervision of Dr. Brown, a *cousin of old John Brown*—quite a reverse of fortune and change of control in three years.

Supt. Sikes, who has charge of the contrabands here, in a visit to Portsmouth found some old papers and documents in a house once occupied by the descendants of Com. Barrow,[117] of the frigate Chesapeake, of the U.S. navy in the old revolution; his descendants are now in the confederacy. One of these papers he kindly gave me, as a relic of "antiquity;" it is a "Journal of the House of Delegates of the Commonwealth of Virginia, held at the Capitol in the city of Richmond," Dec. 8, 1803. He also found a Norfolk newspaper of June 13, 1808, about the time of trouble with Great Britain which began the war of 1812, and has a notice of an attack by us upon a British boat trading with Indians at Niagara; another document which I saw was an original manuscript binding 40 slaves for 21 years; this agreement was made by a brother of Com. Barrow.

In looking, the other day, for old documents, relics of secession, I found near Suffolk, several Richmond papers, messages, &c., of this date, also private letters of some interest in being written by rather celebrated men now in the confederacy; as there is no room this time to give detailed account of them, and something in regard to the rebel-inclined city of Suffolk, I will leave that till my next.

We are all hearty, and generally enjoying good health, and any who happen to be on the sick list are "brought about" in a hurry by our experienced hospital physician, Dr. John Snively. Yours, &c., J.T.F.

Friday, 27th.—Another fine, warm day. Skirmish drill 9 A.M. Took back the paper I borrowed from Corp[ora]l Sykes & found him at Uniontown sorting clothes sent from the North for contrabands. Saw piles of books sent for the same. Walked with the corp[ora]l to the hospital of the 2d & 4th Wis[consin] Battery & int[roduced] myself to R.D. Bullard—hospital steward who showed me over the house formerly occupied by one of the F.F.V. Nice fire places & no very sick men. A fine location, over the river & well shaded. Was vexed when he told me that Mr. Baker, of Brockport, had been at this place 10 days & left last Monday for home. Int[roduced] to a German cor[respondent] of a Milwaukie German paper. Stopped & bo't pie & talked with a darkey, then on to camp after a fine walk. Wrote to mother.

Saturday, 28th.—Pleasant but cold. Pass & went to Suffolk & waited a long time for Nelson [Ely] but he did not come. Girl riding alone & driving a horse in a 2 wheeled cart—pine box. Officer riding about. Walked about with some of our boys. Left overcoat at store. At market saw fresh fish by the load &c. Bo't cup coffee (4c) & cakes. At the camp of the 4th Wisconsin Battery found Mr. Chauncey Baker, Wagon-master & act[in]g Q[uarter]-master. His father lives in Brockport, N.Y. He put up his horse & asked me to take dinner with him, which I did. Had a pleasant talk & he showed me the stable & horses. Back to S[uffolk] in the rain. Stew of oysters. Get overcoat & staid in store talking with men till 5 mail. Bo't paper; rec[eive]d Unc[le] T[om]'s C[ab]in[118] from home, also letters from Father, M[ary] & sis[ter] also H[enr]y [C. Murray] & Aunt C., P., & Walter. Back to camp in rain. Coffee & bread for supper. Sent bread by Peter [Ely]. Reading in tent all eve. Rainy. Heavy thunderstorm & lightning.

Sunday, 29th.—Weather variable—windy, cloudy, then pleasant. Warm, then cooler. Regular March weather. Polished brass & packed knapsacks for inspection. Drummer in the tent. Shaved by [Jonas H.] Kocher. Wrote. Mr. Chauncey Baker, Sergeants Clark & [blank space] of the 4th Wis[consin] Battery came to see me. I showed them our rifles &c. They only staid a short time. Finished letter to Aunt C. Rec[eive]d letter from "Mate A. C." [Mary A. C. French] Bost[on]., a good one, also papers for W[illia]m Price, 8th Co[mpany] & [Rochester Evening] Express of 23rd & 25th. In eve. read Unc[le] T[om]'s

C*[abin]* across the R.R.—they all were much interested in it. After roll call read till 9½

Monday, 30th.—Colder & windy today. On guard, 2nd relief. Sent blossoms of peach in letter. Commenced letter to M*[ary]* A. C. *[French]* & finished after guard on post 1 & seeing game of ball. After being relieved at 7, *[Sampson W.]* F*[ry]* & I went to H*[etty Copeland]*'s & I read U*[ncle]* T*[om]*'s C*[abin]*. Boys from M*[ounted]* Rifles there. Up at 11. On guard & the Grand Rounds came as usual. Rome *[countersign]*.

Tuesday, 31st.—Up at 5 A.M. but as rain poured down, *[Sampson W.]* F*[ry]* & I staid in the tent till nearly 7, then out. Took ration to H*[etty Copeland]*'s— she gave us meal of coffee, hoe cakes, bacon, & fried bread. Good. After boys made arrangements to have cook house built, I wrote to Aunt C. Rainy & chilly. Dinner at 3; salt pork & bean soup. Walked to see Cousin Geo*[rge]* Farnham. M*[oun]*t*[e]*d Rifles & only staid a few minutes. Saw his horse. Back to dress parade. Muddy. Letter from A*[ndrew]* Boyd. Pleasant moonlight eve. In tent talking with J. C*[hauncey]* P*[arker]*, H.Z. & M.M. till 10.

April

Wednesday, April 1st.—Not much fooling this day. Drill &c before breakfast. Windy, cloudy & cold, like northern weather. Read speech of Hon. *[George Washington]* Julian[119] on the Dem*[ocrat]* policy. Good. Rec*[eive]*d *[Brockport]* Republic. At Uniontown Sup*[erintenden]*t Sikes showed me the schoolhouse. Nearly finished. Saw skiffs on the creek. S*[ikes]* told me about marrying contrabands, &c. Called at Wis*[consin]* Hosp*[ital]* & had quite a pleasant time. Back in time for dress parade. Read a little in *[Uncle Tom's Cabin]* & went to bed early. Saw M*[ounted]* Rifle boys who had been on the Blackwater & run the rebs in line of battle.

Thursday, 2d.—Slight wind all day. Warm. Bro't shingles to build cook house. Pass & went to Suffolk. Called at Wis*[consin]* Batt*[ery]* & left paper for *[Chauncey P.]* Baker. Saw *[Major]* Gen*[eral Grenville M.]* Dodge, formerly Col*[onel]* of Mounted Rifles on a gray horse & train start for Norfolk. At Norfolk Market called at store. Walked about. I called to see Dr. Webb, an old resident—inclined to the south—& had talk with him. Oyster stew raised to 20c. Bo't note paper, common, 6 sheets for 9c; gilt edged 2c a sheet. Norfolk Day book of April 30, 1863, & then came back. Laid down. Parade. In the Orderly's tent while he was gone. Read papers. Something warm. A warm night.

Friday, 3d.—Wrote to *[Brockport]* Rep*[ublic]* & mailed. Drill. A heavy wind last night, came very near taking down our tent. Bread to H*[etty Copeland's]* & she cleaned my canteen. Helped work on the cook house & burned brush. Letter from Alfred S. Lewis, Co A., 140th NYV, Capt*[ain Milo]* Starks[120] in Sykes Div*[ision]*. 5th Corps, Army of the Potomac, Washington D.C. At H*[etty Copeland]*'s full of eaters & no chance to read. Bo't stamp of H*[enry C.]* Murray.

Brockport Republic, April 16, 1863

Camp Jericho, near Suffolk, Va., April 3, 1863. Editor Republic:—April has come and we are having her showers. During the past week we have had rain, wind, hail, clouds, and not much sunshine, but rather a chilly time. We cannot expect to have the best of weather about the equinoctial period, and the best of a Southern latitude will soon be upon us. We still occupy our fine camping ground near Suffolk. Health of the company as good as might be expected. Lieut. Hysner is recovering from an attack of rheumatism. Ball playing has been the chief excitement—resulting in a couple of sprained ankles; "Burnside," of the 8th Co., was carried from the field, having met with an accident of that kind.

The Mounted Rifles furnish most of our intelligence of what is going on between the rebel and our lines, in the direction of the Blackwater. They are the outside pickets, and often have a slight brush with scattering parties of the enemy. On Tuesday night last the whole regiment went on a reconnoitering expedition to the Blackwater started about 8 P.M., and arrived at the enemy's lines about 8 o'clock the next morning. The roads, they say, were very muddy, making progress slow. But the rebs; as is always the case, knew of the movement, (probably through rebel friends; who by pulling the "Union" wool over the eyes of our too easy authorities give aid and comfort to our enemies) and our advance guard, one fourth of a mile ahead, came on the rebel pickets back of which could be seen the enemy drawn up in line of battle, ready to dispute the ground. The Lieut. in charge of the advance, on being halted, in a low voice gave the order to his men to "left about," while he kept the picket by advancing a few steps; then all turned about and the whole party returned without any damage on either side, but we got the information that the rebels have fortifications this side of the Blackwater. I suppose we must wait for dry roads and for the water to dry up. In the swamps—for all that region is thickly wooded—before we can advance, if we do at all. Several prisoners, conscripts, have lately been brought in by the Rifles, who say they have enough to eat and wear, "such as it is." The Rifles appear to do all the hard work of scouting and picketing about here. By the way, Judson, better known to readers of story papers as

"Ned Buntline,"[121] once editor of "Ned Buntline's Own," a paper printed in New York, is a member of the Mounted Rifles, and is their scout. Their former Colonel, Dodge, is promoted to Brig. General.

Among the large force of troops here is the 2nd and 4th Wisconsin Battery. In the latter is Chauncey Baker—a son of Mr. Baker, of Brockport—wagonmaster, and acting Quarter-master of the Battery. Mr. Baker informed me that his father had recently been here on a visit of several days. The Battery have a fine hospital on the bank of the Nansemond river, quite a romantic place, and I should think a fine place for the sick to recuperate. It is a former residence of a wealthy Virginian—confiscated property—and before the war a lovely home. To the courtesy of the hospital steward, B. D. Bullard, I am indebted for a view of the interior of the mansion, &c.

Suffolk (**19**) is an old city and formerly contained a population of from 10,000 to 16,000. At one time 10,000 rebel soldiers were here. Two newspapers, whig and Democrat, were printed here several years ago, but after a period of local strife, keeping the inhabitants supplied with topics for discussion, they finally both, died away. A religious paper was since published here. The streets are badly paved, but Main is adorned with comfortable-looking houses, yards of shrubbery and flowers cultivated with taste. The city is 17 miles from Portsmouth, 18 from Norfolk, and 80 miles from Richmond by rail, which latter is of course mostly occupied by the rebels. There are any amount of secesh in Suffolk, and it would seem have a great deal of liberty to go back and forth in the lines, and it is said use their liberty to our disadvantage. At one end of Main street is a square or market, where at stands are sold provisions, vegetables, all kinds of "truck," and on the three market days of the week, is a lively place. Colored people generally attend to the selling of the articles and warm meals, oysters, &c., are served from a few of the stands. I will give you some of the prices; Sweet potatoes; 82 a bushel; cabbage, 5 cents a head; salad, 25 cents a pack; corn meal $2 a bushel; butter, 40 cents; cheese, 25 cents; milk 18 to 20 cents a quart; chickens and ducks, $1.25 a pair; turkeys, $2 each. Fresh fish, perch, chub, shad, mullet, bass, catfish or bullheads and other varieties are numerous. As the mail is going I will close for the present.

[The remainder of the letter in the Brockport Republic of April 16, 1863 was dated April 10 and is included below after the diary entry of that date.]

Saturday, 4th.—Still a heavy wind, north & snow at morning. Cold. Sand flies all over everything. In A.M., heard S[arah] read at H[etty Copeland]'s. In P.M. wrote letter to Father, Mother, then sister C[ordelia] Harvey, & Mrs. S[mith] in Mr. [William] Hue's tent. Rather cold & snow. Sent paper home in A.M. Letter from Father, Mother, & br[other] Harvey, also papers. Read them

& papers & in eve. read U[ncle] T[om's] C[abin]. Heavy snow, cold, storm tonight.

Sunday, 5th.—Pleasant in the latter part of the day & snow 3 inches deep, melted fast. Had breakfast at H[ett]y [Copeland]s, took over meat, bread, & sugar & heard G. read. Rec[eive]d 3 days rations sugar in P.M. No mail. Wrote to A.B., Co[mpany] H. Pleasant eve. & not very cold.

Monday, 6th.—Splendid day. Signed 2 payrolls. Visited Cousin G[eorge Farnham] at Mounted Rifles, saw pay-master. With G[eorge] till 12. Read N[ew] Y[ork] paper. Back & warmed coffee & ate bread with B. for dinner. Took cup & went to Uniontown. In guard house talked with Corporal. Could not get any oysters. At the 4th Wisconsin Hosp[ital]. Visited awhile with the boys, then back; saw Sup[erintend]t Corp[oral] S[ikes] who told me about the contr[a]b[and] school commencing the A.M. Back & read [Brockport] Republic. Letter of 26 M[arc]h—mistakes. Dress parade. Heard today of a murder in 164th N.Y. & that [Major] Gen[eral Erasmus D.] Keys supercedes [Major] Gen[eral John J.] Peck, commanding Gen[eral] here. Warm evening. Across R.R. awhile.

Tuesday, 7th.—Fine day. Drill at 9. Wrote to Alfred Lewis [Company] A, 140th N.Y. Beans & pork & bread. Pass & went to Suffolk with [Jonas H.] Kocher. Bo't 1 quire note paper (25c), package envelopes 25c, bottle ink 15c, scissors (40c). At Battery saw voting & Baker. Heard paymaster was at camp & hurried back but no pay for us. Walked to town again 1¼ miles bo't paper on way. At U[niontown] saw Sup[erintenden]t Corp[ora] S[ikes] & could even get post[age] stamps $90 worth had been sold between 4½ & 5 o'c[lock]. On the way back saw colored half-blood woman with long black curls—splendid! Down & back in 40 minutes. Letter from M[ary]A. C. F[rench], good long one, full. Papers from home. Read C. & Across R.R. saw Lieut[enant]s, 25th C[onnecticut] & read U[ncle] T[om's] C[abin]. Fine evening.

Wednesday, 8th.—Another fine day. On guard, 2[n]d r[elief]. Sent [Brockport] Repub[lic] to M[ary] A. C.F[rench]. Commenced writing to M[ary A. C. French] & then on guard from 11 till 1. Relieved by [Sampson W.] F[ry]. Crowd in the tent to see ball fixed. Rec[eive]d papers, wrote till 5, then on guard till 7. Across the R.R. awhile. Up at 11, guard & loaded my rifle & out to the forage (8) & soon the moon arose & at 12 the Cong roll sounded [general alarm] & all the men were called out under arms & ammunition given out & then boys ordered to pack up every thing & be ready to march at an hour's notice. The moon then could hardly be seen from a thick fog.

Thursday, 9th.—Great excitement in the camp & preparations to leave. At 1 A.M. came off guard & packed knapsack &c. & finished writing to M[ary A. C. French] & put in a few lines to Mother. Rations cooked. Laid down amid noise & confusion till 5 then out till 7 & saw the clouds in the east turn pink, then blood red, & the sun, clear, came up red & the fog passed. Coffee & beef, bread. Then finished getting ready for marching. But soon began to think we might not go today but hear that we are to hold ourselves in readiness. A splendid day. Nothing happened till P.M. Quite a confab in tent. [*Sampson W.*] Fry, Charley Collamer, & [*James R.*] Blood 8th Co[*mpany*] ordered to pack up & go on board gunboat but going out ordered back. Took walk. Letter from Aunt C. After supper took walk on R.R. then across. Fine eve. To bed early. Tired.

Friday, 10th.—Not disturbed last night. Slept well. Fine day. Wrote to Aunt C. Bro't wood. Washed up. Paid $26 by paymaster at midnight. [*Pass*] to the city of Suffolk. Back at 4 P.M. Ordered to march & left overcoat & knapsack at South Key [*Quay*] Battery, 1 mile west of Suffolk on the Nansemond river. Behind the breastworks troops all ready to fight & cannons with horses hitched. Rebels only 4 miles away. Shells fired at rebs—all excitement.

Brockport Republic, April 16, 1863 [*continuation of letter of April 3, dated "Friday Eve., April 10, 1863]*

Editor Republic:—For the first time in the military life of the 6th, 8th, and 9th Companies of the 1st N.Y. Sharpshooters, all camped together here, we are under orders to be in "light marching" condition. In order to attempt a little history of our two past days of our excitement, I must begin at Wednesday night. Up to that time, everything, so far as we are concerned, was "quiet" on the Nansemond. A trifling excitement, though, was caused, on Saturday night last, during a heavy snow storm, a party of the Mounted Rifle pickets, a sergeant, corporal, and three privates, being captured while rowing a boat used by our forces in building a bridge across the Nansemond river, at about six miles from here. The Mounted Rifle Regiment went out to re-take the captured pickets, but the lurking guerillas had scattered. Since then, there have been mysterious movements by our troops to and from the direction of the Blackwater. But to my story.

At midnight of Wednesday, as I was standing guard at the rear of our camp, and the moon just rising above the horizon, a whistle sounded and a drum beat out first stirring "long roll." Next burst forth a bugle blast by Spalding, followed by the order, "Turn out! turn out!" This was promptly responded to by a hurried putting on of garments; a buckling on of harness and a jump for their rifles, and the boys were quickly in line. Then came an explanation:

The order had come—everything must be packed up, ammunition dealt out, two days rations prepared and we hold ourselves in readiness to march at a moment's notice. By this time it was 1 o'clock A.M., Thursday, and all these preliminaries were attended to, for all were anxious to smell powder, and every nerve quivered with patriotic fire. While knapsacks were being packed, many were the conjectures as to our destination for as everything was to be packed it must mean more than a slight march. Well, the night wore on, and many were the short letters hastily penned, for when might there be another opportunity to write? Surely it meant a "right smart chance, I reckon," for a fight, when they should call us out. The morning dawned; the sun, as usual, rose; no booming guns were heard, and quiet reigned supreme. Evidently the rebs had notice of our ready response to the roll, or why did they not come? About noon it was stated that our brigade, Gen. Terry's, had been preparing to go to some distant field. (Charleston was suggested.) but the movement was delayed by an activity toward Blackwater; and we were told that had not our orders of the previous night been given, we should have taken part in a light fight then going on, but we were still under orders *expectant*, for another direction. At 1 P.M. came an order for the Eighth Co., Capt. Robinson, to march to Suffolk, take passage on a gunboat for—no one knew where, but again something mysterious interposed, for after leaving camp with all the "pomp and circumstance of war," with martial tread, amid cheers of the Sixth and Seventh, and followed by the ambulance, meeting a messenger with orders to "hurry," they quickened pace, only alas! To meet just at the village an "order" from the "powers that be," countermanding the previous one. So after a march of 1½ miles, they came back with the consolation that they were once more saved for future glory. As their "rear guard" slowly "toted" in, for a long distance behind the main body, it was evident they suffered a fatiguing march.

Last night a sound sleep partly repaid for the alarm and bustle of the night before, and to-day "wars and rumors of wars," kept up a lively gossip, and if feverish excitement could control the atmosphere, the past day of summer heat can be accounted for. Well, 5 o'clock P.M. of to-day came, and with it another "order" from headquarters, countermanding the one for packing up all our "traps," but instead, we must see that we had a full supply of ammunition, two days rations, rubber and woolen blankets ready, and all this preparatory for an expected trip, in "light marching order." As all this meant that we should leave our heavy knapsacks, (an eyesore to the soldier more dreaded than the bullet,) we must be expecting lively work at no great distance from here, and from good authority I am informed that 28,000 rebels are expected to make an attack upon the city of Suffolk, and two regiments of one brigade, having embarked on the cars here, with tents and baggage, ready to leave toward Norfolk, were at

4 o'clock ordered to disembark, to await the expected attack. So we are all ready and anxious for a "scrimmage," and if we could, would willingly help end this contest in a desperate fight. It may seem to us that during forty-eight hours we have been made to play a farce, but if "strategy" will save us speedily, all right. Whatever happens to us, I suppose we will meet it without flinching. Our officers, Capt. Shipman, and Lieuts. Starkweather and Hysner, are as usual "eager for the fray," with all the rest. Only two in the hospital, John Donelson, of this, sixth Co. Engineer C. N. Collamer, who has long and ably filled the position of Co. Clerk I am sorry to say, will hardly be able to march with us, being physically disabled, but still acts as clerk.[122]

10 P.M.—An important and interesting scene in our military drama is about to be played, to close the performance for the day, and with the exception of having the silence broken by calling the names on the roll, (not the *long* one) we will close with a grand tableau, and try to sustain our part while we receive a few greenbacks from the paymaster, who has just drove up. If he be followed by the grayback enemy, and a tragedy comes next, woe to the rebs on whom we "draw a bead." J.T.F.

Context—The battalion participated in defending Suffolk, Va.,against the Confederate siege, April 11–May 4 and lost one enlisted man killed, one died of his wounds and two enlisted men were wounded but recovered.

Saturday, 11th.—Wrote letter to *[Brockport]* Rep*[ublic]* & home & sent $20 home. $5 to *[Sampson W.]* F*[ry]* for Mr. *[William]* Hues. Rode in boat to gun boat. Signals from station. Shells. All our men in. Slept a little on ground. Fine night. All ready to fight the rebs.

Sunday, 12th.—In the front. Rebs ahead. Building torn down. Contrabands coming in. At 10 rebs seen in distance & on sig*[nal]* station. Our boys go out & pop brings reb down from the top. Skirmishing. Bro't plank from bridge in front. Warm. Over to the rifle pit, by *[Sampson W.]* F*[ry]*, *[J. Chauncey]* Parker shot 1st reb. See them in the distance. Rain in eve. Traded coat for blanket with Capt*[ain]*. For the night. Slept out in the field, blanket over me. Boston papers from M*[ary]* A. C.F*[rench]*. Overcoat bro't.

Monday, 13th.—Buildings burned. Up early & rain cleared at 10. Nothing but a little firing at rebs. Letters from home, stamps. Dug rifle pits on front & bullets whined. Worked till 12 or after. Back & slept well.

Tuesday, 14th.—Fine day. Rebs in sight. Hardtack & coffee. Wrote home, sent $5. *[George]* Waters *[died 4/16]* *[George]* Sherry (arm) wounded. W*[aters]* bro't in on stretcher. Saw it all. *[Brockport]* Repub*[lic]* & *[Rochester Evening]* Ex*[press]* in eve. Back to fort & slept on ground, very well. Bo't envelopes.

Wednesday, 15th.—Up at 4 & stood guard till 7, in rain which lasted most all day. Boys of 7th Co*[mpany]*. kindly let me put my things in their barrack. Coffee & tack. On guard on breastwork from 12 till 2, from 8 till 12 had nap in barrack. Shell made rebs scatter. Some of our boys went to lower Nansemond & I was called out of lines & staid. Whiskey rations & coffee, salt beef & tack. Fired guns & cleaned. Laid down on floor of barrack with Corp*[oral James S.]* Edwards. Pleasant in eve.

Thursday, 16th.—Up at midnight & given 1 days rations & drink. Ordered then to put up earth on breastworks, but carried dirt only a little while. Then on fort, watching. No sleep from 12. Up all the time. Break*[fast]*. Trumbull bro't me my diary. Wrote home & to *[Brockport]* Rep*[ublic]*. Pleasant most of the day. *[Brigadier]* Gen*[eral Henry D.]* Terry here early. Contrabands fixing fort. Firing in P.M. About 4 o'c*[lock]* P.M. detailed with about 50 of 6th, 7th, 8th, & 9th Co*[mpanie]*s to relieve others on L*[ower]* Nansemond river, north-west, to watch rebs opposite. Marched to old camp Jericho, found hat & stockings sent from home, also *[Rochester Evening]* Express. Left dirty ones at Hetty*[Copeland]*'s & soon got to the pine grove after coffee. Laid down at foot of pine with Serg*[ean]*t *[Ira or Dan]* Pool, blankets over us. Slept well. Pleasant & starlight. Bo't cakes.

Brockport Republic, April 23, 1863

Suffolk, Va., April 16, 1863. Editor Republic.—In my last I informed you of an expected attack on our forces here by some 20,000 rebels. Well, they have attempted the thing, and for the first time in our experience, the rebels, or their advance skirmish; are in full view of us, and on three sides of Suffolk, north, west and south, trying to rout us and get possession of the city and Norfolk, and we have sent them many a deadly *[illegible word]*. The telegraph, no doubt, has informed you of what is going on here; so I will tell you of some incidents and accidents of our five days "fight," or siege.

Saturday last, at 4 P.M., our three companies of Sharpshooters had orders to march (20) in light fighting order; so, leaving overcoats and knapsacks in our tents, after a hurried preparation, in half an hour we were on the road, passed through Suffolk on to the west of the city, in the direction of the Blackwater. Troops of infantry were in line before their camps as we passed, and the artillery ready to be drawn to the front. A mile from Suffolk brought us to the Nansemond river (a very crooked stream,) and we joined the Chautauqua County Sharpshooters, 7th Co., Capt. Arnold, at South Key Battery, which is a breastworks between forts Nansemond and Rosecrans, between the Seaboard and Roanoke railroad on the right, and the Petersburg and Richmond railroad on the left. This fortification is on a high bluff, commands the ravine and river below, the open fields in front; woods, one mile beyond. In the Battery, were the 4th Regular Artillery with 4 Parrott[123] guns and 2 brass howitzers. We were immediately posted behind the breastworks; to the right and left, infantry and artillery. The enemy were then 4 miles from us, advancing, and the outer pickets had come in, some on foot, without saber, and some with an extra one. In our front, the Mounted Riflemen, with two brass howitzers, were shelling the advancing enemy, and we could plainly see the shells burst in the air. Evidently we would soon be used, and Gen. Terry coolly gave us orders to load our rifles and keep on the lookout. Contrabands took the alarm and came running in with their bundles. Soon firing of shells ceased, and the enemy had halted, and most of our pickets came in. After dark we could see the light of the rebel campfires they were plainly seen on three sides, and at our signal station (a platform erected on a high pine, over a mile to the west,) our signal corps still remained, waving a light; and this telegraphing was responded to by our headquarters, but soon stopped, and all in front were enemies. A detachment of men were sent out under Lieut. Hysner, and in the darkness, dug rifle pits, commanding the "stashes" or felled timber opposite.—What little sleep we had during the night was taken on the ground, wrapped in a blanket.— Rockets were often fired and shells occasionally flew through the air—all serving to keep up the excitement.

Sunday morning came, and with it a report of a rebel flag of truce, and a demand of a surrender of the *[illegible word]* it would be shelled at 10 o'clock. A large building inside the fortification was pulled down, to prevent being fired by rebel shells.—In the night part of the railroad ties on the bridge had been taken up, and all was ready for an attack. About 10 o'clock rebels were seen in the edge of the woods near the signal station. Soon several rebels ascended the ladder to the top of the signal tower, looking through glasses, and they had a good view of our whole position. All the rebs left the tower but one, and while he was stealing observations, a little squad of our Sharpshooters crossed the river, crept up to within a short distance from the tower—crack! Went a rifle, and the spy came down the ladder from the tower as though his time was short. And since that time no one has been seen in that position. During that day the rebel skirmishers came out of the woods, and there was firing on both sides.—J. C. Parker, of Brockport, in the 6th Co., is acknowledged to have "brought down" the first rebel, who was carried off the field. Skirmishing between us and scattering rebels was all that happened that day on our front. Monday there was no general advance, but a little firing on our right and left in which only the forces on these defenses took part. Orderly Root, of Rochester, however, captured a rebel sergeant, who said there was only a small force on the west, but mostly on the north and south, and he said it was expected by them, that no fighting of any account would be had, and this would be "another Harper's Ferry affair." Several houses were burned on the opposite side of the river, and our boys had any amount of sport going across the river and driving the rebels into the woods. D. A. Dart, of Rochester, had a narrow escape, a rebel bullet grazing the top of his cap, made a small furrow in the edge of it. At night more rifle pits were made by us to protect our men from the rebels skulking in the bushes. None of our men were hurt, (although many had narrow escapes,) until Tuesday, when a party of our men were making a bold drive at the lurking enemy, advanced so near the hiding rebels that they were exposed to a dangerous cross fire and in the excitement unnecessarily exposed themselves. Geo. Walters, of Pittsford, and Geo. Sherry, of Irondequoit, Monroe Co., both of the 6th Company, were badly wounded. A ball hit Walters on the right hip, struck the bone, and forced its way up, and he dropped on the ground. A ball struck Sherry on the right elbow and partly shattered the bone; he walked back, but Walters was brought in on a litter by four men, and they were in much danger while doing so. They had nearly accomplished it, when the rebels fired, and shot one of the four, Garrison, of the 8th Co., in the left leg above the knee—only a flesh wound. Since then our boys have been more careful. The wounded were taken to the hospital and attended to. Walters wound is dangerous, and the ball, which went through his pocket book and contents, has not been found; his recovery is rather doubtful. Sherry is tough, and submitted to an operation with perfect coolness; Will lose the use of the arm, but is doing well.—There have been many narrow escapes from bullets. To-day all is quiet, but the rebels may be working secretly, and we are on the watch. The fortification here is to-day being strengthened, and contrabands are at work upon it. Yesterday a shell was fired from here into a series of rebel rifle pits and bursted at one end of them, making the "grays" scatter from it.

On the Nansemond river, near our old camp both parties are fortifying and there has been sharp work between our own Sharpshooters and those of the rebels. Nothing *[illegible words]* our side *[illegible word]* Although one of our 20-pounders[124] was burst to *[illegible words]* several rebel guns dismounted. One of our gunboats there is said to be damaged. They are trying to get it off to Norfolk that we have a strong *[illegible words]* even if they are not trying to *[illegible words]* Battalion from some other point, we will give them fits. Gen. Terry commands us, and appears to be a fighting man, but cautious. He says, "The Sharpshooters are good shots, but mighty lawless." They *[illegible words]* fighting most of the time yet. Last night about twelve o'clock we formed in line of battle, and were up most of the night. We know now what it is to be soldiers and sleep in the open air, on the ground, wet or dry; that is our five days experience, and how much longer we must stay on the lookout, in rifle pits a good share of the time, I cannot say, but whatever happens, we will continue to punish treason. Wish I had time to tell you of all the exciting *[illegible word]*, but good bye for a week. J.T.F.

Friday, 17th.—Dug rifle pit with several others before day light & piled into it—7 of us. Bullets flow around us some, but I did not get a chance to fire at any of the rebs. Heard some of them talk. Shells flew around into rebeldom. About night left the pit, back to grove & had coffee, tack, beans, &c. Washed at spring & laid down in bough house. Pleasant day.

Saturday, 18th.—After getting coffee & filling my canteen, went to pit alone at 7. Put log on top. About 9 saw reb cross by a tree. Fired at him & he gave me 2 balls in return, but they whizzed over & went spat into a log or tree. I fired several times. He left the tree. Two or three of the boys came into the pit & I looked through Julius Thurston's rifle & fired at the reb when he came back & he got 12 feet up the tree. Soon he left & a man with white gloves, black hat, & snuff colored blouse came to the tree & I exchanged shots with him awhile & the balls flew around thick & fast. Rations of "fluid" *[whiskey]*. At 5 relieved & marched to camp Jericho to stay all night. Pass reg*[imen]*ts of infantry & artillery. At camp had good wash & change. Took sh*[irt]* & dr*[awer]*s to Hetty's, & got socks. Coffee & fried hardtack crackers. Read *[Rochester Evening]* Ex*[press]* which came to-night. Back & com*[menced]* letter home but did not finish. This has been a splendid day. Corp*[oral James]* Pamment shot. *[died 4/18]*

Sunday, 19th.—Fine day. Up early & had good wash. Coffee at H*[etty Copeland]*'s. Put on hat from home. Marched to west of city to river. Passed camp of reinforcements. 141st *[NYVI Regiment]* &c. Found boys on side hill out of fort in bough houses. Talked with them. Tired. Letters from Father, Cor*[delia]*, & Mother & *[Rochester Evening]* Ex*[press]* of 14th. Finished letter & saw lizard. Read &c. Zouaves near us. Looked at rebs across in the distance, in their rifle pits. Beans, & the usual tack &c. Heard Zouave tell of battles by our campfire. Cannon firing rapidly. Laid down in bough house with *[Sampson W.]* Fry & Corp*[oral]* Brackett. Fine eve.

Monday, 20th.—Yesterday did not seem at all like Sunday. A little cloudy this morning & cool breeze. Pleasant after. Wash at spring, then coffee & tack. Hear of our forces last night taking 152 prisoners & 5 cannons, 2 of which they took from us a year ago. Finished letter home. In a bough house with

Cha[u]n[cey] P[arker]. Shouldered all our things & marched to camp Jericho & fixed up. Received *[Brockport]* Republic, letters of 3rd & 10th. Looked over my things &c. Laid down under Presidents Proclamation. Miner, (new recruit) came into our tent. Beans, & made cup coffee for dinner *[illegible word]* for supper, & at 6 P.M. after I had been to H*[etty Copeland]*'s & got h*[an]*dk*[erchie]*f, we marched back to the field near South Quay B*[attery]*.[125] Corp*[ora]*l Brackett fixed up boughs for the night. On guard from 7 till 9, countersign "Cone Hill." Rainy eve.

Tuesday, 21st.—Misty rain. Rifle rusty. Wash at spring. Coffee & *[hard]* tack. Sat around campfire, Capt*[ain]* & boys talking. Report of reconnoiter in force, but it did not come off. *[Major]* Gen*[eral Henry W.]* Halleck came. Helped fix up shelter of boughs & had a cold sleep. Letters & papers from home. Sent paper home.

Wednesday, 22d.—A little rainy & unpleasant. Unwell & a sick headache. In P.M. *[Sampson W.]* Fry & I took our rifles & went to the pits & had a few shots at the rebs. All right. After coffee, beans, & bacon we were ordered to pack up & march to Fort Rosecrans, half a mile from this. All ready & at sundown all went there & slept in the sand, side of a sand bank. Looks like rain. At 11 called up & get w*[hiskey]* rations & packed blanket. Back down & slept.

Thursday, 23d.—Up early & rain all day, showers. Got pretty damp. Coffee in morning. All day bullets whizzed thro', over & above us from reb pits 80 rods ahead of the fort. Rebel flag on pit. Shot at them.(21, 22) At 5 o'clock got soft bread, beef & coffee. Cleaned gun several times. Letter from Aunt C. & Alf*[red]* Lewis. Rebels talking with us across the river. No one could go to the spring without being shot at. Damp bed, in sand bank.

Friday, 24th.—Cold & wet when I got up. Sun shone a little &c. Double rainbow. Wash, then poor coffee, meat & soft bread around the fire. Put overcoat & blanket out to dry. Wrote to the *[Brockport]* Repub*[lic]* & to Mother. Sun, then rain, wind. A damp nap, then beans, coffee & beef. Paper from Aunt C. More rain, but cleared up at dark. Dried feet & got water in canteen. After in bed, heard rebel brass band serenading;—good music. Starlight & warm.

Brockport Republic, April 30, 1863

Fort Rosecrans, Suffolk, Va., April 23, 1863. Editor Republic:—After twelve days watching the enemy before Suffolk, in fort and in the field, and in rifle pits, tasting the excitement and the bitter part of a soldier's life, we are today in the above-named fort, the Nansemond river a few rods before us, and beyond the ravine about 60 rods are a few rifle pits occupied by a few of the rebel sharpshooters who keep up a brisk firing at the head of anyone who may peep above the breastwork of this, Fort McClellan to our right and South Quay Battery to our left, about 60 or 70 rods apart, all on Gen. Terry's front. We came in here last evening and to-day the balls whiz, buzz and sound like humming birds or bumble bees as they fly about us and *spot* into a tree behind or over our heads. Such has been the way all the day long and such a bobbing of heads to escape the bullets is amusing. From the top of the breastwork we get occasionally a shot at a rebel head above their pit, but we both have the faculty of dodging at the smoke of a gun, there is no particular damage done to either. A rebel flag or rag floated from each end of one pit, but now only one remains, the other probably having been shot away, as the 6th Co., telescope rifles make close work among the graybacks, while an occasional shell or solid shot makes them "hunt their holes." We are pretty well drenched to-day by April showers, and inside the fort the sand has been plowed into channels along which simulate want [?], making a perfect wand of water, where they all flow into one. Our tents are still at Camp Jericho, and we have made funny shelters in the fort. I am writing in a hole scooped in a mud bank, roof of sand, and boughs half way across the opening—a good shelter and rather romantic.

On our side, among the Sharpshooters, our company, sixth, is the only one that has lost, and two of our men have been laid low. On Friday last, private George Walters, of Pittsford, died of a wound received while scouting and on Saturday last Corporal James S. Pammont was killed while standing in the rear of South Quay Battery by a chance rebel shot. The ball passed through his head and he lived but a few minutes. They were both good soldiers and are sensibly missed by the company; each was active and lively. In the death of corporal P., we lose one of our most able-bodied men. Both bodies have been embalmed,[126] and await the wishes of their relatives. Our company contributed $10 for the embalming of the late corporal.— Private Geo. Sherry, of Irondequoit, badly wounded in the right elbow, at the time of Walter's, is doing well, but will never be able to join his friends in this company,—with one or two trifling exceptions, the remainder of our company are doing duty.—Private May, of the eighth Co., was wounded quite badly on the arm, while scouting.

You can get the news of the "Suffolk siege," by New York city papers, which give a very accurate general account of our accidents, incidents and doings. It is at present very dull about this vicinity, and what the next move is it is hard to guess, but at any rate there are troops enough centered here to accomplish something; a good share of them are from New York State.

Who knows but in a few days we may be on the way to Richmond! If the rebels are in any great form before us they kept very quiet and make no demonstration; nor do they trouble us with heavy shot or shell—it is a regular *hunt* something like watching for four footed game. Monroe county sportsmen would find plenty of employment here—the buzzing might tickle their ears at first, but they would soon get over that.

A little Union expedition went across the Nansemond last Sunday night, and surprised a rebel battery and some infantry while our gunboats were attracting their attention in another direction. Without much resistance 150 rebels (some of them "Louisiana tigers"[127] with Austrian rifles)[128] and 5 cannon, were taken. Our loss 6 killed and 30 wounded. Two of the cannon were among those taken at Harper's Ferry, a year ago. A few nights after this a spy attempting to pass our pickets was fired at and badly wounded.

At a point on the Nansemond, about two miles below Suffolk, the rebels in the woods on the opposite bank of the river troubled us some, and on Thursday night last fifty men of the different companies went out there to relieve those who had been there several days, and I was among the number. Just a few rods before we came to the bank of the river, was a nice thick grove of young pines, and on the ground at the foot of a pine, I rolled up in my blanket and there being an infantry picket in front, we all slept till about 3 A.M., next morning, when several of us dug a rifle pit in the shape of a half circle on the top of the river bank. Other pits were dug. This all had to be done before daylight enabled the rebs to bring their guns to bear on us, and at dawn we had a pit about three feet deep, dirt thrown up in front, and brush and leaves upon the top to screen our heads.—then we were ready for operations. Seven of us were in the pit that day, but could get no good shots as the rebs kept close, though the balls whistled just a trifle to keep us on the alert. Saturday morning filling my canteen with coffee and also fortified with a few hard tack, with rifle and accoutrements I again appeared in the pit and with one exception was alone during the pleasant day. About nine o'clock the bullets flew, whizzed and spat, and I had the satisfaction of exchanging shots with several rebs who came to a certain tree opposite and they each left in a hurry. But I will not brag of having killed any of them "severely." At last a reb with black wide-brimmed hat, snuff-colored blouse, and *white gloves* came to the tree, and I could see all his motions distinctly, when he raised his rifle to fire. He could see nothing but the smoke of my rifle as I fired; that and the pit itself were the only target for him. After exchanging a few shots with him, he left the tree. As white gloves can hardly be afforded by the rebel rank and file, I flatter myself that I had a little skirmish with one of the confederate "chivalry."—Saturday night the fifty who had been there two days at the point, were relieved by others who are there yet, and we all staid in our tents at old Camp Jericho, close by, for the first time in a week, and had a good rest. J.T.F.

Saturday, 25th.—At 12 A.M. helped carry sand bags to put on breastwork (23) & fort. It was good work. Lunch of coffee & beef. Back to bed at 2. Up before sunrise & had good wash & cleaned gun before coffee. Fine day. Hung out things to dry. Saw rebs in pit. Wrote letter to Aunt C. in sun on fort. Bullets whistle overhead. Men playing cards. Darkies shooting at rebs [illegible word] Letter from home, M.C. H & L.—M[ary] A. C. F[rench] & Roch[ester Evening] Ex[press]. Cooler & moonlight. Rebels came to the river & our men talked with them. They said Stonewall Jackson commanded them. Wanted to know what a shilling was. Backwoods. War ought to close. Enough. Sick of large guns. Where's Peck. 44th Alabama brass band from Arkansas. Come to breakfast. We'll exchange papers. Plenty, plenty "yes" interesting. Detailed for guard, all of to-morrow A.M.

Sunday, 26th.—On guard on parapet from 12 till 3½. Chilly. Guns & lights. Laid down, up, then down again. Coffee & w[hiskey] in rations. Wrote to M[ary] A. C.F[rench]. Rice & molasses. Breezy. Shot at rebs who stick up heads. [Brockport] Republic with let[ter] of 16th. Rebs came down & talked. Longst[reet] under arrest in Richmond. The war ought to stop. Only talked a little. Fine evening. Moonlight.

Monday, 27th.—Pleasant day. At 12 o'c[lock] waked up & went to Fort McClellan & shoveled, picked, carried sand in bags & helped place them on the top of the parapet with barrels filled with dirt. Hard work. Corp[ora]l Pool bro't coffee at 3 & we quit; to bed, then up just in time to get coffee, a wash & we all went to Camp Jericho. Had good wash, then to the M[ounted] R[ifles] camp, but Cous[in] Geo[rge Farnham] not there. Back with C[harles W.] Spaulding, & C[harles] Collamer. Boiled eggs, 40 cts a dozen. At H[etty Copeland]'s took po[tato] & b[ee]f & had a good meal. Wrote home to sister & sent sketch. Had nap & woke up boys all gone back to Fort R[osecrans]. Started & half way so tired sat down, then came back to camp to stay all night. Helped make coffee with Jack[son] N[ichols] & the Trumbulls. Walked to [?] & back, big grind. Saw [Major] Gen[eral John J.] Peck. Borrowed blanket of Dr. [John] Snevely at Hosp[ital]. Saw sick boys. At H[etty Copeland]'s for a little while. Staid with Jack[son] N[ichols].

Tuesday, 28th.—Had good sleep last night in tent. At day light heard shells rapidly flying, the rebs were firing on our gunboat in water, & we replied— no damage of consequence. A little rain today. Cleaned gun. Good breakfast of fritters, butter & molasses, bacon, coffee, & hoe cakes at Nelson [Ely]'s. About noon fried or cooked some potato in ham at cook house. Laid down. At 3 P.M. started for Fort. Capt[ain Thomas S.]. Bradley walked down. P.O. Got letters &c for boys. Bo't cakes & had lemonade. On to Fort thro' gulley, bullets whistling. In all right. Fixed "cane" &c. coffee, tack & cake. Saw ex*[cerpt]* of my 16th letter in the Roch*[ester]* Union. Heavy firing & shells whizzing thro' the air & bursting among the rebs. A little talking with the rebs in eve. but no exchange of papers. Rain.

Wednesday, 29th.—On guard from 1 till 4 in the rain. Laid down awhile then without eating anything went to camp with boys & packed up tents & everything. Clothes at H*[etty Copeland]*'s. Bo't pie. Broke camp at 12 & under hot sun marched, pitched tents just back of So*[uth]* Quay Battery, 1 mile west of Suffolk, where bullets fly. After pitching laid down. O, how warm. Soon cloudy. Back to Fort R*[osecrans]*, coffee, then rain & for an hour the hardest lightning & thunder I ever saw, continual for over an hour, rather damp in my "cave". L*[ieutenan]*t *[Philip]* Hysner came—bro't me 2 rubber blankets & I wrapped up good. W*[hiskey]* rations. *[Sampson W.]* F*[ry]* drew them for me. Rain pounds but it's warm.

Thursday, 30th.—Still cloudy & rainy all day. Warm. After coffee &c went to camp, bullets flying. Back to Fort to get my portolis. On way back got glass ale. Drew pair stockings. Called to see Cha*[u]*n*[cey]* *[Parker]*, sick in hospital. W*[hiskey]* rations & had sling. Wrote to *[Brockport]* Rep*[ublic]* & marched back to Fort. Wrote to Bro*[ther]*s Alonzo & Harvey. Rec*[eive]*d *[Rochester Evening]* Ex*[press]*. Man shot in Redan. Pleasant eve. Drew sketch of our front of our battle ground. Filled canteen at spring. Letter from Mother, sister, & Harvey.

Brockport Republic, May 7, 1863

Fort Rosecrans, Suffolk, Va., April 30, 1863 Editor Republic:—During the past week nothing sufficient to change the aspect of affairs had occurred. New forts are being thrown up and artillery planted, and old ones finished. The rebs are working slyly. We are well-fortified, reinforced and in good spirits anxiously looking for an advance of the enemy, who are upon three sides of us, in what force is not exactly known, but all think the rebs are about us in considerable numbers, but keep very quiet, excepting the sharpshooters, who, in rifle pits just in front of us keep up a continual (though harmless) firing. This is replied to by our sharpshooters, and shells from our forts, keep up a fire. With our telescope rifles, the sixth company can see a rebel's head above a pit when the eye alone could not see it—but the "grays" are "artful dodgers," and at every flash, down goes a head. This dodging bullets is a common thing where we hear so many noises in the air like humming birds, or steam escaping from a boiler; those are from bullets, for no rebel shot or shell disturbs our front. Rebel bullets are often picked up, battered out of shape, mostly, and men are rarely hit. No accidents have occurred among our sharpshooters this past week, but some are in the hospital, usually from indisposition, caused by the exposure through which we have passed during our three weeks in the defense of Suffolk; and we have helped finish the forts, carried dirt, &c. May the enemy soon appear that we can have a good fight if necessary, and end this suspense to ourselves and friends.

On Tuesday morning last a gunboat escorted a transport down the Nansemond from Suffolk, and before proceeding far was opened on by rebel batteries hid near the north bank of the river, and solid shot flew into the water all about the vessels. Our own forts then threw shot and shell into the rebel batteries, and for a time the sound of booming cannon was exciting. But the rebels were silenced, and the gunboat and transport passed to safety down the river which empties into the James ten miles south of Suffolk.

On Friday morning last we were serenaded by a good rebel brass band; apparently about a mile from us, and they played almost everything except "Yankee Doodle" and "The Star Spangled Banner." Rebels have on several evenings come to the river bank from their rifle pits and conversed with us, but they appear to fear their officers, and for a few evenings have not done so. So far as the privates are concerned they will talk and exchange papers; the latter had been done. Some appear to be quite honest, while others are the opposite. They tell us Stonewall Jackson is in command, some of them are from the 44th Alabama, others from "Arkansas" and Virginia. Longstreet is under arrest in Richmond—"Plenty, plenty, O, yes, plenty to eat," but "would like to come over and take breakfast," say "the war ought to stop," one of our boys said to them "I am getting mighty sick of hearing those big guns and shells," to which the reb replied, "I am getting mighty sick of them myself," one asked where Gen. Peck was—thought he must be on the other (safe) side of Suffolk; talking of the price of sugar, said they paid five bits (5 shillings) a pound, and when told that we pay one shilling, one of them said "we belong to the backwoods—don't know what a shilling is "What is it?" They exchange tobacco for coffee.

We have moved our camp from Jericho to west of Suffolk, in the rear of South Quay Battery; most of the sixth company still help defend Fort Rosecrans. We are in Gen. Terry's front. Gen. Corcoran defends the south front, and Gen. Getty the north. The Republic is received with pleasure every Sunday afternoon. While we patiently await the enemy's advance, I remain Yours, &c. J.T.F.

May

Friday, May 1st.—A fight.—Killed—6, badly wounded 36. Splendid day. All to camp after break*[fast]*. Wrote to Cous*[in]* Albert Allen & sent documents to

Father. Visited C*[hauncey]* P*[arker]* at hospital. Pretty warm. Nap. All went back early at 3 to help sustain a skirmish. Only 280 infantry, 99th NYV*[I Regiment]* deployed, went out over river & were fired on my rebs in rifle pits & replied to musketry & began hot fire & our artillery threw shell rapidly & the air was full of music for two hours. *[Sampson W.]* F*[ry]*'s gun hammer came off. Kept up. Reb's rec*[eive]*d reinforcements & shell burst among them. We first fired from the parapet of Fort R*[osencrans]*, then too late went into rifle pits to the left of Fort, nearer the engagement & banged at them till about dark when it all dried up before our skirmishers came back without driving the rebs from the pits. None of our men hurt. All back & got supper & at 8 to bed. Pleasant.

[The following note is at the end of Farnham's diary.]

Fight. Reconnoissance. Friday May 1. Weather. Called up in alarm early. Sunday 3rd reb flag of truce &c. In hospital. Cease firing & no shots on either side. *[illegible word]* Zouaves salute &c. Leaves in orchard & green grass refreshing. Rebs laying around. *[Brevet Major]* Gen*[eral George W.]* Getty & *[Brigadier General John]* Cochran going out with force, see them in distance, ambulances &c. Fire in brush. Our loss 60 killed & w*[ounded]*. Col*[onel]* of 103rd mort*[ally]* w*[ounded]* & since died. Monday morn rebs all gone, we ordered to get 3 days rations & two reg*[imen]*ts out & rebs gave up & bro't in. 100 rebs killed left by rebs. buried by our men. Man drowned.

Context—Union forces were defeated in Battles of Chancellorsville and Fredericksburg, May 1–4.

Saturday, 2d.—Fine day, but heavy mist as every morning. Wash then to camp & breakfast. Headache. Run bullets & patched balls. Had good wash cleaned gun. Warm. Rec*[eive]*d *[Brockport]* Rep*[ublic]* 23rd paper from Lon, last one. At hospital. Bo't sugar, baked dried apples—nice. No mail. Back to Fort—in via large rifle pit & from port hole through parapet saw stuffed clothes over reb pit tied to tree, imitation of a man for us to shoot at. Saw a reb shot as he was throwing stone from pit to pit. Shell town. Detailed on guard but kept off. To bed & at 10 o'c*[loc]*k all alarmed—called up under arms. Sat around on ground an hour. Capt*[ain]* singing & boys joking. About 11 *[o'clock an]* officer rode up & we went back to bed, ordered to sleep on arms. Moonlight.

Sunday, 3d.—Another hot day. Up again between 3 & 4 alarmed—stood on the parapet in fog or heavy mist till after sunrise, then to camp & had breakfast coffee. Saw reb flag of truce & rebs standing & sitting on pits & exchanged papers. Want to cease firing during the day. Hawkins Zouaves[129] leave camp for home— most of them. Reb's give them a salute. Went to Fort Seward & saw 84 pounder guns,[130] large fort nearly completed. Visited Geo[rge] Sherry, wounded in elbow nearly 3 weeks ago. Pale, & elbow swelled & looks like proud flesh, smells bad. Pleasant room. A man of 99th reg[imen]t wounded on 1st, thro' left leg grazing bone—flesh wound. Flowers—wild. Refreshing green leaves on apple trees. Nap. Steak at noon. Back to fort at 1½ o'c[loc]k. A force of inf[antry] & art[illery] are out & we are expecting to fight. Opposite fort see rebs reclining outside pits & walking about waving hats. See our forces in distance, ambulances reserves &c. Shell flying, our boys sitting & lying on top of fort. About dark a reb fired a ball & then we opened up on them. One ball came thro' port hole & struck cannon, glanced & hit Corp[oral] of Artillery on left shoulder, not badly. Fire started in brush by shell or wad starting it & burned brightly in eve. Rebs shelled, trying to put it out. On guard at gun from 7 till 10 & saw light of shells. Warm.

Monday, 4th.—A fine day. Shower about 1 P.M. Very warm. Just after sunrise we went to camp as usual but then went back after blanket & overcoat & back to camp. Ordered to have [knap]sack & 3 days rations, ready to march, as the rebs had retreated to the (Blackwater) rear in the night. All ready to march. Wrote home. Our forces go out reconnoitering & the rebs, a good quantity, give themselves up as prisoners & are bro't in, dirty & lean. [Brigadier] Gen[eral John] Corcoran & [Brevet Major General George W.] Getty both went out & the lost was 60 killed & wounded, & the rebs skedaddled. Saw some of the gray backs[131] pass & have a buckshot & ball from one of their cartridges. Some negroes bro't in who had been fighting against us. Will not go off on march today. Read book, Harpers. Fixed for a good rest to-night. Every thing pleasant & seems like being near the woods at home.

Tuesday, 5th.—A hot pleasant day. Up early, after refreshing sleep. Bro't water for cooking break[fas]t. After washing cleaned gun. Had taste of N.Y. maple sugar. All quiet. Sat in shade by brook in hollow. Had good wash up &c. Read a N.Y. story. O! how warm. Rec[eive]d paper & env[elope] inside, then letter from Mother & Harvey & lock of hair from sister. Read them by candle light. Heavy rain tonight, thunder & lightning.

Wednesday, 6th.—Cloudy, chilly & rainy all day. Read N.Y. daily & good news from [Major] Gen[eral Joseph] Hooker's army in the Rappahannock.[132] Bro't wood. Copied letter from Georgia girl to her secesh brother.[133] Wrote to Rep[ublic]. Damp in tent to-night. Letter from M[ary] A. C.F[rench].

Brockport Republic, May 14, 1863

Near Suffolk, Va., May 7th, 1863. Editor Republic:—Of course you and your readers have been informed by telegraph that the rebels have at last given up their plan of taking Suffolk; and on Sunday night the last of them evacuated their position in front of us. So it is, and they are now mostly on the further side of the Blackwater, on the road to Richmond, and our pickets now occupy their former advanced positions. I will endeavor to tell of some incidents of late occurrence, though it will not be given in as glowing or startling a style as some of the New York daily correspondents, who have nothing else to do.

On Friday afternoon last a skirmish occurred, in which the Sharpshooters had the honor of assisting, but the management and result of which no one can consider as entirely *successful,* and perhaps it would not be "policy" to discuss the affair in detail, critically. The rebels in rifle pits just in rifle range of us partially concealed by brush thickly hedged a few yards before them to impede a charge, had been pitching their balls promiscuously about for several days, and at 4 o'clock on Friday afternoon a mere 280 of the 99th N.Y. were sent out across the river to reconnoiter, and, I suppose, drive the rebs from the pits as it was thought the enemy were scarce in the vicinity, and no great resistance was anticipated. The 99th, banner flying, advanced to the opposite side of the river, and deployed to the right and left, and the centre at the same time commenced the charge, reserving fire. Our company and two companies of infantry were at Fort Rosecrans on the right, back of the scene of action, and waiting for a chance to pitch in. All was excitement. Several pieces of artillery were belching forth their thunder, and shell was thrown into the woods before a musketry commenced. Only a slight advance was made when smoke in the rebel pits told us the way was disputed. Volley after volley was poured into the advancing infantry, and we saw reinforcements coming to the relief of the enemy, from the woods. Then commenced the shelling into the pits and they did good execution and we at the fort were ordered to fire on the rebels advancing, which we did at a three-fourths mile range and threw bullets over the heads of our infantry, who were now within 20 yards of the rebel pits, and no reinforcements went to them, and of course the enemy hid, had a good mark while themselves secure. The color bearer of the 99th was shot, and a corporal took up the colors, was struck by two bullets, when the flag was borne by a Lieutenant. Shell from us told effectually and one bursting in the centre of a line of rebels, broke the line, which was immediately reformed and the enemy came on, then the retreat for the gallant 99th was sounded, as it was seen they could not easily charge the pits, though one of them gained the ditch and bayoneted a rebel at the same time receiving several rebel bullets, and fell. We were then ordered to go into our own pits on the left, and nearer the action (where we should have been placed before) to sustain the return of the infantry, who brought in about 30 wounded and 4 killed, (6 since died) leaving a much larger rebel loss, mostly from the effect of our deadly shell. From the pits we then "took charge" of the enemy and poured into them leaden messages to our best advantage, until nearly sundown with no loss on our part, but had the satisfaction of seeing many a traitor tumble in the dust. At sundown all was quiet and thus ended our principal Sharpshooter fight, as yet. Thus we are gradually gaining a battle experience and we are now better prepared for a closer trial of "argument" to convince the "erring chivalry" of their blind and stubborn treason. Our boys and officers, we believe, were as cool as could be expected. About the *coolest* scene *I* noticed, during the roar of artillery, &c., was several quails a few rods in front of us, quietly eating in the grass, entirely undisturbed by the confusion.

All was quiet till Sunday, when early in the morning a rebel flag of truce (**24**) appeared and they proposed to suspend the useless random shooting for the day on our front, which we agreed to. Then for the rest of the day the rebels lounged on the outside of their pits and our men on the walls of the fort talked to them. Was not that a *peaceful* scene? Some of the rebels said they would be in Suffolk on Monday, and that the war would be over in two weeks. The first part of their assertion proved true on Monday, for they were *brought* in by our men. The last prophecy may not prove true, though, *I* sincerely hope the rebels may be brought to terms speedily, and if the good news we now hear from all parts, continues to record victory to our righteous cause, and not till then, peace will soon gladden thousands of true and patriotic hearts. Early on Sunday, Generals Getty and Corcoran went out with a large force to the north, down the river, and we could see the reserve in the distance, and ambulances running to and fro. An engagement was had, and the rebels driven towards the Blackwater, and they left a large number of wounded in a church which our forces took charge of, also 100 rebel dead, which my own infantry buried. Shell were thrown from the fort on our front here, to prevent the enemy flanking; otherwise all was quiet with us, though battle raged down the river, and during the day our loss was some 10 killed and 50 wounded. Our whole loss in killed, wounded and missing up to this time is said to be below 300, while the rebels have lost much more severely.

A Richmond paper speaks discouragingly of Gen. Longstreet's "siege" of Suffolk—which they say only covered a foraging expedition into North Carolina—and does not like the loss of rebel deserters, prisoners, killed and batteries captured, and closes an article by saying, "Confederate sieges appear unprofitable—very."

On Monday morning the rebels were minus, and they had gone beyond, or to the Blackwater. Two regiments were out several miles from Gen. Terry's front, and came upon great numbers of the enemy left behind to throw obstructions in our way, and who without resistance gave themselves up, without seeming to care for the Confederacy, and said that after serving treason voluntarily one year, they were not allowed to go home, but conscripted—therefore became dissatisfied. One, a Northern man from St. Lawrence Co., N.Y., said he would not get away from them, having been conscripted, and was glad to get under the stars and stripes. He found a brother in a regiment here, and joined him "for the Union." A large number of gray-backs, dirty and wearing a rainbow colored uniform, came in during the day, two or three hundred altogether.

We had orders in the morning to prepare three days rations and pack for a march, but did not go, and for several days, have rested in our new camp but old tents, which seem like home after a rough and exciting campaign in the field. We are expecting to get marching orders every hour. Several regiments of artillery have advanced already, and we may change positions with the rebs for a little time, and attack them in their entrenchments on the Blackwater. Many of them were taken off to reinforce the rebels opposed to Hooker. A number of rebel letters from the South were found in the rebel pits, and all of them of a desponding style. Shall we not close up the game the present season? I think so, for the rank and file of our army are in good fighting spirits, and fighting officers can lead them to victory.

Sunday last, part of Hawkins Zouaves, whose two years service has expired, were striking tents to leave for home, and the rebs hearing of it, *fired a salute* in their honor.

On Monday, L. B. Leffingwell, of the 8th Co., S.S. from Ohio, assistant in our hospital, died suddenly, and was buried on Wednesday.

It is rumored that our two first company officers are about to offer a resignation.

All quiet.   J.T.F.

Thursday, 7th.—Weather as damp & heavy as yesterday. Drew shelter tents & I don't feel well. Went across the river & examined reb rifle pits, found pieces of letters, papers, & shell (Union) partly burst. Lots of bullets battered in ravine. Reb P.O. stamps—Jeff[erson Davis]'s photo. Back, tired. Pills from Munson. Wrote to M[ary] A. C. F[rench]. Feel very ague-ish. Letters from Aunt C.

Friday, 8th.—Had two shakes last night. Weather no better. At hospital Dr. Hasbrouck gave me pills operated & quinine which I took during day. No better. 2 papers from home & package of envelopes suspender handk[erchie]f & comb. Good. [J. Chauncey] Parker made me gruel. Glad to sleep to-night. Have been in tent all day with my own & Sam[pson W. Fry]'s 2 blankets over me.

Saturday, 9th.—A little pleasanter but damp & chilly. Slept most of the day. Eat hardly anything. Wrote to Aunt C. & others. Blowed up [at] Hernes who were talking secesh & about the fighting for the niggers. Quinine at hospital. Better at night.

Sunday, 10th.—Summer warmth & fine breeze. Very weak. Cleaned out tent. At hospital & talked with Dr. *[John]* Snevely. No medicine today. Ate little in the morning but no more till —. Wrote to sister. Had wash. C*[hauncey]* P*[arker]* made me some good tea in A.M. Brush & woods burning & rebel pits filled. Very warm in tent. A little breeze. *[Brockport]* Repub*[lic]* & *[letter]* of Ap*[ril]* 30 in eve.

Monday, 11th.—Sent to City for milk, 1 pt & 1 pt for C*[hauncey]* P*[arker]* (15c a qt). Feverish in P.M. Dr. H*[asbrouck]* gave me corn starch which I made with milk. Lemonade. Bo't lemon (5c), white sugar (20c). Fever in P.M.—hot. Good some starch made with milk. Sat on barrel in front of tent in cool of eve. Don't feel like making my bed. Wash at spring at noon.

Tuesday, 12th.—Last night for 1st time in over 3 mo*[nth]*s slept with vest pants & stockings, & rested well. Feel better this morn. Up, wash at spring after change und*[er]* clothes. Canteen of water. Saw Dr. H*[asbrouck]* at hosp*[ital]* & he gave me 3 doses cay*[enne]* pep*[per]* to take ev*[ery]* 3 or 4 hours. C*[hauncey]* P*[arker]* took my canteen to get milk & also got me fresh lemon & orange. Dr. S*[nevely]* bro't me starch. Very faint. Shower bath at spring at noon. Very warm. Not able to make starch & *[Jonas H.]* Kocher made it for me & twas nice with lemon in. Made lemonade & broke raw egg into it. Hardly got up all the P.M. Sent clothes to wash (1 shirt 1 drawers 1 pr so*[cks]*). Letter from Andrew Boyd, 108th *[NYVI Regiment]* dated 8th. Roch*[ester]* Un*[ion]* from Aunt C. & 2 *[Rochester Evening]* Ex*[presses]* from home. Out some about sundown but weak. Strong breeze most of the day.

Wednesday, 13th.—Restless last night, outside clothes off. Not so well as yest*[erday]* morn*[ing]*—sore & tired. Fine morn, every thing green & invigorating breeze. Wash at spring. Ate remainder of starch. A little diar*[rhea]*. At hosp*[ital]* Dr. H*[asbrouck]* whirled & shook me & gave me 3 powders of hashish & opium to take ev*[ery]* 4 h*[ou]*rs. Cleaned haver*[sack]* cut cane. In P.M. sat with H in shade of pine in grass. Cool breeze. Made starch of water & put in egg. Also made little lemonade. Nice cool eve.

Thursday, 14th.—Spr*[ing]*. Wash. Cloudier & cooler this A.M. Feel brighter. Gave up our short swords last evening. D*[octo]*r gave me 5 pow*[ders]* of hash*[ish]* & cay*[enne]* p*[epper]*. Wrote to Father & Mother. Ate bal*[ance]* of last night's starch, made lem*[onade]*. Sent by C*[hauncey]* P*[arker]* for milk, lem*[on]* & eggs. Came at last & I made starch & lem*[onade]*. Little shower.

Woman bro't my stock*[ing]*s & shirts, wash *[illegible word]*. Faint in P.M. Paper from home with tea in & letter from Mother, Sister, Cous*[in]* Al*[bert]* Allen & Nell S. Feel very weak to-night & get into bed as soon as made. Wind blew the tent terribly. Quickly asleep.

Friday, 15th.—Cool & breezy. Not so well this day. D*[octo]*r gave me 2 pills, operated; wash; ate a little starch. *Sampson W.]* F*[ry]* cleaned out tent. In most of day, lying down. Very faint. Lieut*[enant]* gave me his *[illegible word]*. Had good beds in dispensing tent with Dr. *[John]* Snevely & slept well.

Saturday, 16th.—Cool breeze all day. D*[octo]*r gave me 5 pow*[ders]* 3 kinds of med*[icine]* in each, one in 4 hours. Capt*[ain]* S*[hipman]* came in & told me of Col*[onel Thomas J]* Thorp, 130th NY*[VI Regiment]* preferring charges against him for refusing to order out the men to do fatigue while at Fort R*[osecrans]*. Shaved. Faint. Bo't cakes. Went out to river with *[Sampson W.]* Fry to river bank, in shady place & he fished. It was pleasant. Could see boys swimming & horsemen passing across the plain, also *[Major]* Gen*[eral John J.]* Peck's carriage & escorts. Back slowly & got whis*[key]* of L*[ieutenan]*t *[Philip]* Hysner, made egg nog. A little milk of Munson & *[Sampson W.]* F*[ry]* made me some starch. Letter from Aunt C. In eve. went to sleep at d*[ispensar]*y tent.

Sunday, 17th.—Sultry. Some better to-day. D*[octo]*r gave me 3 pow*[ders]*. 3 kinds in each. Ate a little starch. In the shade of tree sev*[eral]* hours. In tent all P.M. & hot, flies biting hard. Had 2 ripe strawberries. Made Lem*[onade]*. Sam*[pson W. Fry]* made tea for me. Received let*[ter]* from M*[ary]* A. C. F*[rench]*, Sent paper to M*[ary]* A. C. F*[rench]* & short letter to Mother. Felt pretty languid all P.M. but towards night, cool, feel better. Kind of row caused by whiskey in Co*[mpany]*. At spring. D*[octo]*r's tent to sleep early. D*[octo]*r read from Mrs. Martineau's[134] travels in the U.S.

Monday, 18th.—Still gaining slowly, but weak. Cool morning. Up early. Down to spring, washed & filled canteen. Drank a little coffee & ate a cake. At 7 the D*[octo]*r (H*[asbrouck]*) gave me sour drops in a bottle; filled with water & sweetened to drink ev*[ery]* 3 hours a tab*[le]* spoon, tastes some like lemonade. Report of Mounted Rifles losing most of 2 Co*[mpanie]*s last night. Out in the grass looking for strawberries but could not find hardly any *[not]* many ripe yet. Blackberries in blossom & berry forming. Wild flowers in blossom some time. In the tent most of remainder of day. Pretty warm, pleasant. No milk today. Letter from Aunt C. & Mrs. S*[mith]*, also Dem*[ocrat]* from Aunt & 2 papers from home & tea. Wrote to Aunt. Bo't eggs, 35c a doz. Made tea & boiled an egg, breaking it in boiling water—good, also hard tack, ate very lightly. At dark went to our tent, made bed & took a drink of whiskey—8 yrs.

old. (Medical Director, Hand *[?]* captured by the rebels). Dr. H*[asbrouck]* in tent just as I had gone to bed.

Tuesday, 19th.—Very cool & breezy. Still gaining. No more med*[icine]*. Light diet. Up early & at the spring. Break*[fast]* of tea, tack & egg "boiled". Aired things. Laid down. Heavy wind—Feverish this P.M. Dr. P*[urchase]* gave me drink whiskey. No mail. Made tea & boiled egg. Scoured tinware & eating tools. Sat & saw the boys playing ball. Have not felt so well today. Weak. At the D*[octo]*r's tent & to bed in good season. D*[octo]*r reading my 13th letter.

Wednesday, 20th.—Very warm, sultry. Had dose of w*[hiskey]* early. Washed at the spring. Waited for the surg*[eon]* an hour & tried to get order for w*[hiskey]*—could not. Serg*[ean]*t *[Robert]* McPherson gave me piece ham from N.Y. State which I cooked with 2 eggs, but only ate 1/3 of it. Also made home tea. Dr. S*[nevely]*. kindly sold me 1 qt whi*[skey]*, & *[Sampson W.]* F*[ry]* dug some wild cherry for me. Just as I was taking the bot*[tle]* of it out of D*[octo]*r's tent, it slipped & the w*[hiskey]* bottle broke into *[in two?]* spilling all the w*[hiskey]*. Dr. gave me another bottle & I bro't it to tent safely! Washed cher*[ry]* root & boiled it with some w*[hiskey]*(which got afire) & had bitters. D*[octo]*r got anxious & thought I had got the wrong root but O.K. Made lemonade. Drank little cold tea. O how warm. Wash in brook & shower bath. *[Brockport]* Rep*[ublic]* from office. Egg & spoon bl*[ack]* tea for supper. We have tea instead of coffee altogether, as many of the boys are sick with diar*[rhea]*. Down to river at sundown with *[Sampson W.]* F*[ry]* to see him fish. D*[octo]*r fixed bed better & I now sleep comfortably.

Thursday, 21st.—Pretty warm. Weak. Tea & 1 egg. Bitters 4 times to-day. At hosp*[ital]* got pill & read Vallandigham[135] indignation meeting in *[New York]* City & disgraceful, treasonable speeches against the Gov*[ernment]* & Pres*[iden]*t. Cous*[in]* Geo*[rge]* F*[arnham]* came to see me & bro't me oranges. Glad to see him. Staid with all day. Boiled fresh beef for dinner. Game enchere under tree. Few strawb*[errie]*s. Letter from Mother & F*[ather]* & papers. Ans*[were]*d. I made g*[reen]* tea & boiled 1 egg. Col*[ored]* woman bro't my stockings, washed & mended 3c. Canteen of water & went to bed at D*[octo]*r's tent early. Dr. S*[nevely]* reading Vicksburg reported evacuated by rebs.[136] Dr. H*[asbrouck]* in tent. Warm night. Latter part cool & breezy.

Friday, 22d.—Cool & breezy early then hot. Up early. Wash at spring. Bitters. Warmed tea left last night & boiled 2 eggs. Felt better after break*[fas]*t. Sent by S*[ampson W.]* F*[ry]* to get eggs, milk apples, crackers, lemon, good java coffee & to get crystal in watch. Swept in front of tents which tired me. Sent Brock*[port]* paper to M*[ary]* A. C. F*[rench]*. Bro't water. Crystal broken 1 hour after rec*[eive]*d. Struck the standard—too flat. Milk & crackers for dinner. Scald rem*[aining]* milk. Roasted lb. coffee & ground in milk at commissary. Paid Dr. S*[nevely]* $1.50. In tent awhile & its awful hot & flies thick. Alex*[ander]* Carmichael give me piece of nice fish. Rubbed body with wet towel at brook—felt better. Nothing by mail. Made part cup java coffee & had milk in—first—ate egg & piece of sw*[eet]* potato. Sat in front of tent. Wet my hat, soaking, *[illegible word]* sev*[eral]* times. Up to tent early, backache & legs ache—tired. Kept awake till 9½ till Dr. S*[nevely]* came, then slept soundly. Quite warm to-night.

Saturday, 23d.—Terrible hot day. Little air stirring. Sleepy, but got up early & to cool spring. Take bitters regularly. Made cup coffee & milk good at 7 A.M. & the coffee was splendid—reminded me of home, in old times, also the usual egg. Felt faint before, but after breakfast felt better. Capt*[ain Volney J.]* Shipman is today to be tried by court martial for refusing to order our Co*[mpany]* out to do night fatigue duty at Fort R*[osecrans]* while there on command of Col*[onel Thomas J.]* Thorp of 130th NYV Inf*[antry]*, Com*[mander of]* fort. We are not liable to do fatigue duty as inf*[antr]*y & Capt*[ain S[hipman]* was holding to the rights of the men as he supposed. Made corn starch in the milk & put in egg. Roasted coffee more. Cut stick for holding little pail over fire. In H*[ector]*. A. Butler's tent. At noon ate little starch. Made lemonade. Had addition of shelter put on back of tent & it's cooler. Warm. Bo't 2 apples. Sam*[pson W. Fry]* & *[Charles P.]* Tinker, who came back from going home from us at Sta*[ten]* Isl*[and]* & now with us in tent. Put all the shelter tents together making more room & cooler. Will have bunks put up. Capt*[ain]*'s trial postponed. Found wild cherry for Lieut*[enant Alphonso W.]* Starkweather. Wash at brook & change but keep off drawers. Killed 1 foot water snake. *[Sampson W.]* Fry took watch & made man put in another gratis—good one & bo't me some lemon. Coffee & egg for supper. Warmest day yet here. Up to tent & abed early—8. Sultry.

Sunday, 24th.—Another heater. Some air stirring in P.M. Up at 6 & spring. Saw Surg*[eon]* at 7—on light duty. Made cup good coffee & boiled egg no milk. Wrote to Mother in A.M. A little boiled beans at dinner. Cooler in double tents—a little breeze tho'—made lemonade. In tent most of the day. Very warm. *[Brockport]* Repub*[lic]* by mail. Finished letter to mother & wrote to sister. Boiled egg & drank some Gov*[ernment]* Bl*[ack]* tea. *[Sampson /W.]* Fry put up the stakes & sticks for my bunk & I put across them flour barrel staves which makes a spring bed when I get tick on. Ate a little applesauce. Up to Dr. S*[nevely]*'s tent at 8 & sat hearing surgeon H*[asbrouck]* & Dr. S*[nevely]* talk awhile. Light & made bed. Sling *[of whiskey]*. To sleep after talking. Sultry.

Monday, 25th.—Windy, cloudy & very cool—nice. Sling *[of whiskey]* & feel better. Made cup coffee & boiled egg. Weighed today 108½—on March 1st weighed 132½. Lost in 2 weeks. Sent to Suffolk for milk & eggs. Bunk fixed up nicely. Milk & crackers for dinner. Most too cool in P.M. Almost had a chill—laid down with blanket over me & slept. Quite a mist late in P.M. cup of milk & egg & toast. Up to tent early & to bed. Windy & cold. Good night to sleep. 29c.

Tuesday, 26th.—Still cold & windy, chilly. Up as usual & to spring. Made coffee, boiled 2 eggs & had applesauce. Took pill last night & op*[erated]*[137] this A.M. first time in nearly 5 days. 6th Mass*[achusetts]* Inf*[antry]* go home to-day. Ate apple. Wrote to M*[ary]* A. C. F*[rench]*. Boiled beans for dinner. Filled tick with dry pine boughs. Can best green tea & letter from Aunt C. by mail—postage 75c. Also paper from her & one from Father. Made tea for *[Sampson W.]* F*[ry]* & I & twas first rate; also boiled eggs. Then wrote to Aunt C. At spring. News of Vicksburg taken by us & the capture of 10,000 pris*[oners]* & 100 cannon. 2 mo*[nth]*s at least will break the rebellion. Made bed & John——of 8th Co*[mpany]* sick, slept with me at Drs. Tent. Pill op*[erated]* Cold & windy.

Wednesday, 27th.—Did not sleep well. Coffee & eggs. Pass to Suffolk. Broke watch crystal again. Walked to Suffolk with Billy Price. Almost every thing in Suf*[folk]* market. Bo't ½ doz. eggs (12c). 1 qt. strawberries (25c), ½ pint milk (10c), loaf new sweet bread (10c), dish ice cream (10c), 4 little apples (5c), 4 cakes (3c), fig paste (13c). Bo't N.Y. paper (6c), back & feel tired. Had strawberries milk & sugar—a good dish; scalded milk & it partly curdled; scalded canteen. Every thing in S*[uffolk]* looks fresh picked, a nice boquet of roses. Cool but sun shines. Letter from Mother & sister & photograph of Lon—a good one & he has changed much—taller, fleshier & better looking. Made tea for self & Cous*[in]* Sam*[pson W. Fry]* (who has dys*[enter]*y) & egg for self. Also had fine dish strawberries & milk. Mr. *[Andrew A.]* King, a kind friend in 9th Co*[mpany]*, New Lebanon, N.Y. bro't me a little milk fresh from cow. Read news. Blanket from D*[octo]*rs tent. Ans*[were]*d at roll call for 1st time 2 weeks. & six days. Sleep in my own tent. Cool to-night.

Thursday 28th—Sun shines brightly. & it's a warm day. Up at sunrise, roll call & wash. Made coffee for Sam*[pson W. Fry]* & I & boiled eggs, also had milk in coffee, & soft, sweet bread & Dutch cheese of my own make. Sent to Suffolk for fresh bread & Geo*[rge]* Goold paid for it. Wrote to sister. Scalded milk. Also wrote to Bro*[ther]* Lon. F*[ry]* read news in N.Y. Times. Vicksburg not yet taken. Made tea, boiled egg, & ate rest of strawberries. Receipt of box from came *[sic]* to J. C*[hauncey]* P*[arker]* by mail. Played game cards with *[Hector A.]* Tinker. Roll call at 8 & to bed at 9. Cool enough to-night.

Friday, 29th.—A little cloudy. Up early. Sun shine. Weak. Wash at spring & canteen of water. Made coffee for self & Sam*[pson W. Fry]* & boiled egg. Also ate small piece good salt pork with good Norfolk bread. Saw Surg*[eo]*n H*[asbrouck]*. Am very costive[138]—sometimes 5 days. Swept under bunk. Boys in tent. Wrote to Nell S'd. Boiled beef for dinner & good soup. Bo't cakes 15 cts—12 & had bill changed. Very little sprinkle in P.M. which is first drop of rain in 3 weeks. Windy. Lemonade. Pretty good. Gov*[ernment]* bread dealt out made green tea & had good supper. Filled canteen & walk about. After dark. Fine moonlight & pleasant air. Game old sledge, then to bed. Horrible noises by the 8th Co*[mpany]* after I got to sleep. Disturbed.

Saturday, May 30.—Cloudy & windy. Not up to roll call for I was sleepy & they had it at sunrise. Up at 5¼. At spring, boiled eggs & had very good gov*[ernment]* coffee & bread & little pork. Bitters not gone yet. Swept in front of tent. Spoke for new shoes ($1.80). Pass to Suffolk till 6 P.M. 31 men of ours marched to hospital for slight summer complaints. To Suffolk— walked. At depot, train came late & 1 car filled with vegetables—earliest of the season. At market bo't loaf bread & 1 qt strawberries. Lovely in market. Talked with darkey who lost much by rebs in siege of Suffolk. Back at noon. Cous*[in]* Geo*[rge]* Farnham came in from picket on horse & ate dinner with me. Quite warm. Weigh 112. Had strawb*[errie]*s & sugar. Back to Suffolk with *[Chauncey]* Parker, *[Nelson L.]* Butler after box at depot by Express but *[it]* did not come. Heavy shower, first rain in 3 weeks. Dish ice cream (10c). Bo't Phila*[delphia]* paper. Back at 4. Hardtack, rice & new fresh Gov*[ernment]* tea. Read. Took pill as I do not feel right. To bed just after roll call.

Sunday, 31st.—Warm & windy. Not up at roll call as I was up hastily at 3 A.M. (not before in over 4 days). I felt pretty weak. Wash at spring. Gov*[ernment]* coffee, piece steak, potato. For not coming out to roll call at 5 o'clock, ordered me to go after wood with others. Although I could not work, I thought the walk would do me good. So obeyed with others & 6 of us bro't in good sized stock with 3 small sticks under it—I in the middle. Did not hurt myself. *[Chauncey]* Parker & *[Hector A.]* Butler bro't down the box from home (which Lieut*[enant Alphonso W.]* Starkweather had bro't from Norfolk *[last]* night). Had sent from home butter, cheese (wine & sauce from Mrs. Harley Clark, Kendall Mills, cakes, white sugar, crackers, apples, lemons & a spoon, also lint clothes & some papers. I feel very grateful for them. Bread & butter & soup. Drew a little syrup. At spring after putting my home goodies away. Wrote to Father & Mother. Made lemonade. Gave the boys some of my good things. Read. No mail for me. Made tea, had remainder of strawberries, bread or toast, butter, cheese & sauce. Good supper. At spring. Walked around some before roll call, then to bed at 8.

June

Context—The battalion was on the Peninsula, Va., in the 1st Brigade, 1st Division, 7th Corps in June.

Monday, June 1st.—Up at roll call 4¼ A.M. then back to bed & slept till 6. To spring & stopped on the way. Boiled cup home coffee, toast, butter & piece beef. Good breakfast. Sent pants to be washed (10c) & wear drawers as I have but 1 pair pants. Sewed. Coffee for dinner. Made lemonade with w*[hiskey]* & eggs in it. Flies thick. *[Brockport]* Republic paper from home & Dem*[ocrat]* & *[Rochester Evening]* Ex*[press]* from Aunt C. Made tea, & had toast & home things. Pants done, but not quite dry. Fine eve. & warm. Game sledge, then to bed. High wind today & hot.

Tuesday, 2d.—Up to roll call at 4½. As usual at spring. Made coffee then breakfast. Hung clothes out. Played game with Mr. *[William]* Hues. Pass to Suffolk & walked up. Tired me much. Glass lem*[onade]* (5c). At dep*[o]*t saw train come in. Picked roses in yard & pleasant young colored girl offered to & poured water into my little tin pail for my roses. Asked me if I "had not been sick—I looked so pale" & offered to get me a fine boquet next Sunday which kindness I accepted & thanked her. I shall never forget this girl, in my Suffolk remembrances. Bo't loaf bread for H*[enry C.]* Murray. Rested a few minutes then slowly walked back & on way stopped & talked with Surg*[eon]* Hasb*[rouck]*. Says if I get my strength in a month I will do well. Back & ate a trifle. Bathed then made lemonade with w*[hiskey]* in it. Read. Warmer than yesterday. Had a nap. Hot as fury. Heavy breeze in P.M. & flies bite awfully. Made tea & ate nice hominy & syrup with other things for supper. Out for dress parade but none. Rules & regulations or articles of war read by Capt*[ain]* Volney J.] S*[hipman]*. Commissions of Serg*[ean]*ts & Capt*[ain]*s rec*[eive]*d by them last night for first time. At spring took walk with *[Sampson W.]* Fry & *[Charles P.]* Tinker. Games with Sam*[pson W.]* F*[ry]*. To bed. Warm. Sudden call. Rain to-night.

Wednesday, 3d.—Up at 3, then before break*[fast]*. Made tea, toast had steak. Rain & nicely cool today & loud. Wrote to Mrs. Clark & to Mrs. L. & sister. Soup & nice beef boiled for dinner. Washed dishes &c at spring. Wrote & read newspapers. Insurrection.

Thursday, 4th.—Break*[fas]*t as usual for several days. Warmer than yesterday. Cleaned my gun & fired it at target, 20 rods. Struck lower edge of paper 1st time, but unsteady & so weak after that I came wide of the mark. Back, cleaned & greased gun, put tallow on & in & old pair drawers around it to keep the flies & dust off. Fried a little rice in the pan & had dinner. Sewed pants. Finished letter to sister & wrote to Aunt C. Borrowed 3 stamps of S*[ampson]* W. Fry. Rec*[eive]*d letter from sister, bro*[ther]*s Lon & Harvey. Pained to learn that mother is quite sick again. Bo't Philadelphia Inquirer of 3rd & read lots of news—all good. Tea & toast. Inspection & parade—only our own Co*[mpany]*. Tired to-night. Read by candle light. Cool to-night.

Friday, 5th.—Up to roll call, 4½ o'c*[lock]*, & back to bed till 6. At spring. No appetite. Ate nothing till 10½. Spoke to Dr. Hasbrouck of furlough—said he would tell Capt*[ain]* of my condition. Talking in Butler's tent. Most of the boys are talking of our being mustered out at the end of 9 months from Sep*[tember]* 13–June 13. Very or quite warm, though a little wind. Blouse washed (5c). Bought 10 sheets paper (10c). Sent for P*[hiladelphia]* Inquirer (5c). Spoke to Capt*[ain Volney J.]* S*[hipman]* about furlough & he gave me encouragement & said he would give me a high recommended for furl*[ough]* after his court martial came off. Sent paper to Aunt C. Sent poetry on the siege to sister yesterday. Rec*[eive]*d paper, read; good news. Also rec*[eive]*d 2 papers from home. Supper. Lame & not out to so-called dress parade. Washed little things at spring.

Saturday, 6th.—Every thing as usual. Sultry. Cleaned up after coffee & roast. Wrote to Cousin Albert Allen. Gave shirt to colored woman to wash. Barrel to sink in ground. Mended stockings. Borrowed another 3 ct. stamp of S*[ampson]* W. Fry—4. Read. Heavy clouds & brilliant heat lightning which I looked at till 10 o'clock. Rain in night. Cool.

Sunday, 7th.—Cool & breezy from heavy shower last night. First thing after getting breakfast I went to Suffolk—nice walk & waited for Mary Jukes to get me flowers & after I had observed soldiers in shoulder straps going & returning in Sunday rig, Mary *[Jukes]* kindly gave me a fine boquet of roses & would take no pay for them. A fine little girl. With my boquet of roses I walked back to camp & gave Capt*[ain]* part of my roses. Mr. *[Andrew A.]* King, my friend of the 9th Co*[mpany]*. gave me poetry from his daughter on *[Major]* Gen*[eral Joseph]* Hooker's last battle—Chancellorsville. Boiled beef & soup. In the Captain's tent & gave him boquet. Wrote to Mr. *[Horatio N.]* Beach, Ed*[itor]* *[Brockport]* Repub*[lic]*. Sent letter for addition & bor*[owe]*d 2 3 ct. stamps. *[Rochester Evening]* Ex*[press]* from home, also *[Brockport]* Repub*[lic]*. Supper. After sup*[per]* read paper, speech of Gerritt Smith[139] (loyal) & other things.

Talk with a sensible Democrat & a loyal one (unusual now here). Cooler than usual & cloudy.

Monday, 8th.—Sick. Headache this morn & did not get up till 8. Spring. Cleaned up & made cup coffee & had a good little breakfast. Very good. Gov[ernmen]t bread lately from Norfolk, Va. Cleaned gun. Got boiled beans to eat, cool & hardtack crackers. My roses from Mary *[Jutes]*, the kind octoroon, keep nicely & smell sweetly—a rich perfume in the tent. Sun shines brightly but there is a cool breeze. Seventh Co[mpany]. camp with us. Last night chilly—almost if not quite cold; a blanket & overcoat hardly kept me warm. Went with cousin S[ampson] W. F[ry] to get sticks for making stools— also found a stick for cane & saw fine "Devil's Darning Needle"[140] a pretty blue & black insect. Sun wilts me. Back & cleaned up. Rec[eive]d paper & 2 fish lines & hooks from home. Gave *[Sampson W.]* Fry a line & hooks. Read. Washed stockings at dusk. Read in eve. Pleasanat to-night. Seventh Co[mpany] Capt[ain Joseph S.] Arnold camped with us today.

Tuesday, 9th.—Up at 5. Cleaned tent. At spring then got coffee & toast for breakfast. Washed some little things, haversack & cloth—dried clothes. Wrote to M[ary] A. C. F[rench]. Cool & breezy. Started to go fishing but the wind blew so hard gave it up & sat down in the shade awhile. Picked flowers. A splendid cool air to-day. Salt pork—nice for dinner & toast & coffee. Cleaned brass in accoutrements. Read old papers. Finished letter. A.M. having a general clean up! Union of 4th from Aunt C. Borrowed 3 ct. stamp of Munson—4 of S[ampson] W. F[ry] & 3 of Munson. Read news. In eve. a game. Feel more unwell this eve. & to bed early after reading.

Wednesday, 10th.—Sugar drawn. Abed with violent sick headache till 8. Felt bad. Up & at spring, &c. Made coffee & toast. Laid down again. A very hot day. Hardly any wind stirring. Soup & boiled fresh beef—nice—for dinner. Saved some for me to-morrow. Rosebuds blooming yet which I got at Suffolk of kind Mary *[Jutes]*. Reading papers some. Uneasy—flies bother me. Hot as fury is the air. Drew rice—white or light—coffee, sugar—maple flavored. Usual supper—washed dishes. Wrote. Talked with Capt[ain] & *Lieut[enants Alphonso W.]* Starkweather & *[Philip]* Hysner. Pleasant air from 6 P.M. Signed pay rolls.

Brockport Republic, June 18, 1863

Camp South Quay, Suffolk, Va., June 11th, 1863. Editor Republic: Dear Sir:–After an illness and debility of a month, from the weakness attending which I appear to be recovering but slowly, am glad to write you once more.

All quiet in our war machine. Vicksburgh attracts even our attention, while we admire the heroic exertions of the fighting men with gallant Grant, who always asks "unconditional surrender," and who thus far sticks to his text.

In the same column with our good Union news how often we get the proceedings of a meeting of cold-blooded traitors at their vile Tory work. Rash men! It would be well for them, in after years, if history could be blotted out. We might be depressed and disheartened by such rope-deserving conduct, but there is no doubt the government are capable and will hold all Vallandighams in check until the soldiers get home from conquering Southern despotism. When the loyal army returns, a list of "poison," correctly written, "by the ear," will enable the war-stained toiler on the battle-field to give the Coppers a share of their deserts (in a reminding way,) hereafter. Do loyal fathers of the North send their sons to the army, the right sort of papers, and plenty of them?

The weather here is mostly hot—an occasional "cooler" of clouds or breeze. Old Virginia's vegetation has long been rich in its green leaved beauty. Strawberries have passed and black ones are coming—one week will bring the first of the latter. Norfolk vegetables and other delicacies at the Suffolk market are abundant, sold at heavy profit rates. (By the way, the Sharpshooters' fund of war-money is giving out, and in some cases quite at lowest ebb, and Major Smith, our greenback *pay*per man, ought to have toed the mark before this, and may be here any moment.)

Suffolk, by the way, has pleasant streets, aromatic flowers and trees of heavy-laden foliage, adorn the avenues while weary soldiers lounge or rest within their cooling shade. I have picked many fine roses, &c., from untrained shrubs adorning walks, both once well cared for, whose former owners have long since gone. A family owning a fine mansion and grounds, being secessionists and refusing to take the oath of allegiance were rightly moved outside the lines, leaving a lovely home.

Our battalion, the 6th, 7th, 8th, and 9th Co.s, have rather a pleasant camping spot. The 7th Co., Capt. S. Arnold acting Major, have but just encamped with us. All the boys are "fixing up," comfortably for the hotter season, though we may leave at any time.

John Dusenberry, of Rensalaer Co., N.Y., in the 8th Co.,, died lately of brain fever. Our sickness, light, is usually incident to the climate or season. Our hospital department, in charge of Drs. Hasbrouck of New York, and Snevely, of Ohio, is in good hands. The cooking, in charge of Tinder, is cleanly and gives satisfaction.

Our worthy captain, V. J. Shipman, of Carlton, Orleans Co., N.Y., is under charges to be tried by court martial, and the amount of the matter is that, while at Fort Rosecrans, with his company, at the siege of Suffolk, being ordered at night to get his men out to do very heavy work, (plenty of infantry, and Sharpshooters with heavy rifles are not intended to do heavy work,) with an eye to the rights of his men, as he believed, he refused to call them out until he saw Gen. Terry; and the captain in charge of the port gave him the countersign for the latter purpose. Gen. Terry could not be easily found; Capt. Shipman came back and finally consented to calling the men out for accommodation. Lieut. Col. Thorpe, of the 130th N.Y., first ordered our company out and brought men of his own with *fixed bayonets* as though to *force* us out. The charges are "refusing to obey orders," and for "leaving his post in the face of the enemy." The foundation for the latter charge was merely the act of leaving the fort on a password given by the Captain commanding, for a few moments, in order to see Gen. Terry, from whom it seems Capt. S. had orders to report to *no officer* at the fort but to go there and operate *as he thought best.* I have good authority for stating this: the charges were preferred a month ago, nearly, and the trial adjourned yesterday for the second time, and our captain has been free from arrest, and at perfect liberty, commanding us as usual. Capt. S. is sustained in his course, I believe, by every commissioned officer in the battalion.—Should his presence be lost to the company, it will be sadly felt, and it will be a long time ere we forget him. I will say more in my next of this affair, perhaps, or when the court martial is over.

Thursday, 11th.—Up at 5 & drilled with rifle & was "tuckered." Swept up after cleaning my gun. Left pail at water last night & lost it. Steak, potatoes, coffee, toast & butter (25). Saw Capt*[ain]* & wrote to *[Brockport]* Repub*[lic]*. Rain & high wind. Dried apples. Dinner. Tried to sleep but just in a fine nap called up to sign pay rolls. Letter from Mother, sister & Bro*[ther]* H*[arvey]*. M*[other]* better also let*[ter]* from M*[ary]* A. C. F*[rench]*. Bo't Phila*[delphia]* Inquirer (5c) Stamps from home gave Munson (borrowed), S*[ampson]* W. F*[ry]* 2 I bor*[rowe]*d from him; I gave him 2. Lost my little pail. Supper & the black Gov*[ernment]* tea was so miserable I threw it away & made green tea Aunt sent me. Have a regular dish-wash every eve. Read in Inquirer good news. A little walk with *[Sampson W.]* F*[ry]*. Mended blanket—a large hole— put in large piece black cloth. Very warm to-night & the wind has blown clouds of dust all day. Troops started to go out toward Blackwater river but came back. 2 guerillas bro't in for shooting our pickets. Did not send my letters to *[Brockport]* Rep*[ublic]*, Bro*[ther]*s Harvey & Alonzo.

[Continuation of the Brockport Republic publication of June 18]

June 12.—There are indications of something to be done here in front. Several thousand infantry cavalry, artillery and ambulances went out this morning and the paymaster just gave us two months dues. For fear of taking up too much room, I close. Yours, &c. J.T.F.

Friday, 12th.—Payday—$26—to May 1st. Not out to roll call. Cleaned out my part of the tent. Washed. Breakfast: potato, steak, coffee, toast & butter. Put handle in tin cup to use as pail for making tea. Fine day, good fresh breeze. Aired clothes. Washed towels. Capt*[ain]* *[Volney J.]* Shipman's court-martial did not come off yesterday (previous statement in regard to it). Sultry & I am about melted. Heavy force of infantry, cav*[alry]* & ambulances towards the Blackwater. Splendid games with S*[ampson]* W. F*[ry]*. Paper from Aunt C & home. Paymaster came, appearing drunk & paid me $26, up to May 1st. Finished letter to Bro*[thers]* Lon & Harvey & sent $5 to mother, enclosed in letter to the *[Brockport]* Republic, which I sent to-night. Also wrote to Editor Philadelphia Inquirer & sent $1 for 2 months—50c for Geo*[rge]* Goold who is to take the loyal paper with me—50c each. Got my own supper. Made bed & played with Sam*[pson W. Fry]*—only for amusement. Laughed after I got to bed, till I shed tears.

Saturday, 13th—Cloudy & cool. Up at roll & back & laid down. Good breakfast. Pepper from Orderly *[A. L.]* Root. Cleaned up, bro't canteen water & washed little things. Brassy & bare-faced subscription paper for the purpose of buying our lazy bugler a fine keepsake—a key bugle to remember the Co*[mpany]* by. I am done with subscription papers for com*[pany]* privates. Our Co*[mpany]* have been nosed about long enough. Started to go fishing, could get no worms. Again in P.M. dig a few worms & saw large black snake which *[Sampson W.]* F*[ry]* & I lost after all. Caught one fish in 3 hours, no bites. Pleasant. Back tired. Washed self & stockings. Bo't 2 large lemons, 10c, & Julius Thurston treated me to glass pop. Read news to the boys.

Sunday, 14th.—Cloudy, windy & cool. Cooked my own breakfast. Pass & went to Suffolk. Saw my octoroon *[Mary Jutes]* on balcony & boy (black) tossed on blanket—funny. Streets thickly shaded, look pleasant, stoops or verandas in front of houses. Attended church, preaching by a chaplain, 2 young ladies accompanied by soldiers were all the ladies. Common sermon, seat in gallery. Dish of oysters 25c, & pie 10c. Picked roses & on way home found that my roses by M*[ary Jukes]* had picked for me & I was not around to get them. I met Cous*[in]* Geo*[rge]* F*[arnham]* on horseback & he paid me $2 for *[Sampson W.]* Fry. Made lemonade with w*[hiskey]* in it. At Suffolk witnessed 2 little incidents that attracted my attention. A little darkey swung in a blanket by a crowd around the edge of it; he made great plunges & dives in the air—rather ludicrous. On a church steps children, white & black, were playing innocently together without regard or notice of the difference in color.

It illustrates the equality of the colors in childhood, at least. Washed box & dishes. Borrowed N.Y. Herald, the would be Gov[ernor] dictator & political windmill. Hear discussion on liquor in next tent.

Monday, 15th.—A clear & at most cloudless day, cool & breezy. Headache. Made a little coffee & small piece toast. Am very costive—5 days. Aired clothes. A splendid air, not sultry in the A.M. today. Felt faint & weak about noon. Bean soup & saved beans for to-morrow. Made lemonade. Games with [Sampson W.] F[ry]. No mail since Thursday last. Pill I took this A.M. operated to-night (I fear I may have piles). Warm to-night. Made tea for [Charles P.] Tinker.

Tuesday, 16th.—High wind & very blustery. Warm. Up a little after roll call, swept, washed & hung out clothes. Felt better. Washed keg & little box & other things. A fine regimental brass band near us plays excellent music every morning. A general clearing up of brush back of camp & cleaning of spring by our companies. Games with S[ampson] W. Fry & Sergeant [James C.] Noble. Under the shade of a tree. Paper from Aunt C & a [Brockport] Repub[lic]. Drew pair Gov[ernment] shoes as served $1.94. Sent [Brockport] Repub[lic] to M[ary] A. C. F[rench]. Cooked tea & toast. Greased shoes & washed my whole body &c. Read a little & to bed early.

Wednesday, 17th.—Hot as fury. Good Gov[ernmen]t breakfast. Piled a few brick & rails. Good talk with a sensible Democrat of the 8th Co[mpany]. Any am[oun]t of "blowing" about nothing. Soup for dinner. Bo't pie (apple 5c) baked by women belonging to 6th Co[mpany] from Chautauqua Co[unty] N.Y. Dinner, then went in shade on bank of river, made lemonade there had a game with S[ampson W.] F[ry] & read. Letter from Aunt C. Hominy & molasses. Washed shirt. Read of the rebel raid in Pennsylvania, capturing 2 towns.[141] 10,000 extra troops for 6 mo[nth]s called for by the president. Great excitement. Very warm to-night.

Thursday, 18th.—Hot. Up at roll call & back to bed till 9. Washed & wrote home. Drank a little wine. Feel weak & my back is lame. Wrote letter home & send $5. Coffee & toast at 11. Leave to go to Suffolk. Reg[imen]ts of infantry coming back from Blackwater in the hot sun. At jewelry shops in S[uffolk] saw wounded men. Glass lemonade 5c. Bo't $1 in postage stamps. Mailed letter home. Bo't bottle ink (10c) q[ui]re paper & cakes. Heard we are ordered to pack up & march away from Suffolk at 4 P.M. I hurried back to the camp & found most of things packed & did mine up in a hurry. Finished my wine. Two papers & letter from home & letter from Mr. H[oratio N.] Beach as satisfactory in regard to my f[urlou]gh as I had expected. 2 days rations—

1. The Farnham family's entry in the 1860 census.

2. At the time Farnham joined the army, this building, 11 College Street, Brockport, at North (now Utica) Street, somewhat altered, housed the nine-member Farnham family, Charles Farnham's medical office, and three boarders.

3. John T. Farnham's grave in the Morton, NY, cemetery, beneath a beautiful mountain ash tree.

4. This house at the corner of Mechanics Street (now Park Avenue) and High Street was the home of Farnham's "sweetheart", Mary A.C. French, and her parents until their deaths and her removal to Coldwater, Mich., in 1912.

5. A sutler's tent in a camp. Farnham describes one such sutler in his 9/10/62 letter in the Brockport Republic. He refers to sutlers many times. (B&L II 154)

6. Cooper-shop, Philadelphia, as described by Farnham in his Brockport Republic letter dated 2/19/63. (Lossing I 577)

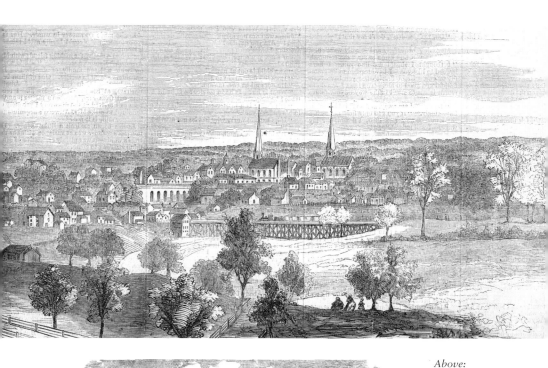

Above:
7. Fredericksburg before the battle. See Farnham's diary for 2/11/63. (HW 1862 777)

Left:
8. The Union assault on Fredericksburg. (Coffin 399)

9. Fredericksburg burning. (Lossing II 490)

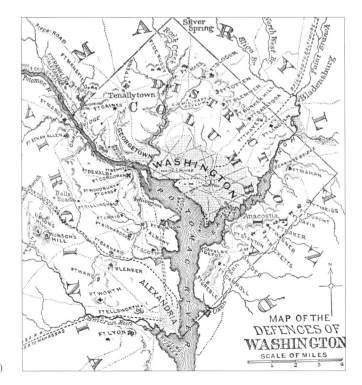

10. Map of Washington and environs, where Farnham was stationed for much of his time in the Army. (B&L II 543)

11. A view of Acquia Creek, which Farnham's unit passed on a rainy march en route to Suffolk, Va. See Brockport Republic 3/12/63. (Lossing I 487)

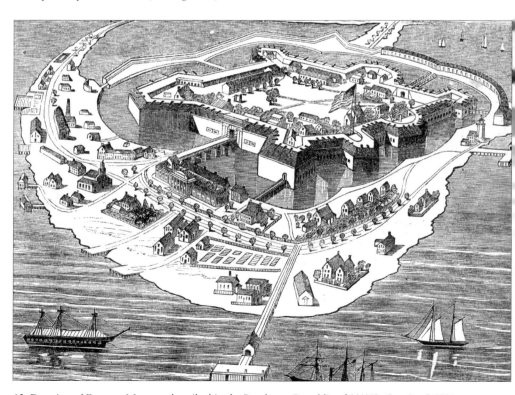

12. Drawing of Fortress Monroe, described in the Brockport Republic of 3/4/63. (Lossing I 499)

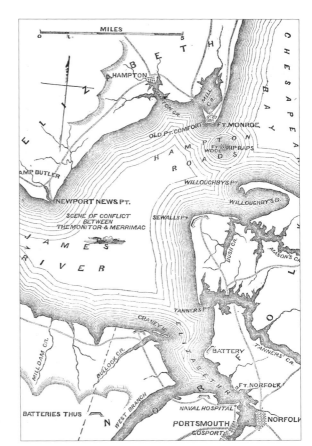

Right: **13.** Map of Fortress Monroe and environs. (Abbott I 345)

Below: **14.** An army field camp of the sort in which Farnham lived for much of his service. (HPH II 517)

15. Confederate prisoners being brought into a camp, as described by Farnham in diary entry 3/17/63, though the number of prisoners was much smaller. (B&L II 156)

16. A "contraband camp" such as Uniontown, which Farnham described in the Brockport Republic of 3/19/63. (Google Images)

17. Some residents of a contraband camp. (Google Images)

18. Foragers. Farnham sometimes went foraging, for instance on 4/8/63. (HPH II 720)

19. Suffolk, Virginia, which Farnham visited often while stationed nearby. See Brockport Republic 4/16/63. (HW 1863 276)

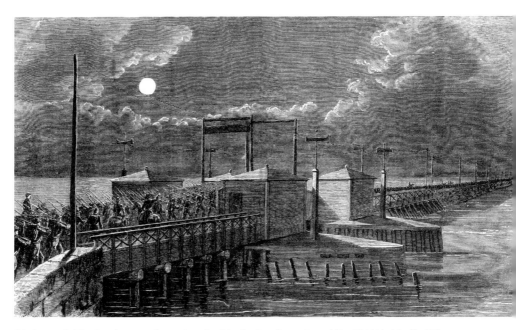

20. A march like Farnham made, as described in the Brockport Republic 4/23/63. (Coffin 73)

21. Armed action short of battle: skirmishing in the woods. Farnham reported many occasions when he and others in his unit skirmished. (HPH I 367)

22. Another armed action short of battle: pickets on duty. Farnham reported many times having been on picket duty, for instance in his diary entry of 10/17/63. (HW 1862 460)

23. Building breastworks. Farnham described doing this in his diary entry of 4/25/63 and, in more improvised fashion, in the 4/30/63 Brockport Republic. (B&L IV 156)

24. A brief, unofficial battlefield truce of the sort reported by Farnham in the Brockport Republic, 5/14/63. (B&L III 139)

25. Mealtime in camp. Drawing rations. See typical accounts of Farnham's meals in his early June 1863 diary entries, for instance 6/11/63. (HW 1863 540)

26. The steamer Columbia that transported Farnham's unit from Norfolk to the Yorktown campaign. See his letter of 6/20/63. (Google Images from Currier & Ives print)

27. Yorktown, Va., as described by Farnham in his 6/26/63 letter. (B&L II 173)

28. A mortar battery during the siege of Yorktown. (HPH I 336)

29. Chesapeake Hospital, where Farnham was a patient, 6/27/-10/9/63. (Miller VII 233)

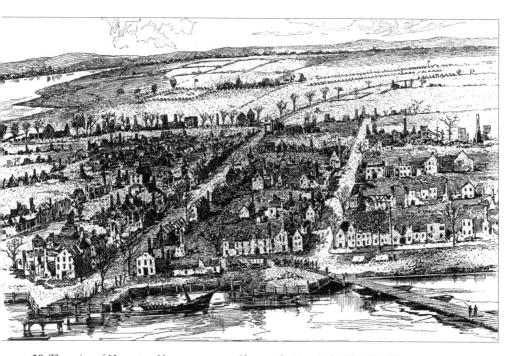

30. The ruins of Hampton, Va., a scene near Chesapeake Hospital. (B&L II 152)

31. The Army of the Potomac at the White House on the Pemunkey, where the sharpshooters camped while Farnham was hospitalized. Letter of 7/9/63. (B&L II 177)

32. Mealtime on the march. See, for instance, his letter of 7/18/63 (B&L II 504)

33. Old Point Comfort, near the Chesapeake Hospital. See his 7/30/63 letter. (HW 1862 604)

34. Former President Tyler's home. See the Brockport Republic, 8/28/63. (HW 1861 406)

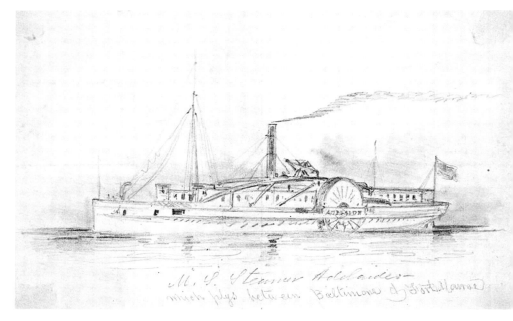

M. S. Steamer Adelaide which plys between Baltimore & Fortill[anvoe]

35. The steamer "Adelaide" that transported Farnham from Fortress Monroe to rejoin his unit after his hospitalization. (LofC DIGppmsca 20974)

36. Crossing a river by pontoon, which Farnham did over the Rappahannock River at Rappahannock Station on 11/9/63. (Elson)

37. An army unit crossing the Rapidan at Ely's Ford. See his 12/5/63 letter. (B&L III 174)

38. Celebrating Christmas in camp on the Rappahannock. See the diary entries of 12/24-25/63. (Coffin 461)

39. Catlett's Station, mentioned by Farnham in his diary on 11/7/63. (Lossing II 451)

40. The section of an army field camp devoted to workshops. (HPH II 622)

41. Building huts in a field camp. Farnham described an example in the Brockport Republic, 2/4/64. (HPH I 168)

42. Warrenton, Va., where Farnham went to bury his younger brother, Charles, who had died of disease in the army. See his 2/25/64 letter. (B&L IV 86)

43. Another view of Warrenton. (HW 1862 581)

44. The ruins of Chancellorsville that Farnham visited 5/7/64. (Lossing III 34)

45. Spotsylvania Court House, where Farnham's unit spent the night of 5/8/63 while fighting in the Spotsylvania campaign. (HPH II 631)

46. Washington's mother's tomb that Farnham visited, 5/19/64. (HW 1862 776)

47. Fighting during the Battle of the Wilderness. See Farnham's letter of 6/16/64. (HW 1864 356)

48. Fire breaks out during the Battle of the Wilderness. (HW 1864 357)

49. In camp on the Chickahominy. See letter of 6/23/64. (HPH I 350)

50. The Union Army advances on Petersburg. See the Brockport Republic 7/14/64. (HPH II 638)

53. City Point, where Farnham convalesced after his hospital stay. See his letter of 7/24/64. (Ellson)

54. The "hospital" at City Point. (B&L IV 583)

OPPOSITE PAGE:

Above: 51. In the Union Army trenches at Petersburg. (HPH II 700)

Below: 52. The occupation of Petersburg. (HPH II 764)

55. Soldiers voting for President. Farnham campaigned for Lincoln in early November 1864. See his diary for 10/20/64. (HPH II 668)

56. A sharpshooter on the prowl. (HW 1863 556)

57. Sharpshooters in action at Petersburg, a similar scene was noted by Farnham on 11/13/64. (B&L IV 560)

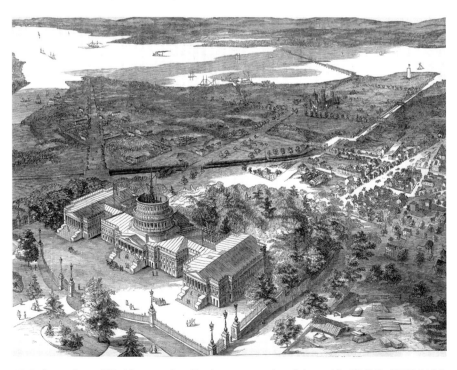

58. Balloon view of Washington when Farnham was stationed there, 4/1-6/16/65. (HPH I 134)

59. The crowd at Lincoln's second inaugural, including Farnham. See diary for 3/4/65. (LoC DIG-cwpb-00601)

60. The War Department building, where Farnham clerked. (B&L II 121)

61. Pennsylvania Avenue, Washington. (B&L I 158)

62. Feminist journalist Jane Swissheim, Farnham's landlady and friend in Washington. See diary for 5/31/65.

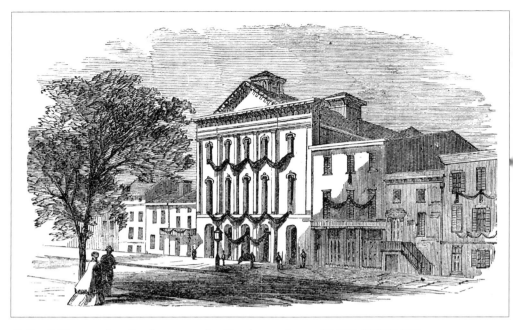

63. Ford's Theater, where Farnham went after Lincoln was shot on 4/14/65. (HPH II 783)

64. Grand review in Washington, viewed by Farnham on 4/18/65. (HPH II 793)

drew sugar for 2 days, salt horse*[radish?]* & meat for 2 days, also hardtack.
Cold beans I had saved at noon I take with me. My knapsack is to be carried.
As much as I wish to attend to carry my rifle & accout*[rement]*s. Every thing
ready & in confusion & at about 6 o'clock we bid adieu to Camp South Quay,
marched to the depot, took cars with 167th N.Y., part of Terry's brigade, bid
adieu to Suffolk amid cheers of the crowd & the music of a brass band on
board, leaving just at dark. I had the pleasure of riding on the open platform
cars, sitting on one & resting my feet on the other. Very good ride through
part of the Dismal Swamp & saw the "Fire Fly Lamps" lighting the solitude
& lone pickets with their fires also lighting up the solitude. Stopped twice to
wood &c. slowly crossed two draw bridges. At last reached the splendid iron
bridge across the water just before entering Norfolk & while on the bridge
a delightful, healthy, invigorating breeze from off the salt water struck us
familiarly in the face. First thing we saw on dock at Norfolk was steamer
Maple Leaf [142] which I had excursion on Lake Ontario 2 years ago—romantic.
Off the cars safely at Norfolk & waiting quite a long time for the baggage to
be transferred to a steamer "Columbia" (**26**) by the light of a glaring pine fire.
A little after 12 we went aboard what proved a poor, dirty craft & too many
piled on—about 500. I with other invalids were shown to the lower cabins or
something but a very foul, hot & close air in it where we had on our overcoats
on the floor, as it had rained some of course as we were on the march while
we waited at dock. In a little time the floor was piled full as though we were
so many sheep or cattle. Started at last & about 3 miles from Norfolk in
Hampton Roads the 2 vessels in company, including ours, ran aground on the
bar in the darkness & nary could get off. Screaming for assistance a tug soon
came to us & pulling awhile gave up hopes of pulling us off. So I made out to
get to sleep in spite of the heated atmosphere & crowded floor. At last every
thing became quiet.

Friday, 19th.—In Hampton Roads between Norfolk & Craney Island on a
sand bar. Awoke sleepy & got a fresh breath of air on the crowded deck & find
we lay where we ran aground, in sight of Norfolk to the south & Craney Island
to the north plainly visible. On all sides pleasant green banks, nicely sloping.
Occasional tug puffing past & occasionally a steamboat, also oyster sloops.
Cloudy & a fine healthy breeze. Good birdseye view of Norfolk. Prospect
this morning of going to Yorktown, Va. At 9 A.M. "Columbia" helped us off
& on we went to Fort Monroe & were signaled to go to Yorktown. Passed
on in rain & nothing of great importance passed. Sun shone as we landed at
Yorktown at 3 o'clock. Drink of cold coffee at guard house. In Yorktown, Va.
(**27, 28**) From the water, heights above Yorktown (a little settlement of old
houses inside heavy breastworks) look fresh & healthy. Lots of negro houses
on hill. Bo't lemonade & biscuit of wenches. Guarded baggage & rode in

ambulance with others to camp thro' Yorktown. New encampments. Our camp is on high hill overlooking a river, good place. Helped put up tent, got water at nearest spring near river, ½ mile. Bo't pie & cakes. Made coffee & had beans with it. Fixed bed, read, & to bed early. All about here lights in camps, looks like streets of a city.

Saturday, 20th.—A good sleep. Roll call. With S*[ampson]* W. F*[ry]* went ½ mile to spring after water & to wash. A fine spring, teams drawing water from them. Made coffee & had fried hardtack. Wrote to *[Brockport]* Republic & home & to Philadelphia Inquirer. Pills of a surgeon, for costiveness. Coffee for dinner. Lemons. Walked to old Yorktown & the houses are old fashioned too, nothing but a little settlement & scattered inside the walls. Stores & groceries selling to soldiers. Got hood & *[illegible word]* cake & ate oysters from the shell in a boat, as they were taken from the shell by darkies who raked them from the bed. Nice large ones. Old graveyard—bodies placed there in 1745 & 1752, one—that of a woman, Susanna Reynolds—with a death's head & cross bones on tombstone. Saw sand bank where Lord Cornwallis dug the 2 rooms in a rock in the war of the Revolution (1776) close by the river. Read the Philadelphia Inquirer (of *[Sampson W.]* Fry's). Rebs mostly out of Pennsylvania. Do not feel very well to-night & it is chilly. Made a little tea & to bed very early. Up at 11 out in the rain 4½ days.

Brockport Republic, June 25, 1863

Yorktown, Va., June 20, 1863. Editor Republic:—Once more on the move, and now 40 miles north of Suffolk, and 60 miles from Richmond. We left Suffolk, after a rather hurried preparation, and only a few hours' notice, on Thursday evening, the 18th, with baggage and two days' rations. Had just put up new summer houses, and everything "at home," in good order, but as soldiers cannot depend upon quiet and ease for any length of time, and as *great things* are about to take place, we cheerfully obey orders. About dark we, with other troops of Gen. Terry's brigade, took cars for Norfolk, and after a slow ride through the Dismal swamp glittering with the light of fire-flies and picket lights, entered Norfolk, fanned by the delicious sea breeze. The first vessel lying at the dock was the noted Maple Leaf, now in the government service, formerly running on Lake Ontario, and which many remember as having conveyed them on holiday excursions from the mouth of the Genesee. Baggage and troops were, at about midnight, put on board the transport Columbia and propeller Eastern State, and on the way to Fortress Monroe. The Sharpshooters were on the latter craft, an old fogy vessel, on which were packed some 500 soldiers with baggage, and the best place provided for invalids was a hole below deck, close, hot and unhealthy.—As usual on our excursions, it was rainy, and, in order to keep dry, your correspondent chose the splendid "state room" just referred to.

Three miles off Norfolk, both vessels ran aground on a sand bar, and, after a long and loud screaming of the whistle, a tug came to pull us off, but no—we must lay there till the tide or good fortune allowed us to get off. About 9 o'clock Friday morning tide arose and the vessels managed to help each other off, and an uninteresting voyage brought us to Fortress Monroe, where we were signaled to go on to Yorktown—then an idea of a march to and capture of *Richmond* entered our heads. Rain and clouds helped to cool us as we gently steamed up Chesapeake Bay, along the green banks on both sides, around to Yorktown, the "city," (poor appellation for an old settlement,) of *[illegible word]* and surrenders, where the sun shone a welcome as we landed at 3 P.M. This heavy fortified stronghold is opposite Gloucester Point and the view while on the water is pleasant—shows green hills, tents, high breastworks, a village, negro huts lining the banks, and an insignificant landing. I have no time to describe the appearance at length in this.

Our camp is to-day in back of the so-called city, and of the breastworks surrounding it, high and dry, near the bank, and overlooking the river, and camps are all about us, but spring water half a mile off—all lively—bands playing, and—well, for short, all the men are in good spirits and expecting orders. I cannot say what all of us are looking forward to, but as this will not be published in time to be strictly "contraband," I will say that men and munitions of war are constantly arriving here. Gen. Keyes is in command at this point. You will get the news by telegraph. Capt. Shipman is left sick at Suffolk, and Lieut. Starkweather has charge of the company. Suffolk is now of no consequence.. Some of our men, in poor condition to march, will be left here, if the order comes for the Sharpshooters to "forward." Excuse more for this week.

Friends in writing to N.Y. Sharpshooters should direct—Yorktown, Va., *Gen. Terry's brigade.* J.T.F.

Sunday, 21st.—Cloudy & cool. Up & out at 7, then abed again. Sick today. At 10 made tea. Sorted over my things in knapsack & gave S*[ampson]* W. F*[ry]* Lin*[amen]*t & bandages. Letter from Cous*[in]* Albert Allen, Parma New York. Am on the list to go to Fortress Monroe. Sultry in P.M. On the hill looking at the river. Made tea. A terrible shower, chilly & cool in eve.

Monday, 22d.—Co*[mpany]* ordered to pack & be ready to march at 9 & leave knapsacks & large tents & take nothing but shelter tents & blanket. Packed up my things & stay, with 8 others in our Co*[mpany]*. A pleasant day. Clouds in A.M. After all the Co*[mpany]* had gone, I went to Yorktown city with Geo*[rge]* Howe, got loaf bread for self, also cakes. Check for rations at commissary. Hot Gov*[ernment]* bread 6 cts. loaf. Saw 3 transports with troops coming in. Back, got water at spring & had fine bath in salt water of the York river, 1st time in salt water. Troops coming in all the time. Read some old papers. Made tea & toast. Fine music by a band all a bustle. Helped bring water. Abed alone in tent early. Drums & bugles of several regiments all beating together, make a horrible din. Quite warm to-night.

Tuesday, 23d.—A fine cool morning. No roll call to get up to this morning. Made coffee. Wrote to Mother. Examined by a head army surgeon who gave me quinine—on sick list. Battery drill on the canvas-covered plain. Carried several letters to the F.C. Very warm in the sun. Bought a copy of the "Yorktown Cavalier" a weekly paper & sent to the *[Brockport]* Republic. Inquired for Dr. Clark at the Medical Directors office & wrote letter to him then. Bought cakes & cheese & a daily at news room where there was a great rush. Made lemonade when I got back. Read. Tea on the river bank. Boys back. Letter from N.S., *[Brockport]* Republic, & 2 Philadelphia Inquirers of 19th & 20th. All right. In tent with *[Theron]* Ainsworth, read.

Wednesday, 24th.—Cool, cloudy. No appetite this A.M. Drills of inf*[antry]* & art*[iller]*y as usual on plain. Sitting on bank of the river look at the transport steamers loaded with troops ready to go up the York river to West Point or White House.[143] Band playing. Saw cannon burst by McClellans troops firing while the rebs had possession a year ago. Bo't pie (25c). Waited for mail. Hot. Drew loaf new bread, had bread & butter & coffee for dinner. Bro't water. Cleaned out tent. Put down boards in tent from house torn down by soldiers. Drew rations sugar 9 oz. Also potatoes. Again on the bank of the river at sunrise.

Thursday, 25th.—Blackberries. Cloudy & rain all day or a kind of drizzle. At 6 o'clock cooked or fried potatoes & pork with hardtack & made our breakfast with that & coffee & toast. Took walk out through the town to see Bates, Wag*[on]* Master of 4th Wis*[consin]*. Battery & met him on horseback & he asked me to go on to his shalet *[chalet?]* or palace, & there I found 2 men of the 4th, 1 cooking breakfast. B*[ates]* came & I tasted some good coffee & had a good few hours visit. B*[ates]* gave me little traveling demijohn with cord attached & lent me overcoat to go back in the rain. Bo't 1 qt nice blackberries of wench. At the P.O. got letter from Dr. A. H. Clark, Surg*[eo]*n Chesapeake Gen*[eral]* Hospital, Fort Monroe & satisfactory. Saw Surg*[eon]* here & showed him letter. Read in *[Theron]* Ainsworth's tent. Drew 1 loaf new bread. Fixed blackberries with sugar, had tea & good supper. Rec*[eive]*d paper from home & the Phil*[adelphia]* Inq*[uirer]*. Dark & rainy night.

Friday, 26th.—Rain all the A.M. Pleasant P.M. four of our boys left to-day for the front on transports with most of the great number here. Gathered some plunder from the deserted camp near us & fixed potatoes & made coffee. Wrote to sister & to *[Brockport] Republic*. Inquired of the D*[octo]*r Sent for paper for Geo*[rge]* Sherry & went to Yorktown with him. Had lemonade & pie. At dock saw transport cars filled with soldiers going up the river. Horses loaded on transports. Men fishing. Bo't a few blackberries of a wench. 22nd Conn*[ecticut]* Reg*[imen]*t on way home. Phila*[delphia]* Inq*[uirer]* of 24th. Supper brisk. Rain to-night.

Brockport Republic, July 2, 1863

Camp "Invalid," Yorktown, Va., June 26, 1863. Editor Republic:—Before this reaches you, it must be generally known that Gen. Keyes, in command of the Yorktown peninsula, is on the road to Richmond, as I intimated last week, with a heavy force, which has been brought via Yorktown, across or up the peninsula, overland or transported up the York or James rivers. Several thousand troops departed here early this morning. How near Richmond the advance is I have no means of stating; they must be well ahead. The quietness of the movement, and its secrecy, so unusual in such matters previously, are favorable circumstances, and the prospect is that the country will shortly have glorious news of a Union victory to offset the Pennsylvania raid.

The 6th Co. of Sharpshooters, with the battalion, (excepting several invalids left behind to take charge of the camp, being unable to march,) went with Terry's brigade on Monday morning last, toward the front, via Williamsburg, twelve miles up the river. They left knapsacks and large tents and all unnecessary baggage, taking shelter tents, &c., with them. Have not heard from the company since they left, only that they were beyond Williamsburg, but they will undoubtedly make themselves known by their rifles, when given a chance.—All were in good spirits when starting and the weather has been mostly cloudy and favorable for marching.

Those of the 6th Co., unavoidably left behind, unable to march, who have not since gone on are: Capt. V. J. Shipman, at Chesapeake General Hospital, Fort Monroe, (in which Dr. A. H. Clark, of Brockport, is stationed), corporal Howe, privates Goold, Smith, Munson, and I am sorry to say your humble servant, J.T.F. All the latter are left at Yorktown for the present. Geo. Sherry, who was wounded and disabled at the siege of Suffolk, is here and will be discharged.

If I were not afraid of a failure, I might try to give you a description of the celebrated "antediluvian city" Yorktown, for I believe it is generally supposed to have some pretensions to notoriety. There is no beauty in the city, rather an ancient mass of crumbling brick, stone and rotten wood, any more than any one sees about the *city* of Redman's Corners, near Brockport. The fortifications are heavy and quite extensive. The ground inside the works is much cut up by ravines, fences here are none, and there is now standing part of the original revolutionary breastwork—the present earth work embracing the dwellings, and is much more extensive than formerly; the whole being high above the landing, and might properly be call the "heights." The contrabands are quite numerous. On the whole, war and its ravages have spoiled what might in the North be made a pleasant village. An old Court-house of brick is now used as an ordnance depot, and the little old jail as a guard house for preserving disorderly soldiers, and unruly secesh, and the grated door is left open for air, with a guard at the entrance. A rickety building which I was satisfied with calling an aristocratic smoke-house, some one told me was formerly a *bank*. There is no accounting for Southern taste. A very ancient black wooden building, once a church, the only one, is on a hill, and near it are indications of a graveyard, laid out, perhaps, by the Puritan fathers. The slabs are defaced and moss-covered, and only two have been placed there within ten years—showing the sparseness of population, or the extreme good health in these parts. One stone bore the inscription—"Thomas Nelson, born 1677, died 1745"—very ancient; "Abraham Archer, died 1753", "Susanna Reynolds, died 1768"; the latter stone was embellished with a skull and cross-bones; what sort of a crime she had committed to deserve the horrid emblem, was not stated. There were other slabs of about the same dates. A large brick building, quite rickety, is said to be Lord Cornwallis' former headquarters, and in the bank of earth fronting the river, are two small rooms, cut in the rock, once occupied by Cornwallis, lately used as a powder magazine, with an underground connection to the center of the town. Threatening cannon and mortars adorn the breastworks, some of which were spiked by the rebels on surrendering to McClellan, and have since been bored out.

Back of the fort is a plain, for several days past covered with tents, and the air has resounded with the sound of drum and bugle, and the tramp of horses carrying messengers with orders. Beyond to the south, extending for miles, are McClellan's earthworks, rifle pits, &c., which were thrown up at the siege of Yorktown, ravines, mounds and undergrowth, then woods beyond. Springs of water are not plenty, and wood is scarce. A regiment encamped here broke up and left this morning, and now there is hardly a board or stick left on the spot, so great was the rush by the darkies for the fuel and leavings of an army.

On the bank of the river, on the height in the grass, one has a fine view of the river's mouth and the transports and sail vessels going up and down, the puffing tugs, oyster boats with men raking for oysters, the pleasant scenery and camps at Gloucester Point, opposite, and the salt water bathers on the beach, altogether, make a lively scene. At sunset it is splendid.

In hope of soon hearing from *[illegible words]* and an entrance to Richmond, *[illegible words]* a condition to go on, I remain, as usual,

Yours truly, J.T.F.

Saturday, 27th.—Pleasant & cool breeze. Fried pork & potatoes. Quinine of surg*[eon]*. Saw Dr. *[Joshua B.]* Purchase. Show him letter of introduction & obtained valuable information of him. Went to Lieut*[enant]* Flynn of 9th Co*[mpany]* who wrote my leave of absence to Fortress Monroe. I wrote letter for Hinman Smith in hospital to his sister. Packed up my things & left camp. Knapsack & haversack with Corp*[ora]*l Delos Howe & at Yorktown the adjutant of Gen*[eral]* King approved my pass & signed it. After seeing Baker & after much trouble (every thing in the boat line going towards Richmond) I succeeded in getting on board *[Major]* Gen*[eral John A.]* Dix's dispatch flag of truce boat. Henry Burden,[144] Capt*[ain]* Cole & had pleasant ride, swift. Met 2 steamboats, south, troops to reinforce Gen. Dix now at the White House. A fine ride & not crowded. From Yorktown to Fort Monroe 30 miles generally run in 2½ hours by the boat. Arrived at Fortress Monroe at 4:25. At Provost Marshall's office then walked 1½ miles with darkey by nice clean street & yards of little cottages, over bridge. Bo't cakes for the darkey & put across at Chesapeake General Hospital (**29**). Found Dr. A.H. Clark, looking fat & hearty. Took me to his room, then to see Capt*[ain Volney J.]* Shipman, sick, then to the 6th ward where I found boys of our Battalion & gave letter to H.H. At supper with all the ward & at long table furnished with fresh bread & butter & blackberries, good enough for anyone. At the D*[octo]*r's. introduced to Dr. Allen & talked a long time with Dr. C*[lark]*. Then in Capt*[ain]*'s room. Occupied bed No. 29 in 6th ward where ill newcomers are furnished with clean cot, shirts & drawers. A nice bed with clean sheets & cover lid. Felt natural. A great number sick & one man died in night. Slept but little as attendants were walking back & forth giving medicine.

Context— George Meade succeeds Joseph Hooker in command of the Army of the Potomac, June 28.

Sunday, 28th.—Up at 5 & washed. Walked about & waked the D*[octo]*r up at 6 & he showed me all about the hospital. Some 700 sick—7 wards, 2 out in the seminary building, neat buildings composed of 4 wings from a square center— counting about 100 patients generally. Female nurse in 6th. Looked into the store room & saw dried apples & other donations. Wash room for washing dishes. Cooking range—a fine thing for baking & making tea & coffee. Ericson engine.[145] Room for cooking low diet for the sickest. Dispensary, took stock of medicines. Store room—provisions. Clerical apparatus & library of Seminary room occupied by Surgeon in charge, Anthony E. Stocker. Drawing room containing piano & melodeon. Four wards in building. 7 in all. Bathing room being fixed. 18 Com[manding] Officers sick here. In the dome of the building had fine view of Hampton (30) village, mostly burned during this war.... View of mouth of James river & the Hampton Roads but the air was foggy & misty & almost rain fell. The Ches[apeake] Hospital building was formerly used as a female seminary & is five stories high, besides the high dome. Large white pillars (built of brick) in front & a fine yard shaded garden with vegetables for the use of Hospital, close by the edge of the water. Breakfast with the boys—coffee, milk, bread & butter & syrup. Bid Capt[ain] good bye, also Dr. C[lark] who gave me letter for Dr. [Joshua B.] Purchase of 130th NYV & bid the boys farewell & was sorry to leave this civilized place. (Forgot to note that I was introduced to Mr. Morehead, nurse at the linen room, where were shelved piles of linen & cotton cloths & garments for invalids; here is also two quilts contributed by some person in Massachusetts which were made & used in hospital at the time of the Revolution in 1776; they have an antique appearance, but have been well preserved). Walked to Fortress M[onroe], show[e]d my pass & got on the mail boat for Y[ork]town. Gen[eral] Dix horse was put on to be sent to him in front. Vessels in the stream with soldiers aboard. Rough passage, windy—just right. At Y[ork]town 1½ P.M. Walked to camp & took letter to Dr. P[urchase], 1 mile, who gave me encouragement. A little rain to-night. Made tea & got supper. In [George] Sherry's tent awhile.

Monday, 29th.—Cloudy & cool, same as for 2 or 3 days. Fried pork & potatoes. Wrote to [Sampson W.] Fry—sent it by Geo[rge] Sherry. Medicine of surg[eon]. Gave a man coffee for oysters, but do not get them to-day. Paid Geo[rge] Goold 25c for his share in the Phila[delphia Inq[uirer] daily. Saw Dr. [Joshua B.] Purchase & he said I go to Ches[apeake] Gen[eral] H[ospital] when the letter as he had written & endorsed Dr. C[lark]'s request. Wrote a word home. Down to town & helped bring up prisoners. At town saw Sam Page a negro 103 yrs old, who remembered the time Lord Cornwallis surrendered his sword at Yorktown. He is yet smart. Cooked oysters & coffee, bo't ½ lb. butter, 20 cts. Aired my knapsack & sorted thro'. Wrote to M[ary] A. C. F[rench]. To bed early.

Tuesday, 30th.—Sick headache. Coffee. Saw Surg[eo]n. High wind but sultry. Bo't pint blackberries, 5c. Gave woman piece of soap & a box for washing shirt, towel & hand k[erchie]f. Finished writing to M[ary] A. C. F[rench]. Mustered for Pay. At the post office & bo't paper in the Yorktown Cavalier office & had a "ration" as the proprietors were jolly. Mustered for pay. Rain a trifle. Lieut*[enant Alphonso W.]* Stark*[weathe]*r back, sick. *[George]* Sherry back & bro't me a letter from *[Sampson W.]* Fry. He gave me sword, short, which I brushed up, also gun &c. Talk with *Lieut[enant]s*. Beef rations— guard from 9 till 1. Pleasant moonlight & hot.

Context—The battalion was in the defenses of Washington 22nd Corps in July and then in the 1st Brigade (Iron), 1st Division, 1st Corps, Army of the Potomac from July until April 1864. Farnham was separated from his unit in the hospital June 27–October 9, 1863. Union forces defeated Confederates in the Battle of Gettysburg, July 1–3, and Vicksburg fell to the Union, July 4.

Wednesday, July 1st.—Sleepy. Break*[fas]*t, then washed up. *[illegible word]* things aired. Sent paper to Father & M*[ary]* A. C. F*[rench]*. Geo*[rge]* S*[herry]* left early today. *[Major]* Gen*[eral George G.]* Meade, successor to *[Major]* Gen*[eral Joseph]* Hooker, commenced to fight *[General Robert E.]* Lee in Penn*[sylvania]* at Gettysburg. Down to the town & carried overcoat to Baker's & saw wenches young & old & heard some dry notes—old lady told some of her experience. Back & stopped at Printing Office & get 2 sticks[146] full—20 or 30 lines *[of type]*—quite natural. Lieutenant *[Alphonso W.]* Starkweather promised to sign me a furlough. Bought Yankee notions & ½ lb. butter (20c) also ale. No returns from Fort*[ress]* M*[onroe]*. Hot in sun, cool breeze. Drew sugar rations for 5 days & coffee & bread for 2 days. Read Yankee Notions.[147] Made lemonade. Slept 2 hours. Tea. Read news of rebs advancing toward & near Harrisburg, Pa. Gen*[eral]* Hooker removed.

Thursday, 2d.—Large fish—18 pounder. Made cup coffee. Warm day, but cool breeze. Wrote to Mother & Father. Saw Surgeon at hospital. Traded coffee for 2 qts blackberries with the darkies. Down st*[reet]* & bo't New York Times (5c). Stewed apples. Berries for supper, also bread & butter, sugar & tea. A large fish, a bass, was caught by the hand of Lieut*[enant Albert N.]* Blinn, 9th Co*[mpany]*, hosp*[ital]* steward Brown & commissary Serg*[ean]*t Starkweather, wedged in a raft. He was a huge one, weighed 18 lbs & came from the river. Bro't a pail water & picked nice shells on the beach. In *[Delos]* Howe's tent till 9½, then commenced letter to *[Brockport]* Repub*[lic]*. Band playing. 11th R*[hode]* I*[sland]*, 9th Mass*[achusetts regiments]* Going home to-morrow. Fine moonlight.

Friday, 3d.—Fall of Vicksburg, 4th Up at 5½ & made coffee. Bath in river after shells. Fine bathing in salt water. Hot—sultry, less breeze than common. Bo't pint of milk 5c. *[Delos]* Howe cooked piece of the 18 lb fish—good. Finished letter to *[Brockport]* Repub*[lic]*. Down to the P.O. Bo't paper for Dr. *[Joshua B.]* Purchase & one for self. Glass ale. Cha*[rle]*s Collamer, Co*[mpany]* Clerk, brought me a letter from Father, Mother, sister & Aunt C. Lemonade. Supper & a walk & sat on the beach on river bank. Read till 10 P.M. Vicksburg surrender by the rebels.

Brockport Republic, July 9, 1863

Camp "Invalid," Yorktown, Va., July 3, 1863. Mr. Editor:—Being left behind with several other "poor invalids," I did not have the pleasure of a march with our battalion of Sharpshooters up the Peninsula to the White House, on the Pemunkey river (31), 20 miles east of Richmond, where at last accounts all our forces under Gen. Keyes lay, waiting for something to turn up. The principal thing accomplished was the capture of 200 rebels in camp, including Gen. Fitzhugh Lee. This was done by the gallant Col. Spear and the 11th Pennsylvania cavalry. All news is contraband, so if I had news I could not communicate it. I understand that all mail for the North from this direction has been delayed at Fortress Monroe and the secret of the expedition toward Richmond has been well kept.

Lieut. Starkweather was here on Wednesday, somewhat unwell, but returned to the company on that day. He reports all the boys feeling as well as could be expected after a march, and in good health and spirits, that not one lagged back after starting from here, every one keeping up, though some had their loads carried. They stood it remarkably. Those on the sick list here in camp are mostly doing well, attended by surgeons Purchase of the 130th N.Y. and G. W. Grosvenor, 11th R.I., and we have a healthy camp back of Yorktown, on the heights. Geo. Sherry, of our company, whose paraents reside in Irondequoit, Monroe county, disabled at the siege of Suffolk, is discharged and has gone home.—Capt. Shipman is doing well at Chesapeake Hospital.

On Saturday last I obtained a pass to Fortress Monroe, through the kindness of Gen. King's aide, and on the flag of truce and Gen. Dix dispatch boat, the Henry Burden, Capt. G. A. Cole, had a pleasant ride of 30 miles, in 21 hours, over the blue waves, and landing at the Fortress, proceeded a mile down the beach, passing by pleasant cottages and the busy streets, and along a not unpleasant road, and halted at Chesapeake General Hospital, a fine, large five story building built in 1850 for a female seminary, and used as such until the war opened, the pen being laid aside for the sword, and science brought to bear in healing sick and wounded. Here I found Dr. A.H. Clark of Brockport, Surgeon in charge of the Sixth ward, which contains all the fever cases. Dr. C. is in good health and spirits, and his parents speak well of him. Through his kindness I enjoyed the hospitalities of the institution, and was shown over its well-regulated and tidy kitchen, mess-room, store-room (and in this room saw some fine, dried fruit among other donations from the ladies of East or West

Clarkson,) room for washing dishes, dispensary or medicine-room, chemical apparatus and library of the former seminary, and the different wards. Seven hundred patients are now under treatment. The main building is well adapted for sick, and a bathing room is being completed. A well-furnished drawing room contains a piano and melodeon. The surgeons occupy pleasant rooms in the second story. Dr. E.A. Stocker is surgeon in charge. Outside the seminary building are two wards, each built in the shape of four long wings, the center of which is built square, with skylights, and the arrangements are neat and tidy. Attendants care for the suffering—all are well taken care of. In one of these wards, the sixth, Dr. Clark has charge and is assisted by a female nurse, who acts the part of "angel of mercy," attending to the little wants with grace and patience. Her presence seems to have a beneficial effect upon the invalids and all is quiet. There is another nurse in the main building—Miss Morehead. When I first entered the ward, the lady was kindly engaged in writing a letter for a weak patient. This ward will accommodate over 100 persons and is now well filled. All are furnished with clean under garments, towels, &c. Those too ill to leave the ward are given a light diet, and those convalescing eat at the mess-room in the main building, where I partook with them of a supper as follows: Tea, fresh wheat bread, nice butter and blackberries; for breakfast, coffee and milk, bread and butter and syrup. The grounds are pleasantly arranged and the institution is fronted by the water of Hampton Roads, with a good view of the Fortress, bay, and for a long distance a fleet of vessels, also Hampton village in the vicinity. This village was mostly destroyed during the present war. From the high dome of the building, I had a glimpse of a church built during the reign of Queen Elizabeth, the timber for which was brought from England, also the former residence of ex-President John Tyler, both these antiquaries are in Hampton. I hope soon to be able to give you a better description of Chesapeake Hospital , Hampton, Fortress Monroe and vicinity. But there is an interesting room in the hospital I had forgotten to mention—it is called the "linen room," and contains wardrobe for patients, as well as linen for wounds, blankets, coverlids, &c, and looks like a well stocked clothing store. The two curiosities now safely kept there are a couple of patchwork quilts made and used for sick in the revolutionary war sent here by some liberal person in Massachusetts who has preserved them well. They are heavy, dark colored, and some of the patches are of buckskin. There is an explanatory inscription upon them, and they have been spread for a short time upon the bed of every patient that all might watch the inspiring "spirit of '76" upon the hallowed patriot quilts.

I see that I have already intruded upon more space than may be spared, perhaps, for this week. I returned on Sunday, after an interesting visit, which, though very brief, was impressive and instructive, owing to the courtesy of the polite surgeon of the 6th ward.

It is to be hoped that the army of Gen. Keyes will celebrate July 4th by an entrance into Richmond, but I fear not. All letters should, until further notice, be directed White House, Va., Gen. Terry's Brigade.   J.T.F.

Saturday, 4th.—Fine day, air hot, cool breeze. Made usual coffee & bo't pint milk, sour. Sent paper & shells to sister. Bath before breakfast, in river. Sling a ration of whiskey, furnished by Lieut[enant Albert N.] Blinn. At the town. All quiet, not even a firecracker—remarkable for Independence Day. At noon National salute from the guns at Fort. Flags of all nations displayed from gun boat & the national ensign from all vessels. No unusual demonstration disturbed the Sabbath quietness. Bo't blackberries. At P.O. & learned of our forces near Richmond. Bo't envelopes & butter. At [Chauncey] Baker's & ate blackberries & had a visit with [Chauncey] B[aker] Crazy man. Heard of midnight court martial of darkies. Fine. Took berries home or to camp. Supper of dutch cheese, tea, bread & butter & berries. On the shore. Cool air & cloudy to-night. Rockets thrown from gunboat.

Sunday, 5th.—Hot & windy.. Bo't pint milk. Near the former rebel fortifications a mile or so, picked 3 pints of blackberries. Bread & milk, b[lack] berries & coffee for dinner. Bo't New York daily Times & read of [Major General George G.] Meade & [General Robert E.] Lee fighting on 2nd & 3rd, a heavy battle. [Lieutenant] Gen[eral] [James] Longstreet (reb) killed.[148] Lay down in P.M. Eggs of darkey for coffee. At town for bread, but got none. Lieut[enant Alphonso W.] S[tarkweather] here.

Monday, 6th.—Eggs for breakfast. Picked blackberries. Surgeon [Joshua B.] P[urchase] here & gave me prescript[ion] of quinine & blue mass pills. Corporal [Delos] Howe went to the Co[mpany] & left me some of his things. Went to town, heard nothing by mail; brought back pail & "buried" it. Took possession of the Corp[oral]'s tent. Lunch. Rations for 5 days. Drew no bread yesterday, but 1 loaf to-day. Wrote to Aunt C. Cool, & little cloudy. Bo't lb butter & heard that Lee's Army is all cut to pieces. Toward eve. salutes were fired at Fort in honor of Meade's victory & rockets thrown up in eve. Game with [George] Bennett & to bed in good season.

Tuesday, 7th.—Picked berries before breakfast. Ate at 10. Eggs, bread, butter, coffee, fried potato & blackberries. Surgeon at hosp[ital]. Finished letter to Aunt C. Warmest day of the season. At town found shackles made to confine slaves. I intend to keep them, tho' rusty & useless as a relic of slavery. No mail for me. A great rush for papers to get the news. Could get none. At [Chauncey] Baker's had piece liver. B[lack]b[erry] pie & had a good time then to supper. At negro town. Staid till dark & went to camp outside of fort. News of Vicksburg fallen! Salutes. N.Y. Herald & to bed early. Hot to-night.

Wednesday, 8th.—Heavy breeze but hot. Breakf[as]t of stewed dried apples. Washed up & took shirt to have it washed down street. Another rush for papers. Bo't Herald & at P.O. rec[eive]d Phil[adelphia] Inquirer of 7th, first one in 2 weeks. Coffee & berries & bread. Rain heavy showers. Some of the boys came from White House, about 6 & I made a bunk in my own tent. Rec[eive]d [Brockport] Republic 2nd. Read till late, but no peace for the bugs flying about, attracted by the lights—annoying.

Thursday, 9th.—Pleasant & warm—a splendid day. Quite a time making coffee for self & Jack Nichols. Cleaned out tent &c. Wrote to sis[ter], [Brockport] Repub[lic] & to Dr. Clark. Ches[apeake] Gen[eral] Hosp[ital]. Drew bread. At town more lively, as all the troops are falling back from White House, or not going to Richmond. At dock with [Chauncey] Baker & saw any amount of officers high & low. (Papers confirm fall of Vicksburg, July 4th. Hurrah! Treason is down.) No Inq[uire]r to-day. Saw Dr. [Joshua B.] Purchase. Bo't butter. Boiled beans of Geo[rge]. B[ennett]. Nap. Supper. Heard negro singing. Read a while.

Brockport Republic, July 16, 1863

Yorktown, V., July 9, 1863. Editor Republic:—Richmond is not taken, and the inhabitants can once more rest in peace, for we have sufficiently alarmed the natives, and the troops of Gens. Dix and Keyes are coming back from the White House. Some of them came in last night, the remainder are expected here to-day or to-morrow. Bridges and all such rebel conveniences were made useless, and how much damage the rebel "communications out of," will be to them is to be guessed. Our damage is of no consequence, and among the rest we have taken prisoners, including a rebel General, W. F. Lee. What use will be made of these troops remains to be seen. There is a report that Norfolk is threatened with a rebel raid. If we are moved from here it must be to the south or west, as Lee is now finished in Pennsylvania, and the rebellion is ere long to be closed up at the southern border. If Vicksburg is really exhausted, as it must be, then treason surely is quaking with terror, and the prospect of peace and a united land is dawning through the mists of blood and slaughter.

The news of the fall of Lee and the taking of Vicksburg was hailed here by artillery salutes and the shooting of rockets. Some were wild with joy at the federal success.

The fourth of July was celebrated in "Quaker style," at Yorktown, with rockets in the evening, and was very dull, not even a fire cracker, though a feeble national salute was fired at noon. Vessels in the harbor were flying the national stars and stripes from the mast head, and a gunboat here was gaily decked out with the many colored flags of all nations, the "palmetto"[149] excepted.

Quite a number of fresh contrabands, male and female, who had just escaped from slavery on the road to (now from) Richmond, came down on the boat lately. They say, "De rebs was mighty scared when de seed de unium comin' and run off and leave der wives and chillum." One Dinah was asked why she did not come away last year, when McClellan skedaddled, replied, "*Did* start to cum but sist we had so many chillen to take care of, and dey cried, and tole me not to lebe dem so, and I went back; but *all hands* come dis year time.—Couldn't fool us, nohow, stayin' der, grubbin', den be toted off to Richmun. Done wid the secehers, sartin." Many from this vicinity, Fortress Monroe and Norfolk, are rapidly recruiting for Uncle Sam's service, and people are rapidly being convinced at this late hour, that the darkey can fight.

Quite a little incident of camp life occurred the other night at the further side of the fort, not far from the headquarters of wagon-master Baker and two others of the 4th Wisconsin Bettery, who are here in charge of some condemned houses. Boards had been frequently taken without leave, from a building near by, and it was resolved to have joke at the expense of the sly rascal. During the night a noise was heard without, and one of the Battery boys rushed out and caught a darkey in the act of making off a load of boards. Sambo was made to dump the property at the door and with great gravity brought before the hastily organized "court martial," inside, who without regard to toilet received the frightened "gemman" with drawn sabers, and in a dignified manner the culprit was informed of the charges, the judge being seated on a box, and the clerk of the court, pencil in hand, noted the evidence. The case was investigated, the frightened African pleading guilty, and expecting a judgment of Rip Raps, at the same time clicking all the money he had. "Ebry cent, massa, only lut me go dis yer time, and dis nigger'll nebber be *[illegible word]* tofin off anudder board." After a serious consultation, sufficiently scaring Ebony, the court with great leniency discharged him with admonition to never again appear in those parts. J.T.F.

Friday, 10th.—Hot but pleasant. A singular funeral. 12 of us buried the body of one of the 8th Co*[mpany]*. Carrying the body on stretcher from hospital to burying ground. 1 mile after putting body in coffin, threw in dirt, & thus ended our duties to the dead soldier. At noon our boys began to come in from the march with sore feet, tired hungry. Made coffee for *[Sampson W.]* Fry. Rec*[eive]*d letter from Francis R. Douglas, 79 North St. Roch*[ester, N.Y.]* It was clever one. Went down town & got *[Philadelphia]* Inq*[uire]*r of 6th & 8th at P.O. Lemonade. Butter, fresh of House. Read news. Warm evening. Visited with S*[ampson]* W. F*[ry]*.

Saturday, 11th.—All to leave for Army of the Potomac, I think. Boxed up some things & sent to Dr. Clark, Chesa*[peake]* Gen*[eral]* Hosp*[ital]*. *[Sampson W.]* Fry also put in some. I put in overcoat, pair boots, short sword (private property), 3 books, brush broom, letters in pocket of coat, India rubber coat, &c. Boy took it down for me to lock. Saw *[Major]* Gen*[eral][Erasmus G.]* Keyes & *[Brigadier General Henry D.]* Terry & Col*[onel George C.]* Spear. Packed my things & carried gun & accout*[remen]*ts to dock—great crowd, & our boys had gone on gun boat transports & we were left. Took my things on board vessel, *City of Albany,* & it started at 2 P.M. Not many on board. Found it going to Fort M*[onroe]* instead of to Washington. At Fort M*[onroe]* went to Med*[ical]* Director *[to]* get pass & from there rode in wagon with all my things to Chesapeake Gen*[eral]* Hospital, saw Dr. Clark who put my rifle in his room & I put my things in the baggage room. Saw boys of Battalion *[long passage illegible because of water soaking.]* Slept in 8th ward among the sick ones.

Sunday, 12th.—Up early. Good wash & breakfast at 7. Coffee, bread & butter & syrup. In Dr. Clark's room & with him to beach of Hampton Roads—saw sand crabs. Dinner plain as all the rest, salt beef, potato, bread, butter, water. Dr. C*[lark]* Gave me letter from home. M*ary A. C.]* F*[rench]* & Cordelia & Aunt C, also from M*[ary]* A. C. F*[rench]* & S*[ampson]* W. Fry of July 7th, also paper from home. Good news. In college or Hosp*[ital]* window, looking at vessels in great numbers on the water of Hampton Roads. A fine view. At the tent of *[Timothy]* Babbitt & Billy *[Price]* glass lem*[ona]*de. Supper &c. Talk with D*[r]*. C*[lark]* & to bed in 6th ward early.

Monday, July 13.—A fine morning, indications of rain. Made up my bed, as all the patients do, although some are too sick for that. Breakfast &c. as usual, I think. At table with *[Timothy]* Babbitt & Billy *[Price]* & divided butter I brought from Yorktown with them. Walked to Fortress Monroe or Old Point Comfort 1½ miles passed again the pleasant cottages & gov't workshop, to Medical Director. Waited, made my business known, & rec*[eive]*d letter to take to Dr. Stocker, Chesapeake Hosp*[ita]*l at landing. Bo't things for *[Timothy]* Babbitt & Billy *[Price]* & this diary & 2 new 2ct postage stamps— first one I had seen they have the portrait of Andrew Jackson. Pie & ice cream of colored lady. On way back bought a soft hab-drab $2. Also envelopes 20c. Brought back some things. Rather a warm walk. Made out to get a dish of pudding after the dinner hour. Washed up & directed to Dr. Clark. Saw Dr. Clark. Put my box in the baggage room. Received paper, *[Brockport]* Republic from B[rock]port. In the hall of the hospital 3rd floor, in the evening listening to music of piano & vocal. Presented letter to Dr. Stoker, Chief Surgeon, & was transferred to the 5th ward, (tent[ative]) A good bed & board floor.

Tuesday, 14th Sultry, but in P. M. wind, rain &c. Reported to Dr. Stoker, who had my name put down to be examined. Had good rest last night. Wrote to S[ampson] W. F[ry], to Father & Mother, & to M[ary] A. C. F[rench] & also reported to Lieut[enant] Alphonso W.] Starkweather. Beans for dinner. At Dr. Clark's room in the P.M., reading & wrote to the Phila[delphia] Inquirer. Nap & almost lost my supper which sour bread & tea, almost made me sick. Three nurses in my tent.—High wind & rain to-night.

Wednesday, 15th.—Up at 6½. Pleasant, tho' scarce any air stirring. Dry bread & coffee with pudding & syrup. Wrote to F[rancis] R. D[ouglas], Roch[ester], in Dr. C[lark]'s room. Hear of the fall Port Hudson[150] on the Mississippi & Charleston[151] almost taken. Riot in N.Y. city.[152] For dinner—peas, beef, pudding & soup. Very sultry no air stirring. Wrote to Nell S. In Dr. C[lark]'s office & read awhile. A poor supper, sour bread & tea—My stomach boils like a soda fountain. In the salt water.

Thursday, 17th—Sultry & I feel languid enough. In the A.M. in the D[octo]rs room & read. Then in Rev[erend] James Marshall's (chaplain) room. Am much pleased with him Saw Brockport Daily. Borrowed "Sylvester Sound, the Somnambulist"[153] by Henry Cockton, & read all the P.M. Rain. Bo't a few cakes. Letter from Aunt C. It seems quite a luxury to get to bed in a decent shape.

Saturday, 18th.– Showery, swept was bad [?], break[fas]t Bor'd in of [Timothy] Babbitt. Wrote to sister C[ordelia]. A splendid morning—nice & cool & reminds me of fine days at home, last summer. Flute & bugles sounding. At No. 56 read news. The N.Y. riot quieting down—a disgraceful affair— perfectly barbarous & bloody. Good war news. In the baggage room looked at my things. Wrote to [Brockport] Republic. Law books drawn at library. Boys cleaned & washed out tent. Read my borrowed novel. A very common supper. Everything dull. In the D[octo]r's room. At sundown looking on the water. Some rain. Peanuts. A little reading by candlelight.

Brockport Republic, July 23, 1863

Chesapeake Gen. Hospital, Fort. Monroe, Va., July 18, 1863. Editor Republic:–I would be glad to give you an account of the doings of the Sharpshooters, but I was detached from them a week ago, and sent to the above hospital, while they went to the vicinity of Washington, in Gen. Meade's army. I can only submit to the separation, knowing that wherever opportunity offers they will show their devotion to the Union and the flag.

On Friday, 10th, Gen. Terry's brigade arrived at Yorktown, having made a hasty and toilsome march from White House, weary and footsore (32). The Sharpshooters, with their usual endurance, came in as gaily as any part of the brigade, no one being seriously ill from the effects of the hard march.

On Saturday morning, after only 24 hours rest, the brigade embarked on transports, supposed to be bound for the Potomac army.—One report since, stated that they were at Frederick, Maryland. At all events, letters to the Sharpshooters with Gen. Terry's brigade, directed to them at Washington, D.C., will not fail to reach them. I hope to be able to give better accounts of them soon.

Chesapeake General Hospital is from its situation well calculated to give new life and health to the sick and weary, not only from being in a healthy location, but has capable Sugeons, among whom is Dr. A. H. Clark, of Brockport, Dr. W. E. Allen, of Scranton, Penn., the Drs. Orton and Strowbridge. The two female nurses, Misses Wolcott and Morehead, are of great service to their department, devoting their entire attention to the humane work of caring for the sick. Another "permanent fixture," is Rev. James Marshall, Chaplain of the Hospital; he is doing much good, going among the host of patients in the different wards, distributing kind words, as well as tracts, books, papers, and writing home for the sick ones. All contributions of books or any reading matter are well taken care of and put to good use, as shown in the labor bestowed in making up a well-appointed library from the miscellaneous lot of books received here during the year. All the patients have the use of the library. At some future time I may give a more extended account of the labors of Captain Marshall, so well appreciated here.—He is a native of Nunda, Livingston Co., N.Y., though later of Syracuse.

The hospital, formerly a female college, stands in a prominent position, overlooking Hampton Roads, is in full view of the vessels passing Fortress Monroe, which is a mile to the left. The mouth of the James river is a little to the right, and vessels guarding this river can be seen from the hospital. Steam transports are at all times in the vicinity.

Quite a celebration was had here on the 4th of July. A flag staff was raised. Among the proceedings the day was a patriotic oration by Surgeon A. H. Clark, and a speech by the celebrated Ned Buntline, who is a patient here. J.T.F.

Sunday, 19th.—Fine day. Coffee, Milk; bread & butter. Cleaned up tent. Called on [Timothy] Babbitt. Weighed 114. Walk about the ground. At preaching in the 6th ward by Rev. Mr. Marshall, on "Hope". Several of the female nurses present—a melodeon, on Inspection. Read [sic] on [or?] Cheese for supper. Walk & talk with [Timothy] Babbitt. On the beach. Boys in swimming. Very sultry night.

Monday, 20th.—Hot as fury. Humid. Wash & breakfast of bread, coffee, mush & molasses. Tent clothes to be washed. Shirt h[an]dk[erchie]f & stockings In Ned Buntline's tent. Wrote to Aunt C. & Cousin H.P.R. [Timothy] Babbitt in tent in P.M. [Brockport] Republic came. In Dr. C[lark].s office showed [Brockport] Republic to him. Read in eve. [Timothy] B[abbitt] called. Heavy wind.

Tuesday, 21st.—Some rain. Read "Little Syracuse Boy"[154] & returned books to library. Talk with Mr. Marshall. Drew Knickerbocker Mag[azine].[155] of 1846. Games in [Timothy] B[abbitt]'s tent. $70 stolen from Billy [Price] last night. Beans, pork & beets for dinner. Mail late. Hard rain & wind tonight.

Wednesday, 22nd.– Rain & cloudy. Break[fas]t 2nd table. Nap after break[fas]t. Read in No. 56. Examined by surgeon McClellan on Monday. Only a few questions. No mail for me. Soup, cabbage & potato. Another nap after dinner. A wash, poured over the Knickbocker & a supper of bread & molasses—tea always. Wrote letter for W[illia]m MacCallister, Pittsburgh, Pa. Read letter from his mother this A.M. or 4 p.m. Cleared off pleasant at night

Thursday, 23d.—Severe headache; & after little breakfast of meat warmed over & good gravy I laid down till 10. Rev. Mr. Marshall Chaplain came & asked me to act as librarian for him while the men drew the books. I did so & soon learned the hang of it, with but few mistakes. Prospect of getting into business when the library or chapel come to which a reading room is to be attached. Wrote to Mother & Ira H[olmes]. Sat in No. 56. in the P.M. & in eve. Fine day. Rec[eive]d letter from Mother & sister & Ira H[olmes], also Frank [Francis R.] D[ouglas], Roch[ester]. Delivered letter to Dr. C[lark] from Father. Became some acquainted with a young man from Mass[achusetts] formerly Dispensary Clerk.

Friday, 24th.—Mush & molasses! Feel first rate today. Pleasant, sultry, but cool breeze in P.M. In Mr. Marshall's room, talking with him, getting items. Wrote to [Brockport] Republic in No. 56. Finished letter to Mother. Wrote to F[rancis R.] D[ouglas] after dinner. Codfish, new corn & potatoes. Read awhile. Had a fine view of the country from the dome of the hospital— very lofty. Heavy breeze. Saw Cape Henry Steamboats coming down the Chesapeake Bay & York river, Sewall's P[oin]t Craney Island, & gunboats &

man-of-war guarding the mouth of James River & sail boats nodding lazily on the unruffled surface of the Hampton Roads.--Could also see the village Hampton, mostly burned by the rebels; ... Supper a grade lower—bad tea, bread & applesauce. (Two rowdys have been down to the Fort & came back drunk.) Strolled to the edge of the water. Changed my bed to tent No. 15; 4 others in same tent.

Brockport Republic, July 30, 1863

Chesapeake Gen. Hospital, Fort Monroe, Va., July 24, 1863. Editor Republic:—In regard to hospitals in general, people are apt to suppose the sick are none too well taken care of and that these are unclean places where time passes wearily under the care of incompetent, careless nurses. If such is the case with most hospitals, Chesapeake is the exception. One has the best of *stranger* care, of course less tender than what would be bestowed by gentle hands at home but far better than generally expected. Not only is everything about the different wards always kept clean, but the rooms are well ventilated. Experienced and attentive surgeons attend the medical wants. The situation of the institution is very healthy, with the benefit of a sea breeze. Groups of men may be seen lounging about on the grass near the edge of the water, or shading themselves under the cooling branches.

No scenery could be more pleasant than that spread out before us. It is the blue water in the famous Hampton Roads. To-day its surface is waveless and flocked with little sail boats and skiffs, slowly making their way along, others seemingly quite lifeless as they lay upon the tide. To the left, near Fortress Monroe, a mile away, are resting transports of various kinds— steamboats and schooners, brigs, sloops and tugs, awaiting government orders. Occasionally, a man-of-war, native or foreign, and often our own gunboats and ironclads add to the liveliness of the Old Point Comfort (33). A little further away to the left are the famous Rip Raps, to which are sent soldiers and others convicted of crimes against the government, punished by hard labor.—Away opposite is Sewall's Point and Craney Island. On the right are vessels blockading the mouth of James river, up and down flag of truce boats go and come, exchanging prisoners at City Point.[156] With such a view before a convalescent, why should he not recover?

Donations of books sent here have been sorted from their chaotic state, rebound, marked and catalogued, and a very good library gotten up, all by individual exertion. Such a work by donations of books in all conditions, should be and, I think is appreciated here.—Further contributions of food for the mind could still be used here to great advantage, and no fears need be entertained that care will be bestowed on them. There are already about 1,000 volumes, which includes several of the leading monthly magazines complete, gathered from scattered numbers such as are often thrown one side, "out of the way," after being once read. The library is free to all invalids and books are drawn three times in each week. Quite an interest is manifested on these occasions, as the men exchange books just read for new ones. A taste for reading is thus formed by those who before spent their time in idleness. In going through the different wards after the drawing, one can see the effect of the good work in the knowledge in this way being diffused as one after another of the invalids looks up from the page he is reading. The effect of many bad habits is thus counteracted.

Partly through the endeavors of Dr. S. L. Abbott, of Boston, a benevolent gentleman, and through private subscription, a patient sectional building, costing $600, is to be sent here for the purpose of use as a chapel. It will be put together by the means of screws, will be 52 feet long, 20 feet wide and 16 feet high. A library and reading room will also be attached to this, for the accommodation of the hospital inmates. It cannot fail to be of great benefit. If the war should soon close this will remain a post hospital or soldier's home.

At present, we are having in the mess-room, some of the luxuries of the season, in the shape of beets, cabbage, new corn and potatoes. The weather is hot—sultry.

A medical examination of the sick here by a medical board among whom was Dr. McClellan, of the Hampton hospital, a brother of "little Mac" will result in many being sent to their regiments, while a number will be placed in the honorable Invalid Corps.[157]

Maj. Gen. John G. Fowler had command of this department, which includes North Carolina. He takes the place of Gen. Dix, who is now in command of New York city. J.T.F.

Saturday, 25th.—High wind latter part of day. Mercury 90° in the shade. Helped scrub out the tent & changed beds. At room 56 wrote to Serg[ean]t A[ndrew] Boyd, Co. H. 108th NY[VI Regiment] Acted as librarian for Mr. M[arshall]. Quite a rush for books. Clothes of washerwoman 10c. Changed clothes on beds. Sent letters—one to F[rancis R.] D[ouglas]. No great news to-day. Read some in Byron. Bo't candy's 5c. Bread, molasses & tea. Lounging about in eve. Very strong wind. Moon shines brightly, & I sleep to-night with my side of the tent open. Hot.

Sunday, 26th.—Still windy. Good wash, teach[?] scrubbed & a slight walk in the wind. (Yesterday had apple from N.Y. State, also juice maple sugar) Put on white cotton shirt last night. In Dr. C[lark]'s room read papers, & book. Inspection very strict 3 P.M. Washed stockings, & h[an]dk[erchie]f. Some of the S[harp] S[hooter] boys left for the Bat[talion]. Read Magazine. On the dome of the building in the cool breeze & shade. Saw a curiosity taken from the water—horseshoe crab. Heavy guns fired from the Merrimac,[158] iron-clad. Laid out on the bank of the "Roads". Fine moonlight & sleep with tent open, air drafting through.

Monday, 27th.—Splendid breeze. Hot as fury. Felt quite natural after breakfast. Gave colored washerwoman shirt. In No. 56. Quite a dash of waves to-day, & white caps run high—the wind whistles. In my tent when the D[octo]r leans in. No med[icine]. Some rain in P.M. In Mr. Marshall's room, & had conversation. On dome of building, looking thro' spy-glass. Gen[eral] orders read at supper. No one can pass outside the guard except men detailed, unless on urgent business. Tyrannical, for a hospital. In Dr. C[lark]'s room saw a Brock[port] paper. Rain. Mosquitoes are a nuisance to-night.

Tuesday. 28th –Dark & cool. Swept out tent. Took book back to library after writing a little in No. 56. Half of a good mince pie in P.M., 13c; & 10 sheets let[ter] paper 10c Acted as librarian. Drew "Life of Benj. Franklin";[159] the model printer & Philosopher. Rec[eive]d letter from home, Mother sister, bro[ther]s L[on] & H[arvey]; it had been to the Co[mpany] & [Sampson W.] Fry sent it back to me & wrote a few words. Read Franklin in P.M. & eve. It is very interesting. Bread & sauce of a N[ew] H[ampshire] man in tent who has a low diet supper brought to him. Our mess table to night is set with old bread & tea. Pleasantly cool to-night.

Wednesday, 29th. –Alternate rain & shine. Sultry. Mosquitoes bothered me much last night. In Mr. M[arshall]'s room, & read news in Dr. C[lark]'s No. 56. The most important of the news is that Napoleon has appointed Duke Maximilian King of Mexico, which I am inclined to think will not work well, & fail to be recognized by other nations, our own at least. Read Yankee Notions. Nice beef & sweet corn for dinner. Read Franklin in P.M. Rain & thunder. Stroll in yard & looked at men swimming & flowers in front of hosp[ita]l. To bed early after read "B[enjamin] F[ranklin]."

Thursday, 30th.—Pleasantly cool. Headache. Meat, potato, & gravy, warmed up for 6. In No. 56 wrote to sister C[ordelia] & Bro[ther] Lon. Read news. Acted as librarian. Heavy showers from 2 till 3½. Letter from Mother & sister. Borrowed tank of Mr. ___. Book from library—novel. Had the pleasure of visiting with Mrs. Dulley.[three lines illegible] Pleasant sociable time. Pleasant eve. A few games with Wil[l] Price. Read Franklin. Cool night.

Friday, 31st.—Fine hot day. [two lines illegible] Mr. Marshall & Dr. S[nevely] detailed me to assist him in the library & I commenced at 9 A.M. by dusting books. After dinner worked in the library till 5. Felt rather tired. Saw Capt*[ain Volney J.]* Shipman who has just returned from visit home. Says he will send me my descriptive list. Letter from Mrs. L. of B*[rockport]* & S*[ampson]* W.F*[ry]*, in Co*[mpany]* & ans*[were]*d it just at dark. Bo't pie, 25c, & 2c stamp & paid one borrowed. Changed from tent No. 15 to 19 & fixed bed after moving things. In *[Timothy H.]* Babbitt's & Billy *[Price]*'s tent & had lots of fun. Looked at moonshine on the water.

August

Saturday, Aug. 1.—Lovely day. Washed out stockings & h*[an]*dk*[erchie]*f before break*[fast]*. Saw Capt*[ain Volney J.]* Shipman & talked with him, & gave him a letter for *[Sampson W.]* Fry. Read the news & went to work in the library, straightening books & dusting them till noon. Letter from Aunt C. Changed bedclothes, shirt, &c. Hair cut 10c, & a general wash. Finished regulating books. After I read awhile in No. 56. Very warm today. Mercury above 90° in the shade.—Molasses for supper. Sat on the beach awhile. Abed early.

Sunday, 2d.—Another hot day. Mush for breakfast. Weight with 3 others—117 lbs., a gain of 3 lbs. in just 2 weeks. In No. 56 wrote to Aunt C. & to Mrs. S*[mith]*. Read in tent. Inspection at 3 P.M. *[word illegible]* Feel pretty languid. Molasses & bread with tea for supper. On top of hospital. No mail. Tired & gone to-night.

Monday, 3d.—Still hot. Mercury above 90° in shade. Game with Billy *[Price]*. In the library all the A.M. & in P.M from 2 till 6, opened box of books & papers & entered German books & marked them. Letter from my friend Serg*[ean]*t A*[ndrew]* Boyd, Co. H., 108th *[NYVI Regiment]* Eighty-five men left the hospital for the Invalid Corps, Dr. S*[nevely]* making a short speech to them. Overhauled my knapsack & took out a woolen blanket & haversack to tent. Dr. C*[lark]* brought me the *[Brockport]* Republic of 30th ult. letter of 24th. Nothing new to-night.

Tuesday, 4th.—Still hot but pleasant. Walk before & after breakfast. In Billy *[Price]*'s tent & in my own read a while before going to the building. Attended to the drawing of books in the library. In P.M. fixed books. Letter from M*[ary]* A. C. F*[rench]* & F*[rancis]* R. D*[ouglas]*. Commenced letter to F*[rancis]* R. D*[ouglas]*. At tent & to bed early. Mosquitoes very thick.

Wednesday, 5th.—In No. 56 finished writing to F*[ather]*. Dr. Allen back. Rec*[eive]*d letter from Sh*[e]*dr*[i]*ck *[J.]* Jackson, 140th *[NYVI]* Reg*[imen]*t

Co*[mpany]* H which I answered immediately. Commenced a letter home. Several games in Billy *[Price]*'s tent. Read after supper. A fine evening & I thought of old times as I saw a couple walking toward the beach. Sultry to-night & I sleep with tent open.

National Fast Day

Thursday, 6th.—Mosquitoes very annoying last night & I was so much bothered by them that I saw the sunrise finely. Washed up & put on clean shirt. Read till 9. Wrote notice for door of Library. At 10½ attended sermon or discourse by Rev. Mr. Marshall, in 7th ward, showing the history of the nation & our successes. Good. Letter from Mother & sis*[ter]*. Finished answer to ib*[id]*. Also *[Brockport]* Repub*[lic]* paper of 23rd, from home. Short nap. Watermelon for supper. Peanuts on my own hook. Very sultry. Mercury 92° at 3 P.M. in shade. A very slight sprinkle of rain. A hot night.

Friday, 7th.—Headache. Same weather continued. Wrote M*[ary]* A. C. F*[ench]*, in No. 56. Read off names for clerk copying the pay roll from 1 till 5. In clerk's room. Learning to consolidate the diet lists. Obtained mosquito net of Mrs. Dulley & Mr. *[James]* Hathaway. Kindly helped me put it over my bed. A walk. Still sultry.

Saturday, 8th.—Cleaned my gun in No. 56 and read daily. Overhauled books in Chaplain's room & took them into the library. Gave out books from 10½ till 12, & in P.M. had quite a time getting books straightened which had been thrown about by men looking them over. Dr. S*[nevely]*. brought me *[Brockport]* Repub*[lic]* 6th. Clean bedclothes & cotton shirt furnished all the men by the Sanitary Commission.[160] Read in clerk's room. Heard of the relief of Dr. Stocker by Dr. Dalton of New Y. City. All seem to rejoice at the removal of this tyrant. In Chaplain's room. Bath in the salt water. A very warm day has this been, merc*[ury]* 93° in shade.

Sunday, 9th.—A very sultry night but am free from mosq*[uitoes]*s by being inside the net. Washed up & "clean boiled over". Washed stockings. After break*[fas]*t wrote to Serg*[ean]*t A*[ndrew]* Boyd. Laid down till noon inside the fly net. Good dinner of corn, beans, potato, soup, &c. In P.M. in room of Chaplain. Drew pants 2's. Another nap, till inspection by Dr. Stocker & Dalton. Walk after supper. Cooler.

Monday, 10th.—Took box of clothes from the baggage room & aired clothes, &c. Sent "Yankee Notions" to Bro*[ther]* Harvey 4 cts. Bo't p. stamps 50c. In Mr. M*[arshall]*'s room & saw his application for leave of absence, which he got at eve. Laid down most of P.M. & read.—Game with Billy *[Price]*. Had fine coffee, biscuit, butter & cheese roasted or fried. Walked around the hospital & to the water. Good breeze tonight. Drew pants.

Tuesday, 11th.—Finished reading "Harry Lorregnor".[161] Washed pants to make them shrink. Also washed h*[an]*dk*[erchie]*f. Glass lemonade 5c. Read daily. Helped Mr. Marshall about getting ready to go away. Agreed to give notice of meetings, take charge of his room & the library, send his letters to him, &c. Opened library & attended to the drawing of books, from 11 till 12. Heavy thunder, but no rain. Wind. Carried Mr. Marshall's carpet bag to the carriage & bid him good by at 3½. In Dr. Clark's room. Fixed up books in Mr. M*[arshall]*'s room. On the dome of the building.—Feel well to-night.

Wednesday, 12th.—Have a cold in my throat—raw. After reading a while, went to 58, (was visited by the steward on account of petty jealousy of a nurse whose dignity I had aroused, in regard to the cleaning of the room & who told a falsehood, tho' one not worth attending to.) Went to my tent & read & laid down till noon, giving them a chance to clean the room. Letter from *[Sampson W.]* Fry. Demanded letter or mail for Mr. M*[arshall]* & directed or remailed it to him at Nunda, Livingston Co., N.Y. Then visited by Ward master of 3rd ward in a contemptible way & saw Mrs. Dulley & foiled his ideas by keeping the key to the room in my possession. In Mr. M*[arshall]*'s room from 1 till 5 looking over library record. Intend to study arithmetic, once more, & thus improve my time here. Read. Bath in eve. Washed shirt. Very warm again to-night.

Thursday, 13th.—After breakfast wrote to sister. Attended a library drawing. Letter from M*[other]* and S*[ister]* & one from S*[hedrick]* J. Jackson, 140th NYV*[I Regiment]*, in regard to the death of my brother in the 108th NYV*[I Regiment]* Nov*[ember]* 16, 1862, of fever. S*[hedrick]* J.J*[ackson]* nobly stood by him till death & helped bury him. Finished letter to Sister, &c. Rec*[eive]*d 2 pens from home. In No. 58. Gave Miss Morehead papers. Read in Dr. C*[lark]*'s room. Fixed backs of books. Wrote a letter to the *[Brockport]* Republic or commenced it but did not finish. Bath. Wind blows.

Brockport Republic, August 20, 1863

Chesapeake Gen. Hospital, Fort. Monroe, Va., Aug. 14, 1863. Editor Republic:—Something to write about is a scarce article in the present dullness of hospital life. "The weather," that never failing topic, might furnish an item were it not "dried up" by the intense heat, as shown by the mercury at 90°

to 95°, during the day, only condescending to stop at 85° at sundown, where it invariably rests till again forced to a scorching reconnoisance among the nineties.

Flies by day and mosquitoes by night are buzzing, biting bothersome pests—but thanks to the Sanitary Commission, inmates here are provided with nets mosquito proof, which entirely cover one's couch, and inside those places of refuge is the only retreat from the assaults of winged insects.

Salt water being near at hand, a briny bath may be brought into requisition, and after the heat of the day never fails to impart renewed energy to the faint and weary.

To us who sojourn in ample canvas houses, enjoying the luxury of a board floor, good bed, mattress, clean sheets, pillows, &c, and a cool cotton shirt, though plain, all furnished by the blessed Sanitary Commission, we ought, I say, to be thankful for such comforts, as a refreshing breeze fans us through the uplifted sides of the tent.

Then from the well-stocked hospital garden the mess table is supplied with the vegetables of the season, and for a variety the "luxury" of mush and molasses is occasionally served up to us.

A change has taken place in the management of the hospital, Dr. A. E. Stocker being removed, gives place to Dr. Dalton, of N.Y. city. A court of inquiry will investigate rather serious charges against Dr. S., including acts of petty tyranny and mis-management which had been submitted to by both officers and patients here, until forebearance ceased to be a virtue.

The able corps of surgeons and nurses are doing their work of relieving the suffering sick, and new arrivals of the latter come in daily. A number of convalescents, since the arrival of Dr. Dalton, have been returned to their regiments, and a number have been sent to the Invalid Corps—among the latter was R. Z. C. Judson, the celebrated "Ned Buntline."

Rev. James Marshall, the worthy young Chaplain, has obtained a thirty days' leave of absence, and on Tuesday started for his home in Livingston Co., N.Y., in order to recruit his health for renewed labor here. Having been appointed librarian, I now have the honor of dispensing books to the invalids from the ample miscellaneous assortment of reading matter gathered here for their use.

National Thanksgiving Day was observed here by a suspension of ordinary business, and a discourse was delivered by the Chaplain.

Capt. Shipman, of the 6th Co. Sharpshooters, after a sick leave home, returned to duty in the company from this hospital two weeks ago, in improved health. From a letter received yesterday I learn that they are at Rappahannock river, lying beside rifle pits, which they had dug. The rebels were only a short distance ahead of them, and it was reported were planting some heavy guns, which our boys were in daily expectation of hearing from.

Lieut. Hysner was sick, also several of the privates, but none dangerously. Their address at present is—"Headquarters 1st Army Corps, Army Potomac, Washington, D.C."   J.T.F.

Friday, 14th.—Not quite so warm as a few days ago. Finished letter to *[Brockport]* Republic. In library room. Read Timothy Litcomb's "Letter to the Young,"[162] a very interesting book of good advice & shows a knowledge of human nature. Took charge of Mr. M*[arshall]*'s mail. On the balcony of building enjoying the cool breeze & a view of the vessels near Fortress Monroe. Am somewhat troubled with a cold in my head. Boys in tent in eve. Telling stories.

Saturday, 15th.—I slept well last night. Cool. A fine cool, healthy, bracing morning. Read a few chapter in "Tim*[othy]* Li*[tcom]b.*" In No. 58 wrote to Sh*[e]*d*[rick J.]* J*[ackson]* & S*[ampson]*. W. Fry. Letter from Aunt C. in library. Changed clothes on bed, &c. Nap & read J. J. Weighed 118 a gain of 1 lb. In 2 weeks. On bank of Roads. Washed towel. To bed in good season. At 10 Mrs. Dulley sent for key to No. 58.

Sunday, 16th.—Up early went to see about having preaching in 6th Ward— not convenient. Just as I had started to leave the ward, some called to me, when I found it to be my friend Chauncey Baker, wagon-master of the 4th Wisc*[consin]* Battery, whom I had left at Yorktown.—He had been here 10 days, sick of inb.[163] fever, now better. At 7th ward in condition to have meeting. I stuck up written notice of the meeting but it turned out that instead of a preacher who came it was the Hon. Mr. Morehead,[164] of Penn, a member of Congress &c. Carried papers to the 7th ward. As I had agreed I went with ink & paper to see *[Chauncey]* Baker & wrote two letters for him, & had a pleasant visit till 11 A.M. A good dinner. Cool breeze to-day, but sultry. After dinner a nap, read "J. J." Cheese Molasses & tea for sup*[per]*. Inspection at 6½. Called on C*[hauncey]* B*[aker]*. About sundown a body floated to the shore. It was decomposed & appeared to be that of a sailor. No clue to his name, &c. A large crowd gathered to see the body. Feel well to-night, & go to bed in good season. Two men have died in the 6th ward today. Applied for pass.

Monday, 17th.—Cool breeze early & looks like rain. Finished reading "J.J." & ready to go out on pass. Called on C*[hauncey]* B*[aker]*. About 9 rec*[eive]* d pass "to Fort*[ress]* Monroe" started for Hampton Hospital & in 10th ward saw Stickle of the 4th Wis*[consin]* Bat*[tery]* who is going home to-day, discharged. At my namesake's President John Tyler's former residence (34), a gothic house, almost square, painted brown, surrounded by traces of former shrubbery & trees of different kinds. In one room of the house is a colored school, taught by an elderly Quaker lady, Miss Eliza Yates, a member of the Society of Friends & here I spend an hour pleasantly hearing the exercises of the colored children of all shades who appeared much interested as well as their benevolent teacher & appeared to make as much progress as white children of the same age. Some very mischievous ones among them. Songs were sung & at the close I had an interesting conversation with the teacher, who introduced me to Rev. Ja[*me*]s P. Stone & lady of Vermont, on a mission here, who are cleaning up the mansion. They courteously showed me the rooms of the house & in the bedroom of Pres[*iden*]t Tyler, I saw the heavy & broad dark Mahogany bedstead where once reclined the venerable (now dead) Chief Magistrate of our country. Also saw his wardrobe of mahogany & another closet all now left of the furniture. The soldiers had rudely defaced some parts of the house. I picked some flowers from bushes in the yard. At Hampton bridge an officer passed me to Hampton ruins. Quite a pleasant village was here burned by the rebel Gen[*eral John Bankhead*] Magruder. This was next to Jamestown the oldest settled place in the United States. Now only inhabited with few exceptions by contrabands who have built rude huts against the walls of ruins. Was once a pretty village. Visited the ruins of an old Episcopal church, built during the reign of Queen Elizabeth of bricks brought from England. It is in the shape of a cross. It is surrounded by a graveyard containing some ancient slabs the oldest of which marks the resting place of one who died in 1701. Most of the mounds & slabs are badly defaced, broken. The once pleasant cemetery is shaded by large willows & contains shrubs of various kinds. A high brick wall encloses the whole. The church was also burned & the walls are crumbling down & the appearance is that of ruin. On my return stopped at a colored (almost—white) house & got a few peaches, the first of the season. Bo't box of blacking, pie 25c & cake. Walked back and got to C[*hesapeake*] G[*eneral*] H[*ospital*] at 5. After supper called on [*Chauncey*] B[*aker*]. Early to bed, tired. Quite a cool day, a light sprinkle of rain & heavy wind to-night.

Tuesday, 18th.—High wind. Slept well last night with clothes over me. Up in 56, read the news.—Attended drawing of books. Had taste of nice wedding cake. Mailed letter to Mr. M[*arshall*]. Took books over to C[*hauncey*] B[*aker*] & found him pretty low. Wrote letter to his brother-in-law, Geo[*rge*] Mott, Oneida Co., N.Y., to him come here to see C[*hauncey*]. Attended [*Chauncey*] Baker till 3. He gave me $104.85 to keep for him. A few games with W[*illiam*] P[*rice*]. After supper called again to see C[*hauncey*] B[*aker*] & he wanted me to stay in the ward near him all night. Prayer meeting in the ward. Went to bed there at 9. Not to sleep very easy, so much running about, & so much light.

Wednesday, 19th.—Up at 2 & found [Chauncey] B[aker] doing well Gave him cold tea. Slept till 5, then up & made bed. [Chauncey] B[aker] rested well & is better. This is a splendid morning, cool & pleasant. Washed shirt, last night. Bought paper with news of bricks made to fly from the walls of Sumter. Nap in tent from 10 till 12. Do not feel so well as I might. Good breeze. Wrote to Mother. Game with W[illiam] P[rice]. Called on [Chauncey] Baker in eve. Heard W[illiam] P[rice] tell "yarns".

Thursday, 20th.—Had good rest last night. Attended to library. Carried books to [Chauncey] Baker who is getting better. Letter & "photo" from M[ary A. C.] F[rench]. No letter from home as I expected. Tent raised.—Good nap from 4 till 6. — In to see Dr. C[lark] & [Chauncey] Baker at eve. On the beach. The weather appears like Fall.

Friday, 21st.—1st anniversary of my enlistment. One year in the service of Uncle Sam. Cool breeze. Finished letter to Mother, wrote to M[ary] A. C. F[rench] & rec[eive]d letter from Nell. S. Nothing from home. Over to see [Chauncey] Baker & wrote letter for him. Had short nap. Warm. Patients came on boat in evening. Attended funeral of a man (John P. Parrish) of 125th Ohio Reg[imen]t Co[mpany] F, drum & fife. Quite a procession. Saw the Hampton Chaplain, who agreed to preach in the 7th ward Sunday.

Saturday, 22nd.—Warmer than before this week. Breakfast at 6½. To see [Chauncey] B[aker]. Wrote notice of meeting. In 56 read news. Attended drawing books. More of a rush than usual. Letters from home & Em[ma] S[mith] & picture (group) of Mother, Father, Sister & bro[ther]s Harvey & Eddie. Also slate pencil from Lon. Very good.—Drew book for [Chauncey] B[aker] & self "Life of P. T. Barnum" & "Bitter Sweet' by Rev[erend] Holland.[165] Over to see [Chauncey] B[aker]. Changed clothes on bed, &c. Baked beans for dinner.—Mush & mol[asses] for break[fast].—All around in P.M. & had a nap as usual. Clam soup, supper.

Sunday, 23d.—Weighed after breakfast—120 a gain of 3 lbs. since a week ago Saturday night. Left papers in 7th ward. Attended preaching there by a chaplain of Hampton Hospital. About 30 men present from outside the ward. [Brockport] Republic of 20th with my letter of 14th. Nap. Inspection at 6½. In Dr. C[lark]'s room and showed him [Brockport] Republic. Pleasant moonlight eve. At [William] Price's tent. Drummers.

Monday, 24th.—Cool breeze. Wrote letter for [Chauncey] B[aker] & to Father for shirt to be sent in box with [Chauncey] B[aker]'s. Borrowed $3 of [Chauncey] B[aker] & with it bought a new jacket of a man going away—$2 less than Gov*[ernment]* prices. Laid down all the P.M. In to see *[Chauncey]* B*[aker]* at eve. Melon for supper.

Tuesday, 25th.—Escorted *[Chauncey]* B*[aker]* from his ward to the 5th, to see sick Orderly. Attended to drawing of books; forwarded letter to Rev. Mr. Marshall. Heavy rain in P.M., & cooler. Read. Put out clothes to air & they got wet. Walk with W*[illiam]* P*[rice]*. Read by candlelight. Gave papers to men in drummer's tent. Piece of cake from N.Y. State. Good cool night to sleep.

Wednesday, 26th.—Very much like fall weather. Breezy & cool. Put on my new jacket this morning. Wrote to N*[ell]* S. Called on *[Chauncey]* B*[aker]*. Let him have 85c.—which belonged to him. Just such weather as makes one feel lively. Pleasant in P.M. Read most of the P.M. 85c peanuts. After supper in 6th ward & had taste of wine. Walk with W*[illiam]* P*[rice]* & heard darkies sing—an unearthy jubilee.

Thursday, 27th.—Another day of cool fall weather. Fine. Wrote to *[Brockport]* Republic. Let *[Chauncey]* B*[aker]* have 50c. News of the fall of Fort Sumter,[166] Charleston harbor. Attended library. Letter from Mother & Aunt C. Also from F*[rancis]* R. D*[ouglas]* with photo. Ans*[were]*d M*[other]*'s & Aunt's. Drink of wine at *[Chauncey]* Baker's & bo't 10 cts. worth of poor peaches. In No. 56 & borrowed paper of Dr. Allen. Thought of going to Portsmouth, but put off. Heavy guns fired at fort. At contraband tents & heard singing. Read by candlelight.

Brockport Republic, September 3, 1863

Chesapeake Gen. Hospital, Fort. Monroe, Va., Aug. 28, 1863. Editor Republic:—We are now, for a few days, enjoying cool fall weather, and the ground has been dampened by abundant rain.

Fortunately "dog days" have passed, and now convalescents can luxuriate in the melons and peaches and an occasional apple, but no such fruit as one would be treated to if at home. Since the change in directing Surgeons (thanks to the exertions of Surgeon A. H. Clark, who has succeeded in having justice done to the patients,) wagons from the country are allowed to bring fruit here, which the invalids can buy and eat.

A few days since, obtaining a pass from Dr. Dalton, the accommodating surgeon in charge, I started on a visit to the ruins of the once pleasant village of Hampton. After stopping at the "McClellan Hospital" to see a sick friend, I passed on to the former summer residence of ex-President John Tyler. It is ... situated on the bank of a Hale Inlet or mouth of a small creek, and commands a good view of the surrounding country. The fence is demolished, a few trees shade the grounds, and the shrubbery is in a dilapidated condition.

As I approached the house I found some colored children playing in an arbor. They belonged in a school which was held in the mansion. It was vacation with the regular school in which three teachers were employed, now home visiting. The present teacher is an elderly lady from Philadelphia, a member of the Society of Friends. Her name is Miss Eliza Yates. She is a volunteer teacher, coming here and now laboring at her own expense, having a primary school from 9 till 11 A.M., and one for "heads of families" in the evening. I passed an hour in the room, listening to the many-hued children, who seemed much interested in the training process. The school was dismissed with a song.

A short time since, Secretary Seward, his son and daughter, a son of President Lincoln and others, payed a visit to the Tyler house and school, and after a brief stop at the latter, Mr. Seward handed Miss Yates a $10 greenback, as an appreciation of her praiseworthy efforts.

After giving me a history of the school, the plain lady in the plain Quaker cap introduced me to Mr. and Mrs. Rev. J. H. Stone, missionaries from Vermont, who occupy part of the mansion, and who were engaged in "cleaning house." A few apologies for the "looks" of things, (as housekeepers know how to do when caught "in the suds,") and I was kindly shown over the house, which had suffered bad usage from the soldiers on the first occupation of the vicinity. There was nothing unusual about the place, more than common houses, until we came to the room once occupied by the venerable chief magistrate. In one corner stood a wide and heavy bedstead of dark mahogany, and in another corner a wardrobe of the same material.

These and a closet in another room, were the only relics of the Tyler family. The old gentleman died a year ago somewhat inclined to secession. His (second) wife lives on a farm twenty miles away. One who knew him says he was a pleasant man, quite unreserved, with light blue eyes.

Picking some flowers, I crossed a long bridge to the nondescript Hampton ...., now all in ruins—burned by rebels under Gen. Magruder. Here are, however, a large population of contrabands who have erected huts, some on the sides of remaining walls. Nearly every other house contains eatables of some kind. One store is rebuilt, "after a fashion," the father of its proprietor having done business on the same spot twenty-five years, and now holds an unpaid bill against John Tyler. Although having the honor of being named after the old gentleman, I hardly felt disposed to take up the account, though it would seem a proper token of appreciation. But I could not help feeling that the old fellow forgot the claims of his country in advocating or favoring secession.

The principal, and in fact the only object of interest among the war's desolation, is the remains of the Episcopal church.... Nothing but the walls are now remaining, surrounded by the desecrated graves and monuments of a cemetery as ancient as itself. The name on the oldest tombstone is effaced, but the figures 1701 are visible. Flower shrubs, bushes and weeds grow in tangled profusion. A few noble weeping willows overshadow the place— sole mourners of the unremembered dead. A high brick wall surrounds the silent city. The only signs of life were numerous juvenile Africans enjoying a sham fight with stones, some of them reveling in a state of nature. All within a stone's throw of this "heathen" desolation, is commencing a new era— the enlightenment of an ignorant race. May success attend the educational efforts of those engaged in the noble work. J.T.F.

Friday, 28th.—Splendid weather. Everything out doors appears like fall weather. Chirping of crickets & the humming of insects generally. At the water saw some crabs just caught. Wrote to F*[rancis]* R. D*[ouglas]* after visiting *[Chauncey]* Baker. Sat on steps of building some time in the evening.

Saturday, 29th.—Feel unwell. Bo't & eat part of watermelon. Attended to books in lib*[rary]*. Talk with Rev*[erend]* Shumway, of Newark, N.Y. Eat only a mouthful of dinner & laid down from 2 till 6. Saw Orderly Sturdevant of 4th Wis*[consin]*. Bat*[tery]*. Feel a little better to-night. Rain & cool, with wind. Sent paper home & little tracts to Harvey & Eddy.

Sunday, 30th.—Good sleep last night. Cool wind this morning. Feel some better. Beef soup for breakfast. Weighed — 120, no change from a week ago. In 6th ward with *[Chauncey]* Baker. Applied for pass to Portsmouth till tomorrow of Dr. Dalton which I received after showing my letter of Mr. *[Horatio N.]* Beach. Letter from Aunt C. & *[Brockport]* Repub*[lic]* paper. Walked to Fort M*[onroe]* at noon. Bo't pie & cake. Pass signed by Prov*[ost]* M*[arshal]*. On the boat City of Hudson[167] at 1 & pleasant ride up mouth of Elizabeth river to the corrupt city of Norfolk, a pleasant city, formerly containing 20,000 inhabitants, after a ride of an hour. Too late for ferry to Portsmouth, till ½ hour & walked about the city.—Saw some of the st*[reet]* sights. Rode in old ferry after a glass of ale & landed at P*[ortsmouth]* another pleasant place, of formerly 15,000 inhabitants. Followed the Suffolk Railroad over a mile from P*[ortsmouth]*, turned to the right on highway, a half mile, & *[illegible word]* pickets. Came to the "Mounted Rifles" camp in a grove of pines. The Reg*[imen]*t had gone & only left a few back, sick. My cousin Geo*[rge]* Farnham was not here, but with the reg*[imen]*t, so I was disappointed somewhat. But boys from the same place, Serg*[ean]*t Francis & Smith & Hedges were very hospitable. Bo't milk & had that & bread for supper. Pleasant eve. With the *[illegible word]*. But O, how the fleas did bite, after I had got snuggly to bunk.

Monday, 31st.—Rain last night. When I did get to sleep slept well. The boys gave me bacon fried, & coffee & bread. Then after a short time I bid them farewell, excepting for Smith, who went with me to Portsmouth, thro' pleasant roads cornfields abundant. Fine cemeterys, closed—locked. Very good looking yards, as there are in Norfolk. Visited the market—very well kept & regulated but not so complete as the one at N*[orfolk]* S*[mith]* crossed the ferry with me & we walked about the city of N*[orfolk]*. Quite a business place. Bo't stockings & brush for *[Chauncey]* B*[aker]* & peaches & figs (green, poor). As it rained I started for Fort M*[onroe]* at 11 A.M. on same boat came on yesterday. Heavy wind. At Fort safe. Bo't cakes & cheese for *[Chauncey]* B*[aker]* & pie for self. Walked to Ches*[apeake General Hospital]*. Saw *[Chauncey]* B*[aker]*. Letter from S*[ampson]*.W. *[Fry]* *[illegible letters]*. Mustered for pay. At eve., talk & some fun.

September

Tuesday, Sept. 1.—Cool & windy. Regular fall weather. Missed the 1st table.; Assisted in making out pay roll. Attended library. Rec*[eive]*d letter from Capt*[ain]* Volney J. Shipman, with descriptive list. $9.90 due on clothing. Gave it to clerk. Ans*[were]*d the Cap*[tain]*'s letter. In tent with *[Chauncey]* Baker. Watermelon, cards, &c. Gave *[Brockport]* Republic to Dr. C*[lark]*. Quite pleasant P.M. Quite a squabble at table with guard. At 6th ward & in one of the tents in eve.

Wednesday, 2d.—Pleasant. Nothing unusual. Helped about pay-rolls 3 or 4 hours. Wrote to sister. No news in papers, only Floyd[168] & Pemberton[169] traitors, reported dead. Saw *[Chauncey]* Baker as usual. Tried to get a pass in P.M. but could not. Saw Sturdevant, Orderly of Battery sick. *[Chauncey]* B*[aker]* treated the crowd in tent to peanuts.

Thursday, 3d.—Misty & rainy in A.M. Pleasant P.M. Helped on pay-rolls & attended library. Letter from Mother & Sister, with $5 & letter from M*[ary]* A. C. F*[rench]*. Ans*[were]*d M*[other]*'s & Sis*[ter]*'s, & wrote some for *[Chauncey]* B*[aker]*, who bought watermelons. Jolly time in tent. Read &c. Up to see Orderly Sturtevant *[sic]*. Saw nice photographs in a tent. At 6th ward & to bed in good season, after rat trap set.

Friday, 4th.—Helped some about pay rolls. Nothing unusual. Up to see Orderly S. & got D*[octo]*r for him. To bed as usual.

Saturday 5th.—Warm again & more like two weeks ago. Attended library & arranged books. Washed up. With *[Chauncey]* Baker in eve. Saw Orderly J. & showed him pictures. Took $13 of *[Chauncey]* B*[aker]*. Bo't pie. Read letters from New York to the boys in eve. High wind.

Sunday, 6th.—Pleasant. Bo't watermelon for *[Chauncey]* Baker & we ate it in tent. {Last night sold my old silver watch to Commiskey for $4.50, but not warrant it to run.} Tried to write to M*[ary]* A. C. F*[rench]* & finished at noon. Paper from Frank & *[Brockport]* Republic with my letter of 28th. Inspection 5 P.M. Called to see the sick orderly, and got D*[octo]*r for him. Sick men from Yorktown. In Dr. C*[lark]*'s room in eve. & left *[Brockport]* Repub*[lic]* for him. High Wind. Visited orderly in eve.

Monday, 7th.—Pleasant. Sent to Fort *[Monroe]* for crackers for Orde*[rl]*y & called on him—better. Sent shirt to be washed. Called on Dr. C*[lark]* & A. & had talk of furlough—looks dubious. Letter from Frank *[Francis R. Douglas]*. In P.M. played games with boys in *[William]* Price's tent. At supper bo't pie. Heard that Dr. Clark is ordered to report to Norfolk. Tried to see him, but wait till to-morrow. At *[Chauncey]* Baker's.

Tuesday, 8th.—Hot day. In Dr. C*[lark]*'s room & talked with him. He gave me order to get box. Yesterday I cleaned rifle & gave sight to the Dr. to have fixed. Wrote to Frank *[Francis R. Douglas]*, but did not finish. Attended to library. Tried to sleep in P.M. but could not. Over to see *[Chauncey]* B*[aker]* & Orderly. (Poor set of nurses) Look for box, but it did not come. In eve. read a while..

Wednesday, 9th.—Weather same as yesterday. Laid abed till second table. Pretty good kind of hash. *[Chauncey]* Baker in tent telling patient right experience. Finished letter to F*[ather]*. yesterday bought 35c worth of stamps & sent *[Brockport]* Repub*[lic]* to F*[ather]*. Wrote to Eng. Smith. Bo't fish of darkey woman. Paid wench 5c for *[Chauncey]* B*[aker]* to get his valise. At 5 P.M. box came for me & *[Chauncey]* Baker, from home & we had a gay time tasting the good things—chicken, butter, cheese, cake, apple-sauce, dried beef & fruit, popcorn, wine, &c. Aunt C. sent me crackers, Father sent me cheese, & Mother cake & two cot*[ton]* shirts, collars, & a nice necktie. Also a letter & paper. Up to see the Orderly & to bed in good season.

Thursday, 10th.—Cloudy, windy & cold. Slept till 8 & had cup coffee & a bite from the box. *[Chauncey]* Baker not well. Put on shirt from home & collar & necktie. Like old times again. Finished writing to Aunt C. & to Mother. Attended to Library. Heavy guns fired from Fort*[ress]* Monroe & replied to by ship off the Roads. Letter from Aunt C. & sister with piece of dress & "Artemus Ward's Letter".[170] Mailed letter to Aunt C. Mother & Em*[ma]* S*[mith]* & saw *[Chauncey]* Baker. Visited Orderly, & took him eatables from box, then to *[Chauncey]* Baker. At supper had box butter & cheese to eat with bread, molasses & tea at table. Fine air. Feel well to-night. Game with W*[illia]*m Price. Over to see *[Chauncey]* Baker a few minutes & glad to get to bed & sweetly slumber again.

Friday, 11th.—Fine day. Aired things. Up to see Orderly who is better. In No. 56 & read of our possession Chattanooga[171] & Morris Island.[172] Bo't a pint of milk & had it with bread & nice coffee for dinner & a slice from the box. Finished chicken. Paper from Frank *[Francis R. Douglas]*. Astonished to find *[Chauncey]* Baker at 1 P.M. with chilled fever. Finished letter & mailed for him, & waited on him all P.M. Bathed his head in ice water. Visited the Orderly. Baker better in the eve. Read awhile.

Saturday, 12th.—Pleasant, & wind in eve. Took *[Chauncey]* B*[aker]*'s break*[fas]*t to him, then ate my own. Gave *[Chauncey]* B*[aker]* $2. Saw Rev. Ja*[me]*s Marshall, Chaplain, who just came from furlough home. Not well. With *[Chauncey]* B*[aker]*'s razor shaved my chin, first time in nearly a year. Attended library. Talk with Chaplain. Called on Orderly. With *[Chauncey]* Baker. Nap from 4 till 6 & came near losing my supper. After giving *[Chauncey]* B*[aker]* something to eat went to bed again at 7, but could not sleep till about 10.

Sunday, 13th.—First anniversary of my swearing into the U. S. service. Same fine weather as for several days. Gave *[Chauncey]* B*[aker]* his break*[fas]*t the first thing. Have a headache. (Expected to be assisted in getting a furlough, but am disappointed, & conclude the best way is to depend on one's self, & put on a bold face, as the most successful way to get along in the world.) Over at *[Chauncey]* B*[aker]*'s in P.M. & he has more fever. Inspection at 3, by Dr. Stocker, who is reinstated.

Monday, 14th.—Did conclude to ask for a furlough, but on hearing that 15 men were out over their time, I wait awhile. Signed pay-roll. In Mr. M*[arshall]*'s room. Saw *[Chauncey]* Baker & carry a few things to him at every meal. Nap in P.M. Read in eve. & walked up into the building where saw a party & about the ground. Warm.

Tuesday, 15th.—Have a bad di*[arrhea]* today, & awoke very early. Only tasted of bread & coffee at break. Bo't milk & scalded it, & at noon with nice crackers of Orderly S*[turdevant]* ate the milk with them. Attended library, but feel weak. A warm day. Gave Ord*[erl]*y a piece of my cheese from home. Read while lay me down almost the *[illegible word]*. Tea and bread for supper. Another lot of sick men from Yorktown. Feel better tonight & visited *[Chauncey]* Baker. To bed early.

Wednesday, 16th.—A heavy shower at noon, the rest of the day pleasant & cool mostly. Feel pretty weak all day, but none of yesterday's trouble. Cream & coffee & crackers for b*[reak]*f*[as]*t. Called on Rev*[erend]* Marshall. Gave *[Chauncey]* Baker his box food from home. Laid down most of the day. Finished Cha*[rle]*s Lever's "Kate Donohue",[173] a good novel. Wrote a letter to Gov*[ernor]* Andrew of Massachusetts for relief of Kelly Chase of South Dennis in Co. A 4th Mass*[achusetts]*. Baker eaten *[?]* with little soup at noon. Played games with the boys. After sup*[per]*. Shaved In eve. called on Orderly S*[turdevant]* & had long chat with him in Chap*[lain]*'s room. Heavy firing in direction of Norfolk. Read some interesting letters aloud to the boys from L. Maria Child's "Letters from N*[ew]* Y*[ork]*."[174]

Thursday, 17th.—Fine day. Visited *[Chauncey]* B*[aker]* before breakfast. After that put on "clean boiled rag" from home, & wrote to sister. Then attended to Library. Letter from Sister, Mother & Bro*[ther]* Harvey, then finished letter home. Also rec*[eive]*d letter from S*[ampson]* W. F*[ry]*, on the Rappahannock. Read some in the P.M. At tent early, & read aloud all the eve.

Friday, 18th.—Heavy wind all night & today, & some rain. 2nd table break*[fast]*, cup coffee & crust. Called to see Mr. Marshall a while. Bo't milk, (8c a qt.) & scalded. Read. Letter from M*[ary]* A. C. F*[rench]*. Called on Orderly. Certified to signature on pay-roll. Stewed berries for *[Chauncey]* Baker. Clam soup for supper. Very heavy storm of wind & rain at sundown—a perfect tempest. Closed all the tent & wrote to Mate *[Mary A. C. French]*, as we (4) sat around the stand & light: A pleasant evening, inside.

Saturday, 19th.—Stormy & disagreeable—apparently the Equinatial. After break*[fas]*t, finished letter to Mate *[Mary A. C. French]*. A chilly day. (Rats made a race course of the floor last night.) Attended Library & afterwards heard Mr. M*[arshall]* read letter confidentially in the 6 ward where the boys are nearly drowned out. Took book to *[Chauncey]* Baker. Found 2 rats in box on overhauling my overcoat in which they had eaten holes. A short nap, but so sound asleep that I missed the first table. At the second found my No. at table was 45. Sour bread & strong butter. So cold to-night am obliged to go to bed to keep warm. A rat trap was baited with cheese, & at 10 o'clock a large rat was caught & killed in a pillow case. Had a hearty laugh as I lay in bed & saw the performance.

Sunday, 20th.—Latter part of the day warmer & pleasant, but cold & disagreeable early. Sour bread & coffee for break*[fast]*. In 6th ward & gave notice of meeting, which failed. In Chaplain's room. Cleaned up things. Paper, *[Brockport]* Repub*[lic]* of 17th. Dr. Clark called, & as he is going home kindly offered to take anything for me. Did up sword & old diary, & book for Eddy, Harvey & Cousin Walter. Also sent $40 to Mother, (which *[Chauncey]* Baker kindly let me have till pay-day) & these the D*[octo]*r kindly took for me. Inspection at 3, & *[Chauncey]* B*[aker]* at my tent, visiting.—Quite frosty this eve.

Monday, 21st.—Pleasant & Fall like. Had a general time cleaning up, rifle, &c. Store my rifle in Mr. Marshall's room now. Tried to buy some milk but could not. Wrote to S*[ampson]* W. F*[ry]*. Bo't Frank Leslie[175] (10c) & 20c post. Stamps. Saved. Saw the Chaplain in eve. & in the 6th ward. Connecticut sick men going home, to hospital. Cold. Moonlight. To bed very early, tired & sleepy.

Paid $52.—To Sept. 1, '63

Tuesday, 22d.—Very cold night. First thing after breakfast appl*[lie]*d for a furlough after showing Dr. S*[nevely]* my letter from Mrs. H*[oratio N.]* B*[each]*. Promised one after a few of those now away get back. Sent paper to Bro*[ther]* Lon. Letter from N*[ell]* S. Bo't 5c worth of milk, & *[Chauncey]* Baker & myself had bread & milk. Attended Library. Dr. Allen gave me rifle sight which Dr. Clark had fixed for me. Paymaster Fletcher paid me Fifty-two dollars which is due Aug. 31. A fine day. Paid col*[ore]*d woman 10c for washing shirt & two collars. In eve. at 6th ward. To prayer meeting. By the side of *[Chauncey]* Baker in bed.

Wednesday, 23d.—Fine day. Tried to get milk, could not. Sent to Fort for 20c worth of pea-nuts. Mr. *[James]* Hathaway gave me nice peach. In Mr. Marshall's room. Nothing unusual in the P.M. Some fun with *[Chauncey]* Baker in tent.

Thursday, 24th.—Bot a pint of milk, had that & milk for dinner. Pass to go to Fort*[ress Monroe]*. Fixed up. In Library, marked new books, &c. Letter from Mother, Father, Sister & Harvey. Ans*[were]*d them. Also rec*[eive]*d letter from Frank *[Francis R. Douglas]*. At 1 P.M. started & walked to Fort*[ress Monroe]*. Pleasant & mild air to-day. Mailed letters for Mr. Marshall & self. Bo't peaches & apples, & honey, cheese & syrup for self & *[Chauncey]* Baker. Spent $1. Sent things to Hosp*[ital]* by wagon including ham, can chickens & fruit for boys. Saw boys about to start on furlough home. On way back had two glasses hop beer & oyst*[er]* fry. Tea break & things with *[Chauncey]* B*[aker]* a kind of private supper. Then stories by *[Chauncey]* Baker. A fine moonlight.

Friday, 25th.—Another splendid day. Slept so soundly that had to be woke to break*[fas]*t. Ans*[were]*d Frank *[Francis R. Douglas]*'s letter. Helped clean up about. Codfish for dinner. In Mr. Marshall's room. Wrote to Nell S. Rather stormy. An unpleasant eve.

Saturday, 26th.—In Library, had call from 2 ladies, who got books to read over Sunday. Letter from Aunt C. & in P.M. answered it, partly. Washed up & a shave by *[Chauncey]* Baker. Shirt from the Sanitary Commission. Yesterday subscribed 50 cts. for copies of sermon by Mr. M*[arshall]* on Thanksgiving day. Cloudy, then sunshine. Made out list of books. Filled bed tick with straw. In 6th ward by fire. Moonlight bright.

Sunday, 27th.—Cold night. Warm & sunny. Had roasted sweet potato after break*[fas]*t. Fixed up. Walk around the grounds. Weighed 126, a gain of about 6 lbs. since last. O' what a lovely day. Attended a sermon by Chaplain Marshall. Letter from Mate *[Mary A. C. French]*. Also *[Brockport]* Republic. Ans*[were]*d M*[ary A. C. French]*'s partly in eve. Sweet potatoes for dinner. Cold tonight. Inspection at 5. Exchanged hats with *[William]* Price.

Monday, 28th.—Another fine Fall day. Finished letter to M*[arshall]*. Tried to get milk, could not. A sweet potato at dinner. Read awhile and was visited by Orderly Sturdevant in P.M. Miserable supper, only dry bread & tea. Washed h*[an]*dk*[erchie]*f & stockings. Cooked berries by red hot coal stove in 6th ward, & finished the day by reading to the "boys" in tent from magazine. Fine moonlight.

Tuesday, 29th.—Fine weather continues. A horrid breakfast of bread & coffee, plain (this must be considered as paying for sweet potatoes.) Did a little work about the tent. Wrote to L*[ewis]*B. Courtney,[176] Co. A, 140th NYV*[I Regiment]* Washington, D. C. Attended Library. Bid Dr. Allen good by. Massachusetts sick man going home.

Wednesday, 30th.—Same weather. Severe headache. Our miserable "grub" rather improved this morning by a little. Butter & sweet potato. Reclined a good share of the day. Bedclothes changed. In P.M. bought a watch $1 of Harwood, to "spec" one a very peculiar kind of thing. Called to see *[Chauncey]* Baker in eve. One of the S*[harp]* S*[hooters]* in our tent with Runies.*[?]* Pleasant evenings.

October.

Thursday, Oct. 1.—A little more cloudy, tho' pleasant. Paid *[Chauncey]* Baker $6, on order, which leaves just $100 of his in my possession. Commenced a letter to Sister. Attended Library. No letter. Paper from Father. Called to see *[Chauncey]* B*[aker]*. Finished letter to sister. Sent.

Friday, 2d.—Cloudy, windy & some rain. Cleared up pleasant & quite warm in eve. Called on Chaplain. Commenced to write letter to *[Brockport]* Repub*[lic]*. Bo't pint milk. Sweet potatoes twice a day. Read some. At *[Chauncey]* Bakers's in P.M. & in eve. made his bed. Wrote application to Gov*[ernor]* Andrew of Mass*[achusetts]* for Mr. *[James]* Hathaway. Felt unwell to-night & to bed early. Paper from "Frank"*[Francis R. Douglas]*.

Saturday, 3d.—Wrote letter to Capt*[ain]* Easterly of 4th Wisc. Battery for *[Chauncey]* Baker, before breakfast, & gave to Lieut*[enant]*. Sweet potato at tent, ate with raw ham. Washed up & shaved, clean shirt, &c. Paid wench 10c for shirt & collar. Orderly in. This is another lovely day. Never finer. At 9 o'clock Dr. Clark came and brought me a letter from Mother & sister. A handkerchief, pens, & a tin of nice applesauce. Also from *[Chauncey]* Baker's people some cake & grapes, which I took to him;. Dr. C*[lark]* is a patient here. In the Library. Rec*[eive]*d letter from "Frank"*[Francis R. Douglas]*. Quite an excitement in the P.M. caused by all the patients being examined, in order to send duty men to their regiments. Saw Dr. Ward & C*[lar]*k about going into the Invalid Corps. Saw a dress parade by the Invalid Corps.—In eve. saw *[Chauncey]* B*[aker]*. & gave him sauce. Poor supper, dry bread, molasses & tea. At the tent read letters, &c.

Sunday, 4th.—Remarkably fine weather continues. Simple bread & coffee for break*[fas]*t. At my tent had cold potato, raw ham, sauce & coffee. Cleaned up tent, & fixed up. Bo't milk. Attended sermon in 6 ward by Rev*[erend]* Stone, at "Tyler House", & spoke with him afterwards. Up to see *[Chauncey]* Baker now in 3rd ward. *[Brockport]* Republic came. Inspection at 3. Attended dress parade of Invalids who are now dressed in new light blue uniforms, trimmed with black; they are armed with sabres & pistols. Spoke with Dr. Clark. Soon after heard that Dr. Stocker is under arrest. All the men seem delighted. Commenced a letter to Frank *[Francis R. Douglas]*. Visited men in building. To bed early.

Monday, 5th.—Chilly & windy, but pleasant. Had picture taken $1. Finished letter to Frank *[Francis R. Douglas]* & sent. Bo't 90c worth of paper & stamps. Saw *[Chauncey]* Baker. No mail for me today. Another miserable breakfast, coffee, bread & mess of slop or slosh. Sweet potatoes for dinner. With [Chauncey] Baker was weighed: 128—a gain of 2 lbs. Also bid Dr. Clark who is maliciously ordered to Portsmouth for treatment, by Dr. Stocker. At supper had tea molas[ses]. bread.—Bro't water. Saw Maj[or] Gen[eral John G.] Foster just before parade. Read awhile in eve.

Tuesday, 6th.—Pleasant. In Mr. Marshall's room, marked books. Arranged Library, attended drawing of books.—Paper from Frank [Francis R. Douglas]. Ready for inspection by Inspector Gen[eral]. Cuyler. Bo't cakes with [Chauncey] Baker. "Grub" same as before. At evening read some. D[octo]r left for Portsmouth. Hosp[ital] inspected by Insp[ector] Gen[eral] Cuyler. Pleasant time in tent.

Wednesday, 7th.—Bo't 2 lbs. of butter for self & 2 lbs. for Mr. H[athaway], at 35 cts. a lb. Pass to Fort[ress Monroe] & went with Mr. [James] H[athaway]. Boots mended capped & heels at [illegible word] Keys, $1.25. Pleasant walk to Fort[ress Monroe]. Left watch at jeweller's to be repaired. Visited Union gun,[177] weighing 52,005 lbs. Carrying a ball weighing 550 4 feet 4 inches in diameter, 16 feet 8 inches long.—rather a huge animal. Saw [Major] Gen[eral John G.] Foster & staff on deck of steamer "Conqueror" & the latter were playing with a gaily dressed feminine belonging to the Gen[eral]. It was amusing to see the performance—bowing & scraping—all trying to hold the attention of the "femin". Bo't apples & ale. Back to a colored man's place & had a glorious, substantial dinner of roast beef, sweet potato, cabbage, cooked tomatos, bread, butter & pie, with all the "fixins" 40 cts. Strolled to Hygeia Hotel, glass of home made beer from woman. Walked up R.R. to Hampton Hosp[ital], saw Rev[erend] Stone, who showed Mr.[James] Hathaway & self over the "Tyler House" for the benefit of Mr. [James] H[athaway]. Pleasant talk with Rev[erend]. then visit to dry dock, after gathering seeds of flowers to send home. Stopped at store saw fem's trading, two gayly dressed looking ones. Paid for boots, saw a little black piccanninny, & got back at 5 P.M. Heard I was to go to Reg[imen]t & found a letter from [Lieutenant Lewis B.] Courtney. Saw [Chauncey] Baker & Serg[ean]t Clark from Gloucester P[oin]t, V[irgini]a. Quite a pleasant day. Social time in tent, in eve.

Thursday, 8th.—Fine day. Prepared my things for going to my Co[mpany]. Let Mr. [James] Hathaway have my rubber coat, & he is to send me $2 for it. Gave him an old shirt. He gave me sand paper. Sent note to jeweller. Sold gloves for 20 cts. Traded a pair with Mr. [James] Hathaway. Attended library. Letter from Mother, Sister & Aunt C., also bro[ther] Lon & "Mate" [Mary A. C. French]. Nice sweet potatoes for dinner. Com. letter to Mother. Bo't apples for [Chauncey] Baker 25c, who spent the P.M. in tent. Notified at eve. that I was to start for Co[mpany] tomorrow. Finished letter home, &c.

Friday, 9th.—Made ready for leaving. Gave *[Chauncey]* Baker $100, which belonged to him. 3 days rations. Left box with some things in it belonging to *[Sampson W.]* Fry & self, (a list of which is in the back part of this book.[178] All ready at 9. Letter from Em*[ma]* Smith. Saw Dr. Ward, & found how it is I am ordered away. 30 of us altogether left at 1 P.M. I bid good by to friends *[Chauncey]* Baker, *[James]* Hathaway, Sturdevant, & others.—Walked to Fort M*[onroe]*, took steamer Adelaide[179] (35) for Baltimore. Started at 5½ P.M. after seeing a crowd of officers on dock. Found drunk in lower cabin, where all the eve. were drunken men carousing, & one knocked down. Noisy. On deck & the stars shone nightly. Fine cabins, &c. Any am*[oun]*t of liquor on board. Got to sleep at midnight.

Saturday, 10th.—Passed Fort Carroll on Ches*[apeake]*. Bay at 6 & arrived at Balt*[imore]*. At 6½. Break*[fas]*t from my rations. Marched to Prov*[ost]* M*[arshall]*'s office then to Union Relief & had breakf*[fas]*t of nice bread meat & coffee. I then hired carriage (coach $1.50) & rode to Fort Federal Hill, & not finding 8th Heavy Art*[illery]* there went to F*[o]*rt McHenry. Saw L*[ieutenan]*t S. Webster, privates Odell & Bills; & a glimpse of Grif*[fin]* Ladue[180] in line Guard mounting by 8th Heavy Art*[illery]*. Band playing. Only a few minutes to stay & I rode back to R.R. But we waited for transportation till about 4 P.M. Dinner at *[Soldiers]* Relief, cabbage. Bo't apples & pie, at market. (Secesh deserters on boat last night who had taken oath of alleg*[iance]*.) Walked along principal business st*[reet]*, saw gay people & fine stores, almost equal to Broadway, N.Y. On cars at 6 min*[utes]* to 4. Rode over grandest looking country I ever saw, autumn foliage & fine valleys, nice residences. Equestrian statue at Bladensburg; bo't N*[ew]* Y*[ork]* Herald. Girls sitting on lawn. Arrived at Wash*[ington]* at 27 m*[inutes]* past 5, & found lodgings at barracks near Depot. Supper at *[Soldiers]* Relief—good bread ham & coffee—rather better than 6 mo*[nth]*s ago. Tried to get pass—Capt*[ain]* not in, so I went to barrack & had good wash. Gaslight. With Corp*[oral Levi M.]* Leroy slept on floor, under blanket. This has been a fine day.

Sunday, 11th.—Another lovely day. Cold & chilly last night. Up early & had wash. Bo't qt. Milk & a paper, which I sent home. Packed knapsack. Break*[fas]*t at *[Soldiers]* R*[elief]*. Took cars on Alexandria R.R., open cars, after having my rifle stock broken by fall on the floor. Crossed the Long Bridge & rode to Camp Distribution near Alexandria. After a few preliminaries we (I & he) at last got settled in a round tent with 4 others. A stove in. Now for camp life in earnest. Dinner of beans & soup. Saw some other S*[harp]* S*[hooters]* & found W*[illia]*m *[H.]* Shaw, from Clarkson, of 140th NY*[VI Regiment]* A great many men in this large camp, conscripts, convalescents, &c. Wrote to Sister. Attended meeting in a rough ch*[urch]*. A very cold night. Had to build a fire in the night.

Monday, 12th.—Fine day. Very chilly in A.M. After coffee I applied for pass to go to Washington & get rifle mended. Got it & started with rifle at 8½. Pleasant walk to Long Bridge & arrived in W*[ashington]* ab*[out]* 10½. Left rifle in gunsmith's shop; it will cost $2.50 to get it mended. At Ordnance office & War Dep*[artmen]*t. Passed in front of President's White House. Fine grounds. Very lively in Wash*[ington]*, st*[reet]* cars, &c. Saw Treaty building, *[Major]* Gen*[eral Samuel P.]* Heintzyelman, &c. Oysters & coffee at saloon 85c. Walked to P.O. & visited Patent-office, which is a museum of curiosities & worth seeing, nearly everything ever made is here. Articles of foreign manufacture; Gen*[eral]* Washington's dress, camp furniture, equipage, sword, saddle, writing case, & chest of medicine & dishes & tent. A walking stick of Benj*[amin]* Franklin's & any amount of old relics.—Then went to Capitol. In front is a fountain & pond containing gold fish. The Senate Chamber looks dreary with no desks & the Rep*[resentatives]* Hall is being newly carpeted. Tried to get pass extended & could not, so would not leave rifle. Bro't it back. Bo't mol*[asses]* candy. Strolled down Penn*[sylvania]* Avenue, took another look at the White House... . Started back at 4, overtook & passed the 2d D*[istrict of]* C*[olumbia]* Reg*[imen]*t, & after a toilsome march, tired & weary, arrived in camp at 6. Must have walked 15 miles today. A battle was fought in the front on Sat*[urday]* & Sunday & we lost some killed & w*[ounded]*. Our army fell back to the Rappahannock Station. Cup coffee & bread. Five in tent. New ones came in—10 in tent now. Funny German & a "citizen". To bed early, feeling sore.

Tuesday, 13th.—Seemed very cold last night. I feel very sore this morning. Bo't papers. Walked about the grounds. Came near going to work. Wrote Mate *[Mary A. C. French]*. Also to Capt*[ain]* Volney J.] Shipman, Mr. *[James]* Hathaway or *[Chauncey]* Baker. Finished after dark. At barracks 39, saw *[William H.]* Shaw & a sergeant of the 8th N.Y. Cavalry whom I saw at Camp Porter. Some cavalry & others came into the tent, making 14 in all in the tent. Warmer than last night.

Wednesday, 14th.—Misty all the morning. Warm & pleasant later. Lame & sore to-day. Sent letters. Left my rifle at the Arsenal, & took a receipt for it. Sent in to the Q*[uarter]* M*[aster's]* office a specimen of writing for clerk. Walked about the grounds. Transferred to 1st corps tents, in with three gay Zouaves, 14th N.Y. (Brooklyn). Bo't apples. Also butter for supper. Cart wood. Heard band play & stories in the tent. Warm to-night.

Thursday, 15th.—Rain in P.M. Warm. Called at Q*[uarter]* M*[aster's]* office. *[William H.]* Shaw in tent with me. More fun today in tent by the Zouave boys. Beans, pickled beets, bread & butter for dinner. Conscripts & deserters came in with guard from Balt*[imore]*. In barrack a while. Boys playing in tent & having fun of all kinds. Helped get wood. After supper on top hill. In eve. came near bursting with laughter at the gay Zoo-zoo's telling stories & singing in the tent.

Friday, 16th.—Rain a good share of the day; warm. Got some pills in A.M. In the jolly tent most of the day. Coffee & bread for breakfast & supper generally good beef soup & onions for dinner. Some more convalescents in tent. Very dull here. At eve. bo't piece pie. Fine in one tent, & a great yelling. To bed at 7, & talking till 9. Heavy shower in eve.

Saturday, 17th.—Pleasant. Got 1 ration, to go out on fatigue duty, but did not go. At surgeon's. Bo't butter 20c. Do not feel well. Wrote to Mother. Splendid in P.M. At Library. Saw several feminines about the camp. Had a gen*[era]*l cleaning up & change. Bo't bolognas 5c. Laid down. Saw *[George H.]* Fitch *[deserter]*, who left our Co*[mpany]* a year ago. Another gay time in eve.

Sunday, 18th.—Sunny. Failed to go out on fatigue. Looking about the grounds & reading. Bo't pint milk & had bread & beef at Convalescent mess. Quite unlike a Sunday at home. Only two went to dig on entrenchments from our tent. Artillery passed on the way to the front. Heard cannonading in P.M. Supper, then a pleasant chat with Phil Brennan of Co*[mpany]* C., Brooklyn 14th. To bed at 7½.

Monday, 19th.—Rainy till 9, then pleasant. Break*[fas]*t same. To see *[William H.]* Shaw. Read. Talk with *[George H.]* Fitch. A great many doing police duty: cleaning grounds. Saw review of guard Reg*[imen]*t for the camp. Supper at conv*[alescent]* camp: bo't pint milk & had mush, sugar & coffee. Good. Good fire & stories in eve. At story time *[illegible word]* lecture by old Mr. Allen.

Tuesday, 20th.—Cold last night & this morning. A guard around the camp. Drew 1 ration of sug*[ar]* & coffee. Then went out with large squad of men, 3 miles, beyond Fairfax Seminary to work on battery. Fine day. Took ration in co*[mpany]* with *[William]* LeRoy. Good view of the hills & valleys. Firing at target with shell. At work with a shovel till 11½. Then went with L*[eRoy]* & an Irishman to house, where were two ladies, washing. They got us coffee & we had a good meal of cof*[fee]*, milk bread & butter. 10c Back & worked after a fashion till 4. Then a good tramp back, tired. Supper. Wash. Shirt from wash. 5 Five in tent. Boys telling stories. To bed early.

Wednesday, 21st.—Another day of good, sunny weather. First thing after break*[fas]*t a guard around the camp & a ration taken for work 3 miles out.

Luckily I did not go. Quite a scene by boys anxious to escape the "draft". About the grounds. Nothing unusual. Saw a D[octo]r in P.M., as feel lame & sore. Boys in tent telling stories. Pleasant evening. Dish of ice cream, & cake. To bed, 7.

Thursday, 22d.—Same weather continued. Up at 5. Guard all about till nearly all gone to work, then off. At surg[eon's] call. Poor result. Disappointed in getting no letter. Bo't butter ½ lb. 10c. Read news. Laid down in tent in P.M. Supper at conv[alescent] barracks: muster usual time in barracks.

Friday, 23d.—Cloudy but not unpleasant. Not well today. Headache. Up at 1. Swept on st. Some went out to work. Nothing at all new. No letter. Dinner at "conv[alescent]" beans.—Laying down most of P.M.

Saturday, 24th.—Rain all day. Unpleasant. Wrote to Mother. Read. No letters. Dinner coffee, bread & beet. Report that we are to leave for the front to-morrow. Made some arrangements for going. Called on [William H.] Shaw, bid him good-bye. Supper at conv[alescent] camp. Helped get rations—drew hard tack for 4 days. Rain, rain. All the boys in tent, jovial. Good fire in tent.

Sunday, 25th.—Cleared off pleasant. Up early, break[fas]t, & ready for leaving: beef & pork. A little milk. At 9, all ready & 200 of us marched 4 mi[les] to Alexandria. Pleasant village or city. Woman selling pies. Girls standing on corner on way to church. In an enclosure awhile. At 11:20 on roof top of cars rode to Manassas Junction, passing edge of Bull Run battleground— desolate. On the way engine off track; 10 engines close together. We ran so fast almost thrown off the car tops—dangerous. Many curves, hills & valleys. Chilled through. Marched through pleasant country 3 mi[le]s to Bristow Station, where R.R. had been torn up. After waiting awhile at last found the Co[mpany] 1st Corps 1st Brig[ade] 1st Div[ision]. In a nice grove of young pines. Cordial greeting. Also saw boys from K[endall] Mills, in 147th [NYVI Regiment] Our boys in shelter tents. Made coffee. Found letters from home. M[other], Nell, Aunt C. & Mr. [James] Hathaway. Saw Capt[ain] & all. In shelter with Cous[in] Sam[pson W. Fry], [William] Hues [Jonas H.] Kocher & [Theron] Ainsworth, for the night. Pleasant eve.

Monday, 26th.—Pleasant. At roll call.—Cooked coffee, had tack & salt junk. [Brockport] Republic. Capt[ain Volney J.] S[hipman] gave me rifle to carry, which I cleaned. Requisition for tent. Read letters. Wrote to Mate [Mary A. C. French]. Over a mile for water, & muddy at that. Lots of troops all about. Talk with H[enry C.] Murray—family matters. Walk around. Day bright & pleasant—camp fires. Ordered to pack up all but shelter tents, ready to march at moment's notice. At last laid down with boots on, overcoat under, 2 blankets on top, jacket on. Cold night.

Tuesday, 27th.—Chillier than yesterday, but fair. Almost froze my feet last night. Ice in canteen ¼ inch thick. Cooked coffee. Visit with *[J. Chauncey]* Parker, & chat. Rations of fine tack,[181] coffee & sugar for 3 days. Red badge for my hat. Also drew ration of pork. After water which I get from the cleanest mudhole I could find. This is the first time in my life I have used such muddy water. *[Sampson W.]* Fry found 10 bumblebees hid in a hole they bored in a little tree for the winter. Wrote to Frank *[Francis R. Douglas]*. Quite chilly & cloudy before night. Felt rather unwell. Cup of tea. W*[illia]*m LeRoy called three boys of the 14th Brooklyn (Zouaves). Fine cold morning. Drew beef. Heavy cold. Hoarse.

Wednesday, 28th.—Pleasant night & morning & day. Have to go a long distance for water, and muddy at that. Cooked meat & coffee. Read. Got word the boys made beef soup. Traded my flask for a canteen, 5 cts. to boot with *[Lieutenant Alphonso W.]* Starkw*[eather]*. Wrote to *[Brockport]* Repub*[lic]*. Signed for pants on clothing book for Sept*[ember]* 20 $3.00. Pepper & potatoes. Cold night. By the fire in eve.

Thursday, 29th.—Fine weather continued. Went over a mile to get water from a puddle. Heavy frost. Removed camp a short distance in open place. Pitched tent with *[J. Chauncey]* Parker & *[Albert S.]* Knowles. Wrote to sister. Whis*[key]* ration & some men tight. Bro't wood. Wash & supper. Soft bread. Guard on. Pleasant fire in front of tent. S. Delorme, 24th Mich reg*[imen]*t of B*[attery]* formerly. To bed early & very comfortable, 3 blankets.

Friday, 30th.—Cloudy but warmer. Great time all around with whiskey-farce *[force?]* A long distance for water & wash. Breakfast with *[J. Chauncey]* Parker. Grim. *[sp?]*. Gave 10 cts. for beef, extra, & made soup with bones. Drew pork, crackers & soft bread. Also beef. Bo't apples 2—10c, ½ lb. butter (1 lb.—50c), condensed milk at 60 cts a can ($1.15). Walk to Bristow Station. Made good fire for eve. Baked sweet potatoes.

Brockport Republic, November 5, 1863

6th Co. N.Y.S.S., 1st Corps, Bristow Station, Va., Oct. 30, 1863. Editor Republic: After a long silence, having recruited my health at Chesapeake Hospital, Fort Monroe, I had the pleasure of joining my company a few days ago. A night trip up the Chesapeake Bay brought us to Baltimore at 6 in the morning. Made a short visit to Fort McHenry, and found friends in the

8th N.Y. Heavy Artillery, from Lockport. Lieut. S. Webster, of Kendall Mills is commissary of prisoners. Lieut. *[Stephen R.]* Stafford, of Brockport, had gone home on furlough. Part of the regiment were on detail duty at Harper's Ferry. Fort M*[onroe]* is finely situated on a bend of the river.

Baltimore is a pleasant city, and quite busy at present. Contains some elegant residences and stylish stores, hardly surpassed in New York city. Its principal business street is as gay and lively as Broadway, and has well patronized horse cars; lovely ladies and children, advertising fall fashions, parade the thoroughfare, and idle shoulder-strapped Governmental bloodsuckers swing pompously to and fro as in Washington, and other like places.

The ride from B*[altimore]* to Washington by railroad gave a view of magnificent scenery, nature showing her most lively fall color. Hills, valleys, and cottage homes are well interspersed, and indicate nothing of the ravages of war.—For loveliness of scenery this route is unsurpassed.

Washington is the same as usual, but the war draws many army officers to the capitol, and the press of business makes it appear lively, especially Pennsylvania Avenue, which is well sprinkled with every class of society, from President to bootblack, from nobleman to serf. Some of the public buildings are being improved. The dome of the capitol is being finished, and nearly ready for the Goddess of Liberty, (statue.) In front of this noble building the fountain and gold fish attract the passers attention. The Senate Chamber looks desolate in the absence of all furniture, and the Representative Hall appears comfortable with its attractive new carpet. Preparations are making in both rooms for their occupation by Congress in December.

The Patent office building contains curiosities without number, of almost every invention from a tin whistle to a locomotive, also presents to our government from foreign countries and many relics of antiquity.... Nothing short of a visit can give you an adequate idea of this national museum. The White House is a quiet, neat and home-like building well shaded. I had the pleasure of seeing President Lincoln. He was standing on the steps, talking with one of his sons, a boy of 17 or 18 years. The President looked care worn and unwell. Also saw Secretary Seward, Gen. Hentselman, Lord Lyons, Admiral Milne, returning from a visit to the fortifications of Washington.

From W*[ashington]* I went to Camp Distribution near Alexandria. This belongs with Convalescent Camp. Soldiers sent to the Potomac army from hospitals, are received here, and if able to join their regiments are placed in the former camp in tents, till a large number congregate. If unable to go, they are placed in barracks of a hospital close by. At Camp Distribution are a large number of conscripts and substitutes, some under guard. There are in both camps nearly 4,000 men most of the time. Many are given the opportunity of working lightly on the fortifications being completed in the vicinity. Wm. Shaw, of Co. A, 140th regiment, from Clarkson, is detailed as Convalescent Camp assistant ward master.

In the railroad ride from Alexandria here the other day, I had a view of the edge of Bull Run battle ground. It looks desolate enough, and there is many a ruined house, on the field enriched by the blood of heroes.

The Sharpshooters are in very good spirits and condition, after marching all over this part of Virginia since July. Have had a rough time of, especially since the retreat from Rapidan, where they were helping guard fords on the river, and have the name of doing their full duty. We are now in the 1st corps, 1st brigade, 1st division. This is called the "Iron Brigade," mostly composed of veterans. I cannot tell you much news at present, but will try to give you something interesting next time. A fight was had on this ground a week ago, with only slight loss.—The 1st corps are guarding the railroad, which was somewhat disturbed by the rebels. We are liable to fight at any time, and are expecting marching orders. The weather is fine. Nights frosty. Ice one-eighth of an inch thick can be found in the morning. Our address is 6th Co., N.Y. Sharpshooters, 1st army corps, Washington, D.C.

The country here is pleasant. Our camp is surrounded with pines. Our greatest drawback is want of water for which we are obliged to go a mile, and often take it from a mud hole at that. As publication of our position might be contraband information, no more at present. J.T.F.

Saturday, 31st.—Rainy in A.M. Cooked coffee & roasted beef, &c. Unpleasant in A.M. Traded pocket boxes with *[Albert S.]* Knowles. Made bean soup. Drew soft bread. Detailed for guard, to commence at 4 P.M. Bo't ticket of C*[hauncey]* P*[arker]* 25c. Pleasant in P.M. On guard, post 1, road, no orders.—On post 2 was Geo*[rge]* Marlett, of Union, Rock Co*[unty]*, Wis*[consin]* of Co*[mpany]* H 2nd Wis*[consin]*, who knows the Devereauxs. Talk with him. My first duty since May 7. At 6 off & to tent, supper. Back to guard Quarters & laid down on ground with *[Sampson W.]* Fry, boots under our heads. Windy. Quite comfortable on the ground near the fire.

November

Sunday, 1st.—Sunny but chilly. At 12 A.M. up & on post.—till 4. (by fire) To tent & laid down by the side of *[J. Chauncey]* Parker. Up at 7 & *[Chaiuncey]* P*[arker]* had coffee, meat & fried b*[rea]*d ready with milk & butter—Back to guard q*[uarte]*rs at 9. Cleaned same. On guard from 10 till *[?]*. Hot coffee at camp. (saluting officers) Bro't water. Good dinner, coffee. Drew 5 days extra rations of sugar & cof*[fee]*. Also regular rations of them & tack & beans. Let

[Albert S.] Knowles have 2 3ct stamps and Geo[rge] Kelly 1. Back to guard & wrote letter to Aunt C. Pleasant. Discharged from g[uar]d at 4. Bro't water. Sup[per]. Cold night.

Monday, 2d.—Lovely weather. Heavy frost. Break[fas]t early. After water. Tack rations. Washed up & put on clean clothes (drawers first this fall). Tore my blouse & sewed it. No mail. Report that we are to leave to-morrow. Stood guard for J. C[hauncey] P[arker], then [illegible word] supper. Saw [Edwin] Franklin, who left us [transferred out] a year ago. Just back. Warmer than last eve. To bed early & talked of old times with P[arker].

Tuesday, 3d.—Unusually fine weather, still. After break[fas]t made bean soup for dinner. Bro't water & was fed. Drew 3 day's rations pork, tack cof[fee] & sug[ar] & soft b[rea]d. Bo't Herald. Cleaned gun. Packed haversack. Wrote to Em[ma] S[mith]. After water just at night. Sweat after going to bed.

Wednesday, 4th.—Still Pleasant. Finished E[mma]'s letter. Drill at 9½. Read. Nap. [J. Chauncey] P[arker] taken to [illegible word] guard while hunting. Cof[fee] for dinner. Roll Call several times each day, now. No hunting allowed. For water with [Sampson W.] Fry. Saw reg[imen]tal drill. Read papers. Wood. Supper. Started to take blanket to Parker & prohibited by Capt[ain Volney J.]. S[hipman]. Bright fires to-night. Plenty of room in tent.

Thursday, 5th.—No change in weather. Wrote to Lon. Drill. Drew ration of beef.. Letter from Mother, sister & bro[ther] Harvey. Read Wash[ington] Chronicle. At 2 P.M. ordered to pack up tents & march. Put [J. Chauncey] Parkers things in wagon. Started in rear of brigade, & halted on hill near R.R. where a battle had been fought (Bristow Station). (Saw P's in distance.) Ordered to fall in after 45 wagons from 19th M[arylan]d reg[imen]t. Filled canteen with muddy water. After dark in rear of wag[on] train, as guard. Immense train of wag[on]s. Jolted along by hitches, marching a few rods, then stopping, caused by the wagons getting stuck in mud holes. Some bad crossings of small streams in mud. In this slow manner we dragged along, every minute or 2 throwing ourselves on the ground to rest, then up. Had quite a heavy load, knapsack, &c. Loaded rifles. Heavily loaded trains passing on R.R. Nap a half hour.

Friday, 6th.—About 3½ A.M. after 4 miles march, halted in open lot & bivouacked with [Albert S.] Knowles on rubber blanket 2 woolen blankets over us, just as the moon rose or little after. The ground felt as soft as a good bed usually. Water is a hearty beverage on a march. At sunrise woke up, found wind blowing under blankets. Up. Ready for march. Found clean water near.

[Albert S.] K*[nowles]* fried beef, & I made coffee. Good break*[fas]*t. Fine day, light breeze. Men running to & fro. Secesh houses near by; good fenced up, an unusual thing. Flock of sheep grazing. Army cattle feeding. Pleasant scenery. Men busy getting water in canteens. Feel well this morn, after last night's tramp & load. At 10½ heard rapid firing & were all got in line for action, but soon ordered to break ranks. Very high wind on us on hill. Some put up tents. Read. At noon helped M. tent. Gave *[Chauncey]* P*[arke]*r letter & in P.M. he came back. Drew 2 days rations sug*[ar]* & tack. Cars passing nearby remind me of home near the old N.Y. Central RR.—Plank for tent sides. Boys all around fires, talking. Cozy bed & lay warm *[J. Chauncey]* P*[arker]* & *[Albert S.]* K*[nowles]* between.

Saturday, 7th.—Bugle for getting up sounded at 4 A.M. & orders to get ready to march at 6. Chilly. Moon fine.... Canteens of water in dark. Coffee & meat. Packed up & in line at 6½.—Sun rose bright & warm. All troops seemed in motion & over hills & through runs & mud we went. Passed Catlett's Station & Warrenton Junction. Saw cav*[alry]* & art*[iller]*y by the side of *[illegible word]* A stop of 15 min*[utes]*. At noon stopped near a white house. Just tired out, the Capt*[ain]* taking my gun a few rods: halted 15 m*[inutes]*, & ate bacon & crackers. On again, 2 miles, & so tired I could go no farther without resting, & sweat terribly. Capt*[ain]* carried my gun a short dist*[ance]* & he & D*[octo]*r gave me pass to ambulance & I fell out. Ambul*[ance]*s full. Dragged along after resting. Troops passing. Water at well. Overtook amb*[ulance]* train in woods on hill. Men cooking cof*[fee]*. Managed to get in amb*[ulance]* with 2 S*[harp]* S*[hooter]* 7th Co*[mpany]*. Rough. Broke down whiffletree in trying to cross mudhole, leaving amb*[ulance]*. Stuck, unhitched. *[Brevet Major]* Gen*[eral John]* Newton & staff came along & ordered us out of the a*[mbulance]*. Artillery passing, horses tugging. A*[mbulance]* soon repaired & we went on thro' thick woods, "parked". Made cof*[fee]*. Bo't paper. Went to Co*[mpany]*, & helped fix tent, camp in a little valley. My feet are sore. Never was so tired as to-day. Letter from Frank *[Francis R. Douglas]*. Heard heavy firing just before sundown.

Sunday, 8th.—Up at 4 & went thro' same performance as yesterday A.M. Lessened my baggage some. Put bullets in cap box. Started little after sunrise—same fine weather tho' a little sprinkle at 10. Thro' woods to Kelly's Ford on Rappahannock a little stream. Brick house with rebel & Un*[ion]* wounded, (here today our troops captured 500 pris*[oners]* & several guns, & yesterday at Rap*[pahannock]*. Station they capt*[ure]*d 1,100 *[illegible word]*) In line of battle in woods just after 14th NY*[VI Regiment]* passed. Cooked coffee. Rabbit chased by the boys. An hour & we marched on, to R.R. Almost tired out. L*[ieutenan]*t *[Philip]* Hysner carried my rifle. Met *[Major]* Gen*[eral*

George G.] Meade & numerous staff. Gen*[eral]* looks well, rather sedate, tall, wears specs, hair sprinkled with gray. At last poking along, halted on hill just at dark in und*[er]* growth, rabbits plenty. Foot sore & tired. Fire. Long ways to fill canteens. Wrote note to friend Orderly A*[ndrew]* Boyd, Co*[mpany]* H, 108th NY*[VI Regiment]*. Coffee. Beef rations. Andrew B*[oyd]* & Frenchman (shopmaker) came; look natural & glad to see them & had short talk with A*[ndrew]* B*[oyd]*. Heard cannon firing during the day. Sat by fire. Greased blistered feet, then made bed on ground with *[J. Chauncey]* P*[arker]* & *[Albert S.]* K*[nowles]*. Cold. Camp near Brandy Station.

Monday, 9th.—Good breakfast of beefsteak & cof*[fee]* which I cooked. Feel sore. Wash. Saw D*[octo]*r & took salts. Saw Asa Northrop, 94th NY*[VI Regiment]*. Dinner of beef & cof*[fee]*. *[Brockport]* Repub*[lic]*. By mail with lett*[er]* of 30th ult. At 1, to 105th NY*[VI Regiment]* & visited with A*[ndrew]* Boyd. Saw Charley & Trum*[bo]* Miller, Co. E. & talked with them about Bro*[ther]* Ch*[arles]*. Saw King,[182] of Brock*[port]*, co*[mpany]* B. Snow squall, slight. Back to camp & we started 4 P.M. on retreat. I tried to keep up with Co*[mpany]*, but they went so rapidly I failed. D*[octo]*r gave me pass to amb*[ulance]*. when I went 1 mile. Went on another mile, troops passing & so tired I stopped at dusk after some trouble, sat in amb*[ulance]* 3 mi*[les]* glad to rest & had a rough ride, over pontoon on Rappa*[hannock]* Station (36). First snow. Pleasant A.M. About 9 P.M. train halted & parked in woods, & I got out to warm by fire. Squall of snow. Cold. 1st Brig*[ade]*. At Beverly Ford, Rap*[pahannock]*. River. Put up piece shelter tent on brush to keep off wind piled up leaves, laid by fire with overcoat on & blankets over, boots off, nightcap on. Slept quite comfortably. No water or should have made coffee. Am*[bulance]* drivers by same fire.

Tuesday, 10th.—Up at daylight. Fire. Feel better than last eve. tho' sore. Got water & made cof*[fee]*. With tack. Quite pleasant, windy. Saw *[Harry]* Peachy & *[Oscar]* Ov*[erto]*n *[of 147th NYVI Regiment]* in amb*[ulance]*. Sick man lying on gr*[ou]*nd (147th Mass*[achusetts]*, bad. Waiting for orders. Lieut*[enant]* of a train told me to stay with amb*[ulance]*. See troops in distance. Left home Nov*[ember]* 11, '62. About 11, an amb*[ulance]* started, rode 2 m*[iles]* & the train left sick men at a large brick house (to be used as division hosp*[ital]*) surrounded by old outbuildings & orchard of young apple & peach trees. Rode on 2 m*[iles]* to camp in woods on hill where the boys were putting up tents & eating dinners. Cooked meat, & helped *[Albert S.]* K*[nowles]* put up tent. C*[hauncey]* P*[arker]* on picket. Old camp near us. Drew beef ration. Letter from Fath*[er]* & Moth*[er]*. Good camp fire, leaves burning. To bed, & up & draw 6 days tack, sug*[ar]* & cof*[fee]*. For duty from camp.

Wednesday, 11th.—At 5½ o'c[loc]k up and nearly got breakfast, but ordered to get ready, & had to pack up things, then off, without eating at sunrise. Heavy frost, ice ½ inch thick. 6 days rations. A large no. of men joined 14 of us detailed from each co[mpany] in the brigade. Thro' woods & over fields & gulleys we went with a major 5 m[iles] to R.R. at Bealton Station, (no place but a lone chimney.). I fell out on account of my load & they went so fast & caught up. Halted & after a few movements broke ranks, & I made coffee & finished break[fas]t. Chilly, windy. Men at work on R.R. repairing damaged track & teams passing. Pay rolls signed. ($35.82 due) Sent J. [Chauncey] P[arker]'s letters back & write to Mother & sent by [Charles] Collamer. 3 o'c[lock] P.M. cross a field 1 m[ile] & camped in wooded field & put up tent with [Albert S.] K[nowles]. Leaves to sleep on. Water in mud holes, Coffee & bacon. Volunteered as camp guard. Napped till 9, then on duty by blazing fire. Windy & camp fires shining. Read the [Brockport] Rep[ublic]. Pleasantly warm. Plenty of time to think in the starry stillness.—Turned in at 11. Some signs of storm.

Thursday, 12th.—Up on guard from 3 till 5, then down. Up to find break[fast] ready cof[fee] & beef. Washed things. My blistered heel bothers me, & I keep boots off today. Dinner. Boys cutting ties for R.R. Nap. Wrote to Frank [Francis R. Douglas]. Boys bro't rations of potatoes (3 or 4 each), beans, salt & pep[per] & candles & pork. Good supper, fried potato. Bro't wood & water. By the fire & read in eve. To bed in good season. Two months pay 14th.

Friday, 13th.—Same lovely weather. Up & cooked meat & potato. After water, saw rabbit under my feet. Cooked beans. Finished letter to F[ather] & sent it. Packed up & ready to go to new camp. Fired off rifle. Started in advance of the others with 3 stockings on & boot in hand. Along R.R. 1½ m[iles] stopped & when they came along I followed & we camped in woods ¾m. from Rap[pahannock] Station, 2½ m[iles] in all. Men on R.R. preparing track for rails, & laying it fast. After some delay put up tent & went for water, which I found (poor) after walking about till dark. Let H[orace] House have sheet paper & envelope. Found piece of tent. Cof[fee] & fried tack, & pork.— Blazing fire. Candle light, & [Albert S.] Knowles read. Men talking. Notice to-night often a breeze of hot-air, then cool: quite singular. Fixed my feet, then "to bed". Wonder when all this toiling &c, will end.

Saturday, 14th.—Warm. Break[fast]. Bro't wood. Fixed up. Rec[eive]d $35.80, which pays up to Oct. 31, & is balance due on clothing for 1st year. Also letter from Mother, Aunt C. & Mate [Mary A. C. French]. Wrote to Aunt C. & sent $5 in it, home—Ration of pork & beef. Good news, more prisoners. [Albert S.] Knowles paid me 2 stamps. Wrote to Mother. Rain commenced at 4½.

After water. Ration of whiskey. Paper from Frank *[Francis R. Douglas]*. Sitting in tent & rain pouring down & sifting through, very unpleasant. After awhile we get fixed in blankets & slept.

Sunday, 15th.—Rain till late in A.M., but often a lull in the fall & we made out to get breakfast of pork, beef tack & coffee. Detailed to help load ties & went out in rain, but did not work long. Sky cleared up before noon. Made soup. Packed up & ready to march again. Sent M*[other]*'s letter by L*[ieutenan]*t *[William Charles Joseph]* Hall, 7th Co*[mpany]*. Ready to go to camp & started at 4½. Stopped & saw horses killed. Fast march of 3 m*[iles]* & in camp at sundown. Saw calico on a wench. The more I march even a short distance, satisfies me more that I cannot stand it with no more than the light load I have. At camp found a shelter J. C*[hauncey]* P*[arker]* had fixed, & put my things in it. *[Chauncey]* P*[arker]* is off on picket. Got one foot wet coming here. Made coffee, & drew tack. Dried feet, & to bed quite comfortably.

Monday, 16th.—(A year ago to-day my brother Charles died of fever at Warrenton, V*[irgini]*a in the 108th reg*[imen]*t NYV*[I]*. May he rest in peace.) Clouds, then sunshine. Up at sunrise. At spring. Breakfast. Cleaned up things. Washed. Helped *[J. Chauncey]* Parker fix tent for us both & we have a snug shelter. Bo't butter together 12½c. Sup*[per]* by candle light. Then read a story from Frank *[Francis R. Douglas]*'s paper, to the boys. Warmed thro'; then to bed & it is very comfortable.

Tuesday, 17th.—Same as yester*[day]*. Up to roll call before sunrise, then back an hour. Fried tack & beef & cof*[fee]* &c. Cleaned up around & rifle. Shirt to be washed. Jack*[son P.]* N*[ichols]* came. Soft bread potato & pork. Hasty dinner. On picket with *[Sampson W.]* Fry & others, on river Rappahannock by a big tree—pleasant—river not very broad but deep. Crows—birds chirping (My stamps prepaid.) 2 hours on post. Then wrote some to Father. Sup*[per]*. Man across the river taking a sketch on horseback. To camp & rec*[eive]*d forwarded letter from Moth*[er]*, Fath*[er]* & Lon, Oct*[ober]* 22. Read by light of picket fire with S*[ampson]* W. F*[ry]* on with me. Long talk with S*[ampson]* W. Fry*]*. All still & quiet.—Noon from 6 till 10, then laid out on ground together & slept.

Indian Summer.

Wednesday, 18th.—Up at sunrise & cooked break*[fast]* first of any. Finished letter to F*[ather]* & sent $5 in it. Read paper. Officers riding. Fine day. Relieved & back to camp at noon. Helped make fire place & filled bed tick with leaves. Washed up & paid 10c for shirt washable. Bo't paper. After sup*[per]*. with *[J. Chauncey]* P*[arker]* to spring in lot. Moonlight. To bed early.

Thursday 19th.—Perfect summer day. Break*[fast]* early. *[J. Chauncey]* P*[arker]* fried beans in spider[183] & put tin crystal in watch. Burned old letters too much bulk, but hated to throw them away.—Drew soft bread & rice & had boiled rice & sug*[ar]*. Bo't butter, 60 cts a lb. Paid sugar borrowed. Boys singing. O, how warm at noon. Tried to take nap. Powder flask filled. Run 25 bullets, which makes 60 in all. Wrote letter for Serg*[ean]*t *[James C.]* Noble in reply to letter from D*[aniel]* C*[raig]* McCallum, Sup*[erintenden]*t of Mil*[itary]* R.R.s, in regard to position as Engineer. Sup*[per]*. Walk to spring with *[Chauncey]* P*[arker]*. Lovely Moonlight. Express envelope of Capt*[ain]*. To bed in good season.

Friday, 20th.—Same weather. Wrote to *[Brockport]* Repub*[lic]* & to Mother. Sent $20 by Ex*[press]* to Mother. Drew rations of sug*[ar]* cof*[fee]* salt & beef. Cof*[fee]* & toast. Ready for picket & started at 12 for Beverly Ford, ¼ or ½ mile. Take everything with me. In tent with Lieut*[enant Philip]* Hysner. Near the *[illegible words]* On 2nd relief 2 till 4. Saw muskrat eating. Fine sunset. J. C*[hauncey]* P*[arker]* bro't me letter from Moth*[er]* & sis*[ter]*. Laid down with R*[ice]* H. Eaton.

Brockport Republic, November 20, 1863

Camp near Beverly Ford, Va., Nov. 13, 1863. Editor Republic:—We are now doing picket duty at the above ford, on the Rappahannock river, 3 miles from the railroad; also a detail is daily made for fatigue duty, such as working on rifle pits or forts. We assisted a few days in cutting ties for the completion of the railroad track which had been torn up for several miles by the rebs, when they followed our last "fall back." But now the track is in running order to Culpepper, near the Rapidan, and if the unusually pleasant weather continues a few days longer, we expect to move forward, some say to-morrow.—We would prefer to stay and quarter for the winter in our pleasant camp, unless we go directly to Richmond, and make a clean sweep of the rebs this time. Everything is kept so secret, that it is impossible for me to give you much information of movements, which you can get a better idea of from the daily papers.

Two weeks ago we commenced marching from Bristow Station, and for four days were kept on the road, passing Warrenton Junction, and crossing the Rappahannock at Kelly's Ford, where in the early part of the day a fight was had by the advance and several hundred rebel prisoners taken; were drawn up in line of battle once, and then passed on to Brandy Station, 7 miles from Culpepper, where we met Gen. Meade and numerous staff. Gen. M. makes a good appearance on horseback, is tall, appears sober and thoughtful, hair sprinkled with gray and wears glasses.

At Brandy Station we camped over night near the 108th regiment, and I had the pleasure of a brief visit with Orderly A. Boyd, King, and others of Brockport, who were all hearty, and in good spirits, including Lieut. Wickes. The regiment are very much reduced in numbers by the casualties of active field life, and are expecting to go home and recruit, this winter, and its well deserved reputation ought to fill it up rapidly.

From the latter station we fell back here, for guard and other duty, having done some pretty fast marching, and the ambulances were used to good advantage for a few miles by weary and foot-sore ones, loaded with heavy accoutrements, and eight days rations which we must keep on hand for an emergency. Men are generally marched *too fast,* when there is no necessity for it, and not allowed to rest often enough. If one can stand up under the fatigues of such marches, he is indeed a hero. A column is led by officers on horseback, who usually seem to think little of the footman's need of rest. It is no wonder that after a few miles our ambulance trains are so well loaded.

Our own company are suffering somewhat from sickness and other causes of inability to do duty, but the men mostly stand fatigue well. Capt. Shipman and Lieut. Hysner are with the company. Lieut. Starkweather is Battalion Quartermaster. Private Duncan Cameron has been examined by the board at Washington and has received a commission in a colored regiment. Several others from our company are detailed, in various places.

The splendid dry weather is a subject of thankfulness and wonder.

We have lately received our two months greenbacks, and the boys are to-day sending money by Express, and all thus disposed of is kept out of the hands of sutlers, who charge enormous prices for all articles. But no thanks to them, we now have plenty of good army rations. J.T.F.

Saturday, 21st.—Up at 2, & on picket till 6. At 3 cooked meat & cof[fee] & had bread & butter, all by fire light close to river bank. Rather a rustic performance. Sat by fire read letter & talked with R[ice] H. E[aton]. Very dark. Laid down till 9. Sat in tent till 12, & it rained hard. To camp at 1. Cooked rice & had good dinner, Then made bean soup, in rain, which lasted all the P.M. & eve. Quite comfortable in tent. Flag from Frank [*Francis R. Douglas*]. Read. Butter 60 cts lb.

Sunday 22d.—Cleared off. Pleasant, & warm again. Hung things out, & cleaned rusty rifle for inspection, at 9. Boiled beans. Paper, [*Brockport*] Rep[*ublic*] 19th. Drew potatos. Big supper: Beans, pota[*to*], fried tack, pork & cof[fee]. Read in eve. Feel well to-night. Frosty.

Monday, 23d.—Warm till P.M. cloudy. At work on sev[eral] different things during the day. Dinner alone. Boys come building up tents, & at 3 P.M. heard we are to march in the morn*[ing]*. So it always goes: never know what to depend upon. Letter from Frank *[Francis R. Douglas]*. Hair cut by *[Theron]* Ainsworth. Wrote to F*[ather]* sent. Rations for 5 days & we are to be ready to march at daybreak. Packed things, &c. Sugar of Cha*[u]*n*[cey Parker]*. Paid him 50c. Fine eve.

Tuesday, 24th.—Up at 4½, breakfast. Rain all A.M., & pleas*[ant]* P.M. Struck tents, then immediately ordered to put them up again. So goes war: that is the military of it order then countermand. On fatigue all A.M., & helped build picket house. In P.M. helped Cha*[u]*n*[cey Parker]* bring 2 loads of boards & shingles 1 mile. Letter from Frank *[Francis R. Douglas]*.

Wednesday 25th.—Pleasant. Helped *[J. Chauncey]* P*[arker]* put up shanty of boards—took most of the day. Drew pota*[toes]* beans beef &c. A fine house to sleep in & room to stand up in. Cooked beans in eve. Heard firing. Orders to leave in the morn*[ing]*. Just as might have been expected.

Context—The battalion fought in the Mine Run campaign, November 26–December 2 and lost two enlisted men killed and one wounded.

Thanksgiving Day

Thursday 26th.—Up at 4, good dish of beans & pota*[toes]* &c. Packed. Changed boot for shoe on one foot & Capt*[ain]* put boot in wagon. At 6 started & halted 1 mile to hear dispatch read of defeat of *[Confederate General Braxton]* Bragg in Tenn*[essee]*.[184] Band, play. A glorious sunrise, sky clear not a cloud. Several corps moving & cross Rapp*[ahannock River]* on pontoon just after daybreak. Saw star at 8 A.M. east. Not tired till noon. At 3 gave out—tired & sore. Pass of D*[octo]*r could not get in amb*[ulance]*. train till a row walk behind found them halted, made cof*[fee]* & the D*[octo]*r got me in amb*[ulance]* & I rode 3 m*[iles]* getting to camp 8½. Camped on ground with *[J. Chauncey]* Parker.

Friday 27th—Very cold night. Heavy frost. Slept till 2 A.M. Up & made cof*[fee]*–off at 3½. Feel better. Crossed Rapidan on pontoon. Pleasant country. Struck plank road & marched fast till 6½, stopped & made coffee & staid 2 hours or more. Artillery passing. Fodder taken from a barn. Washed. About noon went on along plank very hilly & turned right, loaded guns; right ahead less than ½ mile, guerillas charged on supply train, capturing 12 wagons, killing 1, wounding four men & a mule. Saw dead men on ground. Heard firing. Rested to see what was going on, then forward, right along plank, slowly. Pleasant. Halted at 3½, & cooked sup*[per]*. At 5 waited around about wagon double quick some 6 miles & came on to plank, side of *[illegible word]* wagon train. Very tired & out of breath but caught up at last. Camped at 8, & fire to warm. Feet blistered, "To bed". Woods ablaze with camp fires.

Saturday, 28th.—Cloudy. Up at 3. Coffee. March at 5 to Robinson's Tavern or Grove & with 24th Wis*[consin]* went in woods to left: Just back of picket, at daylight, waiting for skirmishers to *[come back]*. Saw 4 rebs, prisoners, bro't in, talked with them. On skirmish line marched thro' open fields, woods, muddy runs & marshes. Nearly cut off, & a boy pris*[one]*r horse take & guided us thro' the woods, in a hurry. Saw houses & women & girls in the door. Fowls & cotton in field. At last in 2 hours rain, rested, & heard firing of skirm*[ishe]*r. Wet shoes & sock. Reb shell fell 3 rods from me & struck in ground, no damage, but almost took a man of 8th Co*[mpany]*. Battery of (our's) in front of us, & rebs not far off. Coffee, & dried clothes & gun. Wash. Sev*[era]*l Reb pris*[oners]* taken. On hill & saw reb camp fires a mile off. Pork soup. Spread blankets & down. No rain since 3 o'*[cloc]*k.

Sunday, 29th.—Cloudy, chilly. Up at 5. Cof*[fee]*. Gave *[Sampson W.]* Fry sug*[ar]*. Fixed blistered feet. Co*[mpany]*. on brow of hill out of reb shell range, at daylight. Firing of musketry, in front. Drew rations of fresh beef; made soup. Wrote to mother & Lon. Good news from the S*[outh]* W*[est]*. Sup*[per]*. Cold. Smoke in our eyes. Great time getting to sleep.

Monday, 30th.—Sunny. Fine day. Up at 3½ Break*[fast]*. Drew fresh beef. Everything ready to fight & about 9 A.M. heavy cannonading commenced by our artillery. *[Brevet Major]* Gen*[eral John C.]* Robinson com*[mandin]*g Brig*[ade]* gave me permission to go to the top of hill in front for observation & taking notes. Went out & saw shells burst & reb train run off. Also rebs string along breastworks & skirmishers out. Sev*[era]*l buildings together saved burning. Wind cold & biting. Saw *[Major]* Gen*[eral George G.]* Meade & staff, & other Gen*[eral]*s reb prisoner; 14th Brooklyn *[Regiment]* man wounded in foot. All quiet. Back to camp & made beef soup. 12 men & 1 serg*[ean]*t out on skirmish. At 3 P.M. Geo*[rge]*. Kelly, 23 yrs. old, of our Co*[mpany]*. was bro't in dead, on stretcher. Shot while lying down & died instantly. Shot in breast. Buried by the boys as well as could be & grave marked. One of the 8th Co*[mpany]* killed, 1 of 7th *[Company]* wounded. A very cold night. Drew 3 days cof*[fee]*, sug*[ar]*, tack, pork & beef. Put up tents to keep wind off. Men in 9.

December

Tuesday, Dec. 1.—Last night coldest of the season. Water in canteen froze. Did not suffer much. Up & break*[fast]* at daylight. Sun shines. Smoke almost

puts our eyes out. Order from *[Brevet Brigadier]* Gen*[eral Theodore ?]* read
in favor of Capt*[ain]* Volney J. S*[hipman]* obedience to orders yesterday in
charging rebs with our heavy rifles (no bayonet) & driving them. Some one
took money from Geo*[rge]* Kelly's pocket yesterday, while he lay on ground.
Soup. Beef again. 5th Corps came up & we fell back at 4½ & kept going in
dark, don't skedaddle, quick over rough road, in almost every direction till it
must have been 12 P.M. when we halted & back in the woods. *[J. Chauncey]*
P*[arker]* & I fell out, tired & came up. Fire built, & coffee. Moon. Very
cold. Fell in hole & drove stub 5/16 inch thick in my hand, inside an inch,
bled. Plaster of D*[octo]*r. To bed on ground, good. So tired. Forded a stream
to-night.

Wednesday, 2d.—Up a little before day & had meat & coffee. Salve for swelled
hand of *[James C.]* Noble. Marched at 8 across the Rapidan on pont*[oon]*.
Lots of troops. Ambulance nearly upset going down steep hill. Germania Ford.
Halted just on north side, 2 hours. Feel unwell. Coffee. Saw possum. Washed
& off at double quick till noon. Fell ¼ mile behind.—Camped in woods near
Moultons Ford. Supper. Water at pump at house looking old style. Cabbage
leaves. Wash & soap feet. Shelters fixed & a comfortable bed & fire. Fine day
& splendid sunset. Felt pretty well tonight. No mail in a week.

Thursday, 3d.—Up about 7½. Pleasant. Wash & made soup. Yearling beef
captured about noon marched *[illegible word]* jog & saw A*[ndrew]* Boyd,
108th *[NYVI Regiment]*, & talked on road with him. Changed guns with
J. C*[hauncey]* P*[arker]* for awhile. About dark camped near Mt. Run. Fire
sup*[per]* on 2 hard tacks, & to bed. A cough to-night.

Friday, 4th.—Bo't paper. Up early & drew rations of sug*[ar]* & cof*[fee]* & tack
for 5 days. Read news. Marched 1 mile to near Kelly's Ford on Rappahannock,
& some of boys commenced building up, (in woods.) Good supper & camped
on ground. Mail for 1st time since 25th Nov*[ember]*. Letters from home, Aunt
C., Frank *[Francis R. Douglas]*, & 2 home papers. Pins from Mother & pins
& needles from Aunt. Laid on ground. H*[enry C.]* Murray with Cha*[u]*n*[cey
Parker]* & I. Sent letter to mother.

Saturday, 5th.—Good rest last night. Cough.—Soup. Wrote to *[Brockport]*
Republic & to Father about reenlisting & 30 days furlough. Orders to *[be]*
ready to march. Wrote to Hec*[tor A.]* Butler. Water. All ready to go till night.—
Good supper. Fixed boughs to sleep. Paper from Lon. Yesterday agreed take
Sharps breech loading gun & send mine home. Bright fire & talking of old
times. Fixed a bed comfortably. Fine starlight. Chilly.

Brockport Republic, December 10, 1863

Kelly's Ford, Va., Dec. 5, 1863. Editor Republic:—After nine days fatiguing march *[illegible word]* we again rest on the Rappahannock, this time on the south side. On Thanksgiving morning, this corps (1st), started for the Rapidan, which we crossed at Ely's Ford (37), on Friday morning, 27th, at five o'clock. Going on that day, just above us, guerillas attacked a supply train, and we prepared to give them a warm *[illegible word]*, but they skedaddled. After "gobbling" several wagons, burning two. We had one of our men killed, and one wounded and one dead rebel, victims of the raid. Nothing more occurred that day, except that we were rushed through the woods and muddy runs on a double quick, in the dark, for 6 or seven miles, and halted for the night near Robinson's Tavern.

On Saturday 28th, advanced to the front, where a fight was had the day before, and skirmished through the woods and valleys, driving the rebel advance before us. Halted and shell were exchanged by batteries on both sides, several of which struck sufficiently near our company. This was at Nolte Grove, and here we rested for some time, while we supposed preparations were being made for an attack by us. Our artillery were posted in heavy force on hills in front and we could see the rebs half a mile off, watching us, and throwing up breastworks.

On the 29th nothing exciting occurred, but a heavy picket was kept out. On the morning of the 30th a brisk cannonading was commenced and the rebel lines shelled, but no reply of consequence was brought out. Some skirmishing was going on, and an engagement was expected. Obtaining permission of Acting Brig. Gen. Robinson, I visited the hill where a good view of the field could be had if musketry opened. The rebel breastworks could be seen in the distance, also rebs on foot and horseback. Several lines of skirmishers were firing and attempting to drive in the rebel pickets, one of which could often be seen on the retreat. A small stream separated the two parties, the "Johnnies" having a pretty strong position. Several were brought in wounded, but it was evident that there would be no general engagement. Gen. Meade and staff and other generals were inspecting the position. In the afternoon a detail of fifty men was made from our battalion of Sharpshooters, and sent out in charge of Capt. Shipman for the purpose of skirmishing. It was not expected that with our heavy telescope rifles a charge could be made, but it proved to be otherwise, for by some misunderstanding Capt. Shipman received the order to charge after some firing at the rebels and being exposed to to a sharp fire, and *without bayonets* our boys gallantly obeyed the command and made a telescope charge across the ravine, up the hill, and drove the frightened rebs from their rifle pits into the woods, our boys holding the position, the infantry having left them without any support. This daring manoeuvre was afterwards complimented by our division General, Cutler, but the affair cost the lives of two killed and one wounded. Geo. Kelly, of the 6th Co., from Carlton, Orleans Co., was shot in the breast while advancing and instantly killed. Nathaniel Moshier, of the 8th Co., from Columbia Co., N.Y., was killed at the same time: and _____[Martin L.] Moore, of the 7th Co., from Chautauqua Co., N.Y., wounded. Capt. Shipman received a slight scratch on the hand from bullet. We record no other casualty. All the honors which could be done on the occasion were shown our fallen comrades, and they were placed carefully in a soldier's resting place, having done their duty faithfully.

Having, I suppose, accomplished the object for which we went out, on Tuesday evening our forces commenced falling back. We started from the front about five o'clock and made a hasty and hard march through a wooded and rough road, in the dark, halting about midnight, tired and hungry.

It will be late now, for me to give you particulars of the general movement, which you have no doubt read already.

In expectation of winter quarters, the boys have commenced building houses for comfort, pretty well satisfied to rest after a tiresome fall campaign. Finer weather than we have been blessed with for two months never was known, but to-day clouds loom up and a storm is looked for.   J.T.F.

Sunday, 6th.—Sunny & windy. Cough a long time last night. Hated to get up. Drew 2 days rations, tack, pota[to], beans, pork & candles. Saw D[octo]r after break[fast]. Washed dishes. Wrote to Mate [Mary A. C. French]. Bean soup. Skirmishing for "crumbs". Boys building. [Brockport] Repub[lic] 3rd. Helped get supper. Tent put up & good fire. Read. Medicine of D[octo]r for cold.

Monday, 7th.—Very cold night. Ice ½ inch thick. Drew soft bread. Coughed some this A.M. before up. Got water. Beans cooking. Letter to Aunt C. Splendid weather. Private skirmishing. Carried wood. At spring for water & muddy. Bro't boards ¾ mile where houses were being torn down. Bright fire front of tent.

Tuesday, 8th.—Sunny. Very heavy frost. Cough latter part of night. Powders of D[octo]r. Cooked break[fas]t alone. [J. Chauncey] P[arker] at work on road. Drew stove. Read. Took off drawers & shirt. Need tools to build with. Bo't loaf bread 5c, piece cheese of H[enry C.] M[urray] & bo't can milk yesterday, 60c. Parker came at dark & bro't br[ea]d & flour [illegible word] We live well now. Band playing.

Wednesday, 9th.—Very cold. After a good breakfast washed things, cooked beans &c. Fixed up in P.M. Boys (H[enry C. Murray] & C[hauncey Parker]) getting ready for building. Ch*[auncey]* bo't flour. Doing some little above all the while. Boiled potatos. Drew soft B*[rea]*d today. Saw *[Brockport]* Repub*[lic]* & letter of 20th. Laughing after to bed. Not quite so cold tonight.

Thursday, 10th.—No change in sky. Warmer.—Bean soup after Break*[fast]*. Carried clothes to be washed. Bro't back & washed. 10c each. Bo't can oysters 11 shil*[ling]* crackers 15c, sug*[ar]* papers, very busy camp & good time to fix up. My cold is better. 50 cts for 10 pieces washed 3 for J. C*[hauncey]* P*[arker]*. Cooked applesauce.

Friday, 11th.—Bo't papers 5c & read Pres*[iden]*t's message,[185] &c. Cooked while the boys worked on shanty & helped some. Drew pork. Slight sprinkle; little cloudy. Paper from Frank *[Francis R. Douglas]*. On guard, (commissary) in eve., & took blanket to a tent & slept.

Saturday, 12th.—On guard from 2½ till 6, & the stars bright at last. Dog sleeping by fire & mules rattling about. Slept in own tent 1½ hours & found breakf*[as]*t when up. Some rain, & cloudy, temperate. At work on house all day; carried clay for H*[enry C.]* M*[urray]* to put up fireplace & chimney while J. C*[hauncey]* P*[arker]* put up side, windows (16 glass ?) & made bunks. Chimney most done, fire in & tents on for roof at dark. Put all our traps in & got supper, all comfortable & room to stand up in. Nice fireplace. Chaplain & papers. Nice pair socks from home by mail 30c, thread & buttons. Read & wrote in diary a little, Door on house (by J. C*[hauncey]* P*[arker]*.) Everything looks prosperous & comfortable ahead.) Fried potato, pork, flour, gravy, coffee & soft bread which drew to-night. Beef to-day & potatos.

Sunday, 13th.—Cleared off pleasant after heavy rain last night. Everything wet, & water for cooking close by. After break*[fast]* worked a good part of the day claying up between the logs of house. Wrote part of a letter to sister. Busy. Owe *[J. Chauncey]* Parker 55c on eatables of sutler & can milk of *[Henry C.]* Murray 60c. Read news in eve. Bo't N*[ew]* Y*[ork]* Herald 5c. Dried stockings before fire & glad to get in bed.

Monday 14th.—Some rain last eve., cloudy & clear warm, then colder in P.M.; wind. Helped *[Henry C.]* M*[urray]* build chimney most of day. F. bo't 3 lbs. butter 60c a lb. Oysters for supper, & a good dish of soup. Drew beef & soft bread. Received 2 letters from Fa*[ther]* Mo*[ther]* & Sis*[ter]*, 9th & 11th & 2 papers, *[Rochester Evening]* Ex*[press]* & Dem*[ocrat]*. Latter with extract from my letter 5th in *[Brockport]* Rep*[ublic]*. Good news from home & in papers.

Tuesday, 15th.—Detailed & at work laying logs for corduroy road to Brandy Station, sev[era]l miles. At noon to coffee. Quit early in P.M. mule teams hauling logs. Borrowed candle of [Lieutenant Alphonso W.] Starkw[eathe]r. [Brockport] Repub[lic] 10th with letter. L[ieutenan]t [Philip] H[ysner]. in house talking about furlough, 2½ from our Co[mpany]. Up late reading.

Wednesday 16th.—Took [Henry C.] M[urray]'s place on corduroy.—while he staid to help [J. Chauncey] P[arker] put in floor. Very cold last night & to-day. At noon bo't 2 lbs. cheese 40c 80c. Boys bo't 6 lbs. onions, 50c. Pleasant till P.M. cloudy. After quitting P.M. bo't raisins, 10c Drew candle. After sup[per] of cof[fee] butter & soft bread, read important news in Wash[ington] Chronicle.

Thursday, 17th.—Rain heavy. Break[fast] & upset gravy on floor. Squally. Detailed. Onions, for break[fast]. Wrote to Frank [Francis R. Douglas], Father & Em[ma] S[mith]. Corss [?] Robinson [illegible word] Cold to [three illegible words] Detailed for 3 days on corduroy.

Friday, 18th.—Up early & walked sev[era]l miles to work on corduroy, but saw no officers & came back. Witnessed man (Allen) shot for desertion in 76th NY[VI Regiment] Good pluck. Letters from Mate [Mary A. C. French] Aunt & F[athe]r.

Saturday, 19th.—Out thro' woods same as yesterday, built fire & were relieved, back. Wrote to Rev[erend] Marshall & Ja[me]s Hathaway, Ches[apeake General] Hos[pital]. Beans & other rations. Paper from F[athe]r. Cold, freezing.

Sunday, 20th.—Commenced letter to Mat [Mary A. C. French]. Pleasant. Live pretty well now. Headache today. J. C[hauncey] P[arker] sick to-night with cholic. Great flurry. Hot cloths & pepper tea going lively.

Monday, 21st.—Northern weather. "freezy". Inspection of camps. Bo't paper. Took drawers for self, & shirt for Mun[son] to be washed. Yesterday drew new shelter tents. Made into [?] Wrote to Mat [Mary A. C. French]. Serg[ean]t [Lewis C.] Courtney, 140th [NYVI Regiment]. Bean soup. Drew shirt & drawers. Read by good fire.

Tuesday, 22nd.—Good break[fast] of beans, soft b[rea]d, cof[fee], beef, flour, gravy, butter, syrup, &c. Bo't paper. Dug ditch. Potat[o]es. [Mead] Williams & Asa Northrop to [illegible word] Bo't 20c worth of tack 35 cts extra. [11 lines illegible, too faint] On detail to help build mule shelter. Talk with Lieut[enant] Daily of [Brevet Major] Gen[eral John C.] Robinson's staff. At noon orders to be ready to move at moment's notice. Owe J. C[hauncey] P[arker] for 2 loaves soft b*[rea]*d; sold one to J.N.W. Letter to Mother. All for sup*[per]* we could have. Taste of sardines. Hate to leave our pleasant "shanty".

Thursday, 24th—Up at 4, break*[fast]* at 5, packed; heavy load. Off at 4½ to Brandy Station. South on to Culpepper, 1 mile west camped in woods, open. In camp 1 P.M. steady marching, & I fell out, sat down to rest twice. Many stragglers. Fine day. Cold. Fine water close by. Tent up & fire. Leaves & brush for bedding. Spend Christmas Eve (38) by fine fire in open air. Moon clear, air freezing & ate piece b*[rea]*d, little cof*[fee]* & molasses. Read N*[ew]* Y*[ork]* D*[aily]* Herald, Brilliant—camp lights in distance. Slim prospect of a Ch*[ristmas]* dinner to-morrow. (but there's a horse skeleton near, the only spare rib, hardly spared by the crows.) Still we feel in very good spirits & think of the dear ones at home.

Christmas

Friday, 25th.—Slept well & warm between *[Henry C.]* M*[urray]* & *[J. Chauncey]* P*[arker]* on boughs & leaves. 3 blankets & over coats over us. Up & got water. Coffee pork fried tack & soft bread with syrup. Wrote to Aunt C. Steady cold. No snow. Paper from home. See the spires of Culpepper. Apple. Some boys getting boxes. Bo't *[two illegible words]* oysters 1.00 had latter for dinner. *[J. Chauncey]* P*[arker]* owes me 20c. & I owe *[Henry C.]* M*[urray]*. 25c.

Saturday, 26th.—Moved camp ¾m. Helped get logs. Mild. Trees being felled.

Sunday, 27th.—Rain most of day. Bro't a great many logs for building. Sides most up. Laid down. Very disagreeable weather. To bed early, rain falling.

Monday, 28th.—Rain all day. Put up shelter & eat under. *[Henry C.]* M*[urray]* & *[J. Chauncey]* P*[arker]* got boards. Letter from home, box coming.—Stamps 2c. *[Brockport]* Republic. In bed early to get out of the rain.

Tuesday, 29th.—Pleasanter. Headache. Abed late. *[Sampson W.]* Fry coming with us. 1½ miles with *[Sampson W.]* F*[ry]* for barrels & boards, to an old guerilla home. Spoilt book & borrowed shoes.

Wednesday, 30th.—Fine warm day. Bo't paper. Carried stone for chimney. Boys *[Theron]* A*[insworth]* & *[J. Chauncey]* P*[arker]*. at work on house & we moved in at eve. Only partly finished. Bunk with *[Sampson W.]* Fry. All the boys building. Sleep well to-night.

Thursday, 31st.—Rain, drizzle. *[illegible word]* coffee in rain. Wrote to

Mother & sis[ter]. Sent Harvey & Ed. badges. [J. Chauncey] Parker fixing up door, &c. Supper in the rain. In bunk very early. Heard firing of guns at 7½ & expected to be called up. Anxiety soon over. Singing in the camp. A dismal New Years Eve.

January 1864— New Years Day

Friday, January 1st.—The year enters nicely clear & mild till 4 PM wind commenced blowing & ground freezing hard. Carried heavy loads of stone in morning & helped build chimney with [illegible word]. Letter from Mate [Mary A. C. French]. Bro't wood & had fire in chimney at night. Fasted today. No box from home. . Very cold night & we have to huddle around the stove.

Saturday 2nd.—In bed late. Sun shined today but cold & some windy. Breakfast of beef, pork, tack, coffee & condensed milk. Out & bro't wood. Letter & paper from F[athe]r. Beef rations. Look for box. House chinked up with bagging. Potato & ham ration. [top of page: "Box from home" Hett[y Copeland]'s box 130 lbs. with apples, butter, turkey, goose, biscuit, cakes, sausage, &c. Gay, & we had a good supper. Very cold night. Letter from Em[ma Smith] & a paper from Father

Sunday, 3rd.—Cold, but sun shines, freezing all day. Box breakfast late. Cleaned gun & washed dishes. Wrote to Mat [Mary A. C. French]. "Skirmished." Quite like old fashioned Sunday. Rice & cake for dinner. Trees falling or felled. Serg[ean]t [James R.] Blood singing happily. Pleasant evening, but cold.

Monday, 4th.—Detailed for fatigue, clearing piece of ground. Snow commenced falling about 10, continuing all day, About 2 inches deep. Mild. Came in at 2. Washed up feet, [illegible word], handk[erchie]f, towel, night cap in stream out doors. Drew 5 days [illegible word] & cof[fee], dried apples & 2 days soft bread. Box from home for J. C[hauncey] P[arker] & I. After goose & other good things of [Henry C.] Murray's friend our box & found 2 game cocks made of pumpkin seeds in fighting attitude, sent by Harvey. Also socks from Aunt C. & from Mother pincushion for self & Cousin Sam[pson W. Fry] and turkey, pies, frosted fruit cake, butter, cheese, apples, potatoes, candles, pencil, envelopes, illustrated paper from Father & from Mrs. Smith & Emma jug tomato & tomato sauce (catsup), &c. Substantial. For all of which I feel very thankful. Good time eating apples, &c., looking at Pictorial. Think of Mother & all at home for being so kind in sending goodies. To bed without pants & vest.

Tuesday, 5th.—Mild, thawing some. Slept extremely well last night. Sausage, cold goose, baked potato, catsup coffee bread & butter Beef &c. Wrote to F[athe]r. Boys in house to see us. Tomato cooked for dinner, also pie of Mother's make & cheese. Sent paper to Mother. Also wrote to her but not sent today. Cut out pictures of Mine Run & sent home. Duck for supper & Mrs. Smith's cherry preserves, & cheese, & pie, & honey. Good. Quite a stomach pressure, but like New Years usually. Cold, tonight. *[Ernest M.]* Russell spent the eve. with us. Rumors of us going out in the morn[ing] on picket.

Wednesday, 6th.—Some cloudy. Sausage for breakfast. Wrote to Em[ma] S[mith] with letter to Mother. *[Sampson W.]* Fry bo't paper for me. Nothing new with us. Not to go on picket. Beef rations. H[ector] A. Butler came disch[arge]d to visit us before going home. Visit in eve.

Thursday, 7th.—Nothing new. Turkey for dinner. Letter from Reverend Marshall Chesapeake *[General]* Hospital & from Mother & sister & Harvey. Capt[ain Volney J.] S[hipman]. back Drew new woolen blanket & shoes. Lots of talking in house. *[Hector A.]* Butler with us yet.

Friday, 8th.—Snow fell last night. 4 inches deep. Detailed for fatigue & went without breakfast to Culpepper, 1¼ *[mile]* & built 2 bridges over gulleys or runs. Cut logs & carried them. Thaws some. Back about 2 PM. Ate dinner &c. Quite a little "spat" with H[enry] C. M[urray]. Send rifle bullet moulds & "starter" home by *[Hector A.]* Butler. Also watch to Lon. All talking by fire. Ale to drink. Cake of *[William]* Hues & *[Jackson P.]* Nichols box.

Saturday, 9th.—Cold & freezing. *[Hector A.]* Butler left. Wrote to Cous[in Albert] Allen. Fixed boot legs to wear. Steak & toast for breakfast. Things changed in house &c. Cut my nice frosted cake from home, Mother & divided with the boys. Cooked beans & apples. Drew rations of sug[ar] & cof[fee]. Saw Rev[erend] Merrills of Orleans Co[unty] here on visit, pleasant man. Wrote to Aunt C. answering to her letter rec[eive]d this eve. by candle from home.

Sunday, 10th.—Fine day. Last night coldest of the season. *[illegible word]* warm. Cleaned up for inspection. Heard preaching by Rev[erend] Merrill. Very pathetic good. Cake & apples for lunch. Finished letter to Aunt. Good news of reb desertion & a half million men to be drafted![186] Elder M[errill] called. *[Brockport]* Repub[lic] & letter from F[athe]r. Late supper. Heard cavalry going out to the front.

Monday, 11th.—Mild day. Up early. Bad cold. Changed clothes &c. Wrote to F[athe]r & sent $1.50. Nothing new going on in camp. My clothing list already am[oun]ts to $11.30, already drawn. Bro't wood. Cooked beans. In eve. took clothes shirts & drawers to be washed. Walk on road with *[Sampson W.]* Fry & see the Blue Ridge Mountains in distance with snow sprinkled upon them. Signed clothing book & blanks & copied the am*[oun]*ts $11.38 of the clothing I have drawn since the last year was settled. Made up bed & went in early after calling in to Mr. *[William]* Hues' tent.

Tuesday, 12th.—Another fine day, so mild. *[Sampson W.]* Fry & I got breakfast early. To Capt*[ain Joseph S.]* Arnold's tent & saw him eating break*[fas]*t. On fatigue with 30 others. Helped *[illegible word]* log house for brigade headq*[uarte]*rs. At noon cof*[fee]* & toast. Saw Jim Peachy & back. Carried clay for chimney all P.M. till 4. Saw Lieut*[enant D. B.]* Daly on staff of Act*[ing]* Brig*[adier]* Gen*[eral Henry A.]* Morrow who has taken place of Col.*[John C.]* Robinson, & spoke with him. Splendid P.M. Built fire in the new chimney. Drew thro' wrong end of chim*[ney]*. At shanty fried pork, tack & applesauce sup*[per]*. There is talk of our being transferred to cavalry by our aspiring officers & some of the boys are not satisfied with our easy times, doing no picket duty. Only camp guard. Drew one day's tack. No mail to-night. Cars off track.

Wednesday, 13th.—Cloudy. A general wash after breakfast of self some clothes &c. Sewed. Finished cake at noon. Had the pleasure of saluting Capt*[ain Volney J.]* Shipman this A.M. for the first time in long while. Dinner of cof*[fee]* pots. & soft b*[rea]*d. Wrote to Mother. Cooked beans. Two days ration of bread. *[A. L.]* Root telling stories in eve.

Thursday, 14th.—Fine, mild, & spring like. Walk to Culpepper with *[Sampson W.]* F*[ry]*. Saw lots of crows & graves of Union & secesh soldiers; road dry in many places. Culpep*[per]* looks old & as tho' some business had been done, before the savagery *[of]* war. Some modern buildings dwellings & two brick churches with tall spires. Saw Corp*[oral]* Philip Brennan of 14th Brooklyn Zouaves. At depot. Muddy st*[reet]*s & no sidewalks of account. Several women in st*[reet]*. One native walking with sojer, said "I'm a better Yank than she air!" At the Commissary (Brig*[ade]*) *[Sampson W.]* F*[ry]* bo't flour & sugar after some parley. Back & coffee for dinner. Cooked beans. Letter from Em*[ma]* S*[mith]* in eve.

Friday, 15th.—Misty in A.M. Pleasant in P.M. Detailed for getting out sticks for meeting walk for Headq*[uarte]*rs. L*[ieutenan]*t *[D. B.]* Daly superintended the job & took hold of the cross cut saw. Got out 4 loads, quit at 3. Feel better for the work. Soldiers returning from picket. Letter from Mother & sis*[ter]* & paper from Aunt C. Some fun in eve. Finished letter to Bro*[ther]* Harvey & Mother. Wind tonight. Had pancakes for supper.

Saturday, 16th.—Pleasant & too nice for winter. Toast & coffee for break*[fas]*t. Mailed letter to Mother & sent "scrap". Shaved & got ready for inspection at 1½. Put on beef for soup. Drew apples, beans 2 days bread, potatos & beef. Letter from Mat *[Mary A. C. French]*. Boiled beef for supper & potatoes. Wrote some to Mat *[Mary A. C. French]*.

Sunday, 17th.—Windy. Pleasant P.M. Cooked potatoes, made gravy &c. With B*[enjamin]* C. Davis, Capt. Lake & *[Theron]* Ainsworth went to Culpepper but no church till 2 P.M. came back after seeing several native promenaders &c. Finished letter to Mat *[Mary A. C. French]*. Supper. *[Brockport]* Republic 14th came. Read *[Washington]* Chronicle in eve.

Monday, 18th.—Rainy. Up almost after breakfast. Changed clothes & mended. Lots of fun *[J. Chauncey]* Parker & *[Sampson W.]* Fry on duty, came in early. Wrote to Andrew Boyd. Gloomy day. But I am in good spirits.

Tuesday, 19th.—Fixed up things. *[J. Chauncey]* Parker brought up small bunch of *[Rice H.]* Eaton's with tape &c. & most of the day & in eve. was busy printing directions on envelopes for the boys & self. Pretty cold to night.

Wednesday, 20th.—Pretty cold last night. Pleasant today. Up early, fried salt pork &c. Detailed on fatigue, with others. Saw L*[ieutenan]*t *[D. B.]* Daly. Went to Brig*[ade]* Commissary, then with Corp*[oral]* *[Richard C.]* Boyle & *[Rice H.]* Eaton on wagon over to rough road & loaded logs, heavy, 2 loads, while waiting for 2nd load, built fire & found a summer house. After dinner & getting beans ready went & helped finish building fly tent on it. Back at dark. {Woman made fuss about our getting small boards from grape arbor & they were put back!} Bean soup, peach sauce & coffee with soft bread for tea. Bo't 2nd handed blouse of *[J. Chauncey]* Parker, $1. Now owe him 80c. H*[enry C.]* .M*[urray]* owes me 1c on 30 extra Gov't coffee sold; I owed him 25c. Discussion in eve. with H.M. in regard to Gen. *[George B.]* McClellan.

Thursday, 21st.—Moderate. I cleaned up &c. Roll call now at 7 A.M. & 8 P.M. Got breakfast. Boiled beef, soup. Washed a few things. Stewed apples. A rumor that we are to move to the front 5 miles. Fine morn. Commenced letter to Em. S*[mith]*. H*[enry C.]* M*[urray]* paid me 30 cts coffee

Friday, 22nd.—Pleasant in A.M. Cloudy P.M. No move countermanded yet. Drill ½ hour. Wrote to Sister & Em*[ma]* S*[mith]*. In P.M. cooked beans. Can milk 60c. & ½ lb. butter 25c. of sutler & charged. Hear band playing in eve. Letter & paper from Frank.

Saturday, 23rd .—Fine. Mild. So different from cold, freezing weather at home. Drill at 10. I have a side for the first time in long time. Gave note to *[Lieutenant Alphonso W.]* Starkweather for Martha Doug *[sp?]*. Cooked beef, soup. Drew pepper, pork, br*[ea]*d, beans, apples. Police duty. Letter from Lon, Sis*[ter]*, & Mo*[ther]* with slips, & letter from Aunt C. Wrote to Lon in eve. Milk punch by *[James R.]* Blood.

First Frogs 25th

Sunday, 24th.—Mild. Wind from the south. Pleasant. Break*[fast]* in a hurry cof*[fee]*, beef, & soup. Inspection at 8:30. *[Henry C.]* M*[urray]* & *[J. Chauncey]* P*[arker]* off. Very quiet day. Finished letters to Em*[ma]* S*[mith]*, Sis*[ter]*, & Lon. Paid man 10c for washing shirt & drawers. Wash. Chronicle 5c. Cooked beans. Commenced letter to Aunt C. The boys came. Back "gay". *[Brockport]* Republic 21st. Read some. Corp*[oral]* Samedly *[sp?]* told stories. B*[enjamin]* C. Davis in tent reading.

Monday. 25th.—Mild, breeze. Swept up ground. Drew sug*[ar]* & cof*[fee]* to last till Jan*[uary]* 31. By waiting till P.M. & getting soft bread we are only 1 day behind on letter to Aunt & wrote to F*[athe]*r. Paper from Aunt C. First dress parades order read. Pancakes for supper. Drew beans, dried apples & soft bread 2 rations. Also candles 2½. Heard frogs croaking or biting their teeth. Read & played games. Detailed for guard. Boys started for *[illegible word]* in 2nd Div*[ision]*.

Tuesday, 26th.—On guard from 3 to 6 A.M. moonlight. Late break*[fast]*. Boys changed pork for milk. Warm breeze; mild. Read good news in daily. Sent paper home. Finished letter to Aunt C. What singularly fine weather. Cooked beans & apples. Drew beef. Read in eve. To bed early.

Wednesday, 27th.—The almost summer-like weather continues. Up & break*[fas]*t early. Cleaned up for inspection. Mailed letter to F*[athe]*r. Walk to Culpepper. Roads almost dusty. The red-legged Zouaves 14th Brooklyn look gay. Sev*[era]*l Northern ladies on horseback on st*[reet]*s with officers. Soldier on barrel with game board on his back, marked "For Drunkenness". Tried to get meal but found none. Stores open. Saw Ed Lamer *[sp?]* Q*[uarter]* M*[aster]* clerk. Sweat freely walking back. Cleaned up some. *[three illegible words]* Boys playing cards. No parade.

Thursday, 28th.—Summer weather. Hot in tent. Drill. Subscription paper for monument to Maj*[or]* Gen*[eral John F.]* Reynolds killed at Gettysburg, but Capt*[ain Volney J.]* S*[hipman]* succeeded badly, only $2 for the 6th

Co*[mpany]*. Stewed apples. Washed & mended some. Commenced & finished letter to *[Brockport]* Rep*[ublic]* & wrote letter for H*[enry]* C. M*[urray]*. Band playing.

Friday, 29th.—Clear & pleasant. Warm. Police duty—clearing ground. Prepared for inspection by brushing up. [Last evening my box of clothes which I left at Chesapeake *[General]* Hosp*[ital]* in care of Rev*[erend]* Marshall, came by Ex*[press]* paid]. Clothes or little articles for *[Sampson W.]* Fry & mine O.K. Shoes blacked. Attended Divisions Review at 2 P.M. on high ground near Culp*[epper]*. Ladies *[two illegible words]* & many officers spectators. *[Brigadier]* Gen*[eral James C.]* Rice & *[Brevet Major General Henry A.]* Morrow with staffs passed in review. Very warm & we were glad to get back to camp for the sun poured down fiercely. Received cake, apples, a letter, & 3 papers from F*[athe]*r. In A. L. Root's box from home. Got supper. Bo't ½ lb. butter 25c. of sutler charged, $1.10 charged now. Out doors talking; some whiskey afloat. Read papers to the boys in eve. Soft bread, 2 days.

Brockport Republic, February 4, 1864

Camp 6th Co., N.Y. Sharpshooters, Near Culpepper, Va., Jan. 29, 1864. Editor Republic:—Since I wrote you last, we, with all the 1st Corps, moved from comfortable quarters at Kelly's Ford, on the Rappahannock river, Dec. 17, marching 10 miles on ground frozen solid, to this place, over a mile west from the County town of Culpepper, where, after enjoying Christmas in a sort of picnic style in little tents on the ground, we very soon put up houses in the latest approved army styles, which you may imagine are various;(**39, 40**) the one with which I am most acquainted having the luxury of a window consisting of two glasses, being part of a window confiscated from a rebel mansion. It would be worth any person's time to visit the army in winter quarters and see the ingenious contrivances for comfort. In the shanty above spoken of instead of a "crane" for hanging kettles on, in the fire-place, is part of a lightning rod hung across, which was "gobbled" from a house in the vicinity by a representative of Brockport.(**41**) It will be unnecessary for me to state that anything which a soldier finds "lying around loose," is appropriated, if any sort of use can be made of it.

There is no news of importance that I can give you, unless I mention that a cavalry reconnoissance in force has just gone out to "feel" the rebel position in front. Desertions are coming in from the enemy nearly every day. Also negroes in large numbers. On Tuesday 20 came in here. They are often pursued and scattered in various directions, and bring no provisions with them, which shows that the rebels are very saving of their scanty rations.

That eyeopener, the President's amnesty proclamation,[187] has a powerful effect in bringing in those who are sick at heart of southern tyranny.

Last week we were startled by a rumor that we were to move out five miles. But the idea was given up, and it was announced to us that we should hold our present quarters until a general movement of the army in the spring, so we are again contented, but we have cleaned up and made a pleasant camping spot for field life, in an elevated and healthy position, in full view of a long range of the Blue Ridge mountains, in the distance to the northwest.

But such weather! Almost a perfect summer! Are you at home all rubbing your hands and shivering over a blazing fire? We know you *were* only a few days ago. If so, your warm clothing and furs would be cast off should you come here, and enjoy the melting sun which has thrown its cheering influence upon us for one week, causing all nature to laugh snow and jack frost out of existence. The ground is getting quite dry and the dust flying in our faces while we had our daily short drill on the Gordonsville pike or road this morning and yesterday, made us glad to rest and wipe the sweat from our "veteran brows." Indeed, it is so warm in this tent-roofed "mansion" that the breeze, lazily wafted through the open two-glass window, and the open door of our kitchen, sitting room and parlor combined, and up through our neat fireplace and chimney, is not sufficient to keep back the perspiration. We have had only two falls of snow as yet, some six or eight inches in all, and some very cold weather for this region, and we cannot expect the present "dream" to hold us in its genial embrace much longer, and think a storm will shortly break the spell. The army would hardly remain idle with a week more of summer, though to anticipate a continuance of this, would result in a delusion. Frogs in the swamp have been heard to grate or sharpen their teeth, in preparation of a spring campaign, though they are too weak to attempt a song. Ball playing has commenced among the boys, and it may be safe to say that we anticipate *the* ball to open very early this spring, and with a crushing earnestness that will press every remnant of treason from the Southern heart, and give the death blow to the enemies of Union and liberty. This must be done in order to free the deluded people of the confederacy from the unhappy bonds of starvation and misery they are now to a fearful extent laboring under the despotic leaders are desperately striving to overwhelm them in their gulf of despair and wickedness. The end appears, surely and at no great distance, though it comes slowly. With a glorious victory in prospect, the soldiers will cheerfully assist in drawing the cord tightly about the neck of the rebellion, in the hope of smothering the victim before the leaves of autumn strew Virginia's blood-stained soil.

The health of this part of the army is quite as good as possible. In the way of amusements, the 2d brigade of the 1st division have opened a theater for their winter evening pastime. Many other items I am obliged to defer unless our enterprising brother printers, Eaton, Tuttle & Co., issue a sheet with the aid of their little press and type from which they are supplying the boys with small jobs of printing. Thanking you kindly, Mr. Editor, for the Republic so regularly, with home news, I remain, Resp'y,   J.T.F.

Saturday 30.—Changed clothes. A misty day. Slight warm rain. Detailed to finish Surgeon's shanty. Sawed end boards, &c. & nailed them on & closed up cracks, fixed up &c. Observed our Dress Parade. Letter from Father & Mother with 9 3c. stamps & thread; from cousin W. A. Allen & Shedrick J. Jackson, colored, Co*[mpany]* H 140th NY*[VI Regiment]* kindly asking me to come up & go to Warrenton to visit my brother's grave. Also paper from home. Drew rations of pork, beef & molasses. Cooked apples & beef. Read in eve. & talk with *[Jackson P.]* Nichols. Rain in eve.

Sunday, 31st.—Misty. Warm. Insp*[ection]*. Wrote to Father & Mother & Rev*[erend]* Marshall. Sent scraps *[illegible word]* for scrap book Let *[Sampson W.]* Fry have 3 3ct. stamps. *[Corne [sp?]* 5c borrowed. One of the 151st NY*[VI Regiment]* here at dinner. Bo't Sunday *[Washington]* Chronicle. No letter for me today. Hi*[ram]* Williams here. *[Brockport]* Republic came. Read in eve.

February

Monday, Feb. 1st.—Fine rain. Got pants washed 10c. Saw & talked with Capt*[ain Joseph S.]* Arnold also with L*[ieutenan]*t *[D. B.]* Daly in regard to getting a pass to Warrenton. Sent letter home & paper to Mat *[Mary A. C. French]*. Wrote request permission of 2 days leave of absence which Capt*[ain Volney J.]* S*[hipman]* agreed to send on approved to Brig*[ade]* head q*[uarte]*rs. Dress parade. Beans cooked. Drew rations of beans, apples & 2 days soft b*[rea]*d; pepper candles 1½ vinegar. Wrote to S*[hedrick]* J. Jackson 140th *[NYVI Regiment]* Wash. Paper of today. Cleared off very pleasant at 4 o'clock. Good news. Read in eve. *[several illegible words]* in eve.

Tuesday, 2nd.—Heavy mist till 1 P.M. Clear. Mild. Let *[J. Chauncey]* Parker have 3c stamp. Read in A.M. & "skirmished". Brigade Drill at P.M. after *[illegible word]* by Col*[onel Henry A.]* Morrow, Act*[ing]* Brig*[adier]* Gen*[eral]* in regard to our having to do skirmish in which he was quite lenient & mild, we skirmished. Ladies riding horseback. Cooked apples. Strange that I get no letter mail tonight. Heavy sounds of thunder in eve., then a shower of rain, then lightning. Read *[Washington]* Chronicle.

Wednesday, 3rd.—Heavy cold wind all day. Serg*[ean]*ts *[James R.]* Blood & *[James C]* Noble reduced to ranks at roll call: detached to work at some mechanical Gov[ernmen]t work-shop or R.R. started [two illegible words] with pencil a head board for Bro[ther] C[harles]'s grave. Put clothes in salt & water. Cooked apples & beans. Drew pork & bread 1 day. No letter. In eve. wrote to Mat [Mary A. C. French]. Boys had jolly time in P.M. Whiskey.

Reconnoisance

Thursday, 4th—Cold, some wind. Got break[fas]t. Finished & mailed letter to M[other]. Boys drilled, circumstances prevented me. We have permission to shoot at target 30 days. A woman came for [Eli] Barney Barnes to go as safeguard. Brig[ade] drill [illegible word] Cup coffee for supper. Read stories in eve. Drew beef.

Friday. 5th.—Mild. Sick headache. Did not get up till 9. Shot at target in P.M. at 60 rods with rifle never used before. Came near the spot but did not hit it in 9 shots. Cooked beef, soup. Drew tack cof[fee] & sug[ar]. Letters from Mother & Sis[ter] & F[athe]r with photos I sent for. Wrote to [illegible name]. Bo't [illegible word].

Saturday, 6th.—Reveille at 6. orders to pack up & be ready to march in an hour. So we get ready & put lots of things we did not want in a box & nailed. 3 days rations. And without break[fas]t we shouldered *[The following page continues with the preceding script in blue ink, but it is interlined with a script in brown ink in the same hand. The brown script seems to clarify the original blue. This is the transcription of the blue ink script, with such use of the brown as seemed appropriate:]* knapsacks, camp guard left back, then fooling about Headq[uarte]rs about 8½ started on march south toward Rapidan [River]. Quite moderate, but I was easily tired no break[fas]t too. Ate at 11½. 2 tack & small piece of beef. At ½ P.M. we camped near Raccoon Ford in woods after hearing artillery firing. Some mud but roads generally good. Woman & child begging food & the boys gave her plenty of U. S. rations. Made coffee & cooked pork. Once more old type of field life & seems quite fascinating. This A.M. left letter to F[athe]r & one for Mother with photograph in care of Mr. [William] Hues to mail. Foggy & a little rain. Yelling & chasing rabbits in woods. Good work but grass for bed & tents put up. At dark before I had drank coffee was detailed 1 of 6 picked men to go with others every thing of our "traps" on. Put coffee in canteen & [J. Chauncey] Parker took pail stewed berries in hand. In road the Act[ing] Brig[adier] Gen[eral] (Col[onel Henry A.] Morrow) took charge of 25 S[harp] S[hooters] & several hundred infantry & through mud we went 2 miles not a loud word, then stopped, in dark while infantry advanced to a little town in range of enemy's guns, which they found abandoned by the enemy. Most of the houses burned which made a brilliant conflagration & lighted up the country for a long distance. Came back to camp at 12 P.M. by light of fire, shoes full of mud. Rain part of time. Dried clothes by fire & to bed.

Sunday, 7th.—Pork, tack & coffee. Cloudy in A.M. Pleasant in P.M. Sun. Back to camp. Letter from Aunt C. & paper from F[athe]r. Read. Nothing new. Boys having great time cutting down trees for squirrels, chasing them, climbing trees, making them jump off, floating gracefully through the air from high to low trees, but grass for bed. Then the order came at [illegible word] to strike tents & in 5 minutes we were under way back to camp at Culp[epper] double quick, no supper, but hot coffee hastily poured in canteen to drink on the way. Halt in open lot, then on, full tilt. [J. Chauncey] P[arker] Serg[ean]t D[aly] & I got off from the Co[mpany] & floundered on through the mud & uneven ground with heavy load enough to try the patience of Job. Troops scattered in all directions, yelling & joking. Got my shoes filled with mud. At last came to R.R. track & followed it to Culp[epper] & found they had been in a great scare & filling cars with grain to retreat! Town filled with scattering soldiers. At last to camp where most of the Co[mpany] were. Put tents (roof) up, by fire got warm & dry & ready for a sleep. Pants & socks plastered with mud. Found every thing all right. Just about tired out.

(Debts, &c.)

Monday, 8th.—Abed late. Cold. Ration of whiskey. All merry. Commenced letter to Mother. Drew tack & beef. Tired & sore to-day. Letter from Mrs. Mary M. Smith also Repub[lic] 9th with letter of 29th. Bought ½ lb. cheese 20 cts—$1.30 sutler. No roll call to-night boys all enjoying themselves.

Tuesday, 9th.—Mild Sunshine. Washed shirt & dr[awers], socks, h[an]dk[erchie]f, towel & night cap. Greased shoes & had 1 pair tapped paid 50 cts one shoemaker 25 cts. borrowed 50 cts. of S[ampson] W. F[ry] now owe him $1.05. & 10c for [illegible word] [J. Chauncey] Parker 80c, [Henry C.] Murray 25c Borrowed 12ct stamp of George Goold. Parker owes me one 2 ct stamp & one 3 ct. [Sampson W.] Fry owes me one two ct. stamp. I bought bottle ink 10—owe 10 ct. for it. Owe sutler $1.30.} Mailed letter to Mother & Em[ma] S[mith]. with picture to Em[ma Smith]. Also paper to F[athe]r. Cleaned gun. Boiled beef, soup. Bo't candle 10c paid. Dress parade with 24th Mich. [Brevet Major] Gen[eral John] Newton & ladies present. Good supper. Commenced letter to [Brockport] Repub[lic]. Pleasant. New moon. Feel well tonight.

Wednesday, 10th.—Very cold & only slight thaw of mud in sun. Skirmish drill. Hair cut. Wash & change. Put clothes to soak. Drew sug*[ar]* & cof*[fee]* 5 days & part can milk 60c—$1.90. butter charged. Dress parade. Boiled pork &c. Bro't wood. Read in eve S*[tephen]* Delorme, 24th Mich*[igan]* visited us in eve. Saw Capt*[ain Volney J.]* S*[hipman]* about a pass at 7½ & he advised me to wait a day or two. Up till 11.

Thursday, 11th.—Very cold last night. Cold wind to-day. No roll-call. Cleaned up the street. {$5 of *[Sampson W.]* Fry last eve.}Washed shirt dr*[awers]* socks & pants. Shaved. Sewed. Cleaned haversack. Paid *[Sampson W.]* Fry $1.05 cts. making only $5 that I now owe him. Drew pork, beans, apples, onions. Boiled pork & beans. Letter from Mother & Sis*[ter]* also $1, 8 3 ct stamps. Bo't 1 lb. butter. Paper of Lieut*[enant Philip]* H*[ysner]*. Capt. S*[hipman]*. agreed to see Col*[onel Henry A.]* Morrow about my going to W*[ashington]*. Wrote to *[Brockport]* Republic, & to Sister.—Application to go to Warrenton came back approved by Brig]adier] Gen*[eral]* Div*[ision]*& Corps Gen*[eral]*s & *[Major]* Gen*[eral John]* Sedgwick com*[man]*d*[in]*g army Potomac. Up late.

Friday, 12th.—At roll call. Hurriedly warmed beans & took cup coffee. Walked fast 1½ mile to Culp*[epper]*, had leave of absence signed by Provost Marshall. Made mistake, got in officers car at depot then ordered out & got in freight car, started at 8½ five cars full at Brandy Station by men going home on recruiting & re-enlisting; sat by & talked with boy in Co*[mpany]* E. 108th *[NYVI Regiment]*(from Parma) Rough road. At Warrenton Junction 10½. Found camp of 140th *[NYVI Regiment]* & S*[hedrick]* J. Jackson, Co*[mpany]* H. Wait for him to get pass. Saw Maj*[or Milo]* Starks, Lieut*[enant Lewis B.]* Courtney. Pleasant & mild day. Pictures of the quartette, Mate *[Mary A. C. French]* & *[letters illegible]* A*[ggie]* J*[ohnson]*. *[two illegible words]* Well entertained by S*[hedrick]* J. J*[ackson]*. Good coffee, cakes, doughnuts &c. Pleasant visit in L*[ieutenan]*t Court*[ney]*'s quarters; saw fine pictures of the "quartette" Walk with L*[ieutenant Lewis B.]* C*[ourtney]* to depot & fort. Officers playing ball. Talk in quarters of L*[ieutenan]*t *[Henry]* Allen & Capt*[ain]* A*[ugust]* M*[e]*yers[188] in eve. Called on Lon *[Alonzo]* Morehouse Hosp*[ital]* Steward Ed*[gar]* Wadhams, *[Isaac]* Barnes *[Jr.]* & others. Mailed letter home & to *[Brockport]* Republic. Sent photo to Mat*[Mary A. C. French]* & Mrs. Court*[ney]*. Pleasant camp.

Brockport Republic, February 18, 1864

Camp 6th Co. Sharpshooters, Near Culpepper, Va., Feb. 12, 1864. Editor Republic:—Dear Sir:—During the recent fine summer weather, the 1st Division of the 1st Corps had a Review, which, by the way, came off on the very day announced by the Richmond Whig, showing how well the rebels are previously aware of many Union movements. The recent expedition of Gen. Butler on the peninsula was frustrated by the cowardly desertion of a soldier who gave information of the move. The Review of which I have just spoken, was attended by our Battalion of Sharpshooters, now commanded by Capt. Shipman, as actors. The troops generally made a good appearance, and not only were reviewed by field officers, but several ladies from the north, visiting here, honored us by their presence on horseback.—This took place on one of the many hills surrounding Culpepper; and we noticed the citizens gazing at the bright arms, various movements, and especially the gaily dressed 14th Brooklyn Zouaves.

Our officers having obtained permission for target practice, we commenced that necessary preparation for the coming earnest campaign, for we intend to *scare* a few traitors, if not more, with our conical bullets.[189] We had practiced but one day, when on Saturday morning last, long before daybreak, the drums of the surrounding camp beat a hasty reveille, waking us up with the idea that something was "up," which we began to realize when the verbal order came to "pack up and be ready to march in an hour!" In winter quarters so sudden a call usually finds a miscellaneous scattering of articles which a soldier gathers during the winter, and it was no slight job to cull out the most necessary clothing, &c., for a "reconnoisance" toward the enemy which we found was our destiny, and to which we responded with cheerfulness, for it was quite a novelty to strike tents after a rest of nearly six weeks.

Just after daylight, leaving a small guard at camp, (for we only "sacked three days' rations), we marched to Brigade headquarters, joined the remainder of the Brigade and afterward the Corps, and on we tramped. The day was mild and a heavy mist broke into a dull trickling rain at noon. But the spirits of the men were buoyant in the hope of a successful raid. Cheering was the order of the march, though our heavy knapsacks pulled upon the shoulders. The ground was very smooth and dry on the open main road, though soft in the timber, and a halt was ordered at comfortable distances. I do not wish to discourage any friend of the soldier in the kind and appreciate act of sending good things from the well stocked cupboard, but may be pardoned for mentioning that one man in the ranks fell out exhausted on the road shortly after starting, said to be caused by hastily making a breakfast of *three mince pies* received in a box from home the night before. He could not "see the point" of a raid just then, and the result was the box was faithfully guarded from a rebel attack in our absence, by the owner himself.

On the way to the Rapidan a large force of cavalry passed us and we were to support them. About noon, having marched about nine miles, we met a battery of brass pieces which had been speaking to the rebs as their advance pickets retreated across the Rapidan. Then a mile through the forest and we halted in the thick mist, put up shelter tents; then many of us cooked the first meal for the day, some having come off without breakfast and silently gnawed hard tack on the road. Cannonading and faint musketry was heard in the distance. A tall, elderly woman and "little girl," of civilized appearance, came to us, begging food, stating a case quite pitiful, and saying that we were encamped upon her brother's farm, whose rails, their only fuel, the boys were ruthlessly burning to dry their damp clothes. A donation was hastily gotten up, the boys contributing liberally, when the woman and child departed, loaded with the choicest viands of the haversack—hard tack, coffee and sugar. This is the "unmerciful and barbarous manner" in which we treat the families of our enemies.

In the evening twenty-five men from our battalion, in company with an ample force of infantry, led by the gallant Col. Morrow, Acting Brig. Gen., and his efficient aides, Capt. Wood and Lieut. Daly, made an advance beyond the outer pickets for the purpose of capturing some rebels who had made a practice of annoying our pickets by a too free use of the bullet. After being cautioned in regard to silence—not being allowed to speak above a whisper, lest the enemy, whose cannon commanded full sweep of the plain, should discover us and open a deathly shower of artillery—through mud we cautiously advanced till we came near a little village of a dozen houses or more; then a halt was whispered, and in the darkness and drizzling rain we crouched upon the ground, in momentary expectation of being discovered. A small squad of men were detailed to creep to the houses and ascertain if they were occupied. This was successfully conducted while we lay in waiting with finger on the trigger of unerring rifle, ready to meet whatever fate Providence had in store for us. Soon the scouts returned, having found only two negro families and one dead rebel in the town; with that exception deserted. Then the scouts were ordered to burn the building unoccupied with the least delay. And we fell back over the brow of a hill, out of reach of the firelight. Soon a faint light glimmered in one building, then another, and soon a blaze appeared, then came huge volumes of flame, and we saw a conflagration in earnest. It was a grand sight, and the country for miles was lighted by the destruction of this traitor nest, and thus the life of many a patriot picket was saved to the defense of liberty. After watching the pitchy flames until the result of the expedition was fully accomplished, we returned wearily to our comrades in camp, satisfied with the labors of the day.

On Sunday nothing exciting occurred, and having made arrangements for another night's "lodge in the wilderness," at five o'clock we had orders to "strike tents," which was done, and in five minutes we trod on our way back to our old camp and gladly too.

Many troops were out—the second and third corps—and all together had succeeded in driving the rebels to the south side of the Rapidan. Numerous prisoners were taken, and the second corps lost a few killed and wounded, while the first corps met with no loss. There was much cheering on the way back, and most of the men came in about 10 o'clock. Those left behind in camp had quite a "scare" fearing a raid, and many government stores were packed up for a backward move.

Health of the men good. Of our Co., 6th, Collamer, and Sergeants Blood and Davis, have been detailed to work at a government machine shop, where they have gone. Lieut. Hysner is now in command of the company.

[The above letter was published, without "J.T.F." together with the letter, dated February 18 in the Brockport Republic issue of February 25. The latter letter is transcribed below after the diary entry of February 14.]

Saturday, 13th.—By kind inv*[itation]* of Ord*[erly Hubert]* C. Taylor, staid with him last night; good time & slept well. Up at roll call. Break*[fast]* with Ord*[erly]*. Called at Shad's *[Shedrick J. Jackson]*—Fine sunny day. Saw guard mount of the boys in Zouave uniform. Saw Maj*[or Milo]* Starks in regard to S*[hedrick J.]* J*[ackson]*'s pass. Visiting with boys. Fixed head board. Pass from Provost Marshal who refused to sign S*[hedrick J.]* J*[ackson]*'s pass & through kindness & diplomacy of Maj*[or]* Starks we (S*[hedrick]* J. J*[ackson]* & I) got on car at 1:45 by climbing up in rear. Ride on top. Pleasant ride. Halt at Middle Station. On & came to Warrenton Village (**42, 43**); pleasant appearance. Hurried to Presbyterian Church brick, behind which my Bro*[ther]* C*[harles]* was buried. Conversed with two ladys Mrs. Bootwright & sister who live in house adjoining church west side of church. Who talked kindly. Grave is in open lot between 12 & 20 feet back from the north east corner or left hand corner facing the street, nearly on range with the east side of church. Placed the headboard firmly in ground & could do no more. Was told that the board would not be disturbed by the Bootwright family. Had only 50 minutes to stay & could not spend so much time as I would have liked at the dear boy's grave. I had *[Shedrick J.]* J*[ackson]* kindly assisted me. Back at 4½ safely in car. Bo't cake & pie, 50c Saw ball play. Good supper with S*[Hedrick]* J. J*[ackson]*. coffee (splendid) warm buck*[wheat]* cake. Called on L*[ieutenan]*t *[Lewis B.]* C*[ourtney]* & visited in eve. also at Lon *[Alonzo]* Morehouse's hospital & saw sick, funny man with rheumatism. Lon brought out the fine thing right. Staid all night with S*[Hedrick J.]* J*[ackson]*. Talked till late by good fire; pleasant. Mild day.

Sunday, 14th—Visited boys before break*[fast]*. Break*[fast]* with S*[hedrick J. Jackson]*. Saw inspection with L*[ieutenan]*t *[Lewis B.]* Court*[ney]*. Feel well to-day. Sunny & some wind; mild. Think of sending this diary home by L[ieutenan]t [Lewis B.] Court[ney]. So good by diary. I hope in health to see you after the war. Home & friends good by for the present. I never forget all. Think this is the last winter [illegible word]

[End of diary; there is a gap from February 14 through February 29, 1864]

Brockport Republic, February 25, Camp 6th Co., N.Y.S.S., Near Culpepper, Va., Feb. 18, 1864. Editor Republic:—Dear Sir:—At last, waiting for over a month after the usual time for pay day, we received two months' greenbacks, on Monday last from Maj. W. P. Gould, paymaster, who is a very accommodating and gentlemanly official. We are now paid to Jan. 1st and should receive $26 again about the 10th of March.

On the same day we had inspection and Division Review by Maj. Gen. Cutler and other Generals. Several ladies were present, including one acting as officer of the day, having a red sash about her. It was a cold, windy day, and snow fell—a few flakes. Review and inspection are often forerunners of a move, and we looked for it. And at night, as bringing a realization of a change, a rumor came that our pickets were driven in, and we had orders to have everything ready to receive the rebels at a moment's notice. But morning came, and not an enemy. Now we are quiet as to rumors, though a heavy, freezing wind pierces through every garment. Yesterday and the night before the cold was most intense, and wood heaped upon the fireplace makes a most inviting fire, to which we readily turn. Snow can be seen upon the Blue Ridge peaks, but we have none here. Writing, even to most intimate friends, is this day a cold and most unpleasant task, and letters from home and friends, in such times, are agreeably received and read before the warming blaze.—This "freeze" will not hold out long, and there is consolation in feeling that no move will be made while it lasts.

Having obtained a leave of absence in Warrenton, Va., (for the purpose of visiting and marking the grave of a soldier brother lying there, having died and being rudely buried just as the village was evacuated in 1862,) I enjoyed the opportunity, a few days since, of a visit with Brockport friends in the 140th regiment, at Warrenton Junction. I found them in the new and tasty Zouave uniform which they have recently put on, and in which they make a fine appearance. They are making their camp, which they found in the mud, a pleasant one under the regulations of their esteemed Colonel, Geo. Ryan, of the Regulars. The boys are daily at work on the grounds, which are well ditched. The quarters of both officers and men are neat and comfortable, and the men are mostly well and healthy. Several worthy and well deserved promotions have lately taken place; among the rest Capt. Starks is made Major, and shoulders the leaf with all the dignified grace of his accommodating nature. To the Major your correspondent is indebted for an act of "double quick" diplomacy, which enabled him to take the train to Warrenton at a late hour. Friend L. B. Courtney, formerly Sergeant in Co. A, has for strict attention to duty, &c., been honored with the commission of 2nd Lieut., and is transferred to Co. D. He is now visiting his friends at home on a ten days' leave of absence. That he will make an officer of strict sobriety and obtain the confidence of his command there is no doubt. Lieut. Allen, of Co. A (now in command of Capt. Meyer), is in good spirits, though suffering from a chronic complaint brought on while in the service. He is well liked by the men under him. Orderly Serg't Chas. Taylor, good natured as usual, was busily engaged at his duties. Serg't Chas. Perry, of Clarkson, has lately been promoted to Captain, and transferred to the 2nd N.Y. Mounted Rifles. Several non-commissioned promotions have been made, of which I have not time to speak in detail. Alonzo Morehouse, formerly clerk in the Brockport postoffice, has the responsible position of Hospital Steward, which he fills with credit and prompt attention. By his polite invitation I visited the commodious hospital tent, which is a model of neatness and comfort; beds and bedding good, and a large fireplace gives out its warmth to the patients, (only 11 at present,) who were being kept in good humor by the songs, jokes and stories of one of their number, an amusing man in arm chair, troubled excessively with the "rheumatics." The dispensary building and cooking house are well arranged. I may mention here that Dr. Flandran, formerly of Brockport, is Division Surgeon of the division to which the 140th belongs.

The regiment has been recruited by a goodly number of first class drafted men; and turned out a goodly number on Sunday morning inspection. I was impressed with the fact that the officers and privates of the 140th are an agreeable body of men, and are honor to Monroe. I regret that space will not allow a more extended notice of them.

Before returning I visited Warrenton on a sad errand, accompanied by one who would not leave the remains until they had found a resting place, though rude. Warrenton is a pleasant village, with many tasty residences. Gen. Gregg's cavalry are quartered there.

Yours, &c. J.T.F.

VOLUME II
1864

Field Diary from March First, 1864
John T. Farnham 6th Ind*[e]*p*[enden]*t Co*[mpany]* N*[ew]* Y*[ork]* S*[harp]*
S*[hooters]*
5th Corps 4th Div*[ision]*. 1st Brigade
Brockport, Monroe Co., N.Y.

March

Tuesday, March 1st, 1864.—Rain all last night & this A.M. slowly. Pancakes,
cold beef & pork & fried beans with cof*[fee]* for breakfast. Read some & wrote
to *[Brockport]* Repub*[lic]*. Got supper.—Letter from F*[athe]*r with geranium
leaf & L*[ieutenan]*t *[Lewis B.]* Courtney Co*[mpany]* D. 140th *[NYVI Regiment]*
and C's & wrote to S*[hedrick]* J. J*[ackson]* Co. H. 140th. Rain all day, snow
to-night, damp. Drew beans potatos *[illegible word]* & candles &c.

Wednesday, 2nd—Mild, sunny. Very light snow, disappeared. At Culpepper
with Orderly McPherson; heard that *[Major]* Gen*[eral Judson]* Kilpatrick with
cav*[alry]* forces, has gone toward Richmond. Called at Brig*[ade]* Headq*[uarte]*rs.
Let Lieut*[enant D. B.]* Daly & others of staff read my printed letters, he kept
paper. Very good fluid *[whiskey]*. Back in mud. Boiled beef & wrote to F*[athe]*r.
Read. Sewed. Received (after Dress Parade) letter from Mat.*[Mary A. C.
French]* which I shall not forget—satisfactory. Bo't papers 5c. Paid 20 cts for
Map of V*[irgini]*a, in co*[mpany]*. with *[Sampson W.]* F*[ry]* *[Henry C.]* M*[urray]*
& *[J. Chauncey]* P*[arker]*. All quiet. Snow gone. Feel in best of spirits tonight.

Brockport Republic, March 10, 1864

Camp 6th Co., N.Y. Sharpshooters, March 2, 1864. Editor Republic:—Dear
Sir:—At present, things with me are very uncertain. The stir of our south-

western armies luckily appears to rouse the quiet of affairs here, and moves have apparently commenced, taking advantage of the fine weather of late, and good condition of roads. Whether the move will be general at present is to be seen.

On Saturday the 6th corps, followed on Sunday by the 3rd, marched on reconnoisance toward the Rapidan, and were to cross if possible. Our corps (1st) was told to hold ourselves in readiness to support them, but have not yet been called upon, though we have three days' rations, and everything packed, in expectation of moving. All sorts of rumors are afloat as is usual when a stir is being made, one of which is that our forces did cross and fought the enemy on Monday. Another story is to the effect that Longstreet, routed for the hundredth time, is crossing to assist Lee, and that the enemy are moving to flank us on the west. A part of the 5th Corps are reported to be quite a long distance to our right. The truth, reliably, cannot easily be had, so we must wait.

On a visit to the camp of the 8th N.Y. Cavalry, veterans, (from Rochester,) I found them preparing to go home on furlough of thirty-five days—that is, those of them who had re-enlisted, and the old members have mostly done so. On Saturday last they rec'd an order delaying them until the present move should be over, and they good-naturedly, "by special request," consented to see the "scrimmage" out. The 8th are true and hardy, and have done good service. I found them in a good location, only a few rods from the inside of infantry picket line. They deserve a good reception at home, and a bounty-ful supply of recruits. Many changes have taken place among the members. Capt. Barry, as you are aware, is now at home in R., reported discharged by reason of disabling wounds, received in a fight near Culpepper last fall. Brockport is now represented in the 8th by Sergeant Mort. Read, (a brother printer,) who is now attending to duties as Orderly in his Co. Corporal Dan. Nellis, of Clarkson, as well as Serg't R., showed the healthy and toughening effects of active army life. Col. Markell, formerly clerk in Mr. E. Whitney's store, commands the 8th.

There appears still to be a constant drain of desertions from rebellion, a whole picket reserve of forty, including a Captain and Lieutenant, having come into our lines a few nights since, and gave themselves up. Such acts are of frequent occurrence. An Orderly of Gen. Lee is said to have reported himself to our lines and upon giving important information as to rebel affairs was furnished with transportation to Ohio, where he formerly resided. He stated that, all told, Lee's force was only 25,000 men.

Reviews continued to be the order of the day until a few days ago. At the last Corps Review our Sharpshooter Battalion had the praise of making the best line and appearance in marching before Gen. Newton, staff, ladies and spectators. The weather to-day—very moist, a slow rain—admonishes us that parades are over, and time for work in the coming *[illegible words].*

By tne way, our Brigade (called the "Iron") has just been recruited by the return of two regiments, the 6th and 7th Wis., who after re-enlistment and 30 days' furlough, bring with them large numbers of recruits. The 19th Indiana are also expected to rejoin us, with additional men. Col. Morron, of the 24th Mich. retires from the Brigade command, Col. Robinson again taking his place after a visit home. Thus our army is being filled with veteran troops "for the war."

Under the command of Capt. Shipman, this Battalion is prospering. Near us is a photograph and ambrotype tent, doing a heavy business. Also a stationary institution. Our sutler has started a bakery, where dried apples cooked in an iron kettle are made into anything but palatable pies at fifteen cents each. Uncle Sam generously furnishes us with the best of rations, plenty and "to spare." Often they have consisted of coffee, sugar, fresh beef, salt pork, potatoes, onions, dried apples, beans, fresh bread, pickled cabbage occasionally, with pepper, salt, vinegar, and soap highly scented—probably a mistake. We live decidedly well. No chances for grumbling.

Later:—The most reliable news this morning (Thursday 3rd) is that our infantry force is at Madison Court House, north of Rapidan, having found no force of the enemy; but are waiting while Gen. Kilpatrick goes in their rear, with a view of liberating our prisoners at Richmond. Gen. K. has a force of over five thousand cavalry, and up to yesterday had not been heard from. He is no doubt doing desperate work.

Our rain turned to snow last evening , which merely covered the ground, disappearing to-day. The sun shines warmly.   J.T.F.

Thursday, 3rd.—Fine spring day. Birds singing. Cleaned up. Boiled beans & d[ried] ap[ple]s. Every one out of doors, enjoying the sunshine. Bo't paper. Read all news aloud in eve. Chilly nights.

Friday, 4th.—Cloudy, windy, chilly. Capt[ain Volney J.] S[hipman] gone home 4th time. After break[fas]t drill, skirmish. Called on Lieut[enant D.B.] Daly (staff) & got my paper. Lieut[enant] D[aly] informed me unasked that a chance for me at Brig[ade] Headq[uarte]rs would soon be open, &c. In Col[onel John C.] Robinson's saluted room—(fluid)[whiskey] In [A. L.] Root's house, [Charles W.] Spa[u]lding there, awhile. Wrote to Mat.[Mary A. C. French]. With "Fry's joke". Mailed paper (Chronicle) to Mr. [Horatio N.] Beach, [Brockport] Repub[lic]. Showed boys my [illegible word] letters; (House out of humor-pies) Drew rations of potatos & syrup. Also 2 days bread. Letter from home, Mother, sis[ter], Lon E[ddie] & H[arvey]. Bo't paper from "bread fund" 2 loaves 5 cts each sold. Boys fooling in st[reet] Shooting at owl.—Games with S[ampson] W. F[ry].

Saturday, 5th.—Mild, cloud & sun, with sprinkle of rain, came off clear. Birds singing. Rations. Drew pork, dried ap*[ple]*s. Beans, sug*[ar]* & cof*[fee]* Cooked beans. Wrote to mother, Sis*[ter]* & Lon. Bo't cap of *[Jonas H.]* Kocher—$1.50—paid all but 50c. Changed und*[er]* clothes & washed. Ball playing {Clothing drawn by most of Co*[mpany]*.} Bo't box blacking, 5c. Bo't paper. Letter from Serg*[ean]*t A*[ndrew]* Boyd, 108th *NYV[I Regiment]* & Mrs. Smith. Clothes to soak. After dark saw unaccountable flashes of light to the south—like artillery flashes. Read the news.

Sunday, 6th.—Fine day. Inspection. Wrote to Serg*[ean]*t A*[ndrew]* Boyd & to Father. Paid my respects to L*[ieutenan]*t Daly, &c. {Horse threw L*[ieutenan]* t *[Philip]* Hysner.} Walk with *[William E.]* Ferrin & *[J. Chauncey]* Parker to 2 miles out, pleasant dry roads. Saw family in house from road, any quantity of children & an 18 year gal who climbed the fence with agility. *[illegible word]* *[Brockport]* Republic came. Bo't paper for self & H*[enry C.]* M*[urray]*. 10c. Boiled potatos & sausage. Read in eve. Discovered something very like a breach of confidence. Windy.

Monday, 7th.—Before break*[fast]* rolled up my new blanket, which B*[enjamin]* C. Davis is to take home for me 10 day furlough & went to Culp*[epper]* depot with him. A fine walk. Birds lively, singing. A warm day. Whirlwind carried papers hundreds of feet into the air & away out of sight. Washed clothes, aired some & mended. Sent paper to Aunt C. Wrote to Chauncey Baker, 4th Wis*[consin]* Batt*[er]*y Post Hosp*[ital]*, Madison, Wis.[190] Stewed apples. Drew 2 d*[ay]*s. Soft bread. Dress parade. Got supper. Ordered to report to Lieut*[enant D. B.]* Daly now Act*[ing]* A*[ssistant]* A*[djutant]*G*[eneral]* & left my supper to do so, found him on hill, talking to Capt*[ain R. S.]* Dillon, Brigade Inspector Gen*[era]*l on staff to whom I was introduced & after a few questions it was agreed that I should be detailed as clerk to Capt*[ain R. S.]* Dillon. At camp had fun with the boys & read in eve. Detailed to Brig*[ade]* Headq*[uarte]* rs. Lieut*[enant Philip]* Hysner informed me kindly that I was ordered to report to Capt*[ain R. S.]* Dillon for duty to-morrow morn*[ing]* at Brig*[ade]* Headq*[uarte]*rs and at roll-call. Starlight.

Tuesday, 8th.—Rain gone part of the day. Reported to Capt*[ain]* Dillon (after calling by request on Lieut*[enant Philip]* Hysner who appeared glad of my appointment.) Found the clerks just getting up. Instructions from Capt*[ain]* D*[illon]* *[J. Chauncey]* Parker built me a nice table or desk, & I got seat from old quarters, then commenced making lines on ruling paper for making out inspection reports. Took dinner with the clerks—9 in a huddle. Copied 4 orders. Heard interesting arguments, clerks, staff & Col*[onel William S.]* R*[owland]*. A pleasant place. Mail distributed in the office. Letter from

S*[hedrick]* J. J*[ackson]*. Talk with Capt*[ain R. S.]* D*[illon]* who formerly lived in Vienna, N.Y. Supper with the boys *[Chauncey P.]* P*[arker]* *[Henry C.]* M*[urray]* & *[Sampson W.]* F*[ry]*. Bro't water. Called on *[William]* Price 8th Co*[mpany]*. Changed pants & mended; read the good news from England— pirates. (Frogs singing)

Wednesday, 9th.—Bo't breakfast. Pol*[ished]* shoes. Sick headache, slightly. Called at Capt*[ain]* "Dill*[on]*'s" quarters for the marking pencil, ruler, & red ink. At office at Headq*[uarte]*rs found all swept & fine. At work ruling for blanks during the day. Horse race. Pleasant & warm. Made & drank cup tea at my q*[uarte]*rs. Bro't water. Endorsed, backed Capt*[ain]*. D*[illon]*'s papers. Brigade mail small came & was dist*[ribute]*d. Letter from L*[ieutenan]*t *[Lewis B.]* Courtney.—Got thro' at office, 5. Spent day busily & pleasantly. Got sup*[per]* &c. Gave *[Edwin]* Franklin his ball starter. Cleaned teeth. Read. Played game with *[Sampson W.]* Fry. Wrote to Mother.

Thursday, 10th.—Rain all day. Bo't another note book 25c. At office after getting breakfast & made out blanks, also sent notice to Reg*[imen]*t com*[man]* d*[e]*rs. Lots of fun in office. Wrote to *[Brockport]* Repub*[lic]* & mailed letter home & to *[Brockport]* R*[epublic]*. No dinner. Mail at 4½, out at 5. Letter from Mat*[Mary A. C. French]*, Em*[ma]* S*[mith]* *[illegible name]* Al*[bert]* A*[llen]*, & Aunt C. To Co*[mpany]* H*[[eadquarte]*rs to sup*[per]*. Bro't water. Wrote to Mat *[Mary A. C. French]*. Disagreeable weather. No roll call for me, nor drill nor guard. Frogs croaking. Beans cooking.

Brockport Republic, March 17, 1864

Headq'rs 1st Brig., 1st Div., 1st A.C., near Culpepper, Va., March 11, 1864. Editor Republic:—Dear Sir:—You and your readers have no doubt heard the result of Gen. Kilpatrick's raid in the vicinity of Richmond and the damage inflicted on the property of rebeldom. The only regret is that Gen. Butler did not co-operate with the cavalry, in which event our prisoners at Richmond might have been released.

Now the only excitement we have is the welcome with which our soldiers hail the news of the special election on Tuesday, at which the loyal people of New York decided that we in the army shall not be deprived of a voice in choosing competent men to administer our laws, and we can hereafter deposit a ballot against traitors and their agents, Copperheads. With this decision of the Empire State, all necessary for the re-election of President Lincoln, is his nomination by the Baltimore Convention,[191] in June for the general expression of all the soldiers is in favor of the man who has faithfully stood by the Union so long, and they think if he is capable of administering such a complicated mass of affairs as ours have been for the past three years of war, it will be just to trust him with another term, the latter part of which, at least, we hope may be peaceful.

The appointment of Gen. Grant to the principal command,[192] under the President, of our armies in the field, and the arrival in Washington, gives a confidence to the army which is warranted by the successful abilities of "Unconditional Surrender."

Yesterday we had a steady rain all day, and the style of weather for the week past has been one day sun, and storm the next. We will be content to accept one amount of March rain in this way.

The Sharpshooters (in this Brigade), have been entrusted with the guarding of the highway (Sperryville pike), from any sudden attack by guerillas. Some of the men have chosen, in exchange for their heavy rifles, Sharp's breech-loaded rifle, a formidable shooter, without bayonet, and which can be fired while lying on the ground three times at least while a musket can be loaded and fired once. The change will soon be made. Capt. V. J. Shipman is now home on furlough of 15 days, leaving Lieut. McDonald, 6th Co., in command of battalion. Private B. C. Davis is home for 10 days. Several detachments have been made from the 6th (Rochester), Co. In a former letter I stated that Lieut. Davis, among others, was detached and on duty in a government railroad shop: it should have read Serg't Noble, instead of Davis. C. W. Spaulding has been for a long time on duty as Brigade bugler at headquarters; A. L. Root is also on duty there attending to the culinary affairs of the staff officers. Lieut. Starkweather acting as Commissary. Lloyd is Brigade butcher. The 6th Co. has also furnished a Lieut. for a colored regiment, 9th—Duncan Cameron, of Caledonia, N.Y. Several non-commissioned promotions have lately been made. R McPherson is Orderly. J. C. Parker, of Brockport, is acting ordnance sergeant.

I would be pleased to give you a few items of news this time, but cannot well do it.—Having been detached from the 6th Co. S.S., I have the honor at present to be acting as clerk for Capt. R. S. Dillon, Acting Assistant Inspector General of this Brigade at Brig. headquarters, and hope thereafter to be able to give you more interesting letters, with increased facilities. I am already indebted to D. B. Daly, Aid, and others for favors, &c.

Robins and other birds have made their appearance, to say nothing of the evening serenade of frogs, indicating the approach of Spring.

Yours truly, &c. J.T.F.

Friday, 11th.—Rain all day. After going to office called at L[ieutenan]t McDonald's & gave instructions. Rec[eive]d Reg[imen]tal Reports & copied them into Rep[ort] to Div[ision] Inspector, after coffee at quarters: Rule &

fig*[ure]* work. Our boys on picket. Sup*[per]*. Letter from Father, Mother & sis*[ter]* & one for H*[enry]* C. M*[urray]*. In eve. called at office, got papers & candles & at q*[uarte]*rs finished Report.

Sat*[urday]*. 12th.—Very pleasant. Corrected Rep*[ort]* & hurried it to H*[ea]* dq*[uarte]*rs & sent it to Capt*[ain]* Dillon, acting Div*[ision]* Insp*[ector]*: (L*[ieutenan]*t *[A. D.]* Rood having taken Capt*[ain R. S.]* D*[illon]*'s place for a while.) Ruled blanks. Coffee at q*[uarte]*rs. Shaved, washed up & changed. At off*[ice]*. Wrote to L*[ieutenan]*t *[Lewis B.]* Court*[ney]* & commenced to Father. Bor*[rowe]*d envelop. Considerable discussion. Mail sorted, let*[ter]* f*[ro]*m F*[ather]* & photo of self. Returned Clarke Baker his gun. Our Sharp's Improved Rifles are at depot. In eve. had confidential talk with *[Sampson W.]* F*[ry]*. Fine moonlight. Read papers.

Sunday, 13.—Pleasant, high wind. Fixed up. At office. No business today. Saw staff officers & our guard going to picket. Copied letter for *[Sampson W.]* Fry {At q*[uarte]*rs have a paper fund for bread sold.} Wrote to Aunt C. Very high wind. Bo't telescope from R. K., for $4 & owe him. Also bo't rifle marked E. Shulters of H*[enry]* C. Murray for $18 to be paid pay-day: ball-starter, patch-cutter, moulds round & conical, & cone wrench, included with rifle. Paid *[J. Chauncey]* Parker 2 *[?]* toward grine board. At office in eve. Talking at q*[uarte]*rs by firelight. Chance to buy heavy globe sighted rifle for $12.

Monday, 14.—Up & washed clothes before break*[fast]*. After, went to office. Ruled & prepared blanks. No stir (Flannel.) Corporal *[blank space]* of the 9th N*[ew]* Y*[ork]* M*[ilitia]* called, pleasant. Drew b*[rea]*d, pork, ap*[ple]*s & beans. (Made out "Roster" & sealed it to Div*[ision]* Insp*[ector]*. Took report of Brig*[ade]* casualties to copy for L*[ieutenan]*t *[A. D.]* Rood. Mail late. Cars off track. Letter of 2nd *[Brockport]* Republic. {Talk with Capt*[ain R. S.]* Dillon in A.M. My knap*[sack]* to be carried, &c.} Got supper. Read, & played funny game with H*[enry C.]* M*[urray]*.

Tuesday, 15th.—Fine day, as was yesterday. Bird music. Got break*[fas]*t. Wrote to F*[athe]*r. At office. Sent paper to F*[athe]*r. Wrote to Mrs. S*[mith]* & Em*[ma Smith]*. Also sent let*[ter]* to Father. Very cold wind. Wrote Corps *[illegible word]* & Capt*[ain]* Wood, A*[ssistant]* A*[djutant]* G*[eneral]*, signed it. Sup*[per]*. Read, & games in eve. *[Dolphan]* Dort going home tomorrow, furlough Cold night.

Wednesday, 16th.—Cold, freezing & windy. At office. Eaton & Tuttle to Wash*[ington]*. Col*[ore]*d Reg*[iment]*. Swept. In Lt. *[D. B.]* D*[aly]*'s office. Ruled blank & finished for L*[ieutenan]*t *[A. D.]* Rood, casualties of Iron

Brigade, & finished it at q*[uarte]*rs. Insp*[ection]* Arms. Rev. R. M. Hatfield, Preacher *[illegible word]* gave me Testament. Drew pork & a day's s. b'd. At office 4 P.M. Found inspector's portfolio with papers. No mail for me. Sup*[per]*. Rec*[eive]*d 75c for share in extra pork & coffee. Wrote to Mother. In bed early. Pretty cold night.

Brockport Republic, March 24, 1864

Headq'rs 1st Brig., 1st Div., 1st A.C. Insp. Gen'l's Office., March 17, 1864. Editor Republic: Dear Sir—Violent winds are now giving us a taste of the usually most unpleasant month in Spring. Yet we in Virginia have no cause to complain; on the contrary, birds of song and frogs of harsher music, have already shown in all possible ways that Winter's reign is over. Of "rain the wet," we labored under the disagreeable effects of two days' spatter last week. Now, aside from heavy gales, we have quite steady cold weather on a small scale. Several days ago we had the exciting phenomenon of a whirlwind, or "little hurricane," covering only a space of about ten or fifteen circular feet. When first seen it was approaching the camp of the 6th and 7th Wis. Veterans, and in its whirling passage lifted rubber blankets, articles of clothing, caps, dust and sticks high into the air.—Newspapers also were gobbled, and "folded" in no careful manner, taken on toward rebeldom, and may have reached and given "aid and comfort" to the enemy, for the last seen of them was a reflection of the sun on their glistening surface, as at least a hundred feet high, they struggled in the embrace of the mighty element. The rebels have tried kite flying, by which means they succeeded in sending letters to their friends inside our lines, attaching the documents to the kite frame.—But that method soon played out, and "Old Boreas" has allowed himself to become a rebel ally; and while he may endeavor to blow them good news, we are preparing to "blow" lead into them, with a small dose of affective powder, unless they soon turn from the error of their ways and *[illegible word]* the whole Union—nothing else.

Of real news we have none, except that which is already known by yourself and readers. Many results are coming in while the commander and staff officers of this Brigade are doing all in their power to make the men efficient and ready in the coming campaign, which it is said will be superintended by Lieut. Gen. Grant in person, who will return to Washington in a few days, to be followed by a partial re-organization of the Potomac army. The rapid personal movements of Grant at present appear to cause much anxiety among the rebels.

The commander of this Brigade is Col. W. W. Robinson, of the 7th Wis. Veterans. The staff officers are Capt. J. D. Wood, formerly Serg't in the 2nd Wisconsin, and a printer, is A.A. Adjutant General. Capt. R. S. Dillon, of

24th Mich., is A.A. Inspector General of this Brigade, although at present acting as Division Inspector in the absence of Col. Osborn. Lieut. A. D. Rood, of 7th Wis. Vet's, and Lieut. D. B. Daly, of 2nd Wis., formerly private, are Aides-de-Camp. Lieut. T. F. Weldon, of 76th N.Y., 2nd Brigade, is acting Provost Marshal and Aide.

The five regiments of this Brigade are 2nd Wis., 6th and 7th Wis. Veterans, 19th Ind. Veterans, 24th Mich., and 1st Battalion Ind'p't N.Y.S.S. The general condition of these commands, as shown by Inspection Reports, is good.

The Sharpshooters are now furnishing a Reserve Picket, 2 miles from Many [?]—light duty. The Reserve found a few days ago, a few concealed arms at a secesh home, which were seized and properly taken care of. A portion of the Battalion have recently received Sharp's Rifles, and the 6th Co. will soon exchange most of their heavy rifles for Sharp's. Two members of the 6th Co., private B. C. Davis and Corp. D. A. Dart have received 10 days furlough to visit sick relatives at home. A member of the 7th Co., David Burns, of Jamestown, Chautauqua Co., N.Y., died on the 12th of fever. Two members of the 6th Co., Tuttle and Eaton, are before the Board of Evaluation for officers in Colored Regiments, at Washington.

Ladies visiting the army, of whom there are several in this Brigade, have been ordered by the War Department to return, and are preparing to do so, except those who are connected with the Sanitary Commission.

Aside from the nightly Ethiopian entertainments in the 2nd Brigade, an occasional exciting horse race enlivens the dullness of life at headquarters, on pleasant days, Capt. W.'s horse "Charley" usually on time, and "more too."

At Brandy station, 5 miles from here, a few days since, a mail train ran off the track, killing a colored man, and wounding several soldiers. Damage slight.

Under new regulations, our mail arrangements are very good. The mail for this Brigade is distributed to the different Regiments from this office, daily, at 4:30 P.M., and leaves an hour after. Articles of clothing not exceeding two pound weight can now be mailed to privates at the rate of four ounces for eight cents. This includes only cotton and woolen goods.

We have a very good headquarters brass band, which is a decidedly musical "institution." The 24th Michigan also have a brass band.

No more at present.   J.T.F.

Thursday, 17th.—Cold wind. Cloudy. Cooked beans for break. At office. Wrote Circular & sent to Reg[imen]ts. Read Regulations. In A. L. Root's shanty. Feel like sick headache. Brig[ade] drill. At q[uarte]rs made cup tea; laid down an hour. At office. Wrote to [Brockport] Repub[lic] & sent. Lent

L[ieutenan]t [D. B.] D[aly] a 3c stamp. Rec[eive]d papers from F[athe]r. Saw L[ieutenan]t [A. D.] Rood. Capt[ain R. S.] D[illon] in office. Coffee for sup[per]. Bo't ½ lb. butter, 25 ct. Read story & Herald. Com[ence]d writing to Mat. [Mary A. C. French] To bed early.

Friday, 18th.—Very high wind. At office, made out Weekly Rep[ort]s. Called on L[ieutenan]t McD[onald] on business. Very uncomfortable, windy & every thing is blown about. Put out fire. –No dinner. At quarters 3½ P.M. Sup[per]. Headache all day. Sore; have cold. At 5 orders to get ready to move, & in an hour the order was countermanded. Great stir. At office & they were all packed up. Letter from Mother & pr lines & Harvey. Saw [Chauncey] B[aker] [illegible word] Quiet eve.

Saturday, 19th.—High wind most of the day. Mild weather or warm. At office early. Issued Circular requiring Reg[imen]t[a]l Com[mander]s to send in Mo[nthly] Rep[ort]s of absent officers. Sent S.S. back. Made out monthly Rep[ort] of Absent Officers, then assisted L[ieutenan]t [A.D.] Rood in making out Rep[or]ts till dark. Introduced to _____Clerk of Div[ision] Insp[ector]. Paper from Mother with new handkerchief & lines. After sup[per] with J. C[hauncey] P[arker] & bo't paper, back to off[ice]. With L[ieutenan]t [A. D.] R[oot] who is still good humor staid till 9. [Sampson W.] F[ry] & [Henry C.] M[urray] on picket. Windy eve. & warm. Sleep alone tonight. Read some.

Sunday, 20th.—High wind; air mild; Slept add last night; built fire & made coffee, bo't can milk, 60 cts. Washed up & changed. Cooked apples. (Yesterday wrote requisition for pair mounted No. 2 pants & gave to ord[er] ly.) At Headq[uarte]rs saw picket mounted. No Sunday "Work" Read news. Laid down an hour. Read Boston Mag[azine].[193] Cleaned rifle. At H[ea]dq[uarte]rs heard stories & waited for the mail. [Brockport] Republic 17th with letter of 11th, & two additional notices.—Mush, cof[fee] & sug[ar] For sup[per] [Lieutenant Volney J.] S[hipman] & I alone Read news in eve. Windy, windy. To bed early. Shipman returned. Sent [Washington] Chronicle & scraps to Mother.

Monday, 21st.—Windy most of the day. Sun in P.M. Up & washed clothes before breakfast. L[ieutenan]t [Philip] Hysner in at H[ea]dq[uarte]rs. Nothing to do. Cold, chilly. Read a very graphic, funny book. "F. H." [Sampson W.] F[ry] & [Henry C.] M[urray] in from picket. Coff[ee] for din[ner]. At H[ea]d-q[uarte]rs. Drew at q[uarte]rs beef, 2 days soft bread, traded potatoes for beans, sug[ar], & cof[fee]. Cooked beans. Sent paper to [Brockport] Repub[lic] & to Mat [Mary A. C. French]. Letter from L[ieutenan]t. & friend [Lewis B.] Courtney, with photo. Also let[ter] from Mat [Mary A. C. French] 17th.

Bo't *[Washington]* Chronicle. Called on Capt*[ain Volney J.]* S*[hipman]*. Wrote
some to Mat *[Mary A. C. French]*. (Cold & clear.)

Tuesday, 22nd.—High wind., & heavy snowstorm 5 o'c*[loc]*k in P.M. At H*[ea]*
dq*[uarte]*rs at 8½. Col*[onel William S. Rowland]* smoking by fire. Showed
him *[Brockport]* Republic. L*[ieutenan]*t *[D. B.]* D*[aly]* & Capt*[ain]* W. in. At
2nd Wis*[consin]* camp & introduced myself to Capt*[ain]* Perry, by request of
L*[ieutenan]*t *[Lewis B.]* Courtney. Quite agreeable. Other officers in. Capt*[ain]*
P*[erry]* showed me Marlot's q*[uarte]*rs & invited me to stay to dinner which
I declined. Visited an hour with Marlot, then back at H*[ea]*dq*[uarte]*rs found
letter from S*[er]*gean]t A*[ndrew]* Boyd, 10th. Ans*[were]*d it & finished letter
to Mat *[Mary A. C. French]*, mailed & sent photo to M.G. (Cold as fury)
Warmed up beans with bread crumbed in. Sewed overcoat. Shoe mended
15c. At H*[ead]*q*[uarte]*rs in snowstorm, & borrowed Harpers Magazine[194]
of *[Charles W.]* Spaulding. Storm storm. Read & a few games. Indian bread
baked by a cook.

Wednesday, 23rd.—Calm & sunny. Snow a foot deep on level & melting fast.
Indian bread for break*[fast]*, good. At H*[ead]*q*[uarte]*rs, nothing new. Took
papers to Capt*[ain Volney J.]* Shipman for him to sign. Plunges in Virginia
snow. Paymaster arrived. Saw *[Eli]* Barnes, safeguard. Hair cut, 25c. cof*[fee]*
at noon. Birds. Wrote to Cordelia. Signed Pay Roll With J. C*[hauncey]* P*[arker]*
walked to Culpepper, in slush & went to depot, where a great many were
expecting the arrival of Lieut*[enant]* Gen*[eral Ulysses S.]* Grant, but he came
not. Snow balling. Cider. Bo't *[Washington]* Chron*[icle]*. Back to camp; signed
pay roll. To-day saw Capt*[ain Erwin A]* Bowen of Medina, of 151st NYV*[I
Regiment]* Co*[mpany]* of S*[harp]* S*[hooters]*.

Thursday, 24th.—Pleasant. Wrote Circular, then to office, at H*[ea]*dq*[uarte]*rs,
L*[ieutenan]*t R*[oot]* signed circular & I dispatched it to the Reg*[imen]*ts
by Orderly. Finished letter to Sis*[ter]* & to H*[arvey]* & Eddy, also to the
[Brockport] Republic. Lieut*[enant]* A. L. Root paid 35 cts. Made coffee at
q*[uarte]*rs. Talk with *[William E.]* Ferrin. At H*[ea]*q*[uarte]*rs & at 3½ went to
Culpepper. Rec*[eive]*d pay to March 1—$26. Lieut*[enant]* Gen*[eral Ulysses S.]*
Grant had arrived. to his quarters; waiting awhile, I saw him & 3 staff officers
descend the steps walk to the gate, get into a carriage & four & drive away.
{Gen*[eral]* G*[rant]* is a very plain looking man, rather stout medium height,
sandy whiskers well trimmed wearing coat open in front & black hat. No style
or airs about him.} Back to H*[ead]*q*[uarte]*rs. Finished letter to *[Brockport]*
Rep*[ublic]* & mailed. Letter from Aunt C. Rec*[eive]*d $28 & paid H*[enry]* C.
M*[urray]* $18 for rifle. Kelly $4 for telescope & *[Jonas A.]* Kocher 50c balance
for cap. Bo't 1 lb. butter 60c. Made coffee. Read news. (22nd Birthday.)

Brockport Republic, March 31, 1864

Headq'rs 1st Brig., 1st Div., 1st A.C. Insp. Gen'l's Office, March 24, 1864. Editor Republic: Dear Sir—"What a spendid old-fashioned snow storm!" was the general exclamation on Wednesday morning, after the heavy blustering fall of snow of the night before had covered the ground to the depth of a foot, which laid so calmly spread out before the gaze, as of old, before we "came soldiering," in the good old times when cutters were plenty, and dashing horses made the spirits of a young load more merry by the music of bells. Although these "fixins'" were out of the question, especially the feminine and most interesting part of it, we enjoyed a view of dazzling scenery quite rare in this part of Virginia, which was so nicely set off by the pearly snow-clad ranges of the Blue Ridge mountains in the distance. The bright sun, however, which followed, made too warm an impression on the modest element, which is fast disappearing, and in a few days the roads will be dry again, such are the sandy and sieve-like qualities of the soil in this region. This storm was severely felt by our pickets, whose stern and unfaltering duty, as proved by experience, would not allow of being dispensed with even on such an occasion; but I her [?] of no less by exposure.

The rebels along our front, several days ago, were busily engaged trying to find a weak point in our well guarded lines through which a raid might be effected, but without success, although our corps had orders Friday P.M. last to prepare for an alarm which order was countermanded in less than two hours after being issued. "All quiet." Our lines are still steadily being "reinforced" by the application of arranging from five to fifteen rebel deserters per day, seeking refuge from tyranny. On a late occasion a squad of twenty came in which included a captain, lieutenant and an orderly sergeant.

It is quite customary for soldiers to be placed as a "safeguard" at the house of a native who has taken the oath of allegiance, upon the request of such safeguard being made. "Barnie", of the 6th Co., S.S., from Rochester, has for some time held such a position in a family near the picket lines, and appears to be quite a favorite, as when the application was made, the "ladies: said no other than "Little Barnie" would do to guard the mansion. So "Barnie" went and still acts the part of faithful sentinel. Safeguards are respected by both rebel and Union forces and are never harmed. At a native house in this vicinity, a soldier acting as above, having a peculiar appreciation of the (doubtful) charms and graces of a mourning southern widow, took pity on her weeds and the romantic finale of the matter ended in military "vows and victuals," with fluid accompaniments; the soldier was fairly a prisoner of war, and may now ruminate on the fortunes of rebellion. Many affairs of this kind are said to be doing in "Dixie."

The principal topic and looked-for event is the arrival of Lieut. Gen. Grant and staff, who are expected here to-day. Headquarters for the General have been prepared in a fine brick mansion off the main street of Culpepper, where he will hold forth until the opening campaign. We are much pleased with the idea of having this unconquerable hero in our vicinity.

The paymaster of this Brigade, Mr. Goold, is paying off the different regiments. The Brigade is continually receiving recruits.

Later.—5 P.M. Lieut. Gen. Grant and staff arrived in Culpepper, in a special train at 1 o'clock. I did not see him as he was followed from the depot to his headquarters by a large crowd of soldiers, citizens and blacks. An old negress said "nobody couldn't git a peep at de ole man—such a crowd—dey all seemed so happy to see de Gen'l it minded her o' de time de good Lord bress her soul!" Being in town about 4 P.M., I saw Gen. Grant and three members of his staff descend from the high stoop in front of the large brick house which he is to occupy, and walking leisurely down the long avenue to the road, enter Gen. Newton's carriage of four horses, when he proceeded on the way to visit the principal officers quartered in town. The General is the plainest of all plain men, stout, or medium, also, light complexion, sandy whiskers well trimmed; no "airs" or "style" in his appearance, not at all handsome, but rather homely. This is my first impression of the veteran who has won a national reputation as the deliverer of the southwest and who comes to Virginia to conduct, if possible, the war to a close successful and honorable to the good of the Union. May he fully succeed, and ere long, too, is the heartfelt wish of this army, who will fight under him with the greatest enthusiasm, while at the same time they feel a deep regard for our devoted President Abraham.

I hope to soon give your readers more particulars of the General's personal movements. He will to-morrow commence a review of the troops, in detail, and receive a hearty welcome.

Friday, 25th.—Pleasant in A.M. Heavy sleet & rain in P.M. & eve. Sick headache & ate no breakfast till late. Hot punch & chicken. {[Sampson W.] Fry's box came last eve. with lots of good things, fluid [whiskey], &c.} At H[ead]q[uarte]rs Made out Weekly report & sealed it. Wrote to L[ieutenan]t [Lewis B.] Courtney & S[hedrick] J. J[ackson], 140th [NYVIRegiment]. The 1st & 5th Corps are to be consolidated with [Major] Gen[eral Gouverneur K.] Warren as commander, all to be called 5th Corps. 1st Brig[ade] to remain as before. Letter from Father, Mother, & H[arvey]. F[ather] sent me [Samuel P.] Chase[195] anti-administration circular which makes me feel disgusted & insulted almost. Read letters after sup[per] of tea, fried cakes & mince pie. Rain all eve. [A. L.] Root today paid me 30c. Games. Letter from [Chauncey] Baker, 4th Wis[consin] Batt[er]y.

Saturday, 26th.—Feel well. Chicken, bologna &c. for break*[fast]*. At office read Gen*[eral]* Orders from War Department. Bo't 1 quire paper 25c. & bunch envelopes 25c. Coffee. Drew soft b*[rea]*d, cof*[fee]* & sug*[ar]* potatoes, beans, ap*[ple]*s, pork, &c. Wrote to Father, Mother & to *[Brockport]* Repub*[lic]*. Sent. Cold wind. Some changes in Brigade—*[Major]* Gen*[eral Benjamin F.]* Butler to command. Bo't flannel shirt of *[Charles W.]* Spaulding & agreed to pay him on next pay day $2. Oysters for supper. Paid 30c for my share At h*[ead]*q*[uarte]*rs in eve. To bed early after reading. Bo't paper 5c.

Brockport Republic, March 31, 1864

March 26—By order of the President, the number of Corps comprising the Army of the Potomac are, in order to be used with more efficiency, reduced to three—2nd, 5th and 8th Corps. The troops of the 1st and 3rd will be temporarily re-organized and distributed in the first named above. The 2 divisions of the 1st Corps are transferred to the 5th Corps, preserving former badges, &c., and on joining that Corps, will be consolidated into 3, the 5th will then consist of 4 divisions, that as well as the 3rd and 6th forming their present *[illegible word]* organization into two divisions each. The 3rd division of 3rd corps is permanently placed in the 6th Corps, which will leave the remaining two divisions of the 3rd to be placed in the 3rd. There will be no material change in this Brigade. This is no doubt the opening of Gen. Grant's programme for the coming vigorous campaign.   J.T.F.

Sunday, 27th.—Pleasant, windy. Oysters for breakfast. *[Sampson W.]* F*[ry]* on picket. At h*[ead]*q*[uarte]*rs, no news. Gave *[Charles W.]* Spaulding due bill, $2. Wrote to Cha*[rle]*s Miller, 108th *[NYVI Regiment]* & Aunt C. Wash, change, & clothes to soak. With J. C*[hauncey]* P*[arker]* walked out on the Sperryville Pike riding part way in jolting army wagon drawn by mules. Stopped at *[Eli]* Barnes' but he could not pay me the $2. Went on to hill where our Reserve S*[harp]* S*[hooter]* boys were picketing. *[Rice H.]* Eaton told me story of an adventure in Wash*[ingto]*n with a young female "waiter boy". Saw *[Sampson W.]* Fry. Pleasant walk. Walked back & went to H*[ead]*q*[uarte]*rs read paper & rec*[eive]*d letter from F*[athe]*r *[Brockport]* Repub*[lic]* of 24th with letter of 17th. Also paper & note from Mother. Gave paper to *[Charles W.]* Spaulding. Hi*[ram]* Williams in q*[uarte]*rs. In eve. Good visit, &c. Read news. We sold bread today to am*[oun]*t of 40c. 1 paper bo't to-night. Sleep alone tonight.

Monday, 28th.—Pleasant, warm, chilly & windy in P.M. Washed clothes. Signed old pay-roll. Wrote letter to Col. *[illegible name]* for *[Levi M.]* LeRoy.

Talk with Col*[onel John C.]* Robinson, who goes back to his Reg*[imen]*t 7th Wis*[consin]*. Brig*[adier]* Gen*[eral]* *[Lysander]* Cutler takes command of Brig*[ade]*. Showed *[Brockport]* Repub*[lic]* to Cap*[tain]* Wood. L*[ieutenan]*t *[D.B.]* Daly, & others. Prospect of staying at H*[ead]*q*[uarte]*rs. Saw Capt*[ain Volney J.]* Shipman, who gave encouragement in regard to Father applying for position of surgeon to the Batt*[alion]* as the First D*[octo]*r is off drunk, discharged. Wrote to Father to come. Rec*[eive]*d Sharps rifle & turned it in, to one of the boys. At H*[ead]*q*[uarte]*rs mail distributed. At quarters, bread & beans. Sold 7 loaves of bread for 50 cts., making 90 cts. for bread from the qu*[arte]*rs. G. Delorme of 24th Mich*[igan]* bid us good by, as he is disch*[arge]*d or sent to Veterans Reserve Corps. To bed early.

Tuesday, 29th.—Up at 5½ o'clock. At H*[ead]*q*[uarte]*rs at 7. Followed Brigade troop 2½ miles to Review by Lieut*[enant]* Gen*[eral Ulysses S.]* Grant & staff & *[Major]* Gen*[eral George G.]* Meade. Also *[Major]* Gen*[eral]* G*[ouverneur]* K. Warren, com*[man]*d*[e]*r of 5th Corps, also Brig*[adier]* Gen*[eral James S.]* Wadsworth, Divis*[ion]*. Rain & wind came on & all dispersed after the Gen*[eral]*s rode by. Good appearance. Talk with D*[octo]*r of 7th Wis*[consin]* now on duty in Batt*[alion]* at H*[ead]*q*[uarte]*rs & took order for picket to Capt*[ain Volney J.]* Ship*[man]*. Dinner of tea, potatos, steak & b*[rea]*d, Boiled beans & apples, Beef & pork. Disagreeable weather. Ale at *[A. L.]* Roots; saw Maj*[or]* Hall of 23rd Colored Reg*[imen]*t. Sup*[per]*. *[Sampson W.]* Fry in from picket. To bed very early.

Wednesday, 30th.—Rain all night, chilly & cold today. At H*[ead]*q*[uarte]*rs made out blanks for monthly Report. Prop*[erty]* Lost or Dest*[royed]*. *[Brevet Major]* Gen*[eral Lysander]* C*[utler]* sewed buttons on his pants. In good humor. Lieut*[enant A. D.]* Rood gave me 25 cts to buy cap paper. Took document to Capt*[ain Volney J.]* S*[hipman]*. Attempted to turn in flask. Could not. Dinner. In P.M. wrote circular for Weekly Report & made out Roster, then wrote circ*[ular]* & sent for Mo*[nthly]* Rep*[ort]* of Prop*[erty]* Lost & Dest*[royed]*. Quite busy. *[illegible word]* & eating.

Thursday, 31st.—At H*[eadquart]*ers.*[?]* Cold & pleasant. Wrote some. Rep*[ort]*s of Prop*[erty]* Lost &c. came in. At q*[uarte]*rs. Wrote letter for 8th Co*[mpany]* man to Co*[lonel Augustus L.]* McCollum. Cleaned gun. Drew rations bread, sug*[ar]* & cof*[fee]* beans & pork. Took documents to H*[ead]*-q*[uarte]*rs for Capt*[ain Volney J.]* S*[hipman]*. *[Edwin]* Franklin gave me a shelter tent which I am to send home. Made out rep*[ort]* consolidated of Prop*[erty]* Lost & Dest*[ro]*y*[e]*d. Busy all P.M. Letter from Mat *[Mary A. C. French]*. Good. Em*[ma Smith]* & Mrs. S*[mith]*. Bo't paper. In eve. read letter & paper & sat by fire light.

April

Context—The battalion was in the 1st Brigade, 4th Division, 5th Corps of the Army of the Potomac from April to August 1864.

Friday, April 1.—Pleasant. Put up things to send home in box. Cleaned canteen. At H[ead]q[uarte]rs wrote to [Brockport] Repub[lic] & at some business. At office, with papers. Rep[ort] of yest[erday] sent back from Div[ision] for slight correction. Some fooling. Reg[imen]t[a]l weekly rep[ort] rec[eive]d re-made. Prop[ert]y report. Rain in P.M. Full of business in eve. Wrote to Mother & Mat [Mary A. C. French]. After buying candle 10c. Received 20 ct. bread money. Up late & mailed or put letters in tea box. Raining in eve. Unpleasant.

Brockport Republic, April 7, 1864

Headq'rs 1st Brig., 1st Div., 1st A.C., Insp. Gen'l's Office., April 2, 1864. Editor Republic—Dear Sir:—The 4th division, 5th corps, comprising one-half the old 1st corps, now commanded by Brig. Gen. Wadsworth,[196] the extensive land owner of Livingston county, N.Y., was reviewed on Tuesday last by Lieut. Gen. Grant, Maj. Gen. Meade and Maj. Gen. G. K. Warren commanding 5th corps, now consolidated with the old 1st. The weather, from a pleasant sunrise, gradually became unpleasant, and by 9 o'clock settled into a light, misty rain, therefore the review was not fully gone through with. The troops made as fine an appearance as could have been expected. Cavalry and artillery in goodly numbers were present, and the noble hills of the review grounds near Culpepper, wore a lively aspect. The white horse of Gen. Warren bore the gallant soldier swiftly about the field, and the silver-haired Wadsworth was a prominent actor, in arranging the line, as column after column arrived.

All being arranged, the Inspecting Generals with staffs appeared. Grant reminded Warren that owing to the coming storm, it would be necessary to hasten the review, and the party proceeded upon their duty. Gen. Grant's fine dark bay horse, full of spirit, made a number of flourishing antics when nearing the drum corps, as though to show how well the illustrious rider could "sit a steed," and finally knowing the guiding principle of his master, "unconditionally surrendered," and behaved gracefully during the remainder of the performance. Grant appeared to better advantage than when he arrived from his official journeying, toll-worn and jaded; and I must be allowed to say that upon a better view he is not so homely as I first thought.—He bears favorable inspection. Hearty cheering was the welcome given him by the Potomac war-scarred veterans.

The recent army changes have, in this brigade, returned to the 7th Wis. Veterans Gen. Robinson who long and successfully commanded the 1st brigade, Brig. Gen. L. Cutler, previously in command of the old 1st division now has charge of this, the so-called "Iron Brigade." He is an officer of previous military experience, and ripe age. His gray and honorable hairs give him a stern, fatherly appearance; he possesses a military bearing, and is systematic in the administration of brigade affairs.

The change of staff officers consists of Lieuts. T. W. Miller, 55th Ohio, and Wm. M. Ransom Aides, Lieut. D. B. Daily, Aide, is acting Provost Marshal of brigade.—Lieut. A. D. Rood, Aide, in absence of Capt. Dillon, home on leave of absence, is acting Brigade Inspector. Nothing new of importance to inform you of in regard to movements. All quiet.

In the 24th Mich. a few days ago, two deaths occurred, one of private Orville Barnes, Co. K, of Livonia, Mich., of fever. The other was a death of rare occurrence. Private Peter Revar, Co. F, of Detroit, aged 22 years, in company with others, became intoxicated the evening before his death and had a "high old time." During the night while sleeping and powerless from the effects of liquor, his stomach refused to hold the filth which had been forced upon it. Lying upon his back, a reaction of his stomach took place, and being unable to turn over, was choked to death in his own vomit, the windpipe being filled.—This of course was the result of intemperance, and according to the statement of Dr. J. H. Beach, Brigade Surgeon, who made a post mortem examination, "it was a most disgusting case." By the way, Dr. Beach was formerly a resident of Gaines, Orleans county, and is a son-in-law of John Perry, Esq., of Clarkson.

In the absence of a more interesting topic, I affix the following from a late paper which may be of value to some of your wide-awake readers. It is a "hint to farmers."

I notice by the Republic of the 24th of March that the benevolent and patriotic ladies of Brockport and vicinity have prepared a box of clothing and necessities for the army of the Potomac. This is truly humane, and shows an appreciation of the labors of Brockport soldiers and a desire to alleviate their sufferings in the field.

A heavy rain swelling the *[illegible words]* and severely chilling the pickets, gives place to quite mild weather, sun and showers

Yours responsibly, J.T.F.

Saturday, 2d.—Mail failed to go & I took letters out & at h*[ead]*q*[uarte]*rs finished letter to Mother & to *[Brockport]* Repub*[lic]*. Talk with Dr. G. W. Beach Chief surg*[eon of the]* Brig*[ade]* & let him have *[Brockport]* Repub*[lic]* of 24th. *[A. L.]* Root sick. Snow storm sleet & rain all day, nearly. At noon, applied to Capt*[ain Volney J.]* Shipman for recommend*[ation]* for permission to go before Board of Examination for officers for Colored troops, which he gave me & it was approved by Capt[ain Joseph S.] Arnold & I wrote application to Maj[or]. Foster & mailed both, after calling on Dr. B[each] & having pleasant visit. Copied order for clerk. Borrowed Caseys Tactics[197] Vol. 1 of clerk & studied in eve. Mended pants.

Sunday, 3d.—Pleasant, windy. Changed clothes, &c. & read regulations. Saw [A. L.] Root stutter at noon coffee at q[uarte]rs. Laid down & read. H[ead]-q[uarte]rs rec[eive]d [Brockport] Repub[lic] with letter of 24th. Sent paper to John Devereaux, Evansville, Rock Co[unt]y, Wis[consin]. Talked with Bushe about mail carrying. Read in eve., & saw Geo[rge] Goold who is going to Wash[ington] before Colored Board in morning. Sent paper to Mat [Mary A. C. French].

Monday, 4th.—Snow & rain from 12 M[eridian (noon)] & in eve. At H[ead]-q[uarte]rs late & smoke filled room (office) Called on Dr. [G. W.] B[each] & pleasant conv[ersation], left paper at q[uarte]rs. Borrowed "Co[mpany] Clerk" of [Delos] Howe also Atlas & studied. Late in P.M. again at office & read Tactics. Letter dated 1st from Father in ans[wer] to mine of a week today, in regard to surg[eon] com[mission], unfavorably, also anti-Lincoln document. Consulted with Dr. [G. W.] B[each], favorably & in eve. wrote to Father urgently & returned anti-Lincoln document by request. Disagreeable evening. Sleet. Dr. Beach gave me paper back.

Tuesday, 5th.—Rain all day. Poor fire & wet wood. At Serg[ean]t [Delos] Howes q[uarte]rs awhile. Rec[eive]d a document from Capt[ain Volney J.] Shipman, printed pamphlet. At H[ead]q[uarte]rs at 11. Read all day. Co[mpany]. Clerk & Tactics. Officers in office. Letter from Serg[ean]t [Andrew] Boyd & L[ieutenan]t [Lewis B.] Courtney. Carried wood & good supper. At Howe's tent in eve. To bed early.

Wednesday, 6th.—Rain all night, but stopped at 9 A.M. High wind. Cold & chilly. Indian bread for breakfast. Drew sug[ar] & coffee & pork. At H[ead]q[uarte]rs read Tac[tic]s. Carried pass to [Timothy H.] Babbitt 8th Co[mpany]. Let L[ieutenan]t take pen. Wrote to Sanitary Christian Commission, Warrenton, Va., for the purpose of finding out some facts in regard to C[harles]'s burial there. Sun shines. Capt. Wood is a "brick" so is L[ieutenan]t [A. L.] Root, joking & telling lively stories. No mail for me. Bo't paper, 5c. Sup[per] & a little of everything in eve.

Thursday, 7th.—Fine summer day. Calm. Washed clothes. At H[ead]q[uarte]rs & read Roch[ester] Dem[ocrat]. Sent Weekly circular. Horse race at

Stevensburg. Back to q*[uarte]*rs & shaved. Bread & butter. Walk—pleasant, to Culpepper, roads getting dry. Fascinating young ladies on st*[reet]*. Called on Corp*[oral]* Phil*[ip]* Brennan 14th Brooklyn Bo't paper, foolscap 25 cts. At depot saw train come in. Walked back. Letter from Mother & sister & paper from Aunt. *[illegible word]* from Mother also neck tie. Wrote to sister in eve.

Friday, 8th.—Another fine day. Weekly Reports from Reg*[imen]*ts came in. Capt*[ain R. S.]* Dillon returned. Finished one Weekly Report in eve.

Saturday, 9th.—Rain steady from 1 A.M., all day & till about 12 P.M. At office. Permit from War Dep*[artmen]*t to appear before the Colored Board for Ex*[amination]* of men for com*[missions]* in Col*[ore]*d Reg*[imen]*ts came. Also for Serg*[ean]*t *[Delos]* Howe. Finished Weekly Report & sent circular for Rep*[ort]* of Darf. *[Deficit?]* In arms & Accout*[rements]* Wrote to Lieut*[enant]* *[Lewis B.]* Courtney. Sent papers to Mat *[Mary A. C. French]*. Father & *[Brockport]* Repub*[lic]*. Made out another Report of Defic*[it]*s. Read Tactics in eve. Letter from Aunt C. Still rain. *[Sampson W.]* Fry on picket. Drew bread.

Sunday, 10th.—Bright sun & warm—lovely. At H*[ead]*q*[uarte]*rs early. Aired blankets, &c. walked to camp 6th Wis*[consin]* & S*[harp]* S*[hooters]* for reports. Lively at H*[ea]*dq*[uarte]*rs. Birds singing. Expected ride horseback. Did not. Drew cav*[alry]* pants, $3.55. Rain at sundown.

Monday, 11th.—Pleasant & warm. Boxed up rifle, belt, canteen, carb*[on]*. boxes, telescope, shirt, &c, & sent to Washington with things of *[Sampson W.]* Fry & the other boys. At H*[ea]*dq*[uarte]*rs. Wrote Mem*[oir]* Of Regulations all day, nearly for Capt*[ain R. S.]* Dillon. Borrowed Tactics of Capt*[ain]* Arnold. Am getting bad cold. Drew pair of shoes of L*[ieutenan]*t *[Alphonso W.]* Starkw*[eather]*. Studied Tac*[tic]*s late in eve.

Tuesday, 12th. Quite pleasant all P.M. Chilly sprinkle. Windy. Finished writing & blanks for Capt*[ain R. S.]* Dillon. Most sick with a cold. Full of business. Letter from Moth*[er]* Sis*[ter]* Lon. Mat.*[Mary A. C. French]* F*[athe]*r & *[Brockport]* Republic. At work in P.M. Read in eve. & sent paper to F*[athe]*r. Also sent or forwarded letter to *[Albert S.]* Knowles Sig*[nal]* Corps. Saw L*[ieutenan]*t *[Philip]* Hysner.

Wednesday, 13th.—Some writing at office in A.M. Pleasant day. Gen*[era]*l Wash at *[illegible word]*. Wrote to Mat *[Mary A. C. French]* *[illegible word]* permission to ride L*[ieutenan]*t Dillon's *[Daly?]* horse. Wrote circular for Capt*[ain R. S.]* Dillon. Rode on saddle first time in my life, on pike, 2½ miles, to Reserve R*[o]*ckets & return. Like riding. Not natural. Saw Barney

[Eli Barnes], who promised to get me the $2 he owes me. Spoke for position for W*[illia]*m Price to L*[ieutenan]*t McDonald. Officers having a gay time—tight. Cap*[tain]* W. unable to get to H*[ead]*q*[uarte]*rs, &c. Medicine for cough of Dr. *[G. W.]* B*[each]*. Saw Benton Little who just returned & is to have Lieut*[enant]*'s commission in colored reg*[imen]*t & who gave me information. Studied in eve.

Thursday, 14th.—Quite pleasant. At H*[ea]*dq*[uarte]*rs. Wrote circ*[ular]* Weekly & forms for Roster. At H*[ea]*dq*[uarte]*rs Co*[mpany]* Q*[uarte]*rs was examined by Tuttle & concluded my chances are slim. Back to H*[ea]*dq*[uarte]*rs & wrote roster of Brig*[ade]* H*[ea]*dq*[uarte]*rs Officers, & to Bro*[ther]* Alonzo. The clerks Woods & Stillon agreed to write for Capt*[ain R. S.]* D*[illon]* in my absence. Do not feel well. Sutler goods confiscated for selling liquor to privates. Cloudy, but mild. Last night at 12 o'c*[loc]*k some 8th N.Y. Cav*[alry]* came & yelled to us as they were on their way to capture reb signal station. Lieut*[enant]* Ransom Acting A*[ssistant]* A*[djutant]* G*[eneral]* to-day. I at work quite late. Permission to go to Washington. Papers signed & got ready to go.

Friday, 15th.—Fine day. Up & packed knapsack. Break*[fast]* with *[Daniel B.]* Gallatin of 8th Co*[mpany]*. NY S*[harp]* S*[hooters]* started for Culpepper. Left knap*[sack]* & haversack at H*[ea]*dq*[uarte]*rs of Brigade. Took watch for Stillson to be repaired with $2.95 for expenses. At depot, papers marked by Prov*[ost]* Marshal & in 5 min*[ute]*s started on. Soldier of 2nd Penn*[sylvania]* Cav*[alry]* left arm amputated below elbow & suffering from pleurisy. Gave him my overcoat & attended to him. At Warrenton Junction saw L*[ieutenan]*t *[Lewis B.]* Courtney & S*[hedrick]* J. J*[ackson]*. Latter gave me photograph. Also saw others drilling in distance. Saw *[Lieutenant]* Gen*[eral Ulysses S.]* Grant on passing train & at Alexandria saw *[Charles]* Collamer & *[William J.]* Noble at working machine shop. At Washington 2:30. Stopped at Sanitary "Home" 374 N*[orth]* Capitol St. Washed after having name taken by sup*[erintenden]*t. Left overcoat & on st*[reet]* cars rode to 14th s*[reet]*. Bo't 3 collars 15c. Walked over 1 mile to Cliffburne Barracks, saw Mr. *[William]* Hues, Clark*[e R. Baker]* & others but did not find S. S. Lewis. Back by car, 5c. Left watch at 384 P Av. To be repaired. To theatre 50c Ford's, saw Forrest play "Febro, the Broker of Bogota".[198] Very good. Met friend Ord*[erly]* Serg*[ean]*t 9th N.Y. M*[ilitia]*. Previously saw 2 young ladies nearly run over by hack "afraid it would run onto her". Laughable. With my friend of 9th I found good bed quilt, & torn sheets. Found good rest.

Saturday, April 16th.—Rain all day. Up & good wash & good breakfast at 7 cof*[fee]* cold beef & bread. Boys discussing tactics. Vote taken for preference for President. Total 30. A*[braham]* Lincoln 27, *[George C.]* McClellan 3. About

9 A.M. went to War Dep*[artmen]*t, saw *[Samuel E.]* Carrington in A*[djutant]*
G*[eneral]* Dep*[artmen]*t, formerly of 8th Co*[mpany]*. NYS*[harp]* S*[hooters]*.
At P.O. sent paper home, 8 cts. Bo't candy & pies & oranges, 3 for 10 cts. At
[Washington] Chronicle Office set 9 lines *[of type]*. Brevier & disk. Found that
men were detailed to work at Gov*[ernmen]*t Pr*[inting]* Office. Saw local editor
[Washington]Chronicle who is very pleasant man & gave me information. At
dinner potato, roast beef, onions & rice. In P.M. on st*[reet]* car, rode to White
House, but Pres*[ident]* was not in reception order. Shown into Recep*[tion]*
Room. Splendidly furnished. Got watch at jewelers & paid $3 for having it
cleaned & crystal. At Capitol, in Rep*[resentatives]* chamber. A long & tedious
National Bank bill was being read for ½ hour. A bee-hive. Very dull. A citizen
pointed out to me the infamous traitor *[Alexander]* Long[199] of Ohio sending
documents *[Benjamin Gwinn]* Harris of M*[arylan]*d.,[200] Fernando Wood,[201]
N*[ew]*Y*[ork]* city, also James Brooks[202] of same & Madden[203] of K*[entuck]*y.
Attempt to adjourn & left at 5. Sup*[per]*. With *[Daniel B.]* Gallatin called
on *[Samuel E.]* Carrington at 512 G. St. & rec*[eive]*d encouragement in
regard to Gov*[ernmen]*t Pr*[inting]* Of*[fice]*. Ladies & gents in parlor. Walked
down st*[reet]*. with *[Samuel E.]* Car*[rington]* & brother to Metropolitan. To
"Home", then to Express Of*[fice]*. Found *[house]* no. of Rep*[resentative]*
Freeman Clarke, Roch*[ester's]* 28th Cong*[ressional]* Dist*[rict]*. Took car to
13th st*[reet]*, walked up 13th st*[reet]* to K & on corner brown house rang
bell, & was met by the Hon*[orable]* Freeman Clarke who invited me in &
promised to get me detached if possible. Walked down st*[reet]* with me. Went
to "Home", where boys were busily talking & writing. Wrote some in diary &
to bed early. Rain.

Sunday, 17th.—Quite pleasant. Up early. Lost letter of Mr. H*[oratio]* N.Beach.
Busy talking & writing last eve. I called at *[Washington]* Chron*[icle]* of*[fice]*
& gave them the vote Pres*[ident]* item, which appeared in the *[Washington]*
Chron*[icle]* this A.M. Bo't copy. A commissary serg*[ean]*t threw cover of sugar
bowl at head of colored boy at table this morning., hurting him, for which he
was reprimanded & sent away. Walked to capitol & saw Capt*[ain Franklin
D.]* Edwards & brother 22nd N.Y. Cav*[alry Regiment]*. At 1st Pres*[byterian]*
Church, 4½ st*[reet]* Rev*[erend]* Sunderland, chaplain of Senate, who only
spoke a few words. Massachusetts Reverend preached from Ex*[odus]* 31:1.
Very good. In gallery saw *[Samuel E.]* Carrington. Fine dinner beef, hash,
pota*[to]*, beef gravy & apples. Late to dinner & had fun with girls. Two boys
14 y*[ea]*rs came in to dinner from 2nd Massachusetts Cavalry. One with
serg*[ean]*ts stripes & saber had been taken pris*[oner]* & let go, horse taken.
The other had taken sabre from wounded rebel. Smart boys & both had
been out as officers serv*[an]*ts 2 years. Serg*[ean]*t Chambers Morgan, Boston,
Mass., John Lane, Philadelphia. In office saw Walter F. Halleck, formerly of

11th Mich*[igan]*, Co*[mpany]* I wounded in face twice left eye put out & shot in left shoulder, formerly in reb*[el]* army, but now 2nd Lieut*[enant]* Inv*[alid]* Corps & going to S*[outh]* W*[est]* army as union spy. Interesting & sharp. Walked about the town, met *[Samuel E.]* Carrington. Stepped into a hole & hurt my hand. At Depot saw Corp*[oral]* *[blank space]* Inv*[alid]* Corps feeding soldiers at Soldiers Rest.[204] Soldiers coming & going to the front rapidly. At sup*[per]* talk with Husted & in eve. went with him on walk about st*[reet]* in moonlight. Many on walk. At store (stores open) bo't peanuts 10c. Back & to bed early.

Monday, 18th.—Lovely day. Feel well. Sent paper to Mat *[Mary A. C. French]*. Saw pictures of Husted's. To 212 F. st*[reet]* reported & rec*[eive]*d leave to report daily until examined. Serg*[ean]*t *[Delos]* Howe ex*[amined]* & rejected, also 5 others examined & only 1 recommended 1st class 1st L*[ieutenan]*t. At War Department saw Maj*[or]* Breck who said no soldiers were detailed to work in Gov*[ernmen]*t office. I went to Gov*[ernmen]*t office in brick near capitol. No consolation. Citizen printers get $3 a day. At dinner. In P.M. visited photograph establishments & bo't 4 fine pictures. At War Dep*[artmen]*t & Pr*[inting]* Off*[ice]* & told to call at 9 A.M. Good news. (warm day) Sup*[per]*. Saw 10th N.J. Vol*[unteer]*s, recruited nearly full on way to front. To theatre with several boys, crowded house. Heard Forrest play Hamlet. Very good & expressive of human nature. Out at 12. Glad to get in bed. Fine moonlight.

Tuesday, 19th.—Fine day. Up early. Wrote to Capt*[ain R. S.]* Dillon & sent by Serg*[ean]*t *[Delos]* Howe. Reported at *[Major]* Gen*[eral Silas]* Casey's Headq*[uarte]*rs & put off until tomorrow. Saw *[Samuel E.]* Carrington at War Dep*[artmen]*t Pr*[inting]* Off*[ice]* & was promised satisfactorily. Left my name & address. At *[Samuel E.]* Carrington who promised to assist me. Bo't Bryant Poems[205] for Sister, $1 sent to her by mail 12 cts. At home, wrote to Mat *[Mary A. C. Fren ch]* & sent photos. At House, in lobby, interview with Representative Freeman Clarke, 28th Dist*[rict]* N*[ew]*Y*[ork]* after sending in card to him. Gave him my name & he agreed to attend to my detachment to work in War Pr*[inting]* Off*[ice]*. In P.M. visited Senate chamber. Heard *[Charles]* Sumner[206] appeal for repeal of Fugitive Slave bill. Sen*[a]*t*[or]* Sem *[sp?]*[207]*[not in Biographical Directory]* spoke. Quite interesting. In eve. went to last reception by Pres*[iden]*t Lincoln. Immense crowd & was nearly crushed. Shook hands with Abraham, who seemed careworn & tired, hand clammy. Mrs. L*[incoln]* (short) looked lovely & young with low-necked dress (Whew!) Many officers in the finely furnished rooms of the White House. Squeezed out at 9. "Home" & to bed in moonlight.

"Octoroon." Washington.

Wednesday, 20th.—Breakfast. Fine day. Bo't collar 5c. Reported at *[Major]* Gen*[eral Silas]*. Casey's at 8½. Expected to be examined. Was not. Staid from 8½ till 1. 10 exam*[ined]*. 3 rejected. At dinner. Talk with Nellie Fulton, & Mrs. Murray had my handkerchiefs washed nicely. At Senate floor, in lobby. Found old man Jones & went with him in st*[reet]* cars to Sanitary House to see about his pay. 2 dist*[inguished]* young ladies in car. Orange & porter. In eve. became acquainted with young Cheney, Conn*[ecticut]* Vol*[unteer]*s & rode to White House. Back to "Home", to Grovers Theatre & in alley saw the "Octoroon"[208] well played. Staid at hotel with Cheney. Disappointed in the "room".

Thursday, 21st.—Sunny & pleasant. Break*[fast]* at "Home" at 6 A.M. Sent letter to *[Lieutenant Lewis B.]* Courtney by *[Daniel B.]* Gallatin, 2nd Lieut*[enant]* in colored Reg*[imen]*t. Yellow wench on st*[reet]* with broom from Baltimore. Secesh cripples. At *[Major General Silas]* Casey's examined 15 minutes by Gen*[eral]* Casey & a Col*[onel]* & ex*[amined]* by D*[octo]*r. Unfavorable on tactics. No prospect as I expected. In P.M. went with Old Man Jones to assist him in getting pension & succeeded. Back to depot. J*[ones]* gave me 25c. On Capitol grounds sat on seat, people passing. At supper. After sup*[per]* walked with one of the boys & promenaded afterwards to "Capitol Steps", 20c. *[Arthur]* Johnson of 8th Co*[mpany]* S*[harp]* S*[hooters]* gave me bundles to send to Capt*[tain Volney J.]* S*[hipman]* & *[Lieutenant Alphonso W.]* Starkweather & $3.75 balance due to Capt*[ain]* Shipman. Fine moonlight & had good time. To bed at "*[Soldiers]* Home" at 10.

Friday, 22d.—Splendid day. Up before 6. Got transportation at office. Took saddle cloth for Capt*[ain Volney J.]* Shipman. St*[reet]* car to 15th St*[reet]*. At *[Major General Silas]* Casey's office found I had been rejected. Bid the boys good by. At War Dep*[artmen]*t saw *[Samuel E.]* Carrington & car to 10th st*[reet]* through the Smithsonian Institute grounds to depot in hurry. Almost begged before I could get on the crowded train. Rough road. Drunk veterans. Bo't paper. Before leaving Wash*[ington]* wrote & mailed letter to Mother. At Warrenton Junction & stopped with S*[hedrick]* *[J.]* J*[ackson]*. Good dinner & good time with the boys. To R.R. 1 mile saw L*[ieutenan]*t *[Lewis B.]* Courtney & had talk with him. Back at Charley Taylor's q*[uarte]*rs. Staid with Lon Morehouse, Hosp*[ital]* Steward, in good bed.

At Warrenton Junction

Saturday, 23rd.—Windy, mild, pleasant. Good rest. Break*[fast]* with S*[hedrick J.]* J*[ackson]*. Ham. Visit with boys. In Capt*[ain August]* Meyer's q*[uarte]*rs.

With L[ieutenan]t [Lewis B. Courtney intr[oduced] to L[ieutenan]t Buckley & Capt[ain] McMullen. Having a good time. Walk with Cou[r]t[ney] to depot & got transportation. S[hedrick J.] J[ackson] there. Saw Maj[or Milo] Starks. Left at 1½ P.M. after eating roast beef & rice at Serg[ean]t Cha[rle]s Taylors. Good cars to ride in. Sent paper to Father this A.M. Pleasant ride. At Culpepper 4 o'clock. Walked to Brig[ade] H[ea]dq[uarte]rs & reported. Gave Stillson his watch & rec[eive]d change due. Found letter from Father & Mother & Mat [Mary A. C. French] with paper of Texas & paper from Father. Letter from Nell & from S[ister]. Also letter stating that the Christian Commission Warrenton[209] had found my brother's grave & that I could get the body, tho' now our forces have abandoned Warrenton. Also rec[eive]d shirt from mother. Have Capt[ain Volney J.] Shipman saddle cloth & $3 & owe him 70 cts. Took haversack & knap[sack]. To co[mpany] Q[uarte]rs. Supper. Pop corn from Frank [Francis R. Douglas]. Saw Capt[ain R. S.] Dillon & officers at H[ea]dq[uarte]rs. Expect marching orders. To bed at 10, tired, & with bad cold.

Sunday, 24th.—Windy & sun. Up & break[fast]. Called on Dr. Beach, & got cough medicine of him. At H[ea]dq[uarte]rs ruled blanks all A.M. Wrote to Father & Aunt C. Sent letter from U.S. Christian Commission in regard Bro[ther] C[harles]'s grave to Father. Can hardly talk aloud. Hoarse. Nap at q[uarte]rs. Supper. Letter from Mother & sister. Also [Brockport] Repub[lic]. Wrote letter for Dort & letter to Mat [Mary A. C. French]. Diarrhea.

Monday, April 25th.—Windy. Mild & sunny. Washed 12 pieces, shirts, &c. At Brig[ade] H[ea]dq[uarte]s at work most all day. Wrote to Nell S. Have papers pretty well arranged. Wrote for S[ampson] W. F[ry]. Feel tired. Almost as hoarse as yesterday. Not at q[uarte]rs. Drew bread, sug[ar], cof[fee] beans, work. Read in eve. To bed early.

Tuesday, 26th.—Cool. Pleasant. Made blanks. Contrabands & whites coming into our lines.--Wrote to Mrs. & Em[ma] S[mith]. Nap in P.M. At Culpepper with [Sampson W.] Fry, who is waiting for ex[amination] to go to Philadelphia Free Military School.[210] Permit to pass on march with troops or train with out arms, signed by [Major] Gen[eral Lysander] Cutler. In eve. read. Visited some of the boys in 8th Co[mpany].

Wednesday, 27th.—Feel better to-day. Quite warm & summer like. No business in office. Wrote [Brockport] Republic. Game of ball with boys. Knocked out every time. Paper of Dr. B[each] & showed him photographs. Troops drilling & men at work on fortification. Warm. Hot. In eve. visited with Serg[ean]t [Delos] How[e] & Geo[rge] Goold.

Brockport Republic, May 5, 1864

Headq'rs 1st Brig., 4th Div., 5th A. C., Insp. Gen'l's Office, April 28th 1864. Editor Republic: Dear Sir:—Very *important* information at present would be contraband, and it is made so justly; for a premature disclosure has often been fatal to the accomplishment of well-laid plans. However, I will venture to give you a sort of idea of our condition and affairs. It is well known outside of the army that all preparations are being made for an active campaign. Recruits have for a long time been reinforcing our army and still come. Among others, yesterday twenty wild Indians, of the Chippewa tribe, from the far west, joined the 7th Wisconsin Vols. Army supplies with ammunition are piled at no great distance from us, which will supply the forces for a long time. Extensive fortifications are being thrown up in the vicinity of Culpepper, and there will be no more falling back to Centerville as in times past. Gen. Grant evidently proposes to work cautiously, and made sure of every step. All civilians not belonging here, are now away, and Culpepper looks quite deserted. Squads of rebel citizens and deserters, with contrabands, come in daily, and the number of these will increase as the weather grows warmer.

By the way, the temperature is quite like summer, with strong and purifying winds. Roads are becoming dry and in good condition. The fresh green grass is refreshing to look upon, and trees are bursting forth their leaves, while flowers are in blossom. The sultry summer days will soon be with us and war, with crimson dye, will redden many a turf spot with the blood of noble heroes. Music of shot and shell, and musketry, will din the air, and many a bullet will do its mortal work. And then, will treason totter on its throne! We wait to see, while at the North you anxiously await the news that tells the task of blood—of victory that must come to us at last.

During a week in Washington, recently on business, I found the military city bustling with activity. Regiments of troops, many being veterans, just from home, after an enlistment, passed through the streets, bands of music at their head, with no loss of that martial ardor than they felt three years ago, when first they came to glory. To how many was that look at the noble capitol their last one? How many will again return?

Washington is very lively with soldiers, officers, and gaily dressed citizens. The numerous street cars are crowded, theatres jammed full from floor to gallery. Ed. Forrest the distinguished actor, has an engagement there, and of course draws well. Amusements are plenty. In the afternoon, if pleasant, the rush of silked and satined youth and beauty parade the Avenue, and seek the pleasnt walks of the Smithsonian Institute and capitol grounds.

At the House nothing of extraordinary importance was going on, and treason slept quietly. It has the appearance rather of a bee-hive, as one looks down from the gallery. "Our Member," the Hon. Freeman Clarke, of Rochester, glasses in hand, was attentively listening to the debate. He has an influence in the House, and is much respected there. To the latter gentleman I am under obligation for personal favors, &c., while in W[ashington]. The air of quiet in the Senate chamber is remarkable, in contrast to the dizzy rush of House affairs. Chas. Sumner, of Mass., the "lion" of Chamber, with perfect self-control, made eloquent and earnest appeals for the blotting out of the Fugitive Slave bill from the Statute book. He is truly a lover and honest advocate of liberty to all. Reverdy Johnson,[211] able and venerable, of Maryland spoke upon the same subject.—Other notables were there, among others, ex-Gov. Morgan,[212] of good appearance, sat near Mr. Sumner, Judge Harris,[213], tall, grave and stately, cannot be compounded in appearance with any other Senator, and with Mr. Morgan was looking earnestly at some important article in a New York journal.

At the President's last reception of the season, which I had the pleasure (but not comfort) of attending, the jam of people by the thousand was so great that ribs and crinolines were terribly compressed—indeed it was an awful crowd, only equaled by the anxious crowd at Rochester, in 1861, when Uncle Abe passed on his way to the presidency.—Once inside the door, each one in turn grasped the hand of Abraham, weary and weak, apparently from so long standing, and this was evident from the coldness of his hand as he grasped so lightly one's palm, and said, in welcome to all, "How do you do, sir!' The President looked as smiling as possible during the tedious performance. Lady Lincoln, dressed in white satin, low-necked, (!) with fan in hand, looked quite charming for a matron, as she conversed with a naval officer on one side and a military officer upon the other, just in the rear of her husband. A young Lincoln sat upon a couch, wearing a major's belt.— While reflecting upon Abraham's weariness, I wondered why Lady L. did not think to "relieve" him for a while, and was sure the visitors would have been pleased with the change. The drawing rooms, richly furnished, were thronged with promenaders. The principal exit was made from a window to the stoop in front, as the crowd continued to be great. How romantic— leaving the White House by a window.

On my return, I visited the 140th N.Y at Warrenton Junction, where now in the same corps with the sharpshooters. I found them all prospering, still prepared for a move.

At present there is quite a rush of soldiers for examination before Gen. Casey's Board for commissions in Colored Regiments. Many have the advantage of going to the Free Military School at Philadephia. Among others, three of the Sharpshooters have lately been recommended for and will soon receive commissions in the colored service, viz., private Benton Tuttle, of —, and George N. Goold, of Carlton, N.Y. in the 6th Co.; the former as 1st Lieut., the latter as 2nd Lieut. also Ketchell of the 8th Co., 1st Lieut., now on duty with his regiment. J.T.F.

Thursday, 28th.—Windy, cool, pleasant. Feel chilly & cold to-day; overcoat on. Hay at cav[alry] camp to fix bed with a blanket stuff. Nap. Coffee & bread for dinner. Sent circular for W[ee]kly Report. Read papers. At H[ea]dq[uarte]rs no mail for me. Sent paper to Mat [Mary A. C. French]. Had requisition so fixed that I may draw my rations at H[ea]dq[uarte]rs after May 1. Pleasant eve.

Friday, 29th.—Pleasant. After light breakfast found canteen at cav[alry] camp & rinsed it. At H[ead]q[uarte]rs made blanks, for W[eek]ly Report & during day made it out. Bean soup for dinner. Cha[rle]s Spaulding paid me 10c lent him. In P.M. sent Report to Division & did other business. Letter from Mother & Harvey & answered it. Spat with J. [Chauncey] P[arker] in eve. To bed quite early. Warm. Heard of death of Chauncey Baker of 4th Wis[consin] Battery.

Saturday, 30th.—Muster day. At H[ea]dq[uarte]rs made out Report of Enlisted Men, Servants & Property Inspected. Also Roster & issued circular for Prop[erty] Lost or Dest[royed]. Called at 7th Wis[consin] & Capt[ain Volney J.] Shipman , Charley Miller 10th Amb[ulance] Corps visited me, & satisfied me that he & Truman [Miller] did all they could for Bro[ther] Cha[rle]s.—I felt quite badly that a report to the contrary had gone out. There must have been some mistake. I think the D[octo]r was to blame, & careless. Hardly think Bro[ther] C[harles]'s grave was disturbed. Dark & rainy in P.M. Drew rations of sugar at H[ea]dq[uarte]rs for 5 days. Copied orders. Wrote to [Samuel E.] Carrington, Washington. Made arrangements for horse to-morrow. Rec[eive]d copy of order to report to H[ea]dq[uarte]rs in March [May?], 7th. In bed early.

May

Tuesday [?], May 1st.—Breakfast of beans. Fixed up, took haversack to H[ea]dq[uarte]rs where I am to mess with clerks who have a cook furnished. Boy Jim colored got Lieut[enant] Ransom's horse for me & I borrowed Stillson's gloves of him, having [Sampson W.] Fry's revolver, & at 7½ mounted & rode through Culpepper on a very good horse, tho' a little stiff. From dark & cloudy the weather changed & the sun shone out finely & the country looked lovely in her spring array, leaves bursting forth, grass springing up, & blossoms out. As I rode along the many camps across the country & struck the Stevensburg pike at the foot of Pony Mountain, I could not help feeling a pleasant sensation such as in the country at home I have often felt in the field at bursting spring time. P[ony] Mountain looked rich & inviting to the eye. At a short distance from the few old houses called Stevensburg, I found the camp of the 8th N.Y. Cav[alry], & saw Orderly Mort Reed,[214] busy with pay-rolls. Heavy force of cavalry. Further on found ambulance train of the 2nd Corps in line, & saw Charley & Truman Miller, who drive teams. Saw Maj[or] Gen[eral Winfield S.] Hancock, who inspected the train. He looks stern. After 12 M[eridian (noon)] went to the boys' q[uarte]rs. Fed horse & self & getting pass, went with Ch[arles] M[iller] to 8th [N.Y.] Cav[alry Regiment] left overcoat with Mort [Read], & pleasant ride on by pickets, to Stony Mountain, camp of 108th NYV[I Regiment]. Tied horse. Found friend A[ndrew] Boyd, Ord[erly] Serg[ean]t Co[mpany] H & good visit with him & Serg[ean]t King & with them went to top of Stony Mountain where is a signal station—very sightly; saw rebs across Rapidan, near Morton's Ford walking; also rifle pits in extent as far as eye could reach, well fortified; reb wagon train in distance; fine country beyond. Took letter for Haley to Tuttle. Well pleased with visit, & rode back to 8th [NY] Cav[alry] with C[harles] M[iller]. Warm, like summer. Saw Mort's pictures, &c. then on slowly, to return. Enjoyed the varied scenery by sunset & arrived back safely at sundown, having passed one of the most pleasant of my Army days. Quite sore from riding at least 16 miles in saddle. Found letter from Father & Mother with 8 3 ct stamps & a paper from Mat [Mary A. C. French]. At Co[mpany] Q[uarte]rs. Gave letter to Tuttle. Drank coffee. To bed early, after short "spat" with J. C[hauncey] P[arker].

Monday, 2nd.—High wind & warm. Up & to H[ea]dq[uarte]rs, swept & first breakfast at Clerks' mess cof[fee] & pork. Made out Report of Prop[ert]y Lost & Destroyed, for April to be sent May 10th. Dinner of b[rea]d cof[fee] & pork. Drew 2 days' sug[ar]. Wrote to Father & Mat [Mary A. C. French] in eve. Down to Co[mpany] & to rest. Letter from Mat [Mary A. C. French].

Tuesday, 3rd.—Quiet in A.M. Lively in P.M. Pleasant but cold heavy wind. At H[ea]dq[uarte]rs most of day, reading, signed Clothing Book for pants & shoes drawn on April 10, but there was 90 cts. that I refused to sign for as I had drawn no drawers this year. Saw the Q[uarter]M[aster] about it. At night packed up my things & took them to H[ea]dq[uarte]rs & packed tack cof[fee] sug[ar] & pork in haversack. All ready to move. Orders to that effect & we may fight tomorrow. May victory be ours. To bed at 10 at h[ea]dq[uarte]rs prepared, I hope & trust for the coming strife.

Wednesday, 4th.—Could get no sleep. At 12 A.M. midnight, up, & ready for move. At Co[mpany] Q[uarte]rs got my tent of [Sampson W.] Fry. My knap[sack] in wagon; followed it ½ mile, stopped, rested on stoop floor while officers were drinking inside. An hour, up & off a mile, stop by fire an hour waiting for Division train. At 3½ started & went round through Culpepper, 1½ m[ile] from starting point, & at daylight the train was on the road near R.R. & went to Brandy Station. 5th Corps near us. Saw 2 140th [NYVI Regiment] boys. 6th Corps passing with heavy artillery force, cav[alry] & inf[antry]. Rested 2 hours, ate from haversack & on, halting often, in dusk to Stevensburg, slept an hour on ground. On hill near Stevensburg at 2 P.M. wrote this. Deserted camp; fine day. Quite tired. While staying with [Henry H.] Wood who is unwell, the train went on [First day's fight] and left me, I left W[ood] though hated to. Caught train of 6 Corps & went sev[era]l miles before finding the 1st Div[ision], where they had parked not far from Ely's ford, Rapidan. Found coffee. Am very tired. Fixed blanket on ground & with Stillson slept till 12. Starry. Reported that our troops today crossed the Rapidan, without opposition.

Context—The battalion fought in the Battle of the Wilderness, May 5–7, and lost seven enlisted men killed or died of wounds 22 enlisted men wounded, and six enlisted men missing.

Thursday, 5th.—Up at 12. Mules fed & I slept till 1. Coffee. Started a few rods, halted till sunrise by a fire & slept on bare ground [Lee falls back.] with overcoat. After sunrise had cof[fee] pork, & soft b[rea]d by our cook Jim. [Henry H.] Wood came on. Train blocked at mudhole. We wait. Immense trains. Feel refreshed. About 9 o'c[lock] we went 2 miles, to Mine Ford, crossed Rapidan on pontoon & on hill in orchard, where rebs were yesterday, near a gold mill & close to cave where gold dust has been dug & mine worked. Saw man there who had worked on place 16 years. Very warm. Dinner & nap. At mill & house & in yard, in shade lay down & rested. Thought of summer at home while in the pleasant [Second days fight] yard where flower shrubs were plenty. Saw a great distance from the elevated Wyckoff yard. Black woman cooking in kitchen hoped we'd go to Richmond, sure this time. Picked up several pieces of quartz apparent containing gold. Heard heavy musketry firing & occasionally cannonading, 5 miles out—part of 5th Corps engaged; 1st & 4th Divisions; [Brevet Major] Gen[eral Alexander] Hays mortally wounded. Many reports. Several officers killed & wounded. 1st & 4th Div[ision]s of 5th Corps fell back 1 mile & were sup[ported]. by 6th Corps. At 5 o'clock train we went over 1 mile to front, passing gold mills which had been commenced on a large scale. Many holes had been dug.—on the [Vanchie Gold Mine]. we had alarm, & thought the guerillas were coming on, & for a few moments there was a stampede of guards & rear with arms, but it was a false alarm 14th Brooklyn Lon [Morehouse]'s} the guards being wanted in rear. We parked on a fine hill, in open ground, in plain sound of firing. Got rails & built fire.—

Had supper. Heavy musketry & saw flashes. Fixed blankets on ground chilly night & slept at 9 will till.

Friday, 6th.—Lovely day. Up at daylight. Breakfast & cannon opened with musk*[etr]*y. Had wash in brook. No excitement; can plainly hear guns. [Third day's fight] Good day for fight. We are in a fine country. Feel first rate to-day. At a house on Flandin Farm, now occupied by Mr. Bullard, a Virginian, with 6 daughters, a fine family. Guard about the house. Talked with Mr. B*[ullard]* & another. Any am*[oun]*t of reports, flying. Hot day. Ice found & used for wounded. Duck for dinner. Heavy firing & charging. Heard girl singing "When this cruel war is over".[215] Sup*[per]* & at sundown train ordered to hitch up as there was a rumor that our right flank had been driven back; guess not. Fixed [Fourth day fight] bed for night, then took it up & laid on rubber with shelter tent over me. About 12 o'clock we started, went a mile & *[entry ends]*

Context—Sherman begins his Georgia campaign, May 7.

Saturday, 7th.—at 4 o'c*[lock]*[216] jammed on through ruts, wagon stuck, took 4 extra mules (10) to get out. Halted at daylight, saw colored troops 23rd U.S., Maj*[or]* *[blank space]* of 7th *[Company]* S*[harp]* S*[hooters]*. Shells fired ½ mile from us & 50 to 10*[0?]* rebel prisoners taken whom I saw; many with out blue clothes—2 officers; turned to left, on, & saw hospitals on roadside with many wounded & bleeding lying about—some I knew, mostly wounded in hand or arm; a few in face & or leg. Provost guard picking up stragglers. Fine day, & warmer than yesterday—a sweater. About 9 came to plank road where battle of Chancellorsville (44) was fought a year ago. Ruins. Brought water. Dinner of boiled potatos, fried pork & tack, & coffee. First meal 9 A.M. since 6 last eve. Laid down under trees, on ground, then under wagon, rest well in the dirt. Rebels are falling back & we are to go to Fredericksburg. On at 12, 2 miles to the Chancellorsville House where *[Major General Joseph]* Hooker was nearly struck by a shell falling in porch—a brick house. Fortifications all about. Hear firing. Waiting for troops to pass. See many relics of the old battle here in '63. Any quantity of old clothing on the ground. Much is now thrown away by our men. About 3½ cav*[alr]*y passing went half way to Fredericksburg; slowly & on pleasant plank road, in dust, hot. Train parked in open lot on side of road. Sup*[per]* & fixed for night. Hear good [Fifth day's fight] news of rebs retreating, &c. Felt like sleeping & gave myself up to rest at 8½ in night cap made by Mother. Pleasant starlight. Hear no firing.

Context—The battalion fought in the Spotsylvania Court House campaign, May 8-21, and lost one enlisted man killed and two officers and nine enlisted men wounded.

Sunday, 8th.—Lovely day. Birds sing. Slept well. Up at daylight. Break*[fast]*. Changed cap for hat & jacket for blouse & fixed things in wagon. Wounded men dressing wounds. Read some. Saw 5th Corps Amb*[ulance]* train & many boys wounded.—S*[hedrick]* J. J*[ackson]* taking care of Capt. *[William S.]* Grantsyn wounded. Saw Capt*[ain August]* Meyer,[217] printer in *[Brockport]* Rep*[ublic]* office wounded in left breast & low; can hardly survive; breathed hard; said he should die if not better cared for than jolted in amb*[ulance]*. Bad wounds on many. Also saw Ch*[arles]* & Tr*[uman]* Miller, 2nd Corps. Very dusty. Heavy trains. Soup & beef for din*[ner]*. At 3 P.M. train moved 3 or 4 miles, toward Spotsylvania C*[ourt]* H*[ouse]* (45) & parked for night; sup*[per]*& good wash. Laid early on ground. Stories of Union Indians giving no quarter & taking prisoners by stratagem, from wagons. Hear firing. Drew 6 days rations

Monday, 9th.—Good rest. Hot & dusty day. Saw *[William E.]* Ferrin, wounded in foot & after breakfast went with him 3 m*[iles]* to 5th Corps, 1st & 4th Div*[isions]*. Hospitals—horrid sight, & amputation & wounds, men lying about. Held the leg of a Corp*[ora]*l in 9th NYM*[ilitia]* while leg dressed. Saw *[Orrin H.]* Strong, clerk. Also *[Captain Volney J.]* Shipman wounded by him sent letter to Roch*[ester]* Dem*[ocrat]* & letter to Mother. Heard that Col*[onel George]* Ryan & Maj*[or Milo]* Starks were killed body buried this A.M. Saw wounded Gen*[era]*l. Tried to find Brig*[ade]* H*[ea]*dq*[uarte]*rs team; did not. [Sixth days fight] Some trouble in finding my way back to train, did at 2. Waited in run. At 3 train started & 2 miles, parked on plank road 5 m*[iles]* from Fred*[eric]*ksb*[ur]*g. Sup*[per]*. Rations, sug*[ar]* cof*[fee]*. Saw *[Major General Ambrose E.]* Burnsides troops pass & 2nd Corps ambulances come back from taking wounded to F*[redericksburg]*. Wash. Wagon fixed. Cloudy in AM. Bed on ground.

Tuesday, 10th.—Up sunrise. Cof*[fee]*. & crackers. Feel well. (3,000 pris*[oners]* taken yester*[day]*. Saw some.) Saw [Seventh day fight.] flour mill run by steam engine made at Downs Seneca Falls, N.Y. Also "Roch. Cutting Box, pat'd 1856, A. Gordon & Co." with plows & harrows, old & new. Flour mill made by Cross of Roch*[ester]*. 56. 147 Mill & house acres owned by John G. Miller, German, here Fredericksburg, Va. 11 years. Relics from Chancell*[or]*sville Battle field. Find young orchard & garden, lettuce & beans, shrubs & grape vines. Saw *[Albert S.]* Knowles. Mr. Miller gave me old copies of Richmond Daily Sentinel & Engineer. He bought at F*[redericksburg]* 6 bushels corn paying $3.00 in conscript money. Flour from $300 to $500 per barrel. Grain destroyed by cavalry our soldiers, who tore open the house, &c. Rosanna Miller gave me small reb flag, 9 stars, made by rebs in Fr*[edericksbur]*g. Laid down lounge to rest, saw accordion & Mrs. M*[iller]* gave me tumbler of fresh milk. Had good wash. At train had coffee. Put up a tent & had to take it down to pack up as train was expected to [Eighth day's fight] move. Mr. M[iller]'s son gave himself up. At Mr. M[iller]'s bid them good by & filled canteen with water. Quite well impressed by the M[iller] family. Waited for train to move till late, then camped on ground.

Wednesday, 11th.—Warm again. Very few rain drops. Good rest. Break[fast] at 6. Good wash at brook, & for first time left off drawers. Dinner, cof[fee] & tack. At Mr. M[iller]'s, rested in sitting room & read book. They are very much distressed by [Ninth day's fight.] impudent soldiers. Play with dog. Sup[per] at [illegible word] Rain at 5½ & during eve. So cool & nice. In eve. fixed up tent, called short time at Mr. M[iller]'s. Slept at tent with Stillson.

Thursday, 12th.—Rainy most of day. Up at daylight & packed. Sultry. Got bridle & came near getting horse. Train moved 2½ miles nearer Fred[erick] sbb[ur]g. Saw Ord[erly] A[ndrew] Boyd wounded in arm. Also saw 3,300 rebel prisoners—hearty looking men. Pitched tent near plank road. Slept. Trains & prisoners passing. Draw fresh beef. Very heavy & rapid cannonading, shakes the earth, till late & in eve. at 10, musketry or picket firing. Soup for sup[per]. Looked into a house occupied by a poor white family, Mr. man wife daugh[ter], & young sons & a confed[erate]. Widow, near by. Women secesh. Ignorant people & squalid. Old ones cannot read. Good [Tenth day's fight] fire in "place". Soldiers in Left disgusted. Rested.

Friday, 13th.—Rain during night; cloudy today, some rain; mud ankle deep. Slept well; up at 6½. Read some in book. Wrote Mat [Mary A. C. French]. With [Albert S.] Knowles saw several cannon taken from the rebels called at house of Mr. Moore found reb canteen. Read old Law book of Virginia. Mr. & Mrs. M[oore] & daughter (Mrs. Leach) 4 sev[era]l small children, amusing time. Supper at camp. Mule kicked me slightly,. Rain most of day. In eve. dried my feet by fire in stove at Mr. M[oore]'s. Pleasant. Soldiers in, talking. Held little Lily on my knee. Mrs. M[oore] fixed blankets on floor for self & safeguard, where we slept.

Saturday, 14th.—Rainy & cloudy. Trains moving all night. Up early, found train gone & found it 1½ miles nearer Fredericksburg, thro' mud & helped put up tent. Very disagreeable weather. After coffee, had nap. Struck tents & moved few rods at 12, to dryer ground, & again pitched tent; got water. Saw Wash[ington] Chron[icle] first paper in 10 days. Clearing off at 3. Wrote to Mat   [Mary A. C. French] & Mother, & sent. Saw 2nd N.Y. Mounted Rifles, & Mons Grummon of Medina. Saw 130th [NYVI Regiment] boy now in 1st Dragoons once at Chesapeake [General Hospital]. Ate 2 boiled potatos late. Rain till late. To bed in tent.—Had quite a talk with M*[ons]* G*[rummon]* about Medina.

Tuesday, 15th.—Still rainy; pleasant at noon. *[Orrin H.]* Strong came up. Drew 5 days rations of cof*[fee]* sug*[ar]* & pork tack. H*[ea]*dq*[uarte]*rs mail came up first time in long while; letter from Aunt & F*[athe]*r last. The train moved about 10, very slowly. In deep mud. I got ahead of train. Saw secesh woman & heard her talk. Heavy shower & hail. On the Heights of Fredericksburg, at 4 P.M. rested in a barn till the storm ceased. Pitched tent on Heights & had supper cof*[fee]* & tack. Rec*[eive]*d *[Brockport]* Republic of 28th ult. & 5th. Do not feel well tonight. Sleep in damp after drying feet, *[rain]* early cleared off at sundown.

Fredericksburg Heights

Monday, 16th.—Heavy fog cleared at 8, then warm. Pork at break*[fast]*. Moved or changed my quarters & shall be with *[Orrin H.]* Strong, clerk: Took rations & all things but knapsack, including Inspector's portfolio. Built fire & helped S*[trong]* cook meat beef cut from bone lying in field. Good soup & coffee for dinner. Saw S*[hedrick]* J. J*[ackson]*. Strong bought can milk, which I shall share with him. Washed up & went on edge of hill to write, where I can see Fredericksburg full in the face: it looks quite pleasant, churches & buildings old & new. Got sleepy & did not write letter. Nap in tent. At 5 got supper of good coffee, steak & fried crackers. Went to Fredericksburg east part. Looks dirty & torn—ravaged. Some fine residences & churches, mostly occupied by wounded. Band playing in yard & young ladies listening. Found the camp of 22d NY Cavalry *[Regiment]*, but the Brockport Co*[mpany]* had gone on picket. Back & to bed early. *[Orrin H.]* Strong read some from Handy Andy[218] to me.

Tuesday, 17th.—Cloudy. Some rain last night.—Built fire, but had to lay down & go without my breakfast; sick headache hard. Slept & felt better. One of the boys brought me from Headq*[uarte]*rs letter, recommend*[ation]* from Mr. *[Horatio N.]* Beach & letter from mother, Lon, & Harvey, May 4th. Also stamps 2 ct. Cof*[fee]* for dinner & felt better. Boiled beef for soup, bro't water. Wrote to Mother & to Mat *[Mary A. C. French]* sent Mat *[Mary A. C. French]* a reb flag & flowers, also letter to Mother. Pleasant in P.M. Soup with garlick & potatoes in for supper. Also sassafras tea. Went to Fr*[edericks]*b*[ur]*g. Saw 8th NY Artillery *[Regiment]* on way to front, 1,500 strong. Saw Grif L. Davis & Lieut. Westcott, also Alex Odell. Also saw *[Franklin D.]* Edwards Co*[mpany]* E, 22nd N.Y. Cav*[alry]* & boys from *[Kendall]* Mills & Br*[ockport]*. Also Editor C. G. Beach of Orleans Republican here in F*[redericksburg]* as State

Agent, for relief of wounded. Glad to see him & he me. Left note for Andrew Boyd, & escorted Mr. *[C. G.]* Beach to the train. & left him with Lieut*[enant Alphonso W.]*. Starkweather. & "commissary whiskey". Borrow 3 ct. stamp of Stillson. Found S*[tillson]* to bed.

Wednesday, 18th.—Fine day. Up early & breakfast of beef, soup & cof*[fee]*. *[Brockport]* Repub*[lic]*. of 12th. Wrote a little to M*[other]*. & Mat *[Mary A. C. French]* & washed shirt, put on clean pants & new shirt. Down town, Co*[mpany]* C., 22nd *[NY]* Cav*[alry]*. Boys having gay time. Demon whiskey, iced; showed them paper. Found that A*[ndrew]* Boyd had gone. Saw S*[hedrick]* J. J*[ackson]* who gave me nice can butter & I drank coffee with him & Capt*[ain August]* Meyers serv*[an]*t in fine dwelling where family resided. At old school house saw among other wounded, Serg*[ean]*t Delos Howe 6th Co*[mpany]* S*[harp]* S*[hooters]* who is suffering from 2nd amputation of left leg. Many wounded—one in breast—some limbs off. (Sent letters.) Walked about the city some time. Saw Dr. Dalton, formerly of Chesapeake *[General Hospital]*. Women in hospitals, tending wounded. Heard that Deacon *[Israel]* Starks[219] of B*[rockport]* is here.—Not many pretty women in F*[redericksburg]*. Very good flower gardens. Former groceries look gaunt & were gutted by our cavalry when they came into town on 8th. One "store" robbed, proprietor told me, of $2,400 worth of goods, mostly tobacco. One female grocer told me she had only subsistence for corn meal for 2 times or messes—had 5 children, oldest girl of 14—probably good looking. In another place young girl tending old grocery with nothing in it. Back to tent on hill at 5, found soup & made coffee. Finished letter to Mo*[ther]* & Mat *[Mary A. C. French]* & sent them to-night. Rain before dark. Heard of Guerillas & that 2nd Corps took 2 lines of breastworks.

Thursday, 19th.—Fine weather, warm. Breakfast. Went to canal to fish.—only a few bites. At hospital in old building. Saw Serg*[ean]*t Boyle & *[William S.]* Mockford & *[Herbert A.]* Cooley of 140th *[NY VI Regiment]*. Left *[Brockport]* Repub*[lic]*. Women nursing & in good spirits. Wounded boys fishing—1 bullhead. Visited monument to Mother of Washington, (46) which had been sadly defaced by target practice by boys from Fred*[ericksburg]* shooting it.—Back to camp. *[Orrin H.]* Strong gone; packed my things & started for front with 7th Wis*[consin]* boy. Very warm. Found 1st N.Y. Dragoon boys who gave us beef & I got coffee, rested. On we went with train loaded. Slight shower in P.M. About 5 o'clock, on going thro' woods, heard firing close by on right & bullets whistled—firing very close—infantry drawn up in line & cavalry maneuvering. Hardly knew where to go—between skirmishes & line of battle—tight place. Turned to left with wagon which had left sick or dead horse & met Heavy Artillery men going to repel attack in woods. Found our way to *[Lieutenant]* Gen*[eral Ulysses S.]* Grant's H*[ea]*dquarte]rs. Near corps hospital. Musketry & art*[iller]*y banged away & wounded came in & were strung along the road. I followed ambulances & at dark came to cook house of our Brig*[ade]* H*[ea]*dq*[uarte]*rs where the cook & serv*[an]*ts were. Made coffee.—Then with Gid *[Allen]* went back thro' woods by moonlight to transport with ammunition train where found *[Orrin H.]* Strong & bunked in with him, tired, having walked about 10 miles.

Friday, 20th.—Hot. Wash. Break*[fast]* with driver & Gid *[Allen]* & S*[trong]*. Boiled beef. Transport went to Fred*[ericksburg]* after mail. Orderly came from Brig*[ade]*. All quiet in A.M. Moved from train to rear of B*[rigade]* H*[ead]* q*[uarte]*rs. On hill, & on way saw 8th H*[eavy]* A*[rtillery]* & boys; found cousin Lester Farnam *[sic]*, Co*[mpany]* F, who gave me photo of self & wife. Read letters. Finished cooking beef. In ref*[uge]* house, deserted, wounded men; old sew machine—dish sparrowgrass cooked by wench—Beverly place. On to Brig*[ade]* H*[ead]*q*[uarte]*rs. Saw Co*[mpany]* boys & officers—took papers for Capt*[ain R. S.]* Dillon. Col*[onel]* & staff in breastworks. Saw rebs thro' glass—firing. At div*[ision]*. H*[ea]*dq*[uarte]*rs & transport—sup*[per]*. At Co*[mpany]* & to bed in open air with *[Orrin H.]* S*[trong]*.

Saturday, 21st.—Pleasant & very warm.—Went 1½ m*[iles]* to get rations & did not. Back. Packed up. At h*[ead]*q*[uarte]*rs rec*[eive]*d paper, letter from Mo*[ther]* & sis*[ter]*, Mat. *[Mary A. C. French]* & Em*[ma]* S*[mith]*. Troops left to left. Shells thrown & burst. Left my jacket & back 1½ m*[iles]* for it. Up with trans*[port]* broke down. Rest. On; stop often; fine country. Water from pump; good looking women on balcony; yellow roses; ice. R.R. Grimes Station, rest at 5, & saw 140th *[NYVI Regiment]* & L*[ieutenan]*t *[Lewis B.]* Court*[ne]*y. Tired; long halt in road; 75 rebs attempt to destroy bridge repulsed; at 9 crossed bridge & 1 m*[ile]*; halt for night & coffee; sleep on ground; corn taken from barn; very slight shower in P.M. all forces move to left. Some artillery; fine moonlight.

Context—The battalion fought in the North Anna/Totopotomoy/Cold Harbor campaign, May 22–June 12, and lost four enlisted men killed or died of wounds, three officers and 15 enlisted men wounded, and one enlisted man missing.

Sunday, 22nd.—Break*[fast]* before daylight. Brig*[ade]* moved 4 m*[iles]* & commence to fortify in hilly, pleasant country. Lost pen holder. Packed up. Found reb buttons. Laid in orchard; apples. Cloudy & cool. Walked to Brigade H*[ead]*q*[uarte]*rs with S*[ampson]* W. F*[ry]* stopped at house got meal sch*[ool]* books. (Saw *[Lieutenant]* Gen*[eral Ulysses S.]* Grant & *[Major General*

George G.] Meade & staffs at Madison's Ordinary or *[Major]* Gen*[eral Andrew A.]* Humphrey & others. Gen*[eral]*s. G*[rant]*. & Meade smoking cigars.) At house invited to eat & offered milk, could not "see it". Cooked meal after seeing sheep shot at on road. *[Sampson W.]* F*[ry]* & I ate mush & of 4 eggs cooked only 1 was good. Enjoyed mush, butter & sugar. Saw 140th L*[ieutenan]*t *[Lewis B.]* Court*[ney]* & *[Gid]* Allen. Marched at noon, slowly from Flosser (I think) P.O. Caroline Co*[unty]*. Men pushed along by Provost; stopped at *[blank space]* church, on Telegraph road, 13 m*[iles]*. from Hanover Junction. Ice house broken open; found poor water made coffee & cooked bacon with tack—made bed early in good place with *[Charles W.]* Spaulding & *[Orrin H.]* Strong, who drew beef for us. Camp in good place. Warm eve. Letter & photo from home.

Monday, 23rd.—Headache. Great time finding water—scarce. We marched at 6, on tel*[egraph]* road. Fine day. Strong march to within 5 m*[iles]* of H*[anover]* Junc*[tion]* reb pris*[on]*. Halted at 10½ rebs ahead cav*[alry]* out & artillery firing. Coffee for *[Sampson W.]* F*[ry]* & I & laid down. Letter from Father & Mo*[ther]* & paper with my letter in Roch*[ester]* Dem*[ocrat]*. Also good photos of sister. Pris*[oners]* mostly N.O. willing to take oath. About 2 P.M. went on after large no. troops having taken wrong road, go back a little & on in hot sun. Boys turn out spinning *[or spitting]* smoke of cannon on left. Oak timber. Follow artillery. Out of rations. Glad to rest in woods when wagons & troops halt. Carry 3 pint pail full of beef—no time to cook it. Fowls & poultry taken & eaten. Cows driven. Now carry my rubbers & woolen blankets in addition to hav*[ersack]* & can*[teen]*, having become disgusted with meanness of jockey driver &c. & will hereafter travel independently. Officers taking sociable drink. Fight, by 4th Div*[ision]* 5th Corps. Young colts & pups. Secesh women. Rush for water to mud holes. Fine country. 5½ reached North Anna River, crossed on pont*[oon]* Troops across & artillery posted & after skirm*[ish]*. At 6 a shelling was com*[menced]* by r*[ebs]* when stampede in rear by non-coms. Heavy shelling & replied to by our side boys saw bursting; with transport recrossed riv*[er]*. High hills on both sides. Very heavy fighting & charging. Shells burst very near. Quiet at dark. A man tried to gobble my things. Made broth of beef, after labor in getting water. Some wounded our loss slight. Bivouac under trees. Supplies going up to troops. Rebels repulsed.

Tuesday, 24th.—Begged 2 hard tack for break*[fast]*. Very warm. Feel weak to-day. Finished cooking beef & drank broth. Wash. Many stragglers. 6th Corps passing. Drew 6 days rations cof*[fee]*, sug*[ar]*, & tack. Pris*[oners]* come in. Distant artillery all day. Rebs fell back from us in night. At 11 crossed riv*[er]* A mile to div*[ision]* H*[ead]*q*[uarte]*rs & slept in shade till 3 or 4, sup*[per]* of mush, beef, & cof*[fee]*. Wash. Troops move on at 5½. Smokey & cooler.

Boys work at upper end of stream, others fill canteens below. Only move into position for night. Camped & put up tent with *[Charles W.]* Spaulding & *[Orrin H.]* Str*[ong]*. Slight rain. Drew beef. Coffee.

Wednesday, 25th.—Pleasant. Up at daylight & troops hurried off the crossing slowly I made cof*[fee]* & had good break*[fast]*. On with S*[harp]* S*[hooters]* a mile to John Mathew's farm & house, orchard & clearing surrounded by woods. Skirmishing & line of battle formed, & fire continued all day. Bat*[ter]*y in posi*[tion]* & transp*[ort]*'s back ND HILL CITIZEN RUN. Saw Gen*[eral]* *[blank space]* at Ja*[me]*s Mathews house, red-haired lady talked quite secesh to officers, pleasant. Darkies had been told "Yanks" would kill them. Saw dead reb, Tho*[ma]*s Weaver, Co*[mpany]* I, 7th V*[irgini]*a, lying in yard. Made cof*[fee]* at transp*[ort]*. Cooked beef & had wash in spring brook. Put up tent with *[Charles W.]* Spaulding & had nap. Cannonading by us at 3½ a few minutes. Wrote home & sent. Cloudy. Telegraph put up for H*[ea]*dq*[uarte]*rs. *[Lieutenant General Ulysses S.]* Grant & *[Major General Geoge G.]* Meade pass. Saw Lon Morehouse, 140th *[NYVI Regiment]*. Slightly musketry. Teams foraging. Rain & wind. Coffee for sup*[per]*.

Thursday, 26th.—Rainy. *[Charles W.]* Spaulding got break*[fast]* of cof*[fee]* & tack fried, had beef. Art*[iller]*y pass, also secesh female soldier in male dress, long hair, straddling horse, under guard. Cleared up at 10. Saw Lon M*[orehouse]* at Hospital. Wrote for Capt*[ain R. S.]* Dillon. Men going by in ambulances, groaning. Very sultry. Saw *[Major]* Gen*[eral Ambrose G.]* Burnside. Drew beef. Sup*[per]*. Moved at dark about a mile. Rain. Laid down on board in mud while troops pass by to n*[orth]* side N*[orth]* Anna River. On in mud & dark woods, & at 10 o'c*[lock]* halted & laid down for the night with *[Orrin H.]* Strong, troops passing.

Friday, 27th.—Sprinkle. Fine sunrise. Bite of cold meat further on. Wash. Coffee & feel well. On to church after gathering salt in field. Train at church & troops where we passed on Monday. Saw *[Major General George G.]* Meade & *[Lieutenant General Ulysses S.]* Grant early. Found sword. Quite rapid marching & found cherries nearly ripe. Splendid country. Boiled beef & had soup for dinner. Halted often to rest. Going to White House Landing, York River. Fine roads. At 4 halted & slept in shade. Train moving slowly. Made coffee at sundown & went on in cool of eve. Could not get to transp*[ort]* & at dark stopped near roadside & bivouacked for the night, tired.

Saturday, 28th.—Hot. Up at sun. Water at spring & made cof*[fee]* in yard of old lady & daughter & son. Fried pork & tack. Good break*[fas]*t. Went on & found train & had to halt frequently for rest. Once in woods *[sugar & cof[fee]* to June 1st all alone, in P.M. saw gray backs pass & kept quiet. On to grocery;

cof*[fee]* passed Mrs. Dabney's at Enfield & on to Pamunkey. Too tired to go much farther; train & troops camped across pontoons on river & found boys on heights, where troops fortify. Took beef to boys from butcher. Helped cook beef after dark. Line of men taking turns at getting water. Soup & to bed on ground, with *[Orrin H.]* Strong again.

Sunday, 29th.—Up daylight. Soup & cof*[fee]* & beef. Packed up. Plenty boiled beef. All quiet. Strong bracing air, breeze from N.E. Started to top of hill & halted early. Gave E*[dwin]* O. Rich*[ard]*son picture of his captured brother. A lovely morn*[ing]*. Think of home to-day. Colored refugees come thronging in from slavery—old & young. Place called Westwood. Hanover Town near river. Judge Meredith (John) owns 100 slaves. At noon made cof*[fee]* & moved on slowly 1½ miles where many lines of breastworks were thrown up by us, within 2 m*[iles]* of the enemy. A corps eng*[inee]*r says its only 13 m*[iles]* from Richmond. [Rations. Sent letter. Fight.] Citizen troops some mounted from Richmond are in front. Our cav*[alr]*y fought them yesterday. Some musketry in P.M. I feel good spirited & that the end of the rebellion is at hand. Saw *[Major General Ambrose G.]* Burnside & *[Major General Gouverneur K.]* Warren. Earthworks. Telegraph. Music. Rest & supper. Beef killed. Bivouacked in woods when staff & Col*[onel]*. Had fire built & a jolly time. Chilly.

Monday, 30th.—A lovely day. Up early & made coffee in cup. Laid around awhile. Heard cannon. Sent letter to Mat. *[Mary A. C. French]*, one for Capt*[ain R. S.]* Dillon. About 9, on about 2 m*[iles]* slowly, nap in shade & made coffee. Then heavy skirmishing & a small fight, transp*[or]*ts went on, halted at near sound of musk*[etr]*y & can*[non]*, wounded, &c. Turned back ½ mile, a sort of skedaddle to near 5th corps H*[ead]*q*[uarte]*rs. Saw *[Major]* Gen*[eral Gouverneur K.]* Warren. Cool breeze. P*[ennsylvani]*a Reserves said to have run. Also 15th H*[eavy]* A*[rtillery]* N.Y. Mich*[igan]* troops captured 30 pris*[oners]*. Bucktails 11th, 6th, & 1st P*[ennsylvani]*a ran, flanked.—Firing continued till dark. Good supper. Bed on slope.

Tuesday, 31st,—Weather same. Up early, good break*[fas]*t. Firing cannon early, then quiet.

[Editor's note: This concludes this diary. Back pages list casualties in Brockport units & miscellaneous information. Farnham's diary from June 1 through October 9, 1864, if it ever existed, is missing. The following four letters were published in the Brockport Republic in June 1864. None appeared in August or September. The file of the Brockport Republic is missing from October 1, 1864 until September 30, 1866. My transcription of Farnham's diary for October 10, 1864 until June 21, 1865, follows the letters.]

Later Letters to the Brockport Republic

June

Context—The battalion was in the 3rd Brigade, 3rd Division, 5th Corps, August-October. Union siege of Petersburg, Va., began June 15.

Brockport Republic June 16, 1864

On Battle Field, June 2, 1864. Editor Republic: Dear Sir:—Skirmishing along the advancing lines, with an occasional small fight, and we still push nearer to the doomed rebel capitol, by Grant's sidewise and thus far successful plan. The rebel occupation grows beautifully less, with only slight loss to us at present, and prisoners, with deserters, come in hourly.—The weather is dry and hot, roads dusty, while everything works well. Shot and shell are being thrown, the bursting of the latter can be distinctly heard as death is sprinkled among the enemy, but the noise of cannonading and musketry are becoming of so common an occurrence, that it is a matter of course, and we mind it not.—Just above the woods is a light puff of smoke, which denotes that a shell has bursted there. This, too, is often seen. Then is heard the popping of musketry, as the skirmishers advance, with an occasional discharge of artillery, which one can feel, as the ground trembles.

To-day, thus far, has been rather quiet, as the troops are being somewhat changed to new positions. But in the latter part of yesterday, and at evening, along most of the line was heavy roar of battle. The rebels charged repeatedly, but without success, as our men obstinately refused to give an inch, but in spite of the opposing cheers, drove them back. Here, on the main avenue from the front, the number taken to the front numbered but few, but our loss must have been light, as we have the advantage of breastworks of earth and rails, which protect most effectually from the enemy's fire. The whole country since we crossed the Pemunkey, five miles back, is a complete web of earthwork defenses which were hastily thrown up at every halt of the troops. Thus Grant completely leads McClellan in the way of digging into Richmond, apparently.

On Tuesday a portion of the Pennsylvania Reserves in this corps, whose time had expired, left the field on the way home. There were no stragglers then. A part of the 14th Booklyn, Zouaves, have also gone. To balance this, reinforcements are coming in. Yesterday, a large number from the vicinity of Alexandria arrived, and were placed in support of the battle line. Fifteen thousand Heavy Artillery—with muskets, from Baltimore and Washington, came on two weeks ago; among them the 8th and 14th N.Y. The eighth have already been officially praised for bravery. The 22nd N.Y. Cavalry, Col. Crooks, were on duty at Fredericksburg, where I saw Capt. Edwards Company. They were all in good spirits. On their way from Washington they were attacked by guerillas; in the melee James Cornes and ——— Mowers, of Edwards Co. were lost. The 2nd N.Y. Mounted Rifles, from Orleans and Niagara counties were in the field acting as infantry—on foot. The army is now stronger than when it crossed the Rapidan.

There can be no mistake this time. Grant will take Richmond, in spite of Lee, who is to be playing sick, leaving the command to Ewell. You need not be disappointed if there no *brilliant* successes—it will be a steady puff—only what has for near two years been so anxiously looked for. If Lee can be cornered in Richmond, so much the better for us. It is feared or supposed he will attempt to evade his doom there, by passing to the right of that city, make a junction on the opposite side in full view of several of their large encampments, and could see several of their signal stations, their lines of pickets, and their trains moving back and forth.—Up to the time of the movement on our part they were continually digging, until they had a complete network of entrenchments, and woe would have been the army to ever have tried to come over there. We remained on Stony Mountain, one day after the army had moved, and it was not till sunset, after the last of our cavalry had been withdrawn from picket, that we mounted our horses and galloped away. At 10 o'clock that night, May 4th, we came up with some of the army trains, in the vicinity of Ely's Ford, when we turned in to the woods for the night. The next morning we crossed the river, followed out the road through the ruins of Chancellorsville, and came up with 3rd corps headquarters at Todd's Tavern. Our Signal Officer, Capt. Taylor, reported to Gen. Hancock, and at 1 P.M., we fell in line with his escort and rode toward the plank road where the 3d corps was forming a junction with the 6th. We rode nearly three miles in a road filled with troops, crowding ahead as fast as possible, and on reaching the plank road found the 6th corps throwing up temporary breastworks of timber and rails and the plank of the road. As soon as the 2nd came up they began the same work, and in an incredibly short time there were three or four miles of these works. At 3 P.M. the order was given to advance down into the woods, and over these works went the old 2nd corps, and in five minutes time came one unbroken roll of musketry, which one need hear only once to remember a life-time. As the fighting was in a hollow, the bullets whistled sharply in the trees over us, and the leaves fell around us like a shower. This was the opening of a fierce campaign, and was but a trifle to what has since followed or will take place before we are done with our summer's work. The country of that region is well named "The Wilderness" (47, 48)—for it is one continuation of forest, with occasional small islands of clearing, and in a place like this neither army could see the other until meeting almost face to face, necessarily making the fighting the closest and most desperate, and not until the enemy were driven from here could any artillery on either side be brought into action. And here for three days the fighting was little more than charging and recharging, our men leaving their entrenchments, charging on the enemy, they repulsisng us and driving us out, following us back, and we driving them back in turn. In one charge of the enemy upon our lines, 450 of their dead were left in front of one division of the 2nd corps. This is only one instance of the terrible slaughters and encounters of the Wilderness battle.

The weather was very hot and dry, and on the second day the woods were on fire and many of our wounded and dead and of theirs lying between the lines that neither side could remove, were consumed by the fire and the living were no light sufferers from the heat and smoke.

It was not till our advance on Sunday across the Po river that we found open country enough to open any communication by signals, and then but little.

In this campaign our corps has been used to ride along the lines in the capacity of dispatch bearers. On Thursday, May 10th, as I was riding through a by-road, going to 2nd Corps headquarters, I came upon two graves that attracted my attention, and halting a moment, judge of my astonishment to read "Col. Geo. Ryan, and Maj. M. L. Starks, killed May 8th, 1864."[220]

I am now with the signal wagon with the 2nd Corps headquarters train, having been sent back some days ago on account of my horse becoming lame. We are 12 miles north from Hanover Court House and 3 from Millford Station on the railroad between Fredericksburg and Richmond. We have crossed the head waters of the Mattapony river, which is formed by four streams named Ma, Ta, Po, and Ny. The line of the army is from 5 to 10 miles south. Supply trains have been sent forward and, as we hear nothing, we judge that all is quiet and that they are waiting the development of some point of strategy.

Our mail wagon has gone out for the first time in several days. It has gone to Port Royal on the Rappahannock and will not return until to-morrow, and so the mail is very irregular these times, it may be some time or days before this can go out.   J.T.F.

Brockport Republic, June 23, 1864

Headq'rs 1st Brig., 4th Div., 5th A.C., Near Bottom's Bridge, Va., June 9th, 1864. Editor Republic: Dear Sir:—On the afternoon of the 7th, we reached the vicinity of the Chickahominy river, (49) and our pickets were posted along the edge of this narrow stream mostly fordable, and said to be entirely dry at the drought season. Its banks are heavily wooded. On our first arrival pickets exchanged shots; but toward evening a mutual agreement was reached to cease firing; following which, "Yanks" and Confeds bathed together in the stream, made peaceful exchanges, while our officers conversed with theirs for a brief time, A rebel Lieutenant, Adjutant of the 15th Va., cavalry, brought over a Richmond paper of that day. Since then, all has been quiet—a relief to the booming of cannon and noise of musketry for so long. Two of our sharpshooters with heavy guns have been sent for, to clear the bridge and railroad. They have dug a large pit, and quickly dispersed a crowd of the enemy looking through a glass, while the road was kept clear during yesterday. From the Division headquarters of Gen. Cutler, in a fine grove, can be seen rebel breastworks, with a provision wagon. They have a heavy cannon placed on a railroad track; this commands our position if they only knew it, but our Division is well screened from them. They are extremely quiet.

We are enjoying the cool breezes of a good location, well shaded and plenty of good water from adjacent wells. The Brigade headquarters are under a large apple tree. The grove within which are the Division headquarters once surrounded a fine mansion burned at the time of McClellan's retreat in 1862. It was used as our hospital and an immense amount of medical stores were burned with it. This vicinity was known as Glasgow, and is 1½ miles from Dispatch Station on the Richmond and York River R.R.—by rail 13 miles and by highway 15 from Richmond On this plantation, now owned by a Richmond machinist named Turner, is 600 acres, adjoining Chickahominy Swamp.[221] Judge Clayton was the former owner, succeeded by Dr. Savage. There is a fine garden here with fruit trees of all kinds, and shrubbery. The chief building on the place is an office formerly occupied by Dr. Savage, but for the last four months occupied by Mr. Wm. H. Harding and wife, who came from Richmond to take charge of the place, rent free. They are very pleasant people, without children, and came from Boston about fourteen years ago, settled in Richmond, where Mr. H. successfully carried on his business, *[illegible word]* and manufacturing pianos, his age and poor health rendering him unfit for military service, which he did not regret, his Northern and Union sentiments made his attachment to old Massachusetts as strong as ever. Having been unable to leave Richmond during the war, except by the risk of blockade running, they patiently suffered the privations of war, until the arrival of Gen. Cutler enabled them to take the oath of allegiance to the Union, preparatory to their leaving for their friends in Boston, which they will do to-day. They are extremely glad at the prospect of leaving their long confederate bondage and only fear lest by some accident they may be left here. They say there are many at Richmond, good Union people at heart, who are smothering their sentiments, hoping for a liberation, which will no doubt be made, slowly now, though surely.—To the kind hospitality of the Hardings I am under many obligations. May they enjoy a rest in the land of plenty.

All the white people about here are those of limited circumstances, and by the recent raids have been mostly reduced to almost wretchedness and beggary for want of food. There has been much destruction of gardens and household property, and the facts cannot be appreciated unless the reality is seen. Last year no crops of account were put in, but having more confidence, many of them recently planted "on shares," and the present indications are that this labor will all be lost, as the occupation by the army prevents a cultivation of the soil, especially at this distance from the rebel capitol, where the ground will be literally stamped down. Corn and potatoes look well, and grain, although light, is quite passable. This country is the garden of Richmond, from which that city has ever been supplied with vegetables and fruits for the table. Even now the officers are luxuriating upon green peas, strawberries, lettuce, and greens, with cherries. Raspberries are just turning color and blackberries will soon follow. Apples and peaches promise an abundance. Attached to most of the residences are ice houses, generally well filled. This luxury is of course not spared. Everything available for *comfort* is confiscated for use. There is much unnecessary destruction by some rascally villains, such as are a curse to the army, and the like of whom can be found in all communities, but these libels on the majority of the army are certainly not authorized by regulations, and the guilty are liable to punishment.

This is the extreme left of the lines of our Corps, cavalry joining us still further to the left. The peaceful calm of a few days indicates a burst of war-like thunder, and the ball may again open after this needed rest.

The 2nd Corps recently came in close contact with the enemy, and the 8th Heavy Artillery suffered considerably, losing their Colonel, Porter, during a heavy fight on the 4th. Friends of the wounded have no doubt learned the particulars. While at the hospital on Monday I heard of the following casualties in Co. K: Lieut. Wallace B. Hard, of Kendall, killed; Lieut. Thos Westcott, of Clarendon, wounded in head; Shaw, Kendall, wounded in both legs; George Walker, Hamlin, wounded in back, seriously; Corp. Ryan A. Barber, missing; Edward Spaulding, Churchville, in arm, slight; Major Willett was wounded. The wounded at the hospital presented a sickening sight, as the day was hot. The sufferers were made comfortable as possible under large tents, lying upon beds of pine boughs, ranged upon each side. The men were uncomplaining and wounds were being dressed.

I learned that Lieut. Stafford had been at the hospital, suffering from chill fever, but did not succeed in finding him. Lieut. Webster remains at Baltimore as Commissary of prisoners.

The 140th N.Y. had an interesting episode in their fatal fighting career last week, June 3, while the right wing of the 5th Corps were brought in. Burnside was to support the movement. By some mistake the 140th were not made aware that the position was to be abandoned, and while the right and left fell back, they unknowingly held their *[ground?][five lines illegible]* and met with only a slight loss, that of Co. A being as follows: August J. Seeley and Peter Shurmer, Clarkson, missing; Henry Kincaid, Clarkson, wounded in both legs; Grove D. Whitney, Lockport, wounded. Lieut. Allen, acting Adjutant, is still uninjured, though with poor health; Lieut. Courtney, reported killed, declines as yet to be numbered in that list, and that the report is untrue I can testify, having, during a halt of this corps on Monday last, partaken of a good soldier's breakfast with the last two officers named.—Lieut. Allen was dealing out shoes to the regiment, which now numbers only 173 muskets and 7 officers. A package of late papers was received from Clarkson on Monday last, by Lieut. Allen. We are having plenty of rations with beef every day. John Lloyd, of Rochester, is now Brigade butcher. Our Brigade band furnishes us with hints of "Home Sweet Home," quite often, but we can't see it yet, and the natives are occasionally astonished with a burst of "Yankee Doodle," which some think is "Right smart of a tune, I reckon."

The Sharpshooters still do picket duty. The report in my last that Serg't Davis was wounded, was a mistake. There are no recent casualties in the 6th Co., though several in the 7th and 8th Co.'s have been wounded.

We hear the booming of heavy guns on the right, near Richmond, and it is reported that Richmond is being sieged.

Respectfully, &c. J.T.F.

Brockport Republic, June 30, 1864

Headq'rs 1st Brig., 4th Div., 5th A.C., Near Charles City C.H., Va., June 15th, 1864. Editor Republic:—Dear Sir: We are lying in camp on the north side of the James, waiting till our turn comes to cross this wide stream on a transport. Then we shall operate on the same side of the river with Gen.

Butler. The manner of our operations you will have learned by the time you receive this. Resting several days near Bottom's Bridge, on Sunday last we moved slowly toward the Long Bridge, lower down the Chickahominy, which we crossed on pontoon Monday morning. After a tiresome march all night, then passing a mile further, halted several hours.—Here the boys made coffee, and found cherries and mulberries along the road. The country looked extremely fine, houses old, and fields of grain and corn looked promising. Fences standing untouched indicated that no force had halted long on the road. It was reported that the picket force left behind, on bringing up the rear on Monday morning, skirmished with 30 rebels who followed them, and leaving a squad of flankers in our rear, the pickets captured the pursuing rebels, without loss to us. In the afternoon troops passed on and part of this Division came to this point about 11 P.M., halting in a clover field. The remainder came on yesterday morning, and part of the 2nd Corps crossed the river yesterday. At this point, Wilcox Landing, the James is said to be about 4 miles wide; at other places it is much more narrow. Transports are numerous. At present we are one mile from the river, on the plantation of John J. Clark, a bitter rebel, who fled to Richmond on our approach, leaving a wife and five daughters, with numerous slaves. A guard is about the well shaded grounds, the front part being occupied as headquarters of General Butler and the 2nd Brigade. Yesterday morning a guard of the 2nd Corps shot at one of our men in a cherry tree, wounding him severely in the leg. Cherries suffered much, also green apples in the orchard, which contained rows of peach and apple trees intermixed. A hollow tree containing a swarm of bees was suddenly relieved of the honey it contained. A young son of Mr. Clark, a rebel soldier, is wounded and in Richmond. The few colored people left here hardly know whether it is best to go north or stay, though they wish to be free, but prefer to remain if they can receive pay for their labor. These appear to be more sensible and intelligent slaves than I have before seen.— Their stories of real slave life correspond to the usual plantation experience of slave driving cruelty. This very ground has been the scene of many of those barbarous transactions, so well described in Uncle Tom's Cabin.

Later—the 23rd—Last evening Sergt. Ira Poole,with N.Y.S.S., was shot while in the act of going into the breastworks in front, and died, almost instantly. He was from Two Bridges, Carlton.

After heavy skirmish firing all night, there is nothing unusually exciting this morning.—Gen. Burnside is reported to have been wounded yesterday.   Yours, &c. J.T.F.

Context—The battalion fought in the siege of and assault on Petersburg, Va., June 16–19, and lost eight enlisted men killed or died of wounds, ten enlisted men wounded, and three enlisted men missing.

Brockport Republic, July 14, 1864

Headq'rs 1st Brig., 4th Div., 5th A.C., Near Charles City C.H., Va., June 20th, 1864. Editor Republic:—Dear Sir:—I will attempt to give you a sketch of our advances from the James river. Cruising the James on the morning of Thursday last, on steamers, the 5th Corps having formed, at 10 o'clock A.M. we marched steadily on the road to Petersburg. Road very dusty and water scarce, country very pleasant. With few halts, at about 9 o'clock we rested in an open field near Prince George Court House, 6 miles from Petersburg. It was splendid moonlight, and we were at least 15 miles from the point where we left the James river. There were many stragglers who had fallen out exhausted, heated and weary, but the forced march was evidently necessary, as we heard the booming of artillery in the direction of R*[ichmond]* and could see the flash preceding each report. In an hour the men had made coffee and were resting, when the order came to advance, and we went two miles nearer Petersburg, halting for the night. The 1st Brigade headq'rs were taken in a large barn, among plenty of cornstalks, and your correspondent, with the Brigade bugler and head clerk, found a pleasant and yielding *[illegible word]* in a large *[illegible word]* was lined with straw. Adjoining the barns remained sufficient evidence of a *[illegible word]* comfortable and lovely southern mansion, well shaded. Early on Friday morning the 5th corps were placed in line fronting the enemy, and during the day threw up breastworks, then towards night the lines advanced and took possession of rebel breastworks which were extremely strong. Nothing but skirmishing that day by infantry. Heavy artillery firing on both sides, shells bursting all about. Some wounded brought in.

On Saturday, in the afternoon, our division charged the enemy's breatworks without much effect, having some killed and wounded. Lieut. Chilson, formerly Adjutant of the 24th Mich. aide to them. Cutler, and a promising young *[illegible line]* relatives in Rochester. Capt. D. B. Dailey, lately promoted, Provost Marshal of Division on Gen. Cutler's staff, was slightly wounded in the ear, losing a small portion of it. Lieut. Rodgers of the 6th Wis., acting aide on the Brigade staff, was slightly wounded, also one of the orderlies, by a spent ball: two orderlies' horses in this Brigade were wounded. The 1st Brigade is now commanded by Col. Bragg, of the 6th Wis. The loss in the Battallion of N.Y.S.S. (3 companies), is said to be 13 killed and wounded. In the 6th Co., losses are follows:

Killed—W. E. Ferrin, Pittsford. Wounded—R. H. Eaton, Henrietta; M. Hennessey, Albion; Wm. McNaughton, Caledonia. Geo. N. Goold, of Carlton, missing.

Wednesday, 23d.—Our front is to-day less than two miles from Petersburg (50, 51, 52). No battle yet. Skirmishing and artillery firing. From a high, heavy fort, once in the enemy's front line of breastworks, can be seen the whole plain below and about the city, with the church spires of the latter, and some buildings. The country is finely diversified with woods, green and golden fields, and earthworks; also the channel of the Appomattox, which runs by the city. We are in a southerly direction from P[etersburg] which is 22 miles from Richmond, 10 miles from James river, and is said to be pleasant; is third in size in the State in businesses and population—latter was about 16,000. Contains several important public buildings, several churches, of which six can be seen, one reduced one-half by a shell; a number of cotton factories, three banks, two ropewalks, woolen factory, iron furnace, wi—— mills, also educational establishments, three newspapers, and a lave pen. The water power is good. The place is in fine range of our guns, which may soon open on the town.

I had the pleasure of witnessing a moderate "artillery duel" this morning, in view of the bursting shell from both sides. It was a *[illegible word]* start for this campaign: the effect of the shells could be plainly seen. The 7th N.Y. Artillery really did the best execution—*[illegible word]* its *[illegible word]* were thrown sufficiently close to the opposing battery to produce a panic among the combatants.

I know of nothing extremely important—Wounded have been removed by ambulance to City Point (**53, 54**) and shipped on steamers to New York. Mail facilities grow better and we get some late papers.

Yours, &c   J.T.F.

Context—The battalion participated in the Weldon Railroad raid, August 18–21, in which one enlisted man died of wounds and three officers and 49 enlisted men were missing. Atlanta fell to Sherman, September 2.

VOLUME III
1864

October

Monday, October 10th. –Some frost last night; to-day sun shines—air cold. Wrote to Frank *[Francis R. Douglas]* & *[Sampson W.]* Fry. Two secesh deserters bro't to H*[ea]*dq*[uarte]*rs, one of them tall (about 7 feet) with a snuff colored suit, or butternut brown. Band practice. Dull quiet continues. Copying in P.M. In eve. wrote some to Em*[ma]* S*[mith]*. Warmed feet by the fire, & the air is more moderate to-night.

Tuesday 11th –Pleasant again. Slept well last night. Feel better than usual to-day. Beef steak for breakfast. Make out a list of the Regimental officers in the Brigade, also copied some orders. Bo't cakes 25c. Sent paper 10c to Mat *[Mary A. C. French]* with programme in it &c. considerable firing of artillery in P.M. & eve. Horse-race. Sent letter to Em*[ma S[mith]*. Fine moonlight again. Dispatch stating particulars of Sheridan's 3rd victory over the rebels on Sunday.

Wednesday, 12th.—Still pleasant—warm. No mail for me and my *[Brockport]* Repub*[lic]* does not come. With *[Charles W.]* Spauld*[ing]*. Went to 140th *[NYVI Regiment]*, to get his *[at top of page: "2 Letters from B[rockport], 13th."]* voting papers signed; 140th moved last night. All of them; Talk with the officers &c., also—Shed*[rick J. Jackson]*, who sent me book called "The Potomac & Rapidan." On way back bought 60c worth of cheese, Roast beef for dinner. Then a wash. Splendid day. Read book, Copied orders. Sprinkle in eve. Read in eve. in my shelter tent by candle. Book is interesting. Serg*[ean]*t *[Andrew]* Boyd called with *[Albert S.]* Knowles & I wrote order for latter to get rifles at City Point.

Thursday, 13th—Cold air & the sun does not give much warmth. The 19th Ind*[iana]* Reg*[imen]*t left the Brigade early A.M., arms reversed to join the

2nd corps. Rec*[eive]*d the P. & R. overcoat—is comfortable, also fives. The most unbearable quiet prevails. Pot-pie for dinner. In eve. copied orders, & sat by the out-door fire. Moonlight. Just after 9 went to bed. *[Orrin H.]* Strong called me; I got up & found at office a letter from Mother, sister & Father, all in one, and one from Mat. *[Mary A. C. French] [at top of page]* "Wrote to Repub*[lic]* 14th. Letter rec*[eive]*d 13th. Sent large hard tack to Fair.]

Friday, 14th. –Pleasant, chilly, sun. Almost finished the book. Helped draw rations, cook away. Some orders to copy. Washed dishes at noon. Pot-pie for supper. By Levingood cl*[er]*k wrote to *[Brockport]* Repub*[lic]* & mail carrier went off before I knew it; I went across ravine and mailed the letter. Change of mail carrier to-morrow. More mild to-night than last. Heard heavy firing of artillery to-day on left. I am reminded of old times by dog barking. Drew mackerel to-day.

Saturday, 15th.—The most lovely weather continues. Some copying. Gave Levingood $1 to buy paper & envelopes for me. Got loaf of bread of Rellon *[sp?]* h*[ea]*dq*[uarte]*rs cook, to whom I gave my old overalls. Apple dumpling for dinner. Sewed overcoat, &c. Went to picket line, & saw rebs & spire in Petersburg. Bo't apples 23c. Fried liver for supper. Sent large hard tack for exhibition to the Brockport Fair. In eve. rec*[eive]*d letter from Em*[ma]* S*[mith]* with a good photograph. Sat up somewhat late, & wrote to Mat. *[Mary A. C. French] [at top of page:]* "Sent 3 letters, 16th Sent 2 letters, 17th"]

Sunday, 16th –Still good weather. Headache this A.M., & slept after break*[fas]*t. Levingood, clerk, went on furlough today. I wrote application for furlough for Mr. Humphrey, fifer, & had L*[ieutenan]*t *[Alphonso W.]* Starkweather sign. L*[ieutenan]*t S*[tarkweather]* has at last returned from home. Copied 4 orders. Finished letter to Mat *[Mary A. C. French]*, & wrote to Father & Em*[ma]* S*[mith]* giving her some good advice. Drew beef. Hear that Sheridan's troops are coming to us from "the Valley,"–some already here. No mail for me to-night. Wrote to H*[enry]* C. Murray.

Monday 17th, —Weather same. Made out report of orders communicated. Also to-day copied report of absent officers. Sec*[retar]*y War *[Edwin M.]* Stanton expected to-day, but did not ride along the lines. Called at the Battalion, talked with the boys. Wrote letter to State Agent for *[Charles]* P. Tinker about his wounded boy at hosp*[ital]*. Roast beef for dinner. Expected the *[Brockport]* Rep*[ublic]* to-night, but it did not come. No mail for me. Dull quiet, but I have plenty to do. Finished report of abs*[en]*t officers. *[at top of page:]* "Sent Ballots, 18th & note to Father."]

Tuesday 18th –No change in the weather. Chilly in the A.M. {Last night about 10 *[Major]* Gen*[eral George G.]* Meade's Band serenaded our Headq*[uarte]*rs playing (to my taste) only 1 good melodious piece in 7, then Hail Columbia, then came the whiskey at the officer's tents, then song comic & patriotic— almost a jubilee. Our H*[ea]*dq*[uarte]*r Band then were called out, both Bands playing some. But word was sent down from Divis*[ion]* H*[ea]*dq*[uarte]* rs to have the noise stopped. How much "wh*[iskey]*" was consumed, can't say. I was glad when the hubbub ended.} Had some splendid beans (baked) for breakfast. They were baked by our excellent cook, Frey, in a bake kettle placed over night in a grounds hole, surrounded by live coals. Took *[Shedrick J.]* Jackson's book to him in 140th *[NYVI Regiment]*, also a mucilage bottle. Saw the last *[Brockport]* Repub*[lic]* my letter of 4th published without an error typographical for a wonder. Procured ballots. Bo't can milk, 75c. & 10 figs, 25c. Found beans for dinner on return. Finished monthly report & sealed up my voting papers sending them by mail to Father. Pasted copy of full ticket which I sent, in back part of this. At Battalion & talked with the boys by the fire on election, &c. Signal rockets & artillery booming. Saw what pretends to be Union tickets, "Little Mac's" portrait on them Some sharp "squibs" in H*[ea]*dq*[uarters]* tent. guns, &c. Again no mail for me.

Wednesday 19th—Good wash. & have my shirt-washed 10c. Splendid day. Bo't cakes 25c. At Battalion attended to boys signing powers of attorney & filled out some blanks, also dealt out tickets to some. Discussion Lieut*[enant Alphonso W.]* Starkweather, who is slightly "copperish". In P.M. went to Corps H*[ea]*dq*[uarte]*rs, but could not find State Agent & get ballot. Saw W*[illia]*m Skillan, 94th NY of Clarkson & gave him Lincoln ballots, complete hoping to gain him over. At 140th *[NYVI Regiment]* & pleasant talk with L*[ieutenan]* t *[Lewis B.]* Courtney Saw Dress parade. S*[hedrick]* J. J*[ackson]* went with me to corps H*[ea]*dq*[uarte]*rs & to "our" H*[ea]*dq*[uarte]*rs with me where I marked some photos in album for him. (Great horse-race to-day) Ate a cold bite late. Obtained Repub*[lic]*. At 140th. Copied order eve. Warmed by fire then to bed. *[at top of page* "Rec*[eive]*d 2 letters 20th. Sheridan's "Victory" yesterday."*]*

Thursday 20th.—Somewhat more chilly weather, though pleasant. Attended the voting business, most of the P.M. Bo't ½ liver, 50c Detected an apparent willful error or gross ignorance in L*[ieutenan]*t *[Alphonso W.]* Starkweather's wrongly signing making out of 13 voting envelopes by which all would have been thrown aside by Inspectors of Election. I put a stop to their being sent & brought the case to the notice of Capt*[ain]* Andrews, A*[cting]* A*[ssistant]* A*[dvocate]* G*[eneral]*, then saw A.D. Waters Cortland Co*[mpany]* N.Y. State Agent & procured ballots of him, which I gave to the S*[harp]* S*[hooters]*.(55)

The election blunder of our "ignorant" A[cting] Q[uarter] M[aster]. Good news in eve. from [Major William T.] Sheridan—another victory yesterday[222]. Letter from Mother & sister with ballots, & letter from Mat.[Mary A. C. French]

Context—Troops led by Cavalry Gen. Philip H. Sheridan won a decisive victory in the Shenandoah Valley over Jubal Early's troops on October 19.

Friday, 21st –Nothing very unusual today. At eve. Lieut[enant Alphonso W.] S[tarkweather] sent for me to go down to the Batt[ery] & I there found him giving a pitiful harangue to the boys on account of their making a fuss about the affidavits & implicating me. I stood up [at top of page: "Wrote letter, 2nd"] to my text & he cooled down. Partly made out weekly report.

Saturday 22d.—Cold, windy, & chilly. Overcoat on all day. Bo't apples, 25c. Finished & sent report. Bo't beef P.M. At 140th [NYVI Regiment] & took sup[per] with [Lieutenant Lewis B.] Courtney & L[ieutenan]t. Campbell, adj[utan]t. Back in dark & took ballots to Battalion. Cold night.

Sunday 23d. —The sun makes everything pleasant again today. Fixed up, had a shave, had pass written, got horse at Batt[alion] borrowed spurs of darkey, then rode with L[ieutenan]t [Lewis B.] Courtney to Fort Morton, near where our Headq[uarte]rs were on July 30th. Had bullets thrown at us in crossing field with 108th [NYVI Regiment] found L[ieutenan]t A[ndrew] Boyd & other officers in bomb proof or cellar. Had pleasant visit & good dinner. At 8th H[eavy] Artillery saw only S. Webster & could not wait for him to do his business. Back at 3½. Fine ride. Sent letter to Mother in [Washington] Chronicle. Read some in eve. Wrote to Mate.[Mary A. C. French] Terribly chilly.

[at top of page: "Sent letter 24th Recd letter 24th Clerks to bear arms and accoutrements 24th"]

Monday 24th.—Sunny again & at noon the chill is off. Took letters to Batt[ery]. Rec[eive]d 3 last [Brockport] Republics this A.M. Mislaid. Finished Mat's [Mary A. C. French] letter. Also rec[eive]d a paper from home. Noise at H[ea]dq[uarte]rs all night. 500 men from the Brigade at work on front line works. Made out weekly report of orders. Fixed up tent. (bedroom). Bo't cakes, 25c. Read papers in eve. Read letter from L[ieutenan]t A[ndrew] Boyd. Appears like snow to-night.

Tuesday 25th.—Heard of order from 5th A[rmy] C[orps] H[ea]dq[uarte]rs that all extra duty men including clerks shall bear arms. Copied orders most all day. Some excitement & bustle as though a move is in prospect. (A petition for the revocation of the clerk order, from the Corps clerks.) Nap toward eve. Late sup*[per]* & made out 2 copies of special report for Capt*[ain]* Osborn. Letter from H*[enry]* C. Murray.

Wednes*[day]*, 26th.—Fine day; cloudy eve. & mild. Order to be ready to move at 5 A.M., 27th. Plenty of copying to do. Clerks to go into the ranks. Took Serg*[ean]*t *[Richard C.]* Boyle heavy rifle, & accout*[re]*m*[en]*ts to carry for him. Packed *[at top of page: "*Wrote letter, 26th Rec*[eive]*d letter 26th Fight. Move.*]* knapsack & put in wagon. Washed up. Wrote to Bro*[ther]* Lon & sent $20 in it to Mother. Most of the Headq*[uarte]*r things are packed including offices, &c. in eve. all quiet. To bed early. Letter from Aunt C. & her photo.

Thurs., 27th.—Chilly, windy, cloudy. Up at 3 A.M., packed up, coffee & the troops to start at 4, which they did. Clerks ordered to go with transport, I as "guard" with heavy rifle. We left H*[ea]*dq*[uarte]*rs at daylight & all the Division H*[ea]*dq*[uarte]*r wagons & pack mules parked at Div*[ision]* Headq*[uarte]*rs. Troops move to left & we hear some firing of art*[illery]* & muskt*[re]*y. Bo't cake & cheese 50cts. Our excellent cook made coffee for us. We wait & listen. Put up tent in rain, had supper, then ordered off the Div*[ision]* Headq*[uarte]*r ground. Were just putting up tent again when orders came for us to move to front, so at dark we started went 8 miles through mud, over stumps, in the darkness, quite fast. At last found corps *[at top of page: "*Rec*[eive]*d 2 letters 28th & sent one. Return. 2nd Corps took 2,000 prisoners 5th C*[orps]* 800 The above is a hoax."*]* Headq*[uarte]*rs about 10 & *[Major]* Gen*[eral Gouverneur K.]* Warren told us not to try & find *[Brevet Major]* Gen*[era]*l *[Samuel W.]* Crawford's Division, but rest till morn. Saw ambulance with wounded, & two very large squads of prisoners going to rear. *[Orrin H.]* Strong & I put up ½ shelter tent against the winds laid on rubber blanket with woolen & poncho over us. Wet with sweat yet slept without unusual chill &c. and the rain came down.

Friday 28th.—Sun shines & a dry wind. Up at daylight, packed up. Found the transport not far off. Filled canteens with water at spring & swamp had coffee. Troops of all kinds in the vicinity & wagons. Saw the 140th *[NYVI Regiment]* pass to rear. About 9 *[Brevet Major]* Gen*[eral Gouverneur W.]* W*[arren]* ordered us to move back to the Yellow House (old 5th C*[orps]* headq*[uarte]* rs) as the troops were to move back to old places & we started moving fast. My rifle made my shoulder lame & before I reached camp again feet were very sore. I halted a mile back & came in behind. Put up tent. Rec*[eive]*d letter from Mother & C*[ordelia]* & Mat *[Mary A. C. French]* & papers from them.

Wrote to Mother. Feel sore all over. Brigade move back into old works. After sup[*per*] I called at Batt[*ery*] & talked with boys who feel well. Took back powder horn. At H[*ea*]dq[*uarte*]rs warmed by the fire & to bed early. The 2nd corps yesterday were outflanked and [*at top of page:* "Sent 1 letter. 9th & 30th"] had heavy fighting & took many prisoners. 1st Div[*ision*] 5th C[*orps*] not much fight. Our Brigade captured about 300 prisoners, skirmishing all day in thick woods & over deep streams, some of the time getting lost. Rebs also were unable to find their way & in trying to take our men prisoners, brought them into our lines & were themselves captured. The absence of the sun led them astray.) Frosty & clear to-night.

Saturday 29th.—Fine day. Did not sleep so warm as usual (only one blanket) Levingood (Insp[*ection*] Clerk) came last eve. Break[*fas*]t. Office tent put up & we do business again. Lent the heavy rifle back to Serg[*ean*]t [*Richard C.*] Boyle. The A.M. passes swiftly. Copied order for Lieut[*enant*] St[*arkweather*] to return to the Battalion & other order in eve. 6 copies. Received [*Rochester Evening*] Express from home saying my vote was rec[*eive*]d. Wrote some to Mat [*Mary A. C. French*]. Had first rate supper to-night. Sat by fire in eve. Levingood paid me back $1. which he forgot to lay out in envelopes & paper, for me.

Sunday, 30th.—Fine day. Copying to do nearly all day. 1st Lieut[*enant Lewis B.*] Courtney called on me in A.M. & showed me photo of Mrs. C., (Nell) Made coffee at noon, as our cook has gone. Finished letter to Mat [*Mary A. C. French*] & called on the 140th [*NYVI Regiment*] a few minutes. On way back saw a dress parade of "Regulars"—so much "style". (An eating house has been built to-day & everything appears as though we were to stay here some time. Sutlers come up. Bo't paper & read Grant's Despatches in regard to the late move, which I cannot "see the point of." Read some in eve. Only my feet are still very sore. (Pretty cold to-night.)

Monday, 31st.—Still pleasant. Orders to copy. In P.M. fixed up my tent warmer & lowered my bed. S[*hedrick*] J. J[*ackson*] & Charley Miller, 140th [*NYVI Regiment*] called on me. Dr. Beach gave me apple & figs & a scrapbook. In eve. read papers. (Gen[*era*]l's house is built to-day.) Bo't fig paste 60cts.—Lent Wood 1 3ct. stamp & Levingood also 1 to Beyers. To bed after mail came in 8½ Mail comes early now.

November

Context—The battalion was unattached in the 3rd Division, 5th Corps from November 1864 until its discharge.

Tuesday, Nov*[ember]* 1—Weather same, though perhaps cooler. Plenty of copying orders. Troops are building huts. Read some to-day. Sent paper to Father with cotton ball in it. Nothing new at all. Bought $1 worth of stamps. Colder than for some time before. (Some men drunk') *[at top of page: "S[harp]* Shooters go to Div*[ision]* Headq*[uarte]*rs 4th. Sent letter home 4th."]

Wednesday, 2d.—Cloudy & rain all the P.M. Some copying to do & it is pretty chilly for writing. Read some. Good dinner, boiled onions & potatoes. (2 of 6th Co*[mpany]* S*[harp]* S*[hooters]* arrested for not reporting as ordered.) Gloomy P.M. Sat by fire in eve., warmed & went to bed early. Rain, rain. Had talk with *[Brigadier]* Gen*[eral Edward S.]* Bragg. Bo't $1 stamps.

Thursday, 3rd—Rain most of the day. Chilly. Copied orders 1st thing before breakfast, & several during day. Our Batt*[alion]* of S*[harp]* S*[hooters]* is ordered to report to 3nd Div*[ision]*. (*[Brevet Major]* Gen*[eral Samuel W.]* Crawford's) Headquarters, to Capt*[ain]* Beckwith, where it is hoped they will be used as sharpshooters. Almost stopped raining in eve. Read some in a rebel copy of "Ovid's Art of Love".[223] Commenced letter to sister & finished it. Up quite late.

Friday 4th.—Cold. Some wind. Not much copying. All busy building houses, though we have no log office built yet & have no fire to work by & the weather is chilly. All the trees are being cut down & I got mad at the darkeys for taking my last tree. Just at *[at top of page: "Sent letter 6th Rec[eive]d* letter, 6th Some one stole our frying pan last night."] dusk I walked to near the Division Headq*[uarte]*rs. Bo't 25c of raisins & had a good time with the boys in the eve. Rec*[eive]*d quite a compliment (*[Orrin H.]* Strong & I) from Capt*[ain]* E.A. Andrews, who volunteered to request *[Brevet Major]* Gen*[era]*l *[Samuel W.]* Crawford to let us remain here & he tells of the Divis*[ion]* "airs". Sat up quite late, read & saw a furlough for a Q*[uarter]* M*[aste]*r's Clerk, who took it. Warmed by a good fire, then laid myself away.

Saturday, 5th.—Very high wind all day, which woke me up very early. This is the most uncomfortable day we have yet had. The chilly wind penetrates every thing, yet my overcoat gives plenty of warmth. Made copy of Casualties of 1st Brigade. Calm at eve. Social chats in eve. in office, by various ones. About 11 P.M. a heavy cannonade opened with musketry & came near startling some. Soon quieted down.

Sunday, 6th—Pretty cold. Heavy frost last night. Band woke me up by solemn airs. Most too chilly in office to copy orders yet I copied 3 or 4. Pleasanter in P.M. & sun shone. Washed up, shaved, &c. Finished letter to Mate*[Mary A.*

C. French], & put it in small box with cotton ball, & photograph of [Major] Gen[eral Gouverneur K.] Warren 25c. Bo't can milk, 75c. After sup[per] went in [at top of page: "Wrote letter, sent 8th General Election."] moonlight to 140th [NYVI Regiment]. Saw S[hedrick J.] J[ackson] & had chat with Lieut[enant Lewis B.] Court[ney] by a warm stove. Pleasant walk back. Found paper from home and note from Mother with goose quill for tooth-pick. Also Repub[lic] & letter from Em[ma] S[mith]. Talk with [Orrin H.] Strong, after he was in bed in office.

Monday, 7th—Rain, rain, warm rain. Half the Brigade ordered to remain under arms during the night. Building still going on. Very dull. Not much to do. Preparations for Election. Paid 25 cts. for flour 4 lbs. & had a pot pie for supper. Bo't 5 apples 25 cts. Wrote to Em[ma] S[mith] in eve. Mild night.

Tuesday 8th.—Election day & all but New York soldiers have polls open in Reg[imen]ts.—No liquor orders signed to-day & all is quiet. Read papers in A.M. Very mild & cloudy. Sent Em[ma]'s letter. Our cook away & I got dinner. Heard of the capture of the pirate Florida[224]. A little work at eve. The vote of our Brigade to-day is as follows: For Lincoln, — Band 9; 6th Wis[consin] 124; 7th Wis[consin] 137; 1st Batt[alion] Wis[consin] 70; 24th Mich[igan] 176; 143rd Penn[sylvania] 186; 149th Penn[sylvania] 188; 150th Penn[sylvania] 110; total, 1,000. For McClellan in same order as above Band 36, 30, 1, 50, 100, 102, 27; total 347. Majority for Lincoln, 653. The soldiers, as a mass, do well for Lincoln. [at top of page: "Army of the Poto[mac] gives 8,600 maj[ority] for Lincoln. Weighed 130½ lbs. 10 oz., a gain of 12½ since Sept[ember] 8."]

Wednesday, 9th.—Fine warm air. Somewhat cloudy. Very little to do to-day. Read some. Pot-pie for dinner. Aired tent & blankets. Good news in regard to the soldiers vote. In P.M. went to 140th [NYVI Regiment] & had pleasant visit with [Lieutenant Lewis B.] Courtney. Came back just in time to catch them eating supper. Issued an order for officer of the Day for to-morrow. Fine moonlight. It is reported that the Potomac Army vote is 19,200—8,600 majority for Lincoln.

Thursday 10th.—Good weather after a sprinkle early A.M. copied 3 orders—14 copies. Had a private skirmish for the first time in long while[225] found plenty of the enemy. Bought another photograph of [Major General Gouverneur K.] Warren 20cts. to send home. Weighed myself. 130½ lbs. We hear that New York State gave 40,000 maj[ority] For Lincoln. Write to Mother in eve. & send photograph of Gen[eral] W[arren]. All quiet. Have the [Washington] Chronicle with Election news. Mailed my letter and one for Dr.

Beach at Division Headq[*uarte*]rs, then back & read awhile. Some of the boys (hostlers) are celebrating the defeat of Little Mac. Letter from home & Mat [*Mary A. C. French*] & paper. [*crossed out:* "let Dr. B[*each*] & Levingood have 1 stamp."]

Friday 11th.—Pleasant. Cold wind. Changed clothes for a wash. Dull in office. One of the Band goes home on 20 days furlough. Have commenced letter to Mat.[*Mary A. C. French*] Pay darkey 15 cts to wash shirt & drawers. In P.M. [*at top of page:* "Rec[*eive*]d 2 letters, 10th & sent one 13th"] we have a Review of our Brigade by [*Brevet Major*] Gen[*era*]l [*Samuel W.*] Crawford. A dull Review. Some work in eve. The Herald having news (contraband) of Gen[*era*]l [*William T.*] Sherman's move toward Charleston, the papers were ordered to be suppressed & were gathered up by officers in eve. and news boys arrested so that the news might not reach the enemy. Pretty cold to-night. About 11 o'clock we had a serenade good instrumental and vocal music.

Saturday 12th.—Quite steady cold. Cleaning up about the camps & Headq[*uarte*]rs. Full of business in A.M. "Lots" of whiskey orders to be signed by Captain E.A. Andrews, A[*cting*] A[*ssistant*] A[*dvocate*] G[*eneral*]. Fixed up about my tent, & went to 140th [*NYVI Regiment*] & sat awhile in S[*Hedrick J.*] J[*ackson*]'s tent, saw Lieut[*enant Lewis B.*] C[*ourtney*] & I made some arrangements for going to 2nd Corps to-morrow. Some rain then the sky cleared off finally after sup[*per*] At Serg[*ean*]t [*Richard C.*] Boyle, tent at Battalion, Div[*ision*] Headq[*uarte*]rs applied for a Sharp's Rifle and trimmings & talked with the boys. The coldest night yet. Had a warm drink.

Sunday 13th.—Fine day but cold & some breeze. Copied two orders & had pass signed then with Lieut[*enant Lewis B.*] Courtney (I having Jack[*son P. Nichols*]'s pony) started for 2nd Corps over same ground as 3 weeks ago, only farther. At last found the 8th N.Y. H[*eavy*] Art[*iller*]y holding breastworks in front of Petersburg, & all without quarters, except underground. Hitched horses & went into L[*ieutenan*]t [*Stephen R.*] Stafford's quarters (underground) then with him to picket line,(**56, 57**) which at one point was within a stone's throw of the rebels through whose works a porthole could be seen. Farther on looked through port holes to Appomattox river below.—in plain sight of the streets of Petersburg. A fine view. Saw darkey pecking on the Railroad. Bullets flew around us. Back and had a good visit, dinner of apple dumpling & came away, though not without a salute of 2 rebel bullets as we galloped across the field harmlessly. Pleasant ride back & paid Jack 50 cts for horse. Finished letter to Mat [*Mary A. C. French*] & sent it. Pretty cold again to-night. In [*Charles W.*] Spaulding's tent & rec[*eive*]d Republic. A clear, cold moon. A cold office tent.

Monday 14th—Cold, yet pleasant. Nothing new. The Pioneers[226] are putting up a house for us & no work of importance is going on in the tent office. House not finished. In eve. at the Batt[alion] & had long visit with the drummer & fifer boys. To bed warm.

Context—Sherman begins the march to the sea, November 15.

Tuesday 15th—Another chilly day, same as yesterday. A chimney is put on our house, & [Orrin H.] Strong & I [at top of page: "Log office built—15th & drew clothing Letters 17th. Sent one 17th"] fixed up bunk in the new house (office), & got to work by the fire at 3½ P.M. In eve copied orders & it seems comfortable in the house. Good warm bed. Rec[eive]d clothing, 1 drawers, 2 p[ai]r stockings.

Wednesday, 16th.—Quite busy in A.M. Pretty cold to-day, but pleasant. Good fire in office. (Florida rebels are deserting—poorly clad.) Did some sewing. Visited the 140th [NYVI Regiment] Bo't leggings of S[hedrick] J. J[ackson], 65c Introduced to Lieut[enant] Locie [sp?], N[ew] Y[ork] Battery. Bo't pair pants 3.27 & jacket 5.50 of L[ieutenan]t [Lewis B.] C[ourtney], & came back in eve. Took trimming from jacket & left it at Band to be fixed. Pretty cold again to-night.

Thursday, 17th.—Splendid day after fog cleared off. Warm. Drew 2 shirts 1 pair drawers & same for [Orrin H.] Strong, let him have white shirt, which he will repay me for by drawing one for me next time. Dull to-day. Had a general wash up & put on new shirt & drawers. Wrote to sister & finished in eve. after receiving letter from home & Mat [Mary A. C. French] & carried letter to Div[ision] mail. Had "A" tent fixed into eating house for us to-day. Mild to-night & looks like rain.

Friday, 18th.—Fine day. Wind in eve. & from [at top of page: "Rec[eive]d stockings from home, 18th Rec[eive]d letter & rec[eive]d [sent?] one 20th."] being warm during day grows colder in eve. Put glass bottle between logs in office for window. Commenced wearing Zouave pants & jacket after having latter fixed—owe 20 cts. Waited at Butchers for beef rations. Hi[ram] Williams, 76th NYV[I Regiment], who had been home to B[rockport] brought me 2 pairs stockings, from Mother. Sprinkle of rain in eve. Reports of some part of the Corps moving. Quiet with us.

Saturday 19th.—Rain. Dark. Some business. Same dull routine. Commenced letter to Mat [Mary A. C. French]. Carried letter to Lieut[enant James K.] McDonald, H[ea]dq[uarter]s Battalion. Wrote to Lieut[enant] A[ndrew]

Boyd, 108th *[NYV]* inf*[antry regiment]*. Copied orders in eve. Rain ceased to-night. Plenty of company in the office, in eve. No mail to-night as the boat is aground.

Sunday 20th.—Rain all day & in eve. Several copies of orders to copy. Brought in wood to last 24 hours. Found my bed dampened from eave-drops & the eaves were repaired during day. Finished & sent letter to Mat *[Mary A. C. French]* & a paper to Grandmother. In eve. the troops had orders to be ready—a scare from *[Brevet Major]* Gen*[eral Samuel W.]* Crawford—countermanded at 7. The mail brought me a *[at top of page; "Mailed letter, 22d."]* paper from home and letter from friend Frank *[Francis R. Douglas]*, who says she is to be married in Jan*[uary]*. I am pleased to know that she is happy in the belief of a wise choice. Read some in eve. The weather is very mild.. We keep the orderlies running some, in the dark, this eve. Sat up late by good fire.

Monday, 21st.—Rain all day & eve. Keep up a good fire in office. Some copying. Wrote letter to Frank *[Francis R. Douglas]*, to send to-morrow. Bo't paper in eve. 10c. Brought in 24 hours wood which Pioneers cut. Nothing unusual & after reading news go to bed early. *[Sampson W.]* Fry continues to give us very good meals and we manage to have soft bread almost every meal.

Tuesday, 22d.—A trifle of sun to-day, then in P.M. grew colder—icy in evening, with wind. Order copying A.M. Borrowed papers of Dr. Beach. Hi*[ram]* Williams called on me. In P.M. called on S*[hedrick]* J. J*[ackson]* & L*[ieutenan]* t *[Lewis B.]* Courtney. Mailed letter after I came back. Brought in wood for night. No mail for me. Took paper to *[Charles W.]* Spaulding & he read me letters. A fire feels decidedly comfortable, while the wind howls without. *[at top of page: "Thanksgiving 24th. Sent letter 24th"]*

Wednesday, 23d.—Froze hard last night. Sun shines today. Dull as usual. We have now come down to hard-tack, no pot-pie lately. In P.M. rigged up Zouave & called on *[Hiram]* Williams, 76th *[NYVI Regiment]*. Had a good visit & rec*[eive]*d much information in regard to affairs there. Saw Capt*[ain R. S.]* Dillon when I came back. At the Battalion. Tack & beef sup. Read in eve. Cold & clear tonight.

Thursday 24th—Splendid day. Sunny. Froze the hardest yet this winter last night. Expected turkeys from the North, but they did not come up to noon & probably halted for officers on the way. At Batt*[alion]* in A.M. Wrote letter to mother. Surprised with turkey for dinner. Pretty quiet about Headq*[uarte]*rs. Music by the Band & some gay dancing in the front yard. Stories in the office in the eve. Went to bed early but no sleep till late.

Friday, 25th.—Splendid weather still. Somewhat busy. Had drawers washed by Solomon, 10c. In P.M. filled out remarks in our Company Descriptive Book at Batt[alion]. Lieut[enant Alphonso W.] Starkweather [at top of page: "Mailed letter, 22nd"] put a bounty & back pay job in my hands, but I couldn't see the point and declined. (Had a slight blow up this A.M. with our "Reverend".) 300 recruits came to our Brigade today. Mild this eve. Froze hard last night. Remarkably quiet. Letter from Mother.

Saturday 26th.—Mild balmy air. Sun in A.M. cloud in P.M. Fixed seat first thing in morning. Copying &c. Placed photographs in blank book by inserting them in the sheet album style. Took letter to Lieut[enant James K.] McDonald, & helped to bring in wood. Some talk of a move. Looks like rain. Letter from Lieut[enant] A[ndrew] Boyd, 108th [NYVI Regiment] & [Brockport] Republic from Brockport. Sat up late writing to Mae [Mary A. C. French]. Sprinkle of rain at 10 P.M.

Sunday, 27th.—Cloudy, mild, misty. Quiet & more like Sunday than for a long while. Last night rec[eive]d morsel of turkey (cooked) from N[ew] Y[ork] State, intended for Thanksgiving. Also 3 apples: Humbug by the time it gets here. Finished letter to Mae[Mary A. C. French], & sent. Have stewed tomatoes for supper.—Read, &c., in eve. A sociable talk & to bed in good season. Letter from Aunt C. [at top of page: "Mailed letter 29th"]

Monday 28th.—Mild. Very pleasant. Considerable writing. Had a slight "skirmish." In P.M. visited 140th. Good dinner with S[hedrick] J. J[ackson]. Roast beef & pudding. Made arrangements with L[ieutenan]t [Lewis B.] C[ourtney] to go riding tomorrow. In eve. wrote to Aunt C. & sent photograph of [Major] Gen[era]l [Gouverneur K.] Warren, which I bought with 3 others in all 55 cts., which I owe to Band boy. A rain breeze to-night. No fire in office—unusual.

Tuesday 29th—Splendid day. Fixed up & looked about for a horse at Batt[alion] & was forced to ask Maj[or] Kerr, 6th Wis[consin] for one, which I obtained & rode with Lieut[enant]s [Lewis B.] Courtney & Wright to 2d Divis[ion], 2d Corps. Found 108th [NYVI Regiment] in Fort McGilvery, had visit with Lieut[enant] A[ndrew W.] Boyd, & dinner then went along lines in sight of rebs & saw man just shot through the head. Found L[ieutenan]t [Stephen R.] Stafford in ground hole. He went back with us to Fort McGilvery, when after looking at the Appomattox & Petersburg, came back, stopping on the way to see Lieut[enant] Webster, 8th H[eavy] A[rtillery] at 2nd Brig[ade]. H[ea]dq[uarte]rs 2nd Corps to move to-night & the [at top of page: "Wrote 2 letters & rec[eive]d one 1st."] 9th Corps met us on the move. Back O.K. Orders to write in eve. and to bed early. Warm.

Wednesday 30th.—Weather never finer. Warm enough to sweat. Saw H*[enry]* C. Murray of 6th Co*[mpany]* S*[harp]* S*[hooters]* who had been home & in Brockport & talked with him. Washed stockings feet & towel &c. Had shirts washed yesterday, 20cts. At Div*[ision]* Batt*[alion]* saw the body of a man who died yesterday, suddenly opened, & a post-mortem examination by 4 surgeons who concluded that death was caused by inflammation of stomach and bowels. Splendid sunset. Good news to-night from Sherman. Very warm in eve. for Nov*[ember]* 30. No letter from Mae *[Mary A. C. French]*, since 17th. Fine starlight and a young moon. After going to bed early heard stories told of deviltry in the wicked west and was much amused. Capt*[ain E. A.]* Andr*[ews]* told some of the most amusing ones. Was introduced to Capt*[ain]* Beckwith of the S*[harp]* S*[hooters]*

Thursday Dec*[ember]*. 1st—Pleasant day. A slight disturbance in the internal region bothered me this morning. Feel unwell. Wrote to Sister C*[ordelia]*. Wrote to *[Brockport]* Republic & sent in same envelope with C*[ordelia]*'s. Hear of Gen'l Scofield's success on the 30th.[227] Fire in eve., and I feel better. Dull. *[at top of page: "December Wrote D——4th"]*

Friday, 2d.—Good weather holds out. Last eve. rec*[eive]*d 2 from home. Hear of Gen'l *[David McMurtrie]* Gregg's destruction of a rebel station, stores, &c.[228] Darned stockings. At Batt*[alion]* in P.M. No mail for me in eve. Prisoners still come in. Brought in wood in eve. To bed very early. Heard more stories by Capt*[ain E. A.]* Andrews, &c.

Saturday 3d—Cloud and sun—mild. Headq*[uarter]*s barn being built. In P.M. at 140th, *[NYVI Regiment]* saw Lon, *[Lieutenant Lewis B.]* Court*[ney]* &c & went to 8th H*[eavy]* A*[rtillery]* & had pleasant visit with Seth Hall & L*[ieutenan]*t *[Stephen R.]* Staf*[ford]*. Also, on way back saw S. Webster, now Capt*[ain]* at Brig*[ade]* Headq*[uarte]*rs. On getting back to office was surprised by seeing young Barlow, the scapegrace, in 94th *[NYVI Regiment]* or 6th A*[dvocate]* General]. Some copying in eve. No letter for me.

Sunday, 4th—A very fine day. At Batt*[alion]* & saw inspection in A.M. Then copied 2 sets of orders, &c. Nap in P.M. Orders to be ready to move, in eve. Wrote *[Brockport]* Repub*[lic]* to-night. Partly packed up. Took letter to Division H*[ea]*dq*[uarte]*rs where they are preparing to get out in morn. The 6th Corps are to relieve ours.

Monday, 5th.—A pleasant day. Some writing. Got all ready to move about 4 o'clock P.M. then the*[y]* agreed to let us stay till morn*[ing]* again. The 1st Division of 6th Corps came up to relieve us before dark. Orders to move to move *[sic]* now at 6 A.M. Bo't paper in eve. & copied some. Some discussion in office in eve. 6th Corps officers camp in our front yard. Mild & hazy. Fine moonlight—waiting to take our places.

Tuesday. 6th –Up at 5. Sprinkle, then cleared off. Lovely day. Moved at 6, or just as day was peeping from the east. Moved 2 miles, to the rear of fortifications, near Jerusalem plank road, & camped on high ground overlooking the plain on which are camped cavalry &c. Near and almost in the woods. Headquarters were put up troops raised shelter tents, & I did the same. Went some distance for water, had wash & finished making out papers for Capt*[ain]* E. A. Andrews, A*[cting]* A*[ssistant]* A*[djutant]* G*[eneral]*. Sent paper to Father. After supper Gen*[eral Edward S.]* B*[ragg]* rec*[eive]*d orders to be ready to move at daylight tomorrow. {It would seem that one more effort is to be made to end the rebellion by a grand blow, & I have faith that it will succeed this time, especially if the present good weather continues.} Band play. All preparations are being made to-night. The army take breath, for the coming struggle. We are to take 4 days rations on person & 2 days in wagon. Every one seems alive to the importance of this move & I have no less of the buoyant feeling than do all to-night. May every energy be exerted bring us victory. Had paper written. Up late.

Wednesday, 7th.—Up at 6. Troops started at daylight. Saw Ed Wentworth of 185th NY*[VI Regiment]* as the 1st Div*[ision]* troops were passing. 2nd Div*[ision]* also passed, & I saw L*[ieutenan]*t *[Lewis B.]* C*[ourtney]* & others of the 140th *[NYVI Regiment]*. The raw recruits of our Brig*[ade]* were left behind. (Last night Wood volunteered to go with the transport & Brigade. *[at top of page:* "Rain, 7th."*]* but I had made up my mind to go.) Rain commenced falling at 9 & we started back to near our old quarters with the train, all of which are parked together. *[Orrin H.]* Strong & I took possession of a large log enclosure & in one corner put up shelter & fixed a comfortable place. Built fire & had a good time. Rain ceased & sun shone at 4. Cooked our own supper & read Dime Novel in eve. Fine moonlight. Made a good bunk & have bough bed. *[at top of page:* "Sent letter 8th Rec*[eive]*d letter 8th"*]*

Thursday, 8th.—Fine day. Breeze. Breakfast of cheese, coffee, pork, fried hard tack. All quiet & we are near R.R. *[Orrin H.]* Strong bo't paper & we read news. Bo't cakes 25c. Got in wood. Wrote to father. Hear rumors of our troops having gone to Weldon, N.C. Had papers in eve. Stragglers from the expedition come in escorted by cavalry—2 to 3,000. Troops had crossed the Nottoway River. Letter from Mat *[Mary A. C. French]*, first since Nov*[ember]* 17.

Friday, 9th.—Very cold last night & we (*[Orrin H.] S[trong]* & I) came near freezing our feet. Ice thick in wash dish & canteens. Cold wind n. Found plenty of wood & kept warm all day. Fried tack & coffee. *[Charles W.]* Spauld*[ing]* called on us. Very game snow birds in out house. Smoky, cloudy. Snow in small quantities and sleet. Went to army H*[ea]*dq*[uarte]*rs. but could get no paper. Had supper of roasted onions cof*[fee]* & rack & a rousing fire. Pretty cold.

Saturday, 10th—Ground & trees covered with ice and icicles abundant. Chunk of ice fell from tree in night & cut hole in our tent. Slept with shoes and overcoat on. Disagreeable day—slosh at Army H*[ea]*dq*[uarte]*rs bo't 2 papers, 15c. Drew *[at top of page: "Sent letter, 10th Rec[eive]d 2 letters 11th"]* 4 days rations—cof*[fee]* sug*[ar]* & tack. Wrote to Mat. *[Mary A. C. French]* Got sup*[per]* wood for eve. Rec*[eive]*d paper from home with stick of gum & quill & note from Mother.

Sunday, 11th.—Cloudy & mud dries up some. By the fire all day, reading. Hear from the troops. Letter from Mat *[Mary A. C. French]*, dated 27th Nov*[ember]*, had been to 2nd Corps. Letter in eve. from Em*[ma]* S*[mith]* and paper from *[Brockport]* Republic with my letter of 1st published. Grows colder to-night & a heavy wind blows.

Monday 12th.—Bright sun. Froze very hard last night, & our feet could not keep warm. *[at top of page: "Letter 13th"]* Early for breakfast. Barlow called. Hung out blankets to dry & washed some things. Read. Cold wind. In P.M. troops returned to their last camping place & we went there & put up tents same as last Tuesday. Found my bed in good condition except full of ice. Boys tell stories of the late raid & the tearing up of the Weldon R.R. & burning of houses, barns, grain, &c. a journey of 50 miles & back. H*[ea]*dq*[uarte]*rs brought back a young contraband. To bed in shelter tent with Wood.

Tuesday, 13th—Cold night last, but I slept quite warm. Quiet to-day. Some work to do in cold office. Letter from A. L. Root. Write *[at top of page: "Sent letter & rec[eive]d one, 14th"]* some to Mother to send next Thursday. 9 months longer only to stay in the Army. Good dinner with bread & beef with gravy, coffee.— Finished Capt*[ain E. A.]* Andrews clothing returns & send them off. Weather is more mild. This eve. sat by fire out doors, talking with the darkies, &c.

Wednesday, 14th—More mild. Sun & cloud. Not very much writing to do. Dull as usual. Plenty of potatoes. Hear heavy cannonading on right. Windy. Wrote to Mother & sent. Nap in P.M. Letter from "Frank" *[Francis R. Douglas]* eve. Sat before fire in the officers chairs as they were all away.

Thursday, 15th.—Colder. Wind. H[enry] C. Murray came to see me. Several orders to copy. Some talk of a change of camp. Nearly ready to move, but wait till to-morrow. Quite mild to-night. Some of the officers feel exhilerated. Some here from abroad. Hear good news from [General William T.] Sherman. Expect stove for tent. [at top of page: "Move Camp, 16th Rec[eive]d 2 letters 16th"]

Friday, 16th.—Splendid day, some like summer. Everything packed & the Brigade move at 9. Office stays till the wagon comes back again. Office left at noon, & we moved 2 miles to near the Jerusalem plank road, in a fine piece of young pines. Put up "A" tent. [Orrin H.] Strong & I making a bed in it & Wood on the other side. Office tent up & all in running order. Rec[eive]d letter from Mat [Mary A. C. French], which had been mislaid, dated 11th. Quite warm to-night. Dr. Beach & Capt[ain E. A.] Andrews in office talking. Very quiet. Men (troops) are going & building winter quarters. Copied order. Letter from Mother & sister. To bed early & a good bed, too.

Saturday, 17th.—Another fine day. Log huts are being put up by troops. A change in our Brigade staff is to be made, some officers leaving. Plenty of orders to copy & I fix up some in tents. Change clothes, &c. Good news from [Major General George H.] Thomas, near Nashville[229].—Fixed up my application for furlough, &c. To bed at 11 P.M. [at top of page: "Sent letter, 18th. Rec[eive]d letter, 18th."]

Sunday, 18th. –Somewhat chilly, cloudy. Had furlough approved by Capt[ain E. A.] A[ndrews] & by Gen[era]l [Edward S.] Bragg] for 15 days. Some copying. Took morning papers to Div[ision] H[ea]dq[uarte]rs & saw the S[harp] S[hooters] boys. Also passed through the 1st & 2nd Divisions, & saw 140th [NYVI Regiment] boys. Back at 2 & made coffee. Felt tired. Finished letter to Mat [Mary A. C. French] & mailed. In eve. rec[eive]d letter from Mat [Mary A. C. French], dated 15th. Warmed feet by fire, & went to bed quite early.

Monday, 19th.—Changeable & warm. Washed clothes in A.M. endorsed orders in P.M. About 4 o'clock my furlough application came back from Division approved for 20 days by Brevet Maj[or] Gen[era]l [Samuel W.] Crawford, but requiring the number of officers & men present for duty, and the same absent on leave or furlough, which I had placed on by the Capt[ain] Com[man]d[in]g Batt[alion] in eve. S[hedrick] J. Jackson, 140th [NYVI Regiment] called on me & I went back with him as far as Divis[ion]. Rec[eive]d [Brockport] Repub[lic] in eve. Some sprinkles of rain in eve. A great fever for furloughs. [at top of page:"Furlough. Stove in tent & sent letter, 20th."]

Tuesday 20th.—Pleasant but cold in eve. Put up sheet iron stove, (Sibley) in tent, & banked up tent with dirt, logs, &c. Sent letter to Mother & finished "filing" orders in eve. Stove heats up like fury. In bed in good season.

Wednesday, 21st.—Rain commenced last eve. & continues till noon. Some writing to do. Stove comfortable. Good news from *[Major]* Gen*[era]*l *[William T.]* Sherman before Savannah, & *[Major General Geoge H.]* Thomas in Tennessee.[230] Very quiet. Cut wood in rain, & wet through my jacket. In P.M. went to Battalion. About 10 in eve. my furlough came, approved by *[Major]* Gen*[era]*l *[George G.]* Meade for 20 days. Got my things together & sat up late.

Thursday, 22d.—Up at 5½ & started for station with Wood, who goes to City Point. *[Brigadier]* Gen*[eral Edward S.]* Bragg, Col. Dana, *[at bottom of page: "Very cold & froze last night."]* & others of the Brigade also rode to the Point on the train. Got my furlough stamped by Provost Marshal & transportation to Wash*[ington]*. On the steamer at 10 & on down river. No good accommodations on the boat. Enlisted men not allowed in upper cabins but I found Bartley of Brockport, (Q*[uarter]* M*[aster]* cl*[er]*k, Ar*[tille]*ry Brigade, 6th Corps) & went up stairs where it is warm. Very cold down stairs & wind blows. Bo't cake & pie, 45c. No breakfast this morning. Just before getting to Fortress Monroe, saw the masts & spars of the sunken pirate "Florida"[231] in the "*[Hampton]* Roads." Soon after sundown the waves began to rise & foam in the Bay, the boat rocked heavily & the passengers could hardly keep their feet. A lamp was knocked from the chandelier to the floor & smashed. Stomaches began to heave & men rushed to the deck & gave way to the tumult raging within. In about an hour the tossing subsided & I only felt a slight effect from the swell—a slight boil at the pit of the stomach, & weakness in my legs did not leave my seat.—made bed on bare floor & slept, warm. *[at top of page: "Washington, Baltimore"]*

Friday 23d—Pleasant day. Cold. Up at 2½ A.M. Ice 1 to 2 inches thick in river which hindered the boat very much & we halted along until 3 o'clock, ice breaking hole in boat side at Alexandria took cars to Washington. Could not find Paymaster at depot after seeing Col*[onel]* Finnicum. Got transportation to Roch*[ester]* & return. Cup coffee & piece bread, 15c, cake of woman, 10c. Helped Capt*[ain]* Barnard, 2nd N.Y.M*[ilitia]* R*[eserve]*, (disabled) into car, & started at 6:45 for Baltimore. Gave a soldier's wife (German) half of my seat. At Balt*[imore]* helped *[at top of page: "Williamsport"]* Capt*[ain]* B. into carriage rode to Penn*[sylvania]* Central Depot & took sleeping car, berth, (top) 50c. Very comfortable, & had good wash. A young man is also with Capt*[ain]*.

Saturday, 24th.—Passed Harrisburg about 2 A.M. Got up soon after daylight; train behind time Wash & we got the Capt*[ain]* into another car—no change from Balt*[imore]* to Elmira. Sleighing on the route to E*[lmira]*. Snow falling. Mountains and fine streams. Left Elmira at 1 P.M., reached Avon at 8 P.M. Bo't supper 15cts. Reached Roch*[ester]* 8½, called at telegraph office, saw *[at top of page:* "(Home, 24th Christmas.)"*]* Jimmy Raleigh; had hair cut & got shaved, 35 cts. Bo't ticket to Roch*[ester]*, 37cts., saw Mary Smith on train & Lib S & Rob. Bond at depot Brock*[port]*, 10 o'c*[loc]*k. Found all abed at home & surprised all of them. Did not see children to-night. Cup of tea & bread. Preferred to sleep on floor after good chat with Mother & Father.

Sunday Christmas—Good sleighing—mild. Abed late. Good breakf*[as]*t. Ready for meeting & wrote note to *Mat [Mary A. C. French]*, (by Eddy) & rec*[eive]*d reply. At church, Presbyterian with Mother & Cordelia, Harvey & Lon, & ran the gauntlet of several "batteries" of eyes, sitting in front, but managed to stand it. *[Professor Malcolm]* McVicar preached. At close of meeting saw & spoke to Ellen Boyd, sister, & Lorna Hutchinson; saw P. Shepard. Pleasant day. With Lon at *[Brockport]* Repub*[lic]* office. Saw Lennie Beach.[232] At sup*[per]* home. After sup*[per]* put on citizen's coat & walked with Cordelia down st*[reet]*. I Called at Mat's *[Mary A. C. French]*. Good reception, & *[at top of page:* "Wrote to Aunt C. & to Frank *[Francis R. Douglas]*, 26th also to *[Orrin H.]* Strong."*]* Passed the evening very pleasantly. Apples & grapes. Splendid time.

Monday, 26th –Breakfast 9. Wrote to Aunt C. & Frank *[Francis R. Douglas]*, &c. Father took my shoes to shop for mending. Have a cold. Sleighing or snow is fast melting. Did not go out of the house till night, except to call on Dr. *[H. C.]* Clark, who was not at home. Had clothes fixed some. Wrote to *[Orrin H.]* Strong & sent $1. which I owe him. Let Lon have $1 for a ride to-night. Bo't 25 cts. worth of pea-nuts. Had shoe mended, 15 cts. Blacking 15 cts. With Cordelia, called on Mat *[Mary A. C. French]* but did not go to Aggie *[Johnson]*'s, as I expected. Music—piano. Did not stay very late. Had mourning envelopes returned, fully. Took some thing vinegar & molasses for my cold—hoarseness. Feels unwell.

Tuesday, 27th.—Sloppy—warm. Hardly out of the house A.M. to-day, & doctored my throat—could not talk loud, till P.M. (My letter came today, dated 20th.) Shaved, &c. Read some. In P.M. went down st*[reet]* with Father; met & *[at top of page illegible word]* spoke to Mr. Barnett.[233] Called on Mr. *[Horatio N.]* Beach & set some type in the *[Brockport]* Repub*[lic]* office, there saw Mr. Northrop, Efner, Avery, & Ch. Palmer. At Randolph's, Fry's, saw Dr. Thacher, Decker, Ed Smith, Randall, & called at Bank, also at Mrs. Beach's, but she was riding, & I saw her in cutter, with Mrs. Williams to whom I was introduced & had a lively chat, 2 minutes, Saw Mrs. Smith at Reeds, also Mrs. R*[andall]* & the baby. At Dr. *[H. C.]* Clark's & had a good time. D*[octo]*r blind, portly. Henry, Amelia, Eva, & introduced to Mrs. Dr. Olden. Baked apples & milk, home. Bo't candy, 5 cts. Feel tired & not extremely well to-night. Have tried to talk so much to-day. Visit at home, eve.

Wednesday, 28th—Feel better to-day. Cold wind & thaws in A.M. Freezes in eve. Rode with Cordelia to Randall's. Saw Henry & all. In a few minutes went on to Uncle Jonah's no one at home except Charley, Hannah & child. Good time.—apples, cider, good dinner. Left at 1 & went to R*[andall]*'s staid till 8 in eve. Good time & supper. *[at top of page:* "Letters rec*[eive]*d—2 on 28th Sent letter, 29th"*]* Dark; rode home safely. Found letter from Frank *[Francis R. Douglas]* & invitation to attend party at Mary Smith's, on Mechanic St. *[now Park Avenue]* to-morrow eve. To bed quite early.

Thursday, 29th.—Colder. Snow flakes, light. Had leggings washed. Rode to John Perry's Clarkson & gave Mrs. Dr. Beach a package—letter & stopped at Steele's—saw Miss F. Little girl rode back to B*[rockport]* with me. Saw several friends. Called at Mr. Baker's—talk with Mrs. B*[aker]*. Saw Mrs. Ch*[arle]*s Taylor. Note from Mat *[Mary A. C. French]* & invitation to dine there on Saturday. Wrote to Mr. Judd, Auburn for Aunt C. to come. In P.M. called at Mr. *[Luther]* Gordon's, & at Smith's on Mechanic St. At *[Brockport]* Repub*[lic]* office read paper with a comp*[limentary]* notice. Spent the P.M. at Mat's *[Mary A. C. French]* Good time—supper. Mrs. F*[rench]* sick. At Presbyterian church, Christmas tree, in eve. with Cordelia & Mary & at *[John]* Getty's Failed to call at Mechanic St. in eve. Up late.

Friday, 30th. –Went to Rochester on 6:45 train, ticket to & return 68 cts. At telegraph office left my over coat. Called at National Hotel. Saw Gallop, clerk. Went to Plymouth Avenue, 2 miles out of my way to find Leopold st*[reet]*. A man helped me to find the way & I at last found the Douglass house, No. 11. Mrs. D*[ouglass]* looking out of the door. Found all busy sewing. Frank *[Francis R. Douglas]* (the to-be bride.) looked well. Showed me photographs & told me of the programme, &c., connected with the approaching marriage; walked back to Arcade with me & we had a pleasant time. She selected a thimble for my mother, $1. Bo't books, $3.50. Photograph album for sister, 2.25 & drew jewelry. Called at Provost Marshall's office, saw Mr. S.H. Clark & Sammy. At Hon. Freeman Clarke's, & he gave me an invitation to write to him in regard to War Department Pr*[inting]* Office. Rode on cars back to Brockport, leaving Roch*[ester]* at noon. Saw Susan Tripp (formerly) on train. In P.M. Cordelia, Mate *[Mary A. C. French]* & I rode in snow storm to K*[endall]* Mills in buggy

— $2. (Bo't chestnuts, 20c. & books for E*[ddy]* & H*[arvey]* & envelopes, 2 letters 80c. At *[Kendall]* Mills stopped at Benedicts, found all at home ex*[cept]* Mr. B*[enedict]* & Fidelia & Melissa, who came in eve. Went on to store, saw old friends, & back to supper at B*[enedict]*'s Good time. "Rast" & wife &c. there. Staid late & pleasant ride back to B*[rockport]* 1 A.M. 31st. Stopped at Mats *[Mary A. C. French]* to warm, then home.

Saturday, 31st.—Pleasant day. Sleepy, A.M. & laid abed late. Set up part of Harvey's Carriers address in office. Saw former Lieut*[enant]* Allen. Met many people in st*[ree]* in P.M., & took dinner at Mat's, *[Mary A. C. French]* with sister Aggie J*[ohnson]*, Mrs. Butler. Splendid table, nice turkey, &c. Did not dare to eat much, but felt distressed bowels in eve., & not well. Down st*[reet]* bo't nuts & got cloves for bad breath. Mate Golden was there when I returned from st*[reet]*, also brother Leon. Had pleasant time, only for my indisposition. So the last night of the year passed in very good style, though not quite so lively as I could *[at top of page: "Last of the Year"]* have wished. Home at 11 P.M., & in a short time felt relieved. Am disappointed in not being able to eat much of the food here so much more hearty than in army. Am in some danger of being killed by kindness. *[at top of page: "——1865.——" 2 letters, rec[eive]d 3rd Sent 1 letter, 2nd"]*

1865

Sunday, Jan. 1st,—Mild. Snow falls. In the house most of the day. Took some medicine for my bowels. Fell like keeping calm to-day. Change clothes. Gave Harvey and Eddy little books. Lie in front room by fire. After supper called at Mates *[Mary A. C. French]*, eve. Good visit.

Monday, 2d.—Pleasant. Cold. Wrote to Hon. Freeman Clarke. Randalls people here. Gave Father $1. At depot, but no one came. Good visit. Supper & Randalls & Walter came. Henry *[C. Murray]* came in eve. (Tim wedding at the college.) Sat up late in eve. & Henry *[C. Murray]* stays with me.

Tuesday 3d.—Pleasant again. Got buggy for Father. H*[enry C. Murray]* goes home. Rode with Father & Mrs. Ball to the *[Kendall]* Mills. Stopped at Goodrich's, H. Clark's (dinner). Bailey, &c. Websters & Benedict's. Home at 6. Letter returned from Headquarters & note from *[Orrin H.]* Strong. Supper. Down st*reet]*. Bo't chestnuts 20 cts. With Mate *[Mary A. C. French]* called at Mr. Williams *[at top of page: "Snow storm, 4th. Sleighride, 5th."]* & Mr. Johnson's, pleasant even*[in]*g. Letter from cousin Albert.

Wednesday, 4th—Blustering storm. Made calls about village. Mrs. Beach, Randolph's Hubbard's & Parker's & Mate's *[Mary A. C. French]*. Read papers at *[Brockport]* Republic office Lost breast pin last eve. at Johnson's & sent for it this A.M. Snow falls all A.M. Shaved & at Mate's *[Mary A. C. French]*, supper. Home in evening.

Thursday 5th—Pleasant. Hired horse & cutter $2 & rode with Cordelia & Mate *[Mary A. C. French]* to Randalls & Uncle Jonah's. All at home. Dinner & good time at Allens, & called at Rs. Sleighing passable. Back at 6½, & made calls. Gave Aggie J*[ohnson]* a ride. At home. With M*[other]* at concert Hall—Chinese Jugglers 70c. Some fun. Thaws tonight. Saw many old faces at the hall. Canteen of cider at Uncle J*[onas]*'s.

Friday, 6th.—Mild; thawing. Up early. Called at Webb's "Wilkie road," & at Dr. Smith's. Well entertained by Mr. S.S. & saw A. B. Miller. On way home saw Mrs. Dr. Beach & rec*[eive]*d package for Dr. B*[each]* In P.M. at Mate's *[Mary A. C. French]* *[Brockp[ort]* Repub*[lic]* office & at Mrs. Butler's. Good time. Saw L*[ieutenan]*t A*[ndrew]* Boyd, & Serg*[ean]*t R*[obert]* Gordon *[Jr.]*. Home to supper. Mr. *[Horatio N.]* B*[each]* gave me ticket to show, & I gave it to Eddy. Some colder to night. With girls at our house. At home all the eve.

Saturday, 7th. —Storm last night & in A.M. Pleasant P.M. On first train to Rochester, 70c. called at Douglass & found Frank *[Francis R. Douglas]* low spirited. Saw Dr. Smith & gave letter of introduction to Mr. King, editor Roch*[ester]* Dem*[ocrat]* & P.M. at home at Washington; he gave me some encouragement in regard to the W*[ar]* Dep*[artmen]*t Pr*[inting]* office. At Powelson's Photo gallery. Saw Mrs. Bills & set for vignettes, ½ doz. $3. Home on 12 o'c*[loc]*k train & saw many friends. Chestnuts, 10c. Daily Democrat, 5 cts. Ale 5c. In P.M. in st*[reet]*, & took tea at Mate's *[Mary A. C. French]*. Saw Mrs. Courtney & Mrs. Williams in eve. Called at Mrs. Baker's. Grapes at Mates, *[Mary A. C. French]* & home quite early.

Sunday, 8th.—Pleasant, mild. Sun. At home all day. *["Not at church" crossed out]* After supper called at Mrs. Smiths, not at home. At Mate's *[Mary A. C. French]* Mrs. Courtney there. Cordelia came & we all went to church (new *[First]* Bapt*[ist]* Church)²³⁴ Union concert. Sat in middle aisle in full view of the congregation. Interesting exercises. Went home with C*[ordelia]* then to Erie st*[reet]* with Nel & Mat.*[Mary A. C. French]*. Pleasant visit, & home not very early.

Monday 9th. —More mild. Cold last night. Abed till 8. At 10 went down street, called at several places: Williams, Johnson's, Beach's, & bid Mrs. Courtney good by.*[at top of page: "Took note of $50 for 6 mo[nth]s, 9th."]* Bo't gum 10*[cts]*, ale 5*[cts]* & agreed to see Mr. *[Horatio N.]* Beach in P.M.

Home to dinner. My last day in B[rockport] for a while at least. Gave Mr. Beach $50 & took his note for 6 mo[nth]s with interest. At Mate's [Mary A. C. French] saw Net. Searles & Reb. brother, also Mrs. Ford & Mrs. Courtney. Mrs. F[ord] gave me some dried cherries. Called at Dr. Clarks, saw Amelia & Eva. Bid Father good bye as he had call to Lake. Pleasant eve. at home. Mrs. Baker & Kitty there. Prepared to go in morn[ing]. [at top of page: "Return to army."]

Tuesday, 10th—Up at 5½. Breakfast. Bid all good bye & Lon went to depot with me at 6½ 35c. Snow falling heavily. Mate [Mary A. C. French] & Mrs. Court[ney] at depot & went to Roch[ester] with me. On st[reet] cars & called on Sarah Lewis, 18 E. Avenue & she went down st[reet] with us. (I first called on the Douglass family.) Bo't 400 sticks of gum mastic (1.50) to take to army, also 2 yds green cord for L[ieutenan]t [Stephen R.] S[tafford] 10 cts. At Powelson's Photo Gallery rec[eive]d 4 of my ½ doz. photographs. Sent 1 to Frank [Francis R. Douglas] & gave the rest to Mat [Mary A. C. French] to take home for me &c. To Genessee Valley Depot with the girls, bid them farewell & left on 10 o'c[loc]k train. Snow fell till we neared Elmira & rain fell. Bo't Democrat 5c. At E[lmira] waited nearly 1 hour for change of cars, very unpleasant. At 5½ left E[lmira] & rode all night & hard time to sleep even with whole seat.

Wednesday, 11th—At 2 engine switched off the track at Little York & we staid there till 8 A.M. On slowly & at Baltimore 11½. Behind [at top of page: "Wrote letter 11th.—Baltimore"] & must stay till 3½ P.M. Pleasant ride through Maryland sun shining. At Soldiers' Rest coffee &c. Walked through st[reet]s & wrote letter at Sanitary Home, to Mate [Mary A. C. French]. Funeral procession &c. across street of eccentric old lady. San[itary] Commission fine thing. Left Balt[imore] at 3:30 ride pleasant. In Washington at 5:30. Went to Sanitary lodge near N[ew] Y[ork] Avenue, left haversack & canteen in bag[gage] room; check & had supper. Tried to find L[ieutenan]t [Alonzo C.] Pickard—had gone to Alexandria. Then tried to find [Samuel E.] Carrington, clerk in War Dept., which did almost at office; he was out, but Britnall clerk went with me to boarding house 275 Vermont Avenue where I had pleasant chat & game checkers. Then at 9:30 went to San[itary] Lodge & found very good bed. To-day lent 50 cts to Frenchman in 108th.[NYVI Regiment].

Thursday 12th—Splendid day—warm. After breakf[as]t went to Willard's hotel registered & did not find Hon[orable] F[reeman] Clarke, but saw young Tousley of Clarkson & a lively rush of gents to & from breakfast. Then at Maj[or] Underwood's rec[eive]d four month's pay, deducting transportation,

$16.16, leaving me $47.50 &c. up to Dec*[ember]* 31. Sent check of $30 in letter to Mother & rec*[eive]*d $17.50 at the Treasury. Saw *[Samuel E.]* Carrington & went to Capitol. Mr. King²³⁵ away on floor of House saw S*[harp]* S*[hooters]*, Stancliff, 8th Co*[mpany]* Also in lobby room, Hon*[orable]* F*[reeman]* Clarke & little encouragement. Pass to City Point of Provost Marshall. Back to War Dep*[artmen]*t *[at top of page: "Washington (58)—sent 2 letters, 12th."]* & saw Mr. W. D. Gourlay, chief of Printing Bureau, who kept my recommend*[ation]* from Mr. *[Horatio N.]* B*[each]* agreeing to let me know the result of my application for transfer to War Dep*[artmen]*t Pr*[inting]* O*[ffice]* in a few days. At Sanitary Lodge wrote to Mr. *[Freeman]* Clarke & to Mother, sending $30 check. Received my baggage & went to steamer by st*[reet]* car on board safely, several rebels on boat, going home to Norfolk. Found 2 "boys" going to Brigade at 7:30 P.M. bo't berth tickets for self (50c) & 2 others & went to bed, finding very good accommodations. *[at top of page: "Join the Army again. At sundown Mud Letter, rec[eive]d 13th, dated 2nd."]*

Friday, 13th.—Pleasant—not very cold. Up at 6. At Fortress Monroe 7½ A.M. Had cup coffee & 2 slices bread & butter, on dock. 25c. Pleasant trip. Many soldiers on board & boat new, large. Bo't N*[ew]* Y*[ork]* Herald, 5c. Nothing extraordinary occurred during trip to City Point, 3 P.M. Had pass stamped by Prov*[ost]* Marshal, & rode on top of car to Hancock station. Weather very mild, Found transport waiting at depot for *[Brigadier]* Gen*[era]*l *[Edward S.]* Bragg, who went on 20 days leave at same time as myself, but he did not come & I rode to Headq*[uarte]*rs. Mud very deep. [Found Wood & Beyer gone on furlough.] Glad to see the office & *[Orrin H.]* Strong & others. Supper. Gave out grapes &c. Saw Dr. Beach & gave him package from his wife; talked with him in tent. Everything same as I left them. Copied orders, &c. Fixed things up. To bed in pretty good season.*[at top of page: "Drew shoes 14th. Sent letter, 14th. Pay for rations, 14th."]*

Saturday, 14th.—Pleasant, warm, windy. Some work to do in office. Saw some of the boys, S*[harp]* S*[hooters]*, paid H*[enry]* C. Murray $1 due for powder flask. Made out papers to draw money value of rations for 20 days absence, which amount at 34c per day to $6.80 & rec*[eive]*d in P.M. after having it signed by L*[ieutenan]*t McDonald & Capt*[ain]* Perry, Starkweather cord 2 yds, rec*[eive]*d 10c. Drew 1 pair shoes (5c) & signed the clothing book. (See clothing acc't at back part of this diary.) Visited the Band boys. No fire needed in office hardly. (The total expense of my trip home, including $16.16 for transportation, amounts to $39.86.) Sold Jimmie Wilkinson, Band, 200 sticks of chewing gum, for $3.00, he to pay me $2.50 on pay day; I owe him 50 cts for photographs. Wrote to Mate *[Mary A. C. French]*; bo't can milk, 75c.

Filed orders, eve. At supper had cold biscuit, sausage, dough nuts, &c. which came to one of the boys in a box. Colder to-night. Made bed & bro't in wood before dark. A rush of orders, & copying to do, till 10 or after. Feel tired to-night. *[Orrin H.]* Strong repaid me shirt lent him in Dec. Paid Solomon 15c for washing shirt & dr*[awer]*s. *[at top of page:* "Sent letter 15th & 16th. Fort Fisher[236] captured 15th & a salute of 100 guns fired here."*]*

Sunday 15th.—Very pleasant. Some wind. Mud drying rapidly. After some work, office visited 140th, 2 miles. Saw S*[hedrick]* J. J*[ackson]*. & gave him photographs. Also saw others. Back at 2 or 3 & on way stopped at Battalion, bought blanket & over coat, nearly new, formerly owned by S*[harp]* S*[hooters]* now prisoners of war, paid for blanket, $3 & for over coat $5. Wrote to sister. Set in wood. Gen*[era]*l *[Edward S.]* Bragg not yet returned from absence of 20 days. Some work in eve. Sent paper to Mate *[Mary A. C. French]*, which I bo't this A.M., 10c.

Monday, 16th.—Weather same. Some one stole our wash dish last night. After the morning business, I changed shoes 5s for 6s with a sojer. There are peace rumors in which Gen'l Crawford is mentioned. Also rumors that the old 1st Corps is to be reorganized. Wrote to Aunt C. in P.M., & had nap. Cut wood for stove. Work in eve. Rec*[eive]*d *[Brockport]* Republic of 12th. In Dr. Beach's office.

Tuesday, 17th.—Some colder, pleasant. Plenty of work. Issued telegram announcing capture of Fort Fisher & a salute fired here, 100 guns! *[at top of page:* "Weighed 125½, 16th. Wrote letter, 18th. Rec*[eive]*d letter, 18th."*]* Fixed overcoat to send to Father by clerk by Express, to-morrow, also an old blanket, rubber, with a broom brush. Wrote to Frank *[Francis R. Douglas]*. Helped *[Orrin H.]* Strong grind hatchet & knife. All quiet again. Issued orders for fatigue & picket details to report in morning, &c. Let the cat out of the bag in regard to my going home on furlough to Capt*[ain]* Andrews & Capt*[ain]* Osborne.

Wednesday, 18th—Weather same. After morning work, make out Roster of Brigade officers. Then wrote to *[Brockport]* Repub*[lic]* & to Alonzo. Gave Dr. Beach my paper. Gen*[era]*l *[Edward S.]* Bragg returned this P.M., & first thing asked me if I "got my wife!" Some work in eve. orders for fatigue & picket. Levingood goes in the morning. Letter from Mother & sister & Father. Lent Levingood my haversack.

Thursday, 19th—Dark, some colder. S. & I alone, have plenty to do. Moved our sleeping tent for new log house to be put up, office. Made out field return,

&c. Bo't Herald 10c. At S*[harp]* S*[hooters]* Batt*[alion]* in P.M., & took down figures *[at top of page:* "New house, or office 21st. Rec[eive]d letter, 20th. Storm, 21st."] at Inspection of 24th Mich*[igan]* by Capt*[ain]* Osborne. Got in wood for night. Very quiet. Gave *[Sampson W.]* Fry 25c for bread.

Friday, 20th.—Busy all the A.M. at Inspector's reports. In P.M., rec*[eive]*d letter from Mr. *[W. D.]* Gourlay, Washington, with instructions in regard to my application for detail to War Dept. Pr. Office. Saw Capt*[ain]* Perry, S*[harp]* S*[hooters]* , & in eve. made application to Gen*[era]*l Meade, through his adj*[u]*t*[ant]* Gen*[era]*l & Dr. Beach gave me good recommend; at Battalion Lieut*[enant]* Starkweather signed my application & Capt*[ain]* Perry approved & forwarded it to Division, 2 letters enclosed. Back to H*[ea]*dq*[uarte]*rs, late, by light of lantern. Worked some on papers, then to bed. Letter from Mate *[Mary A. C. French]*.

Saturday, 21st.—Rain storm all day. Rain froze at first in night. Finished monthly Inspector's Report, & Weekly Report, sent up. Moved into our new log office, covered with thin pine boards, or "shakes". *[at top of page:* "Sent 2 letters, 22nd."] Made good double bed S*[ampson W. Fry]* & I.—Good fireplace. Get fixed up comfortably before dark, & night wood in. Had some of Mother's blackberry sauce for supper. Take comfort in office, eve. Some details to write. Yesterday let Str*[ong]* have 25 cts. for nails, 30c per lb. & paid 25c for 1 lb. Mail behind to-night. Wrote some to Mate *[Mary A. C. French]*, in ans*[wer]* to her splendid letter.

Sunday, 22d.—Had good sleep last night. Late breakfast. Washed up & changed. *[Orrin H.]* Strong plastered up the cracks of house with mud. The usual Sunday office work. Wrote to mother & Mate *[Mary A. C. French]*. Sewed on buttons. Read some in P.M. Orders to write in eve.

Monday, 23d.—Some rain, cloudy, warm. The usual work. No mail to-day or yester*[day]* boat in storm. Our office is finished to-day, mudded, & door put in. Read Dr. B*[each]*'s papers. Felt unwell at 4. laid down & after supper felt better. Hear heavy guns, distant, in eve. *[at top of page:* "Rec*[eive]*d letter, 24th. Sent letter 24th"]

Tuesday, 24th.—Pleasant. Office work. Beyer cl*[er]*k came back last eve. from furlough (a hind quarter of beef was stolen last eve. by guard fraud.) Rec*[eive]* d letter from cousin H. Randall & paper from home with note from mother. Solomon washed my clothes—3 pieces 25c At Battalion & Division H*[ea]* dq*[uate]*rs latter place saw cl*[er]*k about my application, said it was O.K., saw 3 rebel deserters who had just come in with horses—10th Va. cavalry—poor horses. Wrote to Mrs. Marion Bills, Rochester. Work in eve. Colder to-night. Rec[eive]d [Brockport] Republic, 19th.

Wednesday, 25th.—Pleasant. Hardly thawed to-day. Nothing unusual, only heavy firing in James River at rebel gun boats trying to make their way back up. Bo't box blacking, 10c. Very dull. No newspapers lately. In P.M. at Battalion. Wood, clerk, came back this eve. from furlough. Details to write & papers to read. The Richmond Enquirer humbles itself to the U.S. Gov't in a startling editorial on the "situation". Encouraging sign. Very cold to-night. [at top of page: "Sent letter, 27th. Recd letter, 27th"]

Thursday, 26th—Pleasant but cold. After mornings work &c. went to 140th NYVI & not finding Lieut[enant] Courtney, came back—noon. After dinner wrote (partly) a letter to the [Brockport] Republic, & copied some fatigue orders in eve. Cold for this climate. Quinine & whiskey ordered by surgeons.

Friday, 27th.—Clear & cold. Some wind. Plenty of writing. Finished letter to [Brockport] Republic & sent it in one to sister. Weekly Reports to make out for to-morrow. Had the foot orderly get in a 24 hours supply of wood. Snug cold. Hardly thaws. Finished & sent letters in P.M. & read papers. At Batt[alion] & divis[ion] H[ea]dq[uarte]rs. Heard from my application. Finished weekly report in eve. & rec[eive]d letter from Mate [Mary A. C. French]. To bed in good season.

Saturday, 28th—Still colder, O! Took morning papers to Division & could not get the application. Made out some clothing papers for Capt[ain] Andrews. Again at Divis[ion] H[ea]dq[uarte]rs, noon. Only a little [at top of page: "Sent letter, 28th. Rec[eive]d letter 29th. Application to S. Williams, & Brig[adier] Gen[era]l & A[ssistant] A[djutant] G[eneral] Army Potomac for reference."] more mild at mid-day, sun. Write some to Mate [Mary A. C. French], finished & sent. Copying in eve. Discussion in office.

Sunday, 29th.—Quite pleasant & more mild. Sun. Took morn. papers to Divis[ion]. Walked to 140th. Saw L[ieutenan]t Court[ney] & paid him $5.50 due for Zouave clothing bought Nov. 16, '64. Took dinner with him and L[ieutenan]t Wright. Back at 4, found Dr. Beach sick & made out appeal & sent application to Gen[era]l Meade, through Brig[adier] Gen[era]l S. Williams, A[ssistant] A[djutant] G[eneral], for action (by mail) after conferring with Lieut[enant] Starkweather. I do not intend to be bluffed by Brevet Maj[or] Gen[era]l Crawford, after receiving instructions from Adj[utan]t Gen[era]l's office, Washington. Letter from Mother & Sister this A.M.

Monday, 30th.—Pleasant again. {Mrs. F's cherries for sup*[per]* last eve. & breakf*[as]*t this A.M.} Wrote to cousin H.P.R*[andall]*, & filed orders. Daily papers brought around by boy. Nap in P.M. then full of business at sundown & in eve. In Dr. Beach's tent. Peace rumors in great profusion. Note from Mother in a paper. *[at top of page:* "Robins. February. Hair cut, 31ct. Rec*[eive]* d letter, 2nd & sent one."

Tuesday 31st—Splendid day. Reports to make out. Hear English robins whistling & crows cawing. Very busy, P.M. also. Had haircut by Serg*[ean]*t Dick Boyle, S*[harp]* S*[hooter]* —took 1 hour, shears dull &c. Saw several of our Co*[mpany]* for first time in long while—they had been at hospital, &c. Beans, baked, for supper. This is indeed a lovely day—warm. Copying in eve. Up late.

February

Wednesday, Feb. 1.—Spring weather. Very mild. Encountered some whiskey in getting reports signed for Divis*[ion]*. After being through work for A.M. called at Batt*[alion]* & heard that each Co*[mpany]* is to be put with a Brigade, & used as S*[harp]* S*[hooters]*. Had a good wash, in tent. Rumors of a move for us. The weather is too nice to lie still. Wrote some to "Mattie" *[Mary A. C. French]*. No mail for me this A.M. (Last night I called on Dr. J. H. Beach & saw his pet mice in bottles.) At Battalion in eve.

Thursday, 2d.—Still pleasant. Usual routine. Wrote some to Mate *[Mary A. C. French]*. Nap in P.M. Solomon washed 3 pieces for me. Work in eve. & letter from Mother & Sis & Lon, with 6 two cent stamps. Bo't paper, 10c. Sent letter to *[Brockport]* Repub*[lic]*. & Mother. *[at top of page:* "Rec*[eive]*d 3 letters & sent 3 on 4th."]

Friday, 3d.—Dark, cloudy, chilly & tries to snow or rain. After writing some orders in A.M. called on Co*[mpany]* boys at Battalion, S*[harp]* S*[hooters]*. Wrote letter for Dovt. [?] After dinner read, & wrote to Em*[ma]* S*[mith]* & same again to Mattie *[Mary A. C. French]*. Read story & copied in eve. Sobered our young minister clerk *[blot]*

Context—A peace conference between President Lincoln and Confederate Vice President Alexander Stephens at Hampton Roads on February 3 failed. Only Lee's Army at Petersburg and Johnston's forces in North Carolina remain to fight for the South.

Saturday, 4th.—More pleasant still & warm. After break*[fas]*t found letter on desk from Mattie *[Mary A. C. French]*, Aunt C., & S*[ampson]* W. Fry. Sent ans*[wer]* to M*[attie]* *[Mary A. C. French]*. & S*[ampson]* W. F*[ry]*. Also wrote to Mr. W. D. Gourlay, Washington, enclosing 3c stamp. Sent paper & "*[Brockport]* Republic." Bought 2 papers, Herald & Wash*[ington]* Chronicle. 15cts. Paid Sol*[omon]* (dark) 15c for washing, & 25c to *[Sampson W.]* Fry, (cook) for meal or flour for mess. Hung blanket out to air. At S*[harp]* S*[hooter]* Battalion. Birds sing merrily. Orders to be ready to move 4 days rations. No tents or useless baggage to be taken by the troops. Clerks to stay but 1. Guards to be left in camps, &c. A raid, to support cavalry. In eve. orders issued for march, &c. Gen*[era]*l *[Edward S.]* Bragg in office cool as a cucumber. Sat up quite late. Orderlies running. *[at top of page:* "Sent 2 letters, 5th Rec*[eive]*d 1, 5th. Sent 1 letter 6th. A move 5th"]

Sunday 5th—Cloud & sun—mild. Built fire at 6 & break. early. Splendid sunrise. *[Orrin H.]* Strong goes with the transport & troops, who start at 7. I stay, with other cl*[er]*ks. Write a letter to Aunt C. & Lon *[Alonzo]*, to mail to-day both in one. Very quiet. Shovelled & swept the front of office. Letter from Benton Tuttle, Lieut*[enant]* Co*[mpany]* E 108th Reg*[imen]*t U. S. Col*[ore]*d Troops, Rock Island, Ill., (formerly a S*[harp]* S*[hooter]*.[237] Nap in P.M. Heard cannonading, 4 P.M. Read bible in eve. To bed early.

Monday, 6th—Colder. Wrote to Lieut*[enant]* Tuttle, & sent. Heard from troops. The 2nd part of 6th & 9th Corps are also out. Ours, 5th, came part way back, last eve. & on again this A.M.—Read some in papers. At Batt*[alion]* Cut wood. In eve. hear that Mallory (orderly) was killed in fight to-day near Reams Station. To bed very early. Fine moon.

Tuesday, 7th ——Rain & ice freezes on trees, &c. At news depot. Corps h*[ead]*dq*[uarte]*rs & bought "Yankee Notions." *[at top of page:* "Sent letters, 9th."] Back in rain & heard that our Brigade were yesterday engaged in hard fight[238]—many wounded, some killed, among the rest *[*"Holloway (orderly)" crossed out]* Cannot rely on rumors. Dark & cloudy day. Howling wind. Read in eve. Nothing new.

Wednesday, 8th——Pleasant A.M. Chilly wind in P.M. Forage sent to the troops (3 days) No reliable reports yet. Some *[*"many" crossed out]* come in wounded. Sent the "Yankee Notions" to Mate *[Mary A. C. French]*. In P.M. receive *[Brockport]* Repub*[lic]* of 26th & 2nd & paper from Mother, with note & shoe strings.—Read most of the day. Boys in tent, talking, eve., & we hear very heavy cannonading. Not very cold, but clear moonlight. Are reduced to hard tack & mackerel, with coffee.

Thursday, 9th—Somewhat pleasant, Windy. Wrote to *[Brockp[ort]* Repub*[lic]*; & sister, & sent. *[at top of page:* "Leave our good quarters, 11th."] Saw Dr.

Beach from troops. In the house most of the day. At Batt*[alion]* in eve. early &
cut wood during day.

Friday, 10th.—Chilly. Sun & wind. Quite cold nights. Expected troops in
to-day. Read some. Bo't apples & cakes, 30 cts. Mail came in P.M. but nothing
for me. Troops came in at 7, eve. & soon orders came to be ready to move
at 6 A.M. in the morn. to rear line Halifax Road, 5 miles away. Well, this is
a military necessity, & we must leave good winter quarters, for the second
time. They are bound to give us a good taste of rough campaigning for the last
winter in the service. Wrote some to "Mate"*[Mary A. C. French]*. The Band
play a few lively airs. It seems good to have the men (troops) back again.

Saturday, 11th.—Packed up but not very early, as the 6 o'clock order was
countermanded. About 9 *[at top of page:* "off for Baltimore, 11th"*]* order
came to be at R.R. at 2, take cars, then steamers at City Point for Baltimore.
Rode on cars with Gen*[eral Edward S.]* B*[ragg]*. & st*[aff]* off*[icers]*. Waited for
boat till 5½ P.M. Troops took 2 boats, & orders flew. Changes were made &
Bo't cakes & apples, 75c. Wait at dock. In a room with Band & find bed on
floor. Letter to Mat *[Mary A. C. French]* in A.M.

Sunday, 12th.—Baggage came at 2 A.M. & I took mine. Slept again bo't cakes
25c at 9, 7th & 6th Wis*[consin]* ordered off boat. Then we went down river.
[at top of page: "Up Chesapeake Bay 13th"*]* Windy on river—rough. Laid
down some & in P.M. wrote few lines to *[Brockport]* Rep*[ublic]*. & Lon
[Alonzo], off Fort. Monroe at 5 & laid there as the wind was blowing about—
40 laid out in the small room to sleep. Terribly packed, shoved & dovetailed
to-gether.

Monday, 13th.—Pleasant but very cold, like last night. Laid at Fort till 11
then started for Balt*[imore]* then went back till 2 P.M., when wind lowered &
we went across Chesa*[peake]* Bay. Boys have lots of fun. Some sick. Puppy on
board. Coffee & tack during day. Boat quite steady. Ducks on Bay. A foolish
chap drafted who "hopes never to go back to the front again" Have had
headache much since coming on boat. Bed again on floor, but no sleep till
late—so much noise & candle light in face. *[at top of page:* "Annapolis, Md.
Sent 2 letters 14th"*]*

Tuesday, 14th—Colder still last night. Pleasant to-day. Ice in Bay stops us at 7
& we put into Annapolis, Md. Other vessel with S*[harp]* S*[hooters]* on board
behind us. As the 6th, 7th & 8th Co*[mpanie]*s came by mistake they were
put in charge of Pr*[ovost]* M*[arshall]* to be sent back A .SP *[?]*. But *[Orrin
H.]* Strong & I & others stay with Brigade. Walked about the substantial &

apparently wealthy town of brick. Had cup of good coffee, 10c. Mailed letter
[at top of page: "Brigade dissolved 14th."*]* to Lon *[Alonzo]* & one for *[Orrin
H.]* Strong. Glass beer 10c & paper 8c. Back to boat & again in town. In back
room of a store wrote letter to Mr. *[W. D.]* Gourlay, Washington, with ink
from a wine glass. Mailed letter. In P.M. with *[Orrin H.]* Strong had dinner
of ham, beef steak, eggs, fried potatoes, good bread & butter & coffee: 75cts.
Curls &c. apples, 5c. each & 3 for 9c. 24c. Walked to State House. Back to
boat & drew 2 days rations of soft & hard bread pork & coffee, pork boiled.
Then an order came for the 24th Mich*[igan]* to go to Springfield, Ill. the 150th
to N.Y. Harbor, the 143rd & 149th to Elmira to guard drafted men. Then
Gen*[era]*l *[Edward S.]* B*[ragg]* ordered the detailed men belonging to other
regiments to return. Str*[ong]* & I packed up. Gen*[era]*l *[Edward S.]* B*[ragg]*
said he would try to get *[Orrin H.]* S*[trong]* & I to Wash*[ington]*. We (15)
went, — after bidding all good bye to Prov*[ost]* Marshall's & all but myself
went to *[at top of page:* "Sent letter 15th"*]* the front in steamer. I go to the
boat again & sleep in dining room on floor. Warmer to-night.

Wednesday, 15th.—Rain. Gen*[eral Edward S.]* B*[ragg]* gave me leave to go
with troops to Balt*[imore]* & agreed to try & get me a pass to Wash*[ington]*.
Dr. B*[each]* wrote me certificate. At 10 A.M. we left boat in rain, marched to
depot waited 1½ hours. Bo't cakes & cheese 40c. Then went to Barracks, good
shelter & had coffee. Bo't g*[a]*l*[lon]* goats milk 20c. Sent letter to Mother &
Mate *[Mary A. C. French]*. Wait in barracks till o'clock *[sic]* as there are only
12 cars on the horse R.R. to Annap*[oils]* Junction, & a passenger train must
leave at 3. A slow town of 6,000—the capital of Maryland.—A blind horse
& the best conveyance in town requires 3 hours to convey 23 blind singers ¼
mile to depot fast—enterprising. Rested by fire till 9 P.M., then took cars to
Baltimore. Staid on floor of *[Soldiers]* Rest in a regular jam. *[at top of page:*
"Baltimore, 15th, Washington, 16th."*]*

Thursday, 16th—Splendid day. Warm. Bad coffee bread & salt horse, then
gave bundles in charge of darkey. Walked to P*[ost]* O*[ffice]*. Streets slippery &
sloppy. St*[reet]* car to 137 Broadway 6 cts. & bo't linen $1 & leather leggins
50c. Back on car 6c. At Eutaw House saw Dr. B*[each]* & Capt*[ain]* A*[lphonso
W. Starkweather]*. Bo't paper, 5c. At Rest*[aurant]* dinner same as breakf*[ast]*.
Had leggings fixed, 10c. Sent blanket home by Ex*[press]*. Walk with a 24th
man. Bo't dates, 20c. Saw Capt*[ain]* A*[lphonso W. Starkweather]* who gave me
order to Washington Prov*[ost]* Marsh*[all's]* office, & pass to W*[ashington]*.
Ran to depot with bundles & bo't ticket, 1.50, then to W*[ashington]*,
where I arrived at 5½ P.M. At Prov*[ost]* Marshall's. Then to Soldiers Home,
put baggage in room, took check, had good supper of tea bread & butter.
Sup*[erintenden]*t gave me a pass to come in at any time to-night.—Called to

Lee *[Samuel E.?]* Carrington at his rooms & at War Department he was away. Then went to theatre (Grovers) gallery 25c & heard the play of "*Ireland as it was*" by Mr. and Mrs. Barney Williams[239] & 2 other plays. Very good, or passable. Found bed at Home.

Friday, 17th——After break*[fas]*t at 8 went on Penn*[sylavania]* Av*[enure]*. Had shoes blacked 10c. then to War Dep*[artmen]*t saw *[Samuel E.]* Carrington then Mr. *[W. D.]* Gourlay, who told me no one was wanted at his office, so I am again disappointed. Saw *[at top of page: "Sent 2 letters 17th."]* Hon*[orable]* F*[reeman]* Clarke & read papers. At Col*[onel Samuel]* Breck's office.—Wrote to Mate *[Mary A. C. French]* & Sister. Dinner at *[Soldiers]* Rest soup & beef.—changed under clothes & gave 3 pieces to boy. On st*[reet]* cars up 14th & to Mt. Pleasant Hospital. Saw *[Sampson W.]* Fry in cooking room. Had good visit. (A theatre there.) Bought watch of *[Sampson W.]* Fry ($16.50) & now owe him $20. Had tea bread & cheese & went back in rain & snow to *[Sanitary]* Relief. After supper, with West, procured a guard pass & went to Ford's Theatre[240] gallery 25c. & heard play of "*New York Life*", principal actor being Clarke as Tom Badger. First rate the play playing. Saw some "private theatricals". At ¼ to 11 went to bed at *[Sanitary]* Relief.

Saturday, 18th.—Pleasant. Streets full of mud. Walked about st*[reet]*s with J. West, up 4½ st*[reet]*. Back to *[Soldiers]* Rest. Then I went to Surg*[eon]* Gen*[era]*l's office applied for a situation. Examined. Failed at War Dep*[artmen]*t. At 4½ st*[reet]* with West did not go in. At Capitol House & Senate. At 500 6th st*[reet]*., & a little fun. At *[Soldiers]* Relief, sup*[per]*. Then to theatre (Grovers) after paying 30c for 3 pieces washed. Barney Williams & wife played "Lake of Killarney",[241] &c. Good. Bo't apples, 10c.

Sunday, 19th.—Froze last night. Pleasant. On Penn*[sylvania]* Avenue, had shoes blacked 10c. At Central Presby*[terian]* church (Rev. Dr. *[Phineas]* Gurley's *[at top of page: "Wrote 3 letters, 20th & 1 21st."]* where the President attends but was not there to-day. Seat in gallery. Good sermon. Pleasant church & full congregations. After dinner, took nap, till 4½. Oyster stew 40c. Walk about C. & D. st*[reets]* between 12th & 13th. Supper & to church with West (Dr. Gurleys) To bed early, top bunk. Mud freezes to-night.

Monday, 20th.—Pleasant again. After break*[fas]*t, heard national salute fired honor of victory, (Charleston)[242] Wrote to mother, Mr. *[Horatio N.]* Beach & Frank *[Francis R. Dougles]*. At Adams Express office. Bo't ink (bottle) 10c & *[Washington]* Chronicle 5c. soup & beef dinner. On "C" st*[reet]* with West. Gay "millie" Parrot. At pass office & depot. Got pass. After supper at "C". Back & to bed at 8. Bo't collar 5c. Boys full of fun, noisy.

Tuesday, 21st.—Feel first rate; rested. Break*[fast]* at 7½ Wrote letter to *[Orrin H.]* Strong. Salute of 100 *[at top of page:* "Charleston & Wilmington fallen! At Carver Hospital 22nd Ward 43."*]* guns fired—Charleston evacuated Tried to sell watch. Up 14th st*[reet]* in car 5c. to Mt. Pleas*[ant]* Hosp*[ital]*. Dinner with *[Sampson W.]* Fry & after went with Barnes, printer, to hosp*[ital]*. Pr*[inting]* office then to Carver Hosp*[ital]* pr*[inting]* of*[fice]* with him, but could not get a chance for detail. Down in car to Gen*[era]*l Augur's office At *[Soldiers]* Rest. At "C" st*[reet]*, *[illegible word,* "*im?*"*]* At depot & back to *[Soldiers]* Rest. In eve. left diary with Sup*[erintenden]*t & to Canterbury Theatre[243] with West. "Jack Sheppard,"[244] &c. Badly played. Went out at 11¼ *[illegible word]*

Wednesday, 22d—After refreshing nights sleep went to breakfast to "*[Soldiers]* Rest." Sun does not shine this A.M. & some colder.—At Medical Director's & rec*[eive]*d order to be admitted to Carver Hospital 14th St. At Depot 5c. at Mt. Pleasant Hospital 15c & dinner (baked beans) with *[Sampson W.]* Fry. Back & rode down Penn*[sylvania]* Av*[enue]* to depot & rec*[eive]*d pass to front expiring to-morrow. Wrote to Sister. Salute 100 guns fired to-day noon in honor of fall of Charleston. Illuminations to-night. Went to Carver Hospital at 5½ & given a bed in Ward 43; supper, Warmed feet by fire & went to bed tired at 7½ P.M. Good bed. Rain in eve. *[at top of page:* "Wrote 5 letters, 23nd"*]*

Thursday 23d.—Rainy. After break*[fast]* wrote letters to Mother, Mate *[Mary A. C. French]*, Lieut*[enant]* Stark*[weather]*, *[Orrin H.]* Strong & Murray. Surg*[eon]* & Surg*[eon]* in chief saw me. Rec*[eive]*d pass to town to get baggage. Rode up st*[reet]* car 5c. Mailed letters at P*[ost]* O*[ffice]* & had dinner at *[Soldiers]* Rest. At War Dep*[artmen]*t Pr*[inting]* Office at 3½ took knapsack & haversack, canteen, &c. from baggage room of Sanitary Rest. My old haversack is destroyed by rats. Took car to near Carver Hosp*[ital]*. (5c.) where I deposited knapsack, haversack & canteen in baggage room. At Printing office. I was asked to lend my Zouave pants to a man for a performance on stage to-morrow eve. Found powder for my cold. Returned paper & envelopes borrowed. Rain, warm! After *sup[per]* (applesauce) there was card-playing in even*[in]*g. To bed at 8.

Friday, 24th. –Sunshine. Mild. Made up bed at 7. Break. at 8. Dress "Life among the mail-bags"[245] at library. Examining surgeons in at 10 & the ward surgeon, prescribed same as yester*[day]*. Read in P.M. Theatrical company borrowed pants, leggins & jacket for play to-night, & gave me ticket. In eve. at Theatre an hour, but the thing is very stale & too poor view. To bed very early.

Saturday, 25th.—Rain all day. No bread for breakfast. Better dinner. Saw Dr. Sweet at noon & presented credentials, &c., with satisfactory result. Dr. Gray prescribed plaster cantharides (Spanish flies) & the blister was put on at 3. D[octo]r says I have "pleuritis acute" Drew shirts from knapsack. 2 men came in sick. One of them, a tall Dutchman has the bowel complaint to a disgusting degree. Read some after sup[per]. Finished "mail bags" not till I went to bed at 8 did the blister work.

Sunday, 26th—Very pleasant. At 1 o'clock this A.M. I awoke & the nurse took off blister & dressed it. Felt painful. Large blisters. Up just before 7, made bed & changed part of clothes. Bought Herald, 10c. Breakfast boiled corn, whole & gravy with half-baked bread & coffee half sweetened. (Our dirty Dutchman makes a fine mess of himself & creates attention. The [at top of page: "Sent 2 letters, 27th"] surgeons are in at 11 & ward surgeon prescribes. Reference to me in surgeon's consultation. Band play lively. After dinner of potatoes beef & turnips & rice sent paper to Mate [Mary A. C. French]. Laid down a while on floor. D[octo]r of ward came in at 4. Splendid sunset. The "Dirty Dutchman" washes up after much effort. Whew! Boys telling stories. To bed early but blister bothers me. Am taking a pleasant syrup for cold.

Monday, 27th.—Everything much as usual, & weather continues fine, bright sun. Names were taken in A.M. for muster, 28th. D[octo]r said nothing to me on visiting the ward. My blister still troubling me, was dressed with oiled rag at 11. Dr. Sweet, came in to see me at 11 & asked me to call at his office, which I did, & rec[eive]d instructions in regard to copying from large book of surgical operations. dinner (good hash) wrote to Sister, Mr. [Horatio N.] Beach, at 1 o'cl[oc]k commenced operations on Dr. Sweet's book, at his office. Like the job but quit at 4, not feeling well. Sold white leggins [sic] to ass[istan]t nurse for 75 cts. Exchanged library books; obtained "Life of Douglass Jerrold".[246] Feel tired & ache all over me. Read in eve. Had blister dressed & to bed, 8. [at top of page; "Muster-day 28th. Drew clothing –pants. March. Rec[eive]d & sent 1 letter."]

Tuesday, 28th.—Good weather. After usual morning preliminaries, went to work at 9 till 11.—Then drew pair pants (4.75) & took them to tailors for alteration. After dinner mustered for pay by Surg[eon] O. A. Judson, in charge hosp[ital]. At work again in Dr. Sweet's office, copying from 1 till 5 & became acquainted with Dr. S[weet]'s orderly. Dr. S[weet] came from ride at 4½ & talked with me. I am well pleased with him. Tea, bread & applesauce for supper.

March

Wednesday, March 1.—Cloudy A.M. Pleasant P.M. Read & at 9 to work at book, till noon. Rec[eive]d pass to Mt. Pleasant, & was told that in consideration of lending Zouave suit to theatre Capt[ain] McCollum offers me pass at any time. Letter from [Orrin H.] Strong, H[ea]dq[uarte]rs 1st provisional Brig[ade] 3rd Div[ision] 5th A[rmy] C[orps] & paper from home & note of Feb[ruary] 11th, forwarded from front, 2 sticks gum in it. At Mt. Pleas[ant] Hosp[ital]. Gave [Sampson W.] Fry 1st watch & took another at $22. Now owe him $34. to city on st[reet] cars, 5c. Watch repaired, hair spring taken up 50 cts. 5 pens 10cts. Back to Hospital], 5c. Sup[per]. Rec[eive]d altered pants of tailor, 50c.; owe him 5c. At Mt. P[leasant] Hosp. Saw [Sampson W.] Fry, eve. came back by moonlight. Watch stops & goes. Fix buttons on pants & to bed 8½. [at top of page: "Rec[eive]d 4 letters, 2nd Rec[eive]d 4 letters, 3rd"]

Thursday, 2d.—Rain. Had blister dressed; cerate. Feel better. Put on new pants, & shaved. Our Dutchman is a plague, a perfect nuisance. At office from 9 till 12. On way to dinner met Horace House, who belongs to my Co[mpany]; he is nurse in ward 10, here. After dinner I called on him & intend to be transferred to his ward. Rec[eive]d letter from home dated 26th which informed me of the birth of a sister on the 21st. Good news. Also rec[eive]d forwarded 2 letters from home, dated 6th & 13th & one from Henry [C. Murray], dated 10th. But others that I expect do not come yet. At work from 1 till 4½. Read letters. Sup. Called on [Horace] House eve. Rain still falls. Traded watch chains. My watch runs all day.

Friday, 3d.—Rain, rain most of the day. My blister is healing fast. At work, 9 to 12 & examined by Board (weekly.) At noon, dinner, potato & turnip, cold & mackerel. Rec[eive]d paper from home, & letters dated Dec. 4, Feb. 20, & one from Mate [Mary A. C. French] of Feb[ruary] 15, one from [Sampson W.] Fry of Feb[ruary] 20 or 18. Work 1 to 4½, then was trans[ferred] to Ward 10. Had pleasant time in Dr. Sweet's office to-day. Music, &c. In ward 10 to bed early after reading. Blister improving. [at top of page: "Saw Abraham Lincoln Inaugurated, 4th."]

Saturday, 4th.—Rain in A.M. Sky black & wind blew.—Poor breakfast. Rec[eive]d pass. Borrowed 50cts of Horace House. Walked to city. Sky grew lighter at 10, then sprinkle again. The streets full of people, flags flying. Treasury building crowded by gazers & every other building crammed. Horsemen flying, fire & military organizations, & benevolent societies passing, colored troops, printing press on wheels, in operation. Procession, including President passed & I then went on side st*[reet]*, ahead of crowd to capitol. O, what a rush! I tho't of the skedaddle of Bull Run. Helter skelter. Reached Capitol, climbed a tall iron fence, & obtained close view of steps on north side of capitol, middle, where the ceremony was to be. Soon Pres*[iden]*t L*[incoln]*, Vice-President *[Johnson]*, &c. took seats. Mr. Lincoln & Vice Pres*[ident]* Johnson talked pleasantly. Guard formed in front & bands played. Saw foreign ministers. Sun shone brightly 2 or 3 seconds after Mr. Lincoln sat down: had not shone before. Mr. Lincoln read short speech very emphatically, gesticulating bodily always inclining to the left side. Then the oath was administered to Mr. Lincoln by Chief Justice *[Salmon P.]* Chase, (59) Mr. L*[incoln]* bowed to the crowd, turned & Mr. Johnson also bowed politely, &c. Exit the celebrities. Saw Lord Lyons, British Minister, *[at top of page:* "2 letters rec*[eive]*d & 2 sent, 5th."*]* dressed gaily, cocked hat, white plume, lace on coat, scarlet breeches & sash. Salute of 100 guns fired. Bought cake, 5c. & in morn*[ing]* cup coffee, piece pie & 5 cakes 25cts. Bo't paper 5c. President Lincoln & little Tad passed in carriage; also Gen*[era]*l Hooker, Monitor, &c. with printing press, in procession. Great crowd & sun shines pleasantly at noon. On side st*[reet]* saw carriage broken down at Special Relief Sanitary[247], washed, &c. at jewellers had watch regulated. On way to Hosp*[ital]* cap blown into mud & I had to wash it. Supper at 4 of beef & gravy, very little bread at Dr. Sweet's room in eve. to bed early.

Sunday, 5th—Sunny. Wash, change shirts, & black shoes, Bo't paper, 5c. Wrote, (after inspection) to Mother & the *[Brockport]* Republic. Rec*[eive]*d letter from Father, dated 23d Feb*[ruary]* with $1. Also letter & magazine from Lieut*[enant]* Benton Tuttle. Sent paper to Mate *[Mary A. C. French]*. Read & had nap from 3½ to 5. Sup*[per]*, ap*[ple]* sauce, good tea & bread. Read "Doug. Jerrold". Wrote some to Mate*[Mary A. C. French]*. An alarm of fire, nothing but a ward in Colum*[bia]* Hospital. Splendid moonlight night.

Monday, 6th. –Fine day; warm. Hash breakfast. Bought 2 paper collars, 10c., 2 two cent & 7 three cent stamps, 25c. Paid debt of 50cts. At office, writing 9 till 12. *[at top of page:* "Sent 1 letter, 7th"*]* No mail for me to-day. Gen*[era]*l *[Philip]* Sheridan captures reb*[el]* Gen*[eral Jubal Anderson]* Early[248] & men in *[the Shenandoah]* Valley.—Dinner of rice & gravy "mux", tiny piece of beet, &c. Work 1 till 4½. Read some in eve. & write some to Mate *[Mary A. C. French]*. Talking loud in ward. Card-playing, &c. Retire in usual good season, tired.

Tuesday, 7th. –Splendid day. Washed stockings h*[an]*dk*[erchie]*f & towel. At office at work, from 9 to 12, &c., as usual. Quite warm. No mail for me. Sent letter to Mate *[Mary A. C. French]* & paper to Father. Rec*[eive]*d pass

& went to city at 3. Called on Jimmy Edwards, formerly of 6th Co*[mpany]*, now citizen & head clerk at Armory Gen*[era]*l Hospital[249] 7th st*[ree]*t, south. Cordial greeting & he made application to Medical Director for my transfer to Armory *[General Hospital]* & it was signed by the Surg*[eon]* in ch*[arge]* Dr. Bliss. Took sup*[per]* with J*[immy Edwards]*. Biscuit & butter, tea, &c. Was shown around the splendid & tasty hospital, so comfortable. In printing office, &c. Back, & on st*[reet]* saw "2 young ladies." Pleasant walk & visited *[Sampson W.]* Fry before going back to Carver *[Hospital]*. Washed, &c.

Wednesday, 8th.—Pleasant till 5 P.M. when rain set in. Left watch to be repaired, in ward 12, & worked in office 9 till 12. *[at top of page:* "Letters (2) rec*[eive]*d 8th. 2 rec*[eive]*d, 10th. Letters 2 sent, 10th."*]* at noon rec*[eive]* d letter from Mate *[Mary A. C. French]*, Feb*[ruary]* 6, & one from Frank *[Francis R. Douglas]*, Feb*[ruary]* 26. In P.M. office, 1 to 5; slim sup*[per]* taste of cheese, bread & tea. Rec*[eive]*d watch & paid 25c Weather to-day really warm, shower eve. There seems to be prospect of a marriage in the hosp*[ital]* soon. An ass*[istan]*t surg*[eon]*. Watch-cleaner wanted me to pay him $1 but I couldn't "see it." Wrote some to "Frank,"*[Francis R. Douglas]* now Jan*[uary]* 12 married: Mrs. Smith.

Thursday, 9th.—Cloud & sun; some fine rain. Warm. At usual work. No mail. Pleasant day in office, especially some fun when Dr. O. P. Sweet examined 3 or 4 men. Very dull generally to-day. In eve. read "Jerrold".

Friday, 10th.—Cold, rain, freezing, then sun. At work. *[Sampson W.]* Fry called on me. Was informed by Dr. S*[weet]* that the application for my transfer had been approved. At noon rec*[eive]*d letter & $1 from Sister & Mate *[Mary A. C. French]*. Ans*[were]*d each, & sent paper to Em*[ma]* S*[mith]*. After sup*[per]* found that my papers for transfer are being held back in order to keep me here. I found a substitute to take my place in writing, & rode to city in st*[reet]* car 5c. Saw J. Edwards, who assured me of a "good thing", there. Back (5c) at ¼9. In Dr. S*[weet]*'s room. Accomplished nothing there, as Dr. S*[weet]* was out. To bed.

Saturday, 11th.–Pleasant. Cold—freezing. Fixed up bed before break*[fast]* &c. Took book to library. Talked to Dr. S*[weet]* about transfer & he gave me satisfaction (apparently.) At work on book, A.M. & P.M. Good dinner, but none too much of the hash, rice. A little consolation in regard to transfer, but proved to be false when J*[immy]* Edw*[ards]* came with the news that trickery was being played me. I had good chat with J*[immy]* & talk with Dr. S*[weet]* about the affair, who thought there was a mistake & promised to see to it. After sup*[per]* I obtained a pass, walked to town, saw promenading beauty, found J*[immy]* Edw*[ards]* in office Armory Square Hosp*[ital]* then found *["Dr. Judson" crossed out]* that the application was returned with disapproval. So I am wire-pulled out of the good thing, selfishly. In J*[immy Edward]*'s room, saw photo album. Walked back in moonlight, after buying cake 10c. in market. Bursted into Dr. *[O. P.]* Sweet's room, found feminines & music, told Dr. S*[weet]* the result (news to him(?)) backed out, went to ward 10 & to bed. *[at top of page: "Sent 1 letter, 12th. Sent 1 letter 14th."]*

Sunday 12th.—Pleasant. Usual cleaning, break*[fast]* of corn, cof*[fee]* & sour bread, then bought a *[Washington]* Chronicle, 5c. Called at Dr. S*[weet]* room heard some "funny revelations," saw Dr. Craig, who says there may be no objections to transfer on completion of my "book on surgery." Inspection. Wrote to Father & some to Mate *[Mary A. C. French]*. Also wrote letter for sick man. Read some. No mail for me. Dinner of pota*[to]*, turnips, rice. Sent letter to Father & paper to Mate *[Mary A. C. French]*. In Dr. S*[weet]*'s office "Hates to have me leave." Wrote some to Mate *[Mary A. C. French]* in eve., & read magazine.

Monday, 13th.—(6 months from to-day & army life will cease.) Soft air, more like May than March. Washed stockings. Book, "Jerrold" from library. Office work. Heard examination of men for discharge & heard some of the workings of the disch*[arge]* system. After sup*[per]* walked & in eve. wrote to Mate *[Mary A. C. French]*. Read some in book. Saw darkey, old & young, playing. Good dinner today; "Beef mush!" Mild night.

Tuesday, 14th.—Pleasant. sour bread. At work in A.M & till 3 P.M. Dr. S*[weet]* gave me pass & I saw *[Sampson W.]* Fry at Mt. P*[leasant Hospital]*. Supper, then walked to town. Gazed on promenaders & bought pie. 15c Back at 9, tired. Sent letter to Mate *[Mary A. C. French]* at noon. *[at top of page: "Rec[eive]d letter, 17th."]*

Wednesday, 15th.—Warm; sweaty. Cloudy, like rain, in P*[rovost]* M*[arshall]* office A.M. Books inspected in P.M. & I "laid off." Read newspapers in reading room. Had a present of a very good knife by "Sollie," *[Solomon]* fixed up the knife by grinding. Men are being examined for discharge. Good dinner & breakfast to-day, beef "mush" for break. & baked beans for dinner. In our ward is an old chap rheumatic, always "bilious;" full of piety. Good news from Sheridan & Sherman[250]. Too noisy to read in room, & I took book & read in Dr. Beltz' room H*[ea]*dq*[uarte]*rs Traded watches—$10. to boot, for cylinder escapement No. "18629.—C.H." Silver chain.

Thursday, 16th.—Pleasant, cloud & sun P.M. At work as usual. No mail. Peter McNaughton, S*[harp]* S*[hooters]* came over from Alexandria; went to M*[t]*.

Pleas*[ant]* Hosp*[ital]* with him. At sup*[per]* with detailed men. Rode down to city in eve. 5c. Bought hat black $3. Peanuts, 10c. At Arm*[or]*y Sq*[uare]* Hosp*[ital]*. Up 7th to O in wind. Saw nothing much. Walked back to Carver *Hospital]* 8½. Heavy rain, 9½. Has been very warm for March. Last night heard first frogs "singing."

Friday, 17th.—High wind all day. Sun. Chilly.—No fire in room, & did not do much to-day. Read some. Letter from Mother & Sister. Pass at 5. walked to city. Peanuts, pie, &c. 35c. Walk in front of capitol. *[at top of page: "*Sent letter, 20th & 21st*"]*

Saturday, 18th.—Pleasant. High wind. Changed bed clothes (weekly.) In reading room ½ hour 9. (Lent H*[orace]* House, S*[harp]* S*[hooters]*, $1. Paid 5c for washing.) Last eve. bought 25 three cent stamps & 10 two cent ones—95c. At work in P.M. Examined by Board, Dr. *[O. P.]* Sweet & French, who decided to recommend me for Veteran Reserve Corps. No mail to-day. Have more cold. In eve. wrote letter for Larned & read some. A black wedding came off here to-day.

Sunday, 19th.—Pleasant but somewhat chilly. Break*[fast]*, a mixture of beans & corn, boiled, partly, not much of a dish. Bought *[Washington]* Chronicle, 5c. Wrote to Sister & read. At noon Blood & P*[eter]* McNaughton called. Nap in P.M., 2 to 4½. Change of surgeons in ward. Dr. Craig goes. In eve. wrote some to Mate *[Mary A. C. French]*. Wrapped paper, ready to send Mat *[Mary A. C. French]* in morn.

Monday, 20th.—Pleasant, warm. At work as usual. Mailed letter to Sister & paper to Mate *[Mary A. C. French]*. In P.M. worked hard. In eve., gave clothes to Sollie *[Solomon]* to wash. Went to town in st*[reet]* car. Saw *[Lee]* Carrington &____ *[in original]* on avenue & Jimmy *[Edwards]* at Ar*[mory]* Sq*[uare]* Hosp*[ital]*. Peanuts, 5c. cake, 5c., car, 5c. Quite warm in eve. Back to Carver *[Hospital]* just after 9, O.K. Violent toothache.

Tuesday 21st.—Warm sweat. In office all day. Sent letter to Mate *[Mary A. C. French]*. No letter yet. Went after men in wards & heard them examined, pitiful stories. Old white headed man.—Vegetable soup dinner. Some toothache again. Rain in eve.

Wednesday. 22d.—High wind; chilly; at work, took book from library, "Half hours with best authors" by Charl*[es]* Knight[251]. No mail. Pass & walked to Penn*[sylvania]* Avenue. Saw crowd & U.S. Marshal Lawson had pulled a mounted guard from his horse & took him away. No good cause. Paid 25c. for two poor pies for myself & *[Horace]* House.

Thursday 23d.—Chilly. Wind & rain. Copied some in P.M. Rec*[eive]*d *[Brockport]* Republic of 16th, my letter of 5th published. No letter. Ward is white washed & cleaned out to-day. Lost my ring in assisting about the ward. Toothache in eve. Read.

Friday, 24th.—Cold, & high wind. My ring is found. Bought 2 collars paper, 10c. In office. High wind yesterday, blew down flag-staff here & at Mt. Pleasant. At noon, I read 3 *[Brockport]* Republics, of 2nd, 9th, & 16th, latter from Mother, & *[at top of page:* "Rec*[eive]*d letter, 25th & 26th Sent letter 26th."] a Democrat extra—great flood in Rochester. No letter. After sup*[per]* walked to town called on my friends *[Lee]* Carrington & Britnall at 99 F st. Fine rooms. Introduced to a Capt*[ain]* 103rd Ohio, & a citizen. *[Lee]* Car*[rington]*. offered to help me get a clerkship. Got my clothes, 2 pieces washed, 15c. & bought ½ pie, 15c., & 5 cakes, 5c, on 7th st. Home made pie & cake—good. Cold. Back to Carver *[Hospital]* 9.

Saturday, 25th.—My 23rd birthday. Not quite so much wind. Very chilly. Letter from Em*[ma]* S*[mith]* Only a little writing, in P.M. or A.M. Pass. Went to city, car. 5c. At Arm*[or]*y Sq*[uare]* Hosp*[ital]* & called on *[Lee]* Carrington, heard music, & mailed letter to him. At Mt. P*[leasant]* Hosp*[ital]* saw *[Sampson W.]* Fry.

Sunday, 26th.—Cold, wind. Bo't *[Washington]* Chronicle, 5c. Letter from sister dated 23rd. Sent letter to mother & paper to Mate *[Mary A. C. French]*. Nap. J*[immy]* Edwards called. Sent paper to Frank *[Francis R. Douglas]*. Walked to city, & back. Cakes, 10c.

Monday, 27th.—Pleasant. Quite warm in P.M. At work office. Had shoes ½ soled, $1. Good news from N*[orth]* C*[arolina]*. No mail to-day. Read papers, &c. In eve. called on *[Lee]* Carrington. Nothing new.

Tuesday 28th.—At work. Quite warm. Rec*[eive]*d *[Brockport]* Repub*[lic]* of 23rd. In P.M. called on Jimmy Edwards, to see about transfer. Back on car, 10c. Sup*[per]*. Work on the Register from 7 till 9.

Context—Union forces begin Appomattox campaign, March 29.

Wednesday, 29th.—Pleasant, dusty & almost sultry. (Yesterday in W*[ashington]* while walking with *[Lee]* Carrington met *[Brigadier]* Gen*[eral]* E*[dward]* S. Bragg, who stopped, shook hands, & said he would give me a recommend as clerk, Adj*[utan]*t Gen*[era]*l's office War Department (60). *[Lee]* Carrington gave me (form of application at his room.) This A.M. Dr. *[O. P.]*

Sweet endorsed my application by stating that he "fully concurred with the statement of my application & that in his opinion I would not be fit to do field duty during my term of enlistment. I then went by car to [Brigadier] Gen[era]l [Edward S.] Bragg's Military Commission room of which M[ilitary] C[omission] he is President. He was behind time but notwithstanding this, while the military officers & witnesses of the court were waiting he took my application endorsing on it: "This soldier belongs to my command is a faithful soldier and is qualified to perform the duties of the position which he seeks." I then went to the Treasury Department, saw & was well & politely received by Hon[orable] Freeman Clarke, now Comptroller of the Currency[252], who wrote a first-rate recommendation, his clerk copying the same on my application, which Mr. C[larke] signed about as follows: "From personal acquaintance & testimonials furnished I have confidence that John T. Farnham is fully qualified as to character & ability to perform the duties of the place which he requests and recommend him for the same hoping the application may receive favorable consideration." Back on car & had baked beans for dinner. (Mr. Clarke is heavily pressed with business calmly & carefully, to all appearance, discharging his duties.) [Sampson W.] Fry came from Mt. P[leasant] Hosp[ital] & I went with him on st[reet] car to Navy Yard. Visited the Iron-clad Monitor "Montauk"[253] which is a novel sight. This vessel rec[eive]d many hard knocks during engagements with Forts Moultrie & Sumpter [sic] in Charleston Harbor & while engaged in vicinity of Fort Fisher, N.C. Also saw ancient & modern ordnance foreign & domestic with ammunition of all kinds. In the machine shop, I collected shavings from the finishing of brass cannon & the remnant of a sheet of brass after caps had been punched from it. (Ala.) Back on car to Penn[sylvania] Avenue & could not find hot coffee but had pie & glass of milk—total paid today 65c. [at top of page: "Rec[eive]d 4 letters, 30th—Sent 2 letters 30th"] called on [Lee] Carrington, who took my application to deliver to Col[onel Samuel] Breck. Back to Carver [Hospital] at 6½ & wrote on Register from 7 till 9. To bed somewhat tired.

Thursday 30th.—Rain all day, heavy but warm. (Yesterday we had stinking hash for breakfast.) Am told that I cannot be transferred as "Dr. Judson intends to have me detailed as clerk in the office as soon as I get thro' with Dr. [O.P.] Sweet's job." Selfishness or something worse. Letter from Mother, Sister, Mate [Mary A. C. French], Mrs. Bills, H[enry] C. Murray. Ans[were] d M's[Mary A. C. French] & wrote to Mother. Wrote some in P.M. Pass & rode to town, 5c. At [Lee] Carrington's room, he gave me envelop directed to Surg[eon]-in-charge Carver Hospital ordering me to "report to Col. Sam[ue] l Breck Ass[istan]t Adj[utan]t Gen[era]l War Dep[artmen]t if I am unable to do field duty (for duty there.) Mailed letters & called on Jimmy Edwards then bought 2 collars 10c. On car back to Carver [Hospital] & gave Dr. [O.P.]

Sweet my order, which somewhat startled him. To bed in ward, at 9. High wind & rain.

Friday, 31ˢᵗ.—More pleasant. Calm. Fixed up for presentation at War Dep*[artmen]*t Paid 5c for shirt washed. Very good hash. Breakfast. At Dr. *[O.P.]* Sweet's. (Sent letter 31st A*[djutant]*G*[eneral's]* O*[ffice]* War Dep*[artmen]*t April 1st April") office & saw Dr. Gray—satisfactory—Then finished page commenced in book of operations—my last stroke I hope in Carver Hospital. At last 11 A.M. rec*[eive]*d copy of order approved by Dr. S*[weet]* & rode to War Dep*[artmen]*t, A*[djutant]*G*[eneral's]* O*[ffice]* & reported to Col*[onel Samuel]* Breck, & was assigned to room 52; name registered. I am allowed this P.M. to make an arrangement, &c. Looked at several houses & found board at Mrs. Tyler's, (widow) 382 9th st*[reet]* (from Ogdensburg) at $23 per month. Has married daughter whose husband boards there & daughter, (Sarah) & a son, Jimmie, 14. While there, Hon*[orable]* Preston King, ex-Senator N.Y. ²⁵⁴called, & I was introduced to him. A jolly old gent. Found lodging in nice room at O.J. Atwood's 416 G st*[reet]* opposite Patent Office at $13. per month. Wrote to Father. Went to Hosp*[ital]* & took my things to 416 G st. & staid all night, after calling on *[Lee]* Carrington.

April

Context—The battalion fought in the Battle of Five Forks, April 1, and one enlisted man was wounded.

Saturday, 1st.—Pleasant but heavy wind. Up at 7. Break*[fast]* at Mrs. Tyler's at 7½. Good. Coffee especially nice. All family at breakfast. Took lunch of bread & cake for noon. Bought quart bottle, 20c. & had it filled with kerosene oil, 30c. Box matches, &c. *[at top of following page a clipping, apparently from the Brockport Republic obscures part of the diary entry. The clipping reads "We are pleased to learn that our army and Washington correspondent, J.T. Farnham, has been appointed to a lucrative clerkship in the Adj. Gen's Office at Washington." The first legible sentence of the diary follows:]* A man thrown from his horse in the street & horse's ankle put out of joint.—At A*[djutant]* G*[eneral's]* O*[ffice]* promptly 9. Clerks talking. Mr. Hulse undertakes to "break me in." Mr. Hamilton in charge of the room, & 4 other clerks in. This room 52 contains Co*[mpany]* rolls of all Reg*[imen]*ts from M*[ain]*e, N*[ew]* H*[ampshire]*, Conn*[ecticut]*, Vermont, & M*[as]*s*[achusetts]* pension letters & all inquiries to ans*[wer]*. Rolls have to be examined, &c. All the A.M. I was looking over rolls of one Reg*[imen]*t, could not find the name. Lunch & cold water. Tried to get order for my pay. Could not. Like the clerks quite well. Plenty of gossip. Ans*[were]*d letters & signed initials in P.M. till 4, then quit.

(Had ½ hour intermission, 12½ to 1.) Rec[eive]d pass by order Sec[retar]y of War, signed by Colonel Samuel Breck. Supper, after going to room at 4½. Pleasant tea table. Put on overcoat & rode to Mt. P[leasant] Hosp[ital], 5c. (after reading eve. paper at Mrs. Tyler's.) Saw [Sampson W.] Fry & borrowed $20. Now owe him $54. Gave him note, $40. payable May 1 & $14 June 1. Stopped at Carver [Hospital]. Walk to town, 1½ miles. Bought shoe brush 35c. box blacking, 15c. Bottle ink, 10c. At room, heard fire alarm. Saw flame & went. Great crowd & heavy blaze. [Major] Gen[era]l [Christopher Colon] Augur[255] quarters, Q[uarter] M[aster]'s q[uarte]rs, &c. burned. Back & broke lamp chimney, then to bed. [at top of page: "Sent 1 letter 2nd Sent 4 letters 3rd. Fall of Richmond & Petersburg, 3rd."]

Sunday, 2d.—Very pleasant & warm. Late at Breakfast, 8. Bought [Washington] Chronicle, 5c. Wrote to Mate [Mary A. C. French], after walk to Post Office. Also, wrote to Mr. [Horatio N.] Beach, which I mailed. Also wrote to Hon[orable] Freeman Clarke, Controller of Treasury & to [Brigadier] Gen[era]l [Edward S.] Bragg, thanking them for recommending me. At lunch, 1 P.M. introduced to elderly lady. Walked to ruins of last eve's fire. Back to room, &c. Went to Mrs. J.s at 4½, & they had gone to cemetery. Sit by open window looking on st[reet] at 11 to 1. Noisy. Presby[terian] church opposite, also Patent Office. Sweat in my room. At 5:15 went to 382—tea break, butter beef steak & potato mashed, with pickled apple; cakes. Staid during evening; read & talked with Mrs. T[yler] till 9. Then to 416. Mr. Atwood gave me small lamp to use for the eve. Finished letter to Mate [Mary A. C. French].

Context—Richmond and Petersburg fall to Union forces, April 3.

Monday, 3d.—After break[fast] bought a lamp globe, 15c. Sent Mate's [Mary A. C. French] letter, & a paper with letter for Hon[orable Freeman] Clarke. Left [Brigadier]Gen[era]l [Edward S.] Bragg's letter at 470 14th st[reet] for him. At A[djutant] G[eral's] O[ffice] on time. Commenced on a Maine case at 10:30 went with a clerk to Pay masters & rec[eive]d $32, which settles to March 1. At 11 A.M. the news of the fall of Richmond & Petersburg, (the former entered at 8:15 this A.M.) came, & [at top of page: "Paid on 3rd to March 1. "Jubilee"] all the clerks rushed out of the offices. Flags were unfurled & speeches made by Vice-President Johnson, Secretaries Stanton & Seward, Senator Sherman & ex-Sen[ator] Preston King. Great enthusiasm & cheering by the multitude. The elephant "Hannibal"[256] in passing saluted the flag, kneeling. Work is suspended for the day & the deeds of the victorious army celebrated. Cannon roar & bells ring wildly. At 382, gave the news & at 416 wrote a letter to the [Brockport] Republic & to Sister, which I mailed. In the streets men are wild. Some much intoxicated. General rejoicing—Police have their hands full. At the tent of the menagerie & circus. At my room till 4½. Sup*[per]*. 2 papers 15c. Arranged for circus with Mr. & Mrs. Chambers & Miss Sarah Tyler. Bought peanuts, 1 q*[uar]*t 20c. At 7 with the 3 went to store, saw Jimmy E*[dwards]* & concluded to go to Ford's Theater, $1.50 where we saw Miss Laura Keene play in the "Workmen of Washington."[257] Not very extra. Full house. Machinery of a work shop well represented. Some rain. In room at 12 midnight. Found door open or unfastened. *[at top of page:* "Washington Illuminated, 4th."*]*

Tuesday, 4th.—Pleasant. Weather just right. At Breakfast on time. Bought *[Washington]* Chronicle, 5c. Take lunch of bread, butter & cake. At A*[djutant]* G*[eneral's]* O*[ffice]*, 9. At usual work. The "boys" are mostly used up after the "Jubilee." Arrangements for illumination of the public buildings to-night. Went down at noon & had glass of ale; lunch. Quit just before 4 & I went with the clerks to restaurant & "wet my new position" by treating the boys at an expense of $1. At room, supper, ham & eggs, etc. Read paper. At room. At 6:45 go to office, as all clerks are to be there by order of the Sec*[retar]*y of War, to light the candles in each window. (This after sitting by west window of room at 416, looking in st*[reet]*) In our room as in all the upper windows are a locomotive head lights, which at bugle sound, were turned so that the lurid glare shone upon the faces of the crowd in front of the War Department building. Every glass in lower windows burned 2½ candles each. Splendid lights burned in the yard & 5 or 6 Bands followed with successive airs. All gay. And all other public buildings bore various mottoes, with illuminations.— Fireworks were sent up & private houses also blazed with "tallow dips". The streets were crowded with people & speakers addressed a meeting in front of the Pat*[ent]* Office until 11 P.M. I went to room about 10 satisfied. The lights from the Pat*[ent]* Office shone into my room, opposite. Band in the distance, serenading, played me to sleep.

Wednesday, 5th.—Up at 6½ & bought *[Washington]* Chronicle before breakfast, 5c. Still good news. Break*[fast]* on time, & such good coffee. Buttered my bread for lunch! Read & go direct to A*[djutant]* G*[eneral's]* O*[ffice]* via room. On time. Go to work with a will. 6 or 7 cases to-day. Nothing very new. All is pleasant. Jeff*[erson]* Davis reported captured. At 4, "on time" stop work. A 15 minutes brisk walk to 416 Wash. Supper, 382 Plenty of talk, &c. Walk to the Carver Hosp*[ital]*. Call on Dr. Beltz & *[O.P.]* Sweet. At ward 10 see the boys & *[Horace]* House gives me *[Brockport]* Republic of 30th. *[illegible word(s)* "I ult"?*]* (on way up met 19 ambulances which have taken wounded to hospitals.) Walk back, stop at 382, carry in eve. paper & read to Mrs. T*[yler]* & Miss T*[yler]* while Capt*[ain]* & wife are attending to business (law) papers in sit*[ting]* room. Pleasant eve. At 9 to 416,

& soon abed. Hear water running from hydrant. A warm day. *[at top of page:* "Rec*[eive]*d 1 letter, 6th, & 1 on 7th"*]*

Thursday, 6th.—Still warmer and leaves are springing forth.—I had (fresh) for breakfast. Rec*[eive]*d letter from home Father, Sis & Harvey before going to A*[djutant]* G*[eneral's]* O*[ffice]* at 9 & sent *[Washington]* Chronicle to Father. At work on Pension cases & it is more perplexing than usual. Glad to quit at 4. Rebel Band play in front of the War Dep*[artmen]*t. After supper called on *[Jimmie]* Edwards, Arm*[ory]* Sq*[uare]* Hosp*[ital]*. Called at Express office then with Miss T*[yler]*, Mr. & Mrs. Chambers & Jimmie *[Edwards]* to the circus & menagerie; ($1) wild animals—Elephant, Hannibal, &c. Poor circus. Glad to get out again. O, how warm.

Friday, 7th.—Showers & warm. Leaves are springing forth nicely—Up at 6½. Leave off drawers. Shad for breakfast, again. Gave blouse to wench, to wash. A*[djutant]* G*[eneral's]* O*[ffice]*. Do some more work than before, to-day; on pensions. At about 3 rec*[eive]*d my first mail at A*[djutant]* G*[eneral's]* O*[ffice]* letter from Mate *[Mary A. C. French]* dated 6 P.M., 5th. Good news again. Lee & army captured. Hearty sup*[per]* at room & read M*[ary A. C. French]*'s letter, &c. At A*[djutant]* G*[eneral's]* O*[ffice]* again from 7 till 9:30 as work is somewhat pressing. Splendid air to-night.

Saturday, 8th.—Cooler, pleasant. Up early. Read some after break*[fas]* t. Paid girl 15c. for washing my *[at top of page:* "Sent letter 9th. Gen'l Lee surrenders his Army 9th."*]* blouse, which I took to A*[djutant]* G*[eneral's]* O*[ffice]* to wear during the day. Worked into business quite well to-day. Somewhat monotonous. Quit at 4. Disappointed in not finding trunk arrived yet. Sup*[per]*. Called at Express office. Met Capt*[ain Franklin]* Edwards of Brock*[port]*[258]. on st*[reet]* with lady, bonnet trimmed with blue. Asked me to call on him at U.S. Hotel. Bought 2 oranges, 10c. & 2 collars (size 14½) 10c. Walk down Pennsylvania Avenue (61) & back with Miss Tyler. Read awhile & played checkers with Jimmy *[Edwards]*. Looked at game of backgammon & at room at 9½. Very glad to-morrow is a day of rest.

Context—Lee surrenders to Grant, April 9.

Sunday 9th—Chilly. Wind. Up at 5½, & to bed again. Bought *[Washington]* Chronicle, 5c. & read before break*[fast]*. Walked about st*[reet]*, while waiting for room to be cleaned up, &c. (Last night paid Mrs. T*[yler]*. $10 to apply on board.) Wrote to Mate *[Mary A. C. French]*, sent. Also sent paper to sister. Lunch, cake, pie, & a piece of Mrs. Chambers' wedding cake, wine. Nap, 3 till 4½. Sup*[per]*. Called on Capt*[ain Franklin]* Edwards, U.S. Hotel & sent word home. Read papers at 382, then to room & wrote to Aunt C. Put up paper to send to Mate *[Mary A. C. French]*. Rain to-night. *[at top of page:* "Sent 4 letters, 10th. Rec*[eive]*d 1 letter 11th. Another Jubilee"*]*

Monday 10th.—At 10 minutes before 5 A.M. awakened by salute of 2500 guns, fired in honor of Gen*[era]*l *[Robert E.]* Lee's surrender, 9th. At the A*[djutant]* G*[eneral's]* O*[ffice]* we worked from 9 till 11, when a half holiday was announced & we quit. Dissension. The general sentiment seems to be magnanimous toward Gen*[era]*l *[Robert E.]* Lee. Everybody is joyous & some demonstration is made but rain fell all day, making public demonstration doubtful. Bells again ring, & cannon boom. I retired to my quiet room, wrote to the *[Brockport]* Republic, & finished to Aunt C. Sent both in same envelope at 1. An hour at Mrs. Tyler's reading, talking, &c. At 416 wrote to Lieut*[enant Alphonso W.]* Starkweather & H*[enry]* C. Murray. (sent paper to Mate *[Mary A. C. French]* this A.M.) SupI*[per]* 4½. Bought shoes (6c) low, paid $4. pair stocking, 40c. necktie, 50c. Called at *[Lee]* Carrington's & was introduced to Mr. Sleigh, & 2 others. At 382, read eve. paper &c. till 9. Rain. Hear patriotic songs, next house. Band.

Tuesday, 11th.—Rainy, all day. At A*[djutant]* G*[eneral's]* O*[ffice]*. Rec*[eive]* d letter at 10, from Mother of 8th with Express receipt for my trunk sent on 7th. Quit work at 2 to give chance for preparation to be made for illumination to-night. At Adams Ex*[press]* Office. No trunk. Then *[at top of page:* "Rec*[eive]*d letter 12th."*]* at Hamden's Ex*[press]* Office, same result. Showed pass to Prov*[ost]* Serg*[ean]*t, first time in st*[reet]*.—At room. Read at 382 before supper, or "dinner" as they call it here. Saw Capt*[ain]* Chambers & Mr. Platt play chess.—At 7, at A*[djutant]* G*[eneral's]* O*[ffice]*, illumination of all pub*[lic]*. Buildings. Locomotive head lights in our windows & I did not stay in long. Sent Mr. Thatcher $1. In st*[reet]* met Mr. & Mrs. Chambers & Miss T*[yler]* & walked about with them. Fireworks & music. To bed early after reading eve. papers. (Air misty.) Heard President read his speech.

Wednesday. 12th.—Warm, cloudy in A.M. Up at 6½. Some rain during the day, & all the eve. At A*[djutant]* G*[eneral's]* O*[ffice]* about 10. Express man came with my trunk which I ordered sent to 416 G st*[reet]*. At noon I rode in st*[reet]* car to Pat*[ent]* Office, then found & carried trunk up to my room. Found key & everything else O.K. Put on dress coat & went back to office. At 4½ at room. Put on white shirt—again, &c. for tea. Also put on vest. Found letter in trunk, from Mother. Also a cake. Sewed buttons, shaved, &c. Read part of eve. (Life of Grant)[259] at 382. At room put up a paper to send home. Rain this eve. (Thatcher paid me $1. that I lent him last eve. Hear the st*[reet]* cars from my room. *[at top of page:* "Illumination, 13th"*]*

Thursday, 13th.—Pleasant. Sun. Pretty cool breeze. Sick headache most of the day. At A[djutant] G[eneral's] O[ffice], as usual. Quit at 2 to give illumination a chance for the grand city blaze to-night. At room I napped from 2½ till 4. Fixed up, &c. Sup[per]. At room & watched the papers by. Walked on Avenue. Bought Herald 10c. Ale, 5c. Met Vice President Johnson on the walk. Rec[eive]d eve. paper & at 382 with Mrs. & Mr. Capt[ain] Chambers, Mrs. & Miss T[yler], started to see the illuminations. Stopped at Capt[ain]'s office. Introduced to Mr. Reed. On st[reet] a perfect jam of people. Public & private buildings lighted, &c. A splendid sight. Mottoes, transparent, &c. 7:30 note on Treasury—fine representation. Stores decorated. ([Lieutenant] Gen[era]l [Ulysses S.] Grant said to be in town.) Elegant fireworks, in abundance. Sky clear. Air cool.—After leaving the family at 382 at my room I sat in window & looked at brilliant fireworks.

Friday, 14th.—Pleasant. Warm. Worked till 11, & as it is "Good Friday" we were let off to "attend church". I rode to Georgetown (12c) to see Lieut[enant] Col[onel] D[ennis] B. Dailey, but did not find him. Pleasant view of country. Statue of Washington & horse (equestrian). Saw Col[onel Dennis B.] Dailey in st[reet], & spoke with him. [at top of page: "President Lincoln murdered. Died 15th. Rec[eive]d letter 13th."] He is wounded in hand. At Arm[or]y Sq[uare] Hosp[ital] saw [Jimmy] Edwards. At room, lunch. Wrote to cousin H[enry] P. Randall[260] & to "Frank" [Francis R. Douglas]. After supper walked to Mt. Pleasant Hosp[ital]. Saw [Sampson W.] Fry. Then to Carver Ward 10 & saw the boys. Rode on car, 6c & went to Grover's Theatre,[261] gallery (25c.) Saw the brilliant play of "Aladdin & his wonderful lamp"[262] which is indeed a splendid thing. A panic was caused among the audience by the announcement that the President had been assassinated at his box in Ford's Theatre (63) (shot by pistol in head, the assassin escaping through the stage & rode away. A desperate tragedy.) And the audience left Grover's before the play ended. I went to the front of Ford's Theatre, 10th St., & Mr. L[incoln] had been taken across st[reet] to private house, insensible. A crowd stood in waiting in bad humor with rebels. Excited. At 11½, the crowd were dispersed. I saw horse run past, which was said to have been the one used by the murderer.— Secretary [William E.] Seward was also injured by an accomplice stabbed in his house, his sons also badly hurt, & all of them unconscious. An atrocious plot by traitors.

Saturday, 15th—Washington draped in mourning. Andrew Johnson inaugurated President. Rain all day & the heavens are clothed in black. Mr. Lincoln died about 7 a.m.—Bought 2 [Washington] Chronicles 10c, sent one to Mr. [Horatio N.] Beach & 1 to Alonzo, 2c. At A[djutant] G[eneral's] O[ffice], but all work stopped, & on my way back to room saw hearse pass taking the President's body to the White House to be embalmed. Saw Seward house, & the dagger used last eve. found by a colored boy. Bells toll & crape is hung on most buildings.—Rec*[eive]*d letter from Mate *[Mary A. C. French]*— good long one. Commenced to answer it. Bought paper 5c with account of inauguration of Vice Pres*[iden]*t *[Andrew]* Johnson as president, at 11 a.m. Rain, rain & darkness. Every one is sad. Startling rumors. *[Lieutanant General Ulysses S.]* Grant left town last eve. & escaped murder. Wrote some to Mate *[Mary A. C. French]*. In st*[reet]* at eve. read eve. paper to the T*[yler]* family. To bed early. Bought 10 collars, 40c.start here 203

Sunday, 16th.— High wind, sun. Bought *[Washington]* Chronicle, 5c. After break went to A*[djutant]* G*[eneral's]* O*[ffice]*, no mail. On way back, met Mrs. Lathrop on st*[reet]*. White House dismal. At room, wrote to *[Brockport]* Republic. Lunch at 382. Read &c. till 4½ Supper. Walked to A*[rmory]* S*[quare]* Hosp*[ital]*. Saw *[Jimmy]* Edwards & two men who had come to see their wounded sons & found them dead. Sad. *[at top of page: "Sent 3 letters 16th & 17th"]* Back through Smithsonian Institute yard green & nice. At A*[djutant]* G*[eneral's]* O*[ffice]* on duty from 7 till 10. Took the opportunity of writing letters to Mate *[Mary A. C. French]* & to Mother. Then to 416, rang bell a half hour before I could get in. At 11, to bed, tired. Sent paper to Em*[ma]* S*[mith]* to-day.

Monday, 17th.—Pleasant. Up at 6½. Bought paper, 5c. Break*[fast]*. Then left shirt & drawers at National Steam Laundry, for washing. At A*[djutant]* G*[eneral's]* O*[ffice]* on time & on corner met former Lieut*[enant]* C. O. Wickes of Brockport[263] now clerk in A*[djutant]* G*[eneral's]* sO*[ffice]*, had talk with him. Work about as usual & much talk about the murder of President. A statement is required of every clerk as to where he attended church on Good Friday (a ridiculous idea) & I did not hesitate to state that I attended no church. Rumors that the murderers are caught. $20,000 reward offered. At 4, as I left A*[djutant]* G*[eneral's]* O*[ffice]* on passing the White House, accidentally caught a glimpse of Mrs. H. A. Smith, little Kate, & Mrs. Gurley, Mrs. S*[mith]*'s mother, & turned to speak, met them in Jackson Square but they did not at first recognize the "Johnny" who lived with them at Medina in 1857–8. But they seemed quite pleased to see me, & invited me to call on them. At supper *[at top of page: "Rather an eventful day, 17 th 9 A.M. & 4½ P.M. Saw corpse in state at White House."]* then at room "fixed up", on st*[reet]* bought orange 10c. for Kate Smith, & called on them at No. ___ 5th st*[reet]*, between D & E. Introduced to Mr. Dudley, a gentleman & 2 ladies & passed a very pleasant eve., talking upon olden times, &c. Read at room awhile. Very quiet to-night. This A.M. mailed letter to Mother & Mate *[Mary A. C. French]* & paper to Mate *[Mary A. C. French]* Miss Mower & Mrs. Coleman.

Tuesday, 18th.—Quite warm. Bo't [*Washington*] Chronicle & read before break[*fast*]. On way to War Dep[*artmen*]t met Lieut[*enant*] Gen[*era*]l [*Ulysses S.*] Grant, alone. He looked sad, & I only recognized him by the 3 stars on his shoulders. Work as usual. Did not feel well last night or to-day. Rec[*eive*]d [*Brockport*] Republic yesterday. At 8 P.M. clerks all assembled & proceeded to White House, where thousands were waiting to get in. Passed into East room & viewed hastily & unsatisfactorily the face of Mr. Lincoln in splendid coffin placed in a catafalque or arched canopy draped. The features looked rather painful & a white powder had been sprinkled upon the face. A sad scene. On coming out I went to 416, & to sup[*per*]. Read paper. Then strolled through Smithsonian grounds, got shirt & drawers at laundry, paid 25c. At Mrs. T[*yler*]'s [*at top of page:* "Funeral of President Lincoln, 19th."] introduced to Miss Gault. Read eve. paper, had almonds & raisons [*sic*] spilled water on table, then to room & after preliminaries, went to bed, tired. At between 3 & 4 P.M., saw Secretary [*Gideon*] Welles (Navy) & [*Major*] Gen[*era*]l [*Ambrose E.*] Burnside at War Dep[*ar*]t[*ment*]. Gen[*eral*] B[*urnside*] looks "gay". In st[*reet*] to-night saw guard in charge of a woman & some loafers trying to get 2 little boys to fight.

Wednesday, 19th.—Calm, sultry. Violent sick headache, tasted a little coffee & ate part of a biscuit. Quite sick. Mrs. Tyler kindly attended to my comfort & at 8½ I went to A[*djutant*] G[*eneral's*] O[*ffice*] & found there was to be no work done to-day; back to room & on st[*reet*] saw "Cy" Wickes who told me that Lieut[*enant*] Mort Reed [*sic*], 8th [*NY*] Cav[*alry*], Brockport, was looking for me. Left word for him to call at 416. At my room laid down from 9½ to 11, then felt easier, got up, tasted a biscuit & went out as the preparations for the funeral were being arranged. Streets thronged with people. At National Hotel, but could not see L[*ieutenan*]t Reed. Found a standing place on avenue near Capitol & waited until 2:45 when procession appeared. Colored troops leading followed by cav[*alry*] art[*iller*]y inf[*antry*], marines, officers on foot, Bands, then the canopied hearse bearing the magnificent coffin in full sight fringed with silver bullion. Then the distinguished mourners with family, citizens, &c. A jam & so dusty & hot I was glad to return to room & lay down before the procession passed & slept an hour. It was a half hour from the time I saw the head of procession before I could see the hearse which was in the centre of the whole. At 5, at supper, & had some appetite, especially for the custard.—(To-day bought [*Washington*] Chron[*icle*] 5c & a badge of mourning picture of Mr. Lincoln 25c.) At National Hotel saw Lieut[*enant*] Mort Reed, who is here with 52 others (cav[*alr*]y) each having a captured flag to present to Sec[*retar*]y of War to-morrow, then he goes home on leave. Glad to see him; we went to my room & had a social chat, then I accompanied him to A[*rmory*] Sq[*uare*] Hosp[*ital*], he wishing to see an officer there.—Back to room, early, tired. This ends a sad and memorable day in my experience. At National *[Hotel]* to-day met Mr. Ball, formerly "lawyer" in Medina. *[at top of page: "Rec[eive]d 2 letters, 20th & sent 1, 21st."]*

Thursday 20th.—Rainy; not feeling very well to-day. At A*[djutant]* G*[eneral's]* O*[ffice]* & work as usual. Rec*[eive]*d letter from Alonzo, Cordelia & Mother; am astonished that Mr. *[Horatio N.]* Beach is so mean & avaricious as to hire a boy of 3 years experience in printing at 4.50 per week! Have concluded to have no more to do with the *[Brockport]* Repub*[lic]* establishment. Fish for supper. Mud, mud, mud in st*[reet]*. At room, then to Mrs. Smith's, where I saw Mrs. S*[mith]*., Mrs. Gurley, Kate (or Mabel) Miss Mower, Mrs. Coleman of Roch*[ester]*, Mr. Dudley & introduced to Mr. Dean, of Roch*[ester]*. This is an office of Freedman's Relief Association[264]. Saw some relics of Mr. Lincoln's coffin & had a short visit. Back to room, after stopping at Mrs. Tyler's a moment. Waited for Mort Reed, but he did not come. This A.M. bought 2 *[Washington]* Chronicles & sent one home to Harvey 12c. Warm. At room, eve., read, & wrote to Lon, sending him $1.

Friday, 21st.—Cool, damp, some rain, pleasant in P.M. & eve. Nothing unusual to mark the day. Sent letter to Lon. Bought *[Washington]* Chronicle, 5c. & 20 2c. stamps, 40c. At A*[djutant]* G*[eneral's]* O*[ffice]*, & my head felt bad most of the day. Better in eve. After sup*[per]* took walk on av*[enue]* to Capitol; grounds pleasant. *[at top of page: "Rec[eive]d 1 letter, 22nd"]* Then up 7th st*[reet]*, had glass soda water 10c. In room early. (Had soda water at noon, 10c.) Read some, & to bed.

Saturday, 22d.—Feel some better to-day. Pleasant, clear. At A*[djutant]* G*[eneral's]* O*[ffice]* as usual. After quitting work at 4, on way to sup*[per]* bought dose salts (cfr.), 5c. only! Rec*[eive]*d splendid letter from Mate *[Mary A. C. French]*, dated 20th. Came quickly. Read after sup*[per]*. Called at Mrs. Smith, & read Roch*[ester Evening]* Express. While there saw Sojourner Truth,[265] a colored woman quite distinguished, as a devoted worker for the colored people. She talked quite earnestly, & *[at top of page: "Sent 2 letters, 23rd."]* at last sat down to supper. Walked on Avenue, & 7th st*[reet]*. Quite tired to-night. Had a glass ale, 5c. To-day signed rolls for $30 commissary. Lent Hulse $4.

Sunday 23d—Cold. Windy. Abed late. Took salts, good effect.—Bo't *[Washington]* Chronicle. At A*[djutant]* G*[eneral's]* O*[ffice]*, rec*[eive]*d *[Brockport]* Republic & wrote to sister, mailed then wrote to Mate *[Mary A. C. French]*, mailed. After waiting for supper went on st*[reet]* car to Mt. P*[lesant]* Hospital, saw *[Sampson W.]* Fry, then to Carver *[Hospital]* a few minutes. Walked back & to bed after reading Sunday [*Washington*] Chronicle, which I mailed with another, for Mate [*Mary A. C. French*].

Monday. 24th.—More pleasant but chilly breeze in A.M. Mailed papers to Mat [*Mary A. C. French*] & left 2 shirts at laundry, walked up avenue to A[*djutant*] G[*eneral's*] O[*ffice*]. At noon saw Lieut[*enant*] Mort Reed, who had presented flag to War Dep[*artmen*]t. & is going to Brockport. After sup[*per*] at room. Glass ale 10c. Bought N.Y. Herald, 5c. At Columbia Gardens, saw vast amount of human nature & heard music. At Metropolitan Hall[266], heard singing. There saw "Corporal" Fitch formerly of 6th S[*harp*] S[*hooters*]. Home satisfied.

Tuesday, 25th—Warm. Bought [*Washington*] Chron[*icle*], 5c. & mailed to Mr. [*Horatio N.*] Beach after reading it 2c. At A[*djutant*] G[*eneral's*] O[*ffice*] as usual. Rec[*eive*]d notice that I am assigned to Co[*mpany*] "E." War Dep[*artmen*]t Rifles & ordered to report to the Capt[*ain*], which I neglected to do, but they were said to have drilled to-day. After supper went to Sherburne Barracks, beyond the Capitol, saw Hinman Smith, formerly of 6th S[*harp*] S[*hooters*], now in Co[*mpany*] "D." 12th VI[*eterans*] R[*eserve*] Corps[267]. Then on Av[*enue*] to 7th st[*reet*]. Ale, (2) 10c. Also spent 10c more. Promenaded some & at room heard Band play. Made investigation for new rooming place & found one near Capitol for $30 per month, board & lodgings. [*at top of page; "Rec[eive]d $30 Commissary."*]

Wednesday 26th—Very warm. After breakfast had hair cut. 35cts! A[*djutant*] G[*eneral's*] O[*ffice*] as usual. Nothing much new. Saw 9th corps passing. They having just come up from front. At 11½ A.M. rec[*eive*]d $31 commissary pay. After supper went up 7th st[*reet*]. Glass ale 5c. Found boarding & lodging place near 7th & N.Y. Avenue. At $6 per week! At clothing store bought summer coat & pants, $26. Then took bundle of my army blankets (2) & shelter tents, 2 shirts, drawers, canteen,[*illegible words*] pair pants, to [*illegible*] home. [*illegible*] laundry Mrs. T[*yler*]. read [*illegible*] then at 416 early [*at top of page: Rec[eive]d 1 letter, 27th, & sent 1."*]

Thursday 27th.—Almost hot. Heard alarm of fire about 3 A.M., & saw the light. First thing after breakfast went to Adam's Express office & rec[*eive*]d receipt for bundle. Bought [*Washington*] Chron[*icle*] 5c. At A[*djutant*] G[*eneral's*] O[*ffice*]. Rec[*eive*]d letter Mo[*ther*] & Sis[*ter*], from home, also paper with "ang" ointment. Wrote to Mother & mailed at A[*djutant*] G[*eneral's*] O[*ffice*]. After sup[*per*] called to see about board, on H st[*reet*]. Pleasant room & board, $33 per month. On "G" st[*reet*] at Mrs. Abbey's of Geneva, N.Y., good room, with board, $35 per month. Farther on, nearer the

Avenue, house little back from the st*[reet]*, pleasant, will know to-morrow eve. if I can get board & room at $30. per month. (think I can.) Notice a piano (yes, 2) in parlor. 11 boarders there. At another place, the smallest kind of a room for the exorbitant price of $30. per month, & on coming out I met Dr. *[Samuel]* Sweet & Miss Winans! Rather unexpectedly. Looked for Mr. Huer V*[eterans]* R*[eserve]* Corps*]*, but he is home on furlo*[ugh]*. At room, & went to call on Mrs. Smith, not at home. Ale, 5c. At 382, 9th & read eve. paper. Heard the story of the capture of Booth, & his being shot last eve. told by one of the cavalrymen *[at top of page:* "1 letter, 28."*]* who helped corner him. In room early. Band playing.

Friday 28th.—Weather same.—Bought *[Washington]* Chronicle, after getting up at 6½ & read it at 382, at A*[djutant]* G*[eneral's]* O*[ffice]* 9. Rec*[eive]*d letter from Mate *[Mary A. C. French]* before 10 A.M. & one enclosed from Mrs. Courtney. After sup*[per]* "dressed up", went to G st*[reet]* to see about the $30 place. & then called on Mrs. Abbey & made no decision. Ale, 2, 10c. At Mrs. Smith 5th st*[reet]*. Notified Mr. Atwood that I should not keep the present room at $35. Again at Mrs. Abbeys, but not satisfied. At H st*[reet]* where I called last eve., the $33 place, pleasant, & am to know *[at top of page:* "1 letter rec*[eive]*d, 29th."*]* about it in the morn. when I shall no doubt decide on some place. Sweat terribly to-night. In room, 9.

Saturday, 29th.—Warm & rain. At house on H st*[reet]*, but can make no arrangement there. Bo't *[Washinton]* Chron*[icle]* 5c. order that troops be ready for discharge soon & clerical force of Departments to be reduced. The war is virtually over. At A*[djutant]*G*[eneral's]* O*[ffice]*. At noon saw my Co*[mpany]* Rolls. O.K. Letter from Lon. In eve. rain. Called at Mrs. Wimsatt's 31 G. st*[reet]* & looked at room, concluded to go there next month *[at top of page;* "Sent 1 letter, 30th."*]* at $30. Heard Miss Wimsatt play on piano. Ale, 5c. orange, 5c. In room, wrote to Mate *[Mary A. C. French]*. Little Minnie playing. Sky clear at 9½.

Sunday, 30th.—Rigged up early & bought *[Washington]* Chronicle after break*[fas]*t. Bought 20 three c. stamps 60c. Read at 416, then to War Dep*[artmen]*t, rec*[eive]*d paper from home with tooth pick. Saw Mr. *[William]* Hues at V*[eterans]* R*[eserve]* C*[orps]* Barracks 17th st*[reet]*. St*[reet]* car to Wharf, waited an hour & took "Fulton" boat[268] & had a delightful ride to Alexandria, 20c. The rolling land of Maryland looked charming & in Navy Yard the shining heaps of cannon *[at top of page:* "May 1."*]* balls & artillery in yard was quite a sight. Saw fishermen hauling their nets near Giesboro P*[oin]*t, &c. Arlington House on the heights, once the home of the traitor *[Robert E.]* Lee, stand out in bold relief with its pillared portico. At Alexa*[ndria]*, saw

Blood & P. McNaughton, S*[harp]* S*[hooters]*, for an hour & a chat. Then back on steamer "Young America"²⁶⁹ 10c. At 416 at 3:20. Sat in room awhile, supper & paid Mrs. T*[yler]* $13, which makes $23 for the month's board. Packed things in my trunk. To bed early.

Monday, May 1.—Rain. Break. at 321 G street], Mrs. Wimsatt's; passable. Paid 5c. for *[Washington]* Chron*[icle]*. *[at top of page:* "Rec*[eive]*d *[Brockport]* Repub*[lic]* 27th to-day."*]* Paid Mrs. Atwood $13 for room. Paid darkey 25c for taking trunk to 321 G. At A*[djutant]* G*[eneral's]* O*[ffice]*. Pleasant, but chilly in eve. Bought comb, 25c. Ale, 5c.—Called at Mrs. Smith's & took Mabel to see "Aladdin" at Grover's Theatre²⁷⁰, ($1.15) which she enjoyed much. Sleep with Capt*[ain]* McKelvey at 321 G. about 12.

Tuesday, 2d.—Almost a frost last eve. & cold to day. Bought *[Washington]* Chron*[icle]* 5c. Read after very good breakfast. At A*[jutant]* G*[eneral's]* O*[ffice]*. Feel first-rate to-day. After supper, rode on cars, 6c. to Carver Hosp*[ital]* also to Mt. P*[leasant Hospital]*. Rode back on car 6c. at 321 & to bed early with Capt*[ain]* McKelvey. Bo't razor, 50c.

Wednesday, 3d.—More mild. Pleasant.—Took lunch to A*[jutant]*G*[eneral's]* O*[ffice]* after reading the news. Nothing very new at A*[djutant]* G*[eneral's]* O*[ffice]*. On way to supper got 2 shirts & drawers, 35c. at laundry; found *[Sampson W.]* Fry waiting for me at 321. Wrote to Mother after supper. At 416 G. st*[reet]*, & engaged old room & board at the rate of $35 per month. Walked about some. At 7 to A*[jutant]* G*[eneral's]* O*[ffice]* & worked till 10 with the rest of the boys, although it seemed useless. Fine moonlight. *[at top of page:* "Sent 1 letter, 4th."*]*

Thursday, 4th.—Warm & fine. Bo't *[Washington]* Chronicle, 5c. At A*[djutant]* G*[eneral's]* O*[ffice]* only worked till 12, then all quit for P.M. to observe the burial of Mr. Lincoln at Springfield, Ill. Borrowed $5 of Mr. Hulse. At 321 packed up my things & paid Mrs. Wimsatt $4 for board. Had trunk taken to 416 G st*[reet]* 25c. & settled there again. Wrote to Mother & sent. Nap. Supp*[er]* at 321, & an affecting parting! At Jackson Square, then called at Mrs. Smith's Glass ale, 7th st*[reet]*—Called at Mrs. Tyler's then at room. Mr. Atwood gave me a night key. Listened to music. *[at top of page:* "Rec*[eive]*d 2 letters, 5th"*]*

Friday, 5th—Up at 7¼. Breakfast at Mr. Atwood's 416 at 8. Good. Two ladies & 2 gents at table besides family of 4. Bo't *[Washington]* Chronicle, 5c. Read. At A*[djutant]* G*[eneral's]* O*[ffice]*, 9. Rec*[eive]*d letter of 1st from M*other]* & Sis*[ter]* A.M., & in P.M. letter from Mate *[Mary A. C. French]*, of 3rd.

At 1½ rec[eive]d $39.78 Q[uarter] M[aster] pay, making in all, thus, far for last month $69.78. Paid Hulse $5 borrowed. At 4½ good sup. Sweet potato asparagus, lettuce. In room, read. On car 6c. to end of 14th st[reet], & walked to *Mt. P[leasant]* Hosp[ital]. Paid [Sampson W.] Fry $30, & gave him note for $24, payable June 1. Walked back. At Gonzaga Hall[271] (Catholic) Fair. 15c. Fine articles. Saw Mrs. S[tephen] A. Douglas, who looks "sweetly sad", & young. Youth, beauty & "Wont you take a chance" at lottery. Came away satisfied with the brilliant display, came to room & wrote to Mate *[Mary A. C. French]*.

Saturday, 6th.—Air almost hot. Cool breeze in eve. Bo't Baltimore American, 5c. Read. Hot cakes & syrup for breakfast. Lunch. Sent 2 papers to Father & mourning photo of Lincoln to Harvey.—At A[djutant] G[eneral's] O[ffice]. (Took off und[er] shirt today) At 4, room, changed clothes, sup[per] at 4½. On Avenue, car up 14th st[reet], 6c. met Miss San. of Syracuse. At Carver Hosp[ital]. Saw [Horace] House, &c. Called for [Jimmy] Edwards but did not see him. In room at 9. This is lovely weather. Splendid moonlight eve. Band play at Gonzaga Hall. *[at top of page: "Sent 1 letter, 7th"]*

Sunday, 7th—Pleasant. Cool. Up at 6½ *[Washington]* Chronicle, 5c. Read & went to Armory Square Hosp[ital]. Saw *[Jimmy]* Edwards. Back & wrote to Mate *[Mary A. C. French]*, & sent. Read. Dinner at 2; roast turkey; &c. Ice cream & strawberries.) Walked to capitol throng on grounds. Saw Mabel Smith. Mrs. S[mith] has removed to 304, 10th st[reet], bet[ween] N & O. Took observation of people passing on 7th & was especially amused at the darkey couples. Heard one white woman say to another she would "get divorced in spite of everything." Back to room at 8. Sup[per], alone, cool tea, being late. In room, wrote, & prepared for to-morrow. Sat on balcony. *[at top of page: "Rec[eive]d letter, 10th"]*

Monday 8th—Bo't *[Washington]* Chron[icle] 5c. Mailed paper to Mat *[Mary A. C. French]*. Took 2 shirts to laundry. At A[djutant] G[eneral's] O[ffice]. Rec[eive]d *[Brockport]* Repub[lic] of 4th & *[Rochester Evening]* Ex[press] from home Lunch. Rain to-day & eve. After sup[per] worked in A[djutant] G[eneral's] O[ffice] from 7 till 9½. At room read awhile. To bed at 10½. Music in st[reet].

Tuesday, 9th.—Headache all day. Don't feel like reading & hardly like working, but go to A[djutant] G[eneral's] O[ffice]. Lunch. At 2½ was paid $38.50, balance of last month's wages, (including regular pay for March $16 as a soldier & 6.50 due for clothing not drawn, up to March 31.) making my pay for last month, $85.78., altogether.—Cool, almost chilly air. Mud. At sup*[per]*, then sat in room. (On way to sup. saw on st*[reet]* Charley, clerk at 3rd Div*[ision]*, 5th A*[rmy]* Corps H*[ea]*dq*[uarte]*rs) Lent *[illegible word]* A. Thatcher, room 52, $5. Bo't Herald & in room all the eve. reading. Called at Mrs. Smith's, introduced to Miss Knowlton.

Wednesday 10th—Dark. Cold. Slept late. At A*[djutant]* G*[eneral's]* O*[ffice]*. Worked hard & the girl Purdy sick 8th 9th & 10th—Rec*[eive]*d letter *[illegible word(s)]* from Mother & Sis*[ter]* of 8th. Paid 25c. for 2 shirts, washed. After sup*[per]* on avenue & 7th st*[reet]*. Bo't Tribune & in room early. Read & wrote to Sister. *[at top of page:* "Sent letter, 11th. Rec*[eive]*d one 13th."*]*

Thursday, 11th.—Rain P.M. & eve. Did not hear the bell & late at breakfast. At A*[djutant]* G*[eneral's]* O*[ffice]*. Mailed letter to Sister & papers to Father. Rush of work. At sup*[per]*. Walked down 7th st*[reet]*. At work in A*[djutant]* G*[eneral's]* O*[ffice]*, 7 till 10. Got wet in rain. Thunder & lightning. Rode to 416 G. st*[reet]* on car, 7c.

Friday 12th—Splendid day. Clear but cool. At office, after buying & reading *[Washington]* Chronicle 5c. Worked hard to-day. Purdy the disgraced called at office.—After sup*[per]* on Avenue & 7th st*[reet]* met Darling *[sp?]* formerly of Brockport, who treated me to glass ale. Bo't peanuts, 10c. Also bought a modern straw hat, $1.75. Cheap. At room early. Washed stockings & wrote to Mate *[Mary A. C. French]*. No letter to-day.

Saturday, 13th.—Have a heavy cold on my lungs & in my head, which make me feel unwell. Baltimore American, 5c. Read after & before break*[fast]*, as I got up before 6½. Splendid day. Just warm enough. Letter from Mate *[Mary A. C. French]* at 1:45 P.M. *[at top of page:* "Jeff*[erson]* Davis captured, 10th! Good. Sent 3 letters, 14th"*]* Quit work at 4 as usual.—After sup. at Avenue saw Jimmie Edwards & went with him to Arm*[ory]* Sq*[uare]* Hosp*[ital]* where I found Capt*[ain]* (late Lieut*[enant]*) *[Alphonso W.]* Starkweather, in one of the wards with a broken leg caused by a fall from his horse. Also saw Smedley & Hatch, latter wounded & S. taking care of Capt*[ain]* S. Hatch went with me to my room. I then went up 7th st*[reet]*. Ale, 10c. This A.M. bought photograph of Andrew Johnson, President 25c. In room at 9. Head feels badly. Talk through my nose. The 5th & 2nd Corps are near Alexandria, encamped.

Sunday, 14th.—Splendid day.—*[Washington]* Chronicle, 5c. Bad cold in head. No better. Took walk A.M. about town. Wrote to Mate *[Mary A. C. French]* & sent with photograph of President Johnson. Also wrote to

Capt*[ain]* *[Lewis B.]* Courtney & O*[rrin]* H. Strong.—Laid down & read *[Washington]* Chron*[icle]*. Capture of Jeff*[erson]* Davis. Dinner at 2. Walk to capitol & sat awhile with Hamilton & Thatcher, looking at papers by. Then walked with H*[amilton]* around capitol, saw drunken sailors. Down Avenue, to room. Sup*[per]* at 6. Walked after seeing man. *[at top of page:* "Cuff worn by President Lincoln when shot. (Rec*[eive]*d 18th) Sent letter 18th."*]* At Mrs. *[Jane Gray Cannon]* Swisshelm's²⁷² (62) with Miss K. went out with Miss Coleman teacher to Mass*[achusetts]* Avenue, calling at Mr. Slade's private messenger of President L*[incoln]* & Johnson. Introduced to Miss Slade. Glass water. Back with Miss K., on 7th. Bo't 3 oranges & glass soda water, 40c. At 5th st*[reet]*, Mrs. S*[mith]*'s, till 9, then to 416 G. Read & wrote to Father.— Sharp lightning in distance. Saw Gen*[era]*l *[Edward S.]* Bragg & his colored boy, Jake, this eve.

Thursday 18th.—Hot.—Up at 6. *[Washington]* Chronicle 2c. Mailed letter to Father. Splendid morning. After break*[fast]*, sent 3 *[Washington]* Chronicles to Mate *[Mary A. C. French]* & 1 to Father. Bo't 5 two ct. stamps, 10c. At A*[djutant]* G*[eneral's]* O*[ffice]* 9:10. Work as usual. At noon *[Sampson W.]* Fry brought me his telescope rifle which he left. At 4, I took it to 416, to keep for him while he stays in W*[ashington]*. It attracted much attention. Heavy showers in P.M., which cooled the air somewhat. At supper was invited to look at the new house which Mr. Atkins will occupy June 1. (Pineapple for tea.) Pleasant eve. Lent Hulse 50 cts. yesterday. (See page in back of this.) Visited the house, cor*[ner]* 6th & I. Like it well. Called on Miss Coleman, who gave me as a relic of A*[braham]* Lincoln, a cuff cut from the shirt he wore when assassinated. I was glad to get the relic. At room 416, & *[Sampson W.]* Fry came with his knapsack, &c. Heavy *[at top of page:* "Sent 1 letter, 19th Rec*[eive]*d 1 letter 20th"*]* rain all the eve. Went with *[Sampson W.]* Fry to Washington Theatre.²⁷³ ($1) where we saw Miss Maj. Pauline Cushman²⁷⁴ the Federal scout & spy play Kathleen in the Irish piece, "Peep O'Day"²⁷⁵. Very good, though she is rather heavy. Considerable fun. *[Sampson W.]* Fry stays with me to-night.

Friday, 19th.—Pleasant cool. Up at 7, bo't *[Washington]* Chron*[icle]* 5c. & read. *[Sampson W.]* Fry left at 8. Lunch in pocket as usual, to A*[djutant]* G*[eneral's]* O*[ffice]*. At noon wrote to Father subscribing $5 to a fund for erecting a monument to the memory of soldiers killed, &c. on condition that the name of Charles Farnham be placed upon the same. We in office are rushing Descriptive Lists. On way to "dinner" stopped & got my 2 shirts, 25c. Am offered board & room on cor*[ner]* 6th & I at the same rates as I am now paying. Called at Mrs. S*[mith]*'s to see about board next month. Back to room, 8, & found *[Sampson W.]* Fry who stays with me.

Saturday, 20th—Cool. Rain in eve. *[Washington]* Chronicle 5c. at A*[djutant]* G*[eneral's]* O*[ffice]*. Talk of discharging all '62 men on way to supper. Met Capt*[ain]* Simon Webster Brig*[ade]* Insp*[ector]* 2nd B*[attalion]* 2nd D*[ivision]* 2 *[illegible letter]* G. & took glass ale with him *[at top of page:* "Visit to 5th Corps, 21st"*]* After sup*[per]*, called at several hotels on Avenue met Gen*[era]* l *[Edward S.]* Bragg & Maj*[or]* (formerly Capt*[ain]* Osborne) on st*[reet]* & shook hands with them. Saw Adjutant of the 7th Wis*[consin VI Regiment]*. Attended play of "Uncle Tom's Cabin"[276] at Grover's not very good. Out late found S*[ampson]* W. F*[ry]*. in room. Paid $1.55 this eve.

Sunday, 21st—Rainy in A.M. & hindered I & *[Sampson W.]* Fry from going to 5th Corps early as we intended. After break*[fast]* bought *[Washington]* Chronicle 5c. Read some. At 12½ rain mostly ceased. *[Sampson W.]* Fry & I started on st*[reet]* car rode to Georgetown (6c.) crossed the Aqueduct Bridge to Virginia side of Potomac; rain then commenced. I put on my poncho (rubber.) Passed sev*[eral]* forts & at 2½ miles separated. Went 1½ miles to 140th saw Lieutenant Lewis B.] Courtney, who gave me some dinner. Saw *[Shedrick J.]* Jackson, *[Charles W.]* Root, *[Isaac]* Barnes *[Jr.]* & several others. On way back, called on Leon Morehouse Hosp*[ital]* Steward who refreshed me with a drink of wine. Agreed to call on me to-morrow. Walked on to 1st Brig*[ade]* H*[ea]*dq*[uarte]*rs 3rd Div*[ision]* *[at top of page:* "Sent 1 letter, 22d."*]* *[Orrin H.]* Strong had gone to 7th Co*[rps]*. I went on to 3rd Divis*[ion]* H*[ea]*dq*[uarte]*rs. Found the 3 Co's S*[harp]* S*[hooters]* & those of them who had been prisoners. Visit (short) with them. Found *[Sampson W.]* Fry there. Took *[R.C.]* Parker's rifle to send by Express to Brockport, to him. Started (with *[Sampson W.]* F*[ry]*) for W*[ashington]* & caught in rain, stopped till shower was over, in house of a darkey, but could not endure the stench there. Sky cleared before we reached W*[ashington]* riding by st*[reet]* cars to 9th st*[reet]*. I took rifle to room, was not invited to take supper, went to store & bought 5 cakes & bottle of cider, 15c. At room & took off my spoiled collars &c. Rain again to-night. Wrote some to Mate *[Mary A. C. French]*.

Monday, 22d.—Warm & no rain. Put up 2 papers & sent to Mate *[Mary A. C. French]* with letter. Also sent rifle to *[R.C.]* Parker with my overcoat wrapped around it by Hamden Express & took receipt. At A*[djutant]* G*[eneral's]* O*[ffice]*. After sup*[per]* called at Mrs. S*[mith]*'s & agreed to board & room there at $26. per month to commence on June 1. (Bid *[Sampson W.]* Fry good bye as he goes to Rochester. Rec*[eive]*d *[Brockport]* Republic to-day. *[at top of page:* "Army Review, 23rd & 24th. Holidays"*]* Signed rolls for commissary & Q*[uarter]* M*[arshal]* pay) At A*[djutant]* G*[eneral's]* O*[ffice]* at work from 7 till 9½. Then had glass soda water, 10c. To bed, 10.

Tuesday, 23d.—Up at usual time. *[Washington]* Chronicle 5c. (Yesterday paid S*[ampson]* W. Fry $10 & gave him new note for $14, payable July 1, 1865.) After breakfast went to Avenue & found a seat on a plank held up by a rickety barrel, over the crowd & saw the Army of the Potomac pass, except the 2nd Corps: viz: Cav*[alr]*y, 9th 5th & 1 Div*[isions]* of 19th Corps, including a sight of Gen*[era]*l *[William T.]* Sherman, *[Major General George G.]* Meade, *[Brevet Major General George]* Custer & others. Noticed the S*[harp]* S*[hooters]* with their telescope rifles. A grand sight altogether & many people. The troops (art*[iller]*y cav*[alry]* & inf*[antry]*) that I saw were from the 9½ till 1¼ passing one spot, then were to come the 2nd Corps, but I was tired & went to 416 & had a lunch & a nap. Read. Bought 25 stamped Gov*[ernmen]*t envelopes, 80c., 5 two ct. stamps 10c & bottle pomatum[277] 35c. Called to see Lieut*[enant Alphonso W.]* Starkweather. On duty at A*[djutant G[eneral's]* O*[ffice]* 7 till 10. P.M. Saw *[Lieutenant]* Gen*[era]*l *[Ulysses S.]* Grant on horseback with 1 orderly & another officer with 6 or 8 escorts. Seats erected at st*[reet]* for spectators, are finely decorated with flags & mottoes. (Read papers in A*[djutant]* G*[eneral's]* O*[ffice]*, eve.)(On Sunday, one of the 140th boys gave me a piece of the apple tree under which Gen*[era]*l *[Robert E.]* Lee surrendered his army to *[Lieutenant]* Gen*[era]*l *[Ulysses S.]* Grant.) At about 10, went to room, & to bed after hearing band play.

Wednesday, 24th.—Cool & sun shines. Could not have a better day for Review.(**64**) Bought Intelligencer, 5c. Read. Extra No. of people at table. Went to my place of yesterday over rickety barrel & saw Gen*[era]*l *[William T.]* Sherman & part of his army pass & after a horse threw his rider & bounded through a crowd of women, men & children hurting 2 or 3, not badly, I went to room, not caring about seeing the remainder of the army. Wrote to Mother & sent 2 papers to Mate *[Mary A. C. French]*. Nap. Read. Supper, ice cream & cherries strawberries. Walked up 7th saw many soldiers in the st*[reet]*. Called at Mrs. *[Jane Gray Cannon]* Swisshelm's, introduced to Miss Mason. Turned rope for girls to jump & played cards with Capt*[ain]* Greelish, Mrs. S*[mith]* & Mabel, Miss K. & Nettie Swiss'. Till 9, then to 416, to bed early. *[at top of page: "Sent 1 letter, rec[eive]d 1, 25th."]*

Thursday 25th.—Pleasant, warm. Left 3 shirts at laundry. Up Avenue to A*[djutant]* G*[eneral's]* O*[ffice]*. Made out 26 Descriptive Lists today; total in room, 180. Rec*[eive]*d letter from Mother, Sister & Aunt C., written 23rd. Bought *[Washington]* Chronicle this A.M., & Weekly C*[hronicle]*, P.M., 10c. Sultry P.M. After sup*[per]* mailed paper to Father & took walk on 7th. Glass ale 5c. At Smithsonian Institute grounds. Stood on steps of National Hotel & saw J. Clint. Patterson[278], "Esq." Of Brockport, & spoke with him; he & Mr. Latta[279] came here to see the Review but Mr. L*[atta]* had gone back. Streets crowded. At room early; read.

Friday, 26th.—Rain. Cool.—*[Washington]* Chronicle 5 c. At A*[djutant]* G*[eneral's]* O*[ffice]* on time. Hear that all those whose term expires before Oct*[ober]*, 1865 & whose regiments are in the field, are to be sent to reg*[imen]* ts on the 1st June; if so, I am included. Made out 23 descrip*[tive]* lists. &c. to-day. Came from office to room in rain. Dark. Bought ticket to concert $1 & drew a prize, silver call bell. On Avenue. Attended concert. Good. While there had glimpse of a person I had seen a year ago at "Sanitary Home." Pd. $1.15 to-day.

Saturday, 27th.—Cloudy & rain. Sent paper to Mate *[Mary A. C. French]* last eve. At A*[djutant]* G*[eneral's]* O*[ffice]* after break*[fast]* & some reading *[Washington]* Chron*[icle]*, 5c. *[at top of page:* "Rec*[eive]*d 1 letter, 27th. Sent letter, 29th."*]* Spent most of the day in looking for a name on Missouri Rolls. At 11½ rec*[eive]*d $31. Commissary for May. Thacher paid me $5, borrowed. Rec*[eive]*d letter from Mate *[Mary A. C. French]*11 A.M. dated 25th on way to room, at 4¼ o'clock, got 3 shirts, 35c, & saw Ira S. Davis & Dr. Snevely, S*[harp]* S*[hooters]*. After sup*[per]* went on Avenue. Saw J.C. Patterson of B*[rockport]* sitting in U.S. Hotel. Met Lieut*[enant A.D.]* Rood, formerly Brig*[ade]* Inspection, now *[illegible word]* Lieut*[enant]* Co*[mpany]* C. 6th Reg*[imen]*t Hancock's Veterans Corps. Went to Oxford Hall, 25c. saw dancing, singing, & the play of "Forest of Bondy"[280] learned dog. Very good performance. Cleared off pleasant, eve.

Sunday, 28th.—Cool. Pleasant. Sick headache, not very hard.—*[Washington]* Chronicle 5c. Read. Wrote to Mate *[Mary A. C. French]*. Walk to Maine Avenue. Back & nap. Dinner at 2. At Capitol Park, sat on seat & watched the passers by an hour. Called to see Lieut*[enant Alphonso W.]* Starkweather at A*[rmory]* S*[quare]* Hosp*[ital]*. Sup. at 6½. Walked up 10th. Called at Mrs. S*[mith]*'s 304, introduced to Capt*[ain]* Shaw & passed a pleasant eve. Gave Mrs. Smith my photograph for Kate's album. Rain again to-night.

Monday, 29th.—Sent letter to Mate *[Mary A. C. French]*, & 2 papers. Bought 5 two c. stamps.—Left vest at Avenue to be washed. Found *[Brockport]* Republic at A*[djutant]* G*[eneral's]* O*[ffice]*. Did not *[at top of page:* "Changed boarding place, 31st."*]* much work to-day. Some fun. After sup*[per]* promenade. Up 7th & almost called at Mrs. *[Jane Gray Cannon]* Swiss*[helm]*. Played with Mabel & paid Mrs. Smith for 2 strawberry Festival tickets, 50c. At room, 9. A lovely evening.

Tuesday, 30th—Warmer. *[Washington]* Chron*[icle]* 5c. At A*[djutant]* G*[eneral's]* O*[ffice]*, rec*[eive]*d $31.75. Rec*[eive]*d $36.40 for Bens & could not find him. Hulse paid me 50c. After sup*[per]* called to report my income to the U.S. Internal Rev[enue] assessor, but not finding him in & the office house being such that I never can find them in, I tore up my report. Called 304 10th a few minutes & heard singing & playing. Bo't N[ew] Y[ork] Times, 5c. & read awhile.

Wednesday, 31st.—Abed late. At A[djutant] G[eneral's] O[ffice] as usual. Col[onel Samuel] Breck promised that I should be mustered out July 1. Wrote to sister. At sup[per] in new house, cor[ner] 6th & I. Mr. Atkins new home. Paid Mr. A[tkins] $30.50, for board & room to date. Had trunk taken to 304 paid 50cts. & established myself at Mrs. [Jane Grey Cannon] Swisshelm's. From my room fronting on 10th st[reet], have fine view of city & country [at top of page; "Sent letter, June 1. Rec[eive]d letter, June 2."] very warm day. Walked down Avenue. Rec[eive]d vest at laundry 25c. Dish of ice cream 10c. Bought shoes $3.50.—2 Weekly [Washington] Chronicles, 10c. At 304 cooled off on the porch & went to bed early.

Thursday June 1.—Warmer still. Fast day in memory of President Lincoln. No work at the Departments. After breakfast mailed paper to Lon & Mate [Mary A. C. French]. At A[djutant] G[eneral's] O[ffice] but no letter from home. On Avenue, bo't N.Y. Eve[ning] Post, 8c. At room laid down & read. Lunch at 1. Mailed letter to sister at 11 A.M. Nap after playing with Mabel.—After dinner heard music, took a short walk ice-cream, 20c! And to bed early after hearing so much talk about "the strawberry festival." Saw Nat Hulburt[281] on st[reet] this eve. O, how warm.

Friday, 2d.—Almost hot.—Up at 5 by mistake. Break[fast] at 7½. Helped Mrs. Sw[isshelm] move bureau. At A[djutant] G[eneral's] O[ffice], & rec[eive]d letter from Mother & sister. Very warm. Nothing specially new. Left my pocket book at room, to-day. After warm walk from A[djutant] G[eneral's] O[ffice], at 4½, cooled off. At Strawberry Festival & invested 55 cts. at Miss Knowlton's stand, ice cream & strawberrys with Miss Dawby & a bowl of mush & milk at Miss [Jane Gray Cannon] Swisshelm's, 15c. Very pleasant. [at top of page; "Rec[eive]d letter 3rd. Sent letter, 4th."] All shades of color present. An Ass[istan]t Serg[eant] of color, &c. A Band, etc. Came away at 10,—to bed soon as possible.

Saturday, 3d.—Hot again. At A[djutant] G[eneral's] O[ffice]. Rec[eive]d letter from Mate [Mary A. C. French] & the [Brockport] Republic of 1st. Nothing new. At room, 4½ Capt[ain] Greelish now rooms with me, as Mr. & Mrs. Logan & little boy, have taken his room. Cooled off & read Mate's [Mary A. C. French] letter before supper. Last eve. bought 10 collars (paper) 40c. Cut paper for raffle at Festival. Went down with Mrs. Smith on st[reet] car.

At Festival, introduced to Miss Ingersoll, (Treasury Dep*[artmen]*t.) & had ice cream, lemonade & treated Nettie Swiss*[helm]* & Mabel S*[mith]*. Paid $1.29 this evening. At 11 came to 304 with Mabel & a basket on st*[reet]* car, glad to rest. (Took share in raffle for picture, but did not draw.)

Sunday, 4th.—Hotter.—By mistake laid till 9, abed. Break*[fast]* & went in hot sun to P*[ost]* O*[ffice]*, got a *[Washington]* Chron*[icle]*, 5c. Back & stripped.— Wrote to Mate *[Mary A. C. French]*. Lor *[sp?]* how "shiftless hot". Nap most of P.M. awakened by African "Jubilee". After dinner, went to see Lieut*[enant Alphonso W.]* Starkweather, at hosp*[ital]* & he, too, thinks of going home July 1. The 6 Co*[mpany]* S*[harp]* S*[hooters]* went up last eve. to Roch*[ester]*, being mustered out.—Mailed letter to Mate *[Mary A. C. French]*, also papers at Capitol, & sat awhile. Pleasant moonlight. *[at top of page: "Sent letter, 6th."]*

Monday, 5th.—Sultry. No rain, At A*[djutant]* G*[eneral's]* O*[ffice]* & did over 15 Descript*[ive]* lists from 1 to 4. Cooled off in Room (304) at 4½. Left shoes to be mended at darkey's this A.M., & 2 shirts with Mrs. S*[mith]*. Last eve. gave a soldier beggar 10c to get tobacco. Paid $1.50 for shoes, tapped & healed *[sic]*. At P*[ost]* O*[ffice]* bought N*[ew]* Y*[ork]* Herald, 5c. Ice-cream, 20c. In the house early. Read & a band played about 9, & came again at 12 & serenaded with several tunes. A drunken man made the night hideous & altogether a variety of sounds. Warm Distant lightning.

Tuesday, 6th.—Cool, Cloudy & sprinkle of rain. Late breakfast—At A*[djutant]* G*[eneral's]* O*[ffice]* as usual. Wrote to Aunt C. at noon. At 4, walked to room & wrote some. Dinner at 5½.—Mabel S*[mith]*. went with me to P*[ost]* O*[ffice]* where I mailed letter to Aunt C. Bo't candy for M*[abel Smith]* 5 cts. Sat on steps awhile, then up stairs & read.

Wednesday, 7th.—Cool. Cloudy. At A*[djutant]* G*[eneral's]* O*[ffice]*, after reading *[Washington]* Chronicle, 5c. Work on Pensions. On way to dinner bo't 2 *[Washington]* Chron*[icles]* (weekly) 10c. to send Mate *[Mary A. C. French]* & home. Read. Introduced to Capt*[ain]* Phillips (*cavalry*) & lady at dinner. Took walk down 7th. Bo't paper 15c. Weiss Beer, 10c. At capitol saw soldiers pass on cars, going home. Sat on seat awhile. Then at room early. *[at top of page: "Sent 1 letter—rec[eive]d 1, 8th, & 1 on 10th."]*

Thursday, 8th.—Review of 6th Corps. Very warm. Almost rain at 4 P.M. At A*[djutant]* G*[eneral's]* O*[ffice]*, as usual, but quit at 9:15 to see Review. I did not feel well, so went to A*[djutant]* G*[eneral's]* O*[ffice]*, worked, till 4. Rec*[eive]*d $19.50 regular pay &c. for May. Rec*[eive]*d letter from Mother & sister at noon & sent one to Mother in return. After dinner, 6 P.M. walked down 7th. Had a glass bottled Porter, 10c. Back & sat on stoop—heard music. To bed early. A little rain at 6. Sprinkle.

Friday, 9th.—Paid 16cts. for 2 shirts washed. Cheaper than at laundry & they are bro't to house. At A[djutant] G[eneral's] O[ffice]. My watch is out of order. A hot day. (Fuss at A[djutant] G[eneral's] O[ffice] about missing book.— Hamilton implicated, & stays away to-day.) Worked hard. Tried to cool off at room after 4. Walked down st[reet]. At capitol sat awhile. Ale, 10c. At concert (free) bet[ween] 4½ & 6. Singing & dancing. Passed by circus. Back to 304 & found Capt[ain] G. out this eve. saw Lieut[enant Alphonso W.] Starkweather at Hosp[ital].

Saturday, 10th.—Warm Shower in P.M. at A[djutant] G[eneral's] O[ffice], rec[eive]d letter from Mate [Mary A. C. French] & [Brockport] Republic of 8th. Nothing new. Rode to 304 on car, at 4, 6 cts. In room, changed, &c. Headache to-day. Down to Avenue, Ale, 10c. To bed early. [at top of page: "Sent letter, 11th"]

Sunday, 11th.—Cool. Wrote to Mate[Mary A. C. French], A.M. Bought [Washington] Chronicle, 5c.—Splendid day. Read. Nap. Waited till 6 before dinner. Mailed letter & paper to Mate [Mary A. C. French]. Called on Lieut[enant Alphonso W.] S[tarkweather] with Jimmy Edwards at Hospital. Back at 304, early. Had some sport with Capt[ain] G., Mrs. Smith, & Miss Knowlton.

Monday, 12th.—Sick headache all day. Ate no breakfast, hardly. Sent note to Mr. Hamilton, Room 502. Laid down. Not very hot.—At 2 P.M. had cup of tea. Felt better. Nap. Dinner at 6. On 7th st[reet] & had glass ale, 5c. Back & had a "time" with the little girls, candy, 4c. a very warm night. Could hardly sleep.

Tuesday, 13th.—Hot. But a good heavy shower at eve. Headache, some again but went to work after giving colored woman clothes to wash. At A[djutant] G[eneral's] O[ffice] left application for my discharge with Col[onel Samuel] Breck, A[ssistant] A[djutant] G[eneral]. Worked on Pensions most of day. Nap at room before dinner at 6. In eve. walked to 7th glass ale, 5c. back had game euchre & short promenade with Mabel [Smith]. Splendid shower about 1½ hours, eve., but air is none too cool. [Rec[eive]d 1 letter, 15th. Sent letter, 15th."]

Wednesday, 14th.—Cool. No dust. At A[djutant] G[eneral's] O[ffice] as usual. Feel clear headed to-day. Hamilton leaves the office on acc[oun]t of the book affair & obliged to resign. After some "stumbling" Hulse takes charge of the room, which is satisfactory to all parties, though Houghton is senior. Rain at 5. Had nap before "dinner." Bought 2 *[Washington]* Chronicles, 10c. & sent 1 to Mate *[Mary A. C. French]*. Went down 7th, had ale, 5c. & went to Grovers Theatre, 50c. Play of Pocahontas[282]. Ludicrous. Afterpiece of "Loan of a Lover"[283].

Thursday, 15th.—Cool. Little rain to-day. Paid 17cts for 2 shirts washed. At A*[djutant]* G*[eneral's]* O*[ffice]*. At noon made inquiry in regard to my application for discharge, & it was attended to with prospect of my getting order to go to Elmira to be mustered out. Letter from Mother & Sister. At room 4½. Wrote to Mother & Sister. Sent paper to Sister. Down st*[reet]* in eve.—ale, 5c. Heard music. To bed in good season.

Friday, 16th.—Packed trunk. At *[Washington]* Chronicle office & did not subscribe. At A*[djutant]* G*[eneral's]* O*[ffice]* got order for muster out at Elmira. Also rec*[eive]*d $30.50, part pay for June. Transportation of *[Brigadier]* Gen*[era]*l *[E. W.]* Rucker & tickets after waiting in P.M. Col*[onel Samuel]* Breck allowed me to copy recommendation file on March 29 of *[Brigadier]* Gen*[era]*l *[Edward S.]* Bragg, Controller Clarke. Got around to 304 at 4½ after subscribing for the Tri-Weekly Intelligencer, 3 months $1.50. Paid Mrs. *[Jane Gray Cannon]* Swisshelm $13 & had supper. Took biscuit for lunch. Bid all good bye & gave darkey 75 cts to take my trunk to depot, & I start. *[at top of page: "Discharged, June 17th"]* On train met *[Roland]* Houghton[284]. Also had incident with Brevet Brig*[adier]* Gen*[era]*l *[Henry A.]* Morrow who with staff were going to Louisville. Rode from one depot to another on top of omnibus 35c. Had baggage re-checked. Paid 50c. for berth in sleeping car, rested very well.

Context—By the time Farnham's company was discharged, it had lost ten enlisted men killed in action or died of wounds, four other enlisted men wounded, and nine enlisted men died of disease.

Saturday, 17th—Hot. Up early. Washed & took regular car. At Williamsport had two cups coffee. With Mrs. *[Jane Gray Cannon]* Swisshelm's rolls, 20c. On seat with Lieut*[enant]* Thompson of Albion, discharged. Reached Elmira at 12 M. Met Chet Van Tine[285] & mother in st*[reet]*. Waited till 2 P.M. for my discharge which being made out wrong I had to make out myself, but could not get pay to-day.—Called on 2nd cousin Geo*[rge]* W. Farnham, No. 4, William st*[reet]*, who took me to his house, where I was introduced to his his *[sic]* family, Mrs. F*[arnham]*, Miss Ellen Florence Stella, & son. Also two young men. Supper. G*[eorge]* W. F*[arnham]* then called with me at Mr. Fitch's

46 1st st*[reet]*, where cousin Sarah Farnham lives, but she was away. Then called on Aunt Farnham now Mrs. *[sic]* who seemed very glad to see me. Then at Mr. Millins, 87 Gray st*[reet]*, where we found cousin Sarah & Marion. (now Mrs. M*[illins]*) & had a good time till 9. (laughed about the incident of S*[arah]* losing her shoe a long time ago) then went on st*[reet]* called at Mr. Millins store had ale, 10c. Then at barber shop was shaved, paid for by G*[eorge]* W. F*[arnham]*. Then to his house, & to bed. Tired.

Sunday 18th.—Hot. Up early went to depot opened my trunk, took pictures, shirt, &c. changed at house. Breakf*[as]*t. Had sport with little cousin Stella. With cousin G*[eorge]* W. *[Farnham]* walked to barracks where I saw rebel prison & found cousin H. R. Randall, 50th N.Y. Engineers, in soldier clothes about to be discharged. Enlisted in March last $1100 bounty. Lent him $40. Back. Called on Sarah 46 1st st*[reet]* & was introduced to Mr. Fitch Mrs. G. & cousin Geo*[rge]* Farnham, a printer, 15 y*[ea]*rs old. Pleasant time. Dinner. With Sarah & Geo*[rge]* Called on Aunt F. (Mrs. ___) short visit. Then to Mrs. Millin had a fine time in shade of trees. Good supper. In eve. at Mr. Fitch's & introduced to Lieut*[enant]* Fitch & went *[at top of page:* "Bounty & final payments. 19th. Sent letter, 19th.*"]* to church with Cousin Marion, Sarah &c. Heard Rev*[erend]* Beecher, father of Henry Ward B*[eecher]* in an amusing sermon on the subject of negroes voting. Home with Mrs. M*[illins]*. To bed.

Monday, 19th.—Still hot. Up & break. at 6½. Rode to depot with Mr. & Mrs. M*[illins]* & they took cars to Penn Yan. Bo't paper & note paper, 7c. Wrote to Mate*[Mary A. C. French]* at Vantines *[sic]* store about town. Called on Geo*[rge]* Farnham at printing office. In P.M. Paymaster Thurston paid me $107.10, of which $75 was Gov*[ernmen]*t Bounty. This settles my acc*[oun]*t. At G*[eorge]* W. F*[arnham]*'s & tea. Rain. In eve. introduced to Mr. Field & went with him, Ellen & Florence F*[arnhma]* to theatre, $1, heard "Ticket of Leave Man,"[286] Rouse.

Tuesday, 20th.—Rain A.M. Clear in P.M. In house of G*[eorge]* W. F*[arnham]* till 10. Bo't papers 6c. Peanuts 15c. Called on Geo*[rge Farnham]* Jr. At dinner 4 W. st*[reet]*. Then shaved. Called at Aunt Welch's; saw cousin Marion, Mrs. M*[illins]*. Have a horse & buggy, drove about town with Florence & a young *[at top of page:* "Home again, 21st.*"]* lady. At 5, drove to Mr. Fitch's & introduced to L*[ieutenan]*t Guyon. Had supper of strawberry shortcake. Then with Sarah (cousin) rode to Horseheads (6 miles.) Had a pleasant ride. Fine view of the country. Called at Mr. Vantine's *[sic]*; good evening visit. Introduced to three different ones. At 9½ started for Elmira enjoying the ride very much. Rec*[eive]*d photograph of Sarah & Marion. Took horse & stable & paid $5. Went to Hathaway House, paid $1 for bed.

Wednesday, 21st.—Up at 5. at G[eorge] W. F[arnham]'s bid them good bye, went to depot, paid $2.75 for ticket to Rochester, had trunk checked & started on train at 6:30. Changed at Corning, arrived in Rochester at 12:15. Paid 25c. for trunk taken to central depot.—Saw *[Sampson W.]* Fry, who took charge of my haversack. Had ale, &c. 20c. Saw Follett. Called Douglass' corner North St*[reet]*. *[Sampson W.]* Fry not at home. Back & called on Dr. Smith. Ice cream 15c. Bo't ticket to Brockport, 35c. Trunk checked. Left R*[ochester]* at 6, & saw many Brockporters on train. Met Cordelia & Eddy at depot & was escorted to house, glad to meet all again. Supper. Opened trunk &c. Called to see Mate *[Mary A. C. French]*. Also saw Aggie Johnson & Mrs. French. At home early. Tired.

[After the diary entries, there are 18 pages of notes of various kinds, many addresses, financial information, etc.]

Endnotes

1   *Town Clerk's Report.*
2   *Brockport Republic* February 21, 1867.
3   I live at 46 College Street.
4   John Tyler Farnham diary, April 17, 1865.
5   *Ibid.* January 26, 1861. I began my career as a printer at age 13.
6   *Ibid.* August 22, 1862.
7   Horatio N. Beach (1822–96) founded the *Brockport Republic* weekly newspaper as a Republican organ in October 1856. Later, he served as U.S. Consul in Mexico, Venezuela, and Ecuador. He was also active in local politics and business. He served as Village Trustee and Erie Canal Toll Collector, helped found the local gas and electric companies, developed real estate, built houses, and was the prime mover in creating the Brockport Rural Cemetery.
8   John Tyler Farnham diary, August 22, 1862.
9   *Brockport Republic* October 7, 1869.
10 *Rochester Evening Express* October 4, 1869.
11 *Rochester Evening Express* October 4, 1869.
12 A furlough is the military term for taking leave from duty, usually leaving the area for weeks or months.
13 *Brockport Republic*, June 12, 1912.
14 *Ibid.*, July 24, 1917.
15 Escaped slaves from Confederate states who came into the custody and care of the Union Army.
16 John Tyler Farnham diary, August 21, 1862.
17 *Ibid.* December 15, 1862.
18 National Archives.
19 John Tyler Farnham diary, January 30, 1864. SJJ appears in the U.S. censuses from 1860 until 1920 as a resident of Niagara County, NY, a barber by occupation, married successively to three women. In 1910,

an 18-year old daughter lived in their household. His race is given variously as white, mulatto, and black.

20   *Ibid.,* January 30, 1864.

21   Bennett, Brian A., *Sons of Old Monroe, A Regimental History of Patrick O'Rorke's 140th New York Volunteer Infantry,* Morningside, Dayton, 1999, 718, p. 653.

22   John Tyler Farnham diary, June 7, 1864.

23   Village of Brockport, NY, 2005, 248pp.

24   I did use material from many of them in my *Civil War Brockport: A Canal Town and the Union Army,* History Press, Charleston, 2013, 336pp.

25   Frederick Phisterer, *New York in the War of the Rebellion 1861– 1865,*1912, 3d ed. 6 vols., paged continuously, 1,690pp.

26   *Ibid.,* p. 1690

27   *Ibid.,* p. 1691

28   *Ibid.,* p. 1692

29   *Ibid.,* p. 1691

30   *Ibid.*

31   John Tyler Farnham, *Diaries,* January 24, 1863.

32   *Brockport Republic,* December 4, 1862.

33   *Ibid.,* March 5, 1863.

34   Phisterer, *op. cit.*

35   *Brockport Republic* February 25, 1864.

36   ACWRD.

37   Phisterer, *op. cit.,* p. 1693.

38   *Brockport Republic* June 18, 1863; June 25, 1863 and August 20, 1863.

39   *Ibid.* December 10, 1863.

40   *Ibid.,* March 17, 1864, and John Tyler Farnham, *op. cit.,* March 20, 1864.

41   Phisterer, *op. cit.,* p. 1693.

42   *Brockport Republic* November 20, 1863.

43   John Tyler Farnham diary, May 13, 1865.

44   *Brockport Republic* June 25, 1863 and August 20, 1863.

45   John Tyler Farnham *op. cit.,* May 13, 1865.

46   *Brockport Republic* January 29, 1863.

47   Phisterer, *op. cit.,* p. 1692

48   *Ibid.*

49   He was 24 when he enlisted on August 21, 1862.

50   Pond was a lumber merchant in Brockport. He later was second-in-command of the 2nd U.S. Colored Cavalry as a lieutenant-colonel. After the war he was co-owner of the *RochesterDemocrat and Chronicle* daily newspaper.

51 A small sewing kit.

52 A cap cover made popular by Sir Henry Havelock, a British officer. It was made out of white linen or cotton and worn over the soldier's cap with a long flap covering his neck.

53 Used as an aid in the temporary relief of minor soreness and stiffness caused by overexertion.

54 See endnote 12 above.

55 William Joseph Hardee, a career officer, wrote his "Tactics", the standard infantry drill manual for both armies, in 1855. He became a Confederate general.

56 Farnham's youngest brother.

57 Apparently, this is a reference to the Brockport Collegiate Institute. The Archives of its successor institution, the State University of New York College at Brockport has a list of BCI alumni. No one named Farnham is listed. However, the file for 1862 is missing.

58 Persons of both Dutch and German origin were commonly called "Dutchmen" at that time.

59 Some units in both armies adopted the Zouave uniform, consisting of a distinctive jacket, vest, sash, baggy trousers, and fez, based on that of the elite Zouave battalion of the French Army,which was, in turn, modeled after that of Algerian troops in the colonial war of the 1830s.

60 A small backpack with a single shoulder strap.

61 This band was attached to the 140th NYVI regiment.

62 One of the itinerant merchants who catered to the soldiers by selling items not issued by the government. They required permits from unit commanders and were often believed by the men to be exploiting the privilege by overcharging.

63 As is apparent throughout the diaries, oysters were an important—and cheap—part of the everyday diet at that time.

64 One of Farnham's closest friends in the 6th Company and a cousin, age 29.

65 Despite the unconventional spelling of the forename, Francis is a young woman. Also, Farnham sometimes spells the surname with one "s" and sometimes with two.

66 Charles Gayler's (1820-92) *Our Female American Cousin* (1859) was an imitation of Tom Taylor's *Our American Cousin*. Gayler was a prolific actor, playwright, theatrical producer, novelist, and editor. He wrote and produced hundreds of comedies, tragedies, operettas, and melodramas. He has been called "the father of American dramatists", but was also widely accused of plagiarism.

67 Another cousin.

68 A printers measure for the length of lines of type. An "em" is the width of the letter "m".

69   The nineteenth century term for tuberculosis.

70   Two-term mayor of Chicago, and a six-term member of the U.S. House of Representatives,

71   In the 1820s, Richard Hoe invented a printing press with a curved cylinder, rather than a flatbed, and rolls of paper. This was the first major technological advance in presses since Gutenburg and greatly increased printing speed.

72   Or, South in Secession-Time, Carleton, New York, 1862. Kirke was the nom de plume of James R. Gilmore, a wealthy merchant and well-known publicist of mildly emancipationist views who published several novels, containing realistic portrayals of Southern life and feeling, and numerous war-songs and ballads.

73   A close friend of Farnham from Brockport in the 108th NYVI who was wounded at Laurel Hill, but rose from sergeant to captain. After the war, he manufactured carriages.

74   A positive photograph on glass made (1855–65) by a variant of the wet plate collodion process. Like a print on paper, it is viewed by reflected light.

75   A member of the free-reed aerophone family of musical instruments. It is a type of button accordion on which the melody-side keyboard contains one or more rows of buttons, with each row producing the notes of a single diatonic scale.

76   Stafford became an officer in the regular army and served in the Indian Wars after the Civil War.

77   Freeman Clarke was nominated by this Republican Congressional District convention, was elected, and served 1863-65. He also served in the U.S. House of Representatives, 1871–75.

78   Colt five-barreled revolving rifles were the first repeating rifles adopted by the U.S. Government in 1855.

79   The USS *Monitor* was designed by Swedish engineer John Ericson and built during the Civil War, she was the first ironclad steam warship commissioned by the Union Navy.

80   This may be a play based on the life of the French poet, Louise-Victorine Ackermann, who called Berlin "The city of my dreams".

81   A single turreted, coastal monitor-class steamer built by Continental Iron Works, Greenport, NY, under subcontract from John Ericsson, designer of the Monitor, first ironclad warship, and commissioned in November 1862.

82   A cracker or biscuit of flour, water, and sometimes salt. Inexpensive and long-lasting, it was eaten in the absence of perishable foods, commonly during military campaigns. A typical piece measured 3⅛ by 2⅞ inches and nearly ½ inch thick, 9 or 10 constituting a daily ration.

83 *The Colleen Bawn* (sic), *or The Brides of Garryowen* (1860) a melodramatic play by Irish playwright Dion Boucicault.

84 It was. Richmond did not fall to the Union Army until April 3, 1865.

85 In the Civil War, this term was applied to military personnel who were not enumerated among the regular components of a group, in this case, an extra soldier added to the usual complement for a reconnaissance patrol.

86 "Jayhawk" was a term applied to a band of anti-slavery, pro-Union guerrillas in Kansas in the fighting in the years before the Civil War over whether that territory should be free or slave. Jayhawkers were undisciplined, unprincipled, occasionally murderous, and always thieving. So, Jayhawking became a widely used synonym for stealing.

87 Union forces under General Rosecrans defeated a Confederate General Braxton Bragg's army in the Battle of Stones River at Murfeesboro, Tenn. on January 3.

88 On May 19, a fire in Brockport destroyed or badly damaged eight commercial buildings, two offices, three dwellings, four barns, and a furniture manufactory, an estimated loss of $44,565. Dr. Farnham lost some furniture at his office—*Brockport Republic,* May 24, 1862.

89 An acute infection typically with a skin rash, usually on any of the legs and toes, face, arms, and fingers. It is an infection of the upper dermis and superficial lymphatics, usually caused by beta-hemolytic group A Streptococcus bacteria on scratches or otherwise infected areas.

90 The answer to be given when challenged by a sentry.

91 These were long-range rifles manufactured by the British armaments firm, Whitworth and were regarded as superior to any other, but were very expensive and were not purchased for the Union Army in any quantity.

92 He was the son of Elias B. Holmes, former congressman from Brockport, and a banker. He was a captain in the 3rd New York Cavalry from August 1862 until February 1863. After the war he removed to Chicgo and became wealthy as a banker and real estate dealer.

93 William M. Cooper, a merchant, opened his storefront on Otsego Street, Philadelphia, on May 26, 1861, to aid Union troops passing through his city. It was important as a place of rest where soldiers obtained food, drink, places to wash, and medical care. It and similar saloons helped forge a collective war effort.

94 On May 12, 1861, Union troops under General Benjamin F. Butler erected a small fort on this hill in Washington to guarantee the allegiance of the city to the Union.

95 These were facilities provided by female relief workers from the United States Sanitary Commission (USSC)., United States Christian

Commission (USCC), and other private organizations to supply soldiers with food and medical supplies and nursing and religious services.

96 Represented Kentucky in the House, 1839–47, and in the Senate, 1861–67, as a Whig and in the Senate,1867–72, as a Democrat.

97 Apparently, he is referring to the operation by Major General Joseph Hooker's troops to cut the rail line between Fredericksberg and Richmond.

98 Farnham seems to have been misinformed about the origins of the saloon, apparently mistaking the tradesmen for William M. Cooper.

99 Represented Pennsylvania in the House as a Free-Soil Democrat, 1851–57, and as a Republican, 1957–63 and 1894–1903, Speaker 1861–63.

100 A member from Rochester, 1859–63, and suffered the embarrassment of being taken prisoner by the Confederates while watching the First Battle of Bull Run and held for six months.

101 Congress passed the first Conscription Act in February 1863 and Lincoln signed it on March 3.

102 A dispute.

103 The Protestant Episcopal Theological Seminary was requisitioned for this hospital.

104 First Families of Virginia, a popular reference to the leading, old-line families in the Old Dominion.

105 The Sharps Mfg. Co. made a sniper weapon of greater accuracy than the muzzle-loading rifled muskets, due mainly to the higher rate of fire of the breech loading mechanism. However, it was expensive. So, only 11,000 were produced and most were issued to sharpshooters.

106 Democrats in the North who opposed the Civil War. Republicans likened them to the venomous snake.

107 Robert Smalls, a slave serving as the pilot, took over this Confederate armed dispatch boat and transport, steered it past Confederate defenses, and surrendered it to Union Navy forces on May 13, 1862.

108 Fortress Monroe in Hampton, Virginia, at Old Point Comfort, the southern tip of the Virginia Peninsula, guarded the navigational channel between the Chesapeake Bay and Hampton Roads. The seven-sided fort was the largest stone fort ever built in the United States.

109 A 15-acre artificial island at the mouth of the Hampton Roads. Its name is derived from the Rip Rap Shoals in Hampton Roads, which also gave their name to a nineteenth-century criminal gang.

110 A marshy area in the Coastal Plain Region of southeastern Virginia and northeastern North Carolina. At over 1,000,000 acres, it is one of the last large wild areas in the East.

111 A thin, unleavened round made from cornmeal, water, and salt, crisp at

the edges and fried in fat, golden in patches, dense but creamy. "Hoe" was a colloquial term for *griddle* in parts of England.

112 A Confederate soldier.

113 A type of artillery piece with a relatively short barrel and small propellant charges to propel projectiles at relatively high trajectories, with a steep angle of descent.

114 A cotton-wool blend twill fabric, resembling a cross between burlap and dungaree fabric.

115 A person in charge of a group of military police. The title originated with an older term for military police, provosts.

116 A regional expression meaning "to go afoot".

117 Commodore James Barron (*sic*) (1768–1851) commanded the frigate *Chesapeake* on June 22, 1807, when it was captured by a British warship, one of the causes of the War of 1812. He was court-martialed, convicted, and concluded his naval career on shore.

118 The slave life depicted in this best-selling novel by Harriet Beecher Stowe was a very important factor in preparing public opinion to elect Lincoln and precipitate the Civil War.

119 Republican Representative from Indiana, 1861–71; Free Soil nominee for vice president, 1852.

120 Brockport officer who led a charge repelling Texans at Little Round Top on July 2, 1863, and was killed leading a charge at Laurel Hill on May 10, 1864.

121 Pseudonym of Edward Zane Carroll Judson, Sr. (1821 or 1823–1886), a publisher, journalist, writer, and publicist.

122 This paragraph was reprinted in the *Rochester Union & Advertiser* on April 24, 1863.

123 A rifled cannon that fired an elongated shell made specifically for it, designed by Captain Robert Parker Parrott, a West Point graduate.

124 The largest field gun used during the war, with the barrel alone weighing over 1,800 pounds, also invented by Parrott.

125 A fortification near the bridge over the Nansemond river, on the road leading from Suffolk to South Quay. It was designed to repel an infantry assault upon the town from that quarter.

126 "Modern embalming… was popularized in the United States in the Civil War as a means of allowing the bodies of fallen soldiers to last long enough for them to be shipped home for burial." Rebecca Mead, "Our Bodies, Ourselves", The New Yorker, November 30, 2015, p. 29.

127 The common nickname applied to certain infantry troops from Louisiana, eventually all those in the Army of Northern Virginia.

128 The third most widely used weapon of the Civil War, invented in 1854

by Austrian lieutenant Joseph Lorenz.

129   Nickname of the 9th NYVI commanded by Rush C. Hawkins and recruited in New York City.

130   A rifled cannon invented by Charles T. James, a Rhode Island militia general and self-taught mechanic.

131   Confederate soldiers.

132   In fact, at that time, Hooker, after apparent initial success, suffered a serious defeat at Chancellorsville, which was located near the Rappahannock River.

133   Farnham's text of that letter is reproduced in Bennett, pp. 178-79.

134   Mary Ann Mears Martineau and her husband, Peter, were early pioneers in Milwaukee, Wisc. She kept a journal of their experiences from 1834 until the Civil War, which was published.

135   A Congressman from Ohio, 1859–63, and the leader of the anti-war Democrats.

136   Actually, this did not happen until July 4.

137   Had bowel movement.

138   Constipated.

139   Ultra-Abolitionist Congressman, 1853–54, and publicist.

140   Dragonfly.

141   This may refer to Lee's move from the Shenandoah Valley into Pennsylvania in June to begin the Gettysburg campaign.

142   A Canadian-built U.S. Steamer leased by the Army in 1862 to transport people and freight. In March 1864, it struck a Confederate mine in the St. Johns River in Florida and sank with a loss of four lives. The 63 passengers, including many Union soldiers survived. In 1984, the wreck was discovered and excavated. So much material and artifacts were recovered that a National Park Service historian has said, "The wreck of the *Maple Leaf* is unsurpassed as a source for Civil War material culture.... It is the most important repository of Civil War artifacts ever found, and probably will remain so."

143   An unincorporated community on the south shore of the Pamunkey River. White House Plantation, for which it is named, was the home of Martha Dandridge Custis, the widow who married George Washington in 1759. WH was the site of a major Union Army supply base in 1862 during the Peninsula Campaign.

144   Named for the Troy, NY, inventor and manufacturer of farm implements and machinery.

145   One of many engines designed by the Swedish immigrant John Ericson who also designed the ironclad Monitor.

146   Composing sticks, used to set printers type.

147   *Yankee Notions, or, Whittlings of Jonathan's Jack Knife*, an important

satirical, illustrated humor periodical edited and published by Thomas Strong. Each issue contained a motley assortment of comic stories, jokes, doggerel, woodcuts with humorous captions, and a full-page interior and cover cartoon.

148　Another false rumor. Longstreet long outlived the war, dying January 2, 1904.

149　A silhouette of a palmetto appears on the official flag of the State of South Carolina.

150　This important river port, 25 miles south of Vicksburg that had fallen five days earlier, surrendered on July 9 to the forces of Union General Nathaniel P. Banks after a 47-day siege and many casualties on both sides.

151　This city did not fall to the Union until February 18, 1865.

152　Much the worst of the riots protesting conscription. The drawing of the first draftees' names on July 11 touched off three days of violence, especially against African-Americans. An estimated 74 persons died.

153　A humorous novel.

154　Memoir of Scoville Haynes McCollum, the *Little Syracuse Boy*. New York: Board of Publication of the Presbyterian Church, 1861, 324pp., a youthful biography.

155　One of the earliest, long-lived, popular New York magazines (1833–59)

156　A bluff overlooking the confluence of the James and Appommattox Rivers that Grant made the nerve center of his operations when he took command of the Army of the Potomac.

157　The Veterans Reserve Corps, which was composed of soldiers unfit for regular duty but not so disabled as require discharge.

158　This Confederate ship destroyed several Union Navy ships at Hampton Roads in March 1862, before being fought to a draw by the Union's own iron-clad, the *Monitor*. In May 1862, with Union troops advancing on Norfolk, Va., the Confederacy destroyed the damaged ship rather than let it fall into Union hands.

159　Probably *The Life of Benjamin Franklin A Continuation of Franklin's Autobiography* by Jared Sparks (1856).

160　The United States Christian Commission (USCC), was organized in June 1861 by civilian volunteers under Federal legislation to supply sick and disabled soldiers with food, temporary lodging, medical supplies, nursing, and religious services. It supplied more than one million nights' lodgings and gave out supplies valued at $15 million.

161　Charles Lever, an Irish physician and author began publishing *The Confessions of Harry Lorrequer* as a serial in the *Dublin University Magazine* in 1833 and as a volume in 1839. It was a string of Irish and other stories good, bad and indifferent, but mostly rollicking.

162   Josiah Gilbert Holland, M.D., (1819–81) a distinguished educator, editor, publisher and author of many popular books of high moral tone, published *Timothy Litcomb's Letters to Young People: Married and Single in 1858.*

163   Perhaps "inbelch", vomiting.

164   James Kennedy Moorhead, Republican, represented Pennsylvania in the House of Representatives, 1859–69.

165   Also author of *Timothy Litcomb...* (Above).

166   Another false rumor Although the stronghold was attacked by Union forces in early September 1863 it remained in Confederate hands until evacuated as Sherman approached Charleston in February 1865.

167   This boat was built in 1862 by Power, Holmes & Co. of Catskill, NY. Apparently, the boat was requisitioned by the Union Navy shortly thereafter. After the war, it burned at her dock in Catskill.

168   John Buchanan Floyd, a Virginia politician, secretary of war in President Buchanan's cabinet, who resigned to join the Confederacy as a brigadier general, was cashiered for deserting his post in March 1862 and died August 26, 1863, his health having been ruined by his military campaigning.

169   John Clifford Pemberton, a Pennsylvania native and West Point graduate of Southern sympathies who resigned his commission to join the Confederacy and became a lieutenant general and the defender of Vicksburg. He survived the war, dying in 1881.

170   Charles Farrar Browne (1834–1867) was the American humor writer of the "Artemus Ward" series, which, in a collected form, achieved great popularity in both America and England.

171   Union forces under General Grant, retreating from their defeat at Chickamauga, occupied Chattanooga in September1863, where they were besieged by Confederate General Braxton Bragg until November 25.

172   A fortified island in Charleston harbor that was heavily bombarded by Union forces under Rear Admiral John Dahlgren for months and was evacuated on September 6, 1863, by General Pierre G. T. Beauregard's troops.

173   A novel by Charles Lever published in 1845.

174   Lydia Maria Francis Child (1802 –1880), an abolitionist, women's rights activist, American Indian rights activist, novelist, journalist, and opponent of American expansionism, wrote *Letters from New York* as a serial for the Boston *Courier*. They were published as two volumes, 1843–1845.

175   *Frank Leslie's Illustrated Newspaper*, published news and fiction from1853 until 1922. Leslie was a pseudonym for Henry Carter, an engraver and publisher who immigrated from England.

176 Enlisted in the 140th NYVI on September 13, 1862, promoted to Sergeant, 2nd Lieutenant, 1st Lieutenant, and, then, to Captain for gallant and meritorious services at the battles of the Wilderness and of the Weldon Railroad, mustered out June 3, 1865.

177 This may be the 12-inch rifle, tested at Fortress Monroe about this time, that carried a charge of powder weighing fifty-five pounds, and threw a 600-pound projectile.— O. E. Hunt, "The Ordnance Department of the Federal Army", civilwarhome.com website.

178 On one of the end pages of this diary: "things in box—Frys towel things rolled in, bedsack; bag, flask, drawers. Mine: shoes 1 p[ai]r socks, 2 cot[ton] shirts, dress coat, towel. Wm. Fry, Berlin, Worcester, Mass. Co. father of S.W. Fry, James N. Fry, Bolton, Worcester Co., Mass."

179 This sidewheel steamer was built in 1854 by Lupton and McDermott for Cornelius Vanderbilt and chartered by the Union Navy for use as a transport.

180 Resident of Hamlin, in 8th N.Y. Heavy Artillery Regiment.

181 This may have been what is also called sweet bread, slightly softer than regular hard tack due to a higher sugar and shortening content.

182 My roster of Brockport area Union Army members has no one named King in the 105th NYVI Regiment.

183 A frying pan, originally one with legs or feet.

184 This was General Ulysses S. Grant's breaking of the siege of Chattanooga.

185 Lincoln issued his Proclamation of Amnesty and Reconstruction on December 8, 1863.

186 By the President's Proclamation of February 1, 1864.

187 "Lincoln's presidential act of clemency of Feb. 1864 reduced the sentences of deserters condemned to death to imprisonment at Dry Tortugas, Flas., for the duration of the war."—Patricia L. Faust, "Amnesty Proclamations. Federal", in *Historical Times Encyclopedia of the Civil War,* Harper & Row, NY, 1986, p. 12.

188 He was wounded in the Battle of the Wilderness on May 5, 1864, and died on May 24, 1864, of wounds suffered at Fredericksburg.

189 These were the famed muzzle-loading rifle Minié balls invented by Frenchman Claude-Etienne Minié and used extensively in the Civil War. Its design dramatically increased both range and accuracy.—Historynet website.

190 ACWRD says C.B. died April 5, 1864, in Madison, Wisc.

191 The National Union National Convention was the presidential nominating convention held by the main faction of the Republican Party in a coalition with some War Democrats. It nominated Republican

Abraham Lincoln for President and Democrat Andrew Johnson for Vice President.

192   In March 1864, Lieutenant General Ulysses S. Grant was appointed general-in-chief of all Union armies with headquarters with the Army of the Potomac and provided operational direction to Major General George G. Meade, but Meade retained formal command.

193   This may have been the *Boston Review* that was published 1861–71.

194   *Harper's Magazine* was a monthly magazine of literature, politics, culture, finance, and the arts. Launched in June 1850, it is the second-oldest continuously published monthly magazine in the U.S. and is still being published.

195   Secretary of the Treasury in Lincoln's first cabinet. Later Lincoln appointed him to the Supreme Court. All the while, he entertained Presidential ambitions of his own.

196   A member of one of New York State's wealthiest landowning families, he commanded the 4th Division V Corps in the Battle of the Wilderness, where he was mortally wounded, dying May 8, 1864.

197   Major General Silas Casey (1807–1882) chaired a committee that revised the manual of tactics for foot officers. His three-volume *System of Infantry Tactics* expanded William Hardee's two-volume work.

198   A domestic drama, one of many written on commission for Edwin Forrest by Robert Montgomery Bird (1806–1854), an American novelist, playwright, and physician. It was set in eighteenth century Colombia and was considered his best by many critics. Forrest (1806–72), was a prominent nineteenth-century American Shakespearean actor. Beginning in 1860, his performances as Hamlet were the most successful of his life.

199   Democrat served 1863–65.

200   Served 1863–67. Tried and convicted in 1865 of harboring two paroled Confederate soldiers and sentenced to three years imprisonment.

201   Democrat served 1841–43, 1863–65, 1867–81 and died in office, mayor of New York City 1855–58, 1861, and 1862.

202   Whig served 1849–53,Democrat served 1863–66, 1867–73 died in office.

203   Not in *Biographical Directory of the American Congress.*

204   Facilities in various cities that provided food and shelter during brief stays for soldiers who were traveling, some remaining for assignments locally but most passing through by train, boat, or afoot.

205   William Cullen Bryant (1794–1878) was an American romantic poet, journalist, and long-time editor of the *New York Evening Post.*

206   Massachusetts Senator as Democrat/Free Soil served 1851–57, as Republican 1857–74 died in office, was assaulted on Senate floor 1856 and severely injured.

207 Neither that name or any similar to it appears in the *Biographical Directory of the American Congress.*

208 By Dion Boucicault opened in 1859 and was extremely popular. Among antebellum melodramas, it was second only in popularity to *Uncle Tom's Cabin.*

209 The United States Christian Commission furnished supplies, medical services, and religious literature to Union troops, combined religious support with social services and recreational activities, and supplied Protestant chaplains and social workers. One of its 25 stations was located at Warrenton.

210 An institution to instruct applicants for the command of colored troops, 1864–75.

211 Senator from Maryland who served as a Whig,1845–49, and as a Democrat, 1862–68.

212 Republican Governor of New York 1859–62, Major General in the Union Army 1861–63, Union Republican Senator 1863–69.

213 Ira Harris, Republican Senator from New York, served 1861–67; justice on the NY State Supreme Court, 1847–59.

214 1st Lieutenant Morton A. Read as a member of the 8th New York Cavalry captured the battle flag of the 1st Texas Infantry at the Battle of Appomattox Station on April 8, 1865, for which he was awarded the Congressional Medal of Honor.

215 First published in 1862 by J. C. Schreiner & Son, Charleston, with words by Charles C. Sawyer and music by Henry Tucker.

216 This seems to pick up from the previous entry.

217 A Brockport soldier in Company A, 140th who was wounded in the Battle of the Wilderness, May 5, 1864, and died of his wounds May 24, 1864.

218 Charles Lover, the Irish novelist, published the comedy *Handy Andy* in 1842.

219 He had gone there to collect the body of his son who had been killed in action. He was a deacon in the First Baptist Church of Brockport.

220 Actually, they were killed on May 10, 1864, leading successive charges at Laurel Hill.

221 Formed as the Chickahominy River flows through a dense forest of pines and underbrush. The river itself is not over sixty or seventy feet wide, but on each side of it, extending beyond the forest, is a deep marshy swamp considered as practically impassable.

222 On October 19, 1864, Sheridan's forces at Cedar Creek in the Shenandoah Valley were surprised and almost routed by Juban Early's rebels, but Sheridan rallied his troops and turned defeat into victory.

223 Publius Ovidius Naso (43 BC–AD 17/18), a Roman poet during the reign of Augustus, was a contemporary of Virgil and Horace. "The Art of Love" is one of his collections of love poetry for which he is best known.

224 A Confederate warship built secretly in England that attacked Union sea commerce very effectively, capturing 17 ships, until rammed and sunk by a Union warship in the harbor at Bahia, Brazil.

225 Phisterer reports no skirmishing that day.

226 Skilled soldiers detached from their regular units to clear roads, construct bridges, dig trenches, and erect fortifications.

227 His troops destroyed the attacking forces of Confederate General John B. Hood at Nashville, Tenn.

228 Part of the campaign against Richmond.

229 He defended Nashville successfully in two days of hard fighting that earned him the promotion to Major General.

230 The Battle of Nashville began on December 15 and the Confederates evacuated Savannah on December 20.

231 After the sinking in Brazil, the U.S. Navy towed the disabled craft to Chesapeake Bay and sank it again.

232 Horatio's son, Lorenzo, who succeeded his father as publisher of the *Brockport Republic.*

233 Probably George B. Barnett of Whiteside & Barnett, formerly shop foreman at the Seymour & Morgan foundry that manufactured the first reapers.

234 The church had been built recently by Luther Gordon and still stands, though greatly modified in the 1920s.

235 Preston King of Ogdensburg was a U.S. Senator in that Congress.

236 This Confederate stronghold on the North Carolina shore was besieged and captured by a force of 44 ships, 1,600 sailors, 400 marines, and three brigades of infantry after heavy bombardment and an assault that ended with fierce hand-to-hand combat.

237 1st Lieutenant, 108th U.S. Colored Infantry, promoted to Captain; mustered out March 21, 1866.

238 The Battle of Hatcher's Run which was preparatory to the final Union offensive of March.

239 Barney Williams (1824–1876), an Irish-American actor-comedian popular over the mid decades of the nineteenth century, who is probably best remembered for playing Ragged Pat in J. A. Amherst's drama *Ireland as it is* [sic].

240 The theater where Abraham Lincoln was assassinated, built in 1863 on the site of an earlier theater that had burned. It seated 1,700 and was one of the most popular entertainment venues in the city. Lincoln attended eight performances there.

241 President Lincoln attended 37 performances at Grover's Theater between 1863 when it opened and 1865, including *The Lakes of Killarney*, starring Barney Williams on February 24, 1863.

242 the Confederates evacuated Charleston on February 17, 1865, after it had been cut off by Sherman's troops and Union forces entered the city on the 18th.

243 Another theater that Lincoln attended frequently.

244 By American playwright George L. Aiken (1830–76).

245 This seems to be James H. Holbrook (1812–64), *Ten Years Among the Mail Bags: Or, Notes from the Diary of a Special Agent of the Post-office Department*, H. Cowperthwaite, Philadelphia, 1855, an account by a former postal inspector of various offenses committed against the Post Office Department.

246 Douglas Jerrold was the quintessential Victorian. Starting life as a seaman, he turned himself into a famous writer and journalist.

247 The Special Relief Department ran a network of soldiers' homes and lodges, usually at transit points, which provided food and shelter to sick, wounded or exhausted soldiers. Special relief staff assisted soldiers with health needs.

248 In fact, Early was not captured and, after Lee's surrender, escaped via Texas to Cuba and Toronto, Ont.

249 Armory Square Hospital, one of the largest in the area, had 12 pavilions and overflow tents with beds for 1,000 wounded soldiers from the battlefields of Virginia.

250 Sheridan was advancing through the Senandoah Valley and Sherman through North Carolina.

251 An English publisher, editor, and author (1791–1873). He was the editor and author of *Penny Magazine* and *Penny Cyclopedia*, and a great variety of other popular works.

252 He was not a candidate for re-election in 1864.

253 Designed by John Ericson, this ship engaged in the siege of several Confederate fortified ports, especially at Charleston. Farnham saw it at the Washington Naval Yard after its action.

254 Democratic Representative 1843–47, 1849–53; Republican Senator 1857–63, from Ogdensburg.

255 Commandant Dept. Of Washington, October 1863–August 1866.

256 Hannibal was born about 1800 and brought to the United States about 1824. He was the largest animal ever exhibited on this continent. His height was 11 feet 8 inches and he weighed 7½ tons. He had spells of violence and killed several men. He died May 7, 1865, apparently after eating poisonous laurel.

257 As described by an adverting flyer by Ford's Theater: "The new sensational drama, The workmen of Washington! : written and adapted by Miss Keene, the distinguished manageress, author and actress.

258 1st corporal/captain, Company K, 13th NYVI; Captain, Company C, 22nd Regiment of Cavalry; discharged for disability, March 20, 1865.

259 Perhaps *Illustrated Life, Campaigns, and Public Services of Lieutenant General Grant*. Philadelphia: T. B. Peterson and Brothers, 1865; or Headley, Rev. P. C. *The Hero Boy; or The Life and Deeds of Lieut.-Gen. Grant*. 1864.

260 Carriage ironer and general blacksmith in Clarkson, NY.

261 The manager at Grover's National Theatre had invited the Lincolns to attend this performance, but they went instead to Ford's Theater.

262 A musical drama by D. A. Strong.

263 In the 13th NYVI on July 21, 1862, received disability discharge, then enlisted in the 108th NYVI as a sergeant, falsely reported killed at Gettysburg, promoted to 1st Sergeant, 2nd Lieutenant, and 1st Lieutenant, discharged, April 22, 1864.

264 The Bureau for the Relief of Freedmen and Refugees was established by Congress on March 4, 1865, to oversee the welfare of former slaves and provide food and clothing for displaced Southern whites.

265 The self-given name of Isabella Baumfree (1797–1883), an African-American who was born into slavery in Swartekill, NY, but escaped with her infant daughter in 1826, became a prominent abolitionist and women's rights activist, and embraced evangelical religion, and moral reform.

266 A variety theater near the intersection of Pennsylvania Avenue and 11st Street.

267 The units in this army corps were composed of soldiers unfit for regular duty but not so disables as require discharge.

268 This ship, also called the *Dick Fulton*) was a 123-ton stern-wheel steamer used as an auxiliary vessel in the Union Navy's Ram Fleet. Among other things, it had been used to hide Union gold.

269 A Confederate tugboat, commissioned in 1855, that had been captured by the Union Navy in April 1861 in Hamton Roads, Va., as it attempted to help a blockade-running schooner enter the James River with munitions for the Confederacy and had been placed in service in the Union Navy.

270 "Aladdin! or His Wonderful Lamp", a popular play, had also been playing the night of April 14 and Tad Lincoln, the President's son, had been attending.

271 This Catholic high school, founded by a Jesuit in 1821, is the oldest educational institution in Washington.

272 A journalist, publisher, abolitionist, and women's rights advocate (1815–1884), who founded a string of newspapers and wrote for them regularly. She founded her last newspaper, *Reconstructionist*, during the Johnson administration.

273   A small venue that doubled as a dancing hall and saloon that featured dioramas or stereopticon projections.

274   Stage name of Harriet Wood (1833–1897), an actress and spy for the Union Army who was caught by the Confederates and sentenced to be executed, but was saved by the timely arrival of Union troops. She was awarded the rank of Brevet Major by General James A. Garfield and commended by President Lincoln for her services.

275   By Edmund Falconer (*c.* 1814–1879), pen name of Edmund O'Rourke, an Irish poet, actor, theatre manager, songwriter and playwright, known for his keen wit and outstanding acting skills. *Peep o' Day* (1861) is the play for which Falconer is best remembered.

276   A stage adaptation of Harriet Beecher Stowe's abolitionist novel. Although it was the best-selling American novel of the nineteenth century, many more people attended dramatizations of the book than read it—some three million. The most successful of them was George L. Aiken's version which was the most popular play in England and America for 75 years.

277   Hairdressing consisting of a perfumed oil or ointment.

278   A boatman on the Erie canal.

279   A shoemaker.

280   A melodrama, originally French, based on an historic crime, in which a dog witnessed a murder and became a hero by identifying the culprit.

281   A private from Hamlin, NY, in Company A of the 140th NYVI.

282   *The Indian Princess; or, La Belle Sauvage*, a musical play with libretto by James Nelson Barker and music by John Bray, based on the Pocahontas story as recorded by John Smith of early Jamestown.

283   A vaudeville drama by J. R. Planche, first produced in London.

284   A sergeant in Company L of the 20th NY Cavalry.

285   A private in Company F of the 13th NYVI.

286   An 1863 stage melodrama in four acts by the British writer Tom Taylor, based on a French drama, *Le Retour de Melun* concerning the blackmailing of a released convict and his exoneration.